Creating Web Pages For Dummies, 9th Edition

Cheat Sheet

Quick Reference & a Sample Web Page in HTML

```html
<HTML>
<!-- Text between angle brackets is an HTML tag and is not displayed. Most tags,
     such as the HTML and /HTML tags that surround the contents of a page,
     come in pairs; some tags like HR, for a horizontal rule, stand alone.
     Comments, such as the text you're reading, are not displayed. The infor-
     mation between the HEAD and /HEAD tags is not displayed. The information
     between the BODY and /BODY tags is displayed.-->
<HEAD>
<TITLE>Enter a title, displayed at the top of the window.</TITLE>
</HEAD>
<!-- The information between the BODY and /BODY tags is displayed.-->
<BODY>
<H1>Enter the main heading, usually the same as the title.</H1>
<p>Be <B>bold</B> in stating your key points. Put them in a list: </p>
<UL>
<LI>The first item in your list</li>
<LI>The second item; <I>italicize</I> key words</li>
</UL>
<p>Improve your image by including an image. </p>
<p><IMG SRC="http://www.mygifs.com/rose.gif" alt="picture of a rose">
Add a link to your favorite <A HREF="http://www.myfave.com/">Web site </A>.
Break up your page with a horizontal rule or two. </p>
<HR>
<p>Finally, link to another page in your own <A HREF="page2">Web site</A>.</p>
<!-- And add a copyright notice. -->
<p>&#169; Wiley Publishing, 2008</p>
</BODY>
</HTML>
```

Web Authoring Resources

Type of Resource	Name(s)	URL(s)
Web page creation	Google Pages	pages.google.com
Blogging	Blogger, Wordpress	www.blogger.com, www.wordpress.com
Photo sharing	Flickr	www.flickr.com
Video sharing	YouTube	www.youtube.com
Music sharing	MySpace	www.myspace.com
Downloads	CNET, Tucows	www.download.com, www.tucows.com
Paid Web tools	CoffeeCup	www.coffeecup.com
Online HTML reference	HTML Goodies	www.htmlgoodies.com/beyond/reference/article.php/3472851
HTML checker	- W3C Tidy - Tidy notes	cgi.w3.org/cgi-bin/tidy www.w3.org/People/Raggett/tidy/

For Dummies: Bestselling Book Series for Beginners

Creating Web Pages For Dummies, 9th Edition

HTML Tags

This section includes a quick-reference list of the most common HTML tags. To see the tags in use, refer to the sample Web page on the other side of this Cheat Sheet.

See the tables in the section in Appendix B called "A Quick Guide to HTML Tags" for a longer list of the most widely used tags — with examples.

Formatting

Headings: `<H1>Top heading</H1>`, `<H2> Next-level heading</H2>`, ... `<H6>Lowest heading</H6>`

Bold: `<B>text</B>`

Italic: `<I>text</I>`

Paragraph: `<P></p>`

Bulleted List: `<UL> <LI> text</li> <LI> text</li> </UL>`

Numbered List: `<ol> <LI> text</li> <LI> text</li> </ol>`

Linking

Links to external Web pages:

`<A HREF="http://www.dummies.com">The ...For Dummies Web page</A>`

Links within a Web site, same directory:

`<A HREF="myres.htm">my resume</A>`

Links within a page:

`<A HREF="#nextline">Jump</A> to the next line.`

`Here is the next <A NAME="nextline">line</A>.`

Graphics and multimedia

`<IMG SRC="myphoto.jpg" ALT="My photo!"> See the embedded photo to the left.`

`Right-click <A HREF="myphoto.jpg">here </A> to download the photo.`

`<EMBED SRC="mymovie.mov"> See the movie playing to the left.`

Tables

`<TABLE BORDER="1">`

`<TR><TD>First Row, First Cell</td><td> <First Row, Second Cell</TD></TR>`

`<TR><TD>Second Row, First Cell</td><td> Second Row, Second Cell</TD></TR>`

`</TABLE>`

Special Character Codes for Web Page Creators

To put special characters in your Web pages, enter the escape sequence or entity reference shown in the following table. Test your special characters in several current Web browsers to make sure that they display consistently.

Character	Escape Sequence	Entity Reference
"	&#34;	&quot;
'	&#39;	&apos;
$	&#36;	&dollar;
¢	&#162;	&cent;
%	&#37;	&percnt;
@@rm	&#174;	&reg;
&	&#38;	&amp;
@@cw	&#169;	&copy;
<	&#60;	&lt;
>	&#62;	&gt;
@	&#64;	&commat;
à	&#224;	&agrave;
é	&#233;	&eacute;
ê	&#234;	&ecirc;

For more information and a complete list of characters used in different languages, see this Web page: www.bbsinc.com/symbol.html

For Dummies: Bestselling Book Series for Beginners

Creating
Web Pages
FOR
DUMMIES®
9TH EDITION

Creating Web Pages FOR DUMMIES®

9TH EDITION

by Bud E. Smith

WILEY

Wiley Publishing, Inc.

Author's Acknowledgments

The author thanks Steve Hayes, acquisitions editor, and the staff that helped produce this book: project editor Nicole Sholly, technical editor James Kelly, copy editor Barry Childs-Helton, as well as the many other people responsible for page layout, proofreading, indexing, and graphic art.

The Web was initially built more for love than for money, and that tradition has been continued by the many people who have generously given their time and support for this book. I especially thank the providers of Web tools who have supplied the world with an ever-growing range of tools, and the Web authors who have let me use their sites for figures in this book.

Publisher's Acknowledgments

We're proud of this book; please send us your comments through our online registration form located at www.dummies.com/register/.

Some of the people who helped bring this book to market include the following:

Acquisitions, Editorial, and Media Development

Project Editor: Nicole Sholly

Executive Editor: Steve Hayes

Senior Copy Editor: Barry Childs-Helton

Technical Editor: James Kelly

Editorial Managers: Kevin Kirschner, Leah Cameron

Media Development Assistant Project Manager: Jenny Swisher

Media Development Assistant Producer: Angela Denny

Editorial Assistant: Amanda Foxworth

Senior Editorial Assistant: Cherie Case

Cartoons: Rich Tennant (www.the5thwave.com)

Composition Services

Project Coordinator: Erin Smith

Layout and Graphics: Claudia Bell, Ana Carillo, Reuben W. Davis

Proofreaders: John Greenough, Debbye Butler

Indexer: Word Co. Indexing Services

Publishing and Editorial for Technology Dummies

    Richard Swadley, Vice President and Executive Group Publisher

    Andy Cummings, Vice President and Publisher

    Mary Bednarek, Executive Acquisitions Director

    Mary C. Corder, Editorial Director

Publishing for Consumer Dummies

    Diane Graves Steele, Vice President and Publisher

    Joyce Pepple, Acquisitions Director

Composition Services

    Gerry Fahey, Vice President of Production Services

    Debbie Stailey, Director of Composition Services

Contents at a Glance

Table of Contents

Introduction

· ·

*I*t may be hard to remember, or it may seem like only yesterday, but some years ago, the personal computer was introduced. The rise and rise *and rise* of the personal computer — with maybe an occasional stumble but never a real fall — seemed certain to be the most important social and technological event at the end of the twentieth century. From the "two Steves" — Wozniak and Jobs — and their Apple II, to Bill Gates's Windows 95, it seemed nothing could ever be bigger, or more life-changing and important, than PCs.

But people *do* talk. In fact, talking is one of the main things that people are all about, and in the beginning, the personal computer didn't let you interact with others. However, first with modems, and then with networks, and finally through their combination and culmination in the Internet, personal computers became the tools that opened up a new medium of communication. The most visible and exciting part of the Internet is the World Wide Web. Now communication, not computation, is the story. Computers are still important, but mostly as the means to an end; the end result is to enable people to interact.

If the most exciting channel of communication is the Web, the means of communication is the Web page. Ordinary people demonstrate amazing energy and imagination in creating and publishing diverse Web home pages. And although ordinary people have a *desire* to create Web pages, businesses have a *need* to set up shop on the Web. So the rush to the Web continues, often with the same people expressing themselves personally on one Web page and commercially on another.

So you want to be there, too. "But," you ask, "isn't it difficult, expensive, and complicated?" Not anymore. As the Web has grown, easy ways to get on the Web have appeared. And I discuss the best of them in the pages of this book.

About This Book

It's *about* 340 pages.

Seriously, what do you find here? Easy ways to get published on the Web for any kind of Internet user we could think of. Quick ways to get a blog, photos, or videos online. Ways to make your first Web page rich with carefully arranged text, graphics, and multimedia, plus the information you need to go beyond your first Web page and create a multipage personal or business Web site. And free online tools, which we describe in the book, to help you go as far as you want to go in creating a Web site.

Foolish Assumptions

Lots of good information is in this book, but almost no one is going to read every word of it — except our long-suffering editors. That's because we cover Web page topics from beginning through intermediate levels, including how to publish a Web page via Google, how to use several different tools, and some Windows-specific and Mac-specific stuff. No one needs to know all of that! But anyone who wants to get a Web page up on the Web does need to know some of it.

But what do *you* need? We assume, for purposes of this book, that you have probably used the Web before and that you want to create a Web page. We further assume that you are not yet a Web author, or that you're fairly new to the process. To use the information in this book, here's what you need:

✔ Access to a personal computer, preferably one running Microsoft Windows XP or Vista.

The CD-ROM only works with Windows. If you have a Macintosh or a Unix/Linux system and an Internet connection, much of this book works for you as well, but you won't have access to the tools on the CD-ROM, nor to most of the online service or Web-page creation tools that we describe, except those available directly to your user community on the Web.

✔ Access to the Web — either through an online service or an Internet service provider (ISP).

✔ You should be running a Web browser such as Microsoft Internet Explorer, Firefox, or a browser provided by an online service.

✔ You should already have spent at least some time surfing the Web, or be willing to do so as you gather information and examples for your Web page.

In other words, if you're wired, or willing to get wired, you're in. With that, the door to this book is open to you, whether you want to create your first Web page or add new features to one you already have.

The figures in this book show up-to-date Windows screen shots for a consistent appearance. We wrote most of the instructions and steps in this book to work equally well for Windows and the Macintosh, though the CoffeeCup instructions are for a program that runs only on Windows.

Conventions Used in This Book

When our publisher first told us that this book was going to have *conventions,* we got out our silly hats and our Democratic and Republican paraphernalia, but apparently she just meant that we had to be consistent. The conventions in this book are standard ways of communicating specific types of information, such as instructions and steps. (One example of a convention is the use of italics for newly introduced words — as with the word "conventions" in the first sentence of this paragraph.)

Here are the conventions for this book:

- Things that you, the reader, are asked to type are shown in **bold.**

- New terms are printed in *italics.*

- Information used in specific ways is formatted in a specific typeface. In this book, one of the most common kinds of information displayed this way is HTML tags; that is, formatting information used to create Web pages (see Appendix B for a more complete definition). An example of a tag is `<title>`.

  We also use a special typeface for URLs (Uniform Resource Locators), which are the addresses used to specify the location of Web pages. For example, the URL for the For Dummies Web site is `www.dummies.com`.

- The Web is fast-paced and evolving. By the time you read this book, some of the URLs listed in it may have changed.

- Representative browser versions appear among the figures.

- Menu selections look like this: File⇨Save. This particular example means that you choose the File menu and then choose the Save option.

- Related, brief pieces of information are displayed in bulleted lists, such as the bulleted list that you're reading right now.

- Numbered lists are used for instructions that you must follow in a particular sequence. This book has many sequential steps that tell you just how to perform the different tasks that, when taken together, can make you a successful Web author.

  To make the steps brief and easy to follow, we use a specific way of telling you what to do. Here's an example of a set of steps:

  1. **Start your Web browser.**

  2. **Go to the Web site** `www.tryfreestuff.com`.

     Note: This site is not real, just an example.

  3. **Click the link that matches the type of computer you have: PC, Macintosh, or Unix.**

Part-y Time: How This Book Is Organized

We wrote this book to a carefully plotted, precise, *unvarying* plan, with the predictable and predicted result: the book you're holding in your hands now.

Wait a second. Isn't it true that the Web is changing every day, that Web sites appear and disappear like so many jacks-in-the-box — or whack-a-moles, if that's a more familiar example to you — and that Web companies can pop into and out of existence in a few weeks? So, what was that about a plan?

Well, okay, we did change things a little along the way. Maybe a lot. But we *did* have a plan behind the book, even if it was finalized in a conference call at 5:00 this morning. The following sections explain the parts that make up the book.

Part I: Create a Web Page Today

You probably want to dive right into becoming a Web publisher. So we start the book with some ideas about what to do in your Web site, and then give specific instructions on how to get your first, simple Web page up. You can start with Google Page Creator and get a firm handle on designing your Web page, no matter what tools you use.

Part II: Getting the Content Right

What goes into your Web page is the core of your efforts, and you can use newer, social-networking tools to work with all the different kinds of content you might want. For example, consider creating a blog to help you generate interesting text, using Flickr and YouTube to post interesting photos and videos, and more.

Part III: Your Site in WYSIWYG

CoffeeCup HTML Editor (and its many younger brothers and sisters) has been around for years, quietly getting better and better and more and more numerous. CoffeCup is a What You See Is What You Get, or WYSIWYG, tool that helps you work on a screen that looks like your Web page and handle many of the messy HTML details for you. This book includes the excellent CoffeeCup Editor trial software so you can get started today. Now I'm including CoffeeCup tools in this part of the book and on the CD-ROM. If you're running a Windows PC, fire it up and go to town!

Part IV: Your Site in HTML

Many Web developers don't want to use a tool, even a cool one like CoffeeCup HTML Editor, at least at first. They want to dive right into the "bare metal" approach and work with HTML in a text editor. I'm a bit like that myself, and no Web author ever suffered from learning HTML *too well*. Here's where you can develop your skills.

Part V: The Part of Tens

A Top Ten list is a great way to make complex information fun and easy to remember. My Top Ten lists show you key dos and don'ts of Web publishing and more.

Part VI: Appendixes

Appendixes in books are usually like appendixes in people: funny little things that get taken out of the patient in a hurry if they act up. But for this book, I pack in great information that can really help you. In Appendix A, a glossary defines Web publishing terms that may be confusing to you. In Appendix B, you get a comprehensive — yet brief — guide to HTML tags, the most basic tools that developers use to create today's Web sites. Appendix C tells you about the CoffeeCup programs on the CD-ROM.

Icons Used in This Book

All Dummies books include icons that point you in the direction of really great information that's sure to help you along your way. Here I briefly describe each icon used in this book.

Marks information that you need to keep in mind as you work.

Points to things you may want to know but don't necessarily need to know. You can skip these and read the text, skip the text and read these (if you're into geek-style light reading), or go ahead and read both.

Designates the tools included on the CD-ROM.

Flags specific information that may not fit in a step or description but that helps you create better Web pages.

Points out anything that may cause a problem.

Part I
Create a Web Page Today

The 5th Wave   By Rich Tennant

"Great goulash, Stan. That reminds me, are you still scripting your own Web page?"

In this part . . .

Jump right in with simple Web page publishing. Decide what to put on your page, and then use a simple Web-based service to get it online today. Make your page look good. Your reward: Telling your friends, family, and colleagues your Web address tomorrow!

Chapter 1

Web Publishing Basics

The Web is an incredibly easy way to get your message — any message — out to anyone in the world who's interested in it. By putting up a Web page you can stay in touch with friends and family, entertain people, help yourself get a job, or help yourself do your job. You can start a business, grow a business, or just have fun expressing yourself.

Having a Web page is also ever more important as social networking and online selling sites — eBay, MySpace, Facebook, YouTube, Flickr, and many others — continue to grow. You need a base that establishes your online presence, and any online commercial interests you have, across all the "walled gardens" that each want you to spend all your online time within their boundaries.

Nearly a million people have purchased this book since its first edition more than ten years ago; my readers have used every technique I describe in this book — and more — to get their first Web pages up and running. By reading this book, you're starting on a path that many, many people before you have followed to Web-page success.

Web Basics 101

You may have begun using the Internet and the Web without really getting a chance to learn how they work. Knowing how they work can help you become a better Web publisher and Web user. Here's a brief, to-the-point description. For more information, you can search the Web; the World Wide Web Consortium site at www.w3.org is a good place to start. (Start with the HTML section.)

Understanding how the Web works

The Web, formally called the *World Wide Web,* is a collection of a bunch of text and graphics files (plus some other stuff) that make up *Web pages.* Web pages are combined into linked sets of pages called *Web sites.* People often use the term interchangeably, but technically, a Web page is a single HTML text file, possibly with one or more graphics and other features added; a Web site is one or more Web pages linked together. These terms will be explained further later in this book.

Underlying the Web is the Internet. The Web depends on the Internet to connect its many files together and to allow people to get to the Web. E-mail is a separate function that also depends on the Internet. And FTP (file-transfer protocol) is another Internet capability, used to move files from one computer to another.

The Web is defined by two specifications: HyperText Transfer Protocol (HTTP) and HyperText Markup Language (HTML). The underlying idea behind the Web is *hypertext* — text that can contain links to other pieces of text and other files, such as graphics files, stored anywhere on the Internet. The Web got its name from the way all the links connect the pieces of text together like a huge spider's web.

You look at Web pages by using a program called a *Web browser.* A Web browser uses HTTP to request a Web page from a Web server. The Web page, in turn, uses HTTP to request any other files, such as graphics images or ads, that are part of the Web page. After you request a Web page, your Web browser pulls the files that make up the Web page from one or more Web servers and assembles those files into a single page displayed on your screen.

The most popular Web browsers are Microsoft Internet Explorer; Mozilla Firefox (the successor to the once all-conquering Netscape Navigator); Opera, a standards-compliant Web browser from a small company; and Safari, Apple's browser for Macintosh computers.

After a Web browser requests a Web page using HTTP, HTML steps in. Each Web page has as its core a text file written in a format called *HTML* (for HyperText Markup Language), which usually includes links to one or more graphics files. HTML defines a Web page's appearance and functionality. Actually, HTML doesn't precisely specify the Web page's appearance: Different Web browsers display various HTML commands differently. Also, users can specify how they want things to look on their own screen. So what one user sees when she looks at a Web page may be different from what another user sees. (Part IV goes into detail about HTML.)

Getting a Web page up on the Internet is surprisingly easy. In fact, if you're in a hurry, you may want to go straight to Chapter 3 to use Google Page Creator. Follow the instructions there to get your first Web page up in about an hour.

Getting Webbed

This book talks a lot about the Web, but doesn't discuss how to get on the Web as a user. Even if you're on the Web already, perhaps through a connection at work, you may also want to get on the Web from home. How do you do that?

There are a wide variety of broadband offerings — some tied to cable TV or satellite TV services, others to phone offerings, and even a few to mobile phones. There are wireless hotspots that may give you inexpensive (or even free) Internet access. And yes, there are still some dialup — that is to say, slow — offerings left.

The most popular online service is still America Online (AOL). AOL has robust Web-publishing features, coverage around most of the world, good spam blocking, kid-safe controls, and many other good features. However, it tends to be expensive, and is gradually losing subscribers.

It's quite likely that your Internet service provider, whether it's a big name (such as AOL and MSN) or a little guy, offers you space for your Web site — and perhaps helpful support services as well. Check your ISP's offerings as you decide how to get your first pages up on the Web.

Getting up URL-y

The Internet is the giant computer network that connects other computer networks around the world. At its base, the Internet is just a giant mechanism for moving files from one computer to another. It finds files by using a kind of address called a *URL* (Uniform Resource Locator — which sounds like something the Army invented to track down clothes!). The acronym URL is usually pronounced "you are ell," although some pronounce it "earl." Most people today use the term "Web address" or "Internet address" instead of "URL," but as a Web publisher you should know all of the terms.

The address that you type to get to a Web page is a URL. For example, www.dummies.com is the URL for the For Dummies site. A URL consists of three parts (see Figure 1-1):

- **Protocol:** The name of the communications language that the URL uses: HTTP (used on the Web), HTTPS (for secure Web pages), FTP, and so on.
- **Domain name:** The name of the server the file is on, such as dummies.com.
- **Pathname:** The location of the desired file on the server.

Figure 1-1:
URL-y to
Web, URL-y
to rise.

←— Protocol —→   ←— Domain name —→   ←— Pathname —→
http://   www.server.com/   folder/filename.ext

The "For Dummies" Way to Web Publishing

Reading this book is going to make you a Web publisher — because anyone who puts up even a single, simple home page is a publisher on the World Wide Web. Congratulations in advance!

Because there's so much you can do on the Web these days, including on social networking sites such as YouTube (for videos) or Flickr (for photos), I have split the description into two basic pieces: getting your content together (Part II) and getting it up on the Web (Part III or Part IV). Part III describes how to get your Web page up using the tool included with this book, CoffeeCup; Part IV describes how to "go to the bare metal" (well, the bare fiber-optic cable) and use HTML directly.

Given the many ways you can work, and the way different Web sites and different tools handle some of the process for you, but not all of it, it's important to understand the underlying steps that define Web publishing. The steps may have different names, or be intermingled with each other, but they're always basically the same. Here they are:

1. **Create the HTML text file that's the basis for your Web page.**

2. **Create or obtain the graphic images you'll use to spice up the appearance of your page.**

3. **Create a link to the graphics in your HTML text file so they appear where you want them to.**

4. **Preview your Web page on your own machine.**

5. **Find Web-server space.**

6. **Transfer the HTML text file and the graphics files to the Web server.**

7. **Check that your new Web page works correctly now that it's online.**

If you use an easy-to-use tool such as Google Page Creator (see Chapter 3), the steps given here are combined and most of the details are handled for you. However, it's good to know what's happening "behind the scenes," to help avoid problems or to help you tackle a more complicated site later.

Web terms to know

To clear up how I define and use some Web terms, here's a brief primer:

✔ **Web page:** A text document that is published on a Web server, has HTML tags in it, almost always includes hypertext links, and usually includes graphics. When you click the Back button in your Web browser, you move to the previous Web page that you visited.

✔ **Web site:** A collection of Web pages that share a common theme and purpose, and that users generally access through the site's home page.

✔ **Home page:** The Web page that people generally access first within a Web site. You let people know the URL (address) of your home page and try to get other Web page creators to provide links to it.

✔ **HTML tags:** Brief formatting or linking commands placed within brackets in the text of an HTML file. For instance, the <b> tag tells the Web browser to display text after the command in bold type; the </b> tag turns the bold off. (See Part IV for more on HTML.)

These steps are usually simple if you're creating a basic Web page. However, they do get more complicated sometimes, especially if you're trying to create a multipage Web site. This book tells you several different, easy ways to get content up on several different kinds of sites or create a Web page, and gets you started on expanding your Web page into a multipage Web site.

When you create a Web page that has complex formatting, or that mixes text and graphics, you'll want to test it in the most popular Web browsers. You should download Microsoft Internet Explorer, the America Online client, the Firefox browser, the Opera browser, the Safari browser, and/or other tools.

For an example of a good-looking Web page, check out the For Dummies home page, shown in Figure 1-2. It has an attractive layout, interesting information, and links to a great deal more information on the For Dummies site and other sites. The For Dummies Web site is professionally done, but you too can achieve good results with a reasonable amount of planning and hard work. In this book, I concentrate on helping you create a simple, individual Web page and combining several Web pages into a closely linked group of pages called a *Web site,* such as the For Dummies site.

Note: The For Dummies home page is shown in Microsoft Internet Explorer, the most popular Web browser. For consistency, I use Internet Explorer for most of the Web-page images in this book.

Figure 1-2:
The For Dummies home page shows Web-publishing skill.

Making simple things simple

If all you want to do is create a simple "I exist" Web page, either for yourself or for your business, you don't have to go through the rigmarole of figuring out HTML or learning a tool, finding server space, and so on. Chapter 3 helps you use Google Page Creator, a tool from the leaders in Web search, Google. To see how easy publishing on the Web is, just turn to Chapter 3 and get started. You'll be a Web publisher with just a couple of hours of effort.

Making difficult things possible

If you want to concentrate on one type of media at a time, Chapter 4 talks about writing words for the Web and shows you how to create a blog; Chapter 5 talks about creating images, especially photos, that are online-ready, and tells you how to manage photos on Flickr; Chapter 6 discusses making sound files and tunes Internet-friendly, and how to get a tune up on MySpace; and Chapter 7 focuses on videos — how to trim their massive storage requirements and get one up on YouTube.

Seeing HTML

When Tim Berners-Lee invented HTML at CERN (the European particle-physics research facility) in the late 1980s, he probably never imagined that so many people would be interested in seeing it. Today, most browsers include a command that enables you to see the actual HTML source instructions that make the page look and work the way it does.

For example, in Internet Explorer, choose View⇨Source to view the underlying HTML file. You see all the HTML tags that make the Web page look and act the way it does. However, some HTML pages are "cleaner" and easier to read and understand than others. Keep looking until you find some pages that make sense to you.

After you open the HTML file, you can edit the text and the HTML tags, save the file, and then open the file again in your browser to see how it looks with the HTML changes. Don't publish someone else's page, of course — but other than that, experimenting in this way is a good way to learn.

Part III — Chapters 8 through 11 — shows you how to use the CoffeeCup editor to pull your content together into a Web site. Part IV — Chapters 12 through 15 — shows you how to do the same in "pure" HTML.

Types of Web Sites

The Web offers examples of nearly every communications strategy known to humanity, successful or not. But not every example of a Web page that you find online applies to your situation. For one thing, the resources of different Web publishers vary tremendously — from an individual putting up family photos to a large corporation creating an online commerce site. For another, several different types of Web sites exist, and not every lesson learned in creating one type of Web site applies to the others.

The major types of Web pages are personal, picture, topical, commercial, and entertainment sites. Increasingly, you can combine different kinds of sites in *mashups* — sites that combine different kinds of technologies. (The Web itself already does that, but a mashup takes combining technologies to another level.) In the next sections, I describe some of the specific considerations that apply to each type of Web page and not to the others. Decide in advance what type of Web page you want to create, and look for other pages like it online to use as models.

Personal sites

Personal Web sites can have many goals. Often, your goal is simply to share something about yourself with coworkers, friends, family, and others. Personal Web pages are a great way for people to find out about others with similar interests and for people in one culture to find out about other cultures. You can also use a personal Web site to share family photos and events — kind of like a holiday letter that's always up to date. Figure 1-3 shows part of the personal site of Web designer Jeff Lowe, who's piloting a remote-controlled blimp in the pictures. You can find the site at `www.jefflowe.com` and the blimp image among the pictures at `www.jefflowe.com/site/pictures/index.php`.

Creating a personal Web site is a great deal of fun and great practice for other work. But personal Web sites are often left unchanged after the initial thrill of creating and publishing them fades. Be different — keep your Web site updated!

As personal Web sites evolve, their creators tend to add more information about a single key interest, in which case the pages may become topical Web sites (described later). In other cases, the Web site creator adds more information about professional goals and accomplishments, in which case the Web page becomes more like a business Web site.

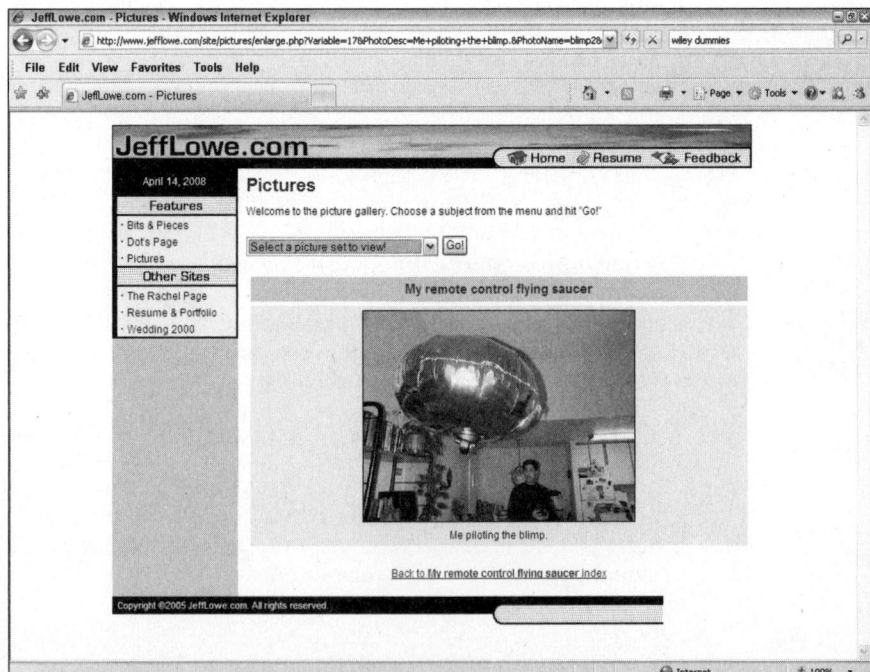

Figure 1-3:
Jeff Lowe pilots the blimp (and posts his résumé too).

Are personal Web sites still relevant?

Most of the activity you hear about on the Web these days relates to large, commercial sites, political sites, advanced technical sites, and so on. Individuals are still contributing a great deal of content but it's through more specialized sites — photo sites, video sites, social-networking sites, and so on. But these tend to appeal to only some people rather than to everyone.

Personal Web sites have gotten somewhat lost in the shuffle as better-funded sites belonging to companies and organizations get all the attention. Never fear; personal Web sites are still fun and easy to create. (And did I mention that they're fun?)

Part of what's driving the continuing interest in personal Web pages is that more and more people all over the world have access to the Web. (The Web passed 1 billion users a few years ago, an important milestone.) The chances are better than ever that a high percentage of your friends, family, and colleagues can visit and appreciate your site. So don't be put off by the tremendous growth of business and large organizational sites on the Web. The personal and fun side is growing, too; it's just getting less media attention than the commercial side.

Following a few simple rules helps make your personal Web site more fun and less work:

- ✔ **What's on first?** No, no. What's on second . . . The upper part of your Web page — the part that appears first when you bring the page up on-screen — needs to make the main point of the site clear. If the main point is "you," the first thing people see should be your name, your photo, and links to some of the things about "you" that are in your site. If the point of your site is a topical interest, business interest, or professional self-promotion, the first area of the home page should make that clear, too.

- ✔ **Keep it simple.** Start with modest goals and get something up on the Web; then create a "To Do" list of ways in which to extend your site. Consider spinning off commercial and topical pages that reflect your desires and interests — into separate sites by topic — rather than creating a sprawling personal Web site.

- ✔ **Provide lots of links.** One of the best ways to share your interests is to share information about Web sites that you like, as well as books and other resources. You can put this list on your one and only Web page or make it a separate page that's part of a personal Web site. If you develop a thorough, carefully updated list of links for a specific interest area, you create a valuable resource for others.

✔ **Consider your privacy.** A Web page is just like a billboard — except that 1 billion or more people can see it, not just a few hundred. Don't put anything up on your Web page that you wouldn't want on a billboard. Identity thieves can do a frightening amount of damage with your full name, your address, the name of your employer and your mother's maiden name. And think twice before putting up information about your kids and other family members: You may well be willing to compromise your own privacy, but you shouldn't make that decision for other people.

Picture sites

Lots of people just want to share pictures online; it's a lot easier to share pictures on the Web than to mail them around, or wait until you get together with people.

You can use any of the Web-page creation tools described in this book to create a photos-mostly Web site, although Flickr (see Chapter 5) is for this purpose alone.

Sharing pictures is often a great joy, but also often quite boring for other people. Here are some tips to help keep your site interesting:

✔ **Get organized.** Think about how photos are going to be organized. Basically, your site should be like a magic photo album — with new content at the front, and as many older photos as you want at the back. So use the home page to highlight the new stuff, and keep the older stuff moving back into archived folders.

✔ **Be a photo editor.** "Less is more," up to a point, even on sites designed to show off the grandkids' latest photos to proud grandparents. Usually, one or two photos of a given spot or event, whether it's a birthday party, a visit to an historic site, or something similar, are enough to give a flavor of it.

✔ **Watch the megabytes.** Use a photo-editing program to save your files as JPEG images with the appropriate degree of compression (Chapter 5 has details). Even though many Web users today have broadband access, you don't want to freeze out the people who don't, and even broadband runs slowly sometimes.

✔ **Protect your identity.** Make sure not to provide identifying information such as anyone's full name, address, or phone number. This helps prevent identity theft.

Getting personal with blogs

A *Web log,* or *blog* for short, is a sort of online diary that usually includes links to Web sites that the user has recently found interesting — thus the term Web log. *Blogging,* or maintaining a Web log, is a whole new form of Web publishing.

You can create a Web page or Web site that's nothing but a blog, or combine blog content with traditional content. Some blogs are extremely personal — sometimes uncomfortably so. Web logs are also used in big Web sites, such as major newspaper sites. In other words, Web logs cross the boundaries between personal sites and other categories — including the topical and business categories — and some of them are pretty entertaining as well!

I have the somewhat old-fashioned view that you probably would benefit from knowing about Web-page creation in general, not just blogging, so I defer a detailed discussion of this larger topic to Chapter 4. But if your whole reason for wanting to create Web pages is to create a blog to call your very own, please skip ahead and read Chapter 4 now, and then come back here when you want to find more about Web pages in general.

Topical sites

That's "topical," not "tropical." A *topical home page* is a resource on a specific topic. A topic can be an interest or volunteer group to which the author belongs, in which case the page may grow over time into something much like a business Web site. (Creating a Web site for a group is a tremendous contribution that you can make, but it can be a lot of work; watch what you may be getting yourself into!) Or your topical Web page can be about any interest, cause, concern, obsession, or flight of fancy that you have. In this sense, the Web is like an out-of-control vanity press, allowing anyone to go on and on about anything — sometimes offering something of great value, oftentimes not.

Making a second career out of maintaining and extending a topical Web site is easy, but the pay is usually low. Here are some things to consider when you create a topical Web site:

- ✔ **What's on first?** As with a personal Web page, the title of a topical Web page and the first screen that users see need to make unmistakably clear the topic that the page covers. And, to the extent possible, they must describe what resources the Web site offers about the topic.

- ✔ **Keep focused.** A topical Web site loses some of its value if it goes beyond a single topic. How many of the people who share your love for Thai cooking also share your abiding interest in rotifers (microscopic creatures that are too small to use in most recipes, Thai or not)? If you have two different interests that you want to share on the Web, consider creating separate Web sites.

✔ **Create a succession plan.** If your Web site grows beyond your capacity to maintain and extend it properly, find someone to help out or to take it over. The first person you should ask about taking over is anyone who's complaining that you're not extending the site fast enough! Decide what role you can handle and then ask for help in doing the rest.

Business sites

Business Web sites, also known as commercial sites, constitute the 50,000-pound gorilla of the Web, with a tremendous amount of time, energy, and money devoted to them. Business Web sites cover a wide range of styles because their goals and the expertise and resources behind them vary so much. This book provides enough information for you to create a competent "Web presence" site with several pages of contact and company information. But even these kinds of sites vary quite a bit, and you need to be sure that your company's page is well implemented.

Figure 1-4 shows the BATCS home page I created along with my wife, Olga Smith, a publisher and tutor. It's created with an online tool provided by the Web host, and is a bit "rough around the edges" from a design point of view, but full of content useful for the purpose. Go surf around the BATCS site to see what a site designed and implemented by someone with a job to do (rather than all the time in the world to show off Web-design skills), looks like: www.batcs.co.uk.

The first question to ask about a business Web site is "Who can access it?" Some sites are intended for the World Wide Web and everyone on it; others are on the World Wide Web but are password-protected or otherwise restricted in access; still others are on private networks and inaccessible to outsiders. These inaccessible networks are described as being "behind the firewall." Any Web page that isn't accessible to everyone is considered to be on an *intranet*, if access is limited to one company, or an *extranet*, if access is limited to a group of companies that are business partners.

Despite the wide variety of business Web sites, following just a few rules can help you create a page that meets your goals:

✔ **What's on first?** A business Web page should make the name and purpose(s) of your business immediately clear. Also, the site should provide easy-to-find information on how to contact your business or organization and what products and services it offers.

✔ **Get the right look.** Telling someone you don't like his Web site is like telling him you don't like his haircut — he's likely to take it personally. But an ugly Web site, like an ugly haircut, can make a permanently bad impression. Make sure that the look of your Web site is up to the professional standards set by other aspects of your business.

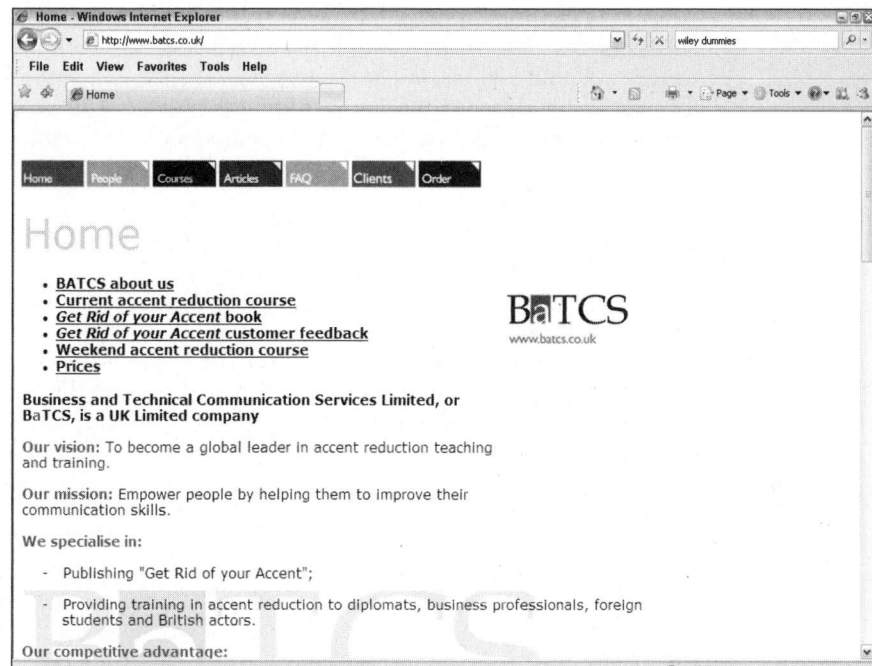

Figure 1-4:
The BATCS home page gets the job done.

✔ **Get permission.** Unless you own the business, you need to ask for permission before putting a company page on the open Web. You also need to make absolutely sure you have the permissions you need for any images or documents that you use before you publish your Web page.

✔ **Inside or outside the firewall?** Deciding who gets access is tricky. For example, a small amount of otherwise-closely-held information can make a site more valuable, but the presence of confidential information *also* prevents you from opening up the entire site to the broader public. Implementing access controls can also be difficult. Investigate how to password-protect a site, or ask a network administrator at your company whether you can physically control access. For instance, you may be able to selectively allow access based on which network the user connects from.

✔ **Find experts.** Businesses similar to yours — or even colleagues, if you're in a large company — likely have Web sites that have a purpose similar to yours. Look to similar sites for guidance and inspiration.

✔ **Monitor usage.** Investing time, energy, and money in a business Web site requires a trade-off among the Web site and other things that those resources could go to. One of the crucial questions you may need to answer in order to justify Web site maintenance or expansion is how much use the site gets. Investigate ways to measure the use of your site. A good way to start is a basic hit counter, such as the free one you can find at the following URL: `www.statcounter.com`.

✔ **Seek out additional resources.** This book focuses on hands-on creation of single Web pages and simple Web sites. For a larger business site, you need access to additional information to help you with the planning, hosting, and maintenance of the site. Consider purchasing *HTML, XHTML & CSS For Dummies,* 6th Edition, by Ed Tittel and Jeff Noble, for more information on the HTML specification, and *Web Marketing For Dummies,* by Jan Zimmerman (both books from Wiley), for more information on planning and creating a business Web site with a marketing bent.

Having a Web site that's too obviously "handmade," rather than professionally created, can be embarrassing for a business. However, many sites are going "back to the future" with a simple, clean look that's light on graphics. So how do you decide whether to make your look fancy or simple? The best way to get a quick reality check is to look at some competitors' Web sites and make sure that your initial site looks roughly as good as theirs. And remember: Often the most embarrassing thing is having no site at all.

Entertainment sites

Entertainment is one of the top few reasons why people use the Web, and the number of entertainment sites continues to grow. Humorous pages and shared games on online services are now a major presence on the Web.

People have high expectations of entertainment sites — which can make them some of the most demanding to create. Here are a few suggestions for creating entertainment sites:

✔ **Don't start here.** Don't try to figure out Web publishing by creating an entertainment site at the outset. It's a very demanding task. Try another type first and edge your way into entertainment.

✔ **Keep it fresh.** How funny is a joke the second time you hear it? You have to either frequently update the content on your entertainment site, or allow participants to provide new content through their interaction with one another — neither option is easy.

✔ **Push the technology.** Interactivity is also key to entertainment, which means going beyond HTML and static graphics. You probably need to figure out and use at least one more advanced Web technology, such as Flash, to make a fresh and interesting entertainment Web site.

Is your page cybersmut?

For most Web page publishers, the best policy with respect to putting anything potentially offensive in your Web pages is to keep your site clean. The use of gratuitous sex and violence in your Web pages will simply put off many people and put you and your Web site in a bad light.

But what if the sex or violence is not gratuitous and is actually central to your point? Then send the author and publishers your URL so that we can see it for ourselves. No, seriously: Be sure to make the first page a home page that specifically warns readers that they may find your content offensive. Doing so lets them gracefully opt out before they view whatever you show.

Also, consider your environment — the site the content appears on. MySpace pages are full of dubious content, whereas YouTube tries to keep things cleaner. A business site should not have anything potentially offensive. Don't have your content violate the local etiquette.

Even this enlightened approach may not be enough, however. Some Web-server owners will drop your page if it violates their rules, and several countries have laws that specify what can and can't be on a Web page. Be sure to find out about the rules and laws that apply to you before you put anything questionable on your Web page.

✔ **Let the technology push you.** The technology can give you ideas that are in themselves pretty funny. Try using Java to create a Three Stooges-type animated routine, or use ActiveX to create a virtual-reality environment that includes funhouse mirrors. (I describe both Java and ActiveX in Appendix A.)

Thinking Your Web Page Through

A Web page or Web site is basically a publication, though an interactive one. Thinking about a few simple principles now, before you start, can help make your Web page much more interesting and useful to the people who see it. You can also revisit this section after you put up your initial Web home page; use these guidelines to revise your page and make it even more interesting and useful!

Ask "Why am I doing this?"

Ask yourself, as you're starting, "Why am I doing this?" (As you do more and more work on your page, your answer to this question may come to have some degree of profanity in it!) That is, why are you creating the page, and not having someone else create it for you? The answer helps you determine some important things about the page. The following list details the most common reasons for people to get involved in creating a Web page:

- ✔ **For work:** More and more people are being asked to create Web pages and Web sites as part of their jobs; for example, they use the Web to communicate with people inside or outside their companies. But unless you plan to be a full-time Webmaster, you need to balance the time you spend developing your pages with the time you spend on the other demands of your job. Be modest in your initial goals, and keep track of each step in creating and modifying your Web pages so that you — or the person who takes over for you — can refer to the records later.

- ✔ **For fun:** Fun sites are a good thing, and they are a lot of what makes the Web worthwhile. But if you create your site for fun, you may find time to work on it only after you spend time on other things, such as work, school, and time with friends and family. So don't be too ambitious in your initial plans, or you may take quite a while to finish and publish your page. (Many bloggers, for one example, now feel that they need to be online 24/7 to keep up.)

- ✔ **As a career move:** So you want to be a full-time, or nearly full-time, Webmaster, blogger, or eBay seller; or you want, in some other way, to make the Internet or Web part of your career? In this kind of situation, you can afford to plan an ambitious Web site that uses advanced tools, tracks usage, and otherwise gets closer to the cutting edge of the Web. To gain experience, create your initial Web page by using the accessible and broad-based tools and approaches I describe in this book. Then take your page closer to the cutting edge by using the more advanced techniques described and taught elsewhere.

- ✔ **Who knows?** As famous baseball manager Yogi Berra once said, "When you come to a fork in the road, take it." You may not have a specific reason for publishing on the Web, but that shouldn't stop you. You may figure out a good reason after you have a little Web experience under your belt. Start simple, so you can score an early success in getting a basic Web page up, and then go from there.

Don't spend too much time on design

Designing a Web page is unlike designing any other kind of publication, because you don't have as much control over the precise appearance of a Web page as you do with other types of publications. Different network connection speeds, browsers, screen sizes, and font and other settings within a browser vary so much that users can have very different experiences with your Web page. Some people may (for example) bring up your page on a personal digital assistant, laptop, Web-connected TV, or mobile phone.

Big issues for big sites

This book focuses on the needs of people who create a single Web page or a small Web site, and who do so on their own. Larger sites, or sites that need to be put up quickly or changed rapidly, need to have additional people working on them.

If you want to create a larger site down the road, start thinking now about what resources may be available to put into it. How many people in your company or other organization work on advertising, public relations, and marketing? How many people question whether those jobs are real work? (Just kidding — the author is a marketer, among other things!)

You may reasonably expect your company to re-target some of its advertising, marketing, and PR resources to support a presence on the Web. And what about sales? Some portion of your company's sales effort is likely to be or become Web-based, necessitating a suitable up-front commitment to bring returns down the road.

Or your company may already suffer from Web burnout. Classic symptoms of Web burnout include massive early investment to create a beautiful site, months of failure to update or maintain the site, followed by finger-pointing about who wasted all that money. Usually the problem is that no one set goals for the site, so no one managed the site's design and construction with those specific goals in mind. Companies often designate too few financial and human resources for maintenance and improvement of the site. If this scenario has happened in your company, you know the problems that result, so be sure to establish clear goals for your own Web efforts.

The most important element in adopting any new technology for business is a successful pilot project. As someone creating a smallish Web site, you're developing important skills and knowledge about the all-important convergence of your business's needs with the Web's opportunities. Set specific goals, strive to meet them, and record both your problems and your successes. By doing so, you position yourself to justify further investment of resources as the Web grows in importance for your company.

With the latest versions of HTML, controlling more aspects of your Web page's appearance is possible. Advanced sites, such as amazon.com, use many different aspects of HTML, as well as programming languages such as JavaScript, to create dense, rich layouts more like a magazine than a typical Web page. However, some aspects of the newest versions of HTML are not yet standard across different Web browsers. In this book, I stick with HTML 4.0, which works the same way for nearly all Web users.

Keep your design simple and don't spend too much time on it initially. A simpler design is more likely to work for everyone — and be easier to update as well. Then improve the design as you find out more about Web publishing and more about how people use your page.

Put the good stuff first

Imagine the Web as a giant magazine rack and the person surfing the Web as someone scanning the front covers of all those magazines. People who see your Web page decide whether to stay at your site — or go elsewhere — based largely on what they see when your page first comes up.

If your purpose is to provide information or links, put that information first. For example, to create a site that provides information about a company, make getting contact information — your company name, address, phone number, and fax number — very easy. To create a personal site that is attractive to potential employers, make clear what employment field you're in right at the top of your Web page and make your résumé easy to access.

If your purpose is to draw people into your site to entertain them, educate them, or expose them to messages from advertisers — or to do all of these things at once — then the first part of the page should make a strong impression and invite the user to go further into your site. Figure 1-5 shows the Fabrik home page, certainly one that catches your attention, located at the following URL: www.fabrik.com.

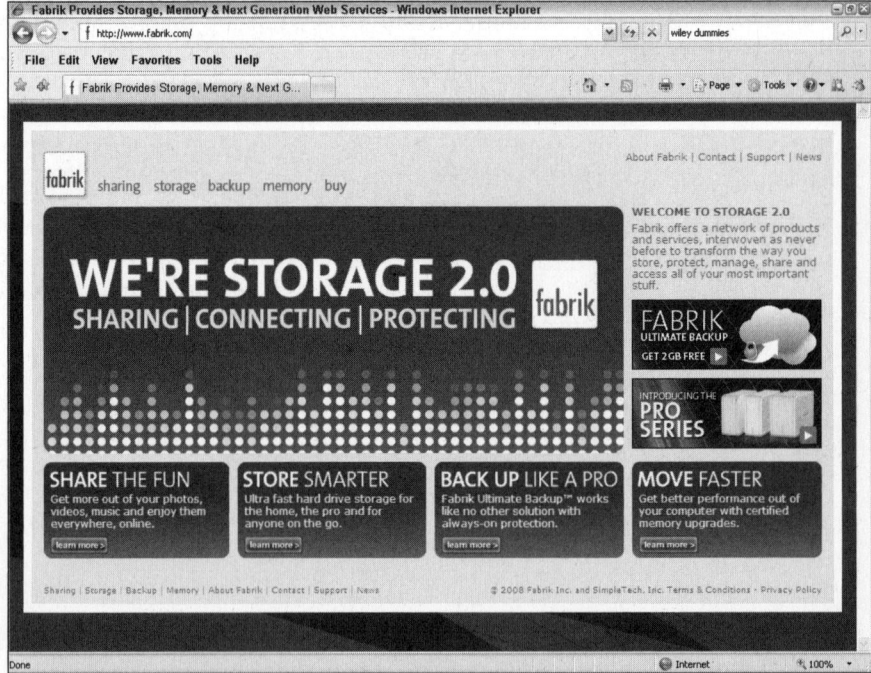

Figure 1-5: Fabrik connects Web users to fast storage.

But, like the Fabrik Web page, your home page also should help people who seek a quick "hit" of information; they're more likely to come back later if you don't waste their time during their first visit.

Think twice about download times

Putting lots of graphics in your pages is time-intensive for you because creating or finding good graphics and placing them appropriately in your Web page can take a great deal of time and effort. Graphics are also time-intensive for those who surf your site because they can take a long time to download.

Many people are ignoring this concern these days because they (and many of their users) are on broadband, so even large images load quickly. There are three problems with making this assumption:

- ✔ Much broadband service has inconsistencies and hiccups that slow speeds at particular times, making that large file download crawl.

- ✔ Even a "fast" download can never be fast enough. A 3-second wait is still annoying, and unnecessarily so if trimming the image size could have taken the wait entirely away.

- ✔ There are still some dialup users out there, and a graphic, say, 1 MB in size, can take several minutes to download on a dialup connection. If you impose this wait, you can unknowingly drive some of your users nuts and put them off your site entirely.

So plan to use *spot graphics* (small images that download quickly) at first. Think twice before creating large clickable image maps or attractive opening graphics like those you find on the sites of large companies, such as General Motors or Apple. If you do use an opening graphic, keep the file size under 20 K or so. See Chapters 2 and 5 for details on the efficient use of graphics, whether they're design elements on your site or stored photos on Flickr.

There has been a good deal of coverage in the computer press, and even in mainstream newspapers and news magazines, about ongoing efforts to make faster access available to ordinary users. But for all the talk about cable modems, Digital Subscriber Line (DSL), and other up-to-date techniques, nearly half of home users in the United States are still on 56 Kbps or slower modems — with even more dialup users in most other countries. (Business users are typically on faster connections.) So ignore the hype — the speed at which the average person accesses the Web is still moving upward gradually, not leaping ahead. For now, be conservative in how much data you put in each page, and test the download times of your pages over a modem-based connection before you publish them.

Know your audience

According to Web researchers, Web users overwhelmingly speak English as either a first or second language. Consequently, the great majority of Web content, Web creation tools, and Web browsers use the English language. More than fifteen years after the birth of the Web — which happened in Switzerland, where there are three official languages, none of them English — the English-speaking world is still considered the "center of gravity" for Web access. This situation will gradually change as other countries catch up to Web penetration in the United States.

Why are people online? Surveys indicate that the top reasons people use the Web are for information-gathering, entertainment, education, work, "time-wasting," and shopping. Which of these purposes do you intend for your site to serve? How do you appeal to people who are online? How do you help them find you? The answers to these questions can help you enhance the appeal and usefulness of your site.

Finally, what kind of browsers are your users running? Surveys indicate that over 90 percent of Web users run Microsoft Internet Explorer; most of the rest use Mozilla Firefox. Both of these browsers (and most others that make up the remaining user base) support graphics, tables, and Cascading Style Sheets — an advanced layout feature. Nearly all users run their browsers with graphics turned on (which doesn't mean that they appreciate waiting for complex images to load — unless those images are *very* cool!).

A still-small-but-increasing percentage of Web access is via "sub-PC" devices such as advanced cellphones. That means relatively tiny screens and slow (and expensive) connections. For more on this kind of Internet use, see *Mobile Internet For Dummies* by Michael O'Farrell, et al, 2008.

Use "text bites"

As mentioned earlier in this chapter, when preparing a Web site, less is more. Saying something with less text makes users more likely to read and remember it. A *text bite* is like a sound bite — it's a short, clearly written piece of text that makes a single point.

Text bites are especially important on the Web because reading from a computer screen is physically less comfortable than reading from a printed page. People tend to end their Web sessions after too much reading. You need to shoehorn your messages into the limited amount of reading time people will devote to your Web site.

Although you can overuse text bites, they're very important in Web-page design. Text bites help you convey as much information as possible in the limited amount of time users spend looking at each Web page. And they help you balance the basic elements of Web page design: text, links, and graphics.

If you want to put long documents on the Web, consider rewriting them as a series of text bites. If rewriting them is too much work to be practical, at least create short, punchy text for navigation and for introductory paragraphs to the long documents. Within a long document, add headers to break up the flow of text and provide pointers on your Web site to key areas within the document. Without such guidance, users may well give up in frustration without reaching the information they're looking for.

Look at sites you like

Look at sites you like and at sites whose purposes are similar to your own. What's good about them? What's not? Imitate successful elements — without copying, which would be a violation of ethics as well as copyright laws — and avoid unsuccessful models. As the development of your site progresses, keep checking it against the sites you previously identified and widen your search to get additional ideas — what not to do as well as what to do.

Few original ideas exist on the Web, so it's no big deal if your initial site contains one or two new ideas at best. The rest of your site may echo things readers have already seen, and you're still better off if your site brings to mind other good sites, rather than bad ones. (But be careful: If you start yelling "Bad site! Bad site!" at your computer screen and swatting it with a rolled-up newspaper, you may not have a working Internet connection much longer.)

Plan for ongoing improvements

As you plan and implement your initial Web page, you will, no doubt, find yourself creating a "To Do" list of things that you can't fit into the original site but want to add later, when time allows. (Creating this list for later use is great protection against trying to create a supersite right off the bat, getting stuck in the creation process, and never getting to a point where you can actually publish your first Web page.) This list is the start of a plan for ongoing improvements.

Some things you put in a Web site need to be kept current. For example, if your business Web page shows your company's quarterly results, be ready to update it quickly when the next quarter's results come out. If it lists company officers, update it as soon as a change takes place. (Unless you're one of the people changed — and then it's your successor's problem!)

Web-site information that is obviously out of date is one of the quickest ways to leave a bad impression of you or your organization or company; it steers visitors right away from your Web site. For business, an out-of-date site can cost you customers.

Not only do you want to update the Web site, but you also want to avoid using "Under Construction" signs and otherwise apologizing for things that aren't there yet. *Everything* on the Web is under construction, which is half the fun of using the Web and creating pages for it in the first place. You get only one chance to make a first impression, and an "Under Construction" sign doesn't count in your favor.

Decide how you define success

Before you design and create your Web page, define what you believe can make it a success. For an initial effort, simply putting up something on the Web that clearly conveys basic information is probably enough. You may just need an online reference point for people who need to get in touch with you by phone or by mail, or want to know a bit more about you or your business.

For follow-up work, get more specific. Are you trying to reach a certain number of people or a certain type of people? Will measuring *page views* — the number of times that people look at one page from your site — be enough, or do you need some other measure of response, such as having site visitors send e-mail or call an 800 number? Do you want to create a cutting-edge site full of bell-and-whistle features like fancy graphics and animation — and if so, are you willing to invest the time and money to make this site happen? Talk to people who do advertising and marketing in the real world, as well as to people who work on the Web; get a sense of what goals they set and how they measure success in meeting their goals.

Chapter 2

Designing Your Online Look

. . . .

. . . .

There are two approaches to a new project — jump in and get your hands dirty, or plan what you're doing first. These could be called the Picard and Riker strategies after the lead characters in the *Star Trek: The Next Generation* TV show and movies.

Captain Picard, famously bald and thoughtful, always seemed to be planning interstellar strategy, even when in the grips of the Borg or other evildoers. Commander Riker, famously hirsute and energetic, was always anxious to lead an "away team" into battle, blasting away more than once right on board the U.S.S. *Enterprise*.

So it is in creating a Web page. If you want to have a clear idea of what you're trying to accomplish before you start, read this chapter first. If you want to get something done right off the bat, then go to Chapter 3, or one of the media-specific chapters in Part II, and get something — anything — up on the Web. Then come back here for a brief refresher on the bigger picture.

You Got the Look

One of the trickiest issues in creating and publishing Web pages is creating and maintaining the overall look of each Web page. Some pages look great. Others look okay. Still others look hokey and amateurish. And how good a page looks varies considerably depending on who's looking — after all, "beauty is in the eye of the beholder." Up to a point, anyway; some pages are so bad, or so good, that everyone agrees on them.

How Web 2.0 simplifies — and limits — design

Web page design is advancing with Web 2.0, which is defined well by Wikipedia: "a trend in the use of World Wide Web technology and Web design that aims to facilitate creativity, information sharing, and, most notably, collaboration among users." (From en.wikipedia.org/wiki/Web_2.)

Web 2.0 designs actually make Web pages simpler by taking away some power from the user — you can't make a very useful blog in YouTube, for instance. And people who spend a lot of time on one type of social networking or e-commerce site — say, Facebook or eBay — tend not to give their blogs as much time and focus to most other bloggers.

In Web 1.0 — what you're doing when you create your own independent Web page — all the power, and all the responsibility, is in your hands. As mentioned before, a standalone Web page of your own is great for supporting and tying together your presence on various social networking and e-commerce sites, serving as a broadly accessible connecting point across different online communities.

You can create a first, "try it" Web page without worrying too much how it looks. But if you're creating a Web page a lot of people will be looking at, or if you're practicing to create a Web page for business or career use, you're going to want it to look good. And explaining how to make a Web page look good is hard.

The overall impression a Web page makes depends on many different factors — the balance of white space (empty space) to text and graphics, the size of text used, the font used, appropriate use of headings versus regular text, and appropriate use of bulleted and numbered lists, hyperlinks, and other eye-catching elements. Each of these factors has to be "right," but "right" is hard to define — you know it when you see it. All the choices you make have to work together as a whole.

It usually takes a professional to make a Web page look really good — so at the end of this chapter, I talk about how to get professional help for the look of your Web page. But it doesn't take a professional to make your Web page look pretty good — or at least to avoid having it be out-and-out ugly. I show you how to make sure your Web page looks at least reasonably good in this chapter.

Three Key Principles of Design

The design of a Web page can be most simply described as the look of the page and how it's perceived by the user — as attractive or unattractive, and as easy to use or difficult to use. Design is artistic and aesthetic; getting it right draws on people's creativity, and judging when it's right depends on people's individual taste. So there are no hard-and-fast rules that always yield a good-looking design. This fact drives some people crazy, but many of the most important things in life — like love, fine food, good wine, and good design — don't operate strictly by specific rules.

In years of work with the Web, I've learned many of the "tricks" of Web design. Instead of relying on the specific and formal rules that some professional Web designers follow, I find that following general principles usually yields good results for smallish Web design projects. Of course, it's good to begin with existing models that most people agree look good, but at carefully chosen times, it's also good to break the rules. The design process is a challenge to anyone's sanity, but mixing and matching is my favored way to consistently create designs that look good.

The design tips in this chapter are based on the author's experience in designing and using many Web sites, not on formal design principles. Furthermore, my advice is just for people doing single Web pages and small Web sites of 5 to 10 Web pages — not large sites that have to be planned carefully from the beginning. All this means that my advice may be infuriating to professionals — but is likely to be very helpful to people just starting out. For detailed information about Web page and Web site design, I recommend *Web Design For Dummies,* 2nd Edition by Lisa Lopuck (Wiley) or the industrial-strength *Building Web Sites All-in-One Desk Reference For Dummies* by Doug Sahlin and Claudia Snell (also from Wiley).

The three most important principles for designing Web home pages and small Web sites are simplicity, predictability, and consistency. It's necessary to follow each principle in order to also follow the others. In the next few sections are pointers showing how to apply these principles.

Achieving simplicity

Simplicity is considered the hallmark of good design. The modern eye is trained to look for and appreciate simple, unornamented designs. Use the simplest design that accomplishes your task, and then figure out how to simplify it further. For Web pages, simplicity means using as few of everything — design elements, graphics, and text sizes — as is reasonably possible.

Simplicity has specific advantages in Web design; in fact, the impact of download time constraints and the differences among users' computer setups make simplicity a necessity. The fact that it takes time to download each element on a Web page means that a simply designed Web page usually loads faster than a complicated one, and users really like fast-loading pages. (Actually, they hate *slow*-loading pages, but I'd rather describe the situation in a positive way.)

The differences among users' computer setups reward simplicity as well. One user can be looking at your Web page on a mobile phone screen; another on a small "sub-PC" screen with 256 colors; another can be looking at it on a large, high-resolution screen with thousands of colors. The simpler your Web page design, the more likely the page will look about the same on all the different computer setups out there.

To you as a novice Web-page author, simplicity is especially important. You don't have the hard-earned experience of having tried many things that didn't work. "Experience," it's been said, "is what you get when you don't get what you want."

Novices also lack the technical knowledge to always do things right, especially when they're trying something new and complicated. The simpler you keep your design, the more likely you are to not mess up.

Simplicity is most important in *content pages,* Web pages where the user is reading an article or looking at a picture. The user doesn't want to be distracted from what he or she is doing. Figures 2-1 and 2-2 show the first and second screenfuls of content for the table of contents of *Dreamweaver CS3 For Dummies* on the For Dummies Web site. Notice how both Web pages allow you to focus on the content.

Figure 2-1: The top of a For Dummies content page is simple, offering tools, navigation, and content.

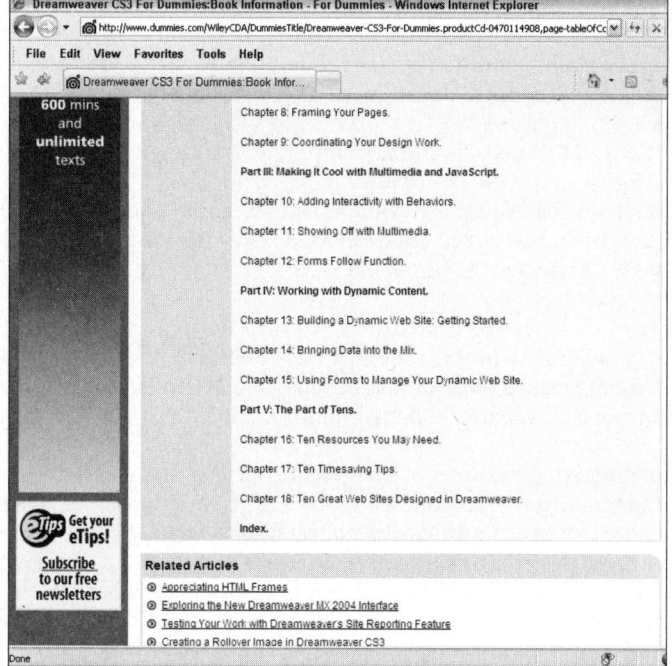

Related Articles
- Appreciating HTML Frames
- Exploring the New Dreamweaver MX 2004 Interface
- Testing Your Work with Dreamweaver's Site Reporting Feature
- Creating a Rollover Image in Dreamweaver CS3

Figure 2-2:
The body of a For Dummies content page is even simpler — just content, thanks.

Producing predictability

Predictability means the user can easily guess where things are on your Web page and how they work. In other words, one of your goals as you design your Web page is to achieve a sense of predictability for the content, layout, and functionality of your page when it's compared to other, similar Web pages.

An important reason that the Web is so popular is that Web pages nearly all look and work alike. Web pages that go too far from the norm tend not to be very popular with users.

Part of the reason this book is called *Creating Web Pages* and not *Creating Web Sites* is that it's focused on people just starting out, who are likely to want to create a single Web page first, and then perhaps expand that page into a small site. But another reason is that users really do experience the Web as a series of individual Web pages. Tests show that many users aren't even aware, when they click a link to a different site, that they've left one site and gone to a different one. People really do experience the Web one Web page at a time.

To understand the value of predictability, imagine what a Web page with a newspaper article on it should look like. The first thing to catch your eye may be a picture — almost always *one* picture, if any. You'd also expect to see the headline describing the article and the reporter's byline.

You would expect to see some navigation at the top of the screen or along the left side. You'd expect a banner ad across the top (but you'd be pleasantly surprised if there wasn't one). The rest of the left side would then be empty below the navigation area. The right side may be empty as well, or have some small ads.

On some sites you may see features, such as buttons for e-mailing and printing the article, somewhere on the first screen. And you may also see a box with headlines for related articles. Figure 2-3 shows a sketch of what the major elements in an article page might look like.

Now imagine if one or more of these features was present but was implemented much differently from what you'd find on other sites. For instance, imagine that the button for e-mailing the article was labeled "Transmit Content." You'd be frustrated and confused. The clever person who put an original label on the button hasn't impressed you — he or she has just made the page harder to understand and use.

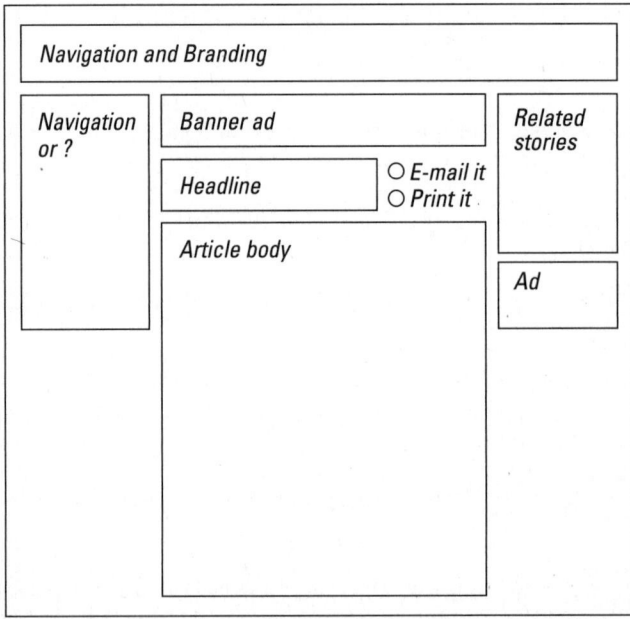

Figure 2-3:
Diagram
of a typical
article page.

That, in a nutshell, is what predictability is about. For any Web page you create, find a few examples of pages on the Web that accomplish something similar to what you're trying to do. See whether your page is similar in content, layout, and functionality. While you're at it, compare the simplicity of your design to the examples you've seen. If your page is different, consider modifying its design to reduce or eliminate the differences. That's predictability.

Creating consistency

Just as every Web page you create should be predictable when compared to the other pages out there on the Web (see the preceding section), each page should also be internally consistent. You shouldn't dramatically change fonts, text size, or layout style within a page.

If you create a multipage Web site (as described in Chapter 11, for use with a WYSIWYG tool, and in Chapter 15 for using HTML directly), all the pages in the site should be consistent with each other as well. Do all you can to help users understand that they're visiting a single, unified Web site.

If your Web pages are simple, and if they're predictable to experienced Web users, consistency becomes one of the easier principles to follow. Here are just a couple of ideas that can substantially improve the consistency of a small site:

✔ Use a repeated navigation block or graphic on each page in your Web site — always in the same position on each page.

✔ Use a consistent background color and foreground color, the same text size for body text, the same or similar image placements, and the same "voice" in the site's writing.

If you create a large Web site (over 20 pages or so), consistency becomes more difficult. The only foolproof way to maintain a consistent approach is to create a template for each of the different kinds of pages on your Web site: navigational pages, content pages (with and without images), forms pages, and so on. Every page in your site will be created from an existing template and then customized for the specific needs of that page. Most really large sites, such as Amazon.com, and most blogging sites automatically "populate" templates with content drawn from a database to create each specific Web page.

No matter what size your Web site is, the easiest way to achieve consistency is to print out every page on the site, then compare the printed pages to each other for consistency in style and approach. This exercise will almost always help you find inconsistencies in design and may expose errors in content as well.

Avoiding Common Design Errors

Simply cruise the Web — especially areas with lots of personal pages, such as the GeoCities site at www.geocities.com or AOL's Hometown area at hometown.aol.com — and you can find many examples of badly designed pages. But what is it that makes these pages bad? Of the many design mistakes you can make, three are common among new Web-page creators: slow-loading pages, ugly color combinations, and small text.

Slow-loading pages

This is the number-one bane of Web-page design, whether amateur or professional. People think they're designing a magazine and throw large, uncompressed graphics around, several per page. An uncompressed screen image of a page at 1024 x 768 resolution — the size used in the screen images in this book — is over 2 MB in size and takes about *8 minutes* to load on a dialup connection. Imagine the uselessness of trying to view that page on your cellphone with a slow Internet connection! The same file, lightly compressed using JPEG compression, is only about 200 KB, one-tenth the size.

Having used large (and perhaps uncompressed) graphics, these same people might add cute little design elements, each of which has to be sent as a separate file by the Web server. As each of the different elements appears on a page, if it's not carefully designed and implemented, the page's content may shift and shimmy in a manner guaranteed to cause motion sickness.

If a page of yours loads slowly, check to see whether you're committing one of two major errors:

- ✔ **A lack of care with one or two individual graphics.** By leaving these graphics files large, you doom the whole page to slow loading. Use the techniques described in Chapter 5 to make your graphics small in their physical size on-screen as well as in their file size.

- ✔ **A profligate use of graphics in general.** Highly designed pages can have lots of little graphical elements that cause many separate file transfers as the page loads. Unless the page is carefully designed, the page actually shifts visibly as each graphic comes in. The overall effect can be quite disconcerting.

Graphics not only can cause your page to load slowly — but they also take a long time to create, tend to have copyright problems and rights issues, and present challenging design and page-layout issues. Keep the use of graphics on your page simple until you get really good at designing with graphics, or until you can get help from someone who has that particular talent.

Ugly color combinations

Many Web page publishers don't much care if the color combinations they use are attractive or not. Others care, but can't critically appraise their own work and see whether the result is ugly and/or difficult to use.

You may understand that certain color combinations can be ugly, but maybe it seems odd for me to say that bad colors can lead to difficult-to-use pages. The reason is that on the Web, color identifies hyperlinks; unused links and recently used links have different colors. The standard colors for links are blue for unvisited links and purple for visited links. If you change these colors, or use the link colors for other purposes, your visitors have trouble identifying which text is links, which links they've visited, and which links they haven't. If you've read the section about creating predictability on your page, you can understand just how major a sin this is!

If you simply must change the link colors, try to use color combinations that are analogous to the standard ones — a lighter, eye-catching color for unvisited links, and a dull color for visited ones. This is at least similar, conceptually, to the standard colors. Then test the design on a few people and see whether they can quickly figure out which links are which.

Now, back to ugly. Just because the Web makes it possible to use various color combinations doesn't mean you should do so. Black text on a white or off-white background is what people are used to, and is always the safest choice. And with this combination, the standard link colors show up really well. You can use a graphical bar at some consistent location on the page and add in one or two useful or interesting graphics per page to give your Web pages a colorful, graphical look without sacrificing predictability and readability within the body of each page.

A few other color combinations work fairly well, but many don't. Remember also that some users run their monitors in 256-color mode and that only 216 colors out of the 256 — the *Web-safe* color palette — are the same on PCs and Macs. So a color combination that looks good on your system may look poor on a system with fewer colors; likewise, colors that look good on a PC may not look so hot on a Mac. Use the Web-safe colors described in Chapter 5 to choose, or cruise the Web looking for an existing Web page that uses a good-looking Web-safe color combination; you can use the same combination for your own site. (This isn't stealing — there are only a few such useful combinations, so the person you're borrowing from didn't exactly invent the electric blender either.)

Small text (and large text, too)

A common mistake people make is to use small text on their Web pages, packed closely together. Small text does look kind of cool, and it allows you to pack in a lot of information. Because of these temptations, even large Web sites (such as early versions of the Microsoft site) have made this mistake. The trouble is that small text becomes *very small text* when viewed on a high-resolution monitor. So small, in fact, that many of the people who visit your Web site may not be able to read the text on your page easily.

It's easy to believe that you've packed in a lot of information when you use small text. But communication is not a one-way street. Written information gets communicated only if it's read. Users will often click rapidly away from dense screens full of text, so nothing gets communicated at all!

Less common, but equally harmful, is text that's too large. You don't need to design Web pages with text that's readable from 20 feet away. Really. (People with true vision problems can use special options in Windows and/or their browser to display text in extra-large size, so they have a way to read text that starts out normal size.) Large text looks awful, especially when viewed on a system with relatively low resolution (such as 800 x 600 pixels).

Both of these problems are made worse by the increasing tendency to embed much of a site's text in graphic images. This text always has a consistent look, because it's treated by the browser as a graphic image, but that look can easily be too small or large. When you save text as image files, the text can't be resized by the browser to accommodate different browser settings. So users can't fix any problems they're having with graphically displayed text.

So what's "normal-size" text? Glad you asked. There's not one exact normal size, but there's a normal range. To find it, match the text size in your Web page to the text size in a few Web pages you like. The current Microsoft page is a good example; though it still uses some small text, and some graphical text, it uses "white" space (that is, empty space) to make it all more readable. See Figure 2-4 for an example.

Once you've compared your site's text size to other sites', ask several people — not all younger and hawk-eyed, nor all older or less visually acute — to tell you if they can easily read the text while sitting comfortably a couple of feet from the computer monitor. If not, fix the problem before it becomes a burden for your Web site's visitors.

Safely Breaking the Rules

A lot of the fun in creating your own Web page is doing what you want to do and not what someone else tells you. Yet you want your Web page to look good. How can you create a design that you like and that also looks good to other people?

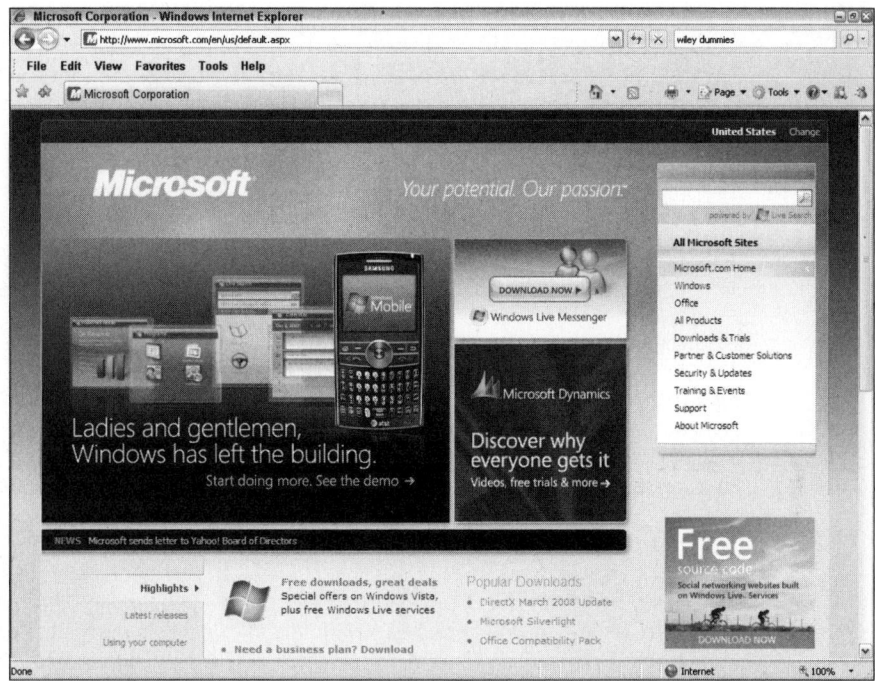

Figure 2-4:
Microsoft is getting religion on text size.

I suggest you follow this five-step process:

1. **Get your Web page up.**

   Include the content and images you want, as I describe throughout this book. Don't worry much about how it looks at first. Just do it!

2. **Find a model page or two that you like.**

   Look for pages that have a similar purpose and content. Make sure that they have a simple, attractive appearance. See the sidebar, "Finding great home pages," for places to look.

3. **Create a new, reduced version of your Web page, using these models as your guide.**

   Get the major pieces — the main text, an image or two, and a list — in place first. Make this basic page look good.

4. **Put additional elements back in, one at a time.**

   By working in this piecemeal fashion, you can prevent your page from becoming a hard-to-fix mess, while still indulging your own creativity.

Finding great home pages

Here are several places you can look to see how others have designed their home pages on the Web:

✔ **GeoCities:** GeoCities is the top provider of home pages for the Web. From the GeoCities home page at `www.geocities.com`, you can access GeoCities Web pages in many different categories. However, there's no "best" or "highly rated" list to help you find the best Web pages. You're going to have to look at a lot of ugly ducklings before you find a swan. And if you're looking for unusual as well as excellent designs, you'll see a lot of white (ordinary) swans before you find a black (unusual) one.

✔ **Tripod:** Tripod is a free Web-hosting company acquired by Lycos, a leading international Web portal. Visit Tripod at `www.tripod.com`. To see cool Lycos Web pages, look in the Member Spotlight area in the Member sites area. The Home and Family area is particularly relevant for personal home pages.

✔ **AngelFire:** AngelFire is the other free Web-hosting company acquired by Lycos.

You can find its home page at `www.angelfire.com`. Click in the Top Member Pages area on the left side of the home page to find links to top sites.

✔ **Hometown:** Hometown is the name of AOL's free Web-page hosting site (see Chapter 4). You can use Hometown even if you're not an AOL member (although only members can use all of the AOL discussion areas and online help that make Hometown a real winner). The Hometown home page at `www.hometown.aol.com` has a list of the most popular categories, but you have to search all the home pages in a category to find the best ones.

✔ **Homestead:** Homestead no longer offers free personal home pages — only business pages, and you have to pay for it. But it offers a lot of support, has some great Web pages, and prominently features some of its customers' better work. Go to `www.homestead.com` and look for customers' sites.

5. **Publish the result and get comments.**

   Let some friends and colleagues see your newly published page, and ask them what they think. Let the site sit for a couple of days, and then take a fresh look at it yourself. Use your own fresh perspective and the comments you get to improve your page further.

You can repeat this process again and again as you improve your Web page and add new pages to create a full Web site. Work through these steps conscientiously, and you may end up with some of the best-looking Web pages around.

Getting design help from the pros

The best way to work with a Web-graphic designer, while keeping your costs under control, is to create your Web site yourself first. Then bring in the designer just to improve the look of the site. Improving the look of your site may take the designer as much as a couple of days and cost you a few hundred dollars — money well spent, if your Web site is going to be part of your career or your business.

The problem is that many of the designers you might talk to will be accustomed to doing the whole job of brainstorming your needs with you, creating content, revising it all to meet your needs, publishing the site, and then modifying it for you. This kind of project could cost you thousands of dollars — which you're going to avoid spending by doing nearly everything yourself for free, by using the information in this book. The one part where you may need help is in getting the look right, so do all the other steps yourself and then bring someone in just for the graphic-design piece.

Organizing Your Page with Tables and Frames

Tables are a layout tool for data tables on Web pages, such as a table in an article or textbook showing the revenues of a company's different divisions each quarter. But the tables capability for Web pages has long been used (misused?) to control the layout of the entire page.

Designers have found that they can make the cells of a table very large, and put large graphics or whole blocks of text in them. You can even resize tables automatically to accommodate various sizes of Web-browser windows — at least up to a point. (I only touch on this advanced use of tables in this section.)

Whether and how to use tables was, for a long time, one of the most controversial topics in Web-page design (not exactly an area where controversies have earth-shattering consequences, but we all need some excitement in our lives).

Frames are more powerful layout devices than tables, but they have fallen into disfavor. They allow separate parts of the Web-browser window to be updated and scrolled separately. However, they produce odd effects; users seem to prefer one unified window to separate "panes" within a window. So I barely mention frames in this book.

Creating simple tables

When used as intended, tables have rows and columns. For each spot where a row and column intersect, you have a table cell. Each cell can have its own formatting — the data in it can be aligned left, center, or right, formatted, and so on. Tables also have header-data cells, in which you put the column headings. Here's the HTML code for a simple table of this type:

```
<TABLE BORDER=2>
<TR><TH><B>Production
         (tons)</B></TH><TH><B>% of goal</B></TH></TR>
<TR><TD><I>>North 40</I></TD><TD>87</TD><TD>102%</TD></TR>
<TR><TD><I>South 40</I></TD><TD>93</TD><TD>110%</TD></TR>
</TABLE>
```

Figure 2-5 shows how this simple table looks in HTML and when viewed in Internet Explorer.

Here's what each part of the HTML code does:

<TABLE BORDER=2>   The TABLE tag begins and ends the table. The BORDER attribute creates a 2-pixel-wide border around the table. Don't forget to include a border, so other text and graphics in your Web page don't crowd too close to the table.

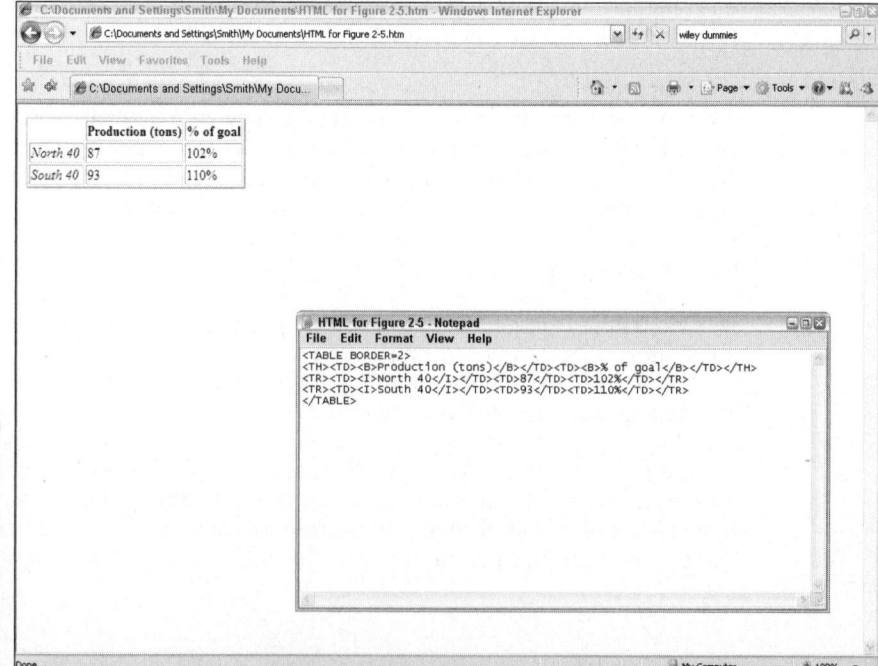

Figure 2-5:
A simple
Web table
and its
simple
HTML
source.

`<TR>`, `</TR>`   Begins and ends the table row.

`<TH>`, `</TH>`   Surrounds table header data. Table header data is automatically formatted as bold and centered.

`<TD>`, `</TD>`   Begins and ends the table data item.

So creating a table in HTML is fairly simple but also fairly tedious. You just create the rows and data items; if you get the data items right, the columns take care of themselves.

Getting the data items right can be a problem, though. To make your table look just right, you have to use a number of alignment and formatting options. Making mistakes becomes way too easy, and updating the table's appearance becomes very hard. That's why so many people use an HTML editor like CoffeeCup to create and manage tables — and then, in some cases, do final tweaking in HTML to get them just right.

Layout with tables

When tables were added to HTML, Web designers quickly figured out how to take them to a whole other level. Imagine making a Web page one big table. Using HTML options, you can suppress the display of the table's cell borders. You can thus create a large grid with invisible separation lines into which you insert chunks of text and graphics. This allows you to create a layout with rows and columns. You can also use tables in this fashion to make sure that a specific block of text stays next to a specific graphic, even if the user makes his Web text large or makes the window extra narrow.

Believe it or not, this whole use-tables-for-layouts thing was a bit controversial at first. Why? Because there were some idealistic motives behind the original design of HTML, such as ensuring that Web pages appear correctly on just about any screen. Table-based layouts, by contrast, only work well on screens of at least a certain minimum size, such as a PC screen rather than, say, a mobile-phone screen.

The controversy largely faded because the people who pay for Web-site development demand that their sites look good on most of the PCs and Macs out there, and tables were for a long time just about the only way to create a complex design that looks good.

For the purposes of designing your own Web page, the key word here is "complex." There are so many different elements that you have to adjust in table-based page design that you need to invest a lot of time and energy to learn how to use tables effectively for layout purposes. And then a whole other set of issues arises about making sure your table-based page design works well on most or all current computer systems and Web-browser setups that are in use.

Figure 2-6 shows an interior page of BATCS. The tool I use to create BATCS uses tables to create a simple, clean layout. Each major horizontal element is a separate table — the navigation is one table, the first area of the content another. Use the View⇨Source or similar command in your Web browser to view the underlying HTML source for this page to see how it's done.

To create your own tables, you can get started by using the Insert⇨Table command in CoffeeCup. However, you really need a more advanced tool to work effectively with tables in your Web pages — something like Microsoft FrontPage or Dreamweaver, both of which give you more direct control over specific options. Of course, your other option is to start doing *a lot* of experimenting in HTML until you learn how to get things just how you want them.

For details on how to use tables for layout, start with this article: www.anownsite.com/web-design/html-tables.html.

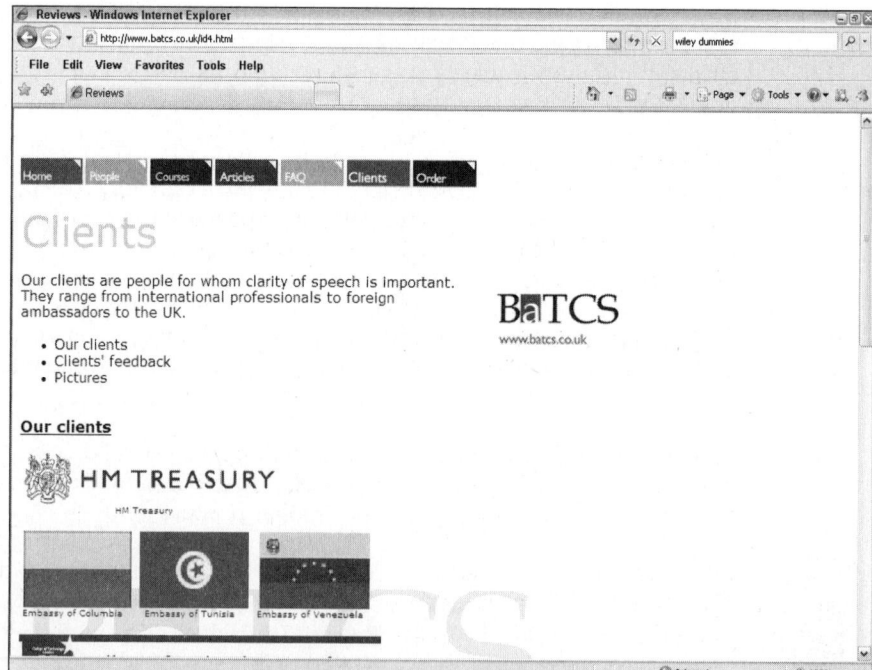

Figure 2-6:
The tool used for the BATCS site uses tables to organize content.

Friends don't let friends do frames

Frames divide a Web page into separate areas which you can then update individually as needed. For example, you can click a link in a frame in the bottom half of a Web page and update it with new content while the other frame stays unchanged. This seems like a powerful capability. However, frames have proven to be less popular than tables.

Why are frames not as popular as tables? Well, frames are hard to create and manage, just like tables. But advanced Web authors are willing to do just about anything to make their Web pages more attractive and more useful, and tables help them do so. With frames, the trouble comes with the "useful" part; users have a hard time using framed Web pages.

For example, when browsing a framed page, users sometimes have difficulty finding where the cursor is. If the user moves the scroll bar, which frame scrolls? Also, going forward and backward in a frame is different from going forward and backward in the overall Web page, so users may get lost easily. And printing a framed page properly requires extra steps — users often try to print the page and end up printing the contents of just one frame instead.

Finally, frames create a functional problem or two. When users resize a browser window, framed pages don't always resize correctly. And designing a framed page to work well for various monitor sizes is even harder than correctly designing pages with tables embedded in them.

Usability tests have shown that users are confused by frames. Some highly controlled framed sites (for instance, those with only one scrollable window) give fairly good results. However, the main purpose of frames on such sites is to allow complex navigation, advertisements, or both to stay in the user's view at all times. Unless you need to offer complicated navigational options that your users can't live without, or unless you have advertisers for your site who demand frames and whose dollars you can't live without, I recommend you avoid frames while creating your initial Web pages or simple Web site.

Still, framed pages can be useful to show complex sets of data and to support navigation. Because creating and managing the HTML for frames is even harder than for tables, I don't describe that process here.

Use an advanced Web-page tool such as CoffeeCup, Microsoft FrontPage, or Macromedia Dreamweaver if you want to use frames in your pages. (Or look up the appropriate HTML tags in Appendix B and start experimenting!)

Chapter 3

A Fast and Easy Page with Google Page Creator

Google has long seemed like the wildest and craziest multibillion-dollar business going. Google was started by two Stanford graduate students, and it grew to hundreds of employees and millions of users before anyone even thought of how it might make money.

Yet Google is now a wildly successful business. Google dominates today's Web, commanding roughly half of all search traffic — and billions of dollars in profits from advertising.

As part of its "ready, fire, aim" approach, Google launches new Web services frequently, usually with a "beta" tag on the new service's Web pages. *Beta* is a computer software term that means "not quite ready for wide release" — it's sort of like a rough draft of a product. Yet the Google mob does release its betas widely, allowing many millions of users to try, and test, a service before it's completed.

Google News, which uses software to make up a newspaper-like front page, was in beta for many months before Google removed the "beta" tag. Google Mail, known as Gmail, which has millions of users, is still in beta at this writing — years after it was first released.

However, the beta status is not experimental enough to accommodate all the great ideas at Google. So Google invented Google Labs, home for ideas that are *really* experimental; "still in an early testing phase", as Google puts it. Google Page Creator is a Google Labs product. (To use Google Page Creator, it's recommended that you sign up for a Google Mail account — "early testing phase" + beta = ?).

The fact that Google Page Creator is still a Google Labs product as this book goes to press — as it was for the previous edition two years ago — shouldn't worry you much. Google has brought many successful products out of the Labs, including Google Maps, Google Scholar (for searching academic journal articles), and Google News Alerts, all products that are widely used and that I've used myself.

All of these applications and many more are considered examples of *cloud computing,* in which purchased software packages are replaced by services offered online via Web sites, often for free. Just think, in using many of the tools described in this book, you're taking part in perhaps the hottest trend in computing!

Google Page Creator is a strategic offering from Google, as it competes with offerings from Microsoft, Yahoo! and others, so you should expect Google Page Creator to go on to ever greater things, whether it's released from Google Labs or not.

We can all join in hoping for a good result here, because Google Page Creator is a slick, easy-to-use service. And it has much room for growth and improvement, given Google's world-class capabilities in search, online commerce, blogging (Google owns Blogger — see Chapter 4), and other Web services.

Getting to Know the Creative Capabilities of Google Page Creator

Google Page Creator has capabilities that seem pretty amazing: You edit your Web page, live, within a Web page! New Web technologies such as AJAX (Asynchronous JavaScript And XML), which incorporates the capabilities of JavaScript and XML — a more advanced relative of HTML — allow Web pages to take on more and more of the aspects of a "real" computer program. (Watch out, Microsoft!)

Google Page Creator includes 100 MB of free storage, automatically saving as you work, and allows you to use HTML tags to directly modify the look of your page. (The overall layout of the page won't be changed, just the details of how the content looks within the page.)

Google Page Creator does have its downside, however. You can't move the site to its own URL, nor include a blog, a message board, or even any kind of form.

The biggest bogeyman of all is advertising. The beta version of Google Page Creator does not, at this point, insert ads into your page. But given that advertising is Google's business, and one it's very good at, you have to wonder whether — or perhaps just when — your page will suddenly have ads added to it. It may be that at some point in the future you'll have to pay to keep your Google Page Creator Web site ad-free.

If you still think Google Page Creator is for you, you should first register with Google, if you don't already have a Google account. You can also register using your mobile phone number, but it's actually easier to manage communications with Google using Gmail than via a mobile phone number that might change (a change which you may well forget to tell Google about).

What's in a Google Name?

Before you begin your Google Page Creator adventure, think a bit about what name you want to use. Your Google account name will be the user name of the e-mail address you use to sign up. (That is, the part of your e-mail address before the @ symbol.) This will also be the default name of your Google Page Creator Web site. If you've been thinking for years that it's funny to have an e-mail address such as redhotkisser@genericmail. com, perhaps you'll find it less funny for your Google Web page to be called redhotkisser.googlepages.com.

However, you can change the Web site name and create more than one Google Page Creator site from your Google account. If you want a unified online identity, though, you may want to create a new Google Mail account with the user name you want and have that be the distinctive part of the name of your Google Page Creator Web site as well. Many desirable Google Mail user names are already taken, so redhotkisser may no longer be available! You may need to be creative to come up with a name you like that's still available.

If you do want to use a Gmail account, it's probably best to set it up first, then follow the steps in the next section to register for your Google account. The Gmail account setup process is pretty simple. Begin by visiting www. gmail.com and follow the instructions, which are similar to those for registering for an account.

One of the first things you can do when creating a Google Mail account is to check the availability of various names. You must enter your first and last names first; you can then enter a suggested username and check its availability. See Figure 3-1 for an example.

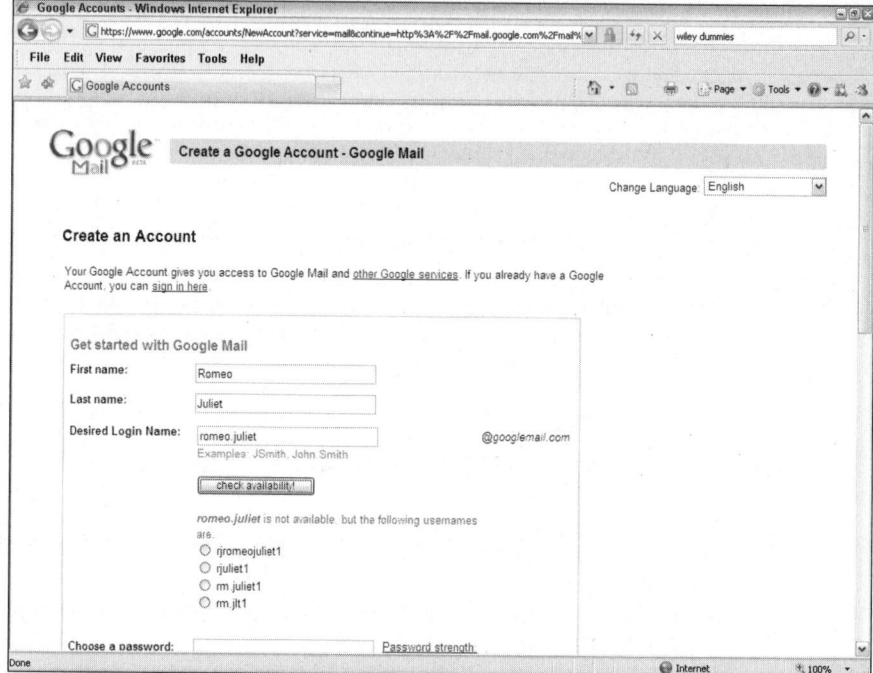

Figure 3-1: An e-mail address by any other name would not smell as sweet.

Gmail is a nice, catchy name for Google e-mail, but the real name, which Google is using and enforcing more and more, is "Google Mail" — possibly under the influence of its attorneys and marketing and branding people. When you create and use your new account, you will want to enter your e-mail address as, say, `iamsocool@gmail.com`. However, Gmail may in some cases actually send this as `iamsocool@google-mail.com`. This disparity can cause problems when, for instance, attempting to unsubscribe from some online services. So either always enter your e-mail address as `@google-mail.com` or be prepared for some possible difficulties.

Registering for a Google Account

To get a Google account, follow these steps. (The idea of Google having user accounts is pretty interesting — Google is beginning to look more like an old-fashioned online service such as AOL or EarthLink.)

1. Open your Web browser.

Google works with any browser and can be used from a mobile phone or other non-computer device. However, you'll need to use a PC ("proper computer," they might say in the U.K.) to create a Web page.

2. **Go to** www.google.com.

   The screen shown in Figure 3-2 appears, with some differences:

   - In most countries outside the U.S., you'll automatically be redirected to a national version of the Google home page, such as www.google.co.uk.

   - If you're already registered as a Google user, your username and additional options appear in the top line on the right.

   - There may be a promotion for a Google service, such as the Google toolbar, on the page. (The Google toolbar is great; it offers quick access to Google search and to features such as pop-up blocking. Try it!)

   - The Google logo is often changed to reflect national or international holidays or events. Find out more at www.google.com/holidaylogos.html.

3. **If you are currently signed in as a Google account holder, your username appears on the Google home. Skip the rest of the steps in this section. Otherwise, click the Sign In link.**

   When you click the Sign In link, the Google Accounts page appears.

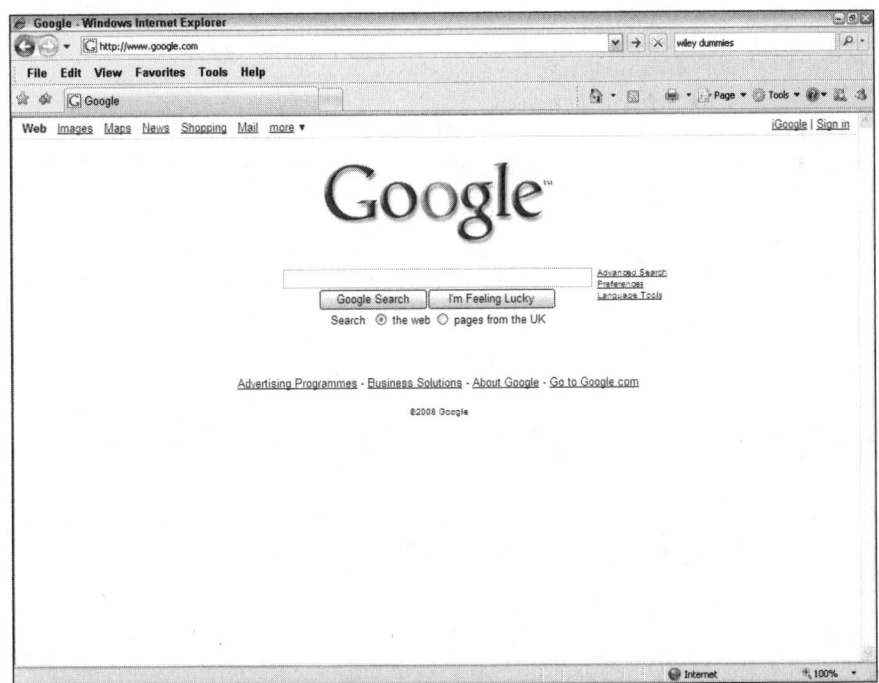

Figure 3-2:
The Google home page is gradually getting busier.

4. If you have a Google account, sign in and skip the rest of the steps in this section. Otherwise, click the link Create an Account Now.

The Create a Google Account page appears, as shown in Figure 3-3.

5. Enter a current e-mail account.

If you don't already have an e-mail account, you need to ask a friend with an e-mail account to work with you on getting signed up for the first time. Or, you can create a Gmail account, as described in the previous section. This doesn't need to be a long-term commitment. After you create your new Gmail account and use it to create your Google account, you can set the Gmail account to automatically forward all incoming Gmail to your existing account. That way you always get your mail from both sources without ever having to check the Gmail account itself.

6. Choose a password, and then re-enter it.

Enter a password for your Google account. The Password Strength meter automatically assesses your password to make sure it fits the rules. However, it will say "too short" until you press the Tab key or click in another area after entering your password. It will then display an assessment of the strength of your password. You can click the Password Strength link for guidance on how to make your password stronger.

Figure 3-3:
Your e-mail address will be part of your Web URL.

[Screenshot: Google Accounts - Windows Internet Explorer]

https://www.google.com/accounts/NewAccount?continue=http%3A%2F%2Fwww.google.co.uk%2F&hl=en | wiley dummies

File   Edit   View   Favorites   Tools   Help

Google Accounts | Page ▾ Tools ▾

Google Accounts   Create a Google Account

Create an Account

If you already have a Google Account, you can sign in here.

Required information for Google account

Your current email address:

e.g. myname@example.com. This will be used to sign-in to your account.

Choose a password: Password strength:

Minimum of 8 characters in length.

Re-enter password:

☑ Remember me on this computer.

Creating a Google Account will enable Web History. Web History is a feature that will provide you with a more personalized experience on Google that includes more relevant search results and recommendations. Learn More
☑ Enable Web History.

Location: United Kingdom

Word Verification: Type the characters you see in the picture below.

walbys

Done   Internet   100%

7. **Click the check box Remember Me on This Computer to automatically log in to your account when you visit Google.**

   You are given this option again in the future when you sign in, so you don't need to click the check box unless you're sure you want this enabled.

8. **Clear the check box Enable Web History if you don't wish to have Google keep a history of your Web searches and Web site visits.**

   Web History allows you to search only on Web sites you've previously visited and improves your search results gradually over time based on your past searches. These probably seem like good things, but there are a few reasons you may wish to avoid Web History:

   • Enabling Web History means Google is gathering data on your searches and Web use, which you may not want.

   • Enabling Web History means that you'll get different search results than other people do; if you're a writer or researcher, for instance, you may want uncustomized search results.

   Of course, if you do enable Web History, you can also get uncustomized results at any time by logging out of your Google account.

9. **Choose your country from the pull-down list.**

10. **Type the verification characters.**

    As with many other sign-ups, Google requests that you type in the characters in the verification graphic.

    If you are visually disabled and using a screen reader, select the image of a person in a wheelchair. The characters are read aloud for you to type in.

11. **Review the terms of service; click the Printable Version link to see an easy-to-read, easy-to-print version in a new window. For details, click the Privacy Policy link or the Terms of Service link.**

12. **Reply to the verification e-mail.**

    A verification e-mail is sent to the e-mail account you entered as part of this process. Retrieve the e-mail message and use the link to verify your account — either by clicking the link, if your e-mail program supports that, or by cutting and pasting the link into the address area of your Web browser.

    After you respond to the instructions in the e-mail, you've finished creating your account.

Private Google on duty

Google's privacy policy is detailed — there are additional, separate details provided for most of its separate services — and easy to understand. Here are some highlights:

- **Combining information:** Google combines information from your registrations for services, cookies, and your visits to Google Web sites.

- **Third parties at arm's length:** Only aggregated, non-personal information is provided to third parties.

- **A different kind of service:** If Google is served with a request for personal information as part of a legal process, they may comply with it.

- **See yourself:** Google commits to efforts to make your personal information available to you, and to allow you to correct or delete it.

- **Yes to opt-in:** In its detailed privacy policy, Google commits to requiring your opt-in consent for the sharing of any sensitive personal information; that means you have to explicitly click a check box before your information is shared.

Creating a Google Page

After you're registered, it's time to start creating your page. Google Page Creator gives you a lot of options; the following steps take you through some of the most important ones:

1. **Go to the Google Page Creator page at `pages.google.com`.**

   If you are not already signed in, the sign-in area appears in the upper-right corner of the page.

2. **If you are not already signed in, enter your password and click the Sign In button.**

   The Google Page Creator start page appears.

3. **Click the link labeled Create a new page.**

   You are asked for a title for your page. This title will be made part of your Web page's URL as follows (if you enter `newtitle` as the title): `newtitle.googlepages.com`.

4. **Enter a title, then click the Create and Edit button.**

   A new page appears, as shown in Figure 3-4. (Your page may look slightly different, but the overall layout of editable areas should be the same.)

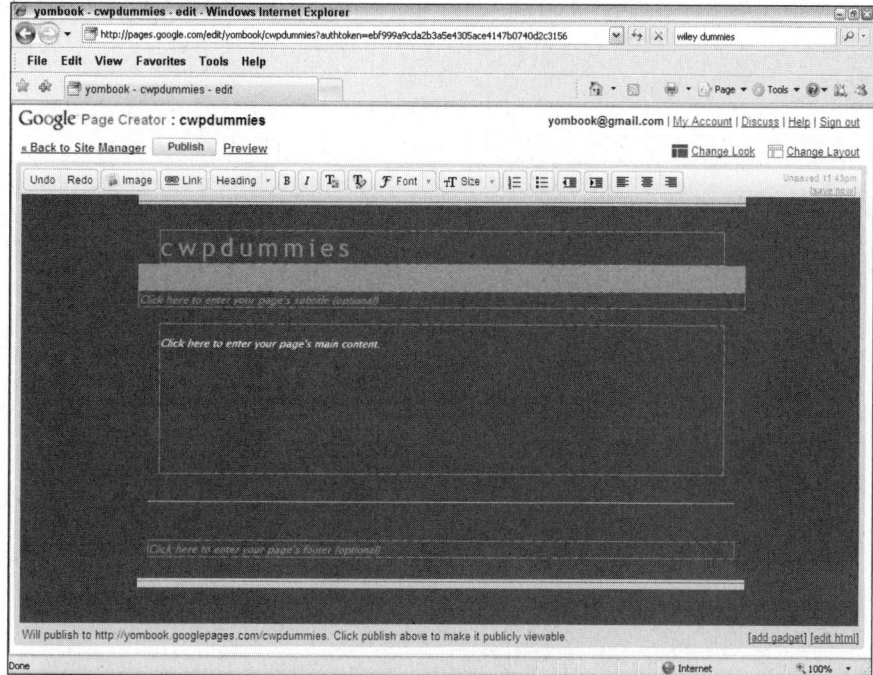

Figure 3-4:
Let there
be —
a blank
page.

5. **Try different layouts by clicking the Change Layout link.**

Although the Change Look button seems to come before it, it's actually better to choose the layout first. The layout underlies everything else, so choosing it early makes it less likely that you'll need to make big changes later.

6. **Click the layout you want.**

At this writing, there are only four layouts, as shown in Figure 3-5. The classic layout for a Web page is the second one, with a title across the top, a navigation area on the left, and a main content area.

When you select a layout, you are returned to the main Google Page Creator page, now sporting your new layout.

7. **Try different looks by clicking the Change Look link.**

Before you start entering content, take a stab at changing the look of the page. When you click the Change Look link, a collection of looks appears — more than 40 at this writing. But the "looks" are a bit generic — they don't necessarily reflect the details of your selected layout.

Google Page Creator - Choose Layout - Windows Internet Explorer

http://pages.google.com/changePageLayout/yombook/cwpdummies?authtoken=35e8354f36b694cbc79d994cff66f7157b7c1 | wiley dummies

File   Edit   View   Favorites   Tools   Help

Google Page Creator - Choose Layout

Page ▾ Tools ▾

Google Page Creator
Choose Layout
yombook@gmail.com | New Features! | Discuss | Help | Sign out

« Back to Page Editor - Select by clicking below.

« Back to Page Editor - Select by clicking above.

You are currently using 0MB (0%) of your 100MB.

Google Labs - Give Us Feedback - Terms of Use - Privacy Policy

© 2008 Google

Done   Internet   100%

Figure 3-5:
Carefully
select the
layout you
want.

8. Try different looks by clicking Preview under each look.

Preview brings up a new window with a sample page, using the
previewed look.

Choose the look carefully; although you can change it later, the look
affects all the other choices you make as you design the page. If
you change it later, you may find yourself wanting to change everything
else on the page as well.

9. Select the look you want.

Choose Select; you'll return to the main Google Page Creator page, with
your page shown in the new look.

10. Edit the page title.

The initial page title is your e-mail address plus the words Home Page.
You'll look like a real amateur if you leave it unchanged, so click the title
and change it.

**11. Highlight the new page title. Try as many formatting options as
possible — bold, italic, header sizes, and more.**

Use every formatting option you can on the title to get a feel for them:

- Bold (the *b* button), italic (*i*).

- Font (*F*) and size (*tT*).

- Left, center, and right alignment.

- Header sizes versus normal text (*A* in different sizes and formats).

12. **Enter new content.**

    Enter your chosen content. Possible topics include

    - Information about your friends and family

    - A description of your work

    - Favorite places on the Web, with links

    Use the formatting options to arrange your content. Be sure to provide plenty of headers to break up long blocks of text; Web visitors tend to scan, rather than read, and headers help make that easy.

13. **Publish your page.**

    Click the Publish button. Your page appears at the URL `e-mail name.googlepages.com`. Click the View It on the Web link to see it. An example is shown in Figure 3-6.

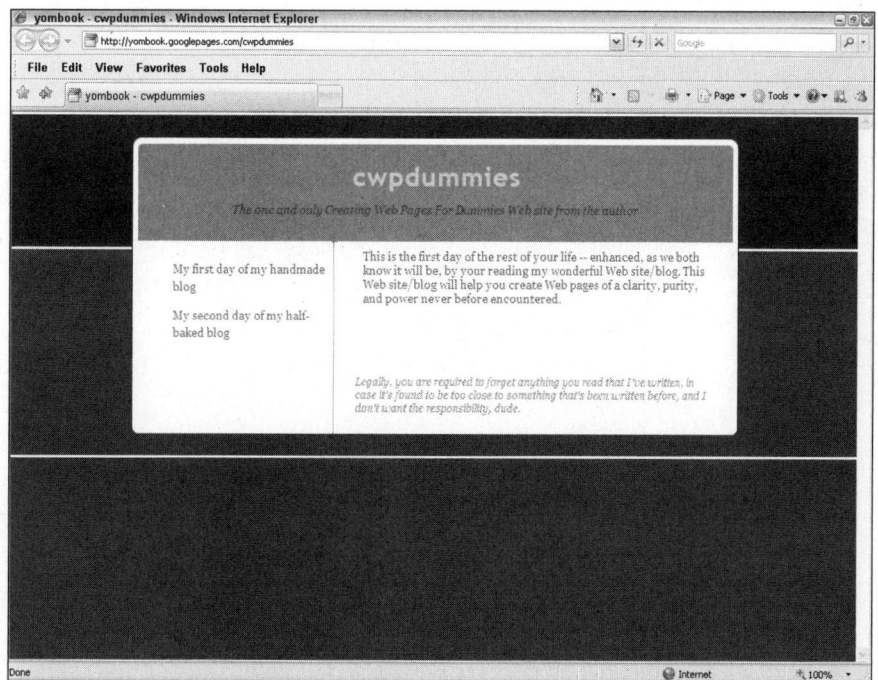

Figure 3-6:
You're a real Google publisher.

Part II
Getting the Content Right

The 5th Wave   By Rich Tennant

"Can someone please tell me how long 'Larry's Lunch Truck' has had his own page on the intranet?"

In this part . . .

Use single-purpose tools to log your journey to stardom and to help your page flicker to life — or to sound off about anything you're interested in. Specialized sites support all these endeavors. Move your entire existence to the Web!

Chapter 4

Words and Blogs

*W*riting for the Web isn't a long-lost art — the Web hasn't been around long enough. It's more an art that hasn't yet been found. With the Web so new, the best way to write for it is still evolving.

Web sites are made up, first and foremost, of words. After all, HTML, the core standard that makes up the Web, stands for HyperText Markup Language. If "hypertext" sounds like words — "text" — on steroids, that's just what it is.

In this chapter, I describe some approaches for effective writing online to make the most of your site visitor's time and attention. I also describe ways to use text you may already have and ways to work *with* the expectations that your Web site visitors have for your site, rather than against them.

Then I introduce the tool that's being used to host huge outpourings of words onto the Web every day — the famous (or infamous) blog. A wonderful thing in itself, and a sort of lab experiment for better understanding the use of words on the Web.

A *blog* — the name is short for *Web log* — is an online journal of a person's thoughts, experiences, and interests. Kept up to date, a blog can help visitors move with the writer through space — well, Web space, anyway — and time.

In a sense, any site can be used as a blog. Just create a new page on your site and write your thoughts for the day. Include links to any site that you visited and want to share with others. Be sure to link to any blog that you find interesting.

Then, a day or two later, add another chunk of text — put the new content on top, pushing your previous work down the page a bit. In your new content, refer to your earlier posting wherever necessary — and, of course, refer to other Web sites and blogs you visit.

But using an actual blogging tool makes this very easy, allowing you — and forcing you — to focus on the content. That blank blogging entry screen can be as terrifying as any blank sheet of paper has been to a non-computer-assisted writer!

Over time, your burgeoning blog may develop into an appealing take on your life and interests — or preoccupations — or even obsessions. You may find that your blog expands so you need to split it up among multiple pages and change your links to fit. Your blog may even get linked to by other *bloggers* (people who keep blogs) and begin to develop a following of its own.

Getting It Write for the Web

Every new medium develops its own style. Magazine articles are often wordy and literary in style. Newspaper articles are usually brief, to the point, and written in a "pyramid" style that puts the most important information first. The Web has its own style. Learning to use it can make your Web page much more interesting and effective.

Web realities

The new style of writing found online is based on four underlying realities about the Web:

- ✔ **The capabilities of HTML:** HTML allows you to specify some simple text formatting, headings, and lists. Newer versions of HTML also allow you to specify fonts and specific text sizes, but these may be displayed differently on different computers, and a user can override these specifications.

  What it means for you: Don't count on complicated formatting and specific layout to get your message across. Keep it simple.

- ✔ **The difficulty of reading from a computer screen:** A computer screen has much lower resolution than a printed page — about 100 dpi (dots per inch), versus anywhere from 300 dpi on up for print. And the computer screen glows, while printed pages use reflected light only. So reading from the screen is harder, and people's eyes get tired when they try to read long blocks of text on-screen. (They often don't consciously note this as they would, say, tired legs from walking a long way; they just stop reading.) Figure 4-1 shows how far on-screen letters are from the smooth lines of printed text.

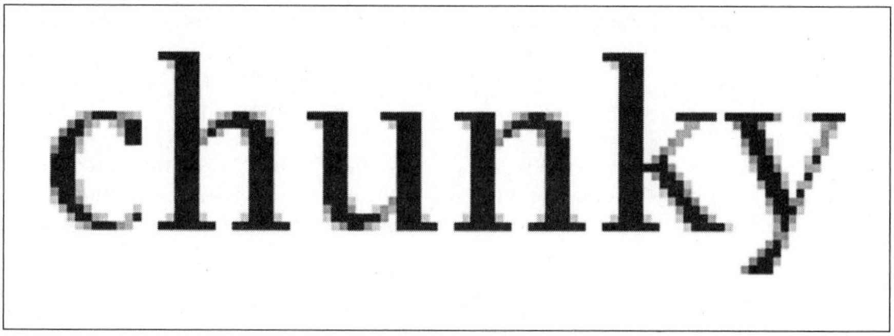

Figure 4-1:
Zooming in
shows how
"chunky"
on-screen
letters are.

chunky

What it means for you: Shy away from long blocks of text. People skim rather than read online, so you are unlikely to have your site visitor's attention for long. Write small chunks of text, then break up what you write using headers, lists, quotes, and other devices. Go through the text again and cut what you write down to the fewest words that do the job.

✔ **The ease of clicking away:** Web surfing, like real surfing, is all about movement. One of the most fun aspects of the Web for users is one of the most vexing for Web publishers: Clicking away to another page or site is very, very easy. Web content is free and voluminous, so users are always enticed to go elsewhere.

What it means for you: In addition to keeping your text brief and broken up, you need to make it as interesting as possible. Take advantage of the ease of clicking away: Include relevant hyperlinks in your Web text.

✔ **Web style:** In response to all this, Web writing has developed its own style. It's characterized by a lack of hype and an informal tone, but a strong need for accuracy — correct facts and no typos or missteaks (I meant to do that). Early Web users were military officers and scientists with Ph.D.s, who set a high standard for correctness that continues, at least on the best Web sites, today.

What it means for you: You need to show people that you're one of the voices on the Web worth listening to. Make sure your grammar, facts, spelling, and punctuation are accurate.

To demonstrate how "sparse" on-screen information is, Figure 4-2 shows a PDF file from the For Dummies site at www.dummies.com with content from a previous edition of this book. It's very well-laid-out online, but the amount of content displayed is only about half of one printed page (remember, a book reader sees two pages at a time). The comparison to the Web is even more unfavorable for magazines or newspapers, which fit even more information on a printed page than a typical book does.

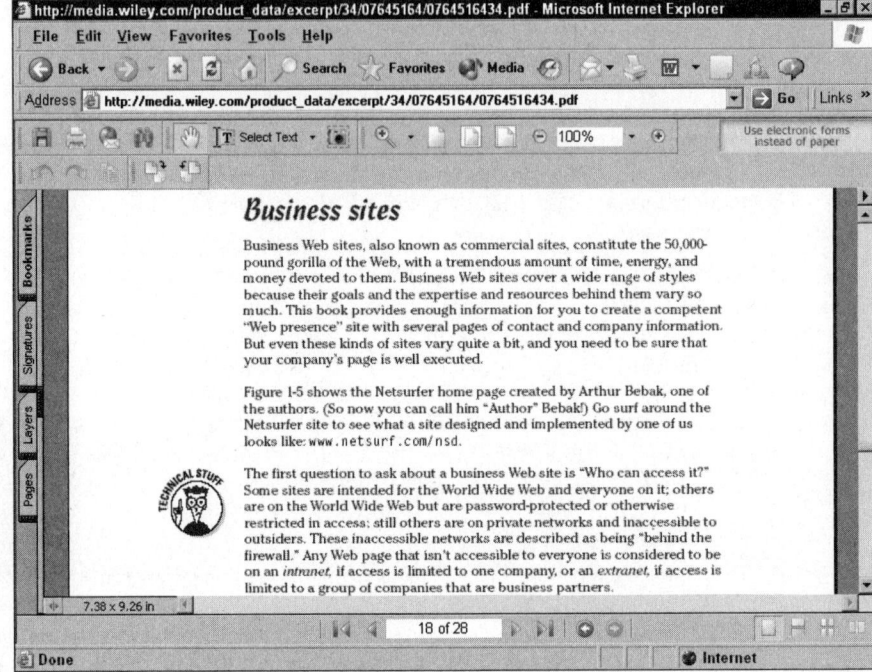

Figure 4-2:
An on-
screen page
has fewer
words than
a printed
one.

If you have something dense and detailed that you really want people to read, put it on a separate Web page and encourage people to print the page out. Or, put it in a PDF file that the user can download and print. (The advantage of a PDF file is that it preserves page layout exactly.) Printing allows users to carefully read the text rather than scan it, as most people tend to do with text on the computer screen, and to mark up the copy with notes and highlighting if they wish.

Even if readers do choose to read online, the use of a PDF gives readers a sense of their place in a document, preserves formatting, and makes resizing easy, making online reading easier than from a typical Web page.

The point is that readers get far more content for a given amount of effort from print than they do from online content. So when writing for the Web, you need to keep your text short, your layout simple, and your content interesting.

Once you think you've got your text short enough, start over. Identify the main point of your piece and make that the first sentence of a rewritten version. Include just enough supporting detail to explain your point. Then include each of your main supporting points, again with just a bit of detail. You should end up with about one-third the words you would use if you were writing for print.

Sources for Web writing

There are many excellent resources for Web writing; just remember that it's still an evolving practice, so don't expect full agreement from various authorities. With that in mind, here are some good resources:

✔ Jakob Nielsen's `useit.com`: This justly famous site has been the leading resource for Web usability information for over a decade. There are many good resources on the whys and hows of writing for the Web at `www.useit.com/papers/webwriting/`.

✔ USC Annenberg Online Journalism Review: This publication of USC's famous Annenberg School for Communication has great general rules, as well as specifics for blogging, at `www.ojr.org/ojr/wiki/writing/`.

✔ Web Reference Writing Well for the Web: These pages on the venerable (by Web standards) Web Reference site are another good source and include special treatment of headlines, particularly important when readers are skimming as they do on the Web. Visit `www.webreference.com/content/writing`.

What HTML Lets You Do with Text

HTML, in its original and most widely supported form, doesn't give you much control over the precise layout of text. In fact, because your Web site visitor may have a different screen size, machine type, and set of available fonts than you're used to, you can only count on a few things:

✔ **Serif or sans-serif text.** You can only count on using a serif font, with little "features" on the characters as you'll see in the text in this book (such as `Courier`), or a sans-serif font such as Arial, which looks cleaner but also cold and inhuman. If you specify a font by name, it's quite likely that some of your site visitors won't have that specific font on their machines, and a substitute font (also either serif or sans-serif) will be used instead.

✔ **Relative size.** You can't control the absolute size of text, only whether it's relatively very large, large, very small, and so on, with seven sizes to choose from. Nor should you want to specify absolute font size — a small font that looks fine on a low-resolution screen may become impossibly tiny on a high-resolution one.

✔ **Headers.** HTML supports seven levels of headers; the biggest headers (H1 and H2, as they're called) render so large on most browsers as to be almost unusable, so a lot of top-level headers get coded as H3 or even H4 headers.

- ✔ **Bold or italic.** Basic HTML includes specific commands for making text **bold** or *italic*. It doesn't support underlining because underlining indicates a hyperlink, not an emphasized word.

- ✔ **Bulleted and numbered lists.** HTML lets you create bulleted and numbered lists, but usually renders them with odd spacing between items — blank space above and below the list, but no extra spacing between items in the list, which to my eye makes the list hard to read.

- ✔ **Relative indent.** HTML lets you indent text from the left-hand margin not at all, some, or a lot.

That's about it. I go into detail in the following Parts on using a *WYSIWYG* (What You See Is What You Get) editor or "straight" HTML, but it's good to know up front what you're getting into.

Figure 4-3 shows these options for Web text formatting in a single example. Use it as a resource when deciding what formatting to use in your own Web page.

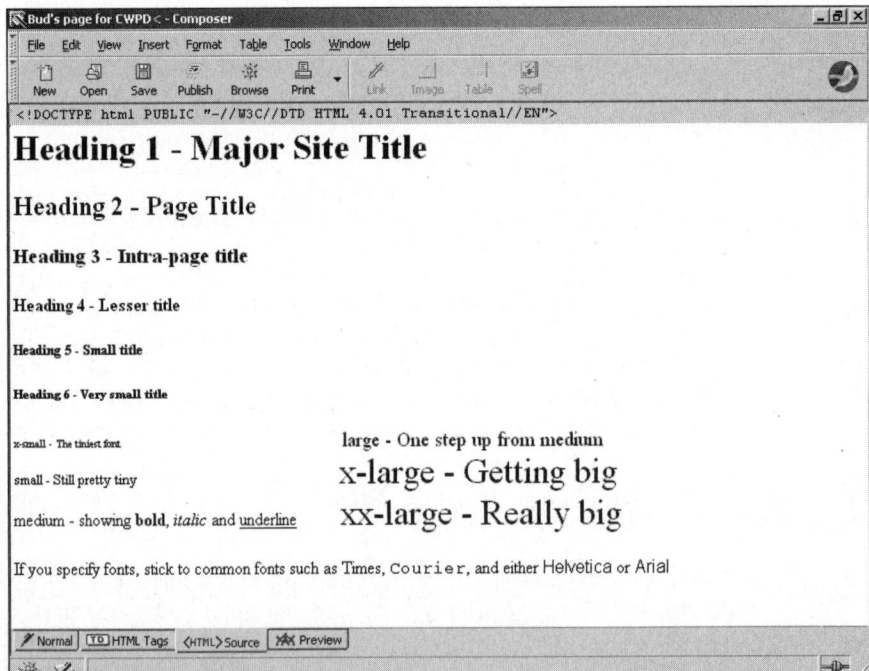

Figure 4-3: Take advantage of Web formatting options.

What color is your hyperlink?

HTML allows you to use colored text on your Web page. I generally don't recommend this.

Why not? (This book is about all the things you *can* do on a Web page, after all!) The reason is that people are very used to monotone text, usually black, on a contrasting background. People have adjusted to the use of colored text on Web pages, but mainly in the form of standard hyperlink colors: blue for a link the user hasn't clicked yet and purple for a recently visited link.

Some Web page authors customize hyperlink colors to fit better with the color scheme of their Web pages. The problem is, research into making Web pages easier to use and less confusing has found that users subconsciously count on blue underlined text to indicated unvisited links and purple underlined text to indicate links the user has already visited. Any change in these colors, or any use of underlining or blue or purple text for other purposes, causes deep confusion.

So I recommend that you don't use colored text, don't change link colors, and don't use underlining except in links. The people who visit your Web page will have a better time using it as a result.

Don't use italics much online; italic text online is very hard to read. Use bold text, but use it in a structural way (as I've done in the bulleted list just shown here) rather than to emphasize some **very important** point or another within a flow of text.

Note that these are the features supported by "straight" HTML, the basic sort that's widely implemented across old and new Web browsers. A newer standard, Cascading Style Sheets (CSS), gives you a great deal more control. However, it's hard to use properly, doesn't work the same on every browser, and can let you do things that look good on your screen but don't work well on all equipment — the opposite of the original intent of the Web. I don't tell you how to use CSS in this book, and I suggest you use it with caution if you do decide to use it.

Using Existing Text

Now that you know what you can do with text, what are the real-world issues that come up when you actually create a Web page or Web site? It's amazing how you can wish for months or even years that you had a Web site or blog — then, when you finally do have one, find looking at that blank screen that needs to be filled so intimidating. One time-honored approach to filling it is to re-use existing content; looking at how to best do so highlights important points about writing well for the Web.

How to reuse right

In many cases, you're actually doing a disservice to your Web site's visitors if you don't reuse things you already have. Your résumé may be of great interest to a visitor to your personal site; the information in your company's marketing brochures is very likely to be relevant to visitors to a company site. If you don't put this information on your site, the visitor will miss out on it.

You shouldn't use the text exactly as is, though, because Web formatting is different and reading from the Web is harder, as described earlier in this chapter. What you need to do is *repurpose* it.

Repurposing has two parts — reformatting and condensing. To reformat text for the Web, you need to tinker with some details:

- ✓ **Break up paragraphs and add some headers.** Since Web users scan, they may get absolutely nothing out of a long flow of, say, 10 or 20 paragraphs of text with no headers or hyperlinks. Paragraphs should be a few sentences long and there should be a header every few paragraphs so users can home in on the things they need to read.

- ✓ **Use lists with bullets or numbers.** People love lists, especially online, as they're easy to scan. Use numbered lists whenever there's a reason for them, such as a set of steps or a ranked list.

- ✓ **Add hyperlinks.** Web users treat hyperlinks as focal points just as they do headers. Hyperlinks also add credibility to your text. So gently introduce a few relevant ones.

- ✓ **Add or update bold, italic, and underlining effects.** If there's bold, italic, or underlined text in your original, consider stripping it all out, then adding bold and italic effects back to the text where appropriate; reserve underlining for hyperlinks.

- ✓ **Add illustrations and photos.** The easy addition and placement of illustrations — especially photos — within a flow of text was what really distinguished the Web from previous hypertext systems. Creating or sourcing appropriate images is a lot of work, but you have to do it if you want interesting Web pages that will get read.

True repurposing requires condensing as well. By the time you've broken up text, hyperlinked it and added graphics, you're almost bound to start shortening it. Because you're going to start developing a sense of what the purpose of the text really is, and all that extraneous stuff from the former version is going to annoy you.

To help with this, and to fit into the online ambiance, add a bit of wit or humor. (Unless you're writing for a medical Web site, in which case you should avoid being humerus.) Web users expect a bit of levity in text. Reading online is hard; humor makes it easier. And research shows that learning is actually helped by laughter. Don't be "another brick in the wall" of boring, hard-to-read online information; lighten the tone of your text.

The text in this book is not a great example for repurposing, because the For Dummies style — designed to be used for reference, easily skimmed and easily read, with icons and illustrations — is already much of the way to good Web-writing style. But take a look at a few pages of a novel and imagine rewriting it for the Web.

As an example, let's take a few sentences from *Moby-Dick, or the Whale* by Herman Melville — a book that's no longer in copyright, so I don't have to get permission to reuse it. (Don't laugh; practical considerations of this type come up all the time in Web writing and Web graphics.) The beginning of the book is:

> "Call me Ishmael. Some years ago— never mind how long precisely — having little or no money in my purse, and nothing particular to interest me on shore, I thought I would sail about a little and see the watery part of the world. It is a way I have of driving off the spleen, and regulating the circulation. Whenever I find myself growing grim about the mouth; whenever it is a damp, drizzly November in my soul; whenever I find myself involuntarily pausing before coffin warehouses, and bringing up the rear of every funeral I meet; and especially whenever my hypos get such an upper hand of me, that it requires a strong moral principle to prevent me from deliberately stepping into the street, and methodically knocking people's hats off — then, I account it high time to get to sea as soon as I can. This is my substitute for pistol and ball. With a philo- sophical flourish Cato throws himself upon his sword; I quietly take to the ship. There is nothing surprising in this. If they but knew it, almost all men in their degree, some time or other, cherish very nearly the same feelings towards the ocean with me."

(From the Project Gutenberg edition of this text at `http://www. gutenberg.org/dirs/etext01/moby10b.txt`.)

Figure 4-4 shows how the same text might look, rewritten for the Web — and updated a bit (with apologies to those who love their Herman Melville straight!) The H1 (header level 1) HTML tag is used for the header; note that it's unattractively large. Although H1 is technically correct, in a real page H3 or H4 would be used instead due to being rendered in a smaller, more appropriate size.

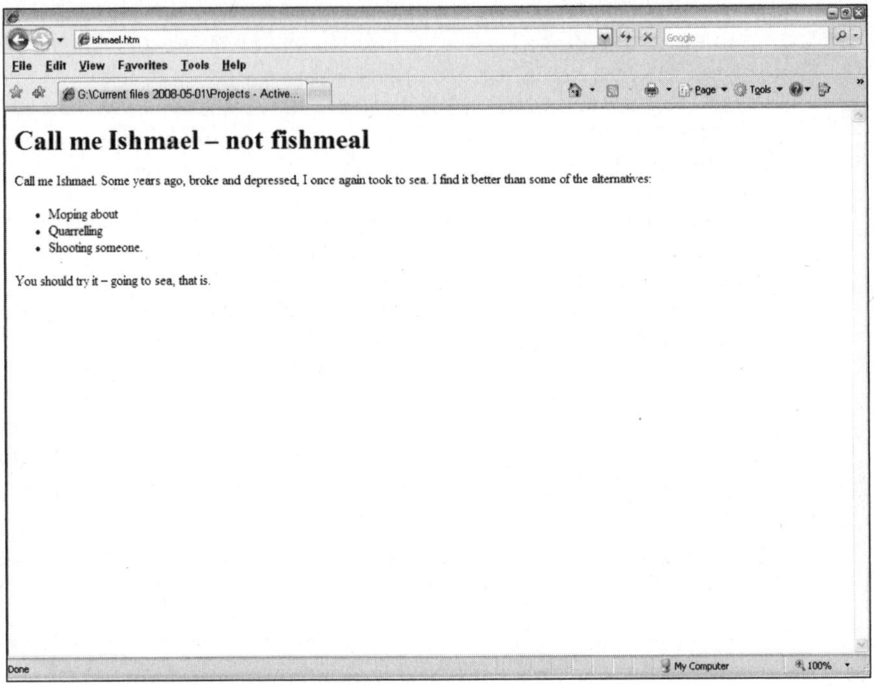

Call me Ishmael – not fishmeal

Call me Ishmael. Some years ago, broke and depressed, I once again took to sea. I find it better than some of the alternatives:

- Moping about
- Quarrelling
- Shooting someone.

You should try it – going to sea, that is.

Figure 4-4:
The opening
lines of
Moby-Dick,
updated for
the Web.

Avoiding existing formatting

If you try to open a formatted word processing file in a Web browser, it will look like gibberish. Or, worse, your browser — specifically Microsoft Internet Explorer — will look for a copy of, say, Word on your hard drive and use it to display the text with correct formatting. I say "worse" because this is a great technique *until* others on the open Web try the same trick in a *different* browser or without the same word-processing program handy. They, unlike you, will see gibberish.

Copying and pasting text from a word-processing file solves some of this, but there's all sorts of garbage — I mean, carefully inserted formatting code — mixed in with the text. Your Web-editing tool may ignore it, try to render it and fail, or successfully render it. In any event, the result is, again, unpredictable on someone else's computer or browser.

For instance, your computer may have the font Arial Narrow. It may display text in Arial Narrow in your word processing program, your Web editing tool and when you test a Web page. But if a visitor to your site doesn't have Arial Narrow, in the size you specified, he'll see some other font that may be different entirely. And your text may not fit in the space you've laid out for it.

The only way to completely avoid such problems is to paste the text into a text-processing program such as Notepad (*not* WordPad) on a Windows PC or BBEdit on the Macintosh. These programs are incapable of coping with formatting and will toss it all out. WordPad, on the other hand, puts formatting codes in your document, just like Microsoft Word and other word processors.

Then, save the Notepad or BBEdit file, just to make sure the former formatting (try saying that three times fast) all disappears. Copy and paste the "clean" text into your Web-editing tool (as described in Parts III and IV of this book). Add formatting there. This process may become quite tedious, especially on long documents, but well-paid professionals spend hours and hours doing it anyway because it's the only sure way to avoid problems.

Getting Copyright Right

It's easy to run into copyright issues with text — and this is a case where perception may matter more than reality.

Copyright only protects one's words against nearly word-for-word copies or very close paraphrases. The old saw, "Copying from one source is plagiarism; copying from three sources is research," captures this reality.

While only a nearly word-for-word copy of someone else's text is likely to get you in trouble legally, people's sense of fairness will kick in quickly if they *believe* you're copying. Text can be different enough from an original to not be legally actionable, but similar enough to bring you unwanted and distracting suspicion from your Web audience as a copycat.

So be careful how you proceed. You may want to tell your Web site's visitors how to add your site to their bookmarks in Internet Explorer — and you may search online to find out for yourself how to do it. The site you find the instructions on doesn't "own" the technique, but it does "own" the specific wording it used to describe how to accomplish that task.

So when you go to put the steps on your Web site, go through each step yourself, then write down what you just did in your own words. Double-check that you haven't unconsciously copied any of the wording you found online. Then put your own, new wording on your Web site. This way you'll be safe from even unintentional plagiarism.

If you do purposefully quote text (as I did in this chapter with *Moby-Dick*) sharply limit the size of your quote. If the text is highly recognizable, or if you go longer, note that the work is no longer in copyright (as I've done before the quotation) or that you've obtained permission (after you've, ahem, obtained permission) so your site visitors know you've done the right thing. Provide a link to the original. If the work is still in copyright, and you can't get permission, don't include the text.

Discovering the Wonderful World of Blogs

One of the best ways to get on the Web quickly is through a blog. A blog is also a great way to practice your Web writing and a great tool for expression in and of itself.

Blogs tend to offer built-in WYSIWYG editors. So Part III of this book, which demonstrates WYSIWYG editing using the CoffeeCup tool, is good background for blogging. And blogs also tend to allow you to touch up your entries with HTML tags, so Part IV of this book, which demonstrates the use of HTML for markup (as well as the Cheat Sheet at the beginning of this book) will also be useful for blogging.

Blogging is not just another tool for generating Web content. Even though it's relatively new, blogging has developed such a following that many people spend hours a day perusing others' blogs and commenting on them as they add to their own blogs. There's even a special word for all this: the *blogosphere,* the world of blogs and commentary about blogs and blogging. (This would be different from *blogosfear;* nobody seems to be shouting "Beware of the blog!") Because some bloggers are also journalists (and vice versa), the blogosphere is intimately tied to the newspapers and magazines that millions of people read daily.

Some blogs are focused on the Web itself, or on technical matters relating to computers — different types of computers, different operating systems, and so on. But some of the most interesting blogs are deeply personal. One blog that's a mix of the two is from the famous, or infamous, Dave Winer, a talented creator and marketer of software who also happens to be a top-notch complainer. You can find his blog at www.scripting.com, which is also a great site for blogging information and tools. You can see a snapshot of it in Figure 4-5.

Blogs have even had a big influence on politics. Remember Howard Dean, the former governor of Vermont who was the leading Democratic presidential candidate in late 2003 and early 2004? His blog was one of the leading tools of his campaign. Through it, people felt they came to know him quickly and well — and wanted to join him in changing the world of politics.

Both Dave Winer and Howard Dean are known for being, well, intense characters — and other people who are into blogging can be very intense about it as well. They tend to talk a lot about blogging and about related topics such as content syndication, collaboration, and online communities. You'll run into this if you search around the Web for blogs and conversations about them (mostly found in other blogs, of course.)

But blogging is now mainstream, having gone well beyond its founding fathers (and mothers, many of whom blog). During the 2008 Presidential campaign, one secret of the surprising success of the Obama campaign was its brilliant use of the Web and e-mail. Any visitor to the Barack Obama Web site can start a personal blog on it!

Figure 4-5:
Dave Winer
is an
über-
blogger.

Finding blogs to read

To find some blogs yourself, you can simply do a Web search using *blogs* as the search keyword. You're likely to run into a lot of stories about blogs and some technically oriented blogs before you find personal or otherwise interesting blogs.

For instance, in one search about blogging, I quickly found a story on a sex-related blog that got a U.S. Senate aide in trouble, a Bill Gates speech about blogging, and some blogging software — but none of the quirky, interesting, if sometimes self-obsessed content that has made blogging a phenomenon found its way to the list of top results.

Here are some list sites that give you a quick peek at what other bloggers are doing:

✔ `www.bloggersblog.com`: If you don't like the sound of "blog," you really may not like the name of this site. But it's a very useful directory of hot blog topics.

✔ `www.weblogs.com`: Some blogs aren't updated much; this list shows only recently updated blogs.

✔ `www.technorati.com/pop/blogs`: A listing by Technorati of the top 100 blogs, great fun to surf and a very useful source for ideas. Also a good introduction to Technorati, one of the most interesting communities on the Web.

Finding software for blogging

Later in this chapter, I show you how to use Blogger, owned by Google. Blogger is one of the easiest and best blogging tools out there — but it's far from being the only tool in town to suit your blogging fancy.

Be warned: I can't promise that you'll ever want to stop blogging once you start. Blogging can be an art form, so if you want to know more about blogs and get your own blog started, here are several top blogging resources you should check out:

✔ `www.typepad.com`: Home for the TypePad Web-logging service.

✔ `www.movabletype.com`: Movable Type is quite technical and quite powerful.

✔ `www.diaryland.com`: Easy, easy, easy is Diaryland's claim to fame.

✔ `www.livejournal.com`: LiveJournal and its users emphasize the community aspect of blogs.

✔ `www.hometown.aol.com`: AOL's Web logging service — free to all, even non-AOL members.

Committing to a blog

A blog takes more commitment than a Web site. The reason is simple: The diary, or "log," aspect of a blog can be time-consuming, day after day after day. An ordinary Web site can still be interesting and useful if it's not updated much for awhile. A blog, by contrast, is valuable precisely because it contains the latest information on a given topic — whether the topic is software, politics, or the daily musings of a bored teenager.

You'll see, as you search through various blogs, that many are started, gain an interesting slant or approach, start to gain regular visitors and fans — and are then abandoned. It's very frustrating to start reading an interesting blog only to see postings slow down and then stop completely. Bloggers burn out — and blog readers also burn out, from keeping up with so many blogs at once. Because bloggers feel compelled to keep up with other blogs as part of making their own blog worthwhile, bloggers can truly find themselves burning the candle at both ends.

An example of blog burnout can be found at `www.britblog.com`, shown in the figure. This formerly brilliant blog — "brill," as Brits would say — was recently shut down due to blogger burnout.

Another thing you may notice is a lot of personal information in blogs. Many bloggers willingly sacrifice some degree of privacy to participate in the blogosphere — but you may want to think twice before following their lead.

So if you're not sure a blog is what you want to do, consider creating a regular Web site first. You can then put the skills you gain creating your initial Web site to good use in creating the world's greatest blog — when you're ready to put in the time to create and maintain it.

Using Google's Blogger.com

Blogger.com, also known simply as Blogger, is the leading blogging site, with the most users and the widest name recognition. The site was acquired by Google in 2003 when Google bought Pyra Labs, the creators of Blogger. At the time it was acquired, Pyra Labs had just six employees — but more than a million registered users for its blogging-oriented Web sites. Now another leading blogging site, LiveJournal, claims over 15 million registered users!

The great thing about Google acquiring Blogger is that it gives ordinary folks — that's you and me — some reassurance that the site will be around for the long term. Many Web sites have come and gone, and when it was owned by Pyra Labs, Blogger wasn't immune to those pressures. Google is a highly profitable Web business, so the chances are greatly increased that Blogger will go on and on.

Blogger gives you the option of having advertising hosted on your page, with you and Blogger splitting the money. This is a great way to do it but Blogger is considered admirably easy, but not as feature-rich as it could be. However, you may want to consider a paid service, such as WordPress (`www.word press.org`), if you want more advanced capabilities in your site.

All blogs that you set up through the process described here are hosted on `blogspot.com` and have similar URLs. If you want to have your site hosted elsewhere, use the advanced blog setup at `www.blogger.com/adv-create-blog.g`. You will need details such as the FTP server to use for transferring content to your blog; get help from the site host if you need it.

Setting up your blog

Since its acquisition by the megalith Google, Blogger has obtained the resources to make blogging easier and faster without quickly pushing its users into paying for services. Blogger has recently updated its interface to make creating an initial blog even easier — a perfect fit with the purpose of this book. Follow these steps to get started:

1. **Go to** `www.blogger.com`.

   The Blogger site appears, as shown in Figure 4-6.

   If you look around the Blogger Web site, you see links to BlogThis, a way to quickly comment on any Web page within your blog.

2. **Click the orange arrow to Create Your Blog now.**

   The Create an Account page appears, as shown in Figure 4-7. Read carefully; just about everything you enter is very important to your blogging happiness.

Figure 4-6:
Blogger
welcomes
you.

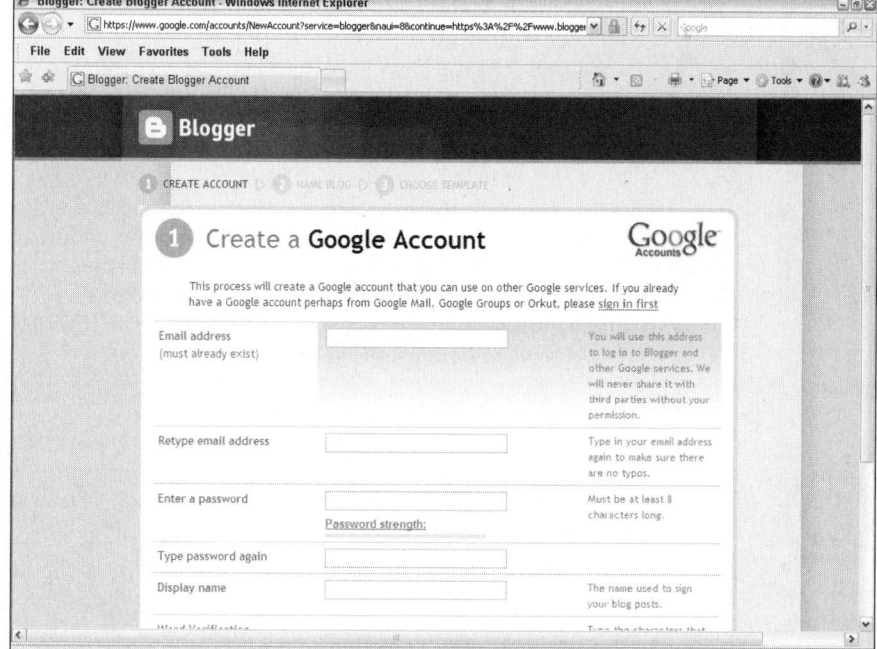

Figure 4-7:
Getting
started with
a Blogger
account
is easy.

3. **Supply a username (it's your e-mail address) and retype the e-mail address.**

   Your proposed username is your sign-on name for Blogger; only you will see it. Because Blogger is so popular, it's quite likely that most of the convenient or funny usernames that you may think of, such as "budsmith" (convenient) or "blogguy" (funny?) are already taken. Choose something you'll find easy to remember, but be ready to enter a second choice if your first choice is already taken.

4. **Enter your password, and then retype your password.**

   Unlike your username, you can enter any password you like — it doesn't matter if someone else has the same one. Just make sure your password is both easy for you to remember and hard for someone else to guess.

   It may seem as if your password is pretty unimportant because your blog is going to be immediately posted on the Web anyway. Okay, that's true, but it's not the point. The point is that if someone guesses your username and password, he can post on your blog (pretending to be you), and people will think the postings are from you — which could get pretty embarrassing!

5. **Enter your display name.**

   You may be tempted to enter your full name here, but with the increasing power of the Internet, it's quite likely that others who have your full name can find out more about you than you might want them to know. Consider using a display name that doesn't give away your complete real name.

   Be careful with putting personal information on the Web; identity theft is becoming a larger and larger problem, and you don't want to make it easy for the fraudsters by giving them a good start on a detailed profile of you.

   Think a bit about your display name; if your blog might cover personal or serious topics, for instance, don't choose a really silly one. (A posting from "wild&crazyguy" about your upcoming big business deal, for instance, may be a bit disconcerting to your blog visitors.) You may also want your display name to relate in some way to your blog title and blog address; see Steps 9 and 10 for details.

6. **Enter the verification characters.**

   Enter the word you see displayed. This is done to verify that you're a human (who can make out the letters displayed) and not a script automatically creating a Web site (which can't "read" such graphical lettering).

7. Click the Terms of Service link.

Before you click to put a check mark in the box that indicates you agree with Blogger's terms, click the Terms of Service link to make sure that you actually *do* agree.

The Terms of Service appear in a new window, so don't worry about losing the data you've already entered.

You should always inspect the terms of service for a Web site if you're going to enter personal information on it, such as your e-mail address. This is especially true with a blogging site — that's because, by nature, blogs require you to put so much data into the service, some of which may be personal. (Some blogs are embarrassingly personal!) Blogger's owner, Google, as a widely respected public company, may be more trustworthy than most — but you should still see what you're getting into.

Courts take Terms of Service seriously — after you agree to them, you're bound by them, whether you've read them or not. Some unscrupulous companies have gotten away with some pretty shady scams this way — and even big, respectable companies have used them to protect themselves from angry users. So give the Terms of Service the once-over.

8. Click the check box to accept the Terms of Service, and then click the Continue arrow.

If you see a new screen called 2: Name your blog (see Figure 4-4), go to Step 9. If you see the same screen as before, with an error message, the error message is most likely to be a caution sign and a warning: "Sorry, this username is not available." If so, enter a new username and reenter your password in both blank areas below it. Then click the Continue arrow.

After your username is accepted, the Name Your Blog screen appears (as shown in Figure 4-8).

9. In the Name Your Blog screen, enter the title for your blog.

You can give your blog any title you want, but give your decision some thought. Ideally, the title should be rare or even unique; should sum up what's different and special about your blog; and should relate to the blog address you'll give it in the next step, which also needs to be unique.

For instance, if you're creating a blog in support of a book about creating Web pages, you might call it "Creating Web Pages Web Log."

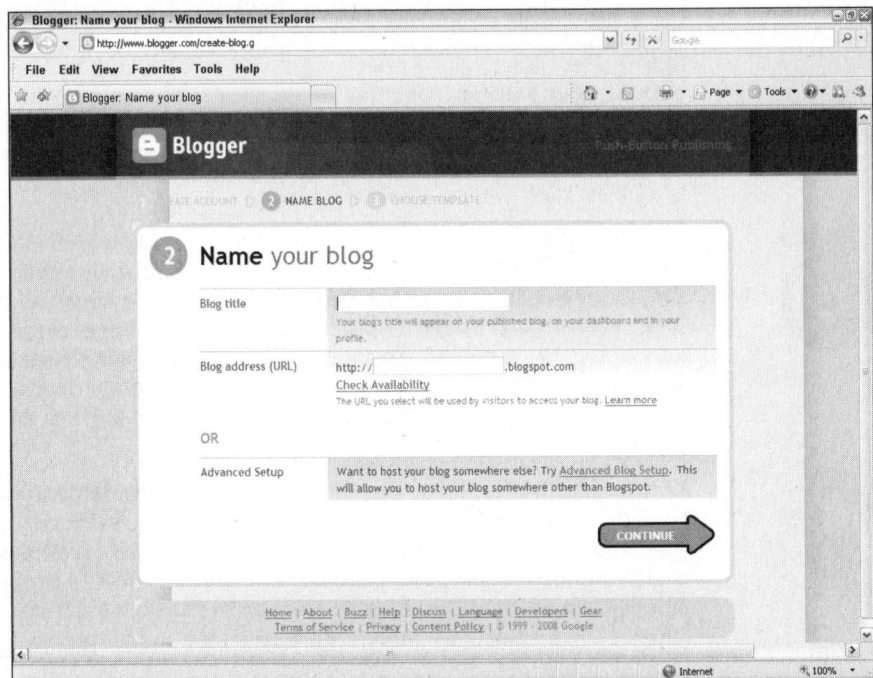

Figure 4-8:
Name your
blog.

10. **Enter the blog address, the first part of the URL for your blog. Click the Check Availability link to make certain it's not already taken and in use.**

    Enter the first part of the blog address for your blog. This portion of the address is used by Blogger to form the first part of your URL for your blog. For instance, if you enter **caveboy4** in the blog address spot, your URL is `caveboy4.blogspot.com`.

    As with your username, your blog address must be unique — if someone else has it already, you won't get it. Believe me — most of the good addresses are taken! So think carefully about a display name (see Step 5), blog title, and blog address that work together and are unique enough to pass muster.

    Google can help you find interesting blogs on Blogger.com — or other interesting content on other interesting sites. If you search for `site: blogspot.com caveboy`, for instance, you're likely to find most of the blogs on Blogger.com that have "caveboy" in their content somewhere. (I say "most of" because Google doesn't index sites instantly, so you may not be able to find something that's moved recently or that has otherwise escaped Google's attentions.)

11. **Click the Continue arrow.**

If you see a new screen called 3: Choose a Template (see Figure 4-9), Step 12. If you see the same screen as before, with an error message, do the following:

The error message is most likely to be a caution sign and a warning: "Sorry, this blog address is not available." If so, enter a new blog address. Then click the Continue arrow. When your blog address is accepted, you see the Choose a Template screen.

12. **Choose a template.**

You'll see a dozen or so templates to choose from — different looks for your blog. Choose one that fits the way you want your site to appear. Click the image of any of the templates to see a larger preview appear in a pop-up window.

It may be tempting to rush this part of the process — especially because Blogger allows you to change your template (by editing the page's HTML) or substitute a different template later, without losing any of your content. But it's worth taking the time now to make a choice you can live with, at least for a while.

Before you click Continue in the next step, be sure to check all your choices by clicking the "preview template" link below a particular template sample; once you click the Continue button your blog is created instantly.

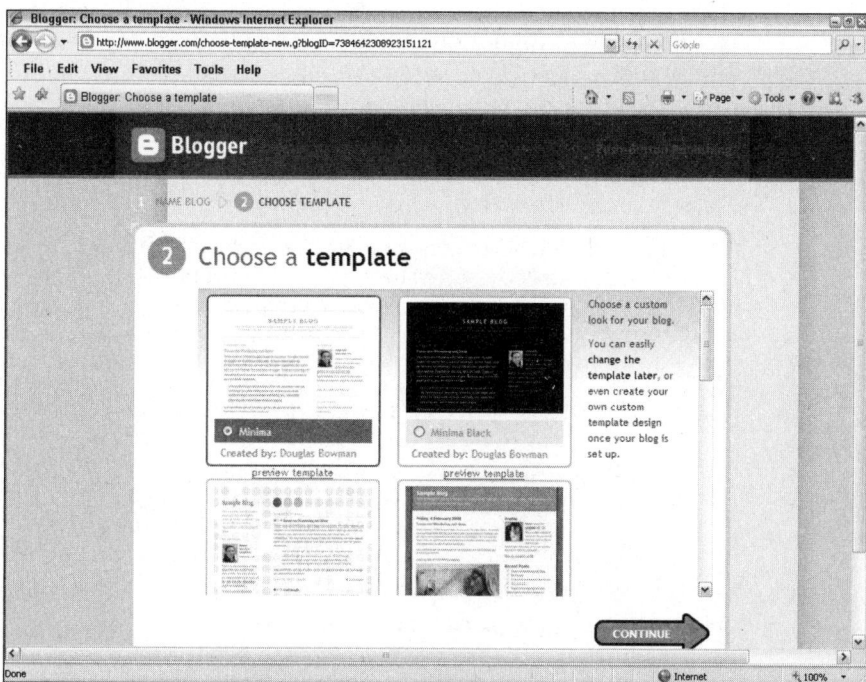

Figure 4-9: Showcase your blog in a template.

13. **When you've made your choice of template by selecting the radio button underneath a template, think about whether you're happy with all the choices you've made so far. If you're happy, and ready to create your blog, click Continue.**

    Your blog is created!

14. **Click the Start Posting button to open your blog so you can start adding content to it. When your blog appears, save the URL in your Favorites list.**

    In Internet Explorer, click Ctrl+D to add the current page to your Favorites.

Adding content to your blog

Adding content to your blog is easy — but doing it just the way you want it can be hard. Not all the options you're used to having for text formatting in, say, a word processor, are available with the Blogger software. You have to experiment to find out what you can and can't do.

From this point, your choices as to what to do, and what order to do it in, are nearly infinite. You may want to create posts right away; on the other hand, you may want to understand everything about your blog page before creating any content — let alone telling anyone how to find it.

To accommodate all the different approaches you can take, the following sections offer highlights of each page you use to edit your blog. Read each section briefly — and then roll up your sleeves and go experiment. That's what Blogger is there for!

Posting and formatting

The Posting page (see Figure 4-10) is where you create the posts that appear on your site. You can always edit, delete, or rearrange posts later, but it all starts here.

If you leave and reenter Blogger, you may find yourself at the Dashboard. To reach the Posting page from the Dashboard, simply click the link labeled New Post.

The Posting page allows you to enter plain text and format it using several options. You can use the easy, word processor–like buttons as shown in the figure, or use HTML directly.

To use HTML directly, simply click the Edit HTML tab. Your content — and the formatting you've applied to it — is displayed in HTML format, as shown in Figure 4-11.

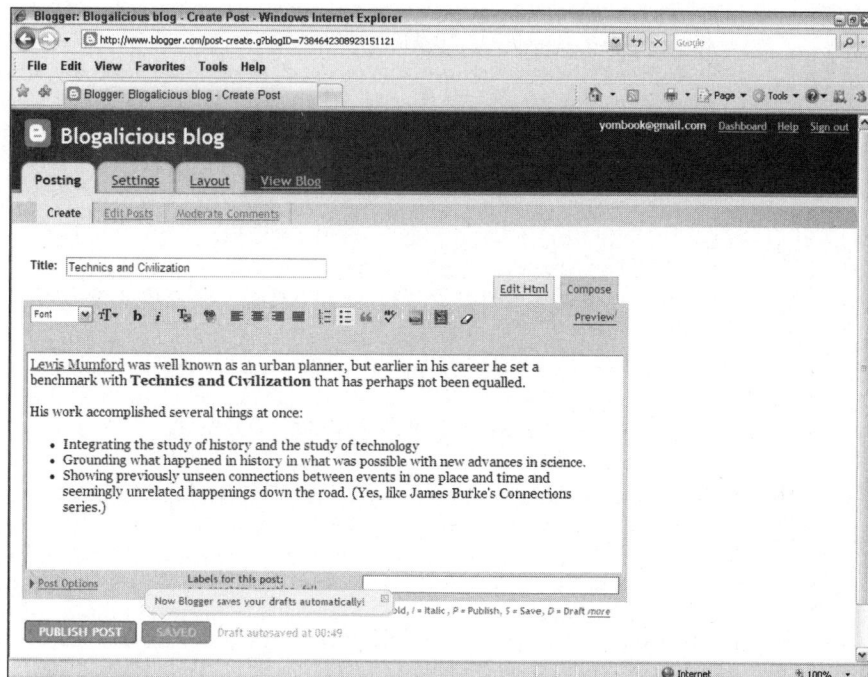

Figure 4-10:
Post to
your host.

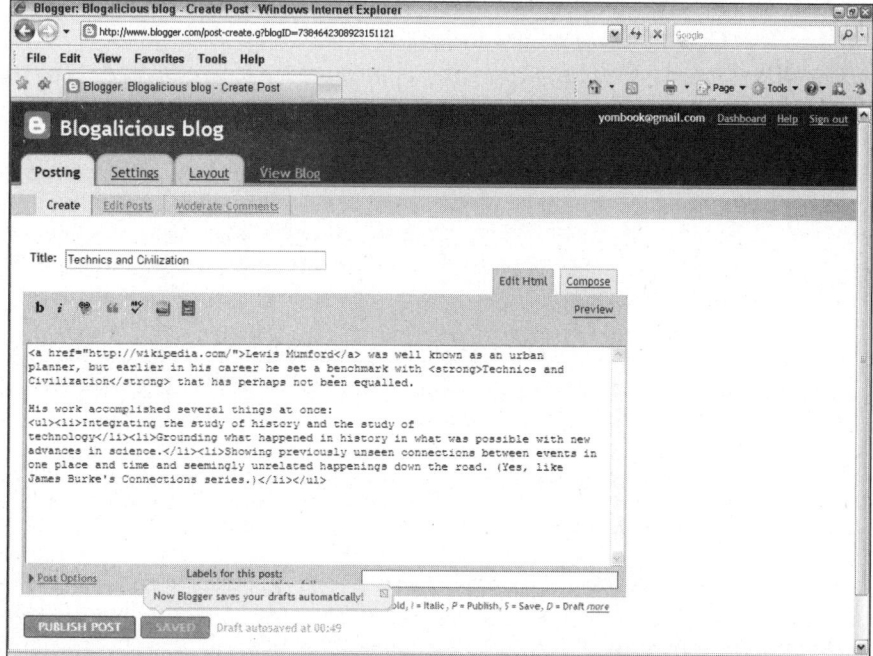

Figure 4-11:
You can dig
right into
the HTML.

Here are a few simple options for using HTML in your text:

- ✔ **Bold:** Makes the text you select bold, as you would guess. You'll see the HTML tags <b> and </b> surround the text, indicating that the bold is beginning (<b>) and ending </b>). Don't overuse bold text (or capital letters) because it looks like you're **SHOUTING.**

- ✔ **Italics:** Also obvious — makes text italic. The HTML tags <i> and </i> surround the text to indicate the beginning and end of italicization. Don't overuse italic text because it makes the text hard to read on-screen. (Printed italic text is much easier to read than on-screen italic text.)

- ✔ **Link:** Here's where you link text to a Web address — a big part of the original purpose of blogging. To use this, highlight the text that you want to have linked, and then click the Globe-and-Chain icon. You'll have the opportunity to link the text. To delete the link, delete the linked text.

Make the linked text short, but at the same time ensure that the users will be able to tell exactly what they'll get when they click the link. It's extremely annoying to see a link called My Favorite Dummies Book, for instance, and click it only to find that the link is to the overall Dummies site, not a description of the specific favorite Dummies book.

You also have the option of spell-checking your content — a capability added since Google purchased Blogger, and for which those of us with bad spelling can be greatful (sorry about that).

Using other Blogger options

In addition to posting — which, I hope, you'll spend the majority of your time doing — Blogger offers many other options. Highlights include

- ✔ **View Blog:** This option pops up a new window with your blog in it as it actually looks to a visitor (Figure 4-12 shows an example). Don't simply do this to view your site after you make changes — you may also want to use this option to see what's currently on your site as you're writing new posts.

- ✔ **Settings:** Settings allows you to change options in separate pages devoted to Basic, Publishing, Formatting, Comments, Archiving, Site Feed, E-mail, and Members options. (The E-mail option lets you post to your blog from an e-mail account.) Carefully check out and test these options, then use the ones that work for you; they support powerful capabilities such as posting to your blog by e-mail.

- ✔ **Template:** Here's where you can see the HTML code for your template — and change it any way you'd like, for better or worse. It requires real HTML skill to navigate through and change the code so it looks exactly as you want it to and doesn't "blow out" part or all of the page, wrecking the "clean" look of your template with content spilling outside the little "box" it's meant to be in.

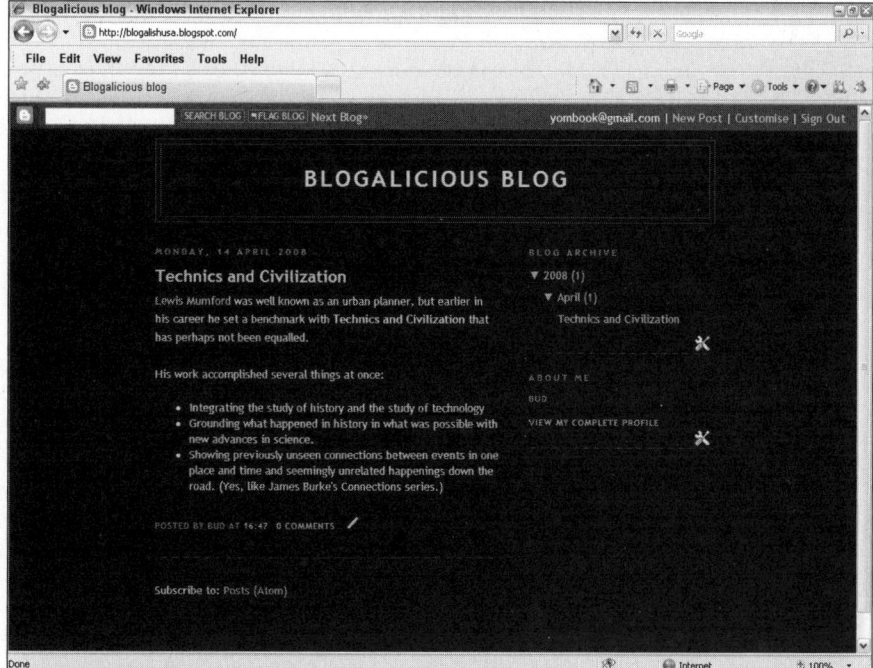

Figure 4-12:
The result
of all that
HTML work
behind the
scenes.

Don't be afraid to ask someone for help if you know a skilled person. You can also choose a different preexisting template here, for which you won't need any special skill.

✔ **Dashboard:** This is the screen you see when you sign in to Blogger in the future. It's your starting point for managing your site.

✔ **Post photos:** Blogger is not as photo-oriented as Flickr (see Chapter 5), but it's pretty good with photos. Click the photo button at any point to add a photo to your blog.

✔ **Post from your mobile:** In the United States, you can post text or photos to your blog from your mobile phone. Just send a message to go@blogger.com from your phone. Blogger creates a blog entry with the text or photo you sent and sends a code to your phone. Sign in to go.blogger.com and enter the code to work on your new blog.

You can do a great deal with your site — allow other people to add comments to it or not, change the look and function of it, and much more. Have fun with it — and keep posting to it every day or two.(You can even post photos to your Google blog from Flickr; see Chapter 5.)

For much more information on how to get the most out of Blogger, go to Blogger Help at `help.blogger.com` or join the Blogger Help Group at `groups.google.com/group/blogger-help`.

There are many options for including blogging capability in a full Web site, but one of the easiest is just to use Blogger for blogging, and then copy and paste the "best of your blog" onto your full Web site — on Google Page Creator (Chapter 3) or anywhere else.

When you have your blog up and running, let people know! Let them add comments if you like. That way, your humble little blog can begin to be the center of a thriving new online community — yours!

Chapter 5

Using Images and Uploading Photos to Flickr

"A picture is worth a thousand words," the old saying goes, and the right picture can convey information or evoke feelings in a way that may take many thousands of words to accomplish.

Having photos and other images as part of the Web seems like an obvious winner now — after all, magazines and newspapers wouldn't work well if you took away photographs, drawings, and all the little graphical page design elements that give each publication its own "look." In fact, including graphics in your Web pages is such a winning strategy that I've coauthored, with Peter Frazier, a companion volume to this one, *Creating Web Graphics For Dummies* (Wiley). You can refer to that book if you need more graphics-related details than you find here.

In the 1980s and '90s, before the Web, the Internet was almost entirely a text-only world. E-mail, Usenet newsgroups, and online service forums were all text-only environments, running mostly on text-only computer systems like UNIX and DOS. The Macintosh and early versions of Windows laid the groundwork for a better, richer way of communicating over the Internet.

Graphics embedded in Web pages made the Web take off — and they are also the most difficult aspect of getting your Web pages right. You can use graphics to convey a thematic "look and feel," to accent certain portions of a Web page, or even to convey the main content of a Web site. Some use of graphics is necessary for just about any site.

In this chapter, I introduce the creating, finding, and preparing of photos and other images for the Web. In later chapters, I describe how to make your images work well within your Web page by adjusting the size of the image; by flowing text smoothly around the image; and by putting a border around it. This is covered in Chapter 10 for using a WYSIWIG Web page editor and in Chapter 14 for using straight HTML.

But what if you just want to put photos on the Web for sharing with other people, without the complexities of creating a full Web page?

Photo sharing is one of the greatest uses of the Web. Flickr is the most popular photo-sharing Web site around, largely because it's so easy to use.

Photo files can be very large. But more and more people have digital cameras and cellphones that take pictures. These pictures are already in digital form — and they can be automatically compressed, using the JPEG standard, from their original size of several megabytes to about 100 KB or so. (A 100KB photo is just a tenth of a megabyte in size, and doesn't take long to upload and download.) These photo files go onto Flickr very easily.

The other technological advance is the increasing number of people who have broadband Web access. *Broadband* is a catchall name for all sorts of faster access, usually at least 1 megabyte per second. At this speed, you can get ten typical JPEG photos uploaded to your Web site — or downloaded to your screen — in a second. Suddenly, adding a reasonable number of photos to your site doesn't slow it to a crawl — *if* they're fairly strongly compressed with JPEG.

The problems of getting photos onto your site and of viewing photos on the Web are steadily getting easier, but "easier" doesn't mean truly easy.

To get to easy, someone has to come along and wrap the technology in a shell that just about anyone can handle — even a *For Dummies* author like me. This happened with the Model T Ford for cars, the Brownie camera for film photography, and the Apple Macintosh for personal computers. Now Flickr has done it for online photos.

Naming of parts for images

Because of the underlying technical realities of using images on the Web, it helps if I use words carefully here. For Flickr purposes . . .

A *photo* is an image captured by a camera from reality. Photos use thousands of shades of color to see the shape and the subtleties of depth in a person's face, a flower, or even a chair, even though the image itself is two-dimensional.

A *photo-realistic image* is a computer-generated image that is so complex that it approaches the subtlety and complexity of a photograph. In this book, when I refer to photos, I include photo-realistic images as well.

The complexity of photos and photo-realistic images makes them hard for a computer to store without making the display size of the image small, then compressing this shrunken image using techniques that make the image less than perfect, but greatly reduce the file size.

The *JPEG,* for Joint Photographic Expert Group, standard uses many subtle tricks to create a highly accurate version of the image in a small file size. JPEG, which has won many awards for the members of the international committees that joined together to create it, is a towering achievement of the human intellect (seriously) and is by far the most popular standard for compressing photographic images.

A *graphic* is an image created by people, and is usually fairly simple in the colors and shapes used; there is rarely a third dimension, just a flat image. Because graphics use few colors and few or none of the subtle shadings needed for three-dimensional reality, they can be compressed to small file sizes with little or no loss of information. The standard used on the Web for compressing graphics with fewer than 256 colors is called *GIF,* for Graphics Interchange Format.

I use the term *image* here to refer to photos and graphics together.

Confusingly, for small images — even photos — either JPEG or GIF may offer a better trade-off between good appearance and small file size. So be ready to experiment with these standards before deciding which one to use for small and very small images.

File size (still) matters

To avoid making big mistakes, you need a general understanding of photo file sizes and the GIF and JPEG graphics standards used on the Web.

To understand just how important compression is, start with the sidebar, "Text files versus photo files." Then read the next section carefully.

Making an image smaller

The first step in making an image file smaller is to decide how big you want the display size to be. There's a tricky distinction here.

Web-safe colors

There are still some computer systems out there that only display 256 colors, and the Web is designed to work with 256 colors as a minimum. There are 256 such "Web-safe" colors for Windows PCs and a slightly different list for Macs; there are only 216 colors that are truly "Web-safe" for both systems at once. If you use colors that aren't Web-safe, then display the resulting image on a 256-color monitor, it will try to create a compromise, using a dithered image mixed from the available colors — sometimes with awful results. However, this only occurs in some cases, and there are now so few users with 256-color-only systems that it's probably not worth boring you with the details of how to avoid this problem. See *Creating Web Graphics For Dummies* (Wiley) or the manual for your image-editing program if you want to learn more.

Using HTML or most WYSIWYG Web page-creation programs, you can downsize the *appearance* of the image on your Web page without changing the image itself. That is, you can display an image whose actual display size is, say, 1024 x 768 pixels in a much smaller window, say, 40 x 40 pixels.

The problem with this is that it leaves the original image, and its file size, unchanged. So the user ends up downloading a 200 x 200 pixel file — which might be, say, 150 KB in size — but only seeing a much smaller 40-x-40 pixel file (one-twenty-fifth the size, if you're counting). Not much bang for your downloading buck.

So what you have to do is use a graphics program to actually resize the image itself to the size you want to display in the Web page. This will get you a file that's no bigger than it needs to be.

Now, you might find as you work on your Web page that you actually need an image size and proportions different from those you originally created — portrait-shaped (like this page) rather than square, for instance. That's fine — just go back to your original image and resize it again.

Always, always, *always* save your original graphics file. Make a copy, and work on the copy, or save it under a name like "Master Image — Me," then under another name like "Working Copy" that you actually work on. While you're at it, always do work on your file, such as applying special effects, adding lettering and so on, to a version of the file that has not been compressed in JPEG or any other type of compression. Doing the compression should be the last step.

To make sure you don't overwrite your original graphic, find its icon in Windows File Manager, right-click the icon and choose Properties, then choose the General tab. Click the Read-Only check box, as shown in Figure 5-1, and save the change. Now, when you open the file, you'll be forced to save it under a new name — you won't be allowed to overwrite the original.

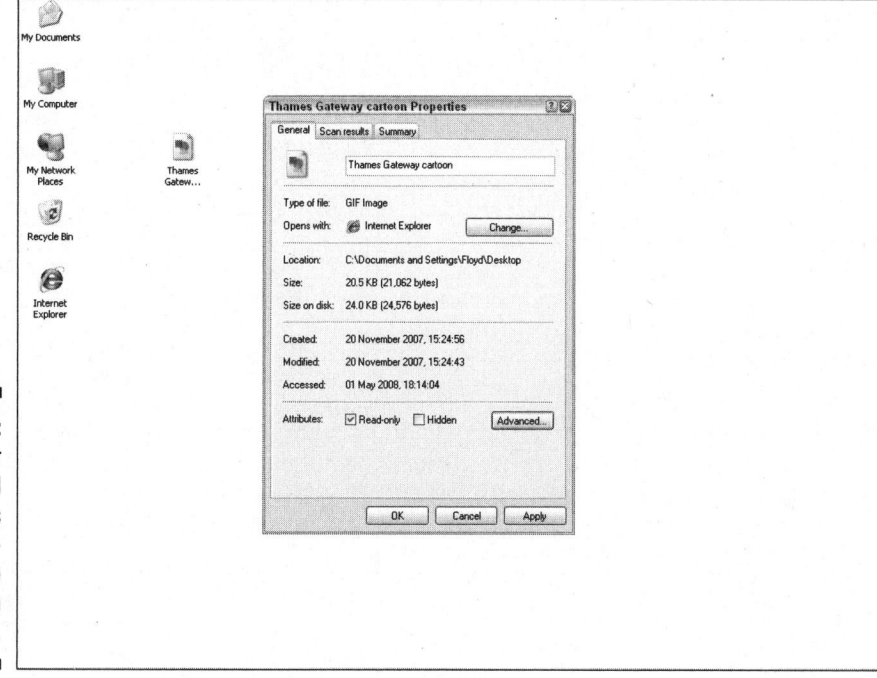

Using GIF and JPEG graphics formats

A graphics program saves files in its own *proprietary graphics format* — the specific arrangement of data that the program uses to save its files. For instance, the popular graphics program Photoshop saves files in the PSD format (for Photoshop Document); Paint Shop Pro, another popular graphics program, saves its files as PSP files. (Guess what "PSP" stands for. Time's up!) Web browsers typically don't know how to display files stored in these formats.

Fortunately, for the purposes of using graphics in HTML, you need concern yourself with only two formats for graphics files — GIF and JPEG — and even then you don't really need to know a lot about the gory details of these formats to use them. See the "Naming of parts for image files" sidebar for details.

GIF, or *Graphics Interchange Format,* is the file format used by most people to exchange most graphics that aren't photographs. That's because people tend to create graphics using just a few simple colors, which GIF handles well. There will be a big block of, say, yellow, then a block of red, then a lot of white. This kind of image compresses very well.

Text files versus photo files

Text files are much more efficient for computers to store and transmit across the network than graphics files. Why? Text is very tightly coded; a typical Web page full of text contains about 1,500 alphanumeric characters, which can be represented in 1,500 bytes, or 1.5 KB, of space. So a full page of text takes about a quarter of a second to transmit on even the slowest standard most people use today, a 56K modem.

Graphics, on the other hand, require a lot of storage. Every graphic has many pixels, and each pixel contains information about the color levels of three colors — red, green, and blue. An uncompressed, full-page, full-color image takes up about 1.5 MB of space — 1,000 times more space than text. This size file takes about 4 minutes (!) to transmit using a 56K modem.

This disparity is why most Web pages are made up of lots of text (which download quickly), fairly large areas of white space (which takes no time at all to download), and small, highly compressed graphics (which still download more slowly).

It's easy to fool yourself about file sizes when you create a Web page on your computer and then test it on a fast connection. Web-page creation programs and HTML make it very easy to make an image *appear* small on-screen while still taking up perhaps 1 to 2 MB. Your computer is perhaps 100 times faster than a 56K modem, and a fast connection is anywhere from five to 20 times faster. So a 1 or 2MB image will *seem* to load fast enough while you're testing.

But when Joe User tries to access your Web page over a slow modem, and it's loaded with 3 or 4 of these 1-MB-plus images, his entire computer may halt. Even fast connections have their hiccups and can be overloaded by too many large files. So sharing your photos may end up burdening your friends, family members, and other viewers of your site or photo page with very long wait times.

There's also potentially a cost issue here. Your free Web page's site may have limits on the number of megabytes you can download per month before it simply halts — or your paid site may charge you by the megabyte. If you get a sudden upsurge in usage, your Web site can stop working for the rest of the month, or you can be hit with a bill for hundreds of dollars, just to download images that were larger than they ever needed to be in the first place.

The answer is that you have to reduce the actual file size of your photos, not just resize the windows in which they display. Okay, it's clearly important. Now this chapter describes how to get it done.

GIF images may contain up to 256 colors, so GIF formatting works effectively for images that have anywhere from a few colors to a few hundred colors. Most simple images — and most images created on a computer — fall into this category.

If an image has more than 256 colors, it loses some color information when you convert the image to GIF. You have to look at the image before and after you convert it to GIF to see if trimming the additional colors noticeably affects the image's appearance.

JPEG, or *Joint Photographic Experts Group* format, compresses complex images, such as photographs, with many color variations. Photographs work by using thousands of different shades to capture (for instance) the subtle differences in color as light falls on a person's face. Photos typically don't have large blocks of a solid color, but instead are filled with subtly varying colors. If you cut down the number of colors in a photo too much, it becomes ugly and cartoonish.

JPEG uses psychological and graphical tricks to create an image that looks as detailed as a photo in much less file space. Even very light JPEG compression, which barely affects the appearance of the image at all, can easily cut the file size of an image by two-thirds. "Stepping on" the image harder, with more compression, begins to introduce visible effects in the image, but at the same time can easily reduce a typical photo to 10 percent of its former file size.

This capability makes JPEG the image format of choice for displaying photographs and other natural-looking images on your Web page. (What makes a photo look natural is that it mimics the way different shades of a color appear as light falls differently on various parts of an object.) These images retain their appearance well when compressed with JPEG.

Figure 5-2 shows a Web page from the NASA Web site to graphically illustrate (pun intended) the difference in GIF and JPEG photo file sizes. Another site you may find useful shows various versions of the same photo of Marc Andreessen, one of the founders of Netscape, to illustrate the various file types and compression options. Here's the URL:

```
cgi.netscape.com/assist/net_sites/impact_docs/e-jpeg.html
```

You can use this GIF/JPEG test page to test the speed of your own Internet connection. The total size of the page with graphics is about 70 K.

For images with lots of large blocks of solid color, GIF file sizes tend to be small. Thus, GIFs are better for banners or images with large areas of solid color, such as bar graphs or icons. In other words, the simple drawings that most of us create work best with GIF. Dense artistic graphics and photos work better with JPEG.

However, there are times when choosing a GIF format for a photo is a good idea. The GIF format gives you some Web page display options that you don't always get with JPEG files. For example, you can make the colors around GIF images transparent to whatever is in the background of the image, and you can save GIF images in *interlaced* format. Images saved in this way, and then downloaded by a browser, first appear at a very low resolution, and then in progressively clearer resolution, until the whole image appears. This feature makes GIF images preferable for quickly displaying a rough-looking graphic that improves with time — and for creating fancy special effects.

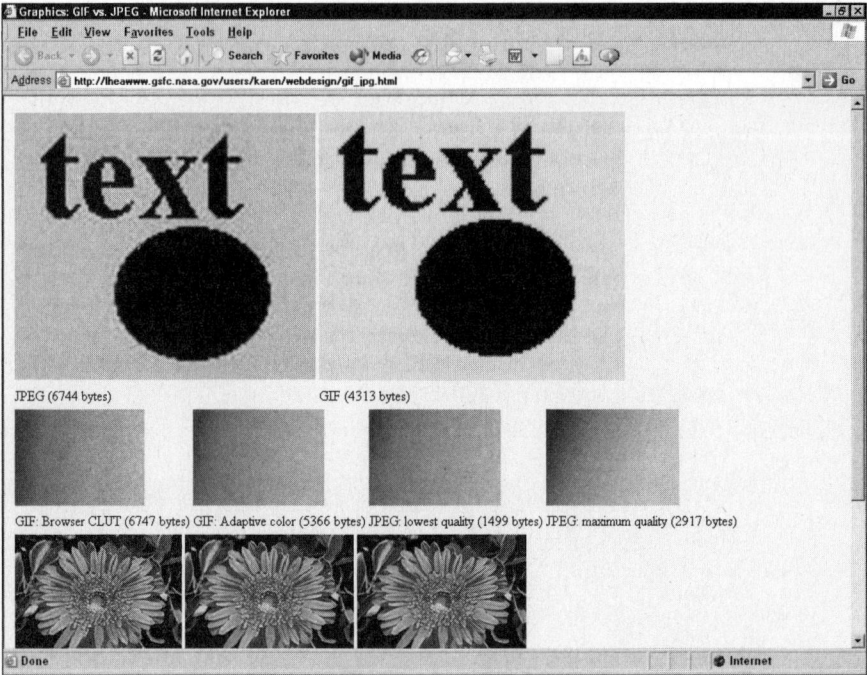

Figure 5-2:
Get an idea
of how
different
graphic
file formats
look.

Transparent images have a clear area surrounding the object of interest. For example, in a photo of a watch, you may not want any background color surrounding the watch, just the watch itself seeming to sit directly on the Web page and its background color. To achieve this effect, you use a transparent GIF, an image with a clear border area. The background color of the overall Web page shows through the transparent area, and the object of interest appears to "float" over the background.

Example: Resizing and saving a screen capture

There's nothing like actually going through the steps to help you gain a practical, not just an intellectual, understanding. These steps will show you how to capture the current image on your screen, resize it, and save it as a GIF and a JPEG, then compare the file size and appearance of the resulting file.

Doing your filing for Web pages

Any up-to-date Web browser can display three types of data: text with HTML tags, GIF graphics, and JPEG graphics. (Some people pronounce GIF as "jiff," others as "giff" as in "gift." I prefer "giff" as in "gift.") A typical Web browser displays HTML-tagged text appropriately, although not all browsers understand all the same tags. A browser also displays GIF and JPEG graphics inline — that is, embedded within the Web page. A Web page with inline graphics looks like a page in a magazine, with text and images mixed seamlessly together. However, each graphics file is stored separately from the HTML-tagged text that makes up the underlying Web page. This makes the Web work better overall, but contributes to some of the problems — such as the difficulty of keeping all your Web files together for proper display — that I describe later in this book.

There are scores of graphics programs out there, many of them completely free, free for a limited time, or relatively inexpensive. (A low-cost version of the industry standard Photoshop program, called Photoshop Elements, retails for less than US$100, and many computers come with a graphics program pre-installed for free.) But there's only one graphics program you can count on finding on any Windows computer, and that's MS Paint.

So, if you use Windows, follow these steps to learn how to capture the current screen image (one of the most useful ways to get graphics, as long as you respect copyright restrictions), resize it, and save it as both a GIF file and as a JPEG. (If you use a Mac, there's no similar standard program, but you might try downloading Ultimate Paint from a source such as www. download.com and following roughly the same steps.)

Always think about rights issues when you're looking for graphics to use. For the example, I'm going to take a PDF file as represented on-screen and make it into a very small image to serve as an example of a PDF on a Web page. I'm going to use a PDF of a page from a For Dummies book I wrote because that way there are no rights hassles. If you follow my example and put a shrunken (but recognizable) image of a PDF file on your Web page, be sure to use a PDF file you have the rights to. It's just good practice if you want to avoid any possible rights problems.

For Windows, follow these steps to capture a graphic from the screen and save it as an uncompressed BMP file, a GIF file, and a JPEG:

1. **Create or find the graphic that you want to use online.**

   This is the fun part! But be careful, any task involving images can somehow magically expand to take hours more than the time you had expected it to. Set yourself a realistic goal with lots of room for error — "a fish," say, not "a green flounder seen from the side."

   In this example, I've navigated to a PDF of a page from *Creating Web Graphics For Dummies* (Wiley).

2. **To capture the entire screen, press the PrtSc key (which may have a slightly different name on your keyboard); to capture the currently active window, press Alt+PrtSc.**

Usually, you will just want to capture the active window.

When you do this, the image is copied to the Windows Clipboard.

The Windows Clipboard and Microsoft Paint store images in BMP format, short for BitMaP format. Every pixel that's captured gets up to four bytes to allow its color to be captured exactly. This produces an exact, completely accurate, absolutely uncompressed image that, like an uncompressed photograph, takes up immense amounts of file space.

Despite the fact that BMP files are large and Windows-specific, you can put them in your Web page and they'll *seem* okay; Internet Explorer running on Windows will display BMP files, and testing on your own machine makes the problem of long download times disappear. But watch out; if you put your page up on the open Web, it will download slowly for users with slow connections, and the image won't even open on many non-Windows systems. A savvy user will look at your HTML source code, see you linked to a BMP file, and conclude that you bothered to read a good book on Web pages (like this one)!

3. **Open Windows Paint by clicking Start⇨Programs⇨Accessories⇨Paint.**

Windows Paint will open.

4. **Resize the image area to the size of the pasted area when you paste in the image:**

   a. *Choose Image⇨Attributes or press Ctrl+E to open the Attributes panel.*

   b. *Enter **1** for the width and 1 for the height.*

   c. *Click the Pixels radio button under Units, as shown in Figure 5-3.*

   d. *Click OK.*

Resizing the working area to one pixel by one pixel, using the Attributes dialog box, will make working with pasted-in images much easier.

5. **Paste the captured image by choosing Edit⇨Paste or by pressing Ctrl+V.**

The captured image appears in Windows Paint. The entire image is selected.

6. **Save the captured image twice: once as an original file, with a name like Screen Capture Original, then as a working copy, with a name like Screen Capture Copy.**

Your changes are recorded in the copy, leaving the original alone.

Consider creating a separate folder for each image you work with to contain the original image and various versions you create.

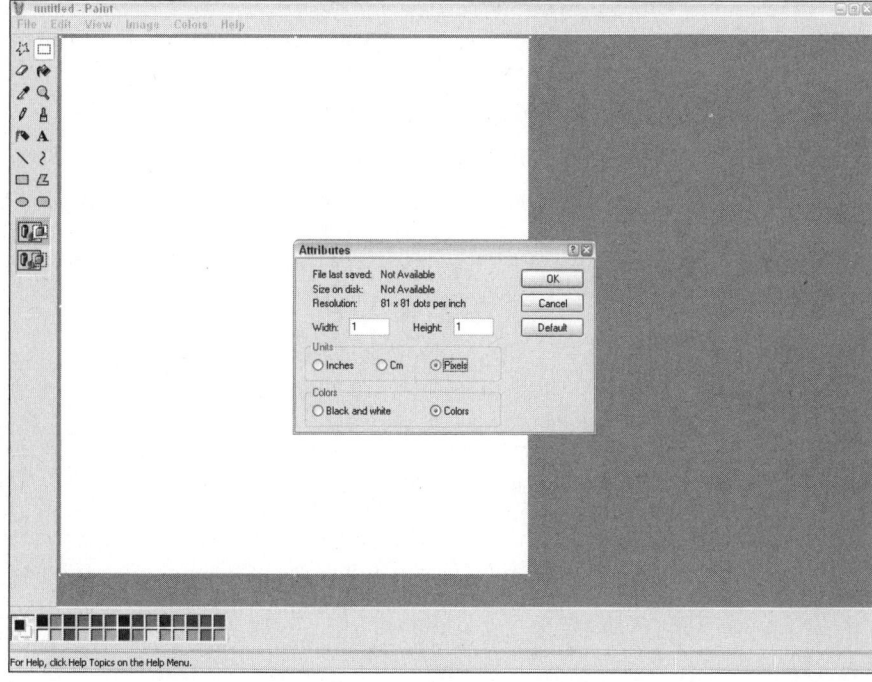

Figure 5-3:
Setting the
working
area size in
Windows
Paint
with the
Attributes
dialog box.

To make sure the original image isn't changed, find the file in Windows Explorer, right-click it, choose Properties, and then change it to a Read-Only file (refer to Figure 5-1).

7. **To see the size of the pasted image, choose Image⇨Attributes or press Ctrl+E.**

    The size of the image will appear in the Attributes dialog box.

Always check the size of the pasted image, and always write it down — on paper, so you have a record, or even in a spreadsheet program so you can calculate the percentage by which to resize it.

8. **To resize the image, choose Image⇨Stretch/Skew or press Ctrl+W.**

    The Stretch and Skew dialog box appears, as shown in Figure 5-4.

9. **Decide on the size you want for the image, calculate the percentage this is of the captured image, and then enter the new size as follows:**

    • Enter the percentage you want to shrink the image by in the Stretch part of the dialog box, entering the same percentage in both the Horizontal and Vertical areas. Click OK. The image will be resized.

    • If the result isn't what you want, press Ctrl+Z to undo and try again.

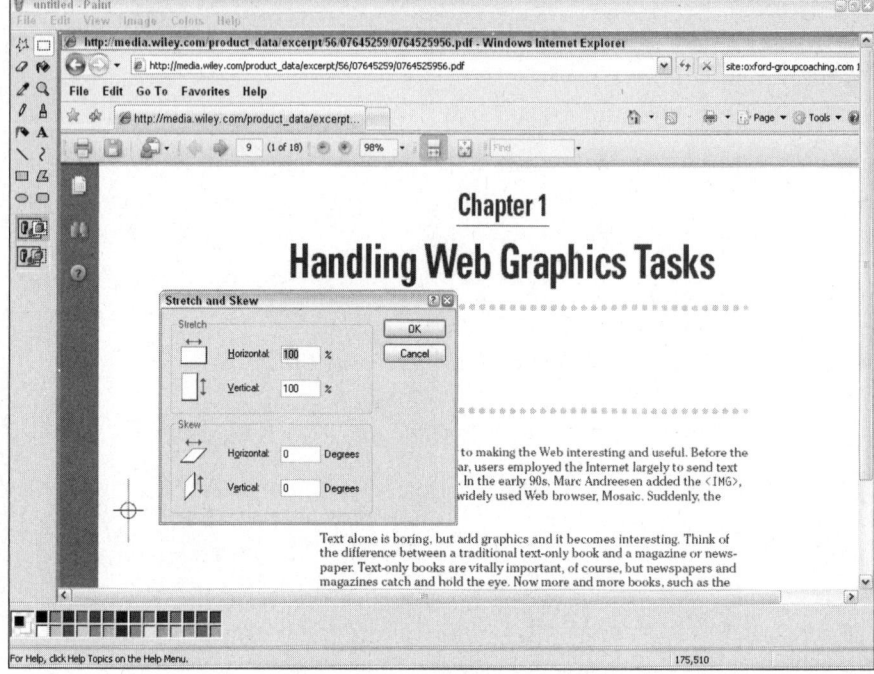

Figure 5-4:
Resizing an image in Windows Paint with the Stretch and Skew dialog box.

- Be sure to enter the same percentage in both the Horizontal and Vertical areas to evenly shrink the image. (If you shrink the image unevenly, it will look very odd indeed, distracting from your Web page's message).

    For this example, I've chosen to shrink the image to about 150 pixels tall, which requires shrinking it to 15 percent of its original size. The width is also 15 percent, resulting (in this case) in a width of 115 pixels.

If you're sure you won't forget the vital step of resizing, you can use the original, very large file when creating your Web page, using commands in your WYSIWIG editor or in HTML to resize its appearance in the Web page until you have it appearing in the size you're happy with. Then go back and *make a resized version of the file* that fits what you need for your Web page.

10. **Save the resized file as a BMP file. Choose File⇨Save As to open the Save As dialog box. For Save as type, choose 24-bit Bitmap from the scrolling list. Enter a name for the file. Click the Save button.**

    The file is saved. It will have the suffix .BMP to mark it as a bitmap file, but you won't see this suffix in Windows, which suppresses filename extensions.

Always save the file as a BMP file first so you have an uncompressed version for later editing.

Consider putting the letters BMP in the main part of the filename so you can easily distinguish the BMP file from other saved versions of the file, and do the same for the GIF and JPEG versions.

11. **Save the resized BMP file as a GIF file:**

   a. *Choose File⇨Save As to open the Save As dialog box.*

   b. *For Save as Type, choose GIF from the scrolling list to save the file in GIF format.*

   c. *Enter a name for the file and then click the Save button.*

   The file is saved.

12. **Save the resized BMP file as a JPEG file:**

   a. *Choose File⇨Open to open the uncompressed BMP file, or choose the BMP file from the list of recently edited files at the bottom of the File menu.*

   b. *Choose File⇨Save as to open the Save As dialog box.*

   c. *For Save as type, choose JPEG from the scrolling list to save the file in JPEG format.*

   d. *Enter a name for the file and then click the Save button.*

   The file is saved.

MS Paint always uses a relatively harsh compression setting for doing JPEG compression, whereas other image programs let you choose how strongly to compress the file. A JPEG created by MS Paint usually doesn't look very good if larger than about 60 pixels in height or width. If the image is too harshly compressed for you, you can still use MS Paint initially, but use a more flexible graphics editor to create the final version of the image.

13. **Check the results of your work:**

   a. *Open the file containing the BMP, GIF, and JPEG versions of the image and note the file size of each.*

   b. *Right-click each image and choose Open with⇨Internet Explorer to see how the image will look in a Web page.*

   c. *Note whether the GIF or JPEG version of the image has the best combination of low file size and acceptable image quality.*

The GIF file will lose some image quality if the original image had more than 256 colors. For large or medium-sized photos, JPEG is almost always better, but for small images only experimentation can tell you which will give better results for a given image.

The danger of re-(re-)compression

If you're a scuba diver, you are likely to have been warned about the dangers of coming up from a great depth too quickly, which can cause a serious condition called "the bends." Unfortunately, it's possible to give your graphical images "the bends" as well — but the cause isn't decompression, it's *re*compression.

When you use GIF or JPEG to save and compress a file, the compressed file is significantly different than the original, in a way designed to maintain the image's appearance while shrinking its size. But if you recompress the compressed file a second (or third, or fourth) time, it gets ugly fast, cluttered with "artifacts" — areas in which poor compression introduces visible "scarring" to the original image. So (it bears repeating) always keep a copy of the original to work on.

There is one exception to this. Some devices (such as digital cameras) always save files in a lightly compressed, still very large, JPEG file. This kind of file can be re-compressed in JPEG to a much smaller image size without visible damage. But this can only be done one time; re-re-compressing the file makes it really ugly. So treat large JPEG files as originals — save them, and only compress them one (more) time before using them in your Web page.

Obtaining and Creating Images

So you want to put various images on your Web page. Great! But, if you can't find the image you need online and use the screen capture method above, how do you create the images you need and get them in the right format (GIF or JPEG)? Fortunately, creating the images you want, or finding some to use, is pretty easy.

The easiest way to obtain graphics is to get access to a clip-art collection. Computer stores sell many inexpensive collections of business and recreational graphics on CD-ROM. You can also access a number of royalty-free graphics and icon collections online.

If you're doing a business or professionally focused Web page, it's important that it have a clean, professional look. To get this kind of look, you have to use attractive images and lay out your page carefully. Chapters 11 (for WYSIWYG editors) and 15 (for straight HTML) tell you how to design your page appropriately for various purposes.

You can spend endless hours looking for art online. To help you get off to a quick start, here's a listing of sites I find especially cool:

- For a large number of different kinds of resources, go to the main WebReference site at www.webreference.com.

- For images of various types, go directly to the images area at www.webreference.com/authoring/graphics/images.html.

✔ For page backgrounds, visit `www.webreference.com/authoring/graphics/backgrounds.html`.

✔ For photographs, try a site with preexisting stock photos — `www.imagestate.com` is one I can recommend. Another choice, popular with professionals, is `www.gettyimages.com`, but these images cost money.

You can find many more sites that offer images and image conversions. Start with the sites mentioned here and expand your search until you find what you need.

Using the Image Search feature on Google or AltaVista is one of the best ways to look for suitable graphics. Be careful, though: Most of the graphics you find are copyrighted; for your Web site, you should only use images that are *explicitly* made freely available.

One of the best places to find images that are free to use is on various government Web sites — with URLs ending in `.gov` in the U.S. and `.gov.uk` in the U.K., just to give two examples. The taxpayers in each country have paid for the images, so they're made available for widespread free use. So government sites are a great resource for free images and, to a lesser extent, sound and video files.

In addition to searching online, another way to get graphics is to whip out any paint program and draw the graphics that you want. For example, you can use the free Windows Paint program (described above) for your initial graphics work. Even inexpensive paint programs today enable you to create some stunning graphics; you're limited mostly by your imagination and artistic ability (which for some of us is a pretty strong limit!).

For big-bucks commercial work and fine art, people regularly use high-end programs such as Adobe Photoshop and Adobe Illustrator. If you lack talent, you can always ask one of your artistically inclined friends to help you, or you can even recruit a starving art student.

Another technique is to use a scanner. You may already have one at home, or have use of a scanner in your office. If not, head to your favorite copy shop or Internet cafe and rent some time on its scanner. Simply scan your graphic or photo, save it in GIF (for graphics) or JPEG (for photographs) format, and slap it on your Web site.

Unfortunately, scanned images tend to have "noise" — little bits of dust, folds in paper, and so forth — that not only mess up the appearance of your image but that also completely undermine compression by breaking up what might otherwise be solid areas of white or some other color. It can take many hours to clean up this noise if you need a high-quality, well-compressed image.

More on graphics

The Graphics File Formats FAQ (Frequently Asked Questions page or area on a site) can answer almost any conceivable question about graphics. For a wide array of information, visit `www.martinreddy.net/gfx/utils-hi.html`. Links from this site lead to detailed technical information about GIF, JPEG, and other file formats. For a detailed description of how to use images well, see `cgi.netscape.com/assist/net_sites/impact_docs/index.html`.

For photos, work with a photo developer, such as a suitably equipped local developer, a chain store such as Wal-Mart or Rite Aid, or a mail-order and Internet operation such as PhotoWorks (`www.photoworks.com`), that can develop your film right to diskette or Photo CD.

A great way to get photographs is to take them with a digital camera. Digital cameras come with cables that connect the camera to your PC to download the photographs onto your computer. They also come with software that enables you to edit the photos on your PC and save them in JPEG format.

Many cellphones in use today take pictures that are good enough for casual Web use. These files are usually stored as JPEGs that you can downsize further for Web use. However, as you put these photos onto your Web site, you may find yourself wishing that your camera had a flash (or a better flash), a little more resolution, zoom, or some other features of a "real" camera.

No matter what format your graphic came in originally, you can convert it to GIF or JPEG by using software that you can easily obtain from the Web. Mac users can run GIFConverter (available at `www.kamit.com/gifconverter`), and Windows users can run the excellent LView program to convert between multiple formats (find LView at `www.lview.com`). Save your graphic as a GIF or JPEG file, and you're ready to incorporate the graphic into your Web page.

Save your image in the program's default format before saving it as a GIF or JPEG. When you save as a GIF or JPEG, the image can lose information. Every time you reopen the GIF or JPEG image, edit the file, and then save it again, you lose even more information. So save your file in its default format to preserve the data in it for later editing, then save a separate copy in GIF or JPEG to use on the Web.

What about rights?

You can find a number of great graphics in books and magazines and on Web sites. Can you just scan or copy these graphics and use them in your own Web site? Should you?

Yes and no. Yes, you can; but no, you shouldn't. Publishers either own the images that they use or obtain a license for them. You can't legally use most images on your own Web site without either buying or licensing them.

For some images on the Web, simply sending a note to the Webmaster gets you a quick okay. But for most Web images and for nearly all images in print, permissions may be very hard to get. Creating a new image that serves the same purpose is often easier than negotiating permissions. And then maybe you can make a little money licensing your new images out to other people!

Designing with Graphics

The most difficult aspect of including graphics in your Web pages is resolving all the design issues that accompany the use of graphics. Creating effective graphics and placing them properly in relation to your text is *not* as easy as boiling water. Although this book doesn't cover all the complexities of graphic design, I can give you a handle on the additional concerns that arise when you use graphics on the Web. That way you can effectively apply your own graphics skills — or those of people who work with you — to your Web pages.

More on download speed

One of the Web's ongoing problems is *download speed* — the amount of time a Web page takes to appear on the user's screen. Download times are especially slow for graphics-rich pages, which, although more interesting to view, can be more frustrating because they appear more slowly. And the trade-off is not simple; lots of variables intervene — these, for example:

- **Access speeds:** Different users access the Web through connections that run at different speeds. And the same server can serve up a Web page at different speeds, depending upon how busy the server is. When you test your brand-new, graphics-rich page on your local machine, everything may run fast. But when you upload that same page to a server and access the page over a 56Kbps (kilobits per second) modem, the page loads much more slowly.

Many more users now have broadband (fast) access at home, as well as at work. The good news is that most users will see your graphics quickly. The bad news is that the still-substantial minority with slow access are getting more and more frustrated as Web authors who have broadband access get careless about page sizes!

✔ **Good and bad graphics:** If you plan to spend your users' time on downloading big graphics, invest some effort up front to make sure that the graphics are as high-quality as possible. People don't mind waiting for a good graphic nearly as much as they mind waiting for a bad one. A good graphic may be a product shot that shows a Web surfer exactly what he or she is going to get. A bad graphic may be a banner that says "HELLO!" in hundreds of rotating fluorescent colors.

✔ **Frustration levels:** The same users who enjoy watching your page appear in the morning while drinking a cup of coffee may be tempted to scream at their browsers when they try to quickly check out your page just before heading home from work — especially if they had a bad hair day, a bad boss day, or even a bad browser day. The better the job you do with your graphics, the more your page will please people.

Table 5-1 shows the time necessary to download 60 K (kilobytes) of data. A text-only page is usually just 2–3K, but pages with graphics are much larger. A complex, quarter-screen GIF image, for example, may be about 60 K, whereas a photo measuring about 150 x 150 pixels would have to be strongly compressed to be that small. Compare the total size of all the elements in your page to the times shown in Table 5-1 to get an idea of how quickly your page loads for the most speed-deficient user, and then design with that person in mind.

Table 5-1	Download Times	
Access Speed	*Description*	*Time to Download 60 K*
28.8 Kbps	Low-end Internet modem	35 seconds
33.6 Kbps	Mid-range Internet modem	30 seconds
56 Kbps	Fast Internet modem	20 seconds
DSL	Special phone line, modem	4 seconds
Cable modem	Special cable hookup, modem	1 second
Ethernet	Standard network	Less than 1 second

Avoiding three big mistakes with images

Don't make these three big mistakes that hamper effective usage of images on the Web:

✔ **No images:** Sorry, but having no images on your Web pages means boring pages, no matter how good the text. Because you're reading this chapter, I assume that you're trying not to make this mistake.

✔ **Too many images:** Using too many large, slow-to-download images may be the biggest newbie Web-author mistake. (A lot of old hands make a similar mistake — everything is well-designed and compressed, but *one* uncompressed or too-lightly compressed photo sneaks through, making the whole page download slowly and shaking the user's confidence in the entire site.)

✔ **No text alternative:** An increasing number of vision-impaired people use the Web, and some users surf Web pages on text-only or slow-connection devices (such as a cellphone's Web browser). You need to accommodate these users by creating your page in a way that supports text-only access as well as graphical access, as described in Chapter 10 (for WYSIWYG Web page editing programs) and in Chapter 14 (for HTML editing programs).

Try an experiment: Go into your browser, turn off the graphics display, and load your Web page. If you can't tell what's on the page or what links go where, you need to redesign your page. (Then, just to blow off steam, or if you don't have a Web page up yet, try the same experiment on some other people's pages and send them a polite note if you encounter problems.)

The usual way to redesign your page for text-only access is to include a textual menu linking to the same places as your graphical menu. Some sites provide a whole parallel set of Web pages that are purely textual rather than graphical. Providing parallel, text-only pages lets the user choose whether to go for the attractive, bandwidth-sucking graphical pages or for the very fast text-only pages, and enables those with visual impairments (or those using other devices such as cellphones) to enjoy the full benefits of the Web.

In the past, many have chosen text-only access because of slow download times. However, because the percentage of users with non-broadband access continues to drop, providing a complete set of text-only pages may be overkill. Consider providing a *text-mostly* version, with limited use of images, simpler layout, and alternative text for images. This option may be just the ticket for users with visual impairments or those who are visiting via limited clients such as cellphones.

Here are the most important rules for supporting text and graphical access:

✔ As you design and create your page, think about how your page will look with all graphic access turned off as well as on.

✔ Test your page with graphics turned off.

✔ Test your page in different browsers.

✔ Include ALT tags — actually, the ALT attribute within the IMG tag — in all images so that explanatory text appears whenever a graphic isn't displayed.

✔ Provide text-only menus in addition to icon-based selections and image maps.

✔ If you want to make everyone very happy, consider creating a separate, text-only version of your site.

If you're considering creating a Web site that's accessible by portable devices such as Windows Mobile-powered phones or the RIM Blackberry line of handheld devices, then creating a text-only version of your site makes a great deal of sense. The text-only version of your site is a good starting point for handhelds.

Flickr forward

Flickr is a great resource for working with images because it's all about photos — and about making photos easy to use online. The home page of Flickr is shown in Figure 5-5.

Figure 5-5:
Flick your photos onto Flickr.

The constant surge of camera phones and digital cameras has created a problem — many photos don't get printed anymore. That's right: The photo gets taken, maybe shown to a couple of people on-screen, maybe e-mailed to a friend or two, and then forgotten in a folder somewhere.

Even the few photos that do get printed have all the limitations of any physical object: They cost money to create, can only be in one place at a time, and have to be stored somewhere or thrown away. All of those limitations can add up to a burden on your wallet and on the environment.

Enter Flickr, which bills itself as "the best way to store, search, sort, and share your photos." (Try saying that three times fast; you'll end up saying "searching, shorting, and sharing.")

As a visitor to Flickr, you can have an awful lot of fun. You can search through photos in a bunch of different ways, from the sensible to the quirky.

But you get the most out of Flickr by using it to store and show off your own photos. When you try this, you find out the really great things Flickr lets you do:

- ✔ **Storing your photos:** You can create a free account that holds hundreds of photos. With a free account, you can upload 20 MB of photos a month, or about 100 reasonably sized JPEG images. The number of photos is also limited — to 200. Or upgrade to a Pro account and store thousands of photos.

   You can simply store all your photos online, at least up to a point. Or you can just store the interesting ones and keep the rest on your PC — or take the opportunity to send them to the great big bit box in the sky.

- ✔ **Sharing your photos:** People can visit Flickr and see your photos — under your control! You can keep private photos confined to a small group of viewers, whereas others can be seen by anyone who visits Flickr.

- ✔ **Sorting your photos:** As your "photobase" grows, you can sort and organize your photos in many ways, making them more interesting and convenient to access for your own use and for others.

- ✔ **Searching through photos:** Labeling and organizing your photos well makes it very easy for you to find just the ones you want — and for others to find the photos you want to share with them as well.

All these uses for Flickr are covered in this chapter. I show you how to get the most out of Flickr and your photos.

In addition to doing these basic things, you can also get involved with the Flickr user community. There are special things you can do with photos on Flickr that you can't do other places. You can

✔ **Add notes to a photo:** For instance, you can name everyone in that picture from the office party.

✔ **Add tags to a photo:** Make it easy for people to find your picture among others like it. For instance, by adding the tag "Golden Gate Bridge" to your photo, you can make it easy for people to find your photo among all those of the famous San Francisco landmark.

✔ **Put a photo in a pool:** Pools of photos are photos linked in some way; if you see an open pool that's relevant, you can dive right in and add your photo to it!

✔ **Engage in discussions about photos:** You can share comments about photos on a message board — even highlight an area on a photo and mark it up with a message. (Yes, you'll see lots of immature "kiss me, you fool"-type messages if you look around.)

✔ **Publish photos to a blog or your Web site:** You can put pictures hosted on Flickr in your blog or other Web site. You can even see recent Flickr uploads on your mobile phone.

I don't describe these additional features of Flickr in much detail here — after you start using Flickr, you can easily (perhaps too easily) spend all your time there. I don't want to be seen encouraging you to do too much of that, or your boss, spouse, kids, and other folks who need your attention might blame me when you "Flickr out" for days on end.

Despite all Flickr does for you, you may want to master one capability for processing images *before* you upload them: making smaller versions of your photos, as described early in this chapter. Many digital camera images are very large, say, 1024 x 768, and with millions of colors, resulting in a multi-megabyte image. This is way more than you need for most purposes (except ordering prints), and means you'll use up your 20MB monthly allotment very quickly. (Mobile phone camera images tend to be much smaller.)

Flickr resizes photos during uploading, but you may want to control the process by doing it yourself.

So, to spare yourself trouble, find an image-manipulation program that you can use to make images smaller. Fortunately, Flickr has good image-manipulation features built into the site. You can also try Photoshop Express, an offering from Adobe (www.photoshop.com/express), though online reviews rated the initial version below Flickr's tools. One very good free program is InsightPoint. You can download a completely free version from sites such as CNET's Download.com (www.download.com). Or, look to see if an image manipulation program was provided with your digital camera.

Flickr flaws

Not everything is perfect in Flickr-land. Here are a few flies in Flickr's ointment that you should be aware of going in:

- **Too adult?** For some potential users, Flickr may have too many grown-up images. Despite strict rules forbidding "frontal nudity, genitalia, and intimate moments" in Flickr photos, it's not hard to find nudity and semi-nudity on the site. If you post family photos on Flickr for your children to view, they may keep looking on the site and find some things you'd rather they not see.

  Flickr's terms of service limit users to those 13 or older, but there's no way for anyone to enforce it — probably, few users even know it. So it's up to you to decide whom you want to encourage to use Flickr.

- **Too easy?** Flickr makes it very easy to upload huge numbers of not-very-interesting photos. (Is *every* picture you take with your mobile phone worth sharing with the world?) You have to exercise considerable restraint to make sure all the photos you upload are worth the time your friends and family might spend looking at them.

- **Too open?** Flickr has excellent privacy protections, but it's still easier to do the lazy thing and make all your photos public — or for passwords to be shared more widely than you planned. Someone putting Tom Cruise's head on your body might be funny — but there are enough weirdos out there that you may want to think twice before letting photos of, say, your kids be widely viewed.

- **Too flexible?** Professional photographers are always careful to get a signed *model release* (permission form) from everyone depicted in a photograph they want to sell or otherwise use. You don't necessarily need to be that careful — but the jury's still out (pun intended) on exactly what the limits are. Be careful, especially about using photos without rights in any way that may help you make money (for instance, on a business's Web site).

- **Too good?** Flickr is so good that it's been acquired by Yahoo! You now need a Yahoo! ID to open a new account. The changes that Yahoo! makes may end up improving it — or not, depending on your point of view.

Think over these concerns before you commit a bunch of time and energy to Flickr. You may prefer to put your photos online some other way. Or, use Flickr to host your photos, but put the best of them on your own site for viewing. No matter what, you have many more options with Flickr than without.

If you share a computer with others, you may not have as much privacy as you think. The History function of your browser can make it easy for others to see Web pages you've visited, and photos get cached in ways that a lot of bright 10-year-olds can figure out. So be very careful if you think you can use "private" areas on Flickr to upload and view highly personal photos, and then let others use your computer and not have access to them. They may see more than you intend for them to.

Uploading a Photo to Flickr

Here's a quick guide to getting a photo onto Flickr. It's amazing how confidence-building it can be just to do something simple like this once.

1. **Get a JPEG photo onto your computer system.**

   The easiest way is to upload or e-mail a photo to yourself from your mobile phone. Or, copy pictures from a digital camera. Find a photo on your hard disk. (Choose Start⇨Search⇨For files or folders, and then choose Pictures, Music, or Video.) Or copy a photo from the Web — use a search engine to find images that are free for use.

2. **Open your Web browser.**

   As is the case with more and more Web sites, Flickr can be used with any kind of PC — or even with a mobile phone. But when you're just getting started, it's best to have a PC with fast Web access to use when you upload photos to Flickr.

3. **Go to www.flickr.com.**

   A screen like the one shown earlier in Figure 5-5 appears, although the screen may change to reflect new quotes, different sponsorships, or increased influence from Yahoo!, Flickr's owners.

4. **Sign in.**

   If you're already a Yahoo! or Flickr member, click the Sign In link on the home page and use your ID to sign in. If not, click Sign up! and create an ID.

   After you're signed in, an opening screen like the one in Figure 5-6 appears. Resist the temptation to explore — it's time to get something done.

5. **Click the link *Upload your first photo* (or *Upload photos* if you've uploaded before).**

   The Upload Photos page appears.

6. **Click the Browse button.**

   The Select File dialog box appears over the Upload Photos page, as shown in Figure 5-7. Note that you can easily specify up to six photos at a time.

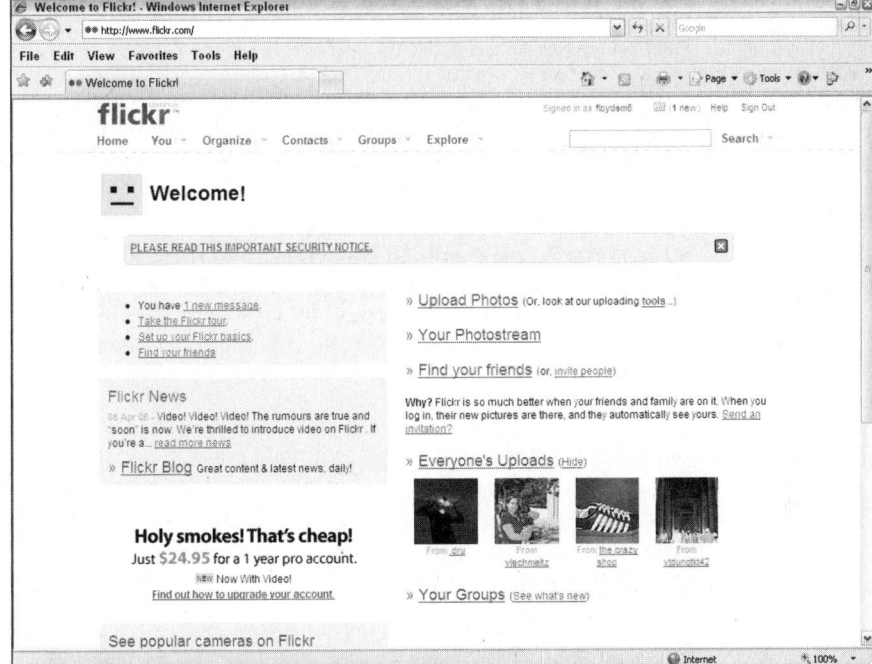

Figure 5-6:
Flickr
invites you
to upload a
photo — or
look around.

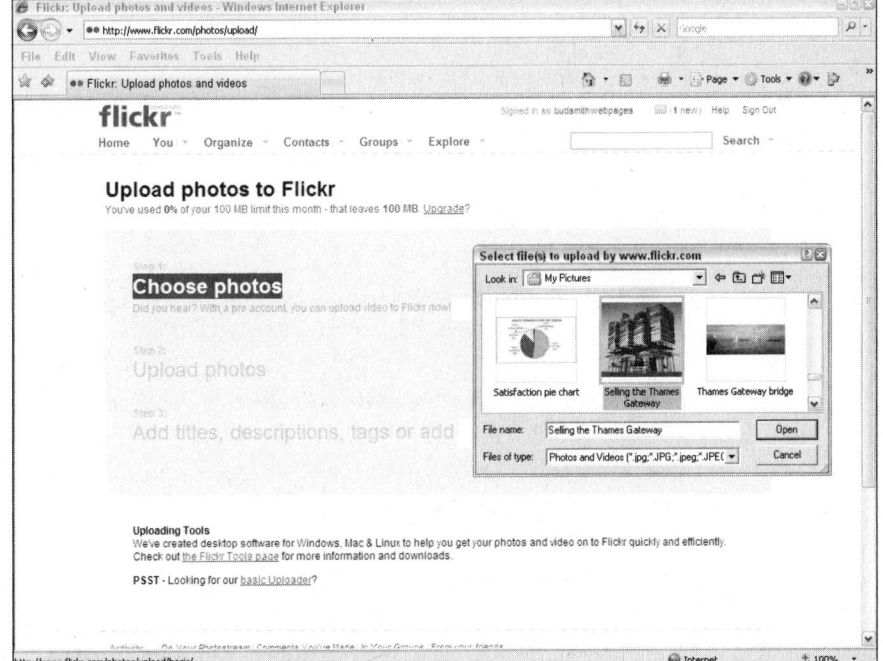

Figure 5-7:
It's easy to
upload a
few photos
at a time
from your
hard drive.

7. **Use the Select File dialog box to locate an image — or several images.**

   Find an image on your PC to upload to Flickr. Repeat to upload multiple images.

   You can avoid the step of copying files to your PC if you can attach your mobile phone or camera to your computer. Just use the Select File dialog box to find the mobile phone or camera as an attached device, and then copy the files directly from there.

   Make sure you *don't* upload an image if you think anyone in the picture may not want his or her face plastered all over the Web. Some people have lost job opportunities (or even jobs they already had) because personal photos that depicted (for instance) drunken behavior at a party were put up on somebody's Web page.

8. **Upload your photos.**

   Click the Upload button; your photos are uploaded, and Flickr creates various preview and thumbnail versions for use in various places. Click the "add a description?" link to bring up the Describe This Upload screen.

9. **Add one or more tags to describe the image(s).**

   Add descriptive words, called *tags,* to describe your pictures. Using tags in a way that makes sense to you, and that fits the way others use tags on Flickr, is a bit of an art — for now, just pick a descriptive word or two. You can always edit tags later.

10. **Choose privacy settings.**

    There are five possible privacy settings in Flickr:

    - **Public:** Everyone can see your photos. Click the Public radio button to choose this setting.

    - **Private: Visible to you only.** To get this setting, click the Private radio button, and then leave unchecked the Visible to Friends and the Visible to Family check boxes.

    - **Private: Visible to Friends.** Click the Private radio button, and then check the Visible to Friends check box. Clear the Visible to Family check box.

    - **Private: Visible to Family.** Click the Private radio button, and then check the Visible to Family check box. Clear the Visible to Friends check box.

    - **Private: Visible to Friends and Family.** Click the Private radio button, and then check the Visible to Friends check box and the Visible to Family check box.

You specify friends and family by adding them to lists. (Yes, you can add one person to both lists, which is sort of like an "all access" pass.) When those folks sign in, they get the access you've specified.

The Private setting visible to you only — which you achieve by choosing the Private radio button and clearing both the Visible to Friends and Visible to Family check boxes — is a bit hidden, but very useful. You can use this setting to store all your photos on Flickr, and then "publish" selected photos to others by changing their privacy settings.

11. **Add titles, descriptions, and tags to your photos.**

    Now's the time! It's easy to skip this step, but if you don't do this now, you may never get around to it — and you may have difficulty finding some of your precious photos again. A typical result is shown in Figure 5-8.

12. **Save your photos.**

    Finally, you're on Flickr! Figure 5-9 shows the first set of photos the author uploaded. Note that the middle picture is sideways — I fix that in the next section.

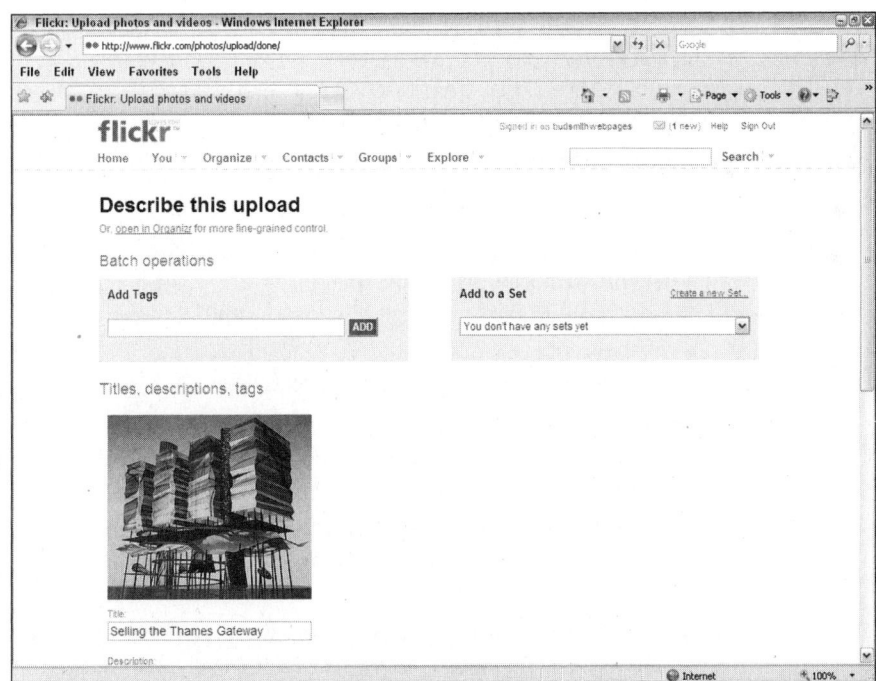

Figure 5-8: Now it's time to title, describe, and tag your photos.

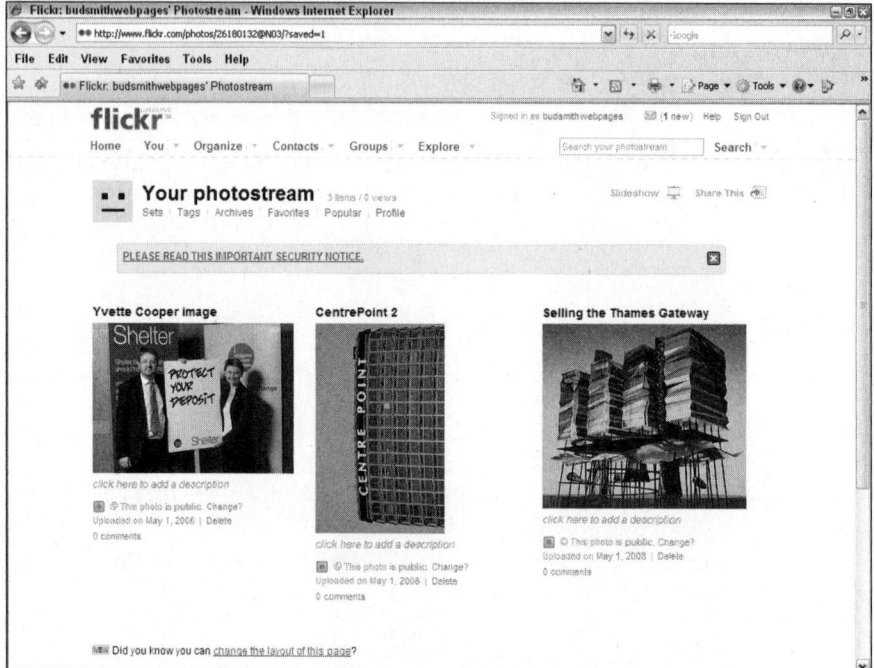

Figure 5-9:
Three's a
lucky
number.

Modifying Photos on Flickr

One of the great things about Flickr is that the people who created it have thought through the whole process. They don't make you fix a photo before you upload it, or figure out every detail of a description the first time — you can change most of those things after you upload a picture.

Here's a quick checklist of things you can easily change after you upload a picture — avoiding, for now, some of the more advanced sharing features of Flickr:

- ✔ **Add note:** You can annotate a picture with a note in a specific location.

- ✔ **Order prints:** You can buy copies of your photos — this works better on photos with relatively high resolution (1024 x 768 or larger), thousands or millions of colors, and taken with a steady hand (not blurry).

- ✔ **Rotate:** My favorite! I like to take pictures at different angles, and Rotate saves me time because I don't have to fix the rotation until after I upload them.

✓ **Change privacy settings:** It's easy to change who can see a picture.

✓ **Change the title, description, and tags:** Easy to do, and redo, and redo — but hard to get around to if you've uploaded a bunch of pictures without giving them meaningful titles, descriptions, or tags.

✓ **Flag as "may offend":** I'm sure that my wonderful readers would never upload a racy image — but in case you do, here's your chance to keep it from vulnerable eyes. Just flag the photo as "may offend" and you keep it from being found on a normal search.

Follow the instructions below to make the preceding changes, or even more, in a photo:

1. **Click a photo you've uploaded to Flickr.**

   Find any photo you've uploaded and click it. You are taken to an editing screen for the photo.

2. **Click the button you want to apply to the photo.**

   You can apply all sorts of changes or actions to the photo (see the preceding list). For example, if you click the Rotate button, a small window appears to preview the rotate operation.

3. **Finish the action you've chosen.**

   Depending on what you've chosen to do — add a note, order prints, and so on — you'll be prompted to take one or more steps to finish the action. Figure 5-10 shows how the screen looks after choosing Rotate for a specific picture, and then clicking the turn-right icon; the preview window shows the rotated photo.

TIP

Flickr-ing photos to your blog

You can "flick" photos onto your blog very easily once you set up a couple of things. Blogger, the blogging service referred to in Chapter 4, is one of the many blogging services directly supported by Flickr. Start by visiting www.flickr.com/blogs.gne to make your blog known to Flickr, enter the password, and so on. Once setup is done, it's just a matter of a couple of mouse clicks to move photos, with comments, to your blog. (Fellow Flickrers who don't want their photos blogged can specify that as well.)

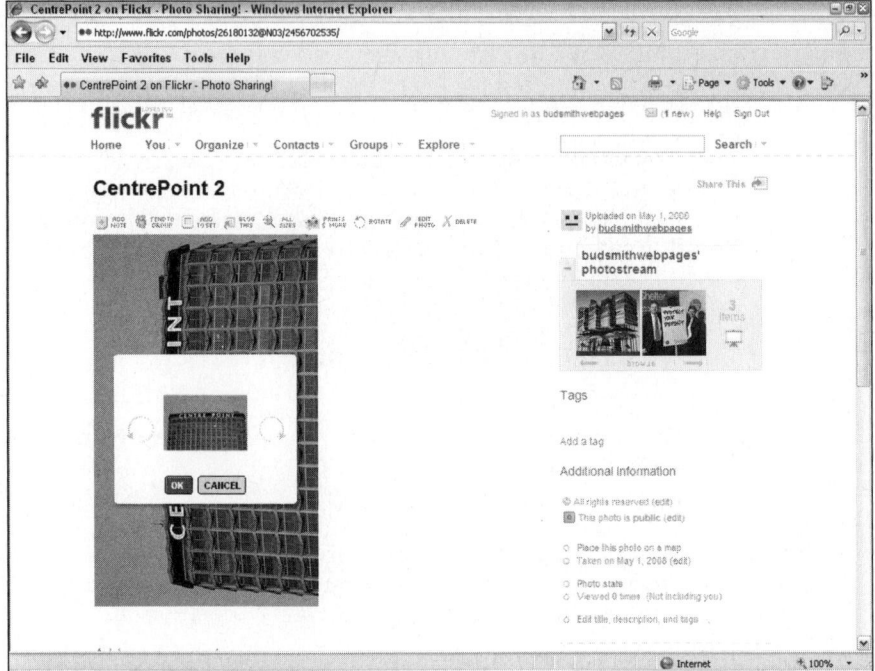

Figure 5-10:
You can make your photos better and more interesting.

4. Click OK to complete the action.

The screen reappears with the update you've chosen.

5. Add comments.

Comments make photos more interesting — and you can use basic HTML to format them, as shown in Figure 5-11. See the Cheat Sheet at the front of this book for some basic commands, or go to Chapter 8 for more information. Here's a brief list of tags:

b. Traditional formatting is `<b>` to start bold text and `</b>` to end bold.

i. Traditional formatting is `<i>` to start italicized text and `</i>` to end italic.

blockquote. Marking out text with `<blockquote>` before and `</blockquote>` after keeps its original formatting and line breaks.

a = href, target. You can use traditional HTML formatting, `<a="www.flickr.com">`. Give a link from the picture to a Web address.

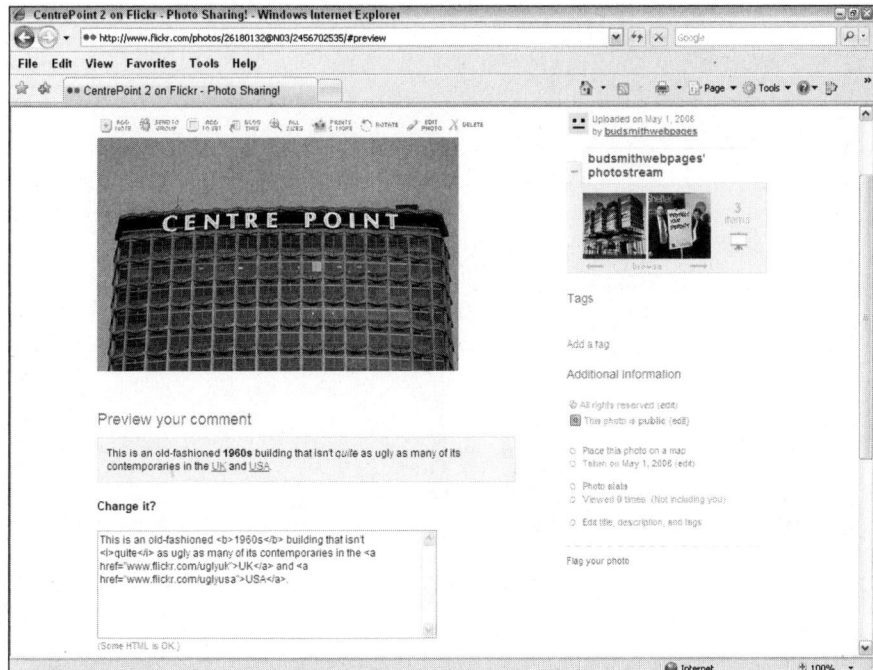

Figure 5-11:
Comments
make
pictures
richer.

Taking Flickr Further

You can do much more with Flickr. Getting experience with uploading, modifying, commenting on, and tagging photos prepares you to take advantage of all of Flickr's features.

You can organize your photos using Organizr, Flickr's photo-file management system. You can change access permission, dates, and tags. You can create sets and modify your Photostream, the log of recently updated photos.

As you do more with photos, even your view of Flickr's home page changes to reflect your work.

Flickr can, all by itself, become a major preoccupation. For example, you can find popular tags on Flickr and set yourself the task of creating and adding new photos that extend your favorite tag sets.

You can also use Flickr to host photos that you then publish on your own Web site or blog, as described in previous chapters — so Flickr can be a resource for all your Web publishing. Enjoy!

Chapter 6

Playing Sounds on Your Site

· ·

· ·

Sound is one of the most important sensory resources we have. It's our early warning system and our primary means of communicating directly with each other. Music is one of the great artistic forms and one of the main pleasures in most people's lives.

Music download sites, for legal, illegal, and gray-market recordings, are among the most popular sites on the Web, consuming huge amounts of bandwidth and attracting usage, attention, lawsuits, and even prosecutions in large numbers. The leading *legal* music-download site, iTunes, is one of the great successes in not only Web but business history.

Yet most Web sites offer only "The Sound of Silence" (to name-drop Simon and Garfunkel). And thankfully so, many of us think; having sound come on suddenly when one visits a Web site is one of the greatest and, often, nastiest surprises that can happen to someone using the Web. (As you'll know if you've ever been embarrassed at work by people turning around to see what the noise suddenly coming from your PC is all about.)

As the example of noisy Web sites illustrates, sound is also very basic and very emotional for people. We have strong reactions to sounds. Teenagers — and, in the U.K. and other countries, soccer fans — often organize into tribe-like groups around music and songs, and music has been used throughout history to organize, direct, and inspire soldiers. So using sound wrongly has penalties that may outweigh the benefits of using it right.

Sound is also a vital — if overlooked — part of video files, the subject of the next chapter. It's the unification of the power of sound with the power of moving images, offering a decent simulation of a real-world scene, that makes video so affecting.

This chapter describes some of the issues around using sound on a Web site — and the much sunnier picture for downloadable tunes, including how to post a tune on MySpace, the extremely popular Web-site host.

Compressing and Decompressing Sound

The human ear is really, really good at distinguishing among different sounds. We can usually spot "foreigners" — whether from another country or maybe just from another neighborhood — by their accents in a second or two, or recognize a favorite tune in just a couple of notes.

This is because there's a tremendous amount of information in the sounds we can hear. To capture this information accurately for computer storage and transmission takes a lot of cleverness — not to mention bandwidth. A relatively uncompressed file format such as the Windows WAV format and the roughly comparable Apple AIFF format take about 170 KB for *each second* of sound, or about 10 MB per minute. Even a fast Internet connection can't deliver "live" WAV sound; users must wait anywhere from several seconds to many minutes before they can hear the sound, depending on how fast the connection is and how long the sound file is.

The most popular compressed file format, the MP3 format — the audio equivalent of the marvelous JPEG photo format described in Chapter 5, using tricks of psychology and physics to capture music in a compressed file — takes about 17 KB per second of sound, or about 1 MB per minute, one-tenth the bit rate of a WAV file. This is just within the capability of most Internet connections to play back an MP3 live, or nearly live, or to download the file within a few minutes for later playback.

Despite its cleverness and success, MP3 may not be as aesthetically successful as its pictorial equivalent, JPEG. Why not? After all, the slight coldness and tinniness of MP3 files is probably, objectively, no worse than the slight visual "noise" found in moderately compressed JPEG files. But because sound is so emotionally involving, MP3 files are perhaps more likely than JPEGS to be experienced as not-quite-good-enough. Two indicators of this dissatisfaction: Vinyl record albums seem to be experiencing a slight resurgence, and there's some support for more precise audio-file formats, despite the cost in file size and transmission time.

Not every computer out there has all the necessary elements to play back sounds in a sound file — a program to decode the sound and play it, sound hardware to deliver sound to output(s), and speakers and/or a headphone jack to actually produce sound the user can hear. Where all the elements are in place, they can be turned off (or the headphones not plugged in), and users may be anywhere from slightly disinclined to absolutely unwilling to turn on the sound gear just to hear the sound you want them to listen to.

Naming of parts for sounds

Here I'm going to refer to *sounds* to mean any of the range of different kinds of sounds you can put on a Web site and *tunes* to mean music files intended for listening, like the kinds of tunes you hear on the radio — including (just to focus on a typical American radio lineup) rock 'n' roll, country and western, classical, Spanish-language, and experimental radio stations!

Using Sound within a Web Page

Many of us would like to have a soundtrack or mood music for our Web sites — that is, a tune that plays continuously while the user surfs around our site. This would make using the site more pleasant — and contribute to its having a personality. Ideally, the user would be able to easily turn the sound on or off — most users would probably prefer being offered this choice before any sound started.

Unfortunately, making this seemingly simple set of desiderata happen in a user-friendly way is just about impossible. You can put a sound file in a Web *page* but not a Web *site*. So you can indeed start a sound playing on a given page of your site. But when the user leaves that page for the next one, sound stops.

On serving the next page, you can play a new sound file — or the same sound file again — but it won't pick up seamlessly from where the sound on the previous page left off. In fact, it's just about impossible to know where the old sound file stopped so as to try to make the sound on the new page pick up again in the same spot.

In the example that follows, I show how to place a sound file in a Web page and attempt to have it start playing automatically. Giving the user a choice before the sound starts playing requires JavaScript or other more advanced Web technologies that are beyond the scope of this book. If you want to offer this capability to the user, see *JavaScript For Dummies* (Wiley) or another source about JavaScript.

Alas, the seemingly unambitious goal of having background music play as the user visits one's Web site is surprisingly difficult to make work consistently.

Using sound on a Web page is easier on any specific type and version of a Web browser, but not easy across different types of Web browsers and different versions. The accepted HTML coding for this capability has changed over the last several years. It used to be that the embed HTML command could, well, embed any kind of multimedia file in a Web site. But EMBED never became an official standard, so Microsoft stopped supporting it, supporting the bgsound (background sound) command instead. Due to popular demand, Microsoft then added support for embed back in, but not all users of Internet Explorer have the fix.

Without embed in Internet Explorer, to make sound work across all types of browsers required that you execute the embed HTML command for some browsers and the bgsound HTML command for others. This can be done by combining the two commands, as I show later in this chapter (and explain in later chapters as well).

Unfortunately, the JavaScript code that could help you make the decision has compatibility problems across early browsers as well. If you made any mistake at all, or were just unlucky, sound would either not play, or the same sound would play twice, with the two instances of the sound slightly out of synch with each other!

Because of all this complexity, few Web sites embed sounds in Web pages. Because it's rarely needed, some users haven't downloaded the software needed to play back sounds from within Web pages. So if you go to the effort, and make it work, you may still be asking the user to go through a difficult and time-consuming program download just to play a background sound in your Web page.

So, believe it or not, there's no simple, reliable, completely user-acceptable way to make a sound play in your Web page. Except by embedding the sound in a video file! No wonder more music videos are now played back on YouTube than on MTV and other music-oriented TV channels.

However, embed is supported widely enough for "fun" use, where it doesn't reflect badly on your professional competence or your organization if it doesn't work for some people. I show how to embed an audio file via MySpace in the example that's coming up shortly.

Getting, Creating, and Including Sound Files by Download

Luckily it's fairly easy to set up a sound file to play by download. If the user has the necessary software and hardware set up and turned on, sound will play. If not, the user probably knows it, and won't click the download link, limiting the impact of any problems on you, the Web-page creator.

Making the user click a link avoids the problem with the conflict between the embed command and the bgsound command described above, so you don't need to use JavaScript or some other technology to try to help your Web page decide what to do.

When standards fail

Early versions of HTML included support for two media types: hypertext and GIF images. JPEG images were not included, and sound and other multimedia files weren't either.

When JPEG files first became popular in Web pages, back in the mid-'90s, you had to download a separate player to view them. Some of these players were pretty good and produced amazingly sharp images; others were crummy. But HTML was still flexible at this time, and JPEG support was added so widely that it became a standard part of the Web browsers that people use today.

Technical Stuff: At first, embedding a multimedia file was easy; the `embed` command was used, usually bringing up Apple QuickTime as the player. But Microsoft quit supporting `embed`, apparently for security reasons. Microsoft recommends the `bgsound` tag instead, but Mozilla — including the currently popular Firefox browser, with about 10 per cent of the user base — doesn't support it.

A similar problem has hampered the physical equipment needed to play back sound. Simply put, sound playback was not part of the PC standard set by IBM back in the '80s, and is still not a completely standard part of a desktop PC, partly because corporations (until recently) have not seen the need for sound, or even actively have discouraged using it. Sound hardware is standard for laptops, but that's still only a part of the market.

For standards to work, all the major players involved have to work together. With Microsoft supporting Windows Media Player, the ex-Microsofties at Real Networks pushing RealPlayer, Apple proliferating its own QuickTime, and the Mozilla people requiring extra steps for any sound support at all, the standards process for sound files within Web pages has broken down. Of course, with universal hardware support lacking, it's little wonder. What is potentially one of the most important tools a Web-page author would like to have in his or her arsenal is missing in action.

Steps shown in Chapter 10 (for a WYSIWYG editor) or Chapter 14 (for "straight" HTML) show how to include a link to an MP3 file. When the user clicks on the link, if everything's set up and turned on, sound will play.

But how do you get a sound file, or create one? I show you here. Then you can make sound available to your users, putting it just a click away.

Getting an MP3 file

At first, it seems fairly easy to find an MP3 file on the Web. However, people know that MP3 files are desirable, so there are a lot of conditions around many of the files out there. Also, some people who want to distribute viruses, spyware, and other malware use MP3 files to attract visitors to their sites — and the innocent visitors leave with more than they bargained for.

Also, the most desirable MP3 files are free copies of hit songs. *These files are illegal* and attract increasingly aggressive litigation and prosecution. So, although they're common on the Web, they tend to be hidden away or only available to those who use file-sharing services (which may themselves carry viruses, spyware, and other such dismal "free gifts").

One trustworthy source for virus-free, legal, free MP3s is the music-download section of CNET's `download.com`, at `music.download.com`. See Figure 6-1 for an example of what's available. Not many hit tunes are there, but not many problems are, either.

Figure 6-1:
CNET's music-download site is a haven, away from MP3-related spyware.

You can search the Web for other sites, many of which are trustworthy — but make sure your virus-protection software is up to date and running first!

Check the permissions on any MP3 file you find carefully. Once you're certain the file is free of copyright problems and available for free use, you can do either of two things:

✔ **Link to it in place from your own site.** This is easy and convenient. If this gives the appearance of the file being on your site, there is the possibility of problems with copyright, as you've made someone else's property appear to be your own, so make sure the file is free to use. If you bring a lot of file downloads to the site, you're also abusing their bandwidth, as someone else's bandwidth is serving your purposes. This is unlikely to be a problem for an occasional download, but for heavy use it's unfair to the file's host.

✔ **Download the file and transfer it to your own site.** If permissions allow this, it gives you control *and* responsibility. It also gives you the bill if there are a whole lot of downloads and you're paying for download bandwidth.

In either case, to make the file available for download, you link to it from your Web page to the location where it's hosted, whether that's on someone else's site or your own site.

The HTML code for this is simple:

To get the latest *a capella* song by me, sung loudly and off-key in the shower,
`<a href=''www.dummies.com/myfile.mp3''>click here</a>`.

I show how to incorporate this functionality into a Web page a little farther along in the book, using a WYSIWYG Web-page creation tool in Chapter 10 and using HTML in Chapter 14.

Creating an MP3 file

It's very satisfying to create and deliver your own MP3 file. In this example, I use the simplest possible tools to create a sound file and convert it to MP3.

The example is a voice file, because that's the easiest to create for the most people and more often useful in a typical, rather than a specialist music, Web site.

MP3 is so good with music that it's a bit of overkill for voice files, which can be encoded and played back with less-powerful compression algorithms. But so many people have set their systems up to play MP3 files these days — both on their PCs and on music players such as the Apple iPod — that you may as well go with the flow and join the crowd (with apologies for using two clichés in a row).

If you have a Mac, it includes well-regarded built-in software to accomplish these tasks called iLife; please refer to the iLife documentation for steps. Follow these steps to create an MP3 file under Windows:

1. **Find the built-in microphone, if your system has one, or attach a microphone to your computer.**

   It's good if you have a built-in microphone or one lying around. If not, try to determine the size of the microphone opening on your PC, or take your PC with you to the shop so you can be sure of getting a fit. Or, if you have an unused USB connector, consider buying a USB microphone, which are well-regarded and are certain to fit.

2. **Open Windows Sound Recorder by choosing Start⇨Programs⇨ Accessories⇨Entertainment⇨Sound Recorder.**

   The Sound Recorder application window is very small and can't be resized. However, like MS Paint (described in the previous chapter), it includes a lot of capability; you can make sounds louder, quieter, faster, and slower, for instance. The Sound Recorder application is shown in Figure 6-2.

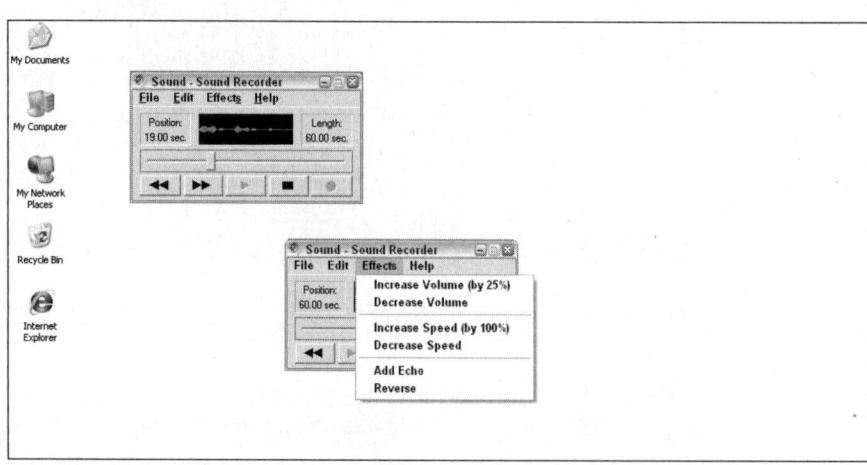

Figure 6-2: Sound Recorder during recording, with editing options showing.

3. **Record your message. Click the red Record button, wait three seconds, and speak. When you're finished speaking, wait three seconds and click Stop.**

   The sound is recorded. The three seconds of "blank tape" at the beginning and end give you room to play with in editing and prevent the recording from seeming to start or stop too abruptly.

4. **Click Play to hear your message. Choose File⇨New and then return to Step 3 to re-record if necessary.**

   When you're happy with your message, go to the next step.

5. Save the file as a WAV file.

This is the only file format supported by Sound Recorder — no tricky choices to make here.

6. Convert the file to MP3.

You may already have a converter program on your PC. If not, search the Web for "MP3 converter" or look for a program of this type on CNET's `download.com`. One well-regarded program that's free is Audacity, which you can download from `audacity.soundforge.net`. It should be quite simple to open the WAV file and save it in MP3 format. You can read the Help file information for instructions on how to edit your file.

7. Play the MP3 file to test it.

You should be able to play the file by double-clicking it. It will play back in Windows Media Player, QuickTime, or another media player you have on your computer.

8. Compare the file sizes of the WAV and MP3 files.

Just to convince yourself of how great MP3 is, do a comparison: In Windows Explorer, navigate to the folder where the files are stored. Right-click each file icon and choose Properties. Inspect the size of each file.

You're done! You now have an MP3 file ready to host on your Web site. And, more importantly, you've learned the process of creating an MP3 file from scratch.

The process is the same for podcasting as for Web-page hosting, so you may have a future in creating your own music or talk show for playback on iPod and other MP3 players.

Posting a Sound File on MySpace

MySpace is amazing, and amazingly popular. It's the graffiti wall for the digital generation, hugely popular with teenagers, young adults, and others who keep up with music, along with smatterings of all kinds of people.

There are a huge number of things you can do on MySpace, but there's one thing it's definitely the best place for: sharing your enthusiasm about music. There are millions of people on MySpace interested in and willing to listen to, comment on, and even become a fan of a new artist or group of just about any type.

MySpace is also famous for being relatively "wild," with lots of, as the Brits would say, "dodgy" (or downright objectionable) videos and other content that only get taken down slowly, and after complaints are made, if at all. Also, even some of the non-obscene content is not for all tastes; when I was logged on, there was a constantly looping video on the home page of two furry toys beating the heck out of each other, which was sort of funny but not what I would have chosen to watch over and over and over. So MySpace is not the place to send your 9-year-old nephew to listen to your latest upload; kids might find lots of objectionable stuff after they view your new cultural contribution.

Join the MySpace cadets

Joining MySpace is relatively simple. Follow these steps:

1. **Go to the MySpace home page at** www.myspace.com **(as shown in Figure 6-3) and click the orange Sign Up button.**

   The Join MySpace Here! Page appears. Click the Sign Up Button to start.

Figure 6-3:
You may
want to
make
MySpace
your space.

2. **Enter login details — a valid e-mail address and a password.**

   The e-mail address you enter will be used to confirm your sign-up and possibly to send you a MySpace newsletter. It may be best to avoid using your work e-mail address, as the MySpace newsletter may not be what your management expects you to be receiving at work.

3. **Note the extra sign-up areas at the right for BAND/MUSICIAN, COMEDIAN, and FILMMAKER members. If you fit in one of these categories, click the appropriate Sign up Here link to sign up.**

   Because MySpace has landed in some trouble for hosting copyrighted material, it limits what users can post. These options allow you to upload files of your own performances — MP3s, for instance, for BAND/MUSICIAN members — but only if you pass MySpace's checks (which can vary from one period of time to the next) that you really do qualify as a BAND/MUSICIAN. Ditto for the other creative categories of members.

4. **Enter personal details — your name, location, birthday, gender, and language. Decide whether you want to allow others to see if it's your birthday.**

   The location info is to allow friends and family to find you on MySpace. On the birthday option, I chose "No," not wanting to get any kind of MySpace spam — or, for that matter, to learn what might be more than I wanted to know about my fellow MySpacers' ideas of appropriate birthday greetings.

5. **Enter the verification text. If you can't make it out, click the Refresh button to bring up different characters.**

   The verification characters prevent automated entry of new MySpace membership details.

6. **Right-click the Terms of Service and Privacy Policy to open them each in a new browser window. Read them, and then close the browser windows. Then click the check box to indicate you've read them.**

   Note that this process may include signing you up for a MySpace newsletter and other materials from MySpace. Refuse this option if you wish.

7. **Click the Sign Up button.**

   The Welcome screen appears, giving you the chance to upload a photo or add friends.

8. **Click Skip this step twice to skip the photo and friends options for now.**

   Your MySpace home page appears.

9. **Click the Edit Profile button.**

The Profile Edit page appears. You can enter HTML or even CSS code here. As you learn more about HTML, you can use your new MySpace page to experiment.

10. **Embed a link to a sound file.**

    All sorts of code to do things in MySpace can be found easily online. Embedding is a bit tricky because of the need to accommodate both the `embed` and `bgsound` commands, but it can be done, as shown in Figure 6-4. (The last part of the command is `</noembed>`.) By placing the commands in the Headline area, the sound plays automatically when the user visits the page.

    One good source I found for MySpace-ready HTML, with plenty of links to other resources, is `www.hypergurl.com`.

11. **Click Save to save your work.**

    You'll return to the MySpace home page.

12. **Visit and test your page.**

    You'll return to the MySpace home page.

13. **Keep updating your MySpace!**

    MySpace is a great place to have fun and to learn Web-page skills as well. Keep having fun with it.

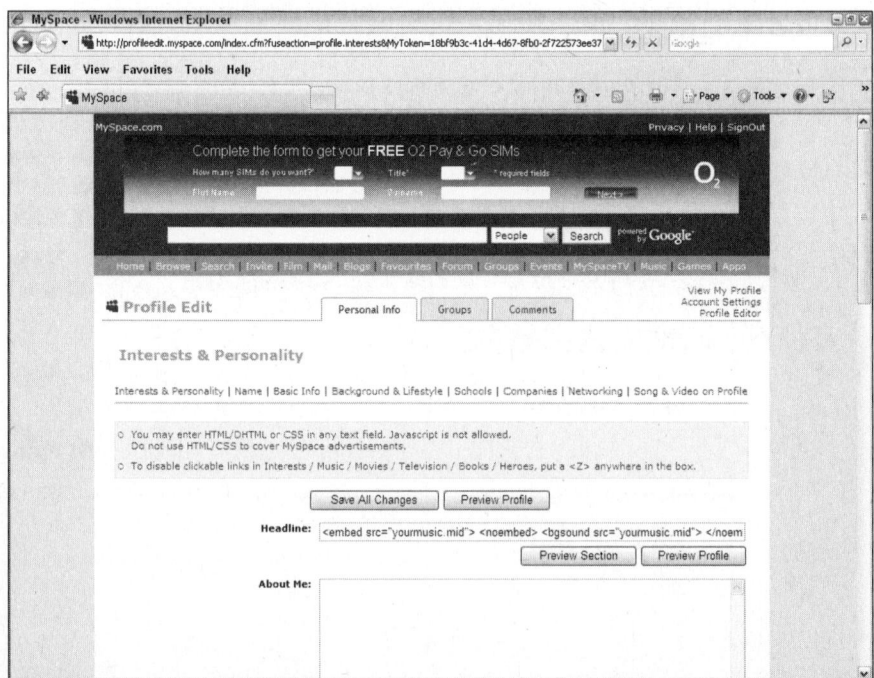

Figure 6-4:
EMBED
links to
music you
like.

Chapter 7

Screening Videos on Your Site

A great deal of derision is poured on television — "a vast wasteland," it was once called, by the chairperson of the Federal Communications Commission, no less. Even the best-known and most widely used Web site for videos, YouTube, gets far more usage than it does respect.

But video is actually the highest form of multimedia. Incorporating images, animation, and sound, it evokes reality better than any other medium. And video is increasingly used even when the primary purpose is to convey sound, as in playing a music video.

Keeping Online Video Small, Short, and Sweet

Pervasive as it is online, video has the potential to impose tremendous burdens on even the most powerful personal computer and the fastest Internet connection. In fact, no one even thinks about recording, transmitting, and playing back uncompressed video full-screen. The bulk of online video you'll see is compressed and concise, for some very good reasons. . . .

Why Web video is compressed

To play back a completely uncompressed widescreen video at 30 frames per second would require a connection with a speed of more than 1 Gb/second (1 gigabit, or one billion bits, per second), more than a thousand times faster than the rated speed of a very fast home or office connection. We're just not there yet. Instead, video is heavily compressed, using a three-stage process:

- **First, video is shown in a small window.** YouTube recently upgraded its offering and began showing most videos in a relatively generous 480 x 360-pixel window, exactly one-fifth the pixels available on a typical 1024 x 768-pixel screen.

- **Then the frame rate is reduced.** Though players are meant to adapt to the bandwidth available, a rate of 10 frames per second — one-third the frame rate of television — is considered acceptable.

- **Then the images themselves are compressed.** JPEG compression, good as it is for images, only works with one frame at a time, so MPEG — Motion Picture Experts Group — video compression is used instead.

MPEG standards are very widely used online (MPEG audio compression is more widely known as MP3), and no wonder: MPEG compression is quite clever. It takes advantage of parts of a scene that don't change from one frame to the next, and only encodes the changed parts. Unfortunately, when part of a scene changes very fast, or all of a scene changes fairly fast, there's often visible distortion in the scene until the compression and decompression can catch up.

For amateur videos such as those seen on most Web sites or on YouTube, this is not a big problem. But for enthusiasts and professionals, image-quality concerns can consume many hours of work and rework.

It's very common for video clips, even on the relatively robust YouTube site, to stall during playback, sometimes for a long time. This is extremely frustrating for users — and for you, if the video is on your Web site. Unfortunately, there is so much variation at all points in transmission, reception, and display of online video — from the servers, across the Internet and on the user's computer — that it's impossible to give users any quick or certain fix for any problems they experience. (Though you can make good money selling more reliable video solutions to corporations and government agencies.)

Keeping your video clips short

Compression helps your video work well on the Web, but to make it sweet, keep it short. Long videos can work (see the accompanying sidebar), but they have some problems that make them the exception rather than the rule:

For typical YouTube-style video clips — medium-size 480 x 360-pixel images, harshly compressed, usually grainy and a bit dim — each 15 seconds of video takes up roughly 1 MB. That's 4 MB per minute. Not too bad a size for a three-minute music video, but that one-hour CEO speech at the annual results announcement is going to take up 240 MB!

✔ **Video can't be searched with the same precision as text.** Searching the video part is tedious, with the necessity to drag the slider back and forth, and searching for a string of words is just about impossible. (If the text has been transcribed quite accurately and made searchable, it becomes possible, but this is rare.)

✔ **Start time is an issue.** If you watch the progress bar on YouTube closely when you watch a video, you'll see that the video begins to download first, then playback starts only after a chunk has downloaded. Basically, the player waits until it can get a head start sufficient that the downloading, as it continues in the background, should complete before the playback in the foreground catches up. If playback overtakes downloading, the video clip must pause for downloading to get ahead of playback again.

For a short video clip, the initial wait for a "buffer" of downloaded video to accumulate is only a few seconds. But for a long clip, the wait may be many minutes.

So keeping your video clips short makes sense for the user, as well as for technical reasons. For that CEO speech, a few minutes of highlights will get a lot more downloads than a full version. Instead of a complete video, the full speech can be delivered in audio as a podcast, perhaps synched with display of any charts or photos that the CEO showed.

If you must deliver a long video — if the CEO wants every moment of his or her precious speaking time to be immortalized in downloadable form for the ages — break up the speech into clips. Preface each clip with a brief description. And hope that at least some of your site visitors have the patience to get through all of it.

Any good long videos out there?

For an example of long video clips that work, visit the U.S. Consumer Product Safety Commission's high-quality MPEG download page at www.cpsc.gov/mpeg2.html. To accompany their press releases, they offer high-quality clips (as an alternative to lower-quality streaming video). Clips available are up to 100 MB in size and take 10 minutes or more to download, even over a fairly fast broadband connection. Yet the playback, while high-quality, is in a much smaller video window than on YouTube. That's a trade-off to keep in mind if you want to go long.

The Role of YouTube

The cost of storing and downloading videos is high enough for even large, well-funded organizations to think twice before posting them, let alone individuals out to have a little fun. This is where YouTube comes in.

YouTube allows you to use its site as a storage site for your video clips. You can store your video clips on YouTube, link to them from your own site, and they play as if you were storing them on your own server. All YouTube gets for this is a YouTube logo showing on the clip and the right to make your videos available on YouTube as well.

This is one of the greatest deals since — well, since Google bought YouTube for $1.65 billion in 2006. That's a lot of money, but for the king of Web search to acquire the king of Web video — as YouTube's founders described it when they announced the deal — for a small fraction of its value today was one of the steals of the Internet's short but exciting history.

YouTube was suffering from increasingly serious service problems before the acquisition, and Google's involvement has been critical to the continued success of YouTube. Google uses proprietary techniques for storing and retrieving large amounts of video quickly and cheaply that were very much needed to support YouTube's continued growth. And Google's deep pockets supported the investment needed to keep the service growing even as some of the sharper business brains around tried to figure out how to make money from it. (In early 2008, YouTube's bandwidth costs alone were estimated at $1 million a day.)

And now that I've brought it up, how *will* they make money from it? The answer, so far, is similar to how Google makes money from search capabilities: by placing small, relevant text ads next to the video when it's played back on YouTube. This kind of thing is a multibillion-dollar business for text search, and may become similarly large for videos. But it's a pretty harmless way for your free video storage and playback to be paid for.

All of this is important to you as a Web-page creator because a potentially huge source of technical problems — and cost for you in using video in your site — is completely solved for you by YouTube. "You" can just put your videos on their site and have them played back for free on any "Tube" on the planet! Pretty cool, huh?

Don't think you're the only one doing this. Governments, political campaigns, and global corporations all host video on YouTube. Figure 7-1 shows the YouTube channel of the U.K. Foreign and Commonwealth Office as just one of many examples. (The clip would have benefitted if they'd given the young woman a bit of frontlighting, as described in the next section.) Join the crowd!

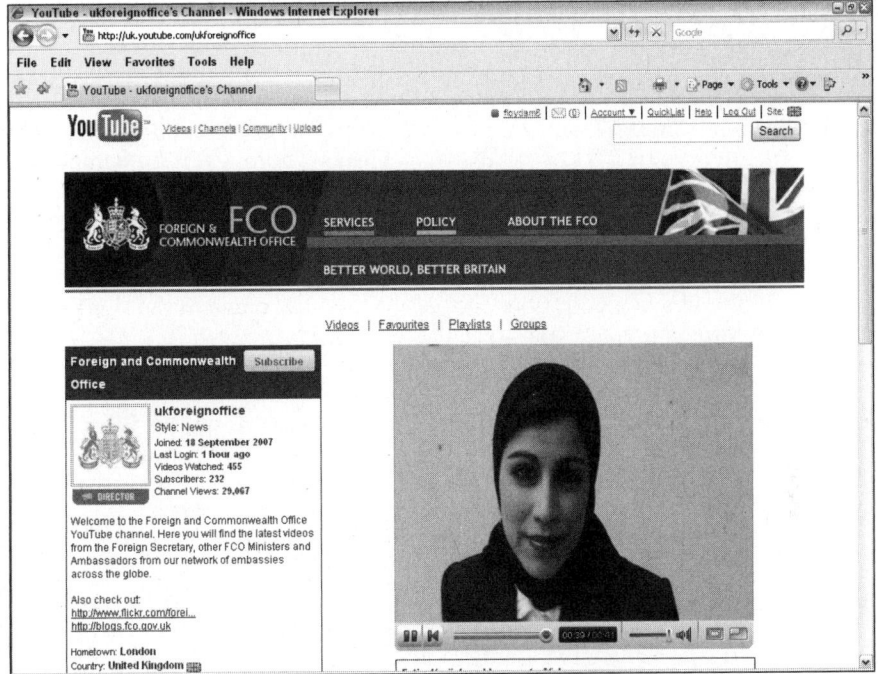

Figure 7-1:
Her
Majesty's
Government
"gets"
YouTube.

Finding Videos for Your Site Online

The easiest way to get video for your Web site is to find a video you like on YouTube, link to it from within your site, and the user will be able to play it while looking at your site, yet all the mechanics are handled by YouTube.

Each video on YouTube is accompanied by the HTML tags for including it in your Web page. Putting YouTube-hosted videos in your Web page is described in Chapter 10, for use with WYSIWYG Web-page tools, and in Chapter 14 for working directly in HTML.

For finding videos for your site, you should use YouTube's Advanced Search, as shown in Figure 7-2.

Searching for specific kinds of videos on YouTube may not always be easy. Yes, it is easy to find music videos by a specific artist, for instance (of course, if the person who posted a video misspelled "Duran Duran" or whatever the band's name is in the posting, nobody's likely to find it!). But the kinds of searches you'll want to do for Web site use might be quite different.

Let's say you want a clip that demonstrates cooking in a wok, just to bring to life the concept of what a wok is for people who may never have seen one.

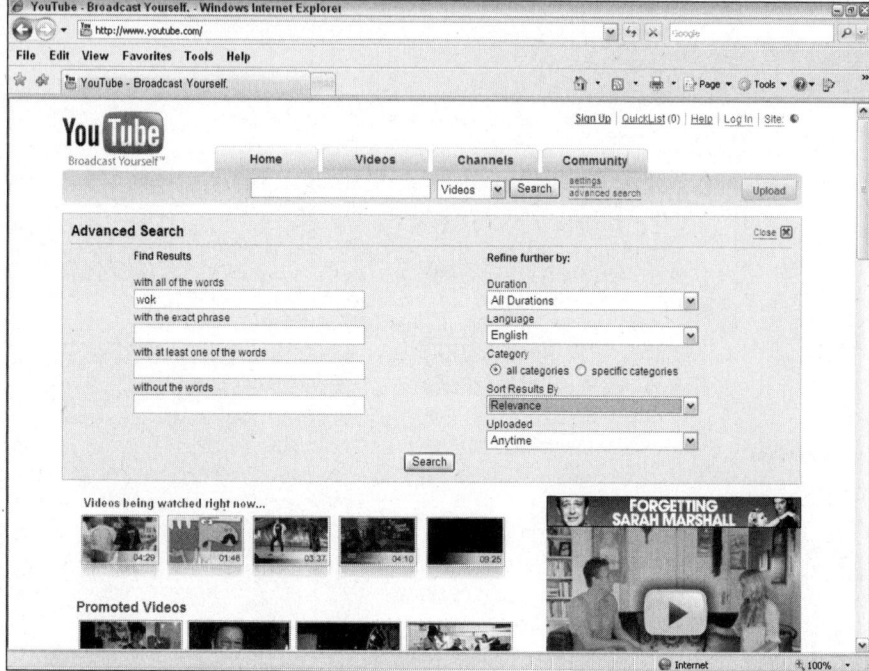

Figure 7-2:
An
Advanced
Search for
video from
every walk
of life.

When I searched for "wok" using YouTube advanced search, I found a couple of clips prominently featuring obscenities, but also several that showed a wok in an interesting way that I could use on a personal Web site.

But let's say I wanted to show using a wok to cook vegetables on a site for vegetarians — so I don't want any meat involved. Typing in "wok vegetables" only got me one suitable clip. And the clip was a bit too long; there was no way for me to edit it down.

Getting a bit creative, and stretching my knowledge of Japanese food preparation to the limit, I tried "wok tempura." This got me a bunch of clips, several of which involved the use of a wok to make vegetable tempura. The word "wok" wasn't mentioned in the words though; I had basically backed into what I wanted, the wok, by association with a dish that's commonly *made* in a wok, tempura.

Inspired (bored? obsessed?), I tried several other combinations of words, dropping "wok" altogether, and got several promising clips I could consider for my intended purpose.

The problem gets even worse if you want to use video, or music attached to a video, to set a mood. The initial results for "peaceful" include a movie trailer for "Peaceful Warrior" and typography relating to "tragic peaceful death."

The first result for "calm" shows two young men playing a war-themed video game in a tournament. Yikes.

However, none of this means the desired results aren't out there, just that they are likely to be hard to find. Set yourself broad goals before looking for a specific piece of video — and be prepared to look at a lot of stuff, not all of it necessarily wholesome, before finding what you want (or settling for something you deem close enough).

If you really want to have a YouTube video on your own hard drive, there are many tools you can find online for grabbing them. Perhaps the simplest is KissYouTube, an online site that makes getting a video clip from YouTube ridiculously easy. You just navigate to the video you want on YouTube, then insert the word "Kiss" into the URL just in front of YouTube. Press Enter, and a download box appears to ask you where you want to save the movie to. (For detailed instructions, visit KissYouTube at www.kissyoutube.com. For a couple of gentle-but-timely caveats, see the next couple of paragraphs and the handy sidebar.)

Be careful how you use the clips you download; the person who uploaded the video to YouTube did *not* thereby agree automatically to your borrowing and re-using it. If you're downloading video because you want to use it on your site, ask the owner first — and abide by the answer you get. If the person got the video from somewhere else, doesn't own it, and can't really give you permission to use it, you're better off *not* using it on your Web page.

You can link to online video clips from many sources besides YouTube, but those hosts may well frown on your linking to their expensively produced, stored, and served clips — especially as they may have rights worries of their own. Be very careful whose online videos you link to from your site, especially if you embed the video clip in your own page. Remember that (as mentioned in Chapter 5) the government is always a good source of free media content.

Capturing Videos from a Camera

You can also capture your own videos for online use. There used to be a lot of things to think about in doing this but, with the availability of YouTube to "launder" your videos into an acceptable format and size, store and serve them for you, and provide you with the HTML to embed them in your Web page, many of those concerns are taken care of.

There are a variety of tools you can use to edit video; if you're using a camcorder, it probably came with one of several available tools. The Macintosh comes with iLife, which includes a well-regarded movie program, and Windows comes with Windows Movie Maker — which you can download for free from Microsoft if you don't have it already. There are also tools available free, or free for an initial trial period, from sources such as CNET's download.com.

Legal concerns for video?

There are huge copyright issues with video and with YouTube. But as I write this, I'm listening to an REM video on YouTube. (The visual part of the video is just a static shot of their album cover; it's the sound I'm interested in.) REM is famously protective of their intellectual property, but they don't object to fans posting a grainy-looking video with somewhat tinny audio on YouTube.

It's possible that someday the band (or their record label) will go after YouTube. But it's pretty unlikely that ordinary people who link to the video from their own Web sites will be involved. However, if your site makes money, or if you have a lot of money that you need to protect, you may want to talk to a lawyer before linking to copyrighted content.

Another similar issue relates to *model releases* — permission forms that say, in effect, "Sure, you can use this image of me for the purpose you've explained to me." Before you use a photograph of someone else for any purpose, but especially before using it to make money, you should have a signed model release listing the rights you have to the image, or the person depicted can come after you legally.

The same reasoning used for photographs applies to video; even if people willingly upload videos of themselves with no thought of compensation, your re-use of such a video on your site could make you liable to compensating the person later.

But, as with music copyrights, these concerns seem to be mostly ignored when it comes to video on YouTube. Again, if your site makes money — or if you, personally, have a lot of money — you may want to talk to a lawyer before linking to content that depicts recognizable individuals who have not given permission for you to use their image.

Overall, such legal worries seem (to me) to favor using YouTube — which encourages the re-use of their videos — as opposed to other online sources for video. Google is big and rich enough to go toe-to-toe with anyone who might come after YouTube for infringement of copyright or image rights. In protecting themselves, they'll be protecting you as well.

I won't describe how to use these different programs here, as there are so many of them; refer to the program's online help file, its manual, or a third-party book on it.

If you're planning to make a habit of making your own video clips and uploading them to YouTube or elsewhere — hey, no copyright worries! — check out *Digital Video For Dummies,* 4th Edition (from Wiley). It covers making video with Windows, Mac, and Linux machines.

Meanwhile, some general steps for capturing video are coming right up.

Whichever program (or platform) you use, don't worry too much about which video format to save the resulting file in. YouTube accepts .WMV (Windows movies), .AVI (a common Windows format), .MOV (QuickTime video), MPEG (the cross-platform standard), and .MP4 formats.

Just for your interest: YouTube will convert the video to a proprietary standard using the Sorenson codec and MP3 audio, controlled by a Macromedia Flash wrapper. Flash does require a plug-in on the user's computer for playback, but most people have it already installed, if only because of previous visits to YouTube. If your users don't yet have Flash installed, it should install automatically when they visit your Web page.

Follow these steps to capture a video for use on your Web site via YouTube:

1. **Set up the shot with strong lighting.**

   All laptop users, and more and more desktop users, have LCD monitors, most of which are a step back in terms of image quality and clarity from the best of the old (expensive, clunky) CRT screens. Also, your video may well be viewed, particularly if on a laptop (or on a mobile phone!), in mediocre or even poor lighting conditions, such as bright room lighting or sunlight. All this means your clip needs to be as bright as possible. Light is the key secret of still photography and one of the two secrets of making video.

2. **Get light onto the faces of people (and animals) and onto the front of objects of interest.**

   See Figure 7-1 at the beginning of this chapter as an example of too little frontlighting.

   If you don't specifically light the faces of people and the fronts of things, they won't be very visible. If you have the background lit but not the foreground — say, if you're filming people with the sun at their backs — the camera will compensate to make the bright background acceptably dimmer, which will make the dim foreground nearly invisible. Although it can be uncomfortable, your subjects should face toward the light (if indoors) or the sun (if outdoors).

3. **Try to capture several seconds of the scene before and after the main action occurs.**

   Having a few quiet seconds of "intro" and "outro" allows the viewer to get used to the scene before anything happens, and to relax afterward before it ends. (People who watch YouTube a lot don't need this cosseting.)

4. **Try to keep motion slow and within a relatively small part of the frame.**

   Because of the way MPEG compression works, fast motion — or motion across the majority of the frame — is likely to cause visible distortion on playback.

5. **Spend extra time and effort on sound.**

   Sound is the other big secret of video. If you're going to use sound picked up during filming, consider using an external microphone — either a lapel microphone on the subject or a boom microphone that can be held close to the subject, but out of the picture. If you're going to add sound after filming, take your time and do it right.

As with light, any sound you don't capture during filming is lost forever.

6. **Try a rehearsal before you shoot the real thing.**

It's surprisingly easy (and surprisingly uncommon practice) to do a dry run before shooting an important scene. Have your kids run around on the grass and film them a few days *before* the big soccer match. Have someone stand onstage behind the podium and try filming her for five minutes a few days *before* the big speech. Go through your entire production process (however simple it might be) and try the resulting video clip on the Web *before* the real event. What you learn will help you improve your final product many times over.

You can use the soundtrack from your video, if it's good enough, as an audio podcast as well.

7. **Think twice before using a Web camera.**

It seems that most of the videos on YouTube and other online video sites are the head of some young person tilting down to talk into the built-in or added-on Web camera on a PC; YouTube makes this very easy with their Quick Capture feature. But (as some of us have found out the hard way) most of us don't look so good from a shooting angle that points halfway up one's nose. Webcams are fun and convenient, and they're fine for young people who may not know each other in any other way except via Webcam conversations. But such clips don't work well for most older people, nor for most halfway serious purposes.

8. **Don't spend too much time in production.**

You can't make a silk purse out of a sow's ear, as the saying goes, and you can't add quality to a video after it's captured — you can only clean it up a bit. (Okay, if you're a pro or a talented amateur, you can clean it up a lot, time and budget permitting.)

Your work is likely to be viewed in a small window on a crowded computer screen in bad lighting and heard over cheap built-in laptop computer speakers (or viewed on a mobile phone screen and heard over a mobile phone speaker!). Don't sweat the small stuff, or even the medium-sized stuff.

9. **Enjoy yourself.**

It's easy to forget, after worrying about legal, technical, and creative concerns, but video is the most natural of media types, and putting video on the Web and playing it back should be fun. Spend some time worrying about the "hygiene" issues described here, but then just relax and enjoy yourself. Any sense of joy and playfulness you bring to your efforts will come through in the result.

TECHNICAL STUFF

Opening up the convert-sation

Even if your video clip is not already in one of the formats YouTube accepts — .WMV (Windows movies), .AVI (a common Windows format), .MOV (QuickTime video), MPEG (the cross-platform standard) or .MP4 — you should be able to convert it to one of the accepted formats.

To find out the file type, look at the icon in Windows Explorer. For details, right-click the file icon in Windows Explorer; choose Properties from the cursor menu. Click the General tab; the file type will appear within a little icon symbol.

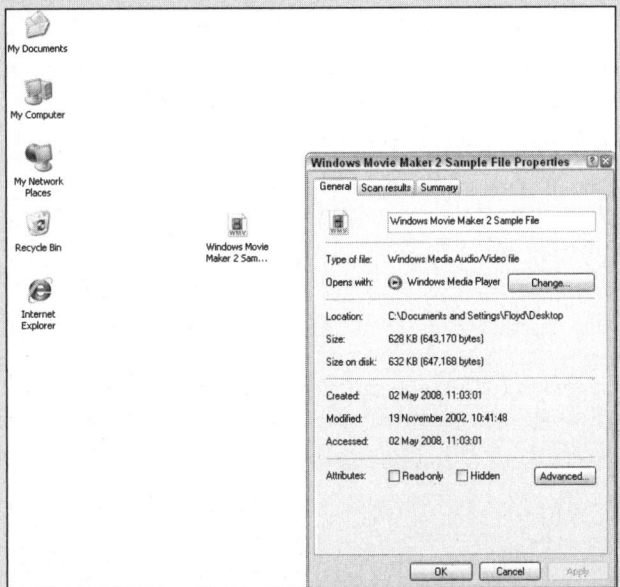

To convert the file, either open it in any program you have that will open it, and try to save it in one of the formats YouTube will accept; or visit www.download.com and search for "file converter" and the actual and desired file types for your file, for example file converter flv wmv. You're likely to find a suitable converter.

Uploading a Video Clip to YouTube

Uploading a video clip to YouTube is almost hilariously easy, as long as it's in one of the right video formats, as it's likely to be. (See the "Opening up the convert-sation" sidebar for what to do if it's not in one of the right video formats.) Follow these steps to put a clip on YouTube:

1. **If you haven't previously joined YouTube or Google, get a Google ID, as described in Chapter 3.**

   A Google ID will not only let you use YouTube, but also all sorts of other cool Google services.

2. **Go to** youtube.com **and sign in to YouTube.**

3. **Click the yellow Upload button in the upper-right corner of the home page (and most other YouTube pages).**

   The Video Upload (Step 1 of 2) page appears.

4. **Enter key facts about your video — think carefully about the right words, as this is how people will search for it. Enter a Title, Description, a Video Category, and Tags.**

   You really want people who know you to be able to find the video, so enter your name in the Title, Description, or Tags area. An example is shown in Figure 7-3. Then a search on your name will find the video. Consider including the name of the place it was recorded and the names of people who helped create it and/or who appear in it. Don't worry about getting this wrong, though; you can always change it.

   Depending on the category you choose for your clip, YouTube offers selected, standard suggested tags that you simply click to add to your Tags list. Use as many of the suggested tags as apply to your posting; experienced YouTube users know these tags and search on them specifically, so you should use them where they make sense.

   A future employer may someday Google your or a friend's name, so be careful if the video is risqué, and don't post it at all if it shows anything that even looks illegal.

5. **To change Broadcast Options, click Choose Options if you want to change your video from Public, the default, to Private — that is, viewable only by a list you specify of up to 25 contacts you have in Google.**

   Try to choose Public if you can to make it easier for people not in your Google contacts list to find and enjoy your video. Also, remember the Private designation is only relative; people on your list can still gather others around their PC to see your clip, or use external programs such as KissYouTube to make a copy and forward it. (Even if it's sent to just one additional person, who sends it to one more, who sends it . . . .)

   If your video clip really needs to be *private,* don't put it on YouTube, or e-mail it, or otherwise share it.

6. **To change Date and Map Options, click Choose Options. Then enter the date the video was recorded and, if you'd like, select where it was recorded.**

   It's quick and fun to enter the date recorded — enter an approximate date if you're a bit hazy — and it's great to have the date with the video for future reference.

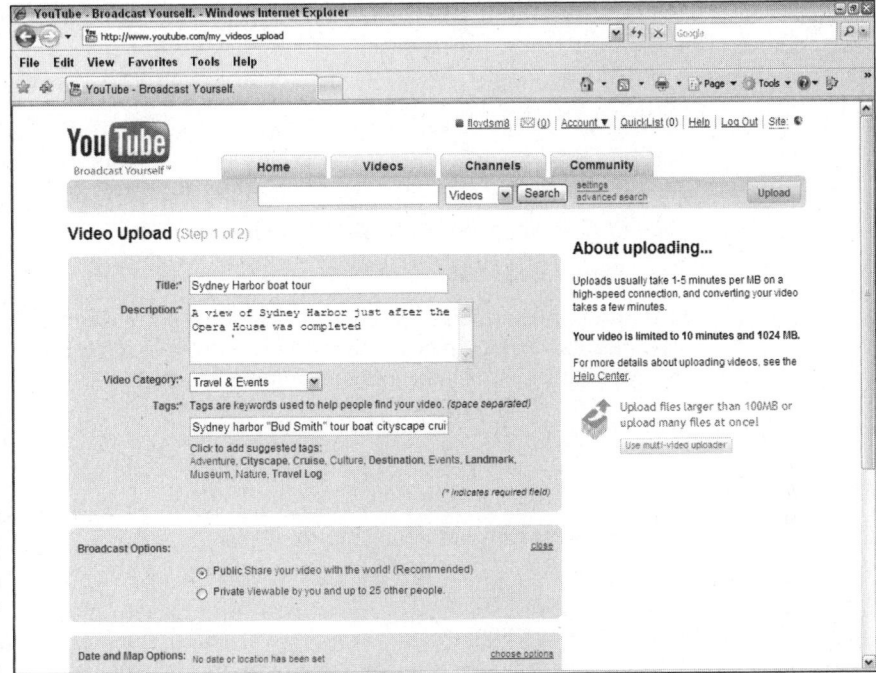

Figure 7-3:
Get ready to
upload your
video.

I found it a bit time-consuming to specify the location for my video on Google Maps, but there are people who spend hours messing around with geocoding information so perhaps it's worth doing this as well.

7. To change Sharing Options, click Choose Options.

Here you have some choices to make (but you knew that) . . .

- You can change comments options so you can moderate or simply block comments; block comment voting; and moderate or block video responses to your own posting.

- You can also block people from using YouTube to rate your video; to embed it in their Web page; and to view it from mobile phones or TV. However, people can still do these things themselves, without YouTube's help.

- As with many sites, this seems like a lot of options, but it will not take you long to go through this once you've done it a couple of times.

- If you're worried about straightforward, rude, or even obscene comments from viewers of your video, then be sure to block or moderate comments as needed — because YouTube users are often straightforward, rude, or even obscene. But unless the video is for work purposes or for family viewing with younger children, consider leaving all options open for now; interaction is what makes YouTube so much fun.

8. Select a video to upload.

To capture a video from a Web camera and then upload it, follow Steps 9 through 13 in this step list.

To proceed with a video you already have, click the Upload a Video button. The Video Upload (Step 2 of 2) dialog box for a video upload appears, as shown in Figure 7-4. Here's the procedure from there:

a. Click Browse and select the video file to upload.

b. Click Upload Video.

Wait until the upload completes before doing anything else. That process can take up to several minutes, depending on the size of the file and the speed of your connection. On a 56K modem (or on a bad broadband day), the upload may take as long as 3 minutes per megabyte. On upload, your file is automatically converted to YouTube's proprietary format, as described above. Eventually, the Video Upload — Upload Complete screen appears.

c. Go to Step 13 in this step list for what to do next.

Figure 7-4:
Find a fine
file to feed
fans.

9. **To capture a video with a Web camera, click the Quick Capture button. (To proceed with a video you already have, go to Step 8.)**

   The Video Upload — Quick Capture (Step 2 of 2) screen for a camera capture appears (as shown in Figure 7-5), along with a request to allow access to your recording hardware (which is necessary in order to complete the process of recording-and-uploading).

10. **Click Allow to allow access to your camera and microphone.**

    The Record screen appears.

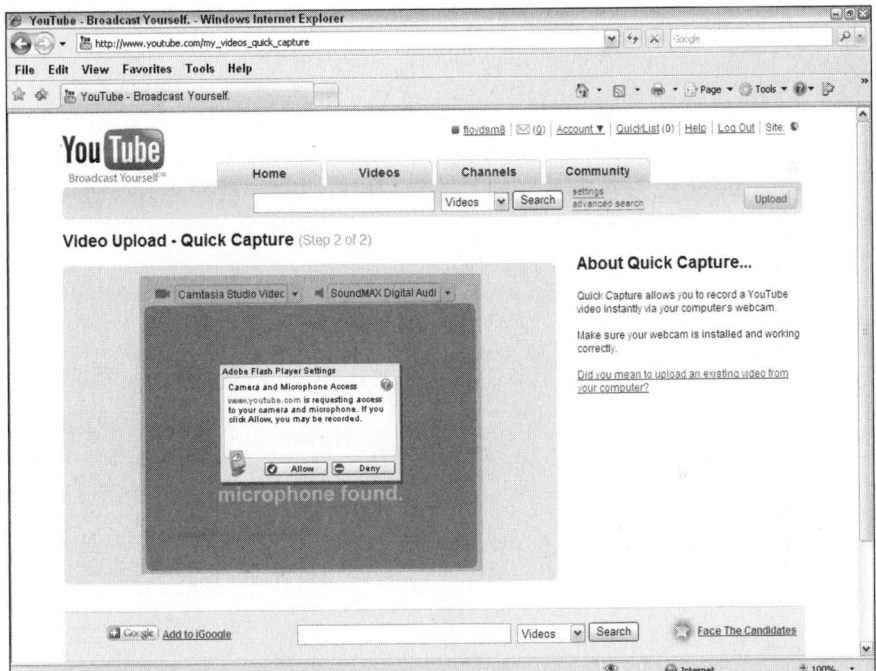

Figure 7-5:
Capture a
cute clip.

11. **Click Record, and wait until the server is ready. Then record up to 10 minutes of action into your Web camera, and click Stop when you're finished.**

12. **From the options that appear, choose what to do next:**

    - Click Preview to preview your video.

    - If you're happy with your clip, click Save.

    - If you want to redo, click Cancel, and then click Record again.

> • Repeat until you're happy with the result; click Save when you have it right.

The Video Upload — Upload Complete screen appears.

13. Complete the upload.

> a. *From the Upload Complete screen (see Figure 7-6), save the Embed code in a word-processing or similar file for later re-use.*
>
> b. *Wait until YouTube finishes processing the video, which may take up to several hours.*
>
> You'll receive an e-mail when the video is up on YouTube.
>
> c. *Click the link in the e-mail to view your video.*

Success — you're now on YouTube!

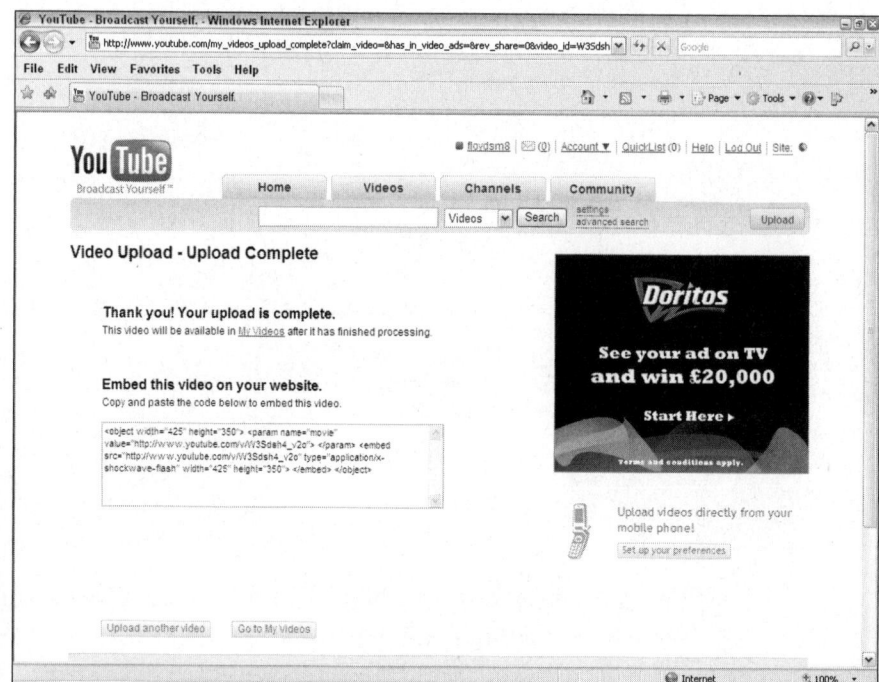

Figure 7-6:
To capture
is human;
to embed,
divine.

Part III
Your Site in
WYSIWYG

The 5th Wave   By Rich Tennant

"Games are an important part of my
Web site. They cause eye strain."

In this part . . .

A What You See Is What You Get, or WYSIWYG, tool will help you work on a screen that looks like your Web page and handle many of the messy HTML details for you. This book includes the excellent CoffeeCup Editor trial software so you can get started today.

Chapter 8

Using a WYSIWYG Editor

In This Chapter

▶ Comparing WYSIWYG editing to plain text

▶ Introducing CoffeeCup HTML Editor

▶ Using CoffeeCup HTML Editor

You can use online tools, such as Google Page Creator discussed in Chapter 3, to create your initial Web page using a template. However, at some point, you will probably want to go further with your Web page than a template allows. To go beyond templates, you have to move away from the online tools and create your own Web page on your own hard drive. Then you can upload tried-and-tested Web pages to any number of different Web hosts, including Google itself.

This chapter describes how to create your initial Web page locally, on your own hard drive, using a WYSIWYG editor. As an example, I use the Visual Editor included in the tool on the CD-ROM, CoffeeCup HTML Editor.

The chapters in this Part describe how to improve your Web page and how to extend your Web page into a multipage Web site using CoffeeCup Visual Editor. Chapter 11 tells you how to publish one or more Web pages that are on your own machine onto the Web.

The next Part tells you how to create and improve Web pages using HTML on its own.

This chapter helps you choose the approach you want to use and then shows you how to create your initial Web page.

Google Page Creator lets you go pretty far with your Web page. However, it locks you into having your hosting done on Google. If you feel comfortable keeping your Web page on the same host for a long time to come, you may want to continue using these tools. The approach I describe in this book, however, gives you more opportunities to keep costs low and flexibility high. You can even edit your pages locally and then upload them to Google for hosting.

Choosing WYSIWYG over Plain Text

You can use a couple of different approaches to create and edit Web pages on your own computer. One approach is to use a WYSIWYG Web page editor. WYSIWYG is pronounced "whizzywig," and stands for What You See Is What You Get. A WYSIWYG Web page editor is like a word processing program — what you see on-screen is at least close to what you get when you publish your Web page and look at it online.

The problem with this is that WYSIWYG doesn't work perfectly on the Web. Different Web browsers can interpret the same HTML tags differently. Also, users can have different browser settings, which means the same page can take on a different look for different users. This variability undermines your efforts to make your Web page look just so. To work around these problems, and to create Web pages that work well on the widest possible range of computers and browser versions and settings, knowing what's going on with the underlying HTML really helps.

For this reason, many Web page publishers work directly with HTML tags. Others work with a WYSIWYG editor, but frequently check what the underlying HTML-tagged text — usually just called "the HTML" — looks like.

Whether you work in HTML directly or in a WYSIWYG editor, your capabilities still reflect what HTML is capable of. The difference is in the ease of working (higher for WYSIWYG) and direct control (higher working directly in HTML).

I recommend that you either work directly in HTML or use a simple WYSIWYG tool that doesn't try to do too much for you, and look frequently at the underlying HTML. If you do want to use a tool, I recommend CoffeeCup Visual Editor, part of the CoffeeCup HTML Editor 2008 package included on the CD-ROM.

Working directly in HTML gives you a great deal of control and helps — okay, forces — you to learn HTML quickly. But there are problems too. Imagining what your Web page is going to look like is quite difficult when you're just looking at text and tags. You can easily make mistakes in the construction of your Web page when you're working directly with the tags — and easily get lost in looking at all that HTML-tagged text when you're trying to remember where to make an addition or change.

As a WYSIWYG tool, CoffeeCup Visual Editor works smoothly with CoffeeCup Code Editor, which lets you work directly with HTML code — as described in Part IV. This gives you the best of both worlds — the ease and speed of working in a WYSIWYG tool, along with the power and precision of being able to work with HTML code directly.

Figure 8-1 shows a simple Web page as it appears when being edited in the CoffeeCup Visual Editor (left) and a text editor (right). You may be able to tell just from looking at the picture which kind of environment you prefer to work in. If not, try both, using the instructions in this chapter, and see which one you prefer.

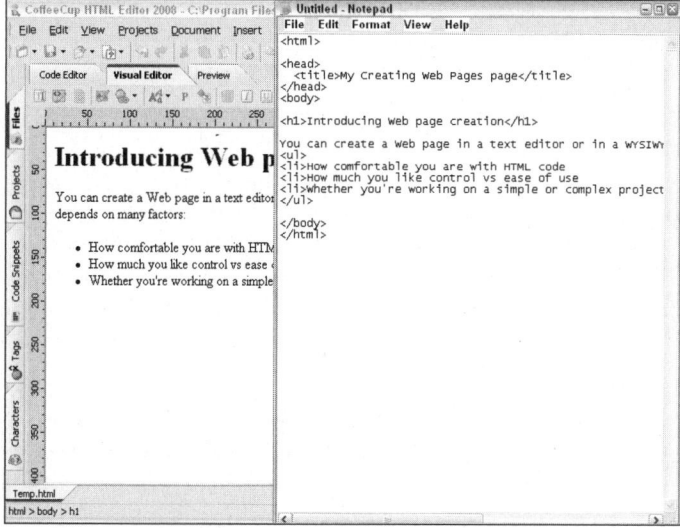

Figure 8-1:
You can compose in a text editor or CoffeeCup HTML Editor.

Why drink from the CoffeeCup?

There are a lot of companies that thought it would be easy to create Web page authoring software — only a few of them have survived and thrived. CoffeeCup Software is one of those few. They've racked up a large number of awards for their dozens of different products, all relating to Web page creation one way or another, from Google SiteMapper, for search engine friendliness, to several Flash tools.

Software companies work in a lot of different ways. The CoffeeCup people have done it the hard way — creating free and low-cost tools, building an audience through word of mouth (and "word of mouse" online), and gradually creating a business around their products. Like a lot of technically based business, they seem to create tools they need for their own use, then turn them into products for others to use.

One very unusual feature of CoffeeCup programs is their lifetime licenses. Once you buy a program, you get free updates for life. Also, today, CoffeeCup programs fill a real gap in the market. Web authoring tools tend to be either unreliable freeware or big, complex, expensive professional tools designed for professional software developers. (Microsoft has even stopped selling its once wildly popular FrontPage program.) CoffeeCup is left standing in the middle, toward the higher end in capability but the lower end in price.

The HTML Editor is the original product from CoffeeCup, so it has over 10 years of development behind it. The new (at this writing), 2008 version has great reviews, well-trafficked message boards (no small thing among such tools), and a whole host of companion tools if your needs grow beyond the core program.

Working within WYSIWYG

As a leading WYSIWYG Web pages tool, CoffeeCup HTML Editor has all the important basic features that you need to build basic Web pages. Using these features, you can:

✔ Create and edit Web pages without seeing HTML tags

✔ Drag and drop links to other Web locations without typing the URL or pathname

✔ Cut and paste graphics into your Web page, resize graphics, and add alternate text

✔ Create and edit tables

✔ Create and edit *forms* — interactive data entry fields commonly found on Web pages

You can also insert multimedia files and computer programs into your Web page. However, not all users can play back those files or run those programs because they may not have the appropriate browser or the right plug-ins installed.

If you add advanced elements, such as multimedia files or computer programs, into your Web page, be prepared to test your pages with several different browsers and to tell your Web visitors what to expect.

CoffeeCup HTML Editor supports forms, but it can't give you the CGI (short for Common Gateway Interface) scripts that you need to make the forms work. These CGI scripts process the data that the user enters into a form; if you can create CGI scripts, you're probably ready for a more advanced tool than CoffeeCup HTML Editor. However, if you don't want to mess with creating these scripts, you can get CGI scripts from others on the Web.

Plusses and minuses of CoffeeCup HTML Editor

CoffeeCup HTML Editor has most of the advantages of an HTML tool, with few of the disadvantages. Here are its six key advantages as an HTML tool:

✔ **CoffeeCup HTML Editor is free to try.** CoffeeCup makes HTML Editor available for free for 30 days — but the version accompanying this book gives you 90 days free. This is long enough to develop a site and stop — or to decide you want to keep using the software.

✔ **It's easy.** CoffeeCup HTML Editor is very easy to use. It leaves out some complex advanced functions in favor of drop-dead simplicity.

✔ **Its functions match HTML tags.** The functions available in HTML Editor are the functions available in HTML — and only those functions. You can't do things in your Web page that aren't supported by Web browsers.

✔ **It uses "generic" HTML.** The only functions available in HTML Editor are those supported by all widely used versions of HTML. Web pages that you create with CoffeeCup are likely usable by all major Web browsers on all computer platforms.

✔ **It lets you see and edit HTML.** HTML Editor gives you one-click access to the HTML tags underlying your Web page, simply by moving between the Visual Editor and the Code Editor. You get ease of editing in WYSIWYG mode but can still always see and edit the underlying HTML-tagged text.

✔ **It's part of a whole suite of programs.** CoffeeCup HTML Editor includes several cool tools, but you can also get a whole bunch more from CoffeeCup. Nearly all of these are available as free trials — which allows you to do just about anything once or twice for free. If it becomes a long-term need, buy the software. Fair's fair.

These features of CoffeeCup HTML Editor place it comfortably between using a text editor and using more advanced HTML editors. The starting and ending points of that spectrum look like this:

✔ **Text editors:** Working directly with HTML tags can be frustrating and lead you to make mistakes in the look and layout of your page.

✔ **Advanced HTML editors:** These programs, such as Microsoft Expression Web Designer and Dreamweaver, may overwhelm you with complex functionality (and certainly will overwhelm you with their price).

I recommend that most beginning Web publishers use HTML Editor in Visual Editor mode and check the underlying HTML frequently to see what's really going on. As you get more knowledgeable with HTML, you may wish to buy and use a more advanced HTML editor — or go the low-tech route (as many Web professionals do much of the time) and use a basic text editor or the Code Editor side of CoffeeCup.

I recommend that you consider using CoffeeCup HTML Editor initially, even if you own a more advanced HTML editor such as Dreamweaver or FrontPage. The functionality of CoffeeCup HTML Editor is simpler, making it easier to learn the core features of HTML, and you can follow along better with this book.

Taking a sip from the CoffeeCup

At this writing, the current version of CoffeeCup HTML Editor is called CoffeeCup HTML Editor 2008. This is also the version on the CD-ROM that comes with this book. Follow the directions in Appendix C, On the CD, to install the software.

To check for an updated version, go to `http://www.coffeecup.com/html-editor/`, shown in Figure 8-2. However, consider using the version on the CD-ROM for your initial work; it has a longer free trial period, and it is sure to match the descriptions and figures in this book. You can then upgrade to the newer version if you decide to purchase the software.

Figure 8-2:
Find the latest version of CoffeeCup HTML Editor.

In order to run CoffeeCup HTML Editor, you need a computer running Windows XP or Windows Vista. It doesn't run on the Macintosh or Linux/Unix operating systems. However, the newer Macintosh computers and many versions of Linux/Unix can run alongside Windows XP or Vista. You can use these compatibility solutions to run CoffeeCup software.

Throughout the remainder of the book, I describe how to use CoffeeCup HTML Editor to make specific kinds of changes in your Web site. But before that, follow these steps to start HTML Editor and get oriented to using it:

1. Start CoffeeCup HTML Editor.

Start the HTML Editor from the Start menu by choosing Start➪Programs➪CoffeeCup Software➪CoffeeCup HTML Editor 2008.

The program opens to the Code Editor window, as shown in Figure 8-3.

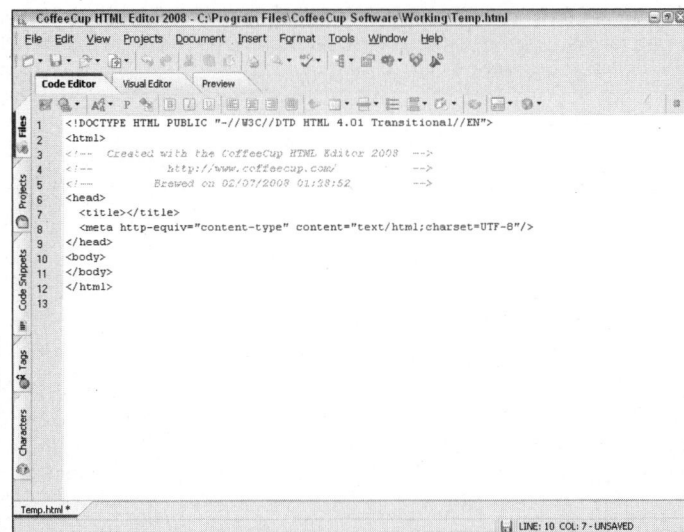

Figure 8-3:
CoffeeCup
gives you a
busy start-
ing page.

2. **Switch to the Visual Editor by clicking the Visual Editor tab.**

   A warning message appears.

   Like many Web editors, CoffeeCup HTML Editor has to change HTML code you write to make it compatible with some of the capabilities it supports in WYSIWYG mode. The reason for saving your code from the Code Editor is so you can return to it if necessary after CoffeeCup changes the version in the Visual Editor.

3. **Click Save & Continue. Save your HTML code — even if you haven't added to it — and click OK.**

   The Visual Editor window opens.

   Buttons along the top of the entry-window area are shortcuts to many of the functions in the Format and Insert menus, introduced in the next two steps. Consider entering a small amount of text (even sample text such as "The quick brown fox jumped over the lazy red dog") for experimentation. You can type in a single sentence, then copy and paste it repeatedly for experimental purposes.

4. **Pull down the Format menu and inspect the options.**

   The Format menu appears, as shown in Figure 8-4. It includes options you can apply to text. Options include changing the font (not to be done without some thought; see Chapter 9); making text bold, italic, or underlined; aligning it left, center, right, or fully justified; indenting text, and other effects.

Consider trying formatting commands on individual characters, words, or a larger block of text.

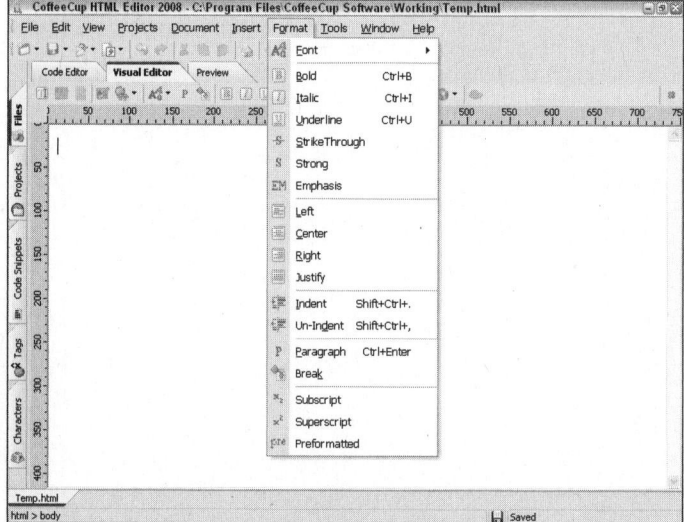

5. Pull down the Insert menu and inspect the options.

The Insert menu appears, as shown in Figure 8-5. It includes different things you can insert into your Web page. Options include inserting a link to another Web page; inserting an image; inserting a horizontal rule; and inserting a title for the Web page.

Consider inserting various options among a few blocks of text. If you do this, note that inserting a link to another Web page works best if you select the text that you want to use as the clickable Link Text *before* choosing Insert⇨Link.

6. Pull down the remaining menus and inspect the options.

It's always good to begin to familiarize yourself with the options in a new program. For CoffeeCup HTML Editor, you'll see that many of the options have to do with managing a project; others relate to spell-checking, testing, and so on. (But try the Special Characters tab under the View menu for one particularly useful feature.) These capabilities, which for the most part allow you to polish your work and to collaborate with others, are not so important right now, but are very much appreciated by CoffeeCup users who work with the tool over time.

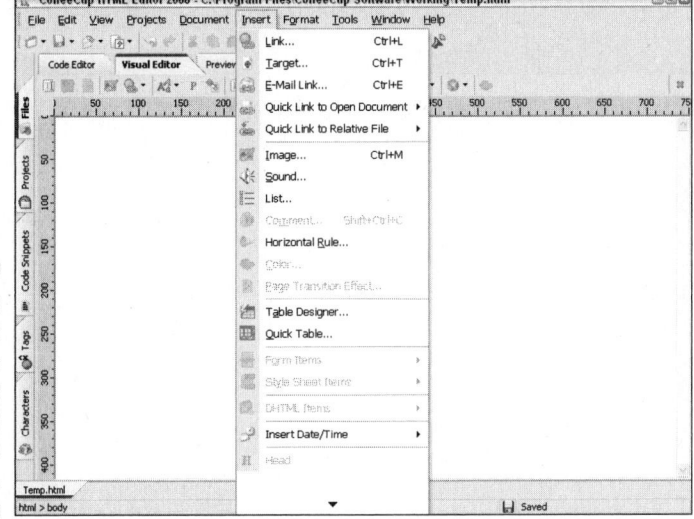

Figure 8-5:
The Insert
Menu helps
you put
things into
your Web
page.

Chapter 9

Creating a WYSIWYG Page

. . . .

In This Chapter

▶ Writing for the Web

▶ Formatting Web text

▶ Using HTML lists

▶ Entering text in HTML

▶ Entering text in SeaMonkey Composer

. . . .

*T*he previous chapter shows you how to get started in a mainstream WYSIWYG editor, CoffeeCup HTML Editor. This chapter shows you how to create your first Web page, put some text in it, and get the text formatted so it looks good.

This chapter draws on the discussion of using text in Web pages in Chapter 4. Review that chapter for information about how to write for the Web. Web writing is a bit different than other kinds of writing. It's also kind of fun, once you get used to it.

Why bother with HTML basics?

Most Web-authoring tools try to hide HTML from the user; you can use one of these tools to create a Web page without knowing a thing about HTML. But CoffeeCup is one of many tools that present HTML right next to a WYSIWYG editor so you can see what you're doing *and* the on-screen results of your actions. Here are some advantages to learning HTML even as you do most of your work in WYSIWYG:

✔ **To understand how the Web works:** This understanding is pretty valuable if you're a heavy Web user (or a light one), especially if you plan to publish on the Web. Some of the Web's limitations, such as "what you see is not (exactly) what you get," are hard to understand if you don't know something about HTML.

✔ **To use free Web tools:** Many free Web tools enable you to enter HTML tags directly to jazz up your text. Knowing a few tags can go a long way.

✔ **To work directly in HTML:** Many Web pros tire of managing HTML tags by hand and start using a tool that hides the tags. Others swear by HTML. (Everyone swears *at* HTML, at least some of the time. But the only way to have a choice is to know some HTML.)

✔ **To do better work using your tool:** When you're using a tool that hides the gory details of HTML from you, knowing enough HTML to understand what's going on "behind the scenes" is an advantage.

Get Ready: A Refreshingly Brief Description of HTML

HTML is a specific way of adding descriptive tags to regular text so that all the formatting, linking, and navigational information you need in a Web page is in text form, contained in the same file with the regular text that appears on the Web page. HTML is designed to be something that humans can read *and* that machines can process, a kind of common ground for human-to-machine communication.

Suppose you want to add bold to a word in your text, such as

```
You can use HTML to specify that a word is bold.
```

To add bold formatting to a sentence using HTML, just take the regular sentence and add a couple of tags to specify where the bold starts and stops. Here's the previous line in HTML:

```
You can use HTML to specify that a word is <b>bold</b>.
```

When you display the sentence with the HTML tags in a Web browser, the browser displays all the words, but not the *tags* — the information between angle brackets. The Web browser uses the tags to do extra things to the text, such as add formatting to it. In this case, the formatting is simple: Start using bold text immediately after the word "is," and stop using bold text immediately after the word "bold."

Because HTML tags exist alongside the text that users see on your Web page, a document with HTML tags in it is called *HTML-tagged text.* A file with HTML-tagged text in it is called an HTML file — but it's really just a specific kind of text file.

An HTML file usually has the extension .htm or .html at the end of the filename. If you look at HTML-tagged text in a text editing program, you see the angle brackets and HTML commands; if you look at it in a Web browser, you see a Web page with formatting, links, and so on.

A document with no formatting — such as italic and other formatting added by a word processor — is called a *plain-text* document. HTML-tagged text documents are considered plain-text documents because they're made up only of text characters, even though some of the characters (the tags) carry formatting information. Word-processing documents that aren't plain-text documents have additional formatting codes embedded in them to tell machines how to display and print the text.

You can add HTML tags to regular text to create your own Web documents in any text editor or word processing program. (However, in a word processing program, you must explicitly save the Web document as a text file.) Or you can use a Web-editing tool that hides the gory details of HTML tags, such as the Visual Editor in CoffeeCup. (The Visual Editor creates an HTML-tagged text file, but displays to you what that file will look like in a Web page. It makes the HTML-tagged text available directly on the Code Editor tab.)

After you publish a few Web pages, you can take the time to find out more about HTML. At that point, you may want to see the full HTML appendix at the back of the book (Appendix B).

If you like to know everything that's going on before you roll up your sleeves and plunge into things, you may want to start by looking at *HTML, XHTML & CSS For Dummies,* 6th Edition, a comprehensive guide to HTML by Ed Tittel and Jeff Noble (Wiley).

Examining the HTML script

Take a closer look at the term for which HTML is an acronym, HyperText Markup Language. You may already know that hypertext is text that has links in it. A *link* is just a connection to another file. So far so good. But what's a *markup language?* (It's not that confusing language that car dealers speak when they decide how high to jack up the price!) A markup language is simply a way to put information about a document — for example, information about hypertext links and formatting — in the document itself. Markup languages often use tags — labels placed within text that give display instructions. So HyperText Markup Language — HTML — is a specific way of using tags to convey information about a document.

Most tags in HTML come in pairs: One starts a change and the other ends it. In the following sample sentence, the first tag, `<b>`, means start displaying text in a **bold** typeface; the second tag, `</b>`, means stop using bold.

Here's how the sentence looks when "marked up" with HTML tags:

```
That's a <b>good</b> idea.
```

Here's how the sentence looks when displayed on-screen:

```
That's a good idea.
```

The browser reads the original, text-only sentence — `That's a <b>good</b> idea.` — and says to itself, "I display `That's a`, turn bold on, display **good**, turn bold off, and display `idea`." The person who created the original sentence puts in the HTML tags, the browser interprets them, and the user only sees the effect — in this case, the word **good** displayed in boldface type.

The `<b>` and `</b>` tags are *formatting tags* that describe how a browser displays text. Another kind of tag in HTML is the *linking tag*. (Links are the basis of hypertext.) Linking tags specify outside information brought into a document. Here's some complicated-looking HTML text that shows examples of formatting and linking tags:

```
To learn about <i>Pokemon</
i>, the "pocket monsters"
that were so popular
with kids, go to the
official Web site for <a
href="http://www.pokemon.
com">Pokemon</a>.
```

The text appears on-screen as follows:

```
To learn about Pokemon, the
"pocket monsters" that
were so popular with kids,
go to the official Web
site for Pokemon.
```

The `<i>` and `</i>` formatting tags specify that the first occurrence of the word `Pokemon` is displayed in italics. The `<a>` and `</a>` linking tags specify that second occurrence of the word `Pokemon` is displayed as an *anchor* — that is, the starting point of a link. On most browsers, as here, anchors are underlined. So what does the extra text — `href="http://www.pokemon.com"` — inside the `<a>` tag mean? `href` is short for *Hypertext REFerence.* If you click the anchor, your browser looks for the URL that serves as the hypertext reference, which in this case is the Pokemon Web-page address that appears after the equal sign.

Viewing HTML documents

You can see HTML anytime you use the Web. Just pull up a Web page in your browser and choose View⇨Source for Internet Explorer, or a similar command for other browsers. A new window opens, the contents of which are the HTML source code that underlies the Web page. Figure 9-1 shows the home page of the *For Dummies* site and its HTML source code as an example.

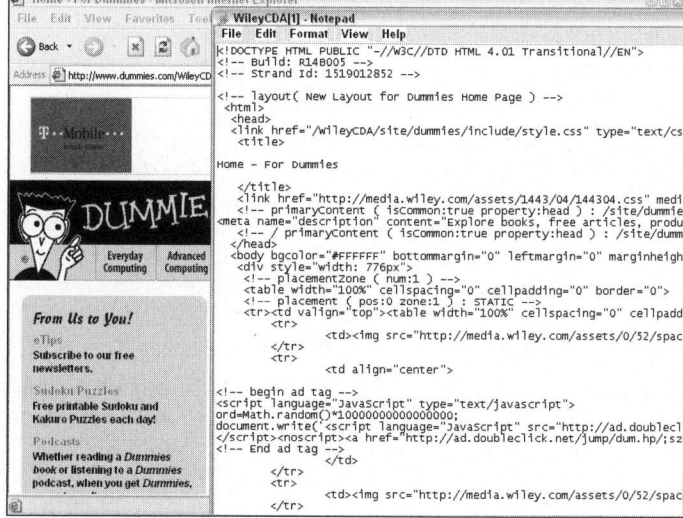

Figure 9-1: The For Dummies site is made of HTML-tagged text and graphics.

Having the ability to view a document's HTML code instantly does naturally lead to the temptation to "borrow" attractive documents from the Web, save them to your hard drive as HTML files, and then use them as templates for your own work — kind of a magpie approach to Web page building. But don't.

Borrowing someone else's material is okay for basic HTML formatting, but for more sophisticated formats that are distinctive and embody a great deal of work, *get permission before you use them* — or don't use them. Simply contact the Webmaster at the site you admire, describe how you want to use the format, and request permission. You may be surprised how many people say yes — without even exacting a promise from you that you hand over your firstborn.

Setting up a Web page

When you first create a Web page, you need to do a certain amount of setup. Luckily, CoffeeCup enters the necessary HTML tags for you (in contrast to having to type them out yourself in a text editor, which Chapter 13 covers).

The needed tags are of five types:

- **Begin and end HTML:** Though your Web page will almost certainly work without them, you really should tell the Internet what protocol your page is made up of. You do this by framing the entire content of your Web page with the `<html>` and `</html>` tags at the beginning and end of the page.

- **Head and body:** The Web page is made up of two blocks of information. Head information is processed before anything visible shows up on the Web page (with one exception, next). The head area is surrounded by the `<head>` and `</head>` tags. Body information is everything you see on the Web page, including text, links, and more. Right after the closing `</head>` tag is the opening `<body>` tag, and the body area is terminated by the `</body>` tag — the last thing in the HTML file except for the `</html>` tag.

- **Page title:** The title of a Web page is meant to be descriptive information for different programs that crawl the Web, such as search engines. But some early Web browsers displayed the contents of the title at the top of a Web page, and now it's noticed by Web users — to the extent that it's important you get it right. The title is in the head area, and is surrounded by the `<title>` and `</title>` tags.

- **Meta tags:** Meta tags are "meta-information", that is, information about the Web page as a whole. For instance, CoffeeCup automatically inserts the standard information, `<meta http-equiv="content-type" content="text/html;charset=UTF-8"/>`. Meta tags were once used heavily by search engines, but now are less used or even ignored. The best way to use meta tags is for the information of yourself or others who might look at the HTML code to tell what the page is about; and if the meta tags help a search engine along the way, great.

- **Comments:** Comments are notes to yourself or future Web authors who might look at the HTML. CoffeeCup automatically inserts a few lines of comments, such as the following: `<!-- Created with the CoffeeCup HTML Editor 2008 -->`. You may wish to add comments in the HTML — there's no way to add them in the Visual Editor.

These tags are demonstrated in CoffeeCup later in this chapter, along with the commands and tags used for formatting Web text.

Formatting Web Text

Whether you use a text editor (as described in Part IV) or a WYSIWYG editor (as described here), the capabilities that HTML makes available for formatting Web text are the same:

- **Headings:** You can specify six levels of headings in HTML, using the tag pairs <h1> and </h1> for the largest, top-level heading; <h2> and </h2> for the next level; and so on down to <h6> and </h6>, the lowest level of headings.

  What it means for you: The ideal way to use headings is as intended — <h1> for the most important heading and so on, down to <h6>. However, you may notice that the heading you're using seems too large in comparison to the text beneath it. Many people use <h4>, for instance, for what's really a second-level heading, or use text size commands and bolding to create their own header styles. Try using the intended headings first, and then use your own formatting if you really need a specific look.

- **Font sizes:** HTML allows you to specify font sizes that are larger or smaller than medium, or standard, size. You can go two sizes smaller or three sizes larger than medium. This formatting works even if users specify a font size or style in their browser setup or in Windows. (As people get older, and their eyes weaken, they resort to various tricks to make using the computer easier — as the author knows from experience.)

  What it means for you: You don't want your Web page to look like a hostage note, with all different styles and sizes of text mixed up, but font sizes can be a good way to make a point (with a larger font size) or fit a lot of text into a small space (with a smaller size).

  Using relative font sizes is one of the few formatting tricks that almost always work well in different Web browsers.

- **Character formatting:** You can make text bold or italic using the <b> and </b> tags to start and stop bold and the <i> and </i> tags to start and stop italic. You can also underline text, but I don't recommend it, because users can easily get confused — because HTML links are usually underlined.

  What it means for you: You should feel free to use bold and italic to emphasize your point, but don't overdo it. Structured use of bold and italic, such as the bold used to highlight items in this list, is one good solution. As for underlining, avoid using it on the Web — people confuse it with the underlining (and use of a color, usually blue) used for hyperlinks. See the "What color is your hyperlink?" sidebar for details.

✔ **Advanced character formatting:** Using tags that aren't supported by all browsers currently in use, you can specify the fonts used in your Web page, as well as font colors. There are problems with doing this, though. Only a limited set of fonts is available for use on all Windows machines or all Macintosh machines. And there isn't much overlap between the specific fonts on Windows and Macintosh, so you won't get the specific effect you desire on the "other" platform. (You can specify backup fonts for use if the desired font isn't there.)

What it means for you: I don't recommend using advanced character formatting because it's complicated and because, just when you start to depend on it, you find it doesn't work for some of your users. Stay away from this kind of formatting unless you're working at a professional level, with the design help and testing resources needed to make it work well for all your users.

Follow these steps to enter and format text in CoffeeCup:

1. **Start CoffeeCup and inspect the HTML in the Code Editor tab.**

   Note the beginning and ending HTML, head, and body tags as well as the Title tag.

2. **Move to the Visual Editor tab.**

   Save the Code Editor contents as prompted.

3. **Choose Insert⇨Title.**

   The Page Title dialog box appears.

4. **Enter an appropriate title, such as My Home Page, and then click OK.**

5. **Move the cursor to a new line.**

6. **Type some text introducing your Web page.**

   When someone searches for your Web page by using a search engine, the search engine may display the Web page title, as described above, and the first few words that appear in the document. So make the first few sentences of text that follow the title an introduction to the entire page or Web site.

   In the document I created for this chapter, I typed:

   ```
   Sierra Soccer Club

   Sierra Soccer Club is a boys' soccer club that
   practices and plays at the highest altitude of any in
   the United States.
   ```

7. **Highlight text that you'd like to make a header.**

   In my document, I highlighted the words Sierra Soccer Club at the beginning.

8. **Choose Format⇨Font⇨Header Sizes and the header size you want, from 1 (largest) through 6 (smallest).**

   The text will change to a header of the selected size. I chose header size 1 as this is the header for all the content that follows.

9. **Highlight other text that you want to format.**

   In my document, I highlighted the word "highest" in the middle of the first sentence.

10. **Click the toolbar button for the formatting style that you want: the B button for Bold, the I button for Italic, or the U button for Underline. Or choose Format⇨Bold, Italic or Underline.**

    The highlighted text takes on the formatting you choose. In my example, I made the word "highest" bold.

    Any HTML styles — paragraph-level formatting commands — that you choose affect the entire paragraph of text in which the cursor rests.

Figure 9-2 shows the CoffeeCup Visual Editor tab with the text formatted as described here. Note that Header 1 may actually be too large for our purposes.

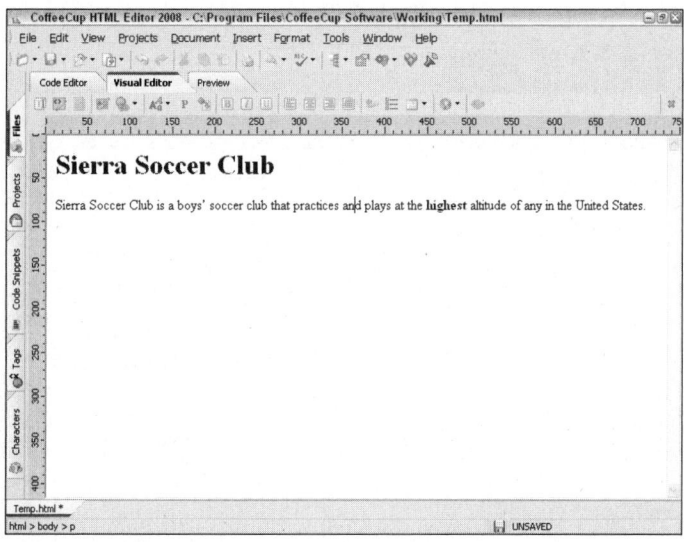

Figure 9-2:
Take advantage of Web formatting options.

What color is your hyperlink?

HTML allows you to use colored text on your Web page and to change the colors used for unvisited, visited, and active hyperlinks. ("Active" means the mouse pointer is over the link, but the mouse button hasn't yet been clicked.) I generally don't recommend this.

Why not? (This book is about all the things you *can* do on a Web page, after all!) The reason is that people are very used to monotone text, usually black, on a contrasting background. People have adjusted to the use of colored text on Web pages, but mainly in the form of standard hyperlink colors: blue for a link the user hasn't clicked yet, and purple for a recently visited link.

Some Web-page authors customize hyperlink colors to fit better with the color scheme of their Web pages. The problem is, research into making Web pages easier to use and less confusing has found that users subconsciously count on blue underlined text to indicated unvisited links and purple underlined text to indicate visited links. Any change in these colors, or any use of underlining or blue or purple text for other purposes, causes deep confusion.

So I recommend that you don't use colored text, don't change link colors, and don't use underlining except in links. (With the exception being if you have the time to come up with a really consistent, carefully thought through and highly usable alternative, which usually requires using a template or a professional level of attention.) The people who visit your Web page will have a better time using it as a result.

Using HTML Lists

People really like lists. David Letterman's Top Ten lists are the highlight of his *Late Night* show and have been the subject of several books. Everywhere you look, you see lists. Here are my top three reasons why lists are a good thing — in a list, of course:

- ✔ **Lists are interesting to look at.** Web pros are always telling people to use lots of white space to vary the appearance of their pages so they're not just featureless blobs of text. Lists do this; they break up text.

- ✔ **Lists are easy to scan.** As I mention earlier in this chapter, people are more likely to scan text on the Web than to read it carefully. Lists are very easy to scan. With the key points highlighted, people can go in depth by carefully reading the points that interest them, and then skim the ones that don't.

- ✔ **Lists make the writer get to the point.** When you write a list, you have to cut and condense what you're trying to say. You may end up editing a page of boring, monotonous text down to three or four points in a bulleted list. All this extra work you have to do greatly benefits the reader, especially the reader who's reading from a computer screen.

HTML and Web-page editing programs based on HTML (such as CoffeeCup) offer three kinds of lists, but only two are used much.

- ✔ **Bulleted lists:** Bulleted lists are by far the most widely used kind of list on the Web. And why not? Bulleted lists are flexible and fun, both to write and, more importantly, to read. You start a bulleted list with the `<ul>` tag, which stands for *unordered list.* You end it with the `</ul>` tag. Each list item is preceded with `<li>`, which stands for — you guessed it — *list item.*

    List items don't have to have an ending tag, though you can add one (it's `</li>`, as you might expect). After your text, the browser expects to see either another `<li>` tag, for the next list item, or the `</ul>` tag to end the list.

    What it means for you: You can convert many, or even most, long blocks of text into a bulleted list — and make the text shorter, easier to read, and more interesting in the bargain. If you have to move existing text to the Web, consider "bulletizing" parts of it as a quick way to make it more Web friendly.

- ✔ **Numbered lists:** Numbered lists look weird when you create them in some Web editing programs — the program puts a number symbol (#) next to each item, and the number isn't assigned until the page displays. (CoffeeCup, fortunately, displays actual numbers.) Numbered lists are very useful, but are found much less often on the Web. Numbered lists begin with `<ol>` for *ordered list,* end with `</ol>`, and — like bulleted lists — use the `<li>` tag to mark the beginning of each list item.

    What it means for you: Any time you have a list that has an order in terms of importance, sequence in time, or any other reason, make it a numbered list. Putting your list items in numbered order makes the list even easier to scan than a regular, bulleted list.

- ✔ **Definition lists:** *Definition lists* give a term and then a definition for the term. They're rarely used, though finding a use for them in your Web page is a good exercise. A definition list starts with `<dl>` and ends with `</dl>`. Each term is preceded by `<dt>`, for *definition term,* and each definition is preceded by `<dd>`, for *definition data.* Again, if you'd like, you can close the tags by adding `</dt>` and `</dd>`, respectively, after the data.

    What it means for you: The appearance of definition lists in your Web page is a bit funny — some Web browsers put the term on one line and then the definition, indented farther in, on the next line. You can help the reader who's scanning find the terms easily by making them bold, as in the definition list you're reading here. People like definition-type lists, but not necessarily formatted the way most Web browsers do it. Use definition lists where you can, or use bold text and bulleted or numbered lists to create your own definition-type list.

✔ **Lists within lists:** You can insert or *nest* one list inside another. The nested list can be the same kind of list, or a different kind, than the list that contains it.

What it means for you: In the limited view offered on most users' screens, users have a hard time keeping track of where they are in the overall list if you start throwing sublists at them as well. I believe that putting one list within another is usually a case of something that's technically possible, but not editorially desirable. (I look forward to one of you proving me wrong by coming up with a good use for nested lists on a Web page.)

Follow these steps to create a list in CoffeeCup:

1. **Add the text for your list in the Visual Editor.**

   In the document I created for this chapter, here's what I typed:

   ```
   If you meet the following qualifications, you may be
   eligible to become a member of Sierra Soccer Club:

   Born in 2000 or 2001. Sierra Soccer Club has played
   together since its founding members were 5 and 6 years
   old and will stick together as they grow up. All our
   club members must be born in 2000 or 2001.

   Some soccer experience. If you have played in organized
   leagues before, or if you're a skilled school player,
   we may be able to help take your game to new levels.

   Good academic record. We are proud that our club mem-
   bers maintain good standing in school as well as in
   soccer.
   ```

2. **Highlight the lines that you want to make into a list.**

   In my document, I highlighted the lines that begin with these phrases:

   ```
   Born in 2000 or 2001

   Some soccer experience

   Good academic record
   ```

3. **Choose Insert⇨List or click the List button in the Visual Editor.**

   The Insert List dialog box appears, as shown in Figure 9-3.

   The Insert List dialog box is a good example of the benefits of using a WYSIWYG editor. It includes options for bullet styles that you might not have known were part of HTML, or for which you might have forgotten the details. With this dialog box, you're not only reminded of the button styles, but also can easily test how they look within your page.

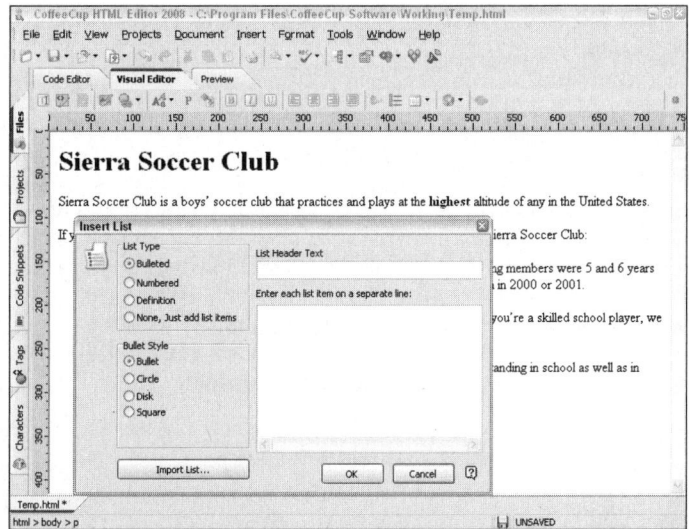

Figure 9-3:
Insert List
gives you
all the list
options.

4. Choose the type of list you want and (optionally) the bullet style.

For this example, I've made a bulleted list of the list items for the soccer club members, and chosen the square bullet style. I then removed extra carriage returns so there would only be three bullets.

Figure 9-4 shows the sample page with all the formatting described in the numbered steps in this chapter applied.

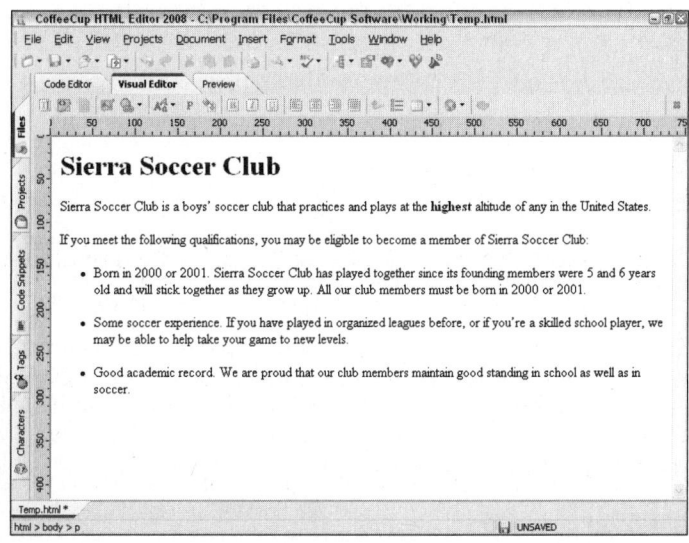

Figure 9-4:
What you
see is what
you get.

5. **To see the underlying HTML, click the Code Editor tab.**

The HTML for your page appears, as shown in Figure 9-5.

When you're working in a WYSIWYG (What You See Is What You Get) tool such as CoffeeCup, you often want to look at the underlying HTML code. Doing so enables you to find out how HTML works and gives you the chance to make adjustments in the HTML tags that affect the way your page looks and works on the Web.

The only problem with looking at the HTML code in CoffeeCup is that you'll be prompted to save the HTML code, even if you haven't changed anything in the Code Editor. However, doing this does give you the opportunity to create a backup of the work you've done in the Visual Editor, even if that wasn't your original intent.

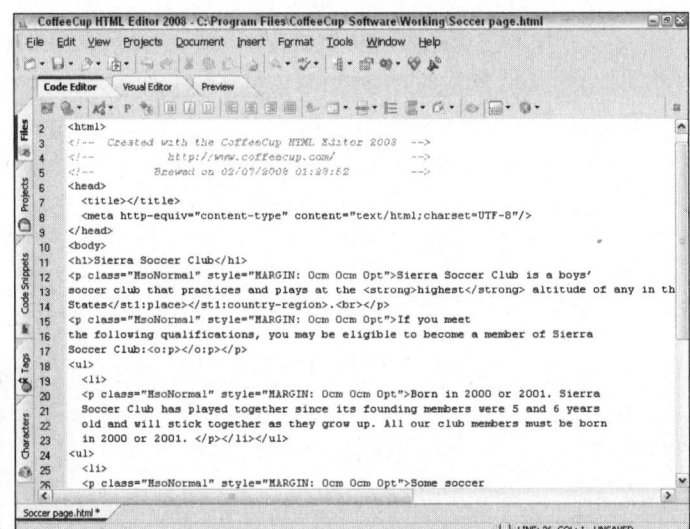

Figure 9-5: How the HTML works.

CoffeeCup or a more sophisticated package?

Although offerings change with time, you can usually get a free trial version of excellent Web-page editing software such as Microsoft Expression Web or Adobe Dreamweaver from the companies' Web sites, or an online download site such as CNET's download.com (at www.download.com, natch). Why use CoffeeCup instead of a free trial version?

✔ **Truly easy:** Because it's designed as an introductory program, CoffeeCup has only basic and intermediate features — not too much complexity, which you don't need most of the time, to make things confusing.

✔ **Far less expensive:** If you choose to pay for CoffeeCup, you'll only pay a small fee, and you'll only pay it once — CoffeeCup includes free lifetime updates.

✔ **Truly HTML-compatible:** As an introductory program, Composer only supports features that work on just about any Web browser out there. By contrast, using all the features in Microsoft Expression Web or Dreamweaver may mean that you add things that don't work in older browsers or across platforms.

In addition, of course, my argument is that you can better follow along with the instructions in this book if you're using the software that I use for many of my examples and figures — either straight HTML or CoffeeCup.

If you're sure that you're going to be using Expression Web or Dreamweaver soon, or if you already have a copy, you may want to use a trial version of the program that's in your future. Even then, you may want to use CoffeeCup for easy work and the full-featured program for advanced features. If you do work in a full-featured Web-page editor, most of the steps in the sections of this book dedicated to CoffeeCup will still work for you — you just need to substitute the specific commands for your program in place of the instructions and illustrations given for CoffeeCup.

Linking to Outside Web Pages

The secret of Web pages is hyperlinks. This is where the phrase "surfing the Web" comes from, with the ease of moving from one page to another and one site to another making the Web easy to use and fun.

This section shows you how to use one form of links: links to totally different Web sites. These are the simplest links, even though they're also the most powerful, allowing you to reach out to any Web site or any Web page on any Web server anywhere in the world.

Hyperlinks are so important that they're reflected in the names of the two key technical standards underlying the Web. *HyperText Transfer Protocol,* the http you see in a Web-page address, is the standard for file transfer used to support Web pages. (When you click a link to a new Web page, an HTML file is transferred to your machine, and links within the HTML file cause graphics to appear within the page.)

HyperText Markup Language, or HTML, is the standard for writing Web pages. While many HTML tags, such as the bold and italics tags (<b> and <i>) are for formatting rather than hypertext, the links described in this section, for linking to outside Web pages, are definitely hypertext markup.

1 link, therefore 1 am

A hypertext link to an outside Web page has two parts: the text that appears as a hyperlink — most often underlined and displayed in blue — and the destination page that appears in the user's Web browser if the user clicks on the link.

The text is made into the starting point of a hypertext link by surrounding it with the `<a>` and `</a>` tags, with a standing for anchor. The link's two ends, the start that the user clicks on and the page that appears as a result, are both called anchors.

The destination of the link is called the `hypertext reference`, or `href` for short. So a link to another Web page in HTML looks like this:

```
Make your own cider with <a href="http://www.ciderspices.com">cider spices</a>.
```

Simple, isn't it? Part of the reason it's so simple is a couple of assumptions: If you use a domain name for a link, such as `www.ciderspices.com`, your Web browser looks for the `index.htm` or similarly named file first, so you don't have to include the filename in the link destination. And the browser further assumes that the destination is the top of a Web page unless you specify a location within the Web page. (I go into more detail on this when discussing links within a Web page and links to graphics and multimedia files in the next two chapters.)

A simple link in a CoffeeCup

Follow these steps to create a simple hypertext link in CoffeeCup's Visual Editor:

1. **In the Visual Editor, highlight the text that you want to make into a hyperlink.**

   In the document I created as an example for this book, I highlighted the words "soccer experience" in the second bullet point.

2. **Click the Links button or choose Insert⇨Link.**

   The Insert Link dialog box appears, as shown in Figure 9-6.

3. **Enter the destination Web address, or URL, in the URL box.**

   Enter the full Web address, including the preceding `http://`, and check whether the address includes `www.` or not; a few Web addresses don't. Also make certain that the site ending really is `.com`, `.org`, `.co.uk`, and so on.

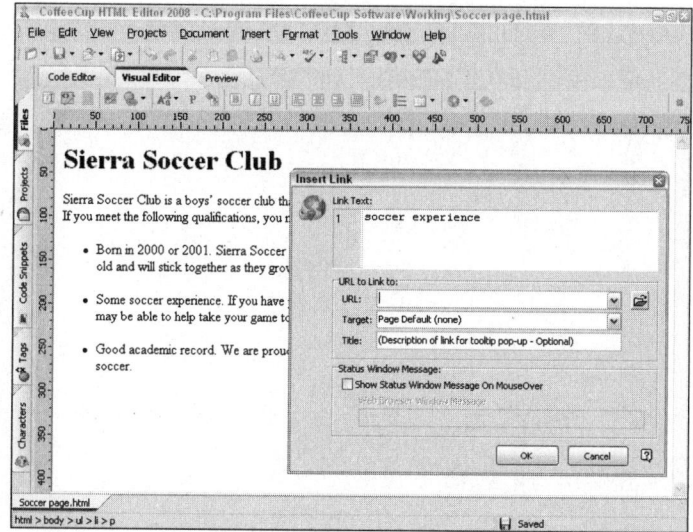

You can open a Web browser to find or check the Web address you need
while the Insert Link dialog box is open.

4. **Enter a title for the link in the** `Title:` **area.**

   The title for the link is text that appears when the user puts the mouse
   pointer over the link. (Text of this sort is called a *tool tip* from its use in
   computer programs.)

   If you leave this area blank, the URL will appear as the tool tip. Often
   this is self-explanatory, as in a link to a Wikipedia entry. You may wish
   to enter the URL, without `http://`, as the link title to make it a bit more
   comprehensible for the user.

   If the URL is long or confusing, enter a simple title that describes the
   page. For instance, the URL for the book *HTML For Dummies,* 5th Edition,
   on `www.dummies.com` is intimidatingly long and confusing:

   ```
   http://www.dummies.com/WileyCDA/Section/id-DUMMIES_SEARCH_RESULT.
            html?queryText=html%20for%20dummies
   ```

   I'd enter a tool tip such as `HTML For Dummies on dummies.com`
   instead.

5. **Click OK to accept the link URL and the link title, if any.**

   The text will appear as link text, underlined and in blue. (Unless you've
   changed the appearance of the links for this page.)

Chapter 10

Graphics and Media, WYSIWYG Style

In This Chapter

▶ Gazing at images in a WYSIWYG editor

▶ Giving voice to your Web page by adding sound

▶ Livening up a Web page with video

*I*n the early days of the Web, it was embedded GIF graphics files that really brought Web pages to life. Then came embedded JPEG files, and more recently downloadable sound files and embedded videos have kept making the Web more and more interesting, relevant, and useful.

Chapters 5, 6, and 7, describe how to create and use images, sounds, and videos (respectively). In this chapter, I show you how to actually put all these kinds of files in your Web page using a WYSIWYG editor, with specific examples using CoffeeCup. By the end of this chapter, you should be able to create very lively Web pages.

Chapter 14 uses this same approach, showing you how to create Web pages "by hand" in Notepad. It looks pretty similar to this chapter; that's intentional. I figure at least some consistency helps shrink confusion.

In the early days of the Web, the only kind of media file that could be really included in a Web page was a GIF graphics file. Though the HTML file itself was text, any GIF file that was linked into the Web page via the IMG tag was displayed as if it were part of the page. JPEG graphics files were included via the EMBED command and were opened with one of a variety of "player" programs that contained the somewhat complex code needed to display a JPEG image.

Fairly quickly, browsers were upgraded to incorporate JPEG files, which can now be handled via the IMG command. PNG graphics files are now fairly widely supported, and even Windows BMP files are supported by Internet Explorer. But GIF and JPEG images remain the only ones that you can really count on including within the "flow" of a Web page.

Web-page authors have had to put up with a certain limitation of standard Web browsers: They can't display or play back sound and video files; for that you need a *player* application such as Windows Media Player, QuickTime, or RealPlayer (to cite three common examples). Even the HTML for including a sound or video file isn't standardized. So if you're going to include these files in a way that most people can use, you have some tweaking and finessing to do. Fortunately, CoffeeCup helps you do it.

Including Images in WYSIWYG

Including images in a Web page isn't all that simple. The complexities of how to create the images themselves are covered in Chapter 5. Linking to images isn't all that easy either. (Similar considerations apply to sound and video, but they're less-used than images.)

There are three kinds of links you can use to include an image in a Web page:

✔ **Linking to a Web URL.** Most every image on the Web has its own URL. So, to include the image in your own Web page, you can just use the IMG tag and give the Web address of the image as the source. When the user sees your Web page, it will look like the image is part of it, even though it's hosted on a different Web site.

Plusses and minuses: This is easy for you as a Web author, but you can't count on the image staying there forever. It also represents the image as your own when it actually belongs to someone else. Finally, it's much slower for the user than hosting the image on your own Web server.

To find the URL of a Web image on a Windows machine, right-click it and choose Copy Shortcut. The URL will then be placed in the Clipboard, meaning you can paste it into a text editor, HTML program or other program.

✔ **Linking to the same folder as your Web page.** If an image file is in the same folder as the HTML file that links to it, you only need to give the name of the image file, no folder or path information.

Plusses and minuses: This is very simple, like linking to a Web URL, fast and easy. When you transfer your files to a Web server, there's no problem with keeping the files in the same relative position. The only disadvantage is that the folder the Web page is in can get quite crowded, especially as many images are used over and over again by different Web pages. So you can end up with one folder containing all the Web pages and images in a site, which can be a mess.

✔ **Linking to a different folder on the same machine as the Web page.** The image file is on the same machine as the Web page, but in a different folder. The link contains either a relative pathway from the Web page to the image file, including moves up and down a tree of folders, or an absolute address relative to the root of the machine.

> *Plusses and minuses:* This is where a lot of problems occur. You have to describe the pathway from the HTML file to the image file, or the absolute location of the file on the machine, and this can easily change or get mangled when files are transferred to a Web server.

> Using a WYSIWYG tool such as CoffeeCup solves many of the possible problems of keeping images in a separate file by automatically generating the path information between the files. CoffeeCup goes one step further and encourages you to arrange the files sensibly.

All the different possible ways of linking an HTML file to an image file are described in Table 10-1. Inspect it carefully now, and use it as a reference when you're creating links to image files. (There's one just like it in Chapter 14 for those hardy folks who've decided to use Notepad instead of CoffeeCup.)

Table 10-1	URL and Web Page Examples		
Location of Target	*URL*	*Web-Page Example*	*Graphics Example**
Same folder	`filename`	`<a href=" mycv.html"> text</a>`	`<img src=" myface.jpg">`
Subfolder at a lower level of the same path	`pathname/ filename`	`<a href=" subpages/ mycv.htm"> text</a>`	`<img src=" grfx/myface. jpg>`
Folder on a different path	`pathname/ filename`	`<a href="../ theother- page/ otherpage. htm>text</a>`	`<img src=" ../sharegfx/ proface.gif>`
Different server, home page (index. htm or index. html)	`domainname`	`<a href=" http://www. largedomain. com">text</ a>`	`<img src=" http://www. largedomain. com/good- face.jpg">`
Different server, interior page	`Domainname/ pathname`	`<a href=" http://www. largess.com/ files/bud. htm">text</ a>`	`<img src= "http://www. largess.com/ gifs/icon27. gif">`

(continued)

Table 10-1 *(continued)*

Location of Target	URL	Web-Page Example	Graphics Example*
Link within a page	Any of the above + #anchor name	`<a name="my anchor"></a>; <a href=" http://www. largess.com# myanchor">Go to my anchor </a>`	Doesn't apply

* These examples leave out the alt option and other important graphics options, described later in this chapter.

Follow these steps to enter and format text in CoffeeCup:

1. **Open the Visual Editor tab in CoffeeCup; move the cursor to the point where you want to insert the graphic.**

   The Visual Editor makes many aspects of linking to a graphic easier.

2. **Click the Image button or click the Insert menu and select Image.**

   The Insert Image dialog box appears, as shown in Figure 10-1.

   Move the dialog box to one side (if possible) so you can see the area where the image is going in.

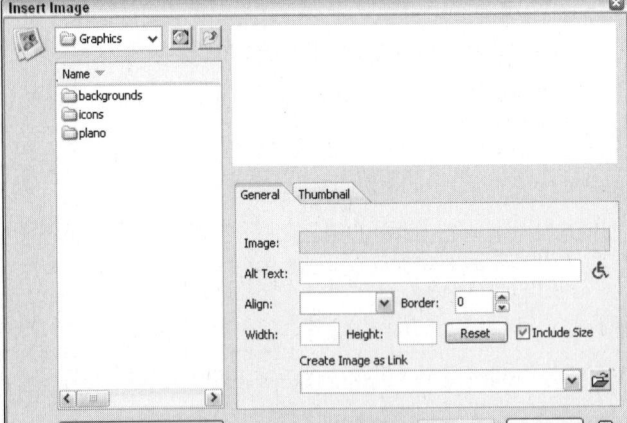

3. **Navigate to the image you want to include and select it.**

   Chapter 5 describes how to create and find images of the right format, adjust image size, and so on. (However, see Step 10 for a quick-and-dirty way to resize an image.)

4. **If CoffeeCup asks you to copy the image to the working folder, say Yes to do so, or No to leave the image where it is.**

   In most cases, it's better to choose Yes; this will place the image in the same folder as the Web page, creating the simplest possible path from one to the other.

5. **Enter** alt **text at the Alt Text prompt.**

   alt text is very important for two reasons. alt text is read out loud by screen readers and other programs for visually disabled users. (The wheelchair image in the dialog box is the international symbol for disability, not specifically for wheelchair use.)

   alt text is also used as a tool tip, text that appears when the user mouses over the graphic. For both purposes, alt text should be a short, simple description of the image, such as the name of a person pictured — or a description, if the image is for the purpose of providing atmosphere.

6. **Choose how the image should be aligned relative to text.**

   The usual choices are for the image to be aligned to the left, with text flowing around it on the right, or on the right, with text flowing to the left of it. This is the magazine or newspaper look, with text and image integrated together.

   Other choices, such as top, bottom, and middle, place a single line of text next to the image and otherwise leave the image on its own. This nearly always looks strange.

7. **Enter a border size for a black border around the image.**

   Adding a thin black border around an image makes it appear sharper and clearer (especially small images). Experiment with border sizes around your image. The Insert Image box will show a preview to help guide you, as shown in Figure 10-2.

   There's an additional attribute that allows you to add blank space around an image that you may want to use; see Chapter 14 for the HTML code to use in the Code Editor to add this padding.

8. **Change the width and height if you want to resize the image in place.**

   Usually you should resize the image before putting it in your Web page. However, you can stretch or shrink the displayed image by changing the width and/or height here.

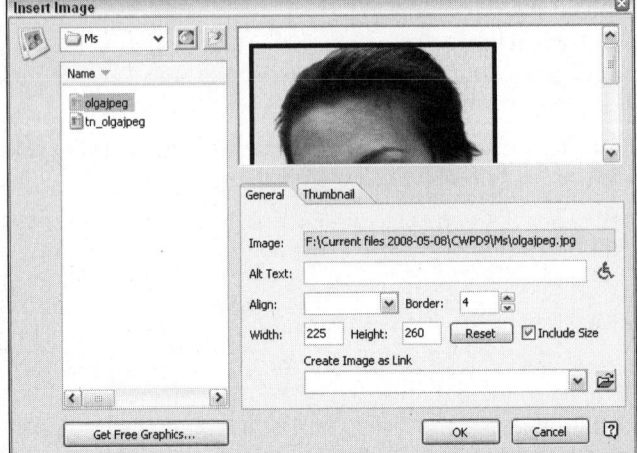

Figure 10-2:
Use the
preview to
set a border
around the
image.

If you want to keep the image in proportion, change both dimensions by the same amount. For instance, if you want to resize the width from 180 pixels to 100 pixels, multiply the height by 100, divide it by 180, and use the result as the new height.

Leave the Include Size box checked so the image size will be included in the HTML code. This allows the Web browser to draw the Web page correctly before the image downloads, preventing different parts of the page contents from lurching about as different elements of the page download.

 9. **To make the image a link, enter a URL, or browse to the destination file on your local machine or network.**

You can link to a Web destination or use images to create an image-based menu.

 10. **To create a smaller version of the image, click the Thumbnail tab, as shown in Figure 10-3.**

You can choose the percentage for resizing, the file format, and the quality setting (for JPEG images).

If you want to give the user the option of clicking the small image to see the larger version, click the Link to Original Image check box.

This is a great feature for creating a thumbnail image, but also a fast and easy way of creating a smaller image "on the fly."

 11. **Click OK to accept the image settings.**

To change the settings later, click the image; the options will show up at the bottom of the Visual Editor area.

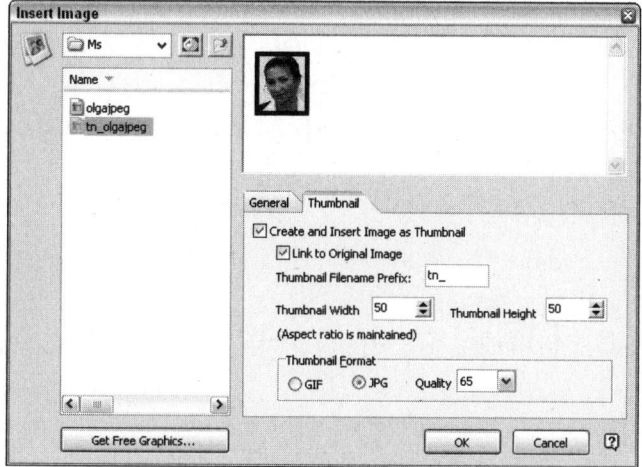

Figure 10-3:
Create a
thumbnail or
just down-
size the
image.

Adding Sound to Your Page

Whether it's a good idea to add sound to your Web page, the plusses and minuses are discussed in Chapter 6. (Also described there are how to host a music file on MySpace.) I mention there that you can't, for instance, have background music for an entire site — sound is controlled one page at a time. But what are the actual mechanics of adding sound?

Because sound is not a standard part of the Web's definition, there are actually two contradictory ways to do it. Briefly, one is with the bgsound tag, and one is with the embed tag.

The bgsound tag works well and has useful options for controlling sound. However, it's not supported by all browsers.

The embed tag is one of the "wild cards" of HTML, not officially supported by the HTML standard at all — but supported by most browsers. One big problem with embed, from a standards point of view, is that the options (officially called attributes) for embed are different for different players. Each player is controlled by a single company — Microsoft, Apple, and Real Networks, for the three major players — and this is not a very standards-friendly situation.

The user can stop sound from playing by clicking the browser's Stop button; you may wish to let your users know this in text on your Web page; many (even most) users don't know it.

Given this confusion, CoffeeCup does an excellent job of supporting the embedding of sounds, but it's still a mess. Follow these steps to add sound to a Web page in CoffeeCup:

1. **Open the Visual Editor tab in CoffeeCup; move the cursor to the beginning of the text.**

   This will put the HTML code for embedding the sound at the beginning of the BODY area of the Web page, where it will be easy to find if you need to modify it.

2. **Choose Insert⇨Sound.**

   The Insert Sound dialog box appears, as shown in Figure 10-4.

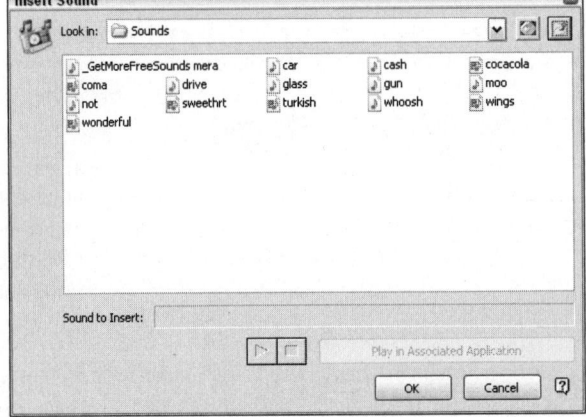

3. **Navigate to the sound file you want to include — one of the sample files included with CoffeeCup (as shown in the figure) or another sound — and select it.**

   The pathway to the file shows up next to the Sound to Insert prompt.

4. **To preview — or "pre-hear" — the sound file, click the green triangle. To open the application that's associated with that type of sound file on your machine, click Play in Associated Application.**

   The sound file will play — without showing the application, if you click the green triangle, or while showing the application, if you click the Play in Associated Application button.

5. **Click OK to accept the sound.**

   A small image will appear in the Web page and the sound will now play whenever the page is opened.

The HTML code generated by CoffeeCup will actually play the same sound twice. To correct this, and to set other options, follow the next steps.

6. Click the Code Editor tab.

The code for playing the sound, both an embed tag and a bgsound tag, will appear.

7. Correct the code to make the sound play only once.

There are three solutions to this:

- Remove the embed tag. This way the sound will only play — once, not twice — on the (many) browsers that support bgsound. Users whose browsers don't support bgsound won't hear anything and won't know what they're missing.

- Remove the bgsound tag. This way the sound will play — only once, not twice — on the (many) browsers that support embed. Users whose browsers don't support embed won't hear anything and won't know what they're missing.

- Surround the bgsound tag with the <noembed> and </noembed> tags. These tags allow the bgsound tag to only execute on browsers that don't support the embed tag; you only hear the sound once, but you miss the loop option of the bgsound tag. Speaking of which . . .

For the bgsound tag only, you can add loop="3", for instance, for the sound to play a total of three times, or loop="infinite" if you want the sound to keep playing. (This can be, well, infinitely annoying.)

Adding Video to Your Page

The whys and wherefores of adding video to your Web page are discussed in detail in Chapter 7, along with the specifics of how to upload a video to YouTube.

You can host a video on your own site or on YouTube. If you use YouTube, you get the advantage of using Google's massive server and processing capabilities — Google owns YouTube — for compressing your video and serving it, all free of charge to you. If you host video on your own site, you may have to pay fees if download activity gets too high.

If a video hosted on a server you pay for "goes viral" — suddenly getting hundreds or thousands of hits — the download charges could scale rather dramatically as well.

YouTube even helps with the mechanics of putting the video in your Web page — which can be done with the same code, wherever it's hosted, except for the contents of the hypertext reference. For every video on YouTube, the code is provided to link to embed that video in your Web page. However, it's not that hard to do the same thing yourself.

Here's a quick example of how to include a video in your Web page, wherever it's hosted:

1. **Open the Code Editor tab in CoffeeCup; move the cursor to wherever you want the video to appear in the Web page.**

2. **If the video is hosted on YouTube, go to the relevant YouTube page and copy the code for the video from there. Paste it into your Web page. Otherwise, type in the following:** `<embed src="path">`.

   If the video is in the same folder as your Web page, the path is just the filename; if the video is on the Web, the path is its URL (of the video, not the page it's on; find this by choosing View⇨Source for the Web page hosting the video). If the file is in a folder on your machine, include the path to it.

   You can figure this out by linking to a graphic in the same folder, using the Insert Image command described earlier in this chapter, then copying the path generated in the dialog box but substituting the video's filename.

3. **Test the video in your Web page.**

   Try the video in your Web page.

   If you're having no luck successfully including the video in your Web page, or if you're worried about download charges, then upload the video to YouTube or another host. Provide a "normal" link to the Web page that hosts the video on your Web page. Users can then return to your site after they've viewed the video.

Chapter 11

Laying Out Your Site in WYSIWYG

In This Chapter

▶ Using mailto links

▶ Linking your Web page internally

▶ Creating a navigation bar

*O*ne of the trickiest things in creating Web pages is going beyond "just putting up a page" to creating a full site. The questions around designing a multiple-page site never get fully answered, even by the experts. (That's oddly reassuring, as it leaves room for creativity.)

In this chapter, I demonstrate how to use links to create first a complex page, then a full site, complete with basic navigation.

Using mailto Links

Oddly, `mailto` links are one of those "simple" things that actually have some complexity to them — complexity that's easy to work around if you know how.

A `mailto` link is a link that has as its destination an e-mail address. If your system is set up properly — a big if — clicking an e-mail link brings up an open e-mail message, already addressed to the e-mail address described in the `mailto` link. (If you're really clever, the subject line of the e-mail can also be pre-filled.) The user just has to enter the content of the e-mail and click Send. See Figure 11-1 for an example of a link and the resulting e-mail message.

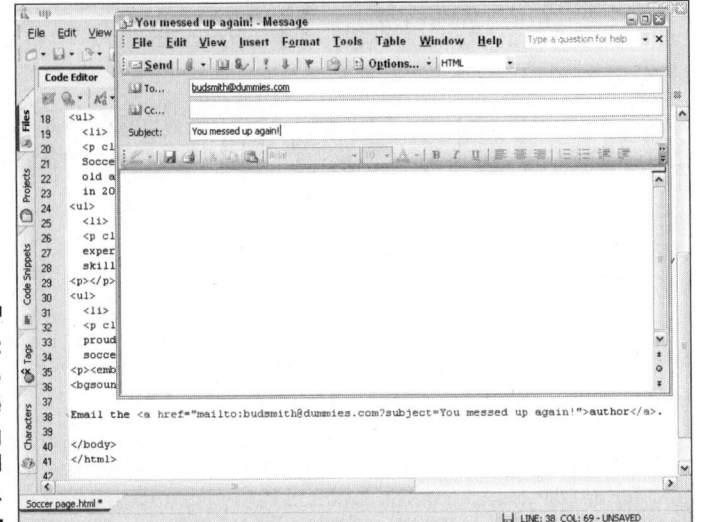

Figure 11-1:
`Mailto`
links make
creating
e-mail
easier.

True enough, `mailto` links are cool, a nice "hack" that makes a difficult problem — getting an e-mail address exactly right — much easier. Unfortunately, there are a few "buts" to take into account before using e-mail links. Here are the problems with them:

✔ `mailto` **links often don't work at all.** Many people don't have their systems set up correctly (that is, so their main e-mail program is recognized by the system and "called" when a `mailto` link is clicked). The result of clicking a link might be that an unused e-mail tool is started, or even that the system asks the user to *find* the e-mail program on the hard drive — not something most people want to do (for one thing, it's annoying).

✔ `mailto` **links often don't work in the way that's wanted.** Different people use different e-mail programs for different purposes. The same person may do e-mail work primarily in Outlook, using his or her job's domain name, may handle personal e-mail through Hotmail or Gmail — possibly through a Web browser window, possibly also in Outlook.

The mailto link can't "know" which e-mail program or source domain the user wants at any given point, but it often guesses wrong. It may (for example) strike the user as strikingly inappropriate to bring up the "work" e-mail when the present objective is to book a vacation. This problem can even contribute to getting the user into difficulty: It's easy to miss an e-mail reply that goes to the "wrong" account or use the "work" e-mail application for inappropriate personal purposes. (Try saying that three times fast!)

✔ `mailto` **links often aren't what the user expects.** When users click a "Contact Us" link, for instance, they want and expect a page of contact information with, ideally, one or more names, addresses, and phone numbers, as well as Web links and e-mail addresses. If, instead, a pre-filled e-mail message to a discouraging address (such as `contact@ wewontanswer.com`) comes up, the user feels cheated.

Luckily, there's a way to use `mailto` links that maximizes their advantages and minimizes their problems. Just follow these rules, which work together to "tame" `mailto` links and make them friendly:

✔ **Never use** `mailto` **links in navigation.** Users expect navigational links to lead to Web pages. Don't surprise them. Use `mailto` links within Web pages, where the user expects them.

✔ **Provide alternatives to e-mail contact.** Don't make e-mail the only way to contact you unless you absolutely have to. Everyone knows that e-mails (especially e-mails to anonymous addresses such as `contactus@...`) often go unanswered. So make the e-mail route just one way to get in touch. (And if you really want to be effective, promise a time frame in which the e-mail will be answered and stick to it.)

✔ **Signal that the** `mailto` **link is present.** Use wording coming up to the `mailto` link that indicates that's what the users will get when they click. Something like this: "To complain, call us at 1 800 555-1212 or send us e-mail...."

✔ **Spell out the e-mail address as well.** Many users are aware that clicking a `mailto` link doesn't work for them. By spelling out the e-mail address as well as providing it in a link, you give them another way to accomplish your shared purpose, which is for them to send you an e-mail. (You also signal that the adjacent e-mail link is just that.)

So a proper use of `mailto` links is within a Contact Us or other page, in a form like the following:

To respond, send <u>e-mail</u> to `wewanttohear@ourcompany.com`.

This will signal the user that clicking the link, e-mail, will bring up an e-mail message addressed to `wewanttohear@ourcompany.com` — and give them a workaround if they want to use the e-mail address themselves.

Creating a `mailto` link in CoffeeCup is just like creating a regular link, only simpler. Follow these steps:

1. **Open the Visual Editor tab in CoffeeCup; move the cursor to the spot where you want to insert the** `mailto` **link. If the text you wish to use for the e-mail link is already present, select it.**

2. **Choose Insert⇨E-mail Link or click the Link button and choose E-mail Link.**

   The Insert E-mail Link dialog box appears, as shown in Figure 11-2.

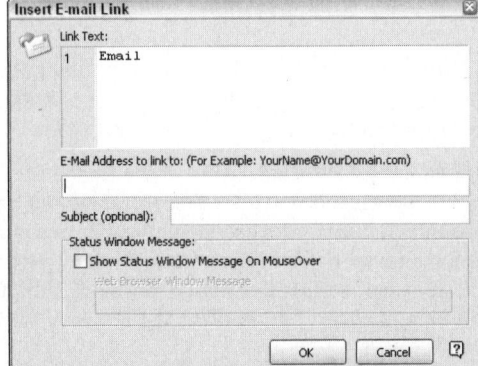

3. **If the Link Text: area is not already filled in with text you selected before opening the dialog box, enter the link text you want to use.**

4. **Enter the e-mail address you want the link to link to.**

   Be sure to get the e-mail address right, and test it after you finish. Nothing is more frustrating to the user than a bad e-mail address in a `mailto` link.

   If there's background work that needs to be done — for instance, if you want to use a generic e-mail address such as `contact@`, but behind the scenes you want to link that to a few people's e-mail In boxes — do that work now so the link works as needed from the beginning, even during testing.

5. **Optionally, enter a Subject line for the e-mail.**

   This can be convenient for both you and the users, but can be changed by the users (or can be ignored completely if users send e-mail to the designated address themselves). So don't count on it working for all e-mails you receive from this `mailto` link.

6. **Optionally, click in the check box to show a status window message when the users move their mouse over the linked text. Then enter the message.**

This option makes a message appear in the status-bar area in the user's Web browser; if you don't enter anything here, the word `mailto:` and the destination e-mail address will appear instead. Unfortunately, most users have the status-bar area turned off (that's the default in recent versions of Internet Explorer, the most popular browser) and, if they do have it on, they expect to be able to see link destinations there when they mouse over a link. So it's probably best not to use this option.

7. **Click OK to accept the e-mail link properties.**

    The appropriate HTML code is added to your Web page.

Internal Links within a Web Page

One of the most productive uses of hyperlinks is to create sets of links that, at first, don't seem all that "hyper": links within a Web page.

One of the cleverest elements of Web pages is that, while they're quite limited in the horizontal dimension — users won't accept having to scroll left and right to read a page — they can be very long indeed in the vertical dimension (up and down). Like an ancient scroll, a Web page can "unroll" to be very long indeed.

But only if you make things easy on the user. You can help a user navigate within a given Web page by using *internal links* — links that go to a specific spot within a Web page.

Internal links are useful for creating a Web site that's made up of a single Web page, divided into sections. Such a page is also a great precursor to a full Web site with multiple Web pages and navigation.

An internal link has two parts:

✔ **A destination anchor:** This is in the form `<a name="targetname"></a>`. Note that there is no text surrounded by the beginning and ending anchor tags. This HTML code simply gives a name to the spot in the Web page where it appears. It's invisible to the user. When a link has the target as a destination, the Web page scrolls upward or downward so that the line is the destination.

✔ **A source anchor:** This is in the form `<a src="#anchorname">text</a>`. This is a typical anchor, but the destination is within a page, as shown by the # character. The source may also include a Web-page name, in which case the target after the # character is a destination anchor within the Web page. If the source doesn't include a Web-page name, the destination must be within the current page.

A classic example of internal links in a Web page that's part of a full site is the familiar FAQ (for Frequently Asked Questions) page. Generally, the questions are all listed at the top, followed by each question with its accompanying (often quite lengthy) answer. Links within the page make it easy to go back to the top of the page whenever you're done reading one of the answers.

Follow the instructions here to create an internal link in a Web page in CoffeeCup:

1. **Open the Visual Editor tab in CoffeeCup; enter some text that includes destinations that you want to link to.**

   The Visual Editor makes the sometimes complicated task of inserting internal links easier. But whether using the Visual Editor or not, it's easier to create the destinations first, then the links that go to them.

2. **Move the cursor to a spot that you want to be the destination of a link.**

   Usually this will be the beginning of a line of text, often a header.

   If you don't have the content of a Web page ready yet, you can just create headers and links; then your navigation system will be ready as you fill in the content.

3. **Choose Insert⇨Target.**

   The Insert Target dialog box appears, as shown in Figure 11-3.

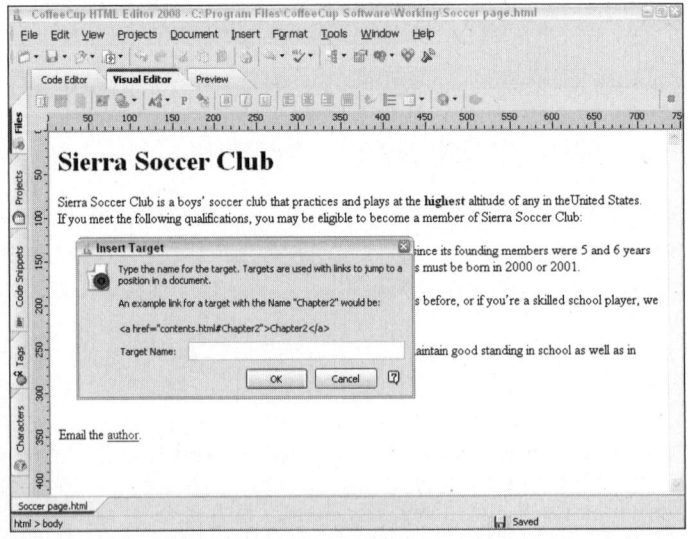

Figure 11-3:
Choose your destination with Insert Target.

4. Enter a target name.

The target name should include some key phrase or words from the text just following the target, but the target name should have no spaces.

5. Click OK.

"Hidden" HTML — HTML that can't be seen in the Visual Editor or in the Web page visible to the user — is inserted, in the following form: `<a name= "anchorname"></a>`. This HTML code simply gives a name to the spot in the Web page where the HTML occurs — a spot that can now be linked to.

6. Repeat for additional internal links.

Create all the additional links you need — if necessary, type in headers or other markers for the internal links to be associated with.

7. Confirm the internal anchors.

To confirm that the internal anchors have been created, choose Insert⇨Quick Link to Open Document and the currently open document. (You can also choose the Link button as the starting point.) The currently defined internal anchors will display, in their order within the document.

The link targets given names in this way are often referred to as anchors, even though technically the beginnings of links are anchors as well. Creating and using these kinds of *anchors* (link destinations) is another area where using a WYSIWYG tool such as CoffeeCup provides a big advantage. Inserting, finding, and using link destinations directly in HTML-tagged text is quite complicated, but in an HTML tool, it's fairly easy with a little planning.

Creating a Navigation Bar Using Text

Navigation bar is a broad term for an area of a Web page that the user recognizes as set aside for links among Web pages. Each separate link or choice in a navigation bar is called a *tab,* whether or not it actually looks like a tab as used in a paper file.

Many more complex sites actually have two or more navigation bars — a *primary navigation bar* for the main areas of the site, which is often graphical and may run down the left side of the site, and a *utility navigation bar* for useful functions such as a site map, contact information, and copyright or legal information. (These functions may be housed on Web pages below the top level of navigation for the site as a whole, or may be separate from the site hierarchy and accessible only via the utility navigation bar.) The utility navigation bar is often text-based (or at least relatively simple) and found in the upper right or across the bottom of each page of a site.

Creating a simple text navigation bar is useful as a precursor to the primary navigation, which may need design input to look good and work well, and also to learn how to create secondary navigation like that often used for simple functions. Even a simple text navigation bar can help enforce useful practices of site design and usability, right from the beginning of creating a multiple-page site.

A text navigation bar is a consistent visual element that appears on every page of the site and that always has the same appearance, the same words, and the same links. It's not an exaggeration to say that a navigation bar of some sort, even a simple one consisting of text, is the difference between a Web *site* and an unconnected mass of Web pages. Creating a navigation bar forces you to start thinking hard about how your site is going to be organized.

Here's an example of a simple text navigation bar for a "personal professional" site, a kind of online super-résumé:

Home I Résumé I Memberships I Publications I Personal I Contact me

Each tab is underlined to reflect that it's a link to that page or multi-page area of the site. Note that the Home tab, as I'll call it, is not underlined. The idea is that, when you're on the home page, you can't click Home to go to the home page — because you're already there.

When you click the word Résumé on the text menu to go to the Resume page, however, the text navigation bar should change to reflect where you are — it's no longer possible to click Résumé, while Home is linked again:

Home I Résumé I Memberships I Publications I Personal I Contact me

To implement this arrangement, you create a "model" navigation bar with *all* the tabs linked — but it's never used in quite that form. For each page on your site, you copy the navigation bar to the page, and then remove the link from the tab that the page in question belongs to.

Follow these instructions to create a text navigation bar:

1. **Open a new, empty page in the Visual Editor tab in CoffeeCup.**

2. **Type in a line of text representing the elements of your site, with a word or two for each page or area.**

   Use the vertical bar to separate the tabs. Examples for a personal/professional site look like this:

   Home I Résumé I Memberships I Publications I Personal I Contact me

   If the vertical bar character is not accessible from your keyboard, it should be available from the Symbol or similar menu. In Microsoft Word, choose Insert⇨Symbol to bring up the Symbol dialog box and select the vertical bar character.

3. **Select the text links and click the Center button.**

   The text menu will be centered.

4. **To link the Home tab to the home page of your site, select the word Home (not the spaces to either side). Choose Insert⇨Link. (You can also start with the Link button.)**

   The Insert Link dialog box appears.

5. **Type in the URL: simply the filename of the home page, `index.htm`, as shown in Figure 11-4. Click OK.**

   You're returned to the Visual Editor.

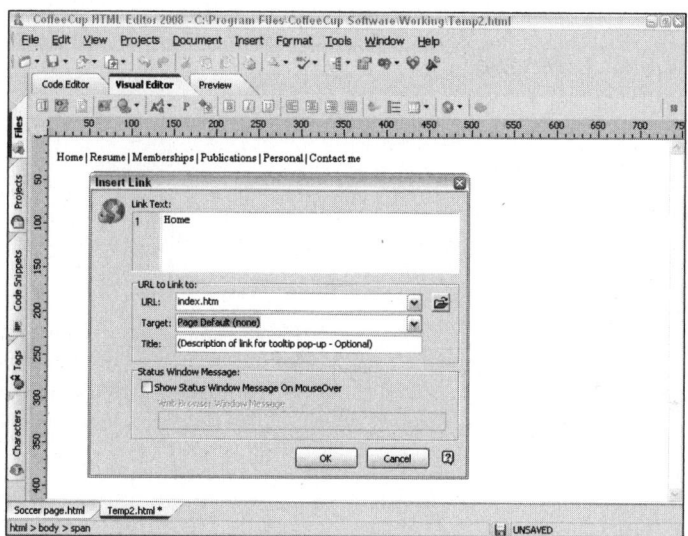

Figure 11-4:
Create the links you need.

6. **For the remaining phrases, repeat this process: Select the tab name (which might have a space within it, but don't select the space before or after); link it to a Web page by name; click OK.**

   By doing it this way, you can put your navigation feature in place; the pages don't even have to exist yet. (When you do create them, however, you must match the names in the text menu exactly.)

   Make the filenames you define here similar to the phrases in the tabs, but don't use spaces or capital letters in the filenames. If you do, the links could break when your Web site is moved to a server for hosting.

   When you're done, you should have a fully linked text menu — every tab linked to a page, even if the page content doesn't exist yet.

   Consider keeping a copy of the complete menu, with all links in place, on your home page or in a working page — so if you make changes later, it will be easier to update the text menu.

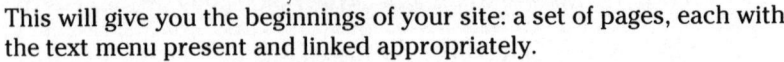

7. **Save the page repeatedly using each of the filenames you've defined. As you proceed, delete the link from the tab representing the page you're about to save, removing the underline and link color from it.**

   This will give you the beginnings of your site: a set of pages, each with the text menu present and linked appropriately.

   You can remove the link from a piece of text by deleting the linked text and then retyping the text, with no link.

Part IV
Your Site in HTML

The 5th Wave   By Rich Tennant

"You know, I've asked you a dozen times <u>not</u> to animate the torches on our Web page!"

In this part . . .

*I*t's always fun to "get right down to the bare metal" in any endeavor, and HTML is no exception. Use free tools available on your computer, such as Windows Notepad, to work directly in HTML, giving you total control over your Web page —and the ability to grow it into an effective Web site.

Chapter 12

Using a Text Editor

*T*he way to really get control of your Web pages is to create and test your Web pages on your own hard drive before uploading them to the Web. Then you can upload tried-and-tested Web pages to any number of different Web hosts, including Google itself. And the way to really, *really* get control is to create or edit Web pages directly in HTML.

Using online tools such as Google Page Creator (discussed in Chapter 3) is a bit like riding a tricycle. Using a WYSIWYG editor, as described in Chapters 8 through 11, is like using training wheels on a bicycle. Using a text editor is like riding on just two wheels, keeping your balance yourself. You can go farther and faster — but it's also more work, and you can crash more spectacularly.

This chapter describes how to create your initial Web page locally, on your own hard drive, using a text editor. As an example, I use Notepad, the text editor included in every version of Windows. If you use a Macintosh, the Simpletext program included with every version of MacOS fills the same role.

The previous Part describes how to create and improve Web pages using a What You See Is What You Get, or WYSIWYG, editor. The chapters in this Part describe how to improve your Web page and how to extend your Web page into a multipage Web site — using Notepad and straight HTML (look, Ma, no hands!). Chapter 15 tells you how to publish one or more Web pages created in a text editor from your own machine onto the Web.

This chapter helps you choose the approach you want to use and then shows you how to create your initial Web page.

As with using a WYSIWYG editor, using a text editor leaves you free to choose your own host for your Web pages. It also adds a powerful tool to your arsenal of Web-page creation and Web-editing techniques.

The good news is, there's no wrong answer; the bad news is, there's no single, simple *right* answer either. Professional Web-page authors often work in a combination of tools: a text editor, a WYSIWYG tool, and a Web browser for previewing. The question isn't really which approach you're going to use in the long run, but how you want to start. Starting in a text editor is a tough school, but a good one.

Choosing Plain Text over WYSIWYG

You can use a couple of different approaches to create and edit Web pages on your own computer. One approach is to use a text editor. A text editor is only partly like a word-processing program: It lets you enter upper- and lowercase letters, digits, and punctuation, but (unlike a word processor) it doesn't give you any way to add formatting such as **bold** characters or bulleted lists.

A core part of HTML (which stands for "HyperText Markup Language," remember) is to "mark up" your text — which means adding formatting to it. So if you're using HTML in a text editor, you're using HTML tags to do part of what a word processor does — to add formatting.

You may have been using computers long enough to remember that early versions of today's word processors worked the same way. In the once-popular WordStar, for instance, you would put special characters before and after a word to make it (for instance) bold. The first versions of Microsoft Word were notable for their heavy reliance on WYSIWYG word processing rather than WordStar-style markup.

What you don't get in a text editor is a preview of what the formatting looks like when it's in effect — and that's the core of WYSIWYG. Using a text editor to work in HTML, however, you can get close. Just enter your text in the text editor, add HTML tags for markup, then save the file and open it in Internet Explorer or another Web browser. What you see when you view your HTML code in IE will truly be what users will get when they view the same Web page in the same Web browser.

While interactive previewing on your own machine is a great way to see what your HTML will really do, this doesn't protect you from all potential problems with your published Web page. In particular, when you transfer your Web page to a host machine, the links that worked so well on your own machine may not work on the new machine. Looking for and fixing these "broken links" is a key concern of Web publishing.

Previewing a Web page in one browser gives you an excellent idea of what it will look like for your Web page visitors — but only the ones who are using the same browser, with the same settings. You must test in a variety of browsers to get good coverage, and always be aware that there's almost always some combination of a Web browser and settings that will cause some user somewhere to have trouble with your Web page.

I recommend that you either work directly in HTML or use a simple WYSIWYG tool that doesn't try to do too much for you, and look frequently at the underlying HTML. If you do want to use a tool, I recommend the CoffeeCup HTML Editor 2008 package included on the CD-ROM and described in Chapters 8 through 11.

Though working directly in HTML in a text editor ramps up your learning curve and gives you a great deal of control, frequent previewing is a tough way to keep on top of the effect your coding will have. It's also very easy to get lost in the HTML-tagged text when you're trying to remember where to make an addition or change.

Figure 12-1 shows a simple Web page as it appears when being edited in a text editor (left) and previewed in Internet Explorer (right). You can see how the same HTML-tagged text looks when seen as HTML and rendered as a Web page.

When you work in a text editor and preview in a Web browser, you'll quickly figure out why so many professional Web-page authors have large screens, multiple screens, or a combination of the two. You want to have enough screen room to put the text-editor window next to the Web browser window, without overlap. A modern, "panorama"-style laptop screen with 1280 x 800 resolution gives you plenty of width for this, though each window is a bit short. Try to get a screen with at least 1280 x 1024 resolution.

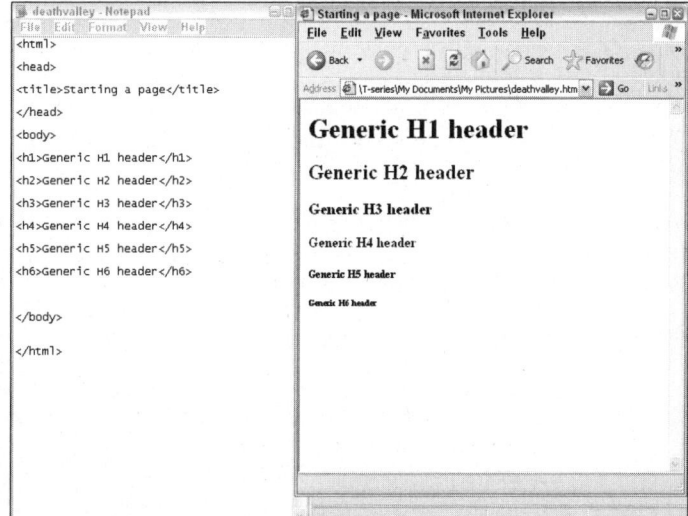

Figure 12-1:
Composing in a text editor and previewing in a Web browser.

Why train in a text editor?

Working in a text editor is great training for drilling the nuts and bolts of HTML into your consciousness, even into your unconscious. (It doesn't even hurt. Much, anyway.)

Every computer you'll ever have access to is likely to include a text editor. So you've got what you need to create or fix a Web page anywhere you are in the world.

You also avoid the problem of having your lovely HTML code messed with when you use a WYSIWYG editor. Most such tools rearrange your HTML code when you bring it into WYSIWYG mode, and the code that such tools create is unlikely to look much like your own. Using a text editor is a "purer" working environment.

However, even the bravest of "bare metal" HTML tweakers have learned their own tips and tricks to make life easier.

One trick is that you can also edit text in a word processor. It's a distracting environment, but the excellent spell-checkers, flexible search-and-replace, and powerful formatting tools in a word processor can help you to tame large or complex HTML files. You just have to remember to always copy and paste the text in and out, without saving — or Word may add its own idea of HTML to your file.

You can also make the initial job of creating HTML files easier by keeping "cut and paste" examples of Web code handy or viewing and retrieving examples from Web-authoring sites as needed.

And knowing enough about how to use an HTML editor to switch into one when needed is always a great help. The CoffeeCup HTML Editor package on the CD is a great tool for such a requirement.

Working within a Text Environment

When you begin using a text editor such as Notepad, it's a good idea to create a sample Web page that includes the major kinds of formatting, so you can cut and paste from it into your own Web page in progress. Some features to include in such a Web page include

- The `html`, `head`, and `body` tags that form a framework for every Web page
- Links to other Web pages on other Web sites
- Links to graphics that accompany your Web page, including size commands and alternate text
- A simple table, or perhaps a few

It's not uncommon for Web-page authors who use a text editor for most of their work to switch to a WYSIWYG tool for creating, filling in, and editing tables, and then switch back to a text editor for their remaining work.

No matter how you edit, if you add advanced elements (such as multimedia files or computer programs) to your Web page, be prepared to test your pages with several different browsers — and to tell your Web visitors what to expect.

As with WYSIWYG HTML tools, you can create HTML forms in a text editor, but this won't give you the CGI (Common Gateway Interface) scripts that you need to make the forms work. These CGI scripts process the data that the user enters into a form. However, if you don't want to mess with creating these scripts, you can get CGI scripts from others on the Web and, after a bit of trial and error, modify them as needed for your Web site.

Plusses and minuses of Notepad as a text editor

Notepad has the advantages of any text-editing tool, with few disadvantages. Here are its four key advantages as a text-editing tool:

✔ **Truly basic.** You don't need to do much to learn Notepad. You do have to learn some things about working in a text editor rather than a WYSIWYG tool, but these aren't imposed by Notepad; they're fundamental to how you're working. If you work in a more powerful tool, any problems you experience could be in your HTML or they could be in the tool.

✔ **No formatting codes.** Notepad is utterly incapable of putting hidden formatting codes into your file.

✔ **Ubiquitous.** Notepad is available on any Windows machine. And because it's so basic, even non-Windows machines are likely to also have basic, Notepad-like tools handy.

✔ **Popular.** Working in Notepad is a popular way to create and edit Web pages, so it's easy to get help from other Web-page authors — anyone who knows HTML well. If you work in a WYSIWYG editor or a more powerful text-editing tool, the only people who can help you are fellow users of that tool.

I recommend that most beginning Web publishers use HTML Editor in Visual Editor mode and check the underlying HTML frequently to see what's really going on. As you get more knowledgeable with HTML, you may wish to buy and use a more advanced HTML editor — or go the low-tech route (as many Web professionals do much of the time) and use a basic text editor or the Code Editor side of CoffeeCup.

I recommend that you consider using CoffeeCup HTML Editor at least occasionally in tandem with editing your Web page in a text editor. The back-and-forth will actually help you learn faster and get more done.

Do I have to use Notepad?

The choice of text editor is up to you. Although I recommend using Windows Notepad, due to its extremely widespread availability, there are many replacement programs for Notepad that have earned fans of their own. There are also Notepad replacements for non-Windows platforms. To see some well-regarded ones, visit CNET's `download.com` site. Search for "notepad replacement" under Windows or Mac software, as your needs dictate. You'll see many highly rated programs, blog posts with reviews, and more.

Hitting the high notes in Notepad

In order to run the one and only Windows Notepad, follow the instructions below. If you want to run a replacement instead, consider using Notepad for the steps below, then repeating them with your replacement program, just to be sure you're completely on top of both programs. (As you may want to use Notepad when using a random Windows machine at a friend's house, Internet cafe, or other location.)

When following the steps below, and in other uses of Notepad, don't open WordPad instead of Notepad. WordPad stores its own hidden formatting codes among the text characters you type, just like Word (but without most of the nice features).

And don't worry about the Font feature in the Format menu in Notepad, a not particularly welcome addition in recent versions of Notepad. The Font option allows you to apply different fonts and a few formatting options (character size, bolding, and so forth) to *all the characters in the document* — not selectively to some characters, words, or paragraphs, and not others. You might even want to use this feature to make your HTML-tagged text easier to read overall, but it's useless for clever tricks like putting your HTML tags in one color and regular text in another. The Font feature in Notepad is so simplistic precisely because Notepad doesn't store hidden formatting codes within the underlying text; the font and other text characteristics are program settings rather than true formatting of the text. That keeps the text itself blessedly plain — and easy for many different platforms to use.

Okay, after all that, it's brass-tacks time. Follow these steps to get started using Notepad as an HTML-editing tool:

1. **Start Windows Notepad.**

   The details may vary slightly across different versions of Windows, but they'll be very close to the following: Start by clicking the Start button (the Vista version sports a Windows symbol, but displays the word Start when you mouse over it.) Choose Start➪Programs➪Accessories➪Notepad.

   The program opens.

2. **Click Save & Continue. Save your document under any name you choose, but don't use the suffix** .txt; **instead, add the suffix** .htm **to the filename.**

   This may seem contradictory, but it works: The file will be saved as a text file, with no formatting codes; the suffix .htm signals to your Web browser (and, after you upload your file, to Web servers and so on) that the file is a Web page.

   It's not your fault if you find this confusing; the role of a filename extension *is* confusing, and Windows makes matters worse by hiding the extension from most views of the file or filename.

   Right-clicking on a file and choosing Properties will reveal the file's suffix.

3. **Pull down the Format menu and inspect the options.**

   The Format menu appears, as shown in Figure 12-2. The Font option, which brings up the Font dialog box also shown in Figure 12-2, lets you change the displayed font, font size, and formatting (narrowly speaking: bold, italic, or bold italic only).

   The Notepad Format works differently from any Format menu in any other program you're likely to use. It changes the way all the text in the currently open file looks on-screen — regardless of whether that text is selected at the time you choose the Format command — and includes options you can apply to text. Options include changing the Font (not to be done without some thought; see Chapter 9) and making text Bold, Italic, or Underlined.

   If you open your Notepad text file on a different machine, it will display using the font, font style, and size in use by that copy of Notepad, neither knowing nor caring what settings you were using in the copy of Notepad you last edited the file in.

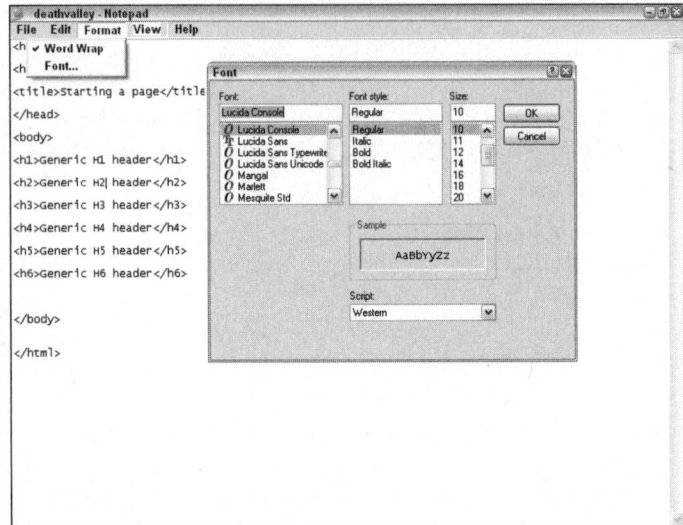

4. **Pull down the other menus and inspect the options.**

   There are very few other options to worry about. And if it occurs to you
   that the Font option should appear under the View menu (since it only
   affects the look of the text), I would have a hard time arguing with you.

Chapter 13

Creating a WYSIWYG Page

*T*he previous chapter shows you how to get started in Windows Notepad as an example of a simple text editor. This chapter shows you how to create your first Web page in a text editor such as Notepad, put some text in it, and get the text formatted so it looks good.

This chapter draws on the discussion of using text in Web pages in Chapter 4. Review that chapter for information about how to write for the Web. Web writing is a bit different from other kinds of writing. It's also kind of fun, once you get used to it.

What the HTML You'll See in a Text Editor

HTML is designed to be something that humans can read *and* that machines can process, a kind of common ground for human-to-machine communication. You begin with regular text, characters that appear directly on your Web page, and add descriptive tags so all the formatting, linking, and navigational information you need is in text form, contained in the same file with the regular text that appears on the Web page.

Suppose you want to add bold to a word in your text, such as you might see in a book, or on the screen of a word processor:

```
You can use HTML to specify that a word is bold.
```

Why bother with HTML basics?

Using a text editor makes the workings of HTML even clearer than using a tool such as the HTML editor within CoffeeCup. To an even greater degree, using HTML in a text editor helps you understand how the Web works, how to use free Web tools that allow you to enter HTML tags directly, and how to use other tools that hide HTML to a greater or lesser degree.

To add bold formatting to a sentence using HTML, you start with the regular sentence and add a couple of tags to specify where the bold starts and stops. Here's the previous line in HTML:

```
You can use HTML to specify that a word is <b>bold</b>.
```

When you display the sentence immediately above in a Web browser, the browser displays all the words, but not the *tags* — the information between angle brackets. The Web browser uses the tags to do extra things to the text, such as formatting it as bold text. In the case of this single-line example, the formatting instruction is simple: Start using bold text immediately after the word "is," and stop using bold text immediately after the word "bold."

HTML tags exist alongside the text that users see on your Web page, so a document with HTML tags in it is called *HTML-tagged text.* A file with HTML-tagged text in it is called an HTML file.

An HTML file usually has the extension .htm or .html at the end of the file-name. If you look at HTML-tagged text in a text editing program, you see the angle brackets and HTML commands; if you look at it in a Web browser, you see a Web page with formatting, links, and so on.

A document with no formatting — such as italic and other formatting added by a word processor — is called a *plain-text* document. HTML-tagged text documents are considered plain-text documents because they're made up only of text characters, even though some of the characters (the tags) carry formatting information. Word-processing documents that aren't plain-text documents have additional formatting codes embedded in them to tell machines how to display and print the text.

You can add HTML tags to regular text to create your own Web documents in any text editor or word-processing program. (However, in a word-processing program, you must explicitly save the Web document as a text file.) Or you can use a Web-editing tool that hides the gory details of HTML tags, such as the Visual Editor in CoffeeCup. (The Visual Editor creates an HTML-tagged text file, but displays to you what that file will look like in a Web page. It makes the HTML-tagged text available directly in the Code Editor.)

When you work in a text editor, such as Notepad, you work directly with HTML from the very beginning. So you might find yourself looking frequently at the full HTML appendix at the back of the book (Appendix B).

If you like to know everything that's going on before you roll up your sleeves and plunge into things, you may want to start by looking at *HTML, XHTML & CSS For Dummies,* 6th Edition, a comprehensive guide to HTML by Ed Tittel and Jeff Noble (Wiley).

Viewing HTML in Web pages

You can see "pure" HTML anytime you use the Web. Open any Web page in your browser and choose the right command — View⇨Source for Internet Explorer or a similar command for other browsers. A new window opens, displaying the HTML source code that underlies the Web page. Figure 13-1 shows a page from the *For Dummies* site and its HTML source code as an example.

What HTML really, really means

HTML is an acronym for HyperText Markup Language. The tags described here are the "Markup" part; the tags are also used to specify hyperlinks to other documents, which is the "HyperText" part.

The way a browser works is described by a mathematical construct called a "finite automaton." Such a construct reads text like a ticker-tape, one character at a time. It can neither store what has already been read nor look ahead beyond the character just in front of it.

Let's see how this works with a Web link, known in HTML jargon as an *anchor*. Here's an example:

```
The <a href="www.
   ninjaturtles.com">Teenage
   Mutant Ninja Turtles</
   a> are becoming popular
   again.
```

The browser begins by reading the first half of the sentence — `The <a href="www.`

`ninjaturtles.com">Teenage Mutant Ninja Turtles` — one character at a time, and says to itself, "I display `The`, begin a link, store the destination, `www.ninjaturtles.com`, and display the following words in blue and with an underline: `Teenage Mutant Ninja Turtles`.

The browser then reads the rest of the sentence — `</a> are becoming popular again.` — again, one character at a time. The browser notes the end of the link, denoted by the close anchor tag `</a>`, and displays each remaining character in normal text.

The anchor tags `<a>` and `</a>` serve as *linking tags,* denoting a hyperlink. They also, in order to do their job, serve as *formatting tags,* changing the way the text they enclose is displayed. The change in how the enclosed text is displayed signals the link to the user.

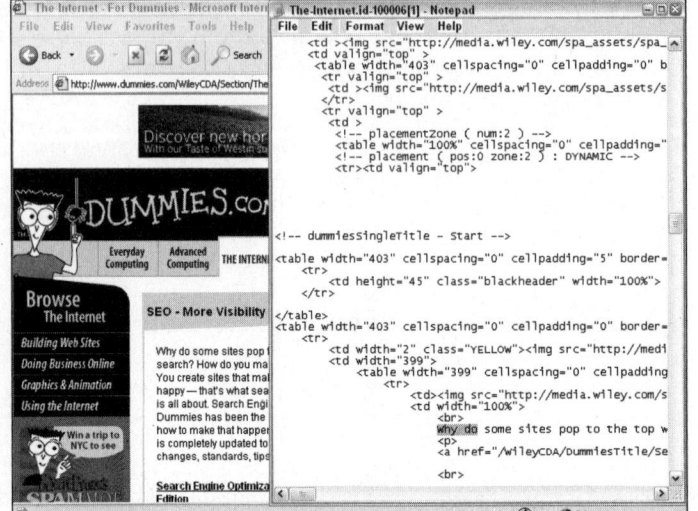

Figure 13-1:
The For
Dummies
site is made
of HTML-
tagged text
and
graphics.

Resist any temptation to "borrow" the HTML from attractive pages on the Web directly. At some point in doing this, you might cross the line into violating the author's copyright. Instead, use existing HTML as a reference, contributing to your efforts to create your own Web page design.

When in doubt, contact the Webmaster at the site you admire, describe how you want to use their code or formatting, and request permission. It's not uncommon to get a positive response — just hope you don't get asked to toss your car keys into the bargain.

Setting up an HTML page

When you first create a Web page, you need to do a certain amount of setup. Working directly in HTML using Notepad, you must enter the needed tags yourself (the CoffeeCup HTML Editor in Chapter 9 sets them up for you, but we're all adventurers here, right?).

The tags you have to create in Notepad are of five types, each serving a distinct function:

✔ **Begin and end HTML:** Though your Web page will almost certainly work without them, it's good form to begin and end your Web page with the `<html>` and `</html>` tags.

✔ **Getting a Head:** Your Web page begins with "head" information, which is information that describes the entire page. With one exception, it's processed before anything visible shows up on the Web page. Surround the head area with the <head> and </head> tags.

✔ **Granting your page a title:** The title of a Web page was originally meant to be descriptive information for search engines and other programs that crawl the Web. But early Web browsers began displaying the title at the top of a Web page, and now it's noticed by Web users, so it's important you get it right. The title, in the head area, is surrounded by the <title> and </title> tags.

✔ **Growing a Body:** Body information is everything the user sees on the Web page, including text, formatting, and links. The opening <body> tag comes right after the closing </head> tag. The body area is terminated by the </body> tag, and the entire Web page is then closed by the </html> tag.

✔ **Meta tags:** Meta tags are "meta-information," that is, information about the Web page as a whole. For instance, CoffeeCup automatically inserts the standard information, <meta http-equiv="content-type" content="text/html;charset=UTF-8"/>. Meta tags, once used heavily by search engines, are now less used or even ignored. Today, the best way to use meta tags is for the information of yourself or others who might look at the HTML code to tell what the page is about. If meta tags help a search engine along the way, great.

✔ **Comments:** Comments are notes to yourself or future Web authors who might look at the HTML. A typical comment is something like <!-Created in December 2008 by Bud Smith>. While it's a good idea to add comments in HTML if you do it consistently, there's also a school of thought that says it's better to put the energy into good, clean, understandable HTML code and a better page design.

These tags are demonstrated in Notepad later in this chapter, along with the commands and tags used for formatting Web text.

Create a model HTML page that you can open anytime you want to start a new Web page without re-entering the "same old" initial tags. To make sure the model HTML page stays unchanged, right-click on the file icon and choose Properties from the menu that appears. In the Properties dialog box that appears, check the Read-only check box. This will ensure that, when you open, change, and then save the file, you're forced to save it under a new name, leaving the original file unchanged.

Formatting Web Text

Whether you use a WYSIWYG editor, as described in Part III, or a text editor, as described here, the capabilities that HTML makes available for formatting Web text are the same:

- **Headings:** There are six levels of headings in HTML that you can use, with the tag pairs <h1> and </h1> used for the largest, top-level heading; <h2> and </h2> next, down to <h6> and </h6> for the lowest (very small) level of headings.

  What it means for you: The intended way to use headings is to start with <h1> for the most important heading right down to <h6> for the lowest level. This kind of usage makes life easier for visually impaired people who use screen readers (which read Web pages aloud). However, the highest-level headings are very large in comparison to regular text. As a result many people use <h4>, for instance, for what's really a second-level heading, or use text size commands and bolding to create their own header styles. Try using the intended headings first, and then use your own formatting if you really need a specific look.

- **Font sizes:** HTML allows you to specify relative font sizes that are larger or smaller than medium, or standard, size. You can go two sizes smaller or three sizes larger than medium. This formatting works even if users specify a font size or style in their browser setup or in their operating system (Windows, Mac, and so on). (As people get older, and their eyes weaken, they resort to various tricks to make using the computer easier — as the author knows from experience.)

  What it means for you: You don't want your Web page to look like a hostage note, with all different styles and sizes of text mixed up, but font sizes can be a good way to make a point (with a larger font size) or fit a lot of text into a small space (with a smaller size). Using relative font sizes is one of the few formatting tricks that almost always work well in different Web browsers.

- **Character formatting:** You can make text bold or italic using the <b> and </b> tags to start and stop bold and the <i> and </i> tags to start and stop italic. You can also underline text, but I don't recommend it, because users can easily confuse text that's underlined for emphasis with text that's underlined because it's an HTML link. The same holds true for using any unexpected colors in your hyperlink text — it's potentially confusing. Best not to go there (see Chapter 9 for a discussion of why).

  What it means for you: Use bold and italic to emphasize your point, but don't overdo it. Structured use of bold and italic, such as the bold used to highlight items in this list, is one good solution.

- **Advanced character formatting:** You can specify the fonts used in your Web page, as well as font colors. But different fonts are available on

Windows and Macintosh computers, so you have to be clever about how you do this. (You can specify backup fonts for use if the desired font isn't there.)

What it means for you: I don't recommend using advanced character formatting when you're starting out because it's complicated and because it won't work for some of your users. You may want to postpone using this kind of formatting until you're working at a professional level, with the design help and testing resources needed to make sure your pages work well for all your users.

Create a model Web page with examples of different kinds of headers, character formatting, and so forth. Then copy and paste from it into your Web page in progress, modifying the model to create your "real" Web page. The model page gives you a way to preview different formats before committing to them and allows you to build your Web page in blocks. Unfortunately, once your Web page is built, all the HTML tends to run together!

Follow these steps to enter and format text in Notepad:

1. **Open Notepad. Enter the beginning and ending** HTML, HEAD, **and** BODY **tags.**

   Make sure to spell the tags correctly and check for matching open and closing tags.

2. **Between the** <head> **and** </head> **tags, add the tags** <title> **and** </title>.

3. **Enter an appropriate title, such as New Home Page, then click OK.**

4. **Move the cursor to a new line after the opening** <body> **tag.**

5. **Type some text introducing your Web page.**

   When someone searches for your Web page by using a search engine, the search engine may display the Web page title (as described earlier) and the first few words that appear in the document. So make the first few sentences of text that follow the title an introduction to the entire page or Web site.

   In the document I created for this chapter, here's what I typed:

   ```
   Death Valley Hockey Club

   Death Valley Hockey Club is a girls' field hockey team
   that practices and plays at the lowest altitude of any
   in the United States.
   ```

6. **Surround the text that you'd like to make a header with the** <h1> **and** </h1> **tags.**

   In my document, I highlighted the words Death Valley Hockey Club at the beginning.

7. **Identify other text that you want to format.**

   In my document, I selected the word "lowest" in the middle of the first sentence.

8. **Surround the text with the tags that support the formatting you want, such as `<b>` and `</b>` for bold or `<i>` and `</i>` for italic.**

   The surrounded text will take on the appropriate formatting. In my example, I made the word "lowest" bold.

9. **Save your file with the extension `.htm` to specify that it's an HTML file.**

   Do this early when working in Notepad so you remember to enter the suffix `.htm`; if you don't, Notepad will use the `.txt` filename extension, and your document won't automatically be treated as a Web page.

10. **Open the file in a Web browser to preview its appearance.**

   Carefully check that each tag you use in the HTML file has the desired effect in the actual displayed Web page. HTML ignores tags it doesn't understand, so if you type `<n>` instead of `<b>`, for instance, the only ill effect will be a lack of bolding (the `</b>` tag you follow it with has no effect); a lack of formatting such as bolding is easy to miss when quickly checking a page, unless you compare your tags with their desired effects.

Figure 13-2 shows Notepad and Internet Explorer with the text formatted as described here. Note that Header 1 may actually be too large for our purposes.

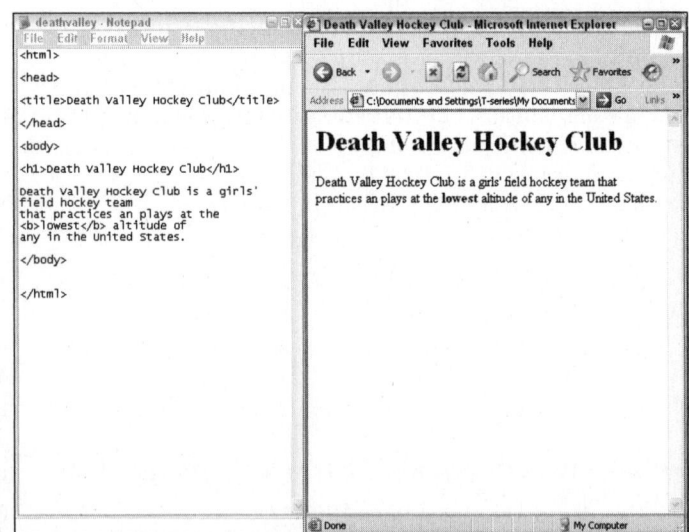

Figure 13-2:
Use HTML formatting options.

Creating HTML Lists in Notepad

As mentioned in Chapter 9, people really like lists such as the Top Ten lists on David Letterman's *Late Night* show. They're interesting to look at, easy to scan, and inspire you to write short, punchy phrases.

HTML offers three kinds of lists, two commonly used and one not so much.

- **Bulleted lists:** "Bulletizing" your text is the quickest way to improve it for the Web. A bulleted list, which HTML refers to as an *unordered list,* is easy to read and easy to write. Start a bulleted list with the `<ul>` tag and end it with the `</ul>` tag. Precede each list item with `<li>` for *list item;* no closing tag is needed. The `<li>` or `</ul>` that follows also ends the list item.

- **Numbered lists:** Numbered lists are useful and should be used more than they are, as they add variety and impose order. Use numbered lists for items that can be ordered in importance, sequence (such as steps), and wherever else you can. A numbered list begins with `<ol>` for *ordered list,* ends with `</ol>`, and — like bulleted lists — uses the `<li>` tag to mark the beginning of each list item.

- **Definition lists:** A *definition list* specifies a term and then the definition of the term. Use definition lists to add more variety — but test the look first, as you may find it a bit odd. Use bold formatting of the term to help. Start you definition list with `<dl>` and end it with `</dl>`. Precede each term in the list with `<dt>`, for *definition term.* Then precede the definition, following the term, with `<dd>`, for *definition data.*

- **Lists within lists:** Inserting a list within another one is called *nesting* it, a favorite programmer's trick when writing code. It may not be your favorite trick, as doubly nested lists can be confusing. You can nest the same or different kinds of lists. A bulleted list within another one will display with a different style of bullets.

Follow these steps to create a list in Notepad:

1. **Add the text for your list in Notepad.**

   In the document I created for this chapter, here's what I typed:

   ```
   If you meet the following three qualifications, most
   important first, you may be eligible to become a member
   of Death Valley Hockey Club:

   8 to 12 years old. Death Valley Hockey Club has girls
   from 8 to 12 years old as members. You must have been
   8, 9, 10, 11 or 12 on January 1st of this year.
   ```

Good in school. We need you to show us you're a good student, and to maintain your academic standing throughout your time with us.

Some sports experience. We would like you to have some previous organized sports experience in any sport.

2. **Surround the lines that will make up the list with the list tags,** `<ul>` **and** `</ul>` **for an unordered (bulleted) list, or** `<ol>` **and** `</ol>` **for an ordered (numbered) list.**

   In my document, I put the `<ol>` tag before the line that begins `8 to 12 years old`, and the `</ol>` tag after the period following the words `in any sport`.

3. **Precede each list item with the** `<li>` **tag.**

   In my document, I put the `<li>` tag before the lines that begin:

   `8 to 12 years old`

   `Good in school`

   `Some sports experience`

With new standards such as XML and XHTML in place, it's considered good form to always close off tags, which means that it's now recommended that you use a closing `</li>` tag after each item. This is good advice, yet there's never enough time to do all one would like to do, and this recommendation may fall into that category.

4. **If you like, for a bulleted list, change the bullet style by adding an additional element, called an attribute, to each** `<li>` **tag.**

   With the attribute added, each `<li>` tag will read in one of three ways:

   `<li type=disc>`, **a filled-in circle or bullet,** the same as if you don't specify the attribute at all

   `<li type=square>`, **a square**

   `<li type=circle>`, **an open circle**

As the example used here is a numbered list, the bullet style options don't apply.

In a good WYSIWYG HTML editor, such as CoffeeCup (see Part III), all the options — including obscure ones like bullet type — are presented to you as options in menus and dialog boxes, so you don't have to remember what the options are (or even that they exist); you just choose them when you need them. This is one advantage a WYSIWYG editor has over working in a text editor such as Notepad.

5. **Save your document — adding** `.htm` **to the filename, if you're saving it for the first time — and open it in a Web browser window (or refresh the window if you already have this document open).**

The list appears in the edited Web page, as shown in Figure 13-3.

The Insert List dialog box is a good example of the benefits that can come from using a WYSIWYG editor. It includes options for bullet styles that you might not have known were part of HTML, or might have forgotten the details of. With the dialog box, you're not only reminded of the button styles, but also can easily test how they look within your page.

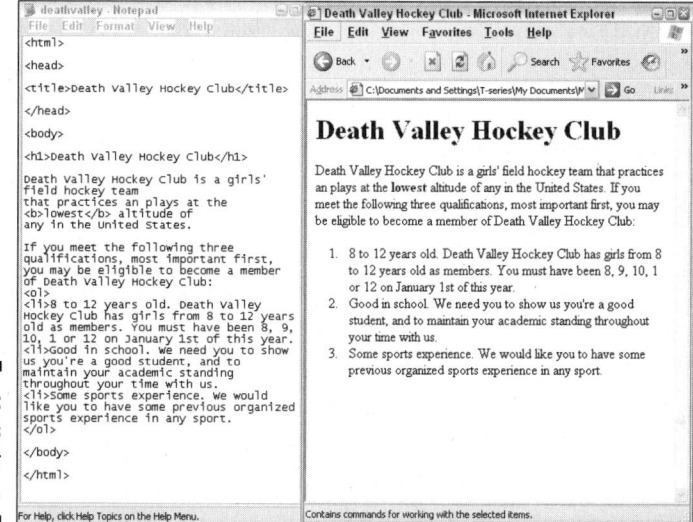

Figure 13-3:
HTML has
your
number.

External Web-page Links

Regardless of the method you use to create your Web page, the secret of moving smoothly from one Web page to another is the use of hyperlinks.

In this section I show you how to create links to totally different Web sites, the simplest kind of links — but the most powerful, as they can take you almost instantly to a page from another computer anywhere on Earth.

Notepad or a more sophisticated package?

Notepad is at the simplest end of the range of ways to edit a Web page, and other options are tempting. Only Notepad, though, is free and available on any Windows PC without downloading, versions, updates, and such. It's a good idea to learn how to work using HTML in Notepad now so you always have the option of doing so later on.

Don't think, just link

If you're building a hypertext link to an external HTML page by hand (so to speak), you should know it's built a bit like an iceberg: It has a visible part (the link text, which appears as blue, underlined text by default) and an invisible-but-impressive part that's normally hidden (the specification of just which file clicking on the link will lead to). The visible part is the friendly, appealing bit; the invisible part will work for you too, but only if it's constructed just right.

Text in an HTML document is made into the starting point of a hypertext link by surrounding it with the <a> and </a> tags, with a standing for anchor. The link's two ends, the start that the user clicks on and the page that appears as a result, are both called anchors.

The destination of the link is called the hypertext reference, or href for short. So a link to another Web page in HTML looks like this:

```
Make your own cider with <a href="http://www.ciderspices.com">cider spices</a>.
```

Oddly enough, this is almost as simple as it looks, and here's why:

- ✔ If you use a domain name for a link, such as www.ciderspices.com, the first thing your Web browser looks for is index.htm or a file with a similar name); you don't have to specify a filename in your link's destination.
- ✔ The browser also assumes that the destination is at the top of a Web page unless you specify a location within the Web page.

That said, the next order of business is to hand-craft a link in Notepad.

So why's everybody all hyper?

Hyperlinks are more than just hype; they're the key to hypertext, which is reflected in the names of the two key technical standards underlying the Web: *HyperText Transfer Protocol,* the http you see in a Web page address, and HTML (HyperText Markup Language). See Chapter 9 for a closer look.

A simple link in Notepad

Follow these steps to create a simple hypertext link in Notepad:

1. **Find the text that you want to make a link.**

   In the document I created as an example for this book, I highlighted the words "Death Valley" in the text before the numbered list.

2. **Surround the text with the** <a> **and** </a> **tags.**

   Getting the end tag in right away will prevent you from forgetting it.

3. **Enter the destination Web address, or URL, by adding** href=*url* **to the** <a> **tag (where** *url* **is a full Web address).**

   Enter the full Web address, including the preceding http://, and check whether the address includes www. or not; a few Web addresses don't. Also make certain that the site ending really *is* .com, .org, .co.uk, or whatever it's supposed to be.

   In up-to-date Web browsers, you can open an additional tab to check your Web address while leaving the first tab for previewing your Web page.

4. **Enter a title for the link by adding the** title **attribute.**

   The title for the link is text that, in some browsers, appears when the user puts the mouse pointer over the link.

   If you leave this area blank, the URL will appear as the title. Often the URL is self-explanatory, as in a link to a Wikipedia entry. You may wish to enter the URL, without http://, as the link title to make it a bit more comprehensible for the user.

   If the URL is long or confusing, enter a simple title that describes the page. For instance, here's the long-winded URL for *HTML, XHTML & CSS For Dummies,* 6th Edition on the For Dummies site:

   ```
   http://www.dummies.com/WileyCDA/DummiesTitle/HTML-XHTML-CSS-For-Dummies-6th-
                        Edition.productCd-047023847X.html
   ```

Using a tool tip — `HTML, XHTML, & CSS For Dummies on dummies. com` — saves your visitors some hassle and you some screen real estate.

Being able to see the URL or title when you mouse over a link is very good for usability. However, in Internet Explorer, the URL or title appears in a strip at the bottom of the screen called the Status Bar — and the Status Bar, in recent versions of IE, is turned off by default. There's not much you can do about this for your users, but at least you can turn on the Status Bar yourself — choose View➪Status Bar in Internet Explorer to turn it on.

5. **Save the Web page to your hard drive and open it in a Web browser to preview and test the link.**

   The text will appear as link text, underlined and in blue, as shown in Figure 13-4, with the URL showing in the Status Bar. Clicking on it should bring up the target page.

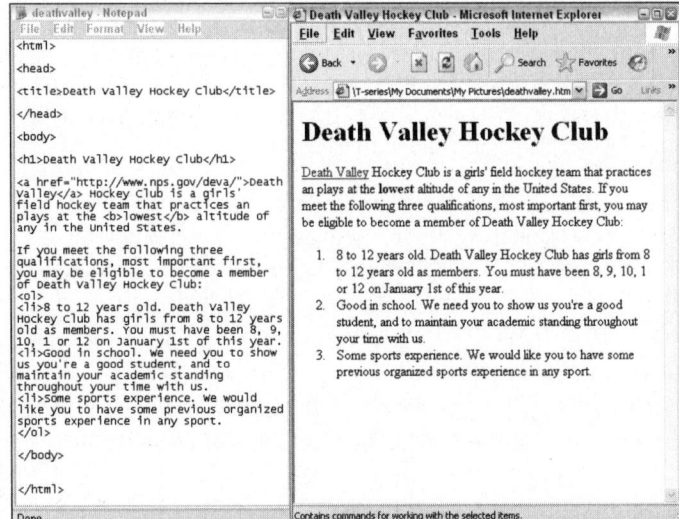

Figure 13-4:
You think
then you
link.

Chapter 14

Graphics and Media in HTML

. . . .

. . . .

The first Web pages supported only one kind of media besides text: GIF graphics files. JPEG images had to be opened in a separate viewer. Now downloadable sound files and embedded videos keep making the Web more and more interesting, relevant and useful.

In Chapters 5, 6, and 7, you learn how to create and use images, sounds and videos, respectively. In this chapter, I show you how to actually put all of these kinds of files in your Web page using Windows Notepad as one example of a text editor. By the end of this chapter you should be able to create very lively Web pages in Notepad.

In case you're wondering, Chapter 10 goes about creating Web pages in much the same way, using the CoffeeCup HTML editor; don't worry if you've read that chapter and feel some déjà vu. Whichever approach you start with, you'll have a consistent idea of the steps involved in Web-page creation.

In the early days of the Web, the IMG command could handle only GIF files. Soon, though, Web browsers were upgraded to include the extra code needed to display JPEG images as well. Before that, JPEG graphics files were included via the embed command and were opened with one of a variety of "player" programs that contained the somewhat complex code needed to display a JPEG image.

PNG graphics files are now fairly widely supported, and even Windows BMP files are supported by Internet Explorer. But GIF and JPEG images remain the only ones that you can really count on including within the "flow" of a Web page.

Unfortunately for us, the Web-page authors, sound and video files aren't included as a standard part of what a Web browser can display or play back. For sound and video files to be standardized, Web browsers would have to include playback code, instead of depending on a separate player engine such as Windows Media Player or the QuickTime player. Not even the HTML for including a sound or video file is standardized. So including these files in a way that most people can use them is hard work and not completely reliable.

Including Images in a Text Editor

Including images in a Web page isn't all that simple, and it is in some ways harder in a text editor than in a WYSIWYG editor such as CoffeeCup. The complexities of how to create images are covered in Chapter 5. Creating links from your Web page to images isn't all that easy either. (Similar considerations apply to sound and video, but they're less-used than images.)

There are three kinds of links you can use to include an image in a Web page:

- ✔ **Linking to a Web URL.** Like every Web page, every image on the Web has its own separate URL. (A URL is just a path to a file, and each image is a separate file, so therefore has its own URL.) To include an image out on the Web in your own Web page, you just use the IMG tag and give the Web address of the image as the source. When the user sees your Web page, it will look like the image is part of the page, even though it's hosted on a different Web site.

  Plusses and minuses: Linking to images that are already out there is easy for you as a Web author, but you can't count on the image staying there forever. Doing this also represents the image as your own when it actually belongs to someone else. Finally, it's much slower for the user than hosting the image on your own Web server.

  To find the URL of a Web image on a Windows machine, right-click on the image and choose Copy Shortcut. The URL will then be placed in the Clipboard, meaning you can paste it into a text editor, HTML program, or other program.

- ✔ **Linking to the same folder as your Web page.** If an image file is in the same folder as the HTML file that links to it, you need only to give the name of the image file, with no other folder or path information.

  Plusses and minuses: This is very simple; like linking to a Web URL, it's fast and easy. And when you transfer your files to a Web server, there's no problem with keeping the files in the same relative position. The only disadvantage is that the folder the Web page is in can get quite crowded, especially as many images are used over and over again by different

Web pages. (Also, Web authors find themselves keeping older versions of a file, or alternate versions, in the Web browser.) So you can end up with one folder containing all the Web pages and images in a site, plus working versions of the files, which can be a mess.

✔ **Linking to a different folder on the same machine as the Web page.** In this way of doing things, the image file is on the same machine as the Web page, but in a different folder. The link typically contains a relative pathway from the Web page to the image file, including moves up and down a tree of folders. The link can also be to an absolute address relative to the root of the machine.

Plusses and minuses: This is the most common kind of linking, as people like to keep different types of files in different folders, but is also where a lot of problems occur. You have to describe the pathway from the HTML file to the image file, or the absolute location of the file on the machine, and the relative or absolute location can easily change or get mangled when files are transferred to a Web server.

Using a text editor such as Windows Notepad exposes you directly to naming hassles. Follow the recommendations in this chapter to manage them more easily.

All the different possible ways of linking an HTML file to an image file are described in Table 14-1 (a duplicate of which appears in Chapter 10 for the folks using a WYSIWYG HTML editor). Inspect it carefully, use it as a reference when you're creating links to image files, and (oh, yeah) double-check your typing in Notepad to make sure it's accurate.

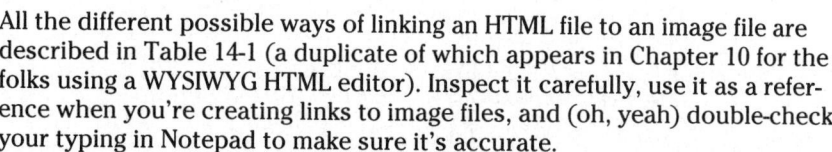

Table 14-1		URL and Web-Page Examples	
Location of Target	*URL*	*Web-Page Example*	*Graphics Example**
Same folder	*filename*	`<a href="mycv.html">text</a>`	`<img src="myface.jpg">`
Subfolder at a lower level of the same path	*pathname/ filename*	`<a href="subpages/mycv.htm">text</a>`	`<img src="grfx/myface.jpg>`
Folder on a different path	*pathname/ filename*	`<a href="../the otherpage/otherpage.htm>text</a>`	`<img src="../sharegfx/proface.gif>`

(continued)

Table 14-1 *(continued)*

Location of Target	URL	Web-Page Example	Graphics Example*
Different server, home page (index. htm or index. html)	*domainname*	`<a href="http:// www.largedomain. com">text</a>`	`<img src " http:// www.large domain.com/ goodface. jpg">`
Different server, interior page	*domainname/ pathname*	`<a href=" http:// www.largess. com/files/bud. htm">text</a>`	`<img src = "http://www. largess.com/ gifs/icon27. gif">`
Link within a page	*Any of the above + #anchor- name*	`<a name= "myanchor"> </a>; <a href=" http:// www.largess. com#myanchor">Go to my anchor</a>`	Doesn't apply

* These examples leave out the ALT option and other important graphics options, described later in this chapter.

Follow these steps to add images to your Web page in Windows Notepad:

1. **Open your HTML file in Windows Notepad. Move the cursor to the point where you want to insert the graphic.**

2. **Enter the** `<img>` **tag where you want the image to appear.**

   Note that the `<img>` tag has no closing tag.

3. **Within the** `<img>` **tag, add the SRC attribute and the pathway, file-name, and extension of the file. (An example is** `src=bigpic.jpg` **for a JPEG file in the same folder as the HTML page.) Refer to Table 14-1 for examples of different kinds of pathways to files.**

   JPEG files sometimes end with the extension JPG and sometimes with the extension JPEG — the same file could be called `bigpic.jpg` or `bigpic.jpeg`. If you get it wrong, the link won't work.

   To find out which extension a given file uses, right-click on the file icon in Windows Explorer, choose Properties, open the Details tab, and note the extension.

4. **Again within the** <img> **tag, add the** alt **attribute and alternate text for the image. (An example is** alt="Grass in Death Valley" **for a scenic image.)**

   alt text is very important for two reasons. alt text is read out loud by screen readers and other programs for visually impaired users. It can also appear in place of the image when the page is viewed on a device that doesn't support graphics, like some mobile phone Web browsers, or even a PC with graphics display turned off.

   alt text is also used as a tool tip, text that appears when the user mouses over the graphic.

   For both purposes, alt text should be a short, simple description of the image, such as the name of a person pictured — or a description, if the image is for the purpose of providing atmosphere.

5. **Then, still within the** <img> **tag, specify how the image should be aligned relative to text.**

   An example is <img align="left">.

   - The usual choices are for the image to be aligned to the left, with text flowing around it on the right, or on the right, with text flowing to the left of it. The values for this are "left" and "right". This is the magazine or newspaper look, with text and image integrated together.

   - Other choices, such as "top", "bottom", and "middle", place a single line of text next to the image and otherwise leave the image on its own. This nearly always looks strange.

6. **To add a black border around the image, add the** border **attribute and specify how many pixels wide it should be.**

   - An example is <img border="2">. Several combinations of image options are shown in Figure 14-1.

   - Adding a thin black border around an image makes it appear sharper and clearer, especially for small images. Experiment with border sizes around your image.

There's an additional attribute that allows you to add blank space around an image that you may want to use; see step 7 for the HTML code to use in the Code Editor to add this padding.

7. **To add a blank area around an image, add the** hspace **and/or** vspace **attribute and specify the number of pixels of horizontal and vertical padding, respectively.**

   The blank area is called *white space,* or *padding.*

   - An example is <img hspace="2" vspace="2">.

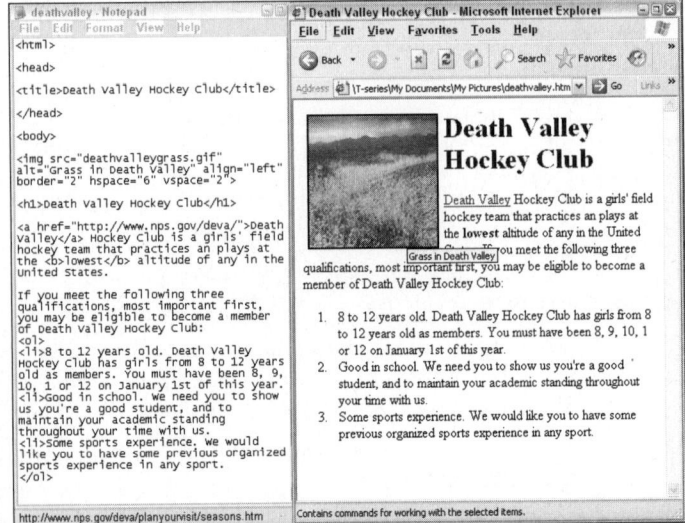

Figure 14-1:
HTML lets
you do a
lot with an
image.

- It's often necessary to add a small amount of padding around an image to keep text from flowing too closely to it. The amount of padding needed can depend on whether an image is near a headline, another image, or such, which can vary as a user makes the browser window wider or narrower. So this attribute is usually specified on a trial-and-error basis.

- Adding more than two or three pixels of padding is likely to make the image appear to float oddly in a "puddle" of blank space around it. Keep the number of pixels of horizontal and/or vertical space very few in most cases.

Figure 14-2 shows various `hspace` and `vspace` settings for the same image.

8. **Add the** `height` **and** `width` **attributes to specify the image size, in pixels, or to change the width and height if you want to resize the image in place.**

Here's an example: `<img height="100" width= "50">`.

- It's usually better to modify the image itself in a graphics program before putting it in your Web page. However, you can stretch or shrink the displayed image by changing the width and/or height here.

- If you want to keep the image in proportion, change both dimensions by the same relative amount. For instance, if you double the width, also double the height.

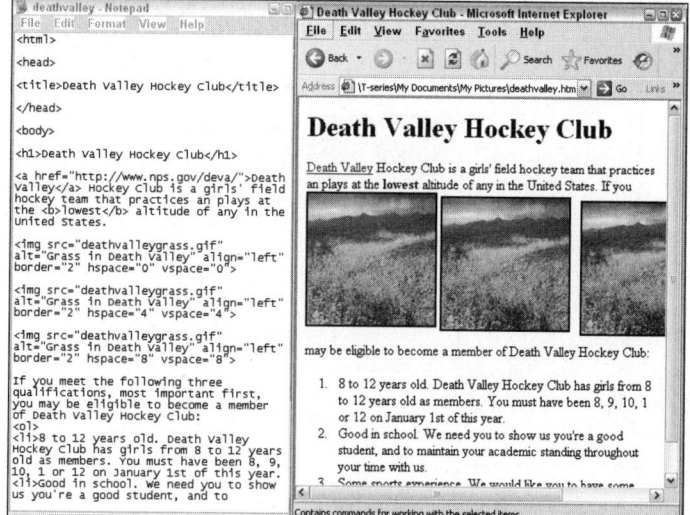

Figure 14-2:
Don't get
lost in
hspace and
vspace.

- Even if you don't resize the image using `<img>` tag attributes, it's good practice to specify the `<img>` tag attributes that fit the image as it is. Why? By "telegraphing" the image size in the `<img>` tag, you give the browser the information it needs to set aside space for the image when downloading the page. This prevents different parts of the page contents from lurching about as different elements of the page download.

9. **To make the image a link, surround it with the** `<a>` **and** `</a>` **tags, and add the** `href=` **attribute to the** `<a>` **tag to specify the link, as described in Chapter 13.**

   You can link to a Web destination or use images to create an image-based menu.

10. **Save the file and preview the results in your Web browser.**

    An example is shown in Figure 14-3.

Adding Sound to Your Page

The plusses and minuses of adding sound to your Web page, as well as how to host a music file on MySpace, are discussed in Chapter 6. But what are the actual mechanics of adding sound?

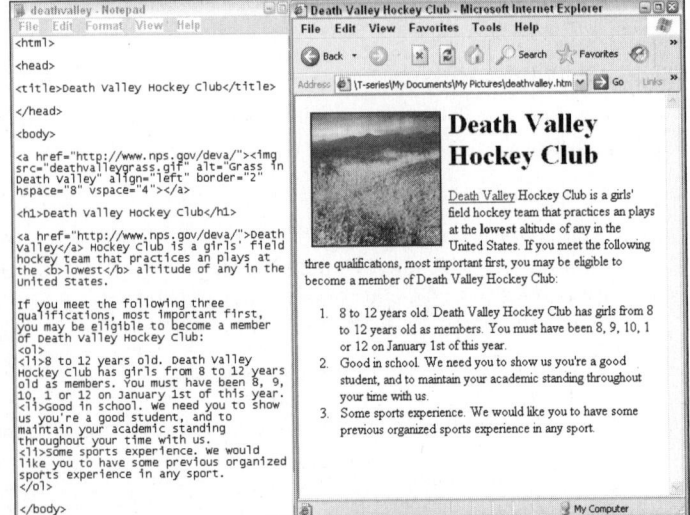

Figure 14-3:
Repeatedly
check
your image
attributes in
your Web
browser.

Because sound is not a standard part of the Web's definition, there are actually two competing ways to do it: with the <bgsound> tag and with the embed tag.

The <bgsound> tag works well and has useful options for controlling sound, but it's not supported by all browsers.

The <embed> tag is not officially supported by the HTML standard at all, but it works in most browsers. <embed> has different options — different HTML attributes — for different media players, such as Windows Media Player or Apple QuickTime. This is a standards-unfriendly situation.

You may want to share a tip with your Web page's users: They can stop sound from playing in your Web page by clicking the Stop button in their browsers.

Follow these steps to add sound to a Web page in a text editor:

1. **Open your Web page in Notepad.**

2. **Enter the** <embed> **tag and a link to the sound file you want to use, as follows:** <embed src="*pathname/filename*">, **where** "*pathname/ filename*" **is a link to the sound file.**

   The rules for creating the link to a sound file are the same as for a link to a graphics file, as shown in Table 14-1. The simplest way to be sure you have the link right is to place the sound file in the same folder as the Web page; that way the link is simply the filename.

3. **Save the file in Notepad and open or refresh it in your Web browser. The sound should play.**

It's important to test the link right away to be sure it will work.

4. **If the sound doesn't play, experiment to make sure you have the path right, and that sound plays on your machine.**

Here are a couple of places to start:

- To make sure you have the link right, put the file in the same folder as your Web page and simplify the link. If this fixes the problem, experiment with having the file where you want it and constructing the link properly, using Table 14-1 as a guide.

- To make sure that sound playback works on your machine, navigate to the file in Windows Explorer and click on it. It should play. If not, identify and fix the files affecting sound playback on your machine.

You can also use the `<bgsound>` tag instead of `<embed>`. (The linking part is the same.) Each will fail to work on some Web browsers and each has options the other lacks; some of the plusses and minuses of each are described in more details in Chapter 10. I tend to favor `<embed>` as it's also useful for video clips and its options, such as showing or not showing a visible player for the file.

Adding Video to Your Page

Chapter 7 describes the plusses and minuses of using video in your Web page and steps you through uploading a video to YouTube.

When you add video to your Web page, the video file can be stored on — that is, be hosted on — your own Web server, some other Web server or, in particular, YouTube. YouTube offers free hosting for videos you upload to YouTube, which can potentially save you a lot of trouble compressing the video, worrying about performance of the server storing the video, and paying for the many megabytes downloaded. (YouTube supports virtually unlimited video downloading for free.) You get the advantage of using the massive server and processing capabilities of Google, YouTube's owner, free — if you don't mind the YouTube logo stamped into the lower-right corner of every frame of your video.

If you host a video on your own site and it becomes a hit, you could be "hit" with very large charges for file transfer. If you link to a video on someone else's site (besides YouTube) and thus drive many hits to it (while making it appear to be on your site), that's very rude of you and you may be found out and charged.

Almost every video on YouTube includes a box with the code you paste into your Web page to play the video there, surrounded by your own content. This code is customized for playback in Flash, a specialized media playback tool:

```
<object width="425" height="344"><param name="movie"
        value="http://www.youtube.com/v/HhcLUF590h4&hl=en&fs=1"></param>
        <param name="allowFullScreen" value="true"></param>
        <embed src="http://www.youtube.com/v/HhcLUF590h4&hl=en&fs=1"
        type="application/x-shockwave-flash" allowfullscreen="true"
        width="425" height="344"></embed></object>
```

Flash was originally used mostly for animations but is increasingly used as a container for video and audio.

Here I'll demonstrate how to include a video in your Web page, wherever it's hosted.

1. **Open your Web page in Notepad.**

2. **Specify the path and filename that allow access to the video you want to use.**

    Here are some commonly used hosting options:

    - If your video is hosted somewhere other than YouTube, type in the following, using the actual path and filename:

    ```
    <embed src="pathname/filename">
    ```

    - If the video is hosted on YouTube, go to the relevant YouTube page and copy the code for the video from there. Paste it into your Web page. (For more about hosting videos on YouTube, see Chapter 7.)

    - If the video is in the same folder as your Web page, the pathname is just the filename; if the video is on the Web, the pathname is the URL of the video. (Find the URL by choosing View⇨Source for the Web page hosting the video.)

    - If the file is in a different folder on your machine than the Web page, include the path to the video. (Refer to Table 14-1 for examples.)

3. **Add the size of the video to your Web page.**

    It's a two-step process:

    a. *Specify the size of the video using the* `<object>` *tag:*

    ```
    <object width="xxx" height= "yyy">
    ```

    b. *Add the same* `width` *and* `height` *attributes to the* `<embed>` *tag.*

The <object> tag tells the user's Web browser that there is something in the Web page, at this spot, of the size you specify. The width and height attributes do roughly the same thing. Specifying the size in both ways, as YouTube does, is a way to make sure that the Web browser sets aside space for the video when it first displays the Web page.

4. **Save the file and open it in a Web browser. Try the video.**

   See the previous section of this chapter, on including an audio file, for what to do if the video doesn't play.

   If you you're having trouble successfully including video in your Web page, or if you're worried about download charges, then upload the video to YouTube or another host. On your Web page, you can provide a "normal" link to the Web page that hosts the video. Users can click the link to see it and then return to your site after they've viewed the video.

Chapter 15

Laying Out Your Site in HTML

In This Chapter

▶ Adding `mailto` links in HTML

▶ Setting up internal links in HTML

▶ Creating a text navigation bar

*E*ven experts have trouble telling people exactly how to go from "just putting up a page" to creating a full Web site. That's because the needs and abilities of people vary so much for each site they create.

In this chapter, I demonstrate some steps along this route: how to use links to create a `mailto` link, a complex page, and a full site, complete with basic navigation.

Using mailto Links in HTML

Although `mailto` links seem simple, actually they have some complexity to them. Here's how to work around it.

A `mailto` link is a link with an e-mail address as its destination. Instead of bringing something into your Web browser (the way most Web links work), it brings up something *outside:* an e-mail message, pre-addressed as specified by the destination given in the `mailto` Link. (If you're really clever, the subject line of the e-mail can also come up already filled in.) The user just has to enter the content of the e-mail and click Send. (See Figure 15-1 for an example of a link and the resulting e-mail message.)

At least this is what's *supposed* to happen. It only works if the user has a default mail program set up in Windows or some other operating system, *and* if the default program is the one the user wants for that particular e-mail message.

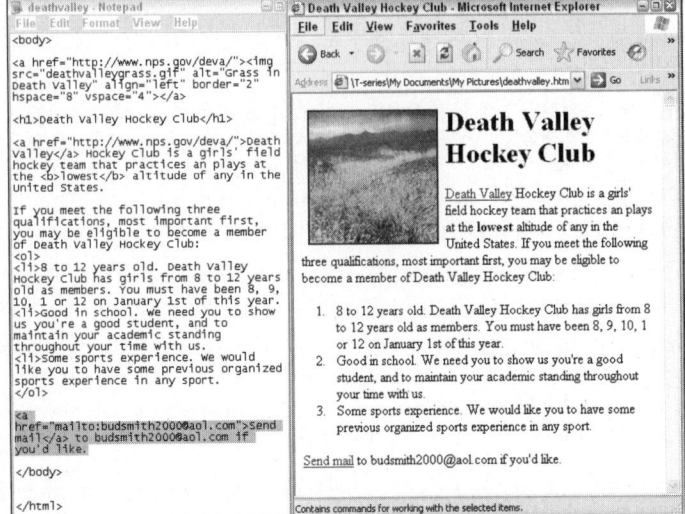

Figure 15-1:
Used
correctly,
`mailto`
links can
make
creating
mail easier.

Often this is not the case. It's quite common for users never to see Outlook Express except when they click a `mailto` link — especially if the manufacturer set up Outlook Express as the default program for that computer, and the user never changed it to full Outlook, Lotus Notes, or the Web-based e-mail program he or she uses.

The other problem is that many users juggle different e-mail systems for different purposes. A user might use Lotus Notes for work but occasionally book a vacation (for instance) on that work computer. For that purpose, someone might want a personal e-mail account (such as a Hotmail account), to appear in response to a `mailto` link.

Also, users know what happens when they click a link: Another Web page comes up. It can be disconcerting when an e-mail message comes up instead. This is even more the case if the `mailto` link is used in navigation — the users think they'll be moved around the site, perhaps reaching a page with all sorts of contact information, and instead they get a partly pre-filled e-mail message that they suspect might never reach a human being.

Here are a few quick hints that should help you use `mailto` links productively:

✔ **Provide means of contact other than e-mail.** Always provide a phone number; many users are visiting your Web page just to find one. If you "hide" it (as the users will see it) and offer only a cold, impersonal electronic replacement, you'll just make them angry.

✔ **Don't use** `mailto` **links in navigation.** Instead of having a Contact tab in navigation, backed only by a `mailto` link, provide a full page of contact information.

✔ **Use the words around the** `mailto` **link to identify it; spell out the e-mail address in the text so users can copy and paste it if they prefer.** A proper use of a `mailto` link is within a Contact Us page, for instance, that includes an address and a phone number as well. The `mailto` link should be in a form like the following:

To reach us by e-mail, click <u>here</u> to send an e-mail message to `yes wecan@thecompany.com`. We'll respond within two business days.

This will signal users that clicking the underlined link (<u>here</u>) will bring up an e-mail message addressed to `yeswecan@thecompany.com` — while also providing a workaround if they want to copy the e-mail address to paste it into a message themselves.

Although the usability concerns around using one can be complicated, creating a `mailto` link in HTML is simple. Just follow these steps:

1. **Open your Web page in Windows Notepad.**

2. **Create the text in which you want to insert the e-mail link.**

   See above for some ideas on getting this right.

3. **Surround the link text, such as** `e-mail us`, **with the beginning and ending anchor tags,** `<a>` **and** `</a>`.

   Entering the closing anchor tag in the beginning ensures that you don't forget later.

4. **Add the** `mailto` **link as a value for the** `href` **(hypertext reference) attribute, in the following form:**

   ```
   href="mailto:username@website.com"
   ```

   Be sure to get the e-mail address right, and test it after you finish. Nothing is more frustrating to the user — and quicker to make you look bad — than a bad e-mail address in a `mailto` link.

5. **Optionally, enter a Subject line for the e-mail. To do so, add a subject to the** `mailto` **value, as follows:**

   ```
   href="mailto:username@website.com?subject=Mail from the site"
   ```

The Web browser will be able to recognize that spaces in the subject line don't mean the end of the value for the attribute, as the spaces are included within the quotation marks around the `mailto` value. But if you forget the quotes, expect problems with how the `mailto` link works.

The subject line can be very convenient for you when you receive the e-mail, but you have to be aware that the user can change it. Because of this, it might be better to create a specific e-mail address used only for this link than to count on the subject line remaining the same for every e-mail sent from this link.

6. **Save the file and open or refresh the Web page in a Web browser. Test the e-mail link, including sending an e-mail, as shown in Figure 15-2. Make sure the message is received where you intend it to go.**

   If you don't discover any problems, your users will!

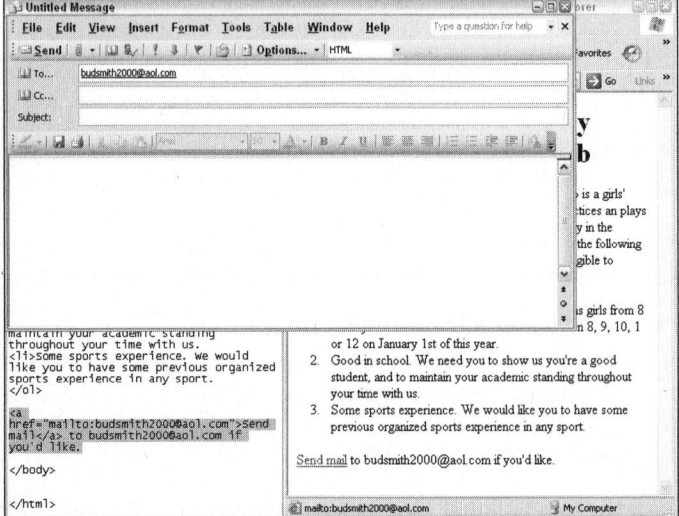

Figure 15-2: A view of the `mailto` code, Web page, and mail message.

Internal Links within a Web Page

Compared to the drama of using a hyperlink to go to a whole new Web site, using a hyperlink to move the user to a new location in the same Web page might seem a bit of a letdown.

But a great advantage of Web pages is that they're vertically just about unlimited, like an ancient scroll. And users are accustomed to moving up and down in long documents, including long Web pages. So a structured way to use this characteristic is welcome.

Having everything about a given topic in one long Web page can be quite helpful to users. They know which page to go to for that topic — and most of them know how to use the search option in their Web browser to get to a particular phrase or word they remember.

Now usability people will tell you that people don't like to scroll unless they're sure of the benefits of doing so. But *internal links* — links that go to a specific spot in a Web page — can use the vertical dimension of the Web page without the user having to scroll. He or she simply clicks links. (Possibly even unaware that they are moving around in a Web page, not moving between one Web page and another page.)

To create an internal link, you have to create a *destination anchor*. The destination anchor marks the spot in the page that the users go to when they click an internal link.

The destination anchor is in the form `<a name="targetname"></a>`. You create your own memorable name to help you organize the page. Note that there is no text surrounded by the beginning and ending anchor tags. This HTML code simply gives a name to the spot in the Web page where it appears.

The destination anchor is invisible to the user. When the user clicks on a link to the destination anchor, the Web page scrolls upward or downward to that line destination.

The link to the destination anchor is a normal link, but the value of the SRC attribute includes the character # followed by the target name of the destination anchor, as in `<a href="planets.htm#mars"></a>`. (That # can be the hardest part of the whole process to remember, so pay special attention to it.)

 You can certainly create a link to an internal anchor that, instead of being on the same page, is on another page. The other page can be on your own site or a distant site. However, users are so accustomed to links going to the top of a page that I suggest alerting them, in the text preceding the link, so that they'll be going to a destination within a page. Here's what that looks like:

> To learn more about ancient Greek cooking oils, you can visit a great page on the subject. To go directly to the entry on Greek cooking oils, in the middle of a long page about cooking oils, click here; to start at the top of the page and survey the entire cooking-oil topic, click here instead.

Wordy, but effective.

A classic example of internal links in a Web page that's part of a full site is an FAQ page, for Frequently Asked Questions. Generally, the questions are all listed at the top (see Figure 15-3), with the rest of the page containing a question, its answer, the next question, its answer, and so on. Links within the page go down to each question and, from the end of each answer, back up to the top of the page.

Follow the instructions here to create an internal link in a Web page in HTML:

1. **Open your Web page in Windows Notepad. Move the cursor to a spot that you want to be the destination of a link.**

    Usually this will be the beginning of a line of text, often a header.

    If you don't have the content of a Web page ready yet, you can just create headers and links; then your navigation system will be ready as you fill in the content.

2. **At the target destination, enter the destination anchor, such as the following:**

    ```
    <a name="UKpolitics"></a>
    ```

    Note there's no text between the beginning and ending anchor tags.

    Make sure the destination is near a recognizable point in your Web page, such as a header, so the link makes sense to you and to users.

3. **Repeat for additional internal links.**

    Create all the additional links you need — if necessary, type in headers or other markers for the internal links to be associated with.

4. **Test the links by linking to them.**

    Here's a typical instance:

    ```
    <a href="#ukpolitics">British politics</a>
    ```

    Create links to each of your destinations, either because you need them now or, if not, to test them.

5. **Save the file and open it in a Web browser. Test the links and fix any that need repair.**

    Internal links cause many problems; it's best to make them your ally, rather than a source of frustration, by getting them working right from the start.

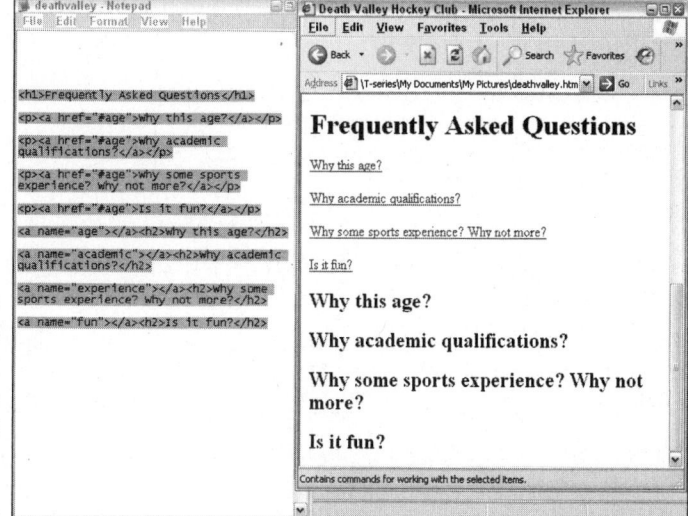

Figure 15-3:
HTML and
the results
for a set
of internal
links.

The link destinations for internal links are often referred to as anchors, even though technically both the beginnings and endings of links are anchors. While a tool such as CoffeeCup, as described in Part III, is good for managing internal anchors, some other tools can't handle them. So if you use a different WYSIWYG tool for Web-page creation, you may still find yourself managing internal anchors directly in HTML.

Creating a Text Navigation Bar

A *navigation bar* is an area of a Web page set aside for links among the pages that make up a site. Each separate link or choice in a navigation bar is called a "tab," whether or not it actually looks like a tab as used in a paper file. A site might have multiple navigation bars that cover content, perhaps in main navigation, and tools or supporting elements, such as a site map and legal reminders, in a secondary navigation bar.

A navigation bar of any type is a consistent visual element that appears on every page of the site and that always has the same appearance, the same words, and the same links. It's not an exaggeration to say that a navigation bar of some sort, even a simple text one, is the difference between a Web site and an unconnected mass of Web pages. Creating a navigation bar forces you to start thinking hard about how your site is going to be organized.

Web-page authors use simple, text-only navigation bars for all purposes during site development — and for several purposes even after creating the graphical main navigation:

✔ To echo main navigation at the bottom of each Web page.

✔ For secondary (or tertiary or — get ready for this one — quaternary) navigation functions on complex sites.

Even the simplest text navigation bar can help enforce useful practices of site design and usability right from the beginning of creating a multiple-page site.

Here's an example of a simple text navigation bar for a small consulting business:

Home | <u>Services</u> | <u>Memberships</u> | <u>Publications</u> | <u>Experience</u> | <u>Contact me</u>

Each tab is underlined to reflect that it's a link to that page or multipage area of the site. Note that the Home tab, as I'll call it, is not underlined. The idea is that, when you're on the home page, you can't click Home to go to the home page — because you're already there. So the area of the site you're already in is not linked.

When you click the word Experience on the text menu to go to the Experience page, the text navigation bar should change to reflect where you are — it's no longer possible to click Experience, while Home is linked again:

<u>Home</u> | <u>Services</u> | <u>Memberships</u> | <u>Publications</u> | Experience | <u>Contact me</u>

To implement this, you create a "model" navigation bar with *all* the tabs linked — but it's never used in quite that form. For each page on your site, you copy the navigation bar, and then remove the link from the tab that the page in question belongs to.

Follow these instructions to create a text navigation bar:

1. **Open a new, empty page in Windows Notepad. Save it under a name of your choice with** `.htm` **as the extension, such as** `navbar.htm`.

2. **Type in a line of text representing the elements of your site, with a word or two for each page or area.**

   Use the vertical bar to separate the tabs. You may find it on your keyboard, or choose Examples for a personal/professional site:

   Home | Services | Memberships | Publications | Experience | Contact me

If the vertical bar character is not accessible from your keyboard, it should be available from the Symbol or similar menu in a word processing program. (There's no such option in Notepad.) You can then copy and paste the vertical bar into Notepad.

3. **Center the navigation bar on the page by using the** center **attribute of the paragraph tag, like so:**

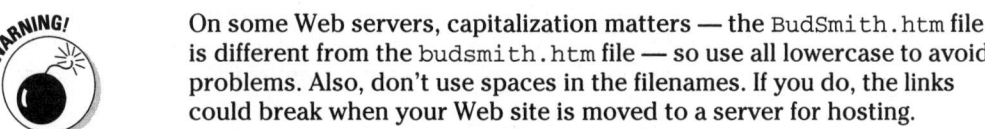

```
<p center>Home | Services | Memberships | Publications | Experience |
     Contact me</p>
```

The text menu will be centered. Note the closing paragraph tag — always a good idea, but especially so in this case, to stop the centering.

4. **To link the Home tab to the home page of your site, surround the word Home with the** <a> **and** </a> **tags. (Exclude the blank spaces to either side). Add the** href **attribute like so:** <a href="home.htm">.

The Insert Link dialog box appears.

5. **Repeat for the remaining phrases — link to the relevant page on your site.**

The pages don't have to exist yet, though of course the links won't work until the pages are there. Whenever you create a page, the name must match the name in the text menu exactly.

On some Web servers, capitalization matters — the BudSmith.htm file is different from the budsmith.htm file — so use all lowercase to avoid problems. Also, don't use spaces in the filenames. If you do, the links could break when your Web site is moved to a server for hosting.

When you're done, you should have a fully linked text menu — every tab linked to a page, even if the page doesn't exist yet.

Consider keeping a copy of the complete menu, with all links in place, on your home page or in a working page — so if you make changes later, it will be easier to update the text menu in one place, then copy and modify it onto all the pages involved.

6. **Copy the menu to each Web page of your site, or create a new file (for any pages that don't yet exist) and put the menu in it. As you proceed, delete the link from the tab representing the page you're about to save.**

Adding this basic (but vital) feature will give you the beginnings of a true site, not just a bunch of pages.

Part V
The Part of Tens

In this part . . .

My Top Tens give you a cache of dos and don'ts for creating Web pages so you can look like a pro your first time out on the Web.

Chapter 16

Ten Web-Publishing Dos and Don'ts

. . . .

*L*ife today is complicated, and so is fiction. Batman has gone from a do-gooder to a "dark knight" (mostly appearing, of course, on dark nights), lately seen in prison right alongside the evil Joker. Ambivalence crops up everywhere.

In the spirit of helping you solve, or avoid, knotty problems, I offer a mixed list of light and dark — ten (plus a couple extra) essential dos and don'ts. Use them to make your site stronger from the start and to help you resist the temptation to let it become hard to use or to fall behind the times.

DO Think About Your Target Audience

Who is your Web site targeting? A little thought along these lines can make your pages much more appealing to your visitors. Before you begin creating your Web site, choose the right look and feel, and a style of presentation that is appropriate for your audience.

For instance, if your target audience is your family, keep your site simple and fun — but if it's a business site, keep the personal stuff well separate.

Include links that *your visitors* find interesting, not just the ones that *you* find interesting — unless "all about you" is the point of your page, of course.

Use good sites as models. Many top-rated sites have settled on relatively simple designs. Identify what works in a site you like. Is it . . .

- ✔ The use of color and the layout of the Web page?
- ✔ The fact that the site loads quickly?
- ✔ The well-organized content?

Google is a good example of a site that is well-focused around a key observation: Speed matters. The Ford site, which could hardly be more different, also does a good job for its customers — by giving cars pride of place.

Research other media, such as newspapers and magazines that have an audience similar to yours (check the articles and the ads to determine this), to find good and bad examples.

But don't overcomplicate things. Stick to basic HTML that works for everyone; try more advanced technologies on "leaves" of your site, on individual pages, before extending their use across your site.

If you want and need to offer something a bit more exciting like a QuickTime movie, help your site visitors by plainly labeling it and offering them any needed support, such as a link to the QuickTime download page on Apple's Web site.

DON'T Forget the Basics

Your site may be the greatest thing since sliced bread, but if you forget to include contact information for yourself in the site, how will you find out that you misspelled "bureaucracy" all over the place?

Similarly, don't put the order form for your spiffy new number-crunching widget five levels down in the "Fruit Bat Guano Statistics — 1876" Web page. If your customers can't find it, they can't buy it.

More basics:

- ✔ Have a useful, search-engine-friendly title (the `title` tag) for each page.
- ✔ Include your e-mail address on your Web page or Web site.
- ✔ If you create a Web site of more than 5 to 7 pages, add a site map.
- ✔ Make the important information prominent.
- ✔ Include a copyright notice, usually in this form: © 2008 MyCo Inc.

DO Think Before You Create

When creating Web pages, a surprising number of people just jump in and start throwing around text and HTML tags with no clue about where they're going or what they want to accomplish. That approach is fine if you just want to play around; in fact, it can be a lot of fun. But if you want to make a good impression on the Web, sitting down and thinking about a few things ahead of time really pays off.

Sketch your ideas on paper. Then describe them to someone else and ask for feedback. This prep work forces you to consider things that you may not think about otherwise:

- ✔ Page layout
- ✔ Graphic design
- ✔ Relationship between pages
- ✔ Target audience
- ✔ Content structure
- ✔ Link grouping

Remember that your Web pages are available and accessible to the whole world. Think a bit about foreign audiences. Do you use colloquialisms that may not be understood by international Net surfers? How do your pages look to your colleagues who view them through a slow Net link? (Fast Internet connections are still very expensive in some places.) Should you include content in multiple languages? Will your humorous or risqué content offend someone in another country or culture?

When you become a Web publisher, you also become a global citizen, and your Web pages play on a global stage. Think through the accessibility and meaning of your pages in advance.

All these issues and more, when properly considered and acted on, can make your site a first-class Web-surfing experience.

DON'T "Borrow" without Asking

Make sure that content you get from the Web to use on your own Web page is labeled as being freely available for reuse, or else get permission to reuse it.

If a Web page doesn't explicitly say that its content can be freely borrowed, assume that it's copyrighted or otherwise protected — which means you should ask before borrowing any of it.

You can easily peek at the HTML source of any Web page, and that's legitimate, and a good way to figure out new design techniques. But you can also easily grab any content that exists on the Web, even privately owned content that belongs to others. However, the fact that you can easily grab others' content does *not* make doing so right or legal. It's also not necessary.

You can find a great deal of public-domain content, and getting permission to use some private content is not all that hard to do. Many people are happy to let you use their content as long as you provide proper attribution and reciprocal links so that they can gain exposure to new Web users who visit your pages. In the process, you may just gain new friends or business contacts, as well as avoid legal problems down the road. (And in case you get tempted to borrow quietly, keep in mind that word of unethical practices gets around quickly on this amazing global network.)

DO Use Links to Outside Sites

No matter how great your content is, you're wasting the most important feature of the Web if you don't include links to sites outside your own. No matter what your topic, you can find complementary sites out there. Giving your visitors links to those sites is not only courteous — it's also part of the foundation on which the Web was built.

If you research your links carefully and organize them well, your links can be a valuable resource for others. In your own Web surfing, you've probably found that one of the best experiences on the Web is the serendipity of stumbling upon some cool site that you had no idea existed. Give your visitors that same experience. Point them to the outside world. That's why it's the Web and not the Hole.

You can use as many links as you like, as long as they fit within a structure. Beginners often organize their pages in ways that make their sites hard to navigate. If your site has more than 5 to 7 pages, you should put some thought into how your visitors navigate it. Nobody likes wandering from page to page with no idea what is where. Likewise, users don't want to follow multiple links to find one piece of information.

Keep the relationship between your pages simple. Make clear which links are internal to your own site and which go out to other sites. Provide a site map or a common menu. And make navigation work consistently throughout the site.

DON'T Abuse Graphics and Multimedia

A prime attraction of the Web is that it's designed to present graphical information. Include pictures, icons, bars, and graphical menus in your Web page. Go ahead, try out transparent GIFs. Multimedia is a great addition, too, where appropriate; one or two sound files, a QuickTime movie, even a simple animated GIF can really liven up a site.

Yet the biggest mistake that some beginning Web authors — and some experts — make is overusing graphics and multimedia on a page. Keep in mind that not everyone has a cable modem or DSL connection wired directly to his or her home PC; many folks around the world still receive Web pages via a more limited 56K or slower dialup connection. For most pages, keep your page size — including both text and graphics — under 50 KB.

People also forget that each separate graphics file linked to in your Web page, no matter how small, generates a separate download request. Because of the nature of IP-based networking (IP is Internet Protocol), a random file access can fail, requiring another request, or take a long time. So it can take a page with a lot of different graphics in it a while to "settle down" even over a fast connection.

Here are ways that you can keep down your page size without sacrificing design flexibility:

- ✔ Resize photos and convert them to JPEG format.

- ✔ Use simple icons and banners — images without very many colors or complex textures — in GIF format.

- ✔ Combine several different small graphics into one physical graphic that includes the white space — a lot of visual impact for one graphics access.

- ✔ Lay out your site to limit the amount of graphics on any one page; add pages if you need to display more graphics.

- ✔ Use <alt> tags to provide text alternatives to meaningful graphics; leave out the <alt> tags for designer elements that improve the look but don't add to the content.

- ✔ Use thumbnail icons to give access to larger images.

The bottom line is that sites that carefully use graphics and multi~ much more interesting than purely text-oriented ones. Give it a ~ prudent.

All these strategies make your pages more interesting, yet ~ Your Web-surfers will thank you.

DO Test Your Pages

You can find so-called "easy-to-use" Web server packages on the market, and Web server capability is now built into many Macs and PCs. But even with these efforts, buying (or using your existing PC), setting up, and maintaining a Web server can become the most expensive, most complicated, and most frustrating part of Web publishing.

Luckily, you can put your content on someone else's Web server using the free services I describe in this book, or you can use an inexpensive paid service while you figure out the other tricks of the trade. Then, as your knowledge and experience grow, consider setting up your own Web server.

No matter where your pages are, you need to test them. Testing your pages is easy. You probably don't send out a memo without spell-checking it. Similarly, you should not put up your Web pages without testing them. That means looking at your pages on your own machine before testing them on the Web — follow links, see how graphics and text fit together, and so on.

Also, looking at your pages in different browsers doesn't hurt. If you can't do it, ask a friend or even a stranger to help. And, of course, don't forget to spell-check your pages.

After you upload your files to the Web, test again on your own machine, your friends' and neighbor's machines, any machine you have access to — you may be surprised by the differences you see. And if you really want a shock, ask a couple of friends or family members to go to your site and click around on it, telling you what they think as they go along; the way they use your site is almost certain to be different from what you expected.

DON'T Break Netiquette Rules

Lapsing into poor *netiquette* — the etiquette, or "Miss Manners" rule book, of the Internet — is too easy to do, and it can bring you a lot of negative attention. If you make any serious offenses against good Internet practices, your Web service provider's server may remove your pages. And you can even get into legal problems.

Avoid the following dubious practices:

- *Spamming,* or sending unwanted e-mail to publicize your site or sell things

› Answers and Explanations

1. **C**—This is the concept of chemiosmosis: the coupling of the movement of electrons down the electron transport chain and the formation of ATP via the creation of a proton gradient. The protons are pushed out of the matrix during the passage of electrons down the chain. They soon build up on the other side of the membrane, and are driven back inside because of the difference in concentration. ATP synthase uses the movement of protons to produce ATP.

2. **B**—This is an important concept to understand. The AP examiners love this topic!

3. **A**—Lactic acid fermentation occurs in human muscle cells when oxygen is not available. Answer choice B would be incorrect because alcohol fermentation occurs in yeast, fungi, and some bacteria. During exercise, if your muscle becomes starved for oxygen, glycolysis will switch over to fermentation. The pain from the cramp is due to the acidity in the muscle caused by the increased concentration of lactate.

4. **B**—Glycolysis occurs in the cytoplasm. All the other statements are correct.

5. **A**

6. **C**

7. **D**

8. **B**

9. **D**—A glucose molecule can net 36 ATP, an NADH molecule can net 3, an $FADH_2$ molecule can net 2, and a pyruvate molecule can net 15.

10. **D**—During glycolysis, a glucose molecule produces 2 ATP, 2 NADH, and 2 pyruvate. The 2 pyruvate then go on to produce 8 NADH, 2 $FADH_2$, and 2 ATP during the Krebs cycle to give the total listed in answer choice D.

❭ Rapid Review

Try to rapidly review the material presented below.

There are two main categories of respiration: aerobic and anaerobic.

Aerobic respiration: glycolysis → Krebs cycle → oxidative phosphorylation → 36 ATP per glucose molecule

Anaerobic respiration (*fermentation*): glycolysis → regenerate NAD^+ → 2 ATP per glucose molecule

Glycolysis: conversion of 1 glucose molecule into 2 pyruvate, 2 ATP, and 2 NADH; occurs in the cytoplasm, and in both aerobic *and* anaerobic respiration; *must* have NAD^+ to proceed.

Total energy production to this point → 2 ATP + 2 NADH

Krebs cycle: conversion of 1 pyruvate molecule into 4 NADH, 1 $FADH_2$, 1 ATP, H_2O, and CO_2; occurs *twice* for each glucose to yield 8 NADH, 2 $FADH_2$, and 2 ATP; occurs in mitochondria.

Total energy production per glucose molecule to this point → 4 ATP + 10 NADH + 2 $FADH_2$

Oxidative phosphorylation: production of large amounts of ATP from NADH and $FADH_2$.

- Occurs in the mitochondria; requires presence of oxygen to proceed.

- NADH and $FADH_2$ pass their electrons down the electron transport chain to produce ATP.

- Each NADH can produce up to 3 ATP; each $FADH_2$ up to 2 ATP.

- ½ O_2 is the final acceptor in the electron transport chain.

- Movement of electrons down the chain leads to movement of H^+ out of matrix.

- Ox-phos *regenerates NAD^+* so that glycolysis and the Krebs cycle can continue!

Chemiosmosis: coupling of the movement of electrons down the ETC with the formation of ATP using the driving force provided by the proton gradient; occurs in *both* cell respiration *and* photosynthesis to produce ATP.

ATP synthase: enzyme responsible for using protons to actually produce ATP from ADP.

Total energy production per glucose molecule to this point → 38 ATP (use 2 in process) → 36 ATP total

Fermentation (*general*): process that regenerates NAD^+ so glycolysis can begin again.

- Occurs in the absence of oxygen.

- Begins with glycolysis: 2 ATP, 2 pyruvate, and 2 NADH are produced from 1 glucose molecule.

- Because there is no oxygen to accept the electron energy on the chain, there is a shortage of NAD^+, which prevents glycolysis from continuing.

Fermentation (*alcohol*): occurs in fungi, yeast, and bacteria; causes conversion of pyruvate to ethanol.

Fermentation (*lactic acid*): occurs in human and animal muscle cells; causes conversion of pyruvate → lactate; causes cramping sensation when oxygen runs low in muscle cells.

Photosynthesis

IN THIS CHAPTER

Summary: This chapter discusses the basics behind the energy-creation process known as photosynthesis. It also teaches you how plants generate their energy from light. You will learn to differentiate between the two stages—the light-dependent and the light-independent reactions.

Key Ideas

✪ Overall photosynthesis reaction: $H_2O + CO_2 + light \rightarrow O_2 + glucose + H_2O$.

✪ Light-dependent reactions: inputs are water and light; products are ATP, NADPH, and O_2.

✪ The oxygen produced in photosynthesis comes from the water.

✪ The carbon in the glucose produced in photosynthesis comes from the CO_2.

✪ Light-independent reactions (dark reactions): inputs are NADPH, ATP and CO_2; products are ADP, NADP$^+$, and sugar.

Introduction

In Chapter 7, we discussed how human and animal cells generate the energy needed to survive and perform on a day-to-day basis. Now we are going to look at how plants generate their energy from light—the process of **photosynthesis.** We stress again in this chapter what we said about respiration—do not get caught up in the memorization of every fact. Make sure that you understand the basic, overall concepts and the major ideas. Remember that most of plant photosynthesis occurs in the plant's leaves. The majority of the chloroplasts of a plant are found in mesophyll cells. Remember that there are two stages to photosynthesis:

the light-dependent reactions and the light-independent reactions, commonly called the "dark reactions." The simplified equation of photosynthesis is

$$H_2O + CO_2 + \text{light} \rightarrow O_2 + \text{glucose} + H_2O$$

The Players in Photosynthesis

The host organelle for photosynthesis is the **chloroplast,** which is divided into an inner and outer portion. The inner fluid portion is called the **stroma,** which is surrounded by two outer membranes. In Figure 8.1, you can see that winding through the stroma is an inner membrane called the **thylakoid membrane system.** This is where the first stage of

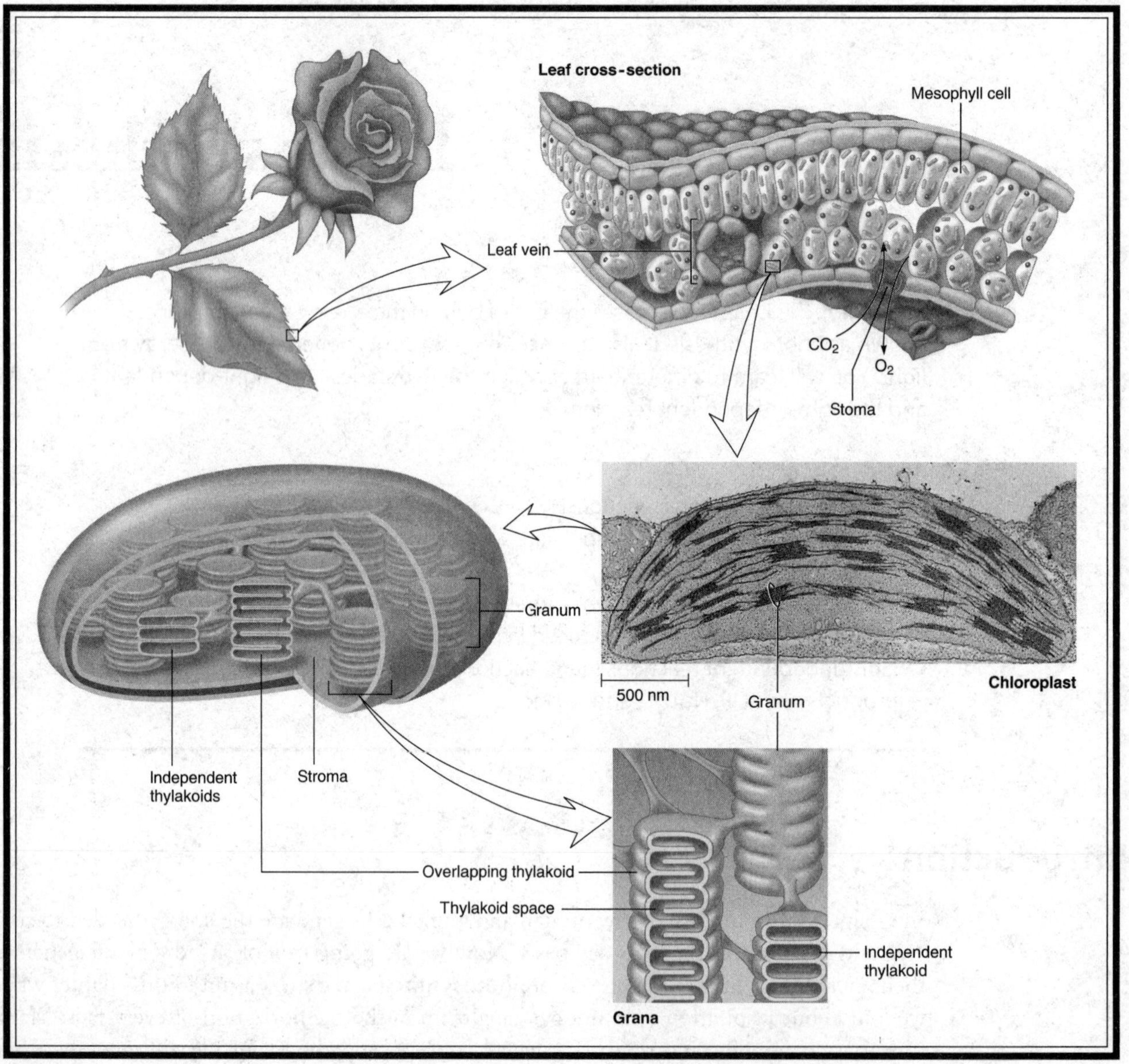

Figure 8.1   An overall view of photosynthesis. (*From* Biology, *8th ed., by Sylvia S. Mader,* © *1985, 1987, 1990, 1993, 1996, 1998, 2001, 2004 by the McGraw Hill Companies, Inc. Reproduced with permission of The McGraw-Hill Companies.*)

photosynthesis occurs. This membrane consists of flattened channels and disks arranged in stacks called **grana.** We always remember the thylakoid system as resembling stacks of poker chips, where each chip is a single thylakoid. It is within these poker chips that the light-dependent reactions of photosynthesis occur.

Before we examine the process of photosynthesis, here are some definitions that will make things a bit easier as you read this chapter.

Autotroph: an organism that is self-nourishing. It obtains carbon and energy without ingesting other organisms. Plants and algae are good examples of autotrophic organisms—they obtain their energy from carbon dioxide, water, and light. They are the producers of the world.

Bundle sheath cells: cells that are tightly wrapped around the veins of a leaf. They are the site for the **Calvin cycle** in C_4 plants.

C_4 plant: plant that has adapted its photosynthetic process to more efficiently handle hot and dry conditions.

Heterotroph: organisms that must consume other organisms to obtain nourishment. They are the consumers of the world.

Mesophyll: interior tissue of a leaf.

Mesophyll cells: cells that contain many chloroplasts and host the majority of photosynthesis.

Photolysis: process by which water is broken up by an enzyme into hydrogen ions and oxygen atoms; occurs during the light-dependent reactions of photosynthesis.

Photophosphorylation: process by which ATP is produced during the light-dependent reactions of photosynthesis. It is the chloroplast equivalent of oxidative phosphorylation.

Photorespiration: process by which oxygen competes with carbon dioxide and attaches to RuBP. Plants that experience photorespiration have a lowered capacity for growth.

Photosystem: a cluster of light-trapping pigments involved in the process of photosynthesis. Photosystems vary tremendously in their organization and can possess hundreds of pigments. The two most important are photosystems I and II of the light reactions.

BIG IDEA 4.C.1

Molecular variation in pigment molecules allows plants to absorb a greater range of wavelengths.

Pigment: a molecule that absorbs light of a particular wavelength. Pigments are vital to the process of photosynthesis and include **chlorophyll, carotenoids,** and **phycobilins.**

Rubisco: an enzyme that catalyzes the first step of the Calvin cycle in C_3 plants.

Stomata: structure through which CO_2 enters a plant and water vapor and O_2 leave.

Transpiration: natural process by which plants lose H_2O via evaporation through their leaves.

The Reactions of Photosynthesis

BIG IDEA 2.A.1

All living things require input of energy.

The process of photosynthesis can be neatly divided into two sets of reactions: the light-dependent reactions and the light-independent reactions. The light-dependent reactions occur first and require an input of water and light. They produce three things: the oxygen we breathe, NADPH, and ATP. These last two products of the light reactions are then consumed during the second stage of photosynthesis: the dark reactions. These reactions, which need CO_2, NADPH, and ATP as inputs, produce sugar and recycle the $NADP^+$ and ADP to be used by the next set of light-dependent reactions. Now, we would be too kind if we left the discussion there. Let's look at the reactions in more detail. Stop groaning . . . you know we have to go there.

Light-Dependent Reactions

BIG IDEA 2.A.2

Autotrophs capture free energy present in sunlight through photosynthesis.

Light-dependent reactions occur in the thylakoid membrane system. The thylakoid system is composed of the various stacks of poker chip look-alikes located within the stroma of the chloroplast. Within the thylakoid membrane is a photosynthetic participant termed **chlorophyll.** There are two main types of chlorophyll that you should remember: chlorophyll *a* and chlorophyll *b*. Chlorophyll *a* is the major pigment of photosynthesis, while chlorophyll *b* is considered to be an accessory pigment. The pigments are very similar structurally, but the minor differences are what account for the variance in their absorption of light. Chlorophyll absorbs light of a particular wavelength, and when it does, one of its electrons is elevated to a higher energy level (it is "excited"). Almost immediately, the excited electron drops back down to the ground state, giving off heat in the process. This energy is passed along until it finds chlorophyll *a*, which, when excited, passes its electron to the primary electron acceptor; then, the light-dependent reactions are under way.

The pigments of the thylakoid space organize themselves into groups called *photosystems*. These photosystems consist of varying combinations of chlorophylls *a*, *b*, and others; pigments called **phycobilins;** and another type of pigment called **carotenoids.** The accessory pigments help pick up light when chlorophyll *a* cannot do it as effectively. An example is red algae on the ocean bottom. When light is picked up by the accessory pigments, it is fluoresced and altered so that chlorophyll *a* can use it.

Imagine that the plant represented in Figure 8.2 is struck by light from the sun. This light excites the **photosystem** of the thylakoid space, which absorbs the photon and transmits the energy from one pigment molecule to another. As this energy is passed along, it loses a bit of energy with each step and eventually reaches chlorophyll *a*, which proceeds to kick off the process of photosynthesis. It initiates the first step of photosynthesis by passing the electron to the primary electron acceptor.

Before we continue, there are two major photosystems we want to tell you about—you might want to get out a pen or pencil here to jot this down, because the names for these photosystems may seem confusing. They are photosystem I and photosystem II. The only difference between these two **reaction centers** is that the main chlorophyll of photosystem I absorbs light with a wavelength of 700 nm, while the main chlorophyll of photosystem II absorbs light with a wavelength of 680 nm. By interacting with different thylakoid membrane proteins, they are able to absorb light of slightly different wavelengths.

Now let's get back to the reactions. Let's go through the rest of Figure 8.2 and talk about the light-dependent reactions. For the sole purpose of confusing you, plants start photosynthesis by using photosystem II before photosystem I. As light strikes photosystem II, the energy is absorbed and passed along until it reaches the P680 chlorophyll. When this chlorophyll is excited, it passes its electrons to the primary electron acceptor. This is where the water molecule comes into play. **Photolysis** in the thylakoid space takes electrons from H_2O and passes them to P680 to replace the electrons given to the primary acceptor. With this reaction, a lone oxygen atom and a pair of hydrogen ions are formed from the water. The oxygen atom quickly finds another oxygen atom buddy, pairs up with it, and generates the O_2 that the plants so graciously put out for us every day. This is the first product of the light reactions.

The light reactions do not stop here, however. We need to consider what happens to the electron that has been passed to the primary electron acceptor. The electron is passed to photosystem I, P700, in a manner reminiscent of the electron transport chain. As the electrons are passed from P680 to P700, the lost energy is used to produce ATP

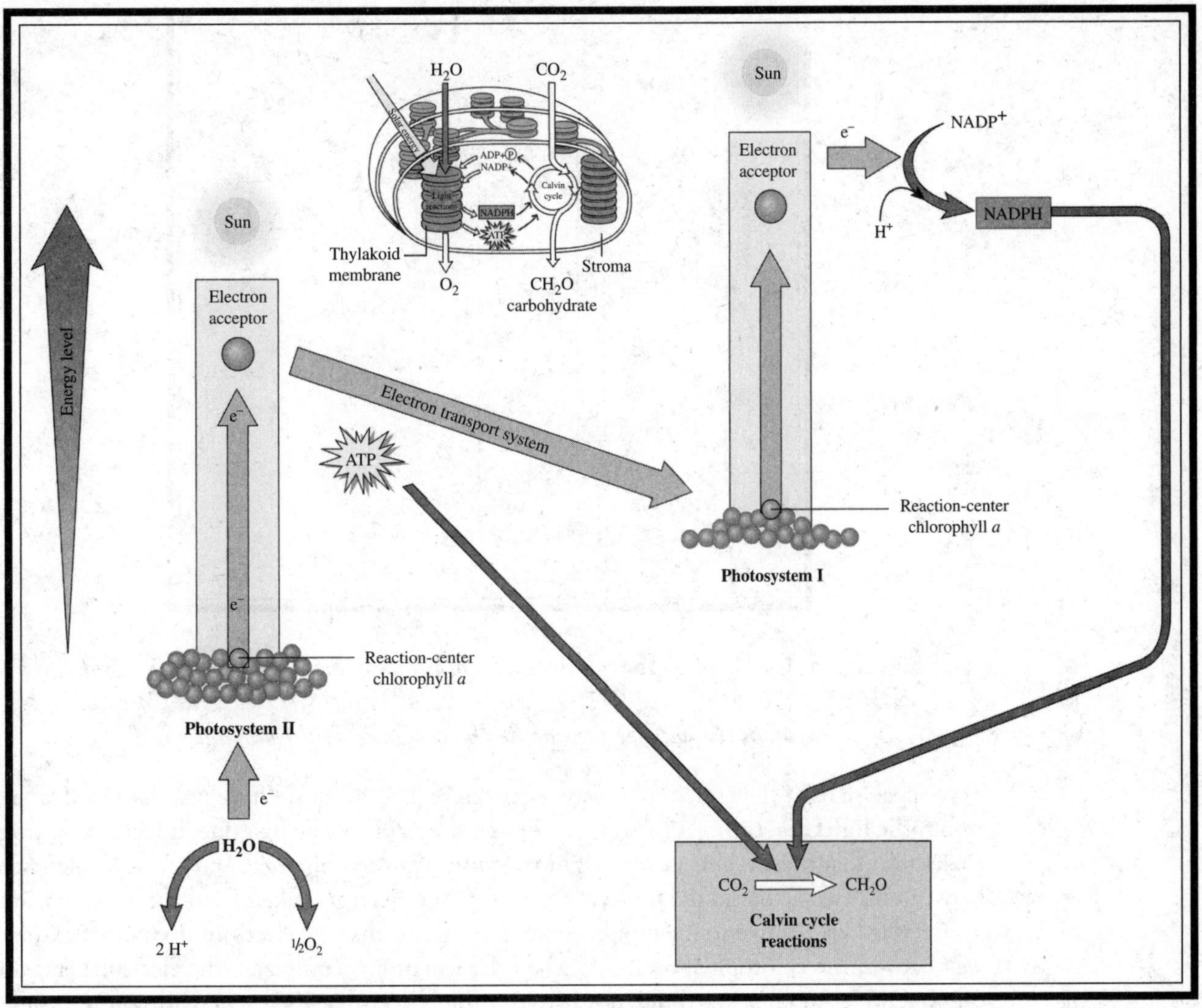

Figure 8.2   Light-dependent reactions. (*From* Biology, *8th ed., by Sylvia S. Mader, © 1985, 1987, 1990, 1993, 1996, 1998, 2001, 2004 by the McGraw Hill Companies, Inc. Reproduced with permission of The McGraw-Hill Companies.*)

(remember chemiosmosis). This ATP is the second product of the light reactions and is produced in a manner mechanistically similar to the way ATP is produced during oxidative phosphorylation of respiration. In plants, this process of ATP formation is called **photophosphorylation.**

After the photosystem I electrons are excited, photosystem I passes the energy to its own primary electron acceptor. These electrons are sent down another chain to **ferredoxin,** which then donates the electrons to $NADP^+$ to produce NADPH, the third and final product of the light reactions. (Notice how in photosynthesis, there is NADPH instead of NADH. The symbol P can help you remember that it relates to photosynthesis. ☺)

Remember the following about the light reactions:

KEY IDEA

1. The light reactions occur in the thylakoid membrane.
2. The inputs to the light reactions are water and light.
3. The light reactions produce three products: ATP, NADPH, and O_2.
4. The oxygen produced in the light reactions comes from H_2O, not CO_2.

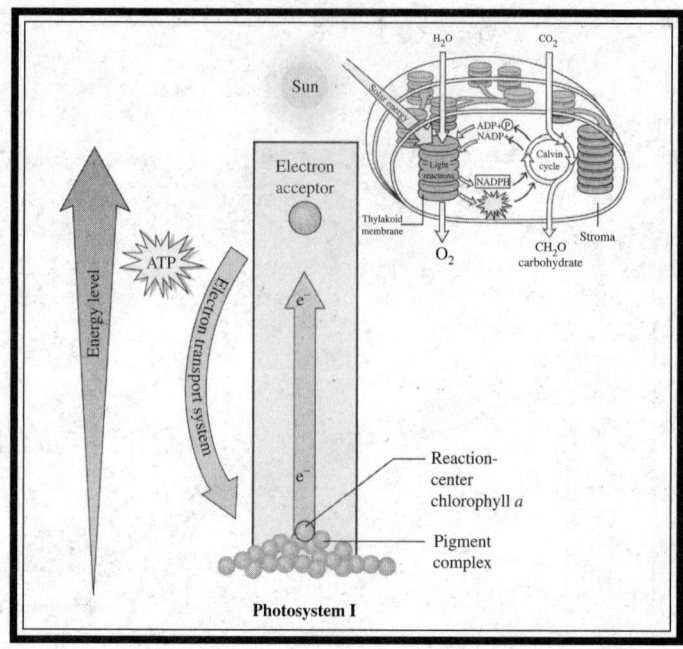

Figure 8.3 Cyclic phosphorylation. (*From* Biology, *8th ed., by Sylvia S. Mader,* © *1985, 1987, 1990, 1993, 1996, 1998, 2001, 2004 by the McGraw Hill Companies, Inc. Reproduced with permission of The McGraw-Hill Companies.*)

Two separate light-dependent pathways occur in plants. What we have just discussed is the **noncyclic light reaction** pathway. Considering the name of the first one, it is not shocking to discover that there is also a **cyclic light reaction** pathway (Figure 8.3). One key difference between the two is that in the noncyclic pathway, the electrons taken from chlorophyll *a* are not recycled back down to the ground state. This means that the electrons do not make their way back to the chlorophyll molecule when the reaction is complete. The electrons end up on NADPH. Another key difference between the two is that the cyclic pathway uses only photosystem I; photosystem II is not involved. In the cyclic pathway, sunlight hits P700, thus exciting the electrons and passing them from P700 to its primary electron acceptor. It is called the *cyclic pathway* because these electrons pass down the electron chain and eventually back to P700 to complete the cycle. The energy given off during the passage down the chain is harnessed to produce ATP—the only product of this pathway. Neither oxygen nor NADPH is produced from these reactions.

A question that might be forming as you read this is: "Why does this pathway continue to exist?" or perhaps you are wondering "Why do they insist on torturing me by writing about all of this photosynthesis stuff?" We will answer the first question and ignore the second one. The cyclic pathway exists because the Calvin cycle, which we discuss next, uses more ATP than it does NADPH. This eventually causes a problem because the light reactions produce equal amounts of ATP and NADPH. The plant compensates for this disparity by dropping into the cyclic phase when needed to produce the ATP necessary to keep the light-independent reactions from grinding to a halt.

Before moving on to the Calvin cycle, it is important to understand how ATP is formed. We know, we know . . . you thought we were finished . . . but we want you to be an expert in the field of photosynthesis. You never know when these facts might come in handy. For example, just the other day one of us was offered $10,000 by a random person on the street to recount the similarities between photosynthesis and respiration. So, this stuff *is* useful in everyday life. As the electrons are passing from the primary electron acceptor to the next photosystem, hydrogen ions are picked up from outside the membrane and brought back into the thylakoid compartment, creating an H$^+$ gradient similar to what we saw in oxidative phosphorylation. During the light-dependent reactions, when hydrogen ions are taken from water during photolysis, the proton gradient grows larger, causing some protons to leave, leading to the formation of ATP.

You'll notice that this process in plants is a bit different from oxidative phosphorylation of the mitochondria, where the proton gradient is created by pumping protons from the matrix *out* to the intermembrane space. In the mitochondria, the ATP is produced when the protons move back *in*. But in plants, photophosphorylation creates the gradient by pumping protons in from the stroma to the thylakoid compartment, and the ATP is produced as the protons move back *out*. The opposing reactions produce the same happy result—more ATP for the cells.

Light-Independent Reactions (Calvin Cycle)

After the light reactions have produced the necessary ATP and NADPH, the synthesis phase of photosynthesis is ready to proceed. The inputs into the Calvin cycle are NADPH (which provides hydrogen and electrons), ATP (which provides energy), and CO_2. From here on, just so we don't drive you *insane* switching from term to term, we are going to call the dark reactions of photosynthesis the *Calvin cycle* (Figure 8.4). The Calvin cycle occurs

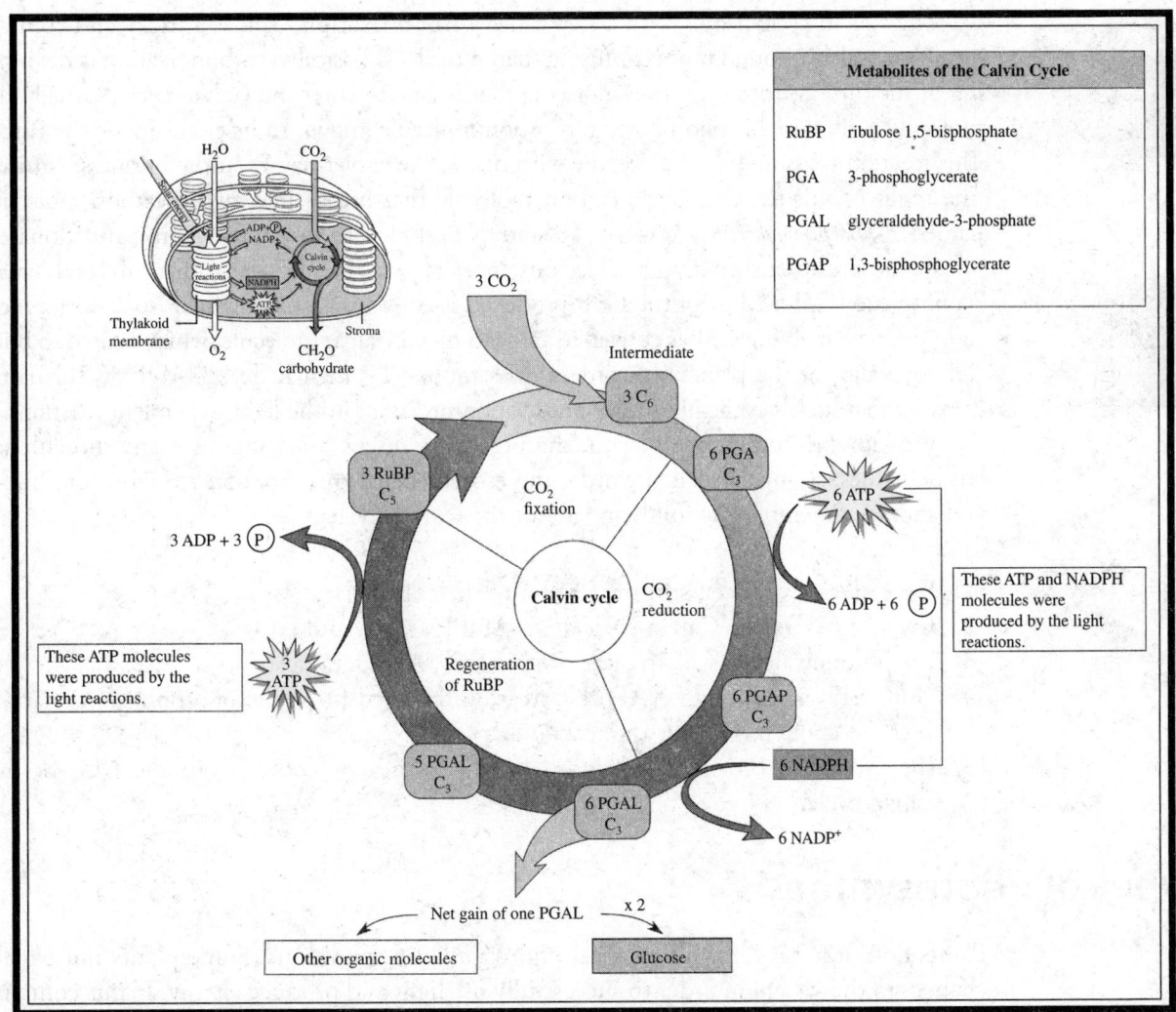

Figure 8.4 The Calvin cycle. (*From* Biology, *8th ed., by Sylvia S. Mader, © 1985, 1987, 1990, 1993, 1996, 1998, 2001, 2004 by the McGraw Hill Companies, Inc. Reproduced with permission of The McGraw-Hill Companies.*)

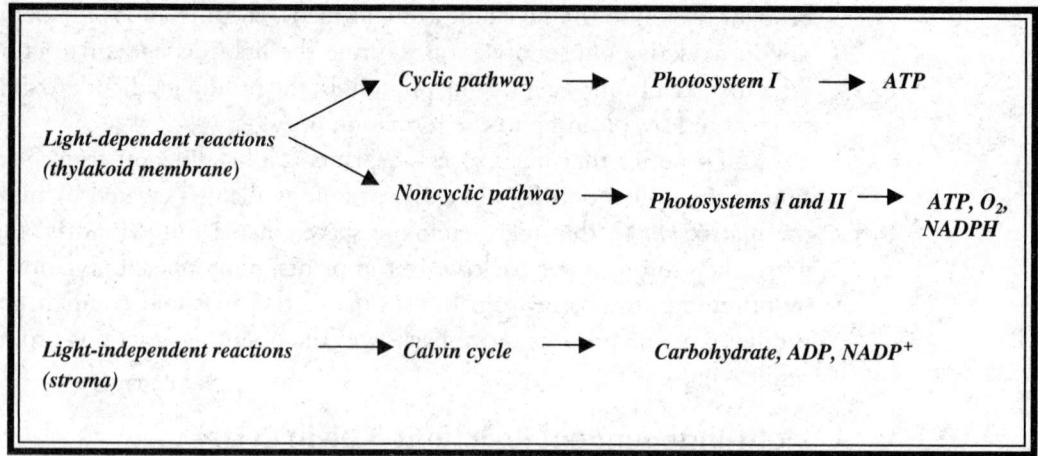

Figure 8.5 Summary of photosynthesis.

in the stroma of the chloroplast, which is the fluid surrounding the thylakoid "poker chips." (For further distinctions among the cyclic pathway, the noncyclic pathway, and the Calvin cycle, see Figure 8.5.)

The Calvin cycle begins with a step called **carbon fixation.** This is a tricky and complex term that makes it sound more confusing than it really is. Basically, carbon fixation is the binding of the carbon from CO_2 to a molecule that is able to enter the Calvin cycle. Usually this molecule is ribulose bis-phosphate, a 5-carbon molecule known to its closer friends as RuBP. This reaction is assisted by the enzyme with one of the cooler names in the business: **rubisco.** The result of this reaction is a 6-carbon molecule that breaks into two 3-carbon molecules named *3-phosphoglycerate* (3PG). ATP and NADPH step up at this point and donate a phosphate group and hydrogen electrons, respectively, to (3PG) to form glyceraldehyde 3-phosphate (G3P). Most of the G3P produced is converted back to RuBP so as to fix more carbon. The remaining G3P is converted into a 6-carbon sugar molecule, which is used to build carbohydrates for the plant. This process uses more ATP than it does NADPH. This is the disparity that makes cyclic photophosphorylation necessary in the light-dependent reactions.

We know that for some of you, the preceding discussion contains many difficult scientific names, strangely spelled words, and esoteric acronyms. So, here's the bottom line—you should remember the following about the Calvin cycle:

1. The Calvin cycle occurs in the stroma of the chloroplast.
2. The inputs into the Calvin cycle are NADPH, ATP, and CO_2.
3. The products of the Calvin cycle are $NADP^+$, ADP, and a sugar.
4. More ATP is used than NADPH, creating the need for cyclic photophosphorylation to create enough ATP for the reactions.
5. The carbon of the sugar produced in photosynthesis comes from the CO_2 of the Calvin cycle.

Types of Photosynthesis

Plants do not always live under ideal photosynthetic conditions. Some plants must make changes to the system in order to successfully use light and produce energy. Plants contain a structure called a **stomata,** which consists of pores through which oxygen exits and carbon dioxide enters the leaf to be used in photosynthesis. **Transpiration** is the natural process by which plants lose water by evaporation from their leaves. When the temperature is very high, plants have to worry about excess transpiration. This is a potential problem for plants because they need the water to continue the process of photosynthesis. To combat this evaporation problem, plants must close their stomata to conserve water. But this solution leads to two different problems: (1) how will they bring in the CO_2 required for photosynthesis? and (2) what will the plants do with the excess O_2 that builds up when the stomata are closed?

When plants close their stomata to protect against water loss, they experience a shortage of CO_2, and the oxygen produced from the light reactions is unable to leave the plant. This excess oxygen competes with the carbon dioxide and attaches to RuBP in a reaction called **photorespiration.** This results in the formation of one molecule of PGA and one molecule of phosphoglycolate. This is not an ideal reaction because the sugar formed in photosynthesis comes from the PGA, not phosphoglycolate. As a result, plants that experience photorespiration have a lowered capacity for growth. Photorespiration tends to occur on hot, dry days when the stomata of the plant are closed.

A group of plants called C_4 **plants** combat photorespiration by altering the first step of their Calvin cycle. Normally, carbon fixation produces two 3-carbon molecules. In C_4 plants, the carbon fixation step produces a 4-carbon molecule called **oxaloacetate.** This molecule is converted into malate and sent from the mesophyll cells to the bundle sheath cells, where the CO_2 is used to build sugar. The **mesophyll** is the tissue of the interior of the leaf, and **mesophyll cells** are cells that contain bunches of chloroplasts. **Bundle sheath cells** are cells that are tightly wrapped around the veins of a leaf. They are the site for the Calvin cycle in C_4 plants.

What is the difference between C_3 plants and C_4 plants? One difference is that C_4 plants have two different types of photosynthetic cells: (1) tightly packed bundle sheath cells, which surround the vein of the leaf, and (2) mesophyll cells. Another difference involves the first product of carbon fixation. For C_3 plants, it is PGA, for C_4 plants, it is oxaloacetate. C_4 plants are able to successfully perform photosynthesis in these hot areas because of the presence of an enzyme called PEP (*phosphoenolpyruvate*) *carboxylase.* This enzyme really wants to bind to CO_2 and is not tricked by the devious oxygen into using it instead of the necessary CO_2. PEP carboxylase prefers to pair up with CO_2 rather than O_2, and this cuts down on photorespiration for C_4 plants. The conversion of PEP to oxaloacetate occurs in the mesophyll cells; then, after being converted into malate, PEP is shipped to the bundle sheath cells. These cells contain the enzymes of photosynthesis, including our good pal rubisco. The malate releases the CO_2, which is then used by rubisco to perform the reactions of photosynthesis. This process counters the problem of photorespiration because the shuttling of CO_2 from the mesophyll cells to the bundle sheath cells keeps the CO_2 concentration high enough so that it is not beat out by oxygen for rubisco's love and attention.

One last variation of photosynthesis that we should look at is the function performed by **CAM** (Crassulacean acid metabolizing) plants—water-storing plants, such as cacti, that close their stomata by day and open them by night to avoid transpiration during the hot days, without depleting the plant's CO_2 reserves. The CO_2 taken in during the night is stored as organic acids in the vacuoles of mesophyll cells until daybreak when the stomata close. The Calvin cycle is able to proceed during the day because the stored CO_2 is released, as needed, from the organic acids to be incorporated into the sugar product of the Calvin cycle.

To sum up these two variations of photosynthesis:

C_4 photosynthesis: photosynthetic process that first converts CO_2 into a 4-carbon molecule in the mesophyll cells, converts that product to malate, and then shuttles the malate into the bundle sheath cells. There, malate releases CO_2, which reacts with rubisco to produce the carbohydrate product of photosynthesis.

CAM photosynthesis: plants close their stomata during the day, collect CO_2 at night, and store the CO_2 in the form of acids until it is needed during the day for photosynthesis.

〉 Review Questions

Questions 1–4 refer to the following answer choices—use each answer only once.

   A. Transpiration
   B. Calvin cycle
   C. CAM photosynthesis
   D. Cyclic photophosphorylation

1. Plants use this process so that they can open their stomata at night and close their stomata during the day to avoid water loss during the hot days, without depleting the plant's CO_2 reserves.

2. Uses NADPH, ATP, and CO_2 as the inputs to its reactions.

3. Photosynthetic process that has ATP as its sole product. There is no oxygen and no NADPH produced from these reactions.

4. The process by which plants lose water via evaporation through their leaves.

5. The photosynthetic process performed by some plants in an effort to survive the hot and dry conditions of climates such as the desert is called

   A. carbon fixation.
   B. C_3 photosynthesis.
   C. C_4 photosynthesis.
   D. cyclic photophosphorylation.

6. Which of the following is the photosynthetic stage that produces oxygen?

   A. The light-dependent reactions
   B. Chemiosmosis
   C. The Calvin cycle
   D. Carbon fixation

7. Which of the following reactions occur in both cellular respiration and photosynthesis?

   A. Carbon fixation
   B. Fermentation
   C. Reduction of $NADP^+$
   D. Chemiosmosis

8. Which of the following is *not* a product of the light-dependent reactions of photosynthesis?

   A. O_2
   B. ATP
   C. NADPH
   D. Sugar

9. Which of the following is an advantage held by a C_4 plant?

   A. More efficient light absorption
   B. More efficient photolysis
   C. More efficient carbon fixation
   D. More efficient uptake of carbon dioxide into the stomata

10. Carbon dioxide enters the plant through the

   A. Stomata
   B. Stroma
   C. Thylakoid membrane
   D. Bundle sheath cell

11. Which of the following is the source of the oxygen released during photosynthesis?

   A. CO_2
   B. H_2O
   C. Rubisco
   D. PEP carboxylase

12. Which of the following is an *incorrect* statement about the Calvin cycle?

 A. The main inputs to the reactions are NADPH, ATP, and CO_2.
 B. The main outputs of the reactions are $NADP^+$, ADP, and sugar.
 C. More NADPH is used than ATP during the Calvin cycle.
 D. Carbon fixation is the first step of the process.

13. Which of the following is the source of the carbon in sugar produced during photosynthesis?

 A. CO_2
 B. H_2O
 C. Rubisco
 D. PEP carboxylase

14. The light-dependent reactions of photosynthesis occur in the

 A. stroma.
 B. mitochondrial matrix.
 C. thylakoid membrane.
 D. cytoplasm.

❯ Answers and Explanations

1. **C**—CAM plants open their stomata at night and close their stomata during the day to avoid water loss due to heat. The carbon dioxide taken in during the night is incorporated into organic acids and stored in vacuoles until the next day, when the stomata close and CO_2 is needed for the Calvin cycle.

2. **B**—The Calvin cycle uses ATP, NADPH, and CO_2 to produce the desired sugar output of photosynthesis.

3. **D**—Cyclic photophosphorylation occurs because the Calvin cycle uses more ATP than it does NADPH. This is a problem because the light reactions produce an equal amount of ATP and NADPH. The plant compensates for this disparity by dropping into the cyclic phase when needed to produce the ATP necessary to keep the light-independent reactions from grinding to a halt.

4. **A**—Transpiration is the process by which plants lose water through their leaves. Not much else to be said about that. ☺

5. **C**—One of the major problems encountered by plants in hot and dry conditions is of photorespiration. In hot conditions, plants close their stomata to avoid losing water to transpiration. The problem with this is that the plants run low on CO_2 and fill with O_2. The oxygen competes with the carbon dioxide and attaches to RuBP, leaving the plant with a lowered capacity for growth. C_4 plants cycle CO_2 from mesophyll cells to bundle sheath cells, creating a higher concentration of CO_2 in that region, thus allowing rubisco to carry out the Calvin cycle without being distracted by the O_2 competitor.

6. **A**—The light-dependent reactions are the source of the oxygen given off by plants.

7. **D**—Chemiosmosis occurs in both photosynthesis and cellular respiration. This is the process by which the formation of ATP is driven by electrochemical gradients in the cell. Hydrogen ions accumulate on one side of a membrane, creating a proton gradient that causes them to move through channels to the other side of that membrane, thus leading, with the assistance of ATP synthase, to the production of ATP.

8. **D**—Sugar is a product not of the light-dependent reactions of photosynthesis but of the Calvin cycle (the dark reactions). The outputs of the light-dependent reactions are ATP, NADPH, and O_2.

9. **C**—C_4 plants fix carbon more efficiently than do C_3 plants. Please see answer 5 above for a more detailed explanation of this answer.

10. **A**—The stomata is the structure through which the CO_2 enters a plant and the oxygen produced in the light-dependent reactions leaves the plant.

11. **B**—The source of the oxygen produced during photosynthesis is the water that is split by the process of photolysis during the light-dependent reactions of photosynthesis. In this reaction, two hydrogen ions and an oxygen atom are formed from the water. The oxygen atom immediately finds and pairs up with another oxygen atom to form the oxygen product of the light-dependent reactions.

12. **C**—This is a trick question. We reversed the two compounds (NADPH and ATP) in this one. More ATP than NADPH is used in the Calvin cycle. It is for this reason that cyclic photophosphorylation exists—to produce ATP to make up for this disparity.

13. **A**—The carbon of CO_2 is used to produce the sugar created during the Calvin cycle.

14. **C**—The light-dependent reactions occur in the thylakoid membrane of the chloroplast. Remember, the thylakoid system resembles the various stacks of poker chips located within the stroma of the chloroplast. The light-independent reactions occur in the stroma of the chloroplast.

❯ Rapid Review

The following terms should be thoroughly familiar to you:

Photosynthesis: process by which plants use the energy from light to generate sugar.

- Occurs in chloroplasts
- Light reactions (thylakoid)
- Calvin cycle (stroma)

Autotroph: self-nourishing organism that is also known as a *producer* (plants).

Heterotroph: organisms that must consume other organisms to obtain energy—*consumers* (humans).

Transpiration: loss of water via evaporation through the stomata (natural process).

Photophosphorylation: process by which ATP is made during light reactions.

Photolysis: process by which water is split into hydrogen ions and oxygen atoms (light reactions).

Stomata: structure through which CO_2 enters a plant, and water vapor and oxygen leave a plant.

Pigment: molecule that absorbs light of a particular wavelength (chlorophyll, carotenoid, phycobilins).

There are three types of photosynthesis reactions:

(*Noncyclic*) *light-dependent reactions*

- Occur in thylakoid membrane of chloroplast.

- Inputs are light and water.

- Light strikes photosystem II (P680).

- Electrons pass along until they reach primary electron acceptor.

- Photolysis occurs—H_2O is split to H^+ and O_2.

- Electrons pass down an ETC to P700 (photosystem I), forming ATP by chemiosmosis.

- Electrons of P700 pass down another ETC to produce NADPH.

- Three products of light reactions are NADPH, ATP, and O_2.

- Oxygen produced comes from H_2O.

(*Cyclic*) *light-dependent reactions*

- Occur in thylakoid membrane.

- Only involves photosystem I; no photosystem II.

- ATP is the only product of these reactions.

- No NADPH or oxygen are produced.

- These reactions exist because the Calvin cycle uses more ATP than NADPH; this is how the difference is made up.

Light-independent reactions (*Calvin cycle*)

- Occurs in stroma of chloroplast.

- Inputs are NADPH, ATP, and CO_2.

- First step is carbon fixation, which is catalyzed by an enzyme named rubisco.

- A series of reactions lead to the production of $NADP^+$, ADP, and sugar.

- More ATP is used than NADPH, which creates the need for the cyclic light reactions.

- The carbon of the sugar product comes from CO_2.

Also:

C_4 *plants*—plants that have adapted their photosynthetic process to more efficiently handle hot and dry conditions.

C_4 *photosynthesis*—process that first converts CO_2 into a 4-carbon molecule in the mesophyll cells, converts *that* product to malate, and then shuttles it to the bundle sheath cells, where the malate releases CO_2 and rubisco picks it up as if all were normal.

CAM plants—plants that close their stomata during the day, collect CO_2 at night, and store the CO_2 in the form of acids until it is needed during the day for photosynthesis.

CHAPTER > 9

Cell Division

IN THIS CHAPTER

Summary: This chapter teaches you what you need to know about cell division in prokaryotes (binary fission), the cell cycle, and cell division in eukaryotes (mitosis and meiosis). In addition, it discusses the life cycles of various organisms.

Key Ideas

- ✪ There are four main stages in the cell cycle—G_1, S, G_2, and M.
- ✪ The stages of mitosis are: prophase, metaphase, anaphase, telophase, and cytokinesis.
- ✪ Crossing over occurs during prophase I of meiosis.
- ✪ Examples of cell division control mechanisms: growth factors, checkpoints, density-dependent inhibition, and cyclins/protein kinases.
- ✪ Sources of cell variation: crossover, 2^n possible gametes, and random pairing of gametes.

Introduction

Cell division, the process by which cells produce more of their kind, can occur in several ways. In this chapter, we discuss cell division in prokaryotes (binary fission), the cell cycle, and cell division in eukaryotes (mitosis and meiosis). After comparing mitosis and meiosis, we will touch on the life cycles of various organisms.

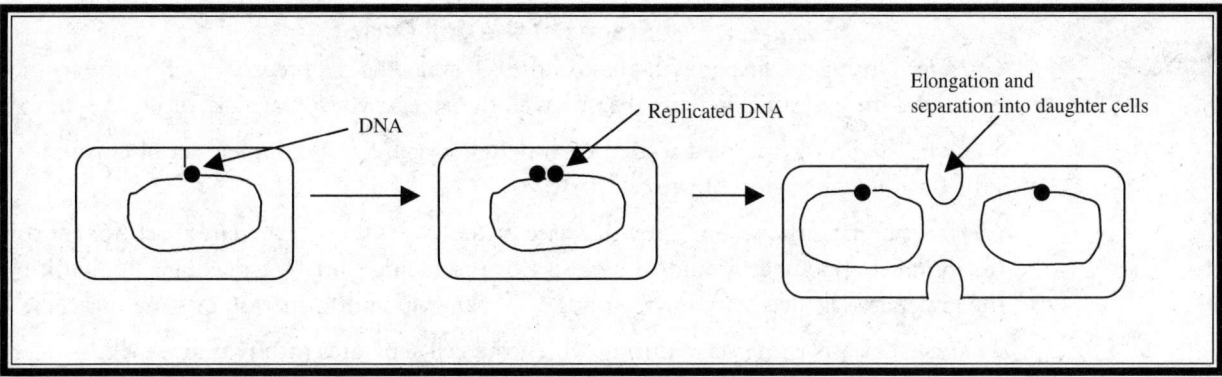

Figure 9.1   Binary fission.

Cell Division in Prokaryotes

Prokaryotes are simple single-celled organisms without a nucleus. Their genetic material is arranged in a single circular chromosome of DNA, which is anchored to the cell membrane. As in eukaryotes, the genetic material of prokaryotes is duplicated before division. However, instead of entering into a complex cycle for cell division, prokaryotes simply elongate until they are double their original size. At this point, the cell pinches in and separates into two identical daughter cells in a process known as **binary fission** (Figure 9.1).

The Cell Cycle

> **BIG IDEA 3.A.2**
>
> *In eukaryotes, information is passed to the next generation via the cell cycle.*

Eukaryotic cell reproduction is a bit more complicated. The cell cycle functions as the daily planner of growth and development for the eukaryotic cell. It tells the cell when and in what order it is going to do things, and consists of all the necessary steps required for the reproduction of a cell. It begins after the creation of the cell and concludes with the formation of two daughter cells through cell division. It then begins again for the two daughter cells that have just been formed. There are four main stages to the cell cycle, and they occur in the following sequence: **phases G_1, S, G_2, and M** (Figure 9.2). Phases G_1 and G_2 are growth stages; S is the part of the cell cycle during which the DNA is duplicated; and the M phase stands for mitosis, the cell division phase.

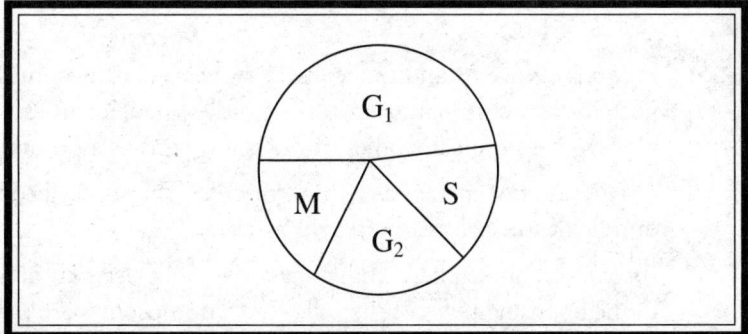

Figure 9.2   Pie chart showing the four main stages of the cell cycle.

Stages of the Cell Cycle

G₁ phase. During the first growth phase of the cell cycle, the cell prepares itself for the synthesis stage of the cycle, making sure that it has all the necessary raw materials for DNA synthesis.

S phase. The DNA is copied so that each daughter cell has a complete set of chromosomes at the conclusion of the cell cycle.

G₂ phase. During the second growth phase of the cycle, the cell prepares itself for mitosis (for producing body cells) and/or meiosis (for producing gametes), making sure that it has the raw materials necessary for the physical separation and formation of daughter cells.

M phase. Mitosis is the stage during which the cell separates into two new cells.

The first three stages of the cycle (G_1, S, and G_2) make up the portion of the cell cycle known as **interphase.** A cell spends approximately 90 percent of its cycle in this phase. The other 10 percent is spent in the final stage, mitosis.

The amount of time that a cell requires to complete a cycle varies by cell type. Some cells complete a full cycle in hours, while others can take days to finish. The rapidity with which cells replicate also varies. Skin cells are continually zipping along through the cell cycle, whereas nerve cells do not replicate—once they are damaged, they are lost for good. This is one reason why the death of nerve cells is such a problem—these cells cannot be repaired or regenerated through mitotic replication.

Mitosis

During mitosis, the fourth stage of the cell cycle, the cell actually takes the second copy of DNA made during the S phase and divides it equally between two cells. Single-cell eukaryotes undergo mitosis for the purpose of asexual reproduction. More complex multicellular eukaryotes use mitosis for other processes as well, such as growth and repair.

Mitosis consists of four major stages: prophase, metaphase, anaphase, and telophase. These stages are immediately followed by **cytokinesis**—the physical separation of the newly formed daughter cells. During interphase, chromosomes are invisible. The **chromatin**—the raw material that gives rise to the chromosomes—is long and thin during this phase. When the chromatin condenses to the point where the chromosome becomes visible through a microscope, the cell is said to have begun mitosis. The AP Biology exam is not going to ask you detailed questions about the different stages of mitosis; just have a *general* understanding of what happens during each step.

Mitosis

Prophase. Nucleus and nucleolus disappear; chromosomes appear as two identical, connected sister chromatids; mitotic spindle (made of microtubules) begins to form; centrioles move to opposite poles of the cell (plant cells do not have centrioles).

Metaphase. For metaphase, think middle. The sister chromatids line up along the middle of the cell, ready to split apart.

Anaphase. For anaphase, think apart. The split sister chromatids move via the microtubules to the opposing poles of the cell—the chromosomes are pulled to opposite poles by the spindle apparatus. After anaphase, each pole of the cell has a complete set of chromosomes.

Telophase. The nuclei for the newly split cells form; the nucleoli reappear, and the chromatin uncoils.

Cytokinesis. Newly formed daughter cells split apart. Animal cells are split by the formation of a cleavage furrow, plant cells by the formation of a cell plate.

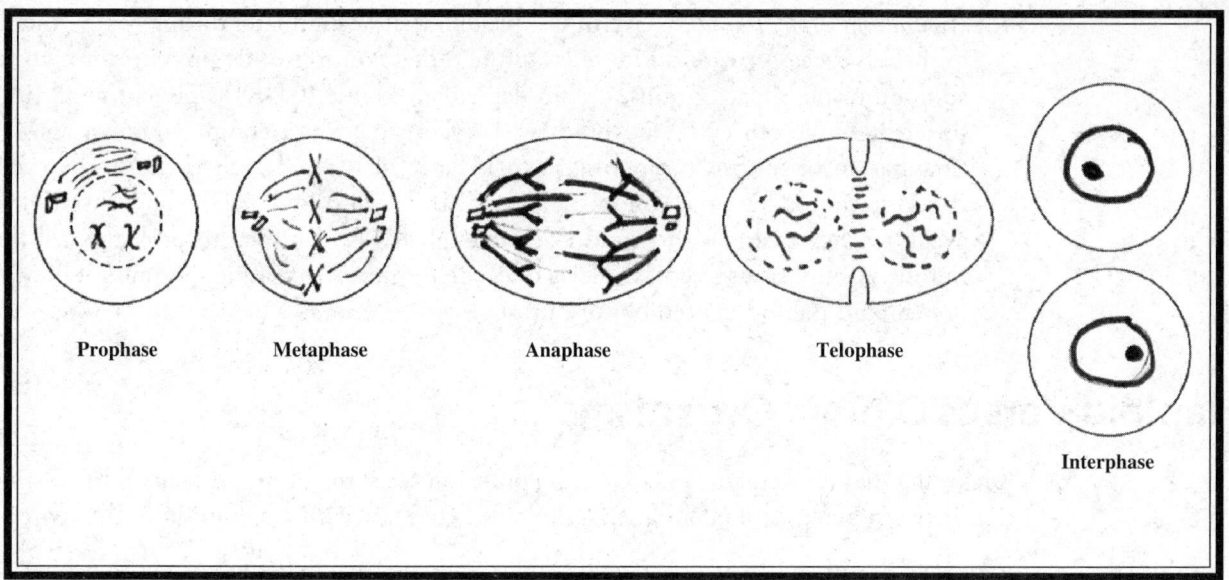

Figure 9.3 The stages of mitosis.

Figure 9.3 is a pictorial representation of the stages of mitosis.

Here are the definitions for words you may need to know:

Cell plate: plant cell structure, constructed in the Golgi apparatus, composed of vesicles that fuse together along the middle of the cell, completing the separation process.

Cleavage furrow: groove formed (in animal cells) between the two daughter cells that pinches together to complete the separation of the two cells after mitosis.

Cytokinesis: the actual splitting of the newly formed daughter cells that completes each trip around the cell cycle—some consider it part of mitosis; others regard it as the step immediately following mitosis.

Mitotic spindle: apparatus constructed from microtubules that assists the cell in the physical separation of the chromosomes during mitosis.

Control of Cell Division

Sam (12th grader):
"Control mechanisms are an important theme for this test. Be able to write about them."

Control of the cell cycle is important to normal cell growth. There are various ways in which the cell controls the process of cell division:

1. *Checkpoints.* There are checkpoints throughout the cell cycle where the cell verifies that there are enough nutrients and raw materials to progress to the next stage of the cycle. The G_1 checkpoint, for example, makes sure that the cell has enough raw materials to progress to and successfully complete the S phase.
2. *Density-dependent inhibition.* When a certain density of cells is reached, growth of the cells will slow or stop because there are not enough raw materials for the growth and survival of more cells. Cells that are halted by this inhibition enter a quiescent phase of the cell cycle known as G_0. Cancer cells can lose this inhibition and grow out of control.
3. *Growth factors.* Some cells will not divide if certain factors are absent. Growth factors, as their name indicates, assist in the growth of structures.

4. *Cyclins and protein kinases.* **Cyclin** is a protein that accumulates during G_1, S, and G_2 of the cell cycle. A **protein kinase** is a protein that controls other proteins through the addition of phosphate groups. Cyclin-dependent kinase (CDK) is present at all times throughout the cell cycle and binds with cyclin to form a complex known as MPF (maturation or mitosis promoting factor). Early in the cell cycle, because the cyclin concentration is low, the concentration of MPF is also low. As the concentration of cyclin reaches a certain threshold level, enough MPF is formed to push the cell into mitosis. As mitosis proceeds, the level of cyclin declines, decreasing the amount of MPF present and pulling the cell out of mitosis.

Haploid Versus Diploid Organisms

One thing that is often a major source of confusion for some of my students is the distinction between being haploid and being diploid. Let's start with a definition of the terms:

A *haploid* (*n*) organism is one that has only one copy of each type of chromosome. In humans, this refers to a cell that has one copy of each type of homologous chromosome.

A *diploid* (*2n*) organism is one that has two copies of each type of chromosome. In humans, this refers to the pairs of homologous chromosomes.

During the discussion of meiosis below, the terms *haploid* and *diploid* will be used often. Whenever we say "*2n*," or diploid, we are referring to an organism that contains two full *sets* of chromosomes. The letter *n* is used to represent the number of sets of chromosomes. So if an organism is said to have *4n* chromosomes, this means that it has four complete sets of chromosomes. Humans are diploid, and consist of *2n* chromosomes at all times except as gametes, when they are *n*. Humans have 23 *different* chromosomes; there are two full *sets* of these 23 chromosomes, one from each parent, for a total of 46 chromosomes. Human sex cells have 23 chromosomes each.

Meiosis

Now that we have armed you with the knowledge of the distinction between haploid and diploid, it is time to dive into the topic of meiosis, which occurs during the process of sexual reproduction. A cell destined to undergo meiosis goes through the cell cycle, synthesizing a second copy of DNA just like mitotic cells. But after G_2, the cell instead enters meiosis, which consists of *two* cell divisions, not one. The second cell division exists because the gametes to be formed from meiosis must be haploid. This is because they are going to join with another haploid gamete at conception to produce the diploid zygote. Meiosis is like a two-part made-for-TV miniseries. It has two acts: meiosis I and meiosis II. Each of these two acts is divided into four steps, reminiscent of mitosis: prophase, metaphase, anaphase, and telophase.

Homologous chromosomes resemble one another in shape, size, function, and the genetic information they contain. In humans, the 46 chromosomes are divided into 23 homologous pairs. One member of each pair comes from an individual's mother, and the other member comes from the father. Meiosis I is the separation of the homologous pairs into two separate cells. Meiosis II is the separation of the duplicated sister chromatids into chromosomes. As a result, a single meiotic cycle produces *four* cells from a single cell. The cells produced during meiosis in the human life cycle are called **gametes.**

Again, the AP Biology exam is not going to test your mastery of the minute details of the meiotic process. However, a general understanding of the various steps is important:

Meiosis I

Prophase I. Each chromosome pairs with its homolog. Crossover (synapsis) occurs in this phase. The nuclear envelope breaks apart, and spindle apparatus begins to form.

Metaphase I. Chromosomes align along the metaphase plate matched with their homologous partner. This stage ends with the separation of the homologous pairs.

Anaphase I. Separated homologous pairs move to opposite poles of the cell.

Telophase I. Nuclear membrane reforms; the process of cytoplasmic division begins.

Cytokinesis. After the daughter cells split, the two newly formed cells are haploid (*n*).

As discussed earlier, meiosis consists of a single synthesis period during which the DNA is replicated, followed by two acts of cell division. With the completion of the first cell division, meiosis I, the cells are haploid because they no longer consist of two full *sets* of chromosomes. Each cell has one of the duplicated chromatid pairs from each homologous pair. The cell then enters meiosis II.

Meiosis II

Prophase II. The nuclear envelope breaks apart, and spindle apparatus begins to form.

Metaphase II. Sister chromatids line up along the equator of the cell.

Anaphase II. Sister chromatids split apart and are called *chromosomes* as they are pulled to the poles.

Telophase II. The nuclei and the nucleoli for the newly split cells return.

Cytokinesis. Newly formed daughter cells physically divide.

Figure 9.4 is a pictorial representation of the stages of meiosis I and II.

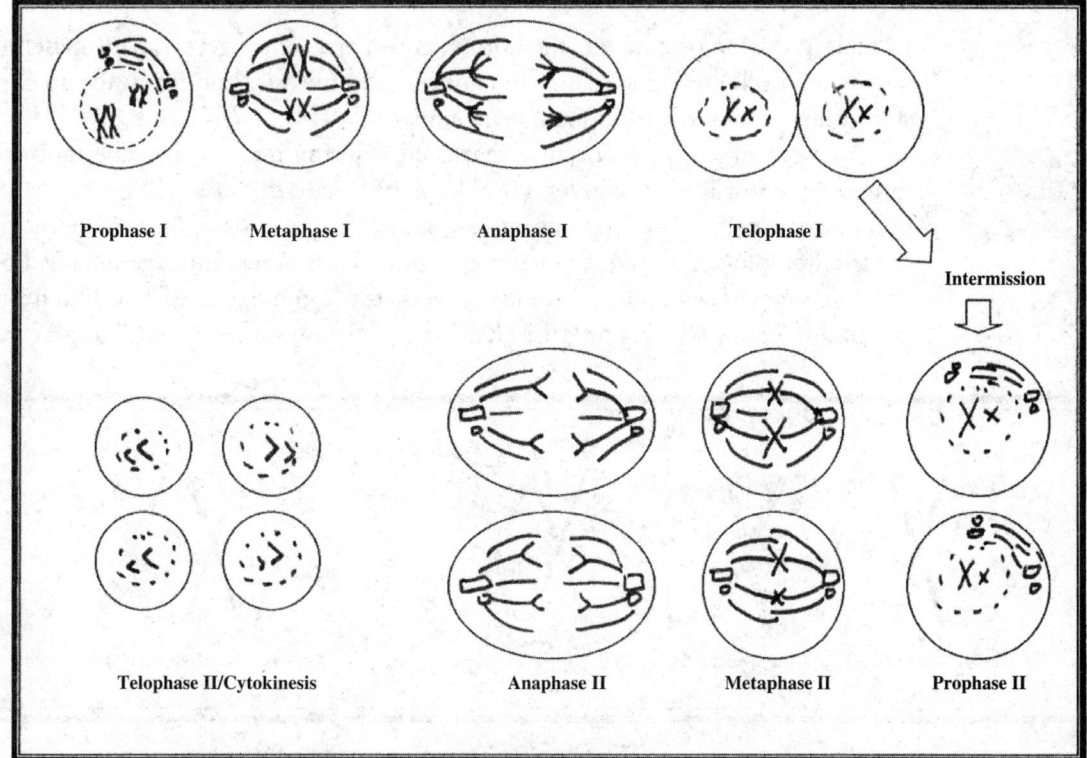

Figure 9.4   The stages of meiosis.

In humans, the process of gamete formation is different in women and men. In men, **spermatogenesis** leads to the production of four haploid sperm during each meiotic cycle. In women, the process is called **oogenesis.** It is a trickier process than spermatogenesis, and each complete meiotic cycle leads to the production of a single ovum, or egg. After meiosis I in females, one cell receives half the genetic information and the majority of the cytoplasm of the parent cell. The other cell, the **polar body,** simply receives half of the genetic information and is cast away. During meiosis II, the remaining cell divides a second time, and forms a polar body that is cast away, and a single haploid ovum that contains half the genetic information and nearly all the cytoplasm of the original parent cell. The excess cytoplasm is required for proper growth of the embryo after fertilization. Thus, the process of oogenesis produces two polar bodies and a single haploid ovum.

To review, why is it important to produce haploid gametes during meiosis? During fertilization, a sperm (n) will meet up with an egg (n), to produce a diploid zygote ($2n$). If either the sperm or the egg were diploid, then the offspring produced during sexual reproduction would contain more chromosomes than the parent organism. Meiosis circumvents this problem by producing gametes that are haploid and consist of one copy of each type of chromosome. During fertilization between two gametes, each copy will match up with another copy of each type of chromosome to form the diploid zygote.

Before moving on, there are a few important distinctions between meiosis and mitosis that should be emphasized.

	MITOSIS	**MEIOSIS**
Resulting daughter cells	Two diploid ($2n$) daughter cells	Four haploid (n) daughter cells
Crossover?	No	Yes—prophase I
Types of cells in which it occurs for humans	All cells of the body other than the cells of the gonads	Cells of gonads to produce gametes

In meiosis during prophase I, the homologous pairs join together. This matching of chromosomes into homologous pairs does not occur in mitosis. In mitosis, the 46 chromosomes simply align along the metaphase plate alone.

An event of major importance that occurs during meiosis that does not occur during mitosis is known as **crossover** (also known as *crossing over*) (Figure 9.5). When the homologous pairs match up during prophase I of meiosis, complementary pieces from the two homologous chromosomes wrap around each other and are exchanged between the chromosomes. Imagine that chromosome A is the homologous partner for chromosome B. When they pair up during prophase I, a piece of chromosome A containing a certain stretch

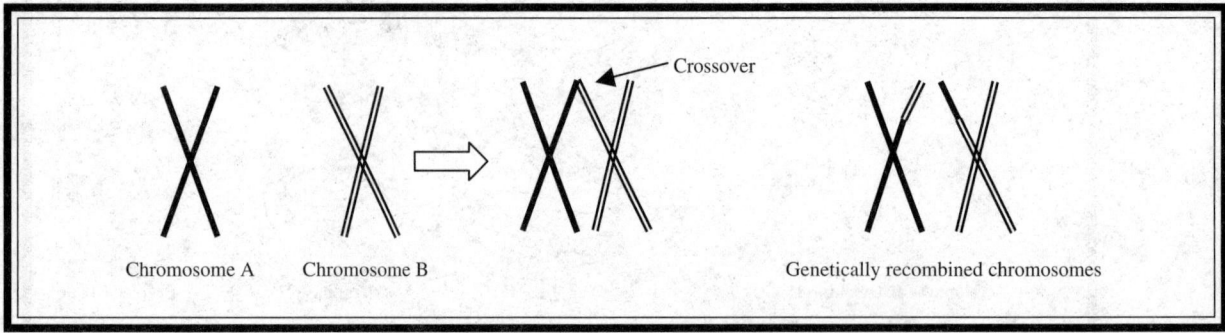

Figure 9.5 Crossover.

of genes can be exchanged for the piece of chromosome B containing the same genetic information. This is one of the mechanisms that allows offspring to differ from their parents. Remember that crossing over occurs between the homologous chromosome pairs, *not* the sister chromatids.

Life Cycles

The AP Biology exam characteristically will ask a question or two about the various types of life cycles for plants, animals, and fungi. A **life cycle** is the sequence of events that make up the reproductive cycle of an organism. Let's take a quick look at the three main life cycles.

The most complicated life cycle of the three is that of plants, also called the **alternation of generations** (Figure 9.6). It is referred to by this term because during the life cycle, plants sometimes exist as a diploid organism and at other times as a haploid organism. It alternates between the two forms. Similar to the other life cycles, two haploid gametes combine to form a diploid zygote, which divides *mitotically* to produce the diploid multicellular stage: the **sporophyte.** The sporophyte undergoes *meiosis* to produce a haploid spore. *Mitotic division* leads to the production of haploid multicellular organisms called **gametophytes.** The gametophyte undergoes *mitosis* to produce haploid gametes, which combine to form diploid zygotes . . . and around and around they go.

The human life cycle (Figure 9.7) is pretty straightforward. The only haploid cells present in this life cycle are the gametes formed during meiosis. The two haploid gametes combine during fertilization to produce a diploid zygote. Mitotic division then leads to formation of

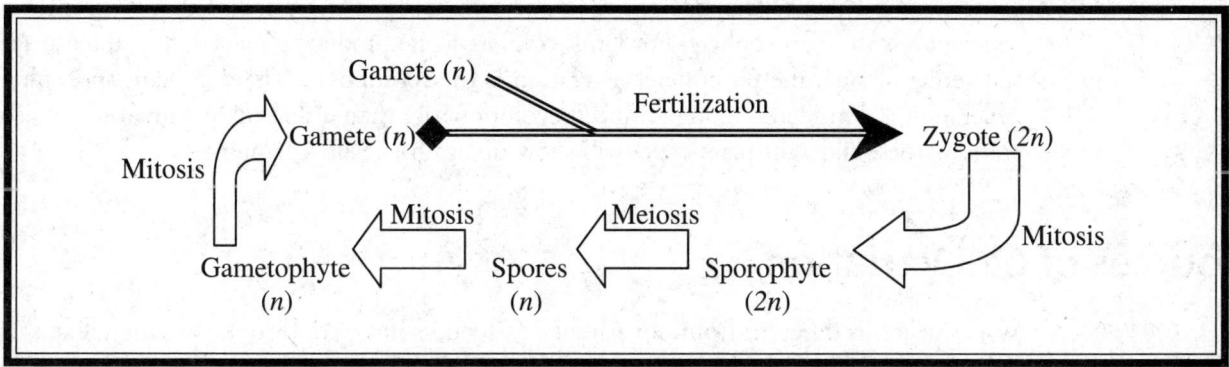

Figure 9.6   Plant life: alternation of generations.

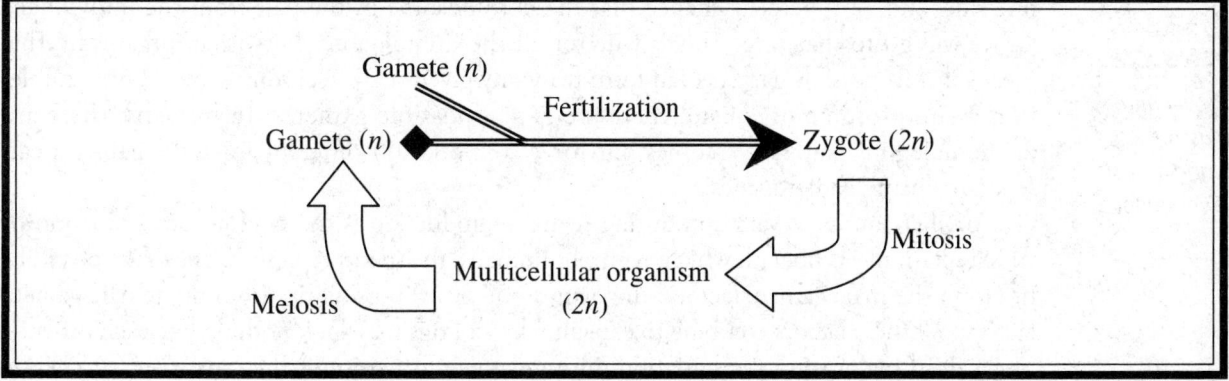

Figure 9.7   Human life cycle.

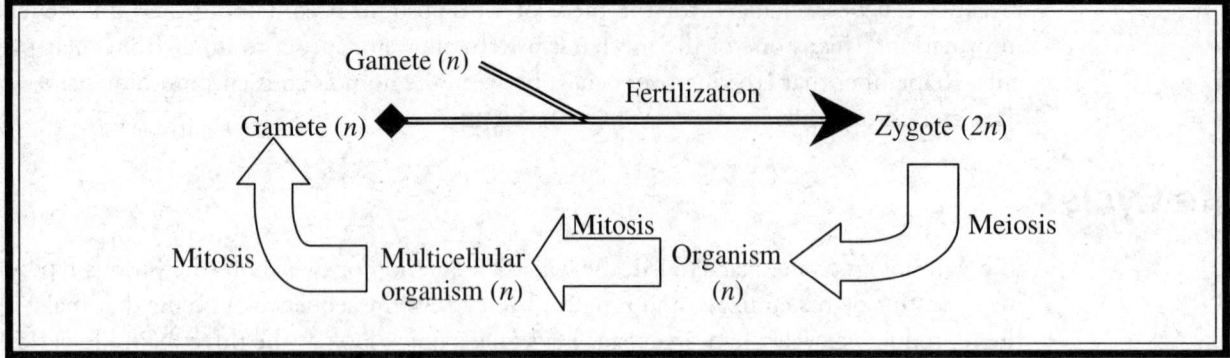

Figure 9.8   Fungus life cycle.

the diploid multicellular organism. Meiotic division later produces haploid gametes, which continue the cycle.

The life cycle of fungi (Figure 9.8) is different from that of humans. Fungi are haploid organisms, with the zygote being the only diploid form. Like humans, the gametes for fungi are haploid (*n*), and fertilization yields a diploid zygote. But in this life cycle, instead of dividing by mitosis, the zygote divides by meiosis to form a haploid organism. Another difference in this life cycle is that the gametes are formed by *mitosis,* not meiosis—the organism is *already* haploid, before forming the gametes.

Here is some trivia about life cycles that might come in handy on the exam. The only diploid stage for a fungus is the zygote. The only haploid stage for a human is the gamete. Of the plant life cycles, the moss (bryophyte) is an exception in that its prominent generation is the gametophyte. For ferns, conifers (cone-producing plants), and angiosperms (flowering plants), the prominent generation is the sporophyte. The dominant sporophyte generation is considered more advanced evolutionarily than a dominant gametophyte generation. These different plant types will show up again later in Chapter 14.

Sources of Cell Variation

NYC teacher: "Knowing the sources of variation is important."

BIG IDEA 3.C.2

Crossing over and random assortment during meiosis increase variation.

What makes us different from our parents? Why do some people look amazingly like their parents while others do not? The process of cell division provides ample opportunity for variation. Remember that during meiosis, homologous chromosome pairs align together along the metaphase plate. This alignment is a completely random process, and there is a 50 percent chance that the chromosome in the pair from the individual's mother will go to one side, and a 50 percent chance that the chromosome in the pair from the individual's father will go to that side. This is true for all the homologous pairs in an organism. This means that 2^n possible gametes can form from any given set of *n* chromosomes. For example, in a 3-chromosome organism, there are $2^3 = 8$ possible gametes. In humans, there are 23 homologous pairs. This comes out to 2^{23} (8,388,608) different ways the gametes can separate during gametogenesis.

Another source of variation during sexual reproduction is the random determination of which sperm meets up with which ovum. In humans, the sperm represents one of 2^{23} possibilities from the male gamete factory; the ovum, one of 2^{23} possibilities from the female gamete factory. All these factors combine to explain why siblings may look nothing like each other.

A third major source of variation during gamete formation is the **crossover** (or *crossing over*) that occurs during prophase I of meiosis. It is very important for you to remember that this process happens *only* during that stage of cell division. It does not occur in mitosis.

〉 Review Questions

1. Which of the following plant types has the gametophyte as its prominent generation?

   A. Angiosperms
   B. Bryophytes
   C. Conifers
   D. Gymnosperms

2. During which phase of the cell cycle does crossing over occur?

   A. Metaphase of mitosis
   B. Metaphase I of meiosis
   C. Prophase I of meiosis
   D. Prophase of mitosis

For questions 3–6, please use the following answer choices:

   A. Prophase
   B. Metaphase
   C. Anaphase
   D. Cytokinesis

3. During this phase, the split sister chromatids, now considered to be chromosomes, are moved to the opposite poles of the cell.

4. During this phase the nucleus deteriorates, and the mitotic spindle begins to form.

5. During this phase, the two daughter cells are actually split apart.

6. During this phase, the sister chromatids line up along the equator of the cell, preparing to split.

7. Which of the following organisms is diploid ($2n$) only as a zygote and is haploid for every other part of its life cycle?

   A. Humans
   B. Bryophytes
   C. Fungi
   D. Bacteria

8. Which of the following statements is true about a human meiotic cell after it has completed meiosis I?

   A. It is diploid ($2n$).
   B. It is haploid (n).
   C. It has divided into four daughter cells.
   D. It proceeds directly to meiosis II without an intervening intermission.

9. Which of the following is *not* true about cyclin-dependent kinase (CDK)?

   A. It is present only during the M phase of the cell cycle.
   B. When enough of it is combined with cyclin, the MPF (mitosis promoting factor) formed initiates mitosis.
   C. It is a protein that controls other proteins using phosphate groups.
   D. It is present at all times during the cell cycle.

10. Which of the following statements about meiosis and/or mitosis is incorrect?

   A. Mitosis results in two diploid daughter cells.
   B. Meiosis in humans occurs only in gonad cells.
   C. Homologous chromosomes line up along the metaphase plate during mitosis.
   D. Crossover occurs during prophase I of meiosis.

❯ Answers and Explanations

1. **B**—Bryophytes, or mosses, are the plant type that has the gametophyte (haploid) as its dominant generation. The others in this question have the sporophyte (diploid) as their dominant generation.

2. **C**—Crossover occurs in humans only in prophase I. Prophase I is a major source of variation in the production of offspring.

3. **C**

4. **A**

5. **D**

6. **B**

7. **C**—The life cycle for fungi is different from that of humans. Fungi exist as haploid organisms, and the only time they exist in diploid form is as a zygote. Like humans, the gametes for fungi are haploid (n) and combine to form a diploid zygote. Unlike in humans, the fungus zygote divides by meiosis to form a haploid organism.

8. **B**—Human cells start with 46 chromosomes arranged in 23 pairs of homologous chromosomes. At this time they are $2n$ because they have two copies of each chromosome. After the S phase of the cell cycle, the DNA has been doubled in preparation for cell division. The first stage of meiosis pulls apart the homologous pairs of chromosomes. This means that after meiosis I, the cells are n, or haploid—they no longer consist of *two* full sets of chromosomes.

9. **A**—CDK is present at all times during the cell cycle. It combines with a protein called *cyclin*, which accumulates during interphase of the cell cycle, to form MPF. When enough MPF is formed, the cell is pushed to begin mitosis. As mitosis continues, cyclin is degraded, and when the concentration of MPF drops below a level sufficient to maintain mitotic division, mitosis grinds to a halt until the threshold is reached again next time around the cycle.

10. **C**—Answer choices A, B, and D, are all correct. C is incorrect because homologous pairs of chromosomes pair together only during meiosis. During mitosis, the sister chromatid pairs align along the metaphase plate, separate from the homologous counterpart.

❯ Rapid Review

You should be familiar with the following terms:

Binary fission: prokaryotic cell division; double the DNA, double the size, then split apart.

Cell cycle: $G_1 \rightarrow S \rightarrow G_2 \rightarrow M$ should be familiar with the following growth$_1$ → synthesis → growth$_2$ → mitosis → etc.

Interphase: $G_1 + S + G_2 = 90$ percent of the cell cycle.

STAGE	MITOSIS	MEIOSIS
Prophase	Nucleus, nucleolus disappear; mitotic spindle forms	—
Metaphase	Sister chromatids line up at middle	—
Anaphase	Sister chromatids are split apart	—
Telophase	Nuclei of new cells reform; chromatin uncoils	—
Prophase I	—	Each chromosome pairs with its homolog; there is crossover

STAGE	MITOSIS	MEIOSIS
Metaphase I	—	Chromosome pairs align along middle of cell, ready to split apart
Anaphase I	—	Homologous chromosomes split apart
Telophase I	—	Nuclear membrane reforms; daughter cells are now haploid (n)
Prophase II	—	Nucleus disappears, spindle apparatus forms
Metaphase II	—	Sister chromatids line up at middle
Anaphase II	—	Sister chromatids are split apart
Telophase II	—	Nuclei of new cells reform; chromatin uncoils

Cytokinesis: physical separation of newly formed daughter cells of cell division.

Cell division control mechanisms:

1. *Growth factors*: factors that when present, promote growth, and when absent, impede growth.
2. *Checkpoints*: a cell stops growing to make sure it has the nutrients and raw materials to proceed.
3. *Density-dependent inhibition*: cell stops growing when certain density is reached—runs out of food!!!
4. *Cyclins and protein kinases*: cyclin combines with CDK to form a structure known as MPF that pushes cell into mitosis when enough is present.

Haploid (n): one copy of each chromosome.

Diploid ($2n$): two copies of each chromosome.

Homologous chromosomes: chromosomes that are similar in shape, size, and function.

Spermatogenesis: the process of male gamete formation (four sperm from one cell).

Oogenesis: the process of female gamete formation (one ovum from each cell).

Life cycles: Sequence of events that make up the reproductive cycle of an organism.

- *Human*: zygote ($2n$) → multicellular organism ($2n$) → gametes (n) → zygote ($2n$)
- *Fungi*: zygote ($2n$) → multicellular organism (n) → gametes (n) → zygote ($2n$)
- *Plants*: zygote ($2n$) → sporophyte ($2n$) → spores (n) → gametophyte (n) → gametes (n) → zygote ($2n$)

Sources of variation: crossover, 2^n possible gametes that can be formed, random pairing of gametes.

CHAPTER 10

Heredity

IN THIS CHAPTER

Summary: This chapter examines Mendel's fundamental laws (law of segregation, law of independent assortment, and law of dominance) as well as some classic exceptions to these laws (intermediate inheritance, multiple alleles, polygenic traits, epistasis, and pleiotropy). This chapter also covers linkage (sex linkage, gene linkage, and linkage maps), and chromosomal errors such as nondisjunction, deletions, duplications, translocations, and inversion.

Key Ideas

✪ Law of segregation: the two alleles for a trait separate during the formation of gametes—one to each gamete.

✪ Law of independent assortment: inheritance of one trait does not interfere with the inheritance of another trait.

✪ Law of dominance: if two opposite pure-breeding varieties are crossed (BB × bb), all offspring resemble the BB parent.

✪ Linked genes that lie along the same chromosome do not follow the law of independent assortment.

✪ Autosomal recessive disorders: Tay-Sachs, cystic fibrosis, sickle cell anemia, phenylketonuria.

✪ Autosomal dominant disorders: Huntington, achondroplasia.

✪ Nondisjunction errors: Down, Klinefelter, Turner syndromes.

Introduction

How many times have you heard someone say as they look at a baby, "Awwww, he looks like his daddy" or "She has her mother's eyes"? What exactly is it that causes an infant to look like his or her parents? This question is the basis of the study of heredity—the study of the passing of traits from generation to generation. Its basic premise is that offspring are more like their parents than less closely related individuals.

In this chapter, we begin by discussing some terms that will prove important to your study of heredity. This is followed by an examination of Mendel's *law of segregation* and the *law of independent assortment,* including how they were discovered and how they can be applied. We will examine the *law of dominance,* which arose from Mendel's work, and we will also discuss some exceptions to Mendel's fundamental laws such as intermediate inheritance (incomplete dominance and codominance), multiple alleles, polygenic traits, epistasis, and pleiotropy.

In the next section, we will examine Thomas Morgan's work on fruit flies, which paved the way for the discovery of linked genes, genetic recombination, and sex-linked inheritance. This discussion concludes with a look at gene linkage and linkage maps.

Finally, since chromosomes carry the vital genes necessary for proper development and passage of hereditary material from one generation to the next, it is important to discuss the types of chromosomal errors that can occur during reproduction. This includes the various forms of nondisjunction, or the improper separation of chromosomes during meiosis (which leads to an abnormal number of chromosomes in offspring). The chapter concludes with an examination of the other major types of chromosomal errors: deletions, duplications, translocations, and inversions.

Terms Important in Studying Heredity

The following is a list of terms that will help in your understanding of heredity:

Allele: a variant of a gene for a particular character. For example, two alleles for fur color could be B (dominant) and b (recessive).

F_1: the first generation of offspring, or the first "filial" generation in a genetic cross.

F_2: the second generation of offspring, or the second "filial" generation in a genetic cross.

Genotype: an organism's genetic makeup for a given trait. A simple example of this could involve fur color where B represents the allele for brown and b represents the allele for black. The possible genotypes include homozygous brown (BB), heterozygous brown (Bb), and homozygous black (bb).

Heterozygous (*hybrid*): an individual is heterozygous (or a hybrid) for a gene if the two alleles are different (Bb).

Homozygous (*pure*): an individual is homozygous for a gene if both of the given alleles are the same (BB or bb).

Karyotype: a chart that organizes chromosomes in relation to number, size, and type.

Nondisjunction: the improper separation of chromosomes during meiosis, which leads to an abnormal number of chromosomes in offspring. A few classic examples of nondisjunction-related syndromes are Down, Turner, and Klinefelter syndromes.

P_1: the parent generation in a genetic cross.

Phenotype: the physical expression of the trait associated with a particular genotype. Some examples of the phenotypes for Mendel's peas were round or wrinkled, green or yellow, purple flower or white flower.

Mendel and His Peas

The person whose name is most often associated with heredity is Gregor Mendel. Mendel spent many years working with peas. It was a very strange hobby, indeed, but it proved quite useful to the world of science. He mated peas to produce offspring and recorded the phenotype results in order to determine how certain characters are inherited. A **character** is a genetically inherited characteristic that differs from person to person.

Before he began his work in the 1850s, the accepted theory of inheritance was the **"blending" hypothesis,** which stated that the genes contributed by two parents mix as colors do. For example, a blue flower mixed with a yellow flower would produce a green flower. The exact genetic makeup of each parent could never be recovered; the genes would be as inseparable as the blended colors. Mendel used plant experiments to test this hypothesis and developed his two fundamental theories: the law of segregation and the law of independent assortment.

When Mendel was observing a single character during a mating, he was doing something called a **monohybrid cross**—a cross that involves a single character in which both parents are heterozygous (Bb × Bb). A monohybrid cross between heterozygous gametes gives a 3:1 phenotype ratio in the offspring (Figure 10.1). As you can see in Figure 10.1, an offspring is three times more likely to express the dominant B trait than the recessive b trait.

	B	b
B	BB	Bb
b	Bb	bb

Figure 10.1   Monohybrid cross.

Mendel also experimented with multiple characters simultaneously. The crossing of two different hybrid characters is termed a **dihybrid cross** (BbRr × BbRr). A dihybrid cross between heterozygous gametes gives a 9:3:3:1 phenotype ratio in the offspring (Figure 10.2).

	BR	Br	bR	br
BR	BBRR	BBRr	BbRR	BbRr
Br	BBRr	BBrr	BbRr	Bbrr
bR	BbRR	BbRr	bbRR	bbRr
br	BbRr	Bbrr	bbRr	bbrr

Figure 10.2 Dihybrid cross.

From his experiments, Mendel developed two major hereditary laws: the law of segregation and the law of independent assortment.

The law of segregation. Every organism carries pairs of factors, called *alleles,* for each trait, and the members of the pair segregate (separate) during the formation of gametes. For example, if an individual is Bb for eye color, during gamete formation, one gamete would receive a B, and the other made from that cell would receive a b.

The law of independent assortment. Members of each pair of factors are distributed independently when the gametes are formed. Quite simply, inheritance of one trait or characteristic does not interfere with inheritance of another trait. For example, if an individual is BbRr for two genes, gametes formed during meiosis could contain BR, Br, bR, or br. The B and b alleles assort *independently* of the R and r alleles.

The law of dominance. Also based on Mendel's work, this states that when two opposite pure-breeding varieties (homozygous dominant vs. homozygous recessive) of an organism are crossed, all the offspring resemble one parent. This is referred to as the *dominant* trait. The variety that is hidden is referred to as the *recessive* trait.

It is time for you to answer a question for us (of course, we have no way of knowing whether or how you will answer this question): Can the phenotype of an organism be determined from simple observation? Yes—just look at the organism and determine whether it is tall or short, has blue eyes or brown eyes, and so on. However, the genotype of an organism *cannot* always be determined from simple observation. In the case of a recessive trait, the genotype is known. If a person has blue eyes (recessive to brown), the genotype is bb. But if that person has brown eyes, you cannot be sure if the genotype is Bb or BB—the individual can be either homozygous dominant or heterozygous dominant. To determine the exact genotype, you must run an experiment called a **test cross.** Geneticists breed the organism whose genotype is unknown with an organism that is homozygous recessive for the trait. This results in offspring with observable phenotypes. If the unknown genotype is heterozygous, probability indicates one-half of the offspring *should* express the recessive phenotype. If the unknown genotype is homozygous dominant, *all* the organism's offspring *should* express the dominant trait. Of course, such experiments are not done on humans.

Remember me!

Mendel discovered many statistical laws of heredity. He learned that a monohybrid cross such as Yy × Yy will result in a phenotype ratio of 3:1 in favor of the dominant trait. He learned that a dihybrid cross, such as YyRr × YyRr, will result in a phenotype ratio of 9:3:3:1 (9 RY, 3 rY, 3 Ry, 1 ry). These two ratios, when they appear in genetic analysis problems, imply mono- and dihybrid crosses.

Intermediate Inheritance

Marcy (college freshman): "Understanding this concept is worth 2 points on the exam."

The inheritance of traits is not always as simple as Mendel's pea experiments seem to indicate. Traits are not always dominant or recessive, and phenotype ratios are not always 9:3:3:1 or 3:1. Mendel's experiments did not account for something called **intermediate inheritance,** in which an individual heterozygous for a trait (Yy) shows characteristics not exactly like *either* parent. The phenotype is a "mixture" of both of the parents' genetic input. There are two major types of intermediate inheritance:

1. Incomplete dominance or "blending inheritance"
2. Codominance

Incomplete Dominance ("Blending Inheritance")

In **incomplete dominance** ("blending inheritance") the heterozygous genotype produces an "intermediate" phenotype rather than the dominant phenotype; neither allele dominates the other. A classic example of incomplete dominance is flower color in snapdragons—crossing a snapdragon plant that has red flowers with one that has white flowers yields offspring with pink flowers.

One genetic condition in humans that exhibits incomplete dominance is **hypercholesterolemia**—a recessive disorder (hh) that causes cholesterol levels to be many times higher than normal and can lead to heart attacks in children as young as two years old. Those who are HH tend to have normal cholesterol levels, and those who are Hh have cholesterol levels somewhere in between the two extremes. As with many conditions, the environment plays a major role in how genetic conditions express themselves. Thus, people who are HH do not necessarily have normal cholesterol levels if, for example, they have poor diet or exercise habits.

One important side note—try not to confuse the terms blending "hypothesis" and blending "inheritance." The latter is another name for incomplete dominance, whereas the former was the theory on heredity before Mendel worked his magic. The blending "hypothesis" says that the HH and hh extremes can never be retrieved. In reality, and according to blending inheritance, if you were to cross two Hh individuals, the offspring could still be HH or hh, which the blending "hypothesis" says cannot happen once the blending has occurred.

Codominance

Codominance is the situation in which both alleles express themselves fully in a heterozygous organism. A good example of codominance involves the human blood groups: M, N, and MN. Individuals with group M blood have the M glycoprotein on the surface of the blood cell; individuals with group N blood have N glycoproteins on the blood cell; and those with group MN blood have *both*. This is not incomplete dominance because both alleles are fully expressed in the phenotype—they are codominant.

Other Forms of Inheritance

Polygenic Traits

Another interesting form of inheritance involves **polygenic traits,** or traits that are affected by more than one gene. Eye color is an example of a polygenic trait. The *tone* (color), *amount* (blue eyes have less than brown eyes), and *position* (how evenly distributed the pigment is) of pigment *all* play a role in determining eye color. Each of these characteristics is determined by separate genes. Another example of this phenomenon is skin color, which is determined by at least three different genes working together to produce a wide range of possible skin tones.

Multiple Alleles

Many monogenic traits (traits expressed via a single gene) correspond to two alleles, one dominant and one recessive. Other traits, however, involve more than two alleles. A classic example of such a trait is the human blood type. On the most simplistic level, there are four major blood types: A, B, AB, and O. They are named based on the presence or absence of certain antigens on the surface of the red blood cells. The gene for blood type has three possible alleles (multiple alleles): I^A, which causes antigens A to be produced on the surface of the red blood cell; I^B, which causes antigens B to be produced; and i, which causes *no* antigens to be produced. The following are the possible genotypes for human blood type: I^Ai (type A), $I^A I^A$ (type A), I^Bi (type B), $I^B I^B$ (type B), $I^A I^B$ (type AB), ii (type O). Type AB blood displays the *codominance* of blood type. As we saw in MN blood groups, both the A and the B alleles succeed in their mission—their antigens appear on the surface of the red blood cell (Figure 10.3). Analyzing blood type can be really complex because human blood types involve not only multiple alleles (I^A, I^B, and i) and codominance (type AB blood), but classic dominance of I^A and I^B over i as well.

Blood Type	Antigens on surface of RBC	Antibodies produced by the body	Can be transfused with which types of blood?	Can be donated to individuals of which type?
A	Antigen A	Anti B	Type A, O	Type A, AB
B	Antigen B	Anti A	Type B, O	Type B, AB
AB	Antigens A & B	None	All Types	Type AB
O	No Antigens	Anti A and Anti B	Only O	All Types

Figure 10.3 Several human blood type characteristics.

If you have ever watched an episode of *ER* on television, you have heard one of the doctors frantically scream, "We need to type her and bring some O blood down here *stat*!" Why is it important for the physician to determine what type of blood the patient has, and why is it okay to give the patient O blood in the meantime? People with type A blood produce anti-B antibodies because the B antigen that is present on type B and type AB blood is a foreign molecule to someone with type A blood. This is simply the body's defense mechanism doing its job. Following the same logic, those with type B blood make anti-A antibodies, and those with type O blood make anti-A *and* anti-B antibodies. People who are type AB make none, and are therefore the universal acceptor of blood. It is important to find out what kind of blood a person has because if you give type B blood to a person with type A blood, the recipient will have an immune response to the transfused blood. Why is O blood given while they wait to see what blood type the patient is? This is because type O blood has neither antigen on the surface of red blood cells. People with type O blood are universal donors because few people will have an adverse reaction to type O blood. Immune reactions are discussed in further detail in Chapter 15, Human Physiology.

Epistasis

In **epistasis** the expression of one gene affects the expression of another gene. A classic example of epistasis involves the coat color of mice. Black is dominant over brown, and brown fur has the genotype bb. There is also another gene locus independent of the coat color gene that controls the deposition of pigment in the fur. If a mouse has a dominant allele of this pigment gene (Cc or CC), it leads to pigment deposition and the coloring of the fur according to the coat color gene's instructions. If a mouse is double recessive for this trait (cc), it will have white fur no matter what the coat color gene wants because it will not put any pigment into the fur. It is almost as if the pigment gene were overruling the coat color gene. If you mate two black mice that are BbCc, the ratio of phenotypes in the offspring would not be the 9:3:3:1 ratio that Mendel predicts, but rather 9:4:3 black:white:brown because the epistatic gene alters the phenotype.

Pleiotropy

In **pleiotropy** a single gene has multiple effects on an organism. A good example of pleiotropy is the mutation that causes sickle cell anemia. This single gene mutation "sickles" the blood cells, leading to systemic symptoms such as heart, lung, and kidney damage; muscle pain; weakness; and generalized fatigue. The problems do not stop there; these symptoms can lead to disastrous side effects such as kidney failure. The mutation of a single gene wreaks havoc on the system as a whole.

Sex Determination and Sex Linkage

Mendel was not the only one to make progress in the field of heredity. In the early 1900s, Thomas Morgan made key discoveries regarding sex linkage and linked genes.

In human cells, all chromosomes occur in structurally identical pairs except for two very important ones: the sex chromosomes, X and Y. Women have two structurally identical X chromosomes. Men have one X and one Y.

Sex-Linked Traits

Morgan experimented with a quick-breeding fruit fly species. The fruit flies had four pairs of chromosomes: three autosomal pairs and one sex chromosome pair. An **autosomal chromosome** is one that is not directly involved in determining gender. In fruit flies, the more common phenotype for a trait is called the **wild-type phenotype** (e.g., red eyes). Traits that are different from the normal are called **mutant phenotypes** (e.g., white eyes). Morgan crossed a white-eyed male with a red-eyed female, and all the F_1 offspring had red eyes. When he bred the F_1 together, he obtained Mendel's 3:1 ratio. But, there was a slight difference from what Mendel's theories would predict—the white trait was restricted to the males. Morgan's conclusion was that the gene for eye color is on the X chromosome. This means that the poor male flies get only a single copy, and if it is abnormal, they are abnormal. But, the lucky ladies have two copies and are normal even if one copy is not.

It is this male–female sex chromosomes difference that allows for sex-linked conditions. If a gene for a recessive disease is present on the X chromosome, then a female must have two defective versions of the gene to show the disease while a male needs only one. This is so because males have no corresponding gene on the Y chromosome to help counter the negative effect of a recessive allele on the X chromosome. Thus, more males than females show recessive X-linked phenotypes. In a pedigree (see Figure 10.6 later in this chapter), a pattern of sex-linked disease will show the sons of carrier mothers with the disease.

The father plays no part in the passage of an X-linked gene to the male children of a couple. Fathers pass X-linked alleles to their daughters, but not to their sons. Do you understand why this is so? The father does not give an X chromosome to the male offspring because he is the one who provides the Y chromosome that makes his son a male. A mother can pass a sex-linked allele to both her daughters *and* sons because she can pass only X chromosomes to her offspring.

Three common sex-linked disorders are Duchenne's muscular dystrophy, hemophilia, and red-green colorblindness. **Duchenne's muscular dystrophy** is a sex-linked disorder that is caused by the absence of an essential muscle protein. Its symptoms include a progressive loss of muscle strength and coordination. **Hemophilia** is caused by the absence of a protein vital to the clotting process. Individuals with this condition have difficulty clotting blood after even the smallest of wounds. Those most severely affected by the disease can bleed to death after the tiniest of injuries. Females with this condition rarely survive. People afflicted with **red-green colorblindness** are unable to distinguish between red and green colors. This condition is found primarily in males.

X Inactivation

Here is an important question for you to ponder while preparing for this exam: "Are all the cells in a female identical?"

The answer to this question is "No." Females undergo a process called **X inactivation.** During the development of a female embryo, one of the two X chromosomes in each cell

---

BIG IDEA 3.A.4

The inheritance of sex-linked traits cannot be explained by simple Mendelian genetics.

Emily (12th grader): "Be able to categorize diseases for this exam!"

remains coiled as a **Barr body** whose genes are not expressed. A cell expresses the alleles only of the active X chromosome. X inactivation occurs separately in each cell and involves random inactivation of one of a female's X chromosomes. But not all cells inactivate the same X. As a result, different cells will have different active X chromosomes.

Why don't females always express X-linked diseases when this X inactivation occurs? Sometimes they do, but usually they have enough cells with a "good" copy of the allele to compensate for the presence of the recessive allele.

One last sex-related inheritance pattern that needs to be mentioned is **holandric traits,** which are traits inherited via the Y chromosome. An example of a holandric trait in humans is ear hair distribution.

Linkage and Gene Mapping

Each chromosome has hundreds of genes that tend to be inherited together because the chromosome is passed along as a unit. These are called **linked genes.** Linked genes lie on the same chromosome and do not follow Mendel's law of independent assortment.

Morgan performed an experiment in which he looked at body color and wing size on his beloved fruit flies. The dominant alleles were G (gray) and V (normal wings); the recessive alleles were g (black) and v (vestigial wings). GgVv females were crossed with ggvv males. Mendel's law of independent assortment predicts offspring of four different phenotypes in a 1:1:1:1 ratio. But that is not what Morgan found. Because the genes are linked, the gray/normal flies produce only GV or gv gametes. Thus, Morgan expected the ratio of offspring to be 1:1, half GgVv and half ggvv. Morgan found that there were more wild-type and double-mutant flies than independent assortment would predict, but surprisingly, some Gv and gV were also produced.

How did those other combinations result from the cross if the genes are linked? **Crossover** (also known as *crossing over*), a form of genetic recombination that occurs during prophase I of meiosis, led to their production. The less often this recombination occurs, the closer the genes must be on the chromosome. The farther apart two genes are on a chromosome, the more often crossover will occur. Recombination frequency can be used to determine how close two genes are on a chromosome through the creation of linkage maps, which we will look at next.

Linkage Maps

A **linkage map** is a genetic map put together using crossover frequencies. Another unit of measurement, the **map unit** (also known as *centigram*), is used to geographically relate the genes on the basis of these frequencies. One map unit is equal to a 1 percent crossover frequency. A linkage map does not provide the *exact* location of genes; it gives only the relative location. Imagine that you want to determine the relative locations of four genes: A, B, C, and D. You know that A crosses over with C 20 percent of the time, B crosses over with C 15 percent of the time, A crosses over with D 10 percent of the time, and D crosses over with B 5 percent of the time. From this information you can determine the sequence (Figure 10.4). Gene A must be 20 units from gene C. Gene B must be 15 units from C, but B could be 5 or 35 units from A. But, because you also know that A is 10 units from D and that D is 5 units from B, you can determine that B must be 5 units from A as well, if A is also to be 10 units from D. This gives you the sequence of genes as ABDC.

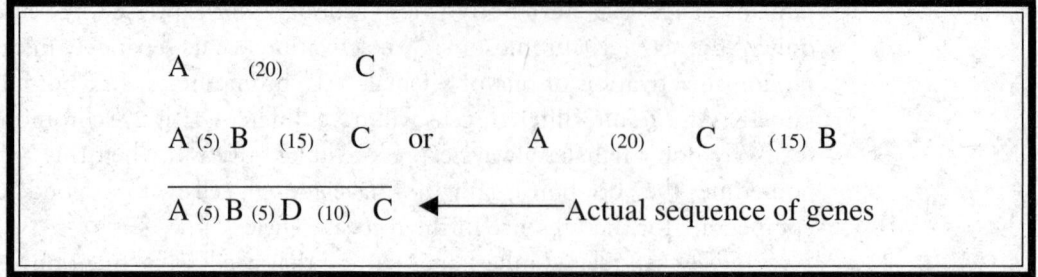

Figure 10.4   A genetic linkage map.

Heads or Tails?

Probability is a concept important to a full understanding of heredity and inheritance. What is the probability that a flipped coin will come up heads? You can answer that easily: ½. What is the probability that two coins flipped simultaneously will *both* be heads? This is a little harder—it is ½ × ½ = ¼. Take a look at Figure 10.5. The first time you toss the coin, there is a probability of ½ that it will land heads and ½ that it will land tails. When you toss it again, it again has a probability of ½ that it will land heads, and ½ that it will land tails. So in the figure, just concentrate on the ½ of the tosses that land heads. Of those, ½ of them will land heads the second time—or ½ of ½. Multiplied together, this results in the ¼ chance of getting heads twice with two coin tosses. This example illustrates the **law of multiplication** with probabilities. This law states that to determine the probability that two random events will occur in succession, you simply multiply the probability of the first event by the probability of the second event.

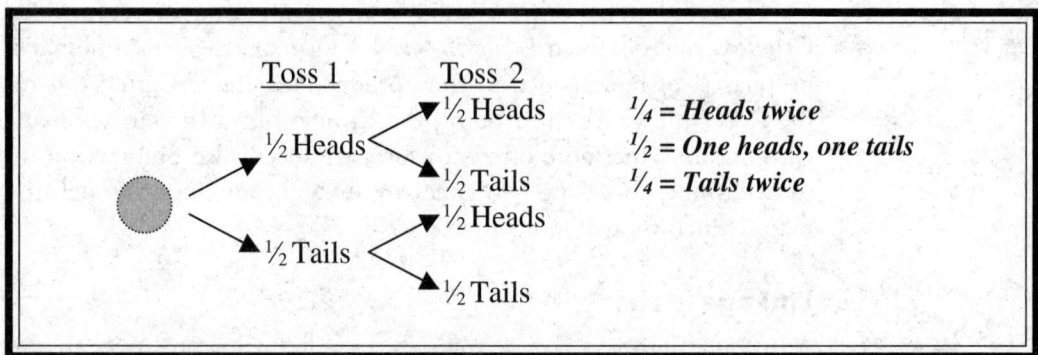

Figure 10.5   Probability in the law of multiplication.

This is the same thought process that we follow to understand Mendel's law of segregation. If you are Aa for a trait, what is your chance or passing on the A? That's right—½. If you are AaBb, what is the chance you pass on both A and B? Clever you are—you multiply ½ × ½ to get ½.

Pedigrees

Pedigrees are family trees used to describe the genetic relationships within a family. Comprehension of the probability concept is important for a full understanding of pedigree analysis. Squares represent males, and circles are used for females. A horizontal line from

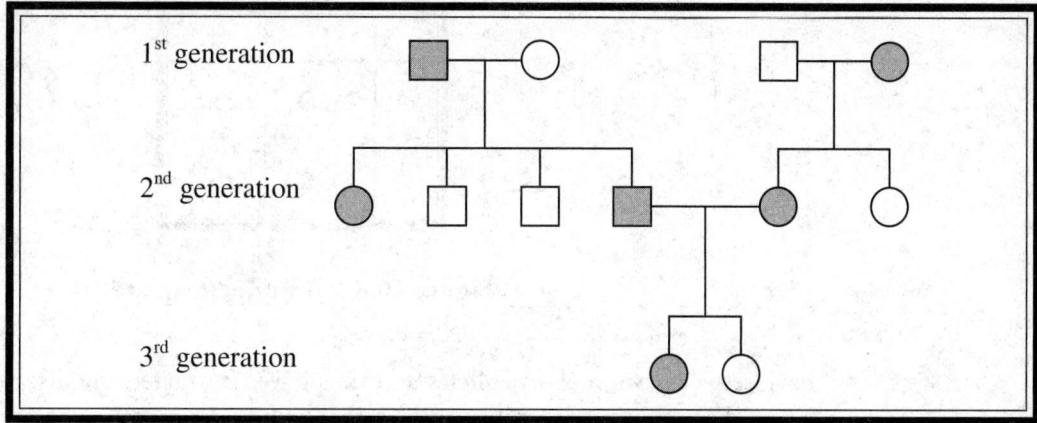

Figure 10.6   Schematic of a pedigree.

male to female represents mates that have produced offspring. The offspring are listed below their parents from oldest to youngest. A fully shaded individual possesses the trait being studied. If the condition being studied is a monogenic recessive condition (rr), then those shaded gray have the genotype rr. If the condition being studied is a dominant condition (Rr or RR), then those that are *un*shaded have the genotype rr. A line through a symbol indicates that the person is deceased. A sample pedigree is shown in Figure 10.6.

CT teacher: "Test almost always has two to three questions about this topic."

   Pedigrees can be used in many ways. One use is to determine the risk of parents passing certain conditions to their offspring. Imagine that two people want to have a child, and they both have a family history of a certain autosomal recessive condition (dd). Neither has the particular condition, but the man has a brother who died of the disease and the woman's mother died of the disease at an older age. They want to know the probability of having a child with the condition. You must first determine the probability that each parent is a carrier, and then determine the probability of the parents having a child with the disease, given that they are carriers. See the pedigree in Figure 10.7.

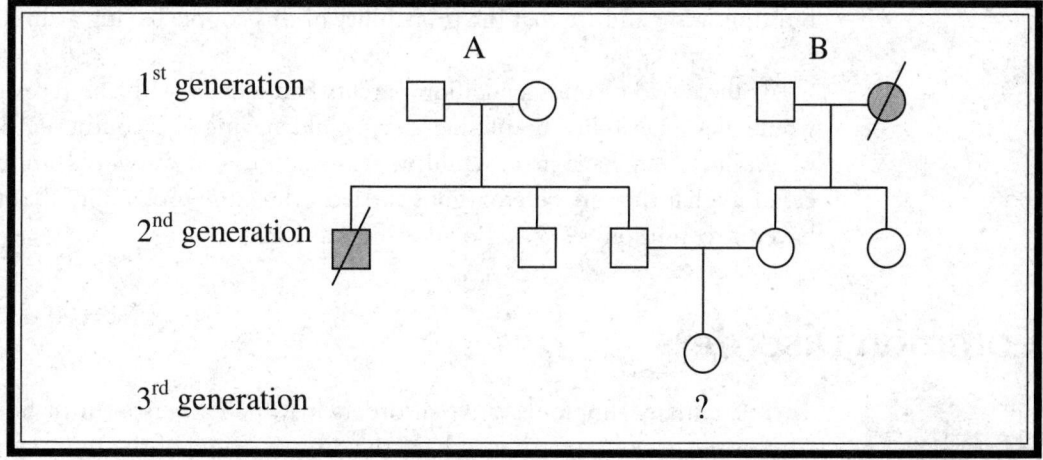

Figure 10.7   Three-generation pedigree indicating probability of inheriting a particular disease.

First, we can determine the father's (second generation) probability of being a carrier. We know that both of his parents must be carriers with a genotype of Dd. Why is this the case? Although neither parent has the condition, they must both be carriers for his brother to

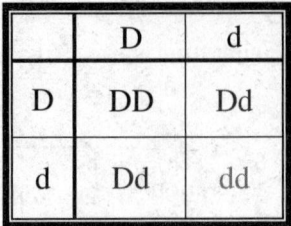

	D	d
D	DD	Dd
d	Dd	dd

Figure 10.8   A Punnett square.

have received two recessive alleles and thus have contracted the disease. How can we calculate the potential probability of the father being a carrier? We construct a Punnett square for a monohybrid cross of the father's parents (first generation) (Figure 10.8).

We know with certainty that he is not dd, otherwise, he would have the condition. This leaves three equally likely possible genotypes for the father, two of which are "carrier" genotypes (Dd). Thus, the probability of his being a carrier is ⅔.

What is the probability that the mother (second generation) is a carrier? We don't even need a Punnett square to determine this one. Her mother (first generation) died of the condition, which means that she must have been dd, and thus must have passed along a d to each of her children. The mother in question does not have the condition, so she must have a D as well. Therefore her genotype *must* be Dd.

To determine the probability that *both* parents are carriers, apply the law of multiplication with probabilities (similar to tossing a coin) and use the following formula:

$$PF \times PM = \tfrac{2}{3} \times 1 = \tfrac{2}{3}$$

(where PF, PM = probabilities of father, mother being carriers).

Now that we have determined the probability that they are both carriers, we need to determine the probability that one of their offspring will have the condition. Their Punnett square would be the same as that shown in Figure 10.8, and we can see that the probability of having a child with the recessive condition is ¼. Again, we use the law of multiplication and see that the probability of this couple having a child with the condition is ⅔ × ¼ = ⅙.

If these two second-generation parents had a child with the recessive condition, what would the probability be of their next child having the condition? It would no longer be ⅙; once they have had a child with the condition, we would know with 100 percent certainty that they are heterozygous carriers. Thus, the probability that their next child will have the condition is ¼, as shown in Figure 10.8.

Common Disorders

There are many simple recessive disorders in which a person must be homozygous recessive for the gene in question to have the disease. Some of the most common examples are Tay-Sachs disease, cystic fibrosis, sickle cell anemia, phenylketonuria, and albinism. These diseases are commonly used as examples on the AP Biology exam and could also aid you in constructing a well-supported essay answer to a question about heredity and inherited disorders.

Tay-Sachs disease is a fatal genetic disorder that renders the body unable to break down a particular type of lipid that accumulates in the brain and eventually causes blindness and brain damage. Individuals with this disease typically do not survive more than a few years. Carriers of this disease do not show any of the effects of the disease, and thus the allele is preserved in the population because carriers usually live to reproduce and potentially pass on the recessive copy of the allele. This disease is found in a higher than normal percentage of people of eastern European Jewish descent.

Cystic fibrosis (CF), a recessive disorder, is the most common fatal genetic disease in this country. The gene for this disease is located on chromosome 7. The normal allele for this gene is involved in cellular chloride ion transport. A defective version of this gene results in the excessive secretion of a thick mucus, which accumulates in the lungs and digestive tract. Left untreated, children with CF die at a very young age. Statistically, one in 25 Caucasians is a carrier for this disease.

Sickle cell anemia is a common recessive disease that occurs as a result of an improper amino acid substitution during translation of an important red blood cell protein called *hemoglobin*. It results in the formation of a hemoglobin protein that is less efficient at carrying oxygen. It also causes hemoglobin to deform to a sickle shape when the oxygen content of the blood is low, causing pain, muscle weakness, and fatigue.

Sickle cell anemia is the most common inherited disease among African Americans. It affects one out of every 400 African Americans, and one out of 10 African Americans is a carrier of the disease. The recessive trait is so prevalent because carriers (who are said to have sickle cell "trait") have increased resistance to malaria. In tropical regions, where malaria occurs, the sickle cell trait actually increases an individual's probability of survival, and thus the trait's presence in the population increases (heterozygote advantage).

Phenylketonuria (PKU) is another autosomal recessive disease caused by a single gene defect. Children with PKU are unable to successfully digest phenylalanine (an amino acid). This leads to the accumulation of a by-product in the blood that can cause mental retardation. If the disease is caught early, retardation can be prevented by avoiding phenylalanine in the diet.

Dominant disorders are less common in humans. One example of a dominant disorder is **Huntington disease,** a fatal disease that causes the breakdown of the nervous system. It does not show itself until a person is in their 30s or 40s, and individuals afflicted with this condition have a 50 percent chance of passing it to their offspring.

Why are lethal dominant alleles less common than lethal recessive alleles? Think about how recessive alleles often are passed on from generation to generation. An individual can be a carrier of a recessive condition and pass it along without even knowing it. On the other hand, it is impossible to be an unaffected carrier of a dominant condition, and many lethal conditions have unfortunately killed the individual before reproductive maturity has been achieved. This makes it more difficult for the dominant gene to be passed along. To remain prevalent in the population, a dominant disorder must not kill the individual until reproduction has occurred.

Chromosomal Complications

We have spent a lot of time discussing how genes are inherited and passed from generation to generation. It is also important to discuss the situations in which something goes wrong with the chromosomes themselves that affects the inheritance of genes by the offspring. **Nondisjunction** is an error in homologous chromosome separation. It can occur during meiosis I or II. The result is that one gamete receives too many of one kind of chromosome, and another gamete receives none of a particular chromosome. The fusing of an abnormal gamete with a normal one can lead to the production of offspring with an abnormal number of chromosomes (**aneuploidy**).

BIG IDEA 3.A.3

Certain genetic disorders can provide understanding of how genes are passed from parent to offspring.

Down syndrome is a classic aneuploid example, affecting one out of every 700 children born in this country. It most often involves a trisomy of chromosome 21, and leads to mental retardation, heart defects, short stature, and characteristic facial features. Most people with trisomy 21 are sterile.

Trisomy 21 is not the only form of nondisjunction caused by error in the chromosome separation process. Trisomy 13, also known as **Patau syndrome,** causes serious brain and circulatory defects. Trisomy 18, also known as **Edwards syndrome,** can affect all organs. It is rare for a baby to survive for more than a year with either of these two conditions. There are also syndromes involving aneuploidy of the sex chromosomes. Males can receive an extra Y chromosome (XYY). Although this nondisjunction does not seem to produce a major syndrome, XYY males tend to be taller than average, and some geneticists believe they display a higher degree of aggressive behavior. A male can receive an extra X chromosome, as in **Klinefelter syndrome** (XXY). These infertile individuals have male sex organs but show several feminine body characteristics. Nondisjunction occurs in females as well. Females who are XXX have no real syndrome. Females who are missing an X chromosome (XO) have a condition called **Turner syndrome.** XO individuals are sterile females who possess sex organs that fail to mature at puberty.

Trisomies are not the only kind of chromosomal abnormalities that lead to inherited diseases. A **deletion** occurs when a piece of the chromosome is lost in the developmental process. Deletions, such as **cri-du-chat syndrome,** can lead to problems. This syndrome occurs with a deletion in chromosome 5 that leads to mental retardation, abnormal facial features, and a small head. Most affected individuals die very young.

Chromosomal translocations, in which a piece of one chromosome is attached to another, nonhomologous chromosome, can cause major problems. **Chronic myelogenous leukemia** is a cancer affecting white blood cell precursor cells. In this disease, a portion of chromosome 22 has been swapped with a piece of chromosome 9.

A **chromosome inversion** occurs when a portion of a chromosome separates and reattaches in the opposite direction. This can have no effect at all, or it can render a gene nonfunctional if it occurs in the middle of a sequence. A **chromosome duplication** results in the repetition of a genetic segment. A **chromosome duplication** results in the repetition of a genetic segment . . . whoops . . . sorry. . . . Duplications often have serious effects on an organism.

These are the major concepts of heredity with which the AP Biology exam writers would like you to be familiar. Try the practice problems that follow and be sure you are able to construct, read, and analyze both Punnett squares and pedigrees, keeping in mind the laws of probability.

❯ Review Questions

1. The following crossover frequencies were noted via experimentation for a set of five genes on a single chromosome:

   A and B → 35%
   B and C → 15%
   A and C → 20%
   A and D → 10%
   D and B → 25%
   A and E → 5%
   B and E → 40%

Pick the answer that most likely represents the relative positions of the five genes.

A. |------|------------|------------|--------------------|
    E   A   D   C   B

B. |------|------------|------------|------------------|
    A   E   C   D   B

C. |------|------------|------------|------------------|
    E   A   C   D   B

D. |------------|------------|------|-------|
    B   C   D E   A

2. Imagine that in squirrels, gray color (G) is dominant over black color (g). A black squirrel has the genotype gg. Crossing a gray squirrel with which of the following would let you know with the most certainty the genotype of the gray squirrel?

    A. GG
    B. Gg
    C. gg
    D. Cannot be determined from the information given

3. From a cross of AABbCC with AaBbCc, what is the probability that the offspring will display a genotype of AaBbCc?

    A. ½
    B. ⅓
    C. ¼
    D. ⅛

Use the following pedigree of an autosomal recessive condition for questions 4–6.

4. What is the genotype of person A?

    A. Bb
    B. BB
    C. bb
    D. Cannot be determined from the given information

5. What is the most likely genotype of person B?

    A. Bb
    B. BB
    C. bb
    D. Cannot be determined from the information given

6. What is the probability that persons C and D would have a child with the condition?

    A. ½
    B. ¼
    C. ⅙
    D. ⅛

7. Which of the following disorders is X-linked?

    A. Tay-Sachs disease
    B. Cystic fibrosis
    C. Hemophilia
    D. Albinism

8. A court case is trying to determine the father of a particular baby. The mother has type O blood, and the baby has type B blood. Which of the following blood types would mean that the man was definitely *not* the father of the baby?

    A. B and A
    B. AB and A
    C. O and B
    D. O and A

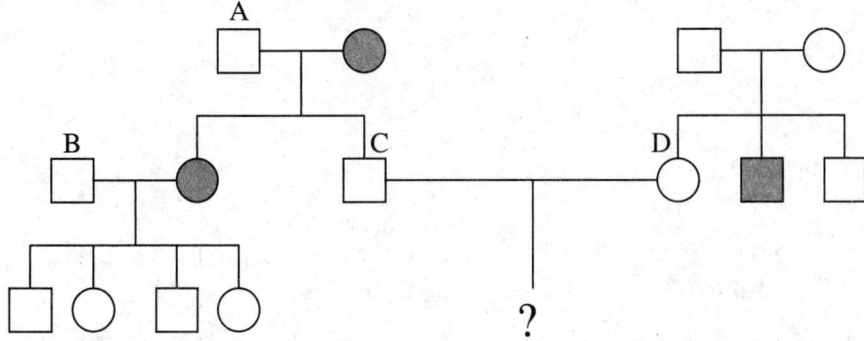

9. Assume that gray squirrel color results from a dominant allele G. The father squirrel is black, the mother squirrel is gray, and their first baby is black. What is the probability that their second baby is also black?

    A. 1.00
    B. 0.75
    C. 0.50
    D. 0.25

10. Imagine that tulips are either yellow or white. You start growing tulips and find out that if you want to get yellow tulips, then at least one of the parents must be yellow. Which color is dominant?

    A. White
    B. Yellow
    C. Neither; it is some form of intermediate inheritance
    D. Cannot be determined from the given information

11. Suppose that 200 red snapdragons were mated with 200 white snapdragons and they produced only pink snapdragons. The mating of two pink snapdragons would most likely result in off-spring that are

    A. 50 percent pink, 25 percent red, 25 percent white
    B. 100 percent pink
    C. 25 percent pink, 50 percent red, 25 percent white
    D. 75 percent red, 25 percent white

12. Which of the following represents the number of possible gametes produced from a genotype of RrBBCcDDEe?

    A. 2
    B. 4
    C. 8
    D. 16

13. Which of the following diseases is *not* caused by trisomy nondisjunction?

    A. Down syndrome
    B. Klinefelter syndrome
    C. Turner syndrome
    D. Patau syndrome

14. The pedigree below is most likely a pedigree of a condition of which type of inheritance?

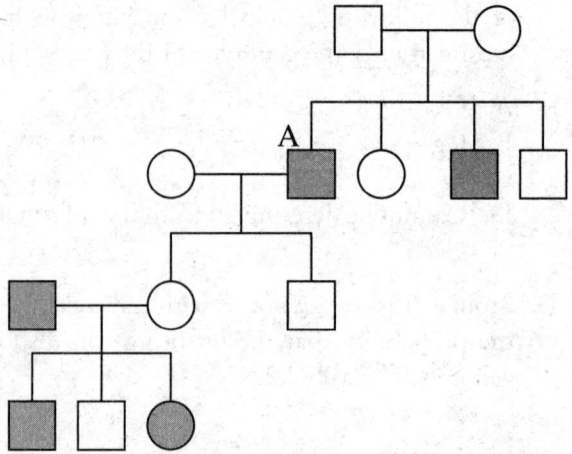

    A. Autosomal dominant
    B. Autosomal recessive
    C. Sex-linked dominant
    D. Sex-linked recessive

› Answers and Explanations

1. **A**—The crossover frequencies are an indication of the distance between the different genes on a chromosome. The farther apart they are, the greater chance there is that they will cross over during prophase I of meiosis. You are first told that A and B cross over with a frequency of 35 percent, so imagine that they are 35 units apart on a chromosome map.

   A (35) B   B (15) C   A (20) C

   We can then tell you that B and C have a frequency of 15 percent. They are 15 units apart on the map,

   but you cannot yet be sure what side of gene A that C is on. Gene A and C cross with 20 percent frequency. This means that gene C must be in between A and B.

   A (20) C (15) B   A (10) D   D (25) B

   Gene A crosses over with D 10 percent of the time, and D crosses with B 25 percent of the time; therefore, D must also be in between A and B. It is closer to A than it is to B. You can use this knowledge to eliminate answer choices B and C.

   A (10) D (10) C (15) B

   Gene A crosses over with E with a frequency of 5 percent. You do not know which side of A gene E is on until you know its crossover frequency with B. Because the question tells you that it has a 40 percent frequency with B, you know that it must be on the *left* of A. This completes your map, leaving A as the correct answer.

2. **C**—This is a test cross. To determine the genotype of an individual showing the dominant phenotype, you cross that individual with a homozygous recessive individual for the same trait. If they have no offspring with the recessive phenotype, then the individual displaying the dominant phenotype is most likely GG. If approximately one-half of the offspring have the recessive phenotype, you know the individual has the genotype Gg.

3. **D**—The Punnett square shown below shows all the possible gamete combinations from this cross. Two-sixteenths or one-eighth of the possible gametes will be AaBbCc. A quick way to determine the number of possible gametes that an individual can produce given a certain genotype is to use the formula 2^n. For example, an individual who is AABbCc can have $2^2 = 4$ possible gametes because Bb and Cc are heterozygous.

	ABC	**AbC**	**ABc**	**Abc**	**aBC**	**abC**	**aBc**	**abc**
ABC	AABBCC	AABbCC	AABBCc	AABbCc	AaBBCC	AaBbCC	AaBBCc	AaBbCc
AbC	AABbCC	AAbbCC	AABbCc	AAbbCc	AaBbCC	AabbCC	AaBbCc	AabbCc

4. **A**—Person A must have genotype Bb because he has some children that have the recessive condition and some that do not. Because his wife is pure recessive, she can contribute only a b. The father must therefore be the one who contributes the B to the child who does not have the condition, and the second b to the one with the condition.

5. **B**—Person B most likely has a genotype of BB. Because he does not have the condition, we know that his genotype is either BB or Bb. If it were Bb, then when crossed with his wife who has a genotype of bb, 50 percent of his children would be expected to have the recessive condition. None of the children have the condition, which leads you to believe that he is most likely BB. (This test is, of course, not 100 percent accurate. Answer choice B is not certain, but is the most probable conclusion.)

6. **C**—We know that neither parent in the question has the recessive condition. We therefore need to calculate the probability that each of them is Bb. The probability that person C is Bb is 1. Because his mother has the condition, she *must* pass a b to him during gamete formation. So the only possible genotypes he can have are Bb and bb. Since he does not have the condition, he must be Bb with a probability of 1. The probability that person D is Bb is 0.67. Neither of her parents has the

condition, but she has a brother who is bb. This means that each of her parents must be a carrier for the condition (Bb). You know that this woman is not bb, because she does not have the condition. As a result, there are only *three* possible genotypes from the cross remaining. Two of these three are Bb, giving her a probability of ⅔, or 0.67, of being Bb. The probability that *both* person C and person D are Bb is (1) × (0.67) = (0.67). Now it is necessary to calculate the probability that two Bb parents will produce a kid who is bb. The Punnett square says that there is a 0.25 chance of this result. To calculate the probability that they will have a child with the recessive condition, you multiply the probability that they are both Bb (0.67) times the probability that two individuals Bb will produce a bb child (0.25). Thus, the probability of an affected child being produced from these two parents is ⅙.

7. **C**—Hemophilia is an X-linked condition. An XY male with hemophilia gets his Y chromosome from his father, and his X chromosome from his mother. All that is needed for the hemophilia condition to occur is a copy of the defective recessive allele from his mother.

8. **D**—Types O and A would prove that he was not the father of this particular child. If the mother has type O blood, this means that her genotype is ii and she *must* pass along an i allele to her child. The baby has type B blood, and her genotype could be I^Bi or I^BI^B. Since the mother must give an i, then the baby's genotype must be I^Bi. It follows that the father must provide the I^B allele to the baby to complete the known genotype. If he is type O, he won't have an I^B to pass along since his genotype would be ii. This would also be the case if he were type A, because his genotype would be either I^AI^A or I^Ai. Therefore, those two blood types would prove that he is not the father of this child.

9. **C**—To figure out this problem, you need to know the genotype of the mother. The father is black, meaning that his genotype is gg. The two of them produced a squirrel that is also black, which means that the gray mother gave a g to the baby. The mother's genotype is Gg. A cross of Gg × gg produces a phenotype ratio of 1:1 gray:black. They have a 0.5 chance of producing another black baby.

10. **B**—According to this scenario, yellow and white are the only colors possible. If white were dominant, and both parents were Ww, you *could* produce a yellow offspring if the two recessive w's combined. If it were intermediate inheritance, you probably would not produce a straight yellow tulip in the offspring because they would either meet halfway (incomplete dominance), or both express fully (codominance). If yellow were dominant, then you could produce a yellow offspring only if there were a Y allele in one of the parents. A cross of yy × yy would produce only white tulips if white were recessive.

11. **A**—This problem involves incomplete dominance. The genotype of the pink offspring from the first generation is RW. When the two RW snapdragons are mated together, they produce the following results:

	R	**W**
R	RR	RW
W	RW	WW

The offspring will be 25 percent red (RR), 50 percent pink (RW), and 25 percent white (WW).

12. **C**—In a problem like this, you will save time by thinking about the laws of probability. The genotype is RrBBCcDDEe. How many possible combinations of the R gene are there? There are two: R and r. How many for B? Only one: B. Following the same logic, C has two and D has one. Now you multiply the possibilities: (2 × 1 × 2 × 1 × 2) = 8. There are 8 possible gametes from this genotype. Another way to arrive at this answer is by use of the expression 2^n, where *n* is the number of hybrid traits being examined. In this case it would be 2^3 or 8 possible gametes.

13. **C**—Down syndrome is most often due to a trisomy of chromosome 21. Klinefelter syndrome is a trisomy of the sex chromosomes (XXY). Patau syndrome is a trisomy of chromosome 15. Edwards syndrome is a trisomy of chromosome 18. Turner syndrome, the only nontrisomy listed in this problem, is a *monosomy* of the sex chromosomes (XO).

14. **D**—This is most likely a sex-linked recessive disease. The father in the first generation does not have the condition, so his genotype would be $X^N Y$. The original couple has four children, two boys with the condition, and one girl and one boy without the condition. The genotype of the boys with the condition would be $X^n Y$. This means that the original mother's genotype would be $X^N X^n$—thus she is a carrier. One of the children who inherited the condition has children with a woman from a different family, and neither of their two children displays the condition. However, the daughter of son A has three children with a man who is $X^n Y$, and she has a daughter and a son who show the recessive condition and one normal son. This means that the daughter of son A is most likely $X^N X^n$—another carrier of the condition. This disease is a condition that is, according to the pedigree, more often seen in men, and passed along to men by the X chromosome from the mother. However, it is important to note that if a father who has the X-linked condition has a child with a female carrier for the condition, that couple can indeed produce a female with the condition.

› Rapid Review

You should be familiar with the following terms:

Character: heritable feature, such as flower color.

Monohybrid cross: cross involving one character (Bb × Bb) → (3:1 phenotype ratio).

Dihybrid cross: cross involving two different characters (BbRr × BbRr) → (9:3:3:1 phenotype ratio).

Law of segregation: the two alleles for a trait separate during the formation of gametes—one to each gamete.

Law of independent assortment: inheritance of one trait does not interfere with the inheritance of another trait.

Law of dominance: if two opposite pure-breeding varieties (BB × bb) are crossed, all offspring resemble BB parent.

Intermediate inheritance: heterozygous (Yy) individual shows characteristics unlike *either* parent.

- *Incomplete dominance*: Yy produces an intermediate phenotype between YY and yy (snapdragons).

- *Codominance*: both alleles express themselves fully in a Yy individual—(MN blood groups).

Polygenic traits: traits that are affected by more than one gene (eye color, skin color).

Multiple alleles: traits that correspond to more than two alleles (ABO blood type: I^A, I^B, i).

Epistasis: a gene at one locus alters the phenotypic expression of a gene at another locus (coat color in mice).

Pleiotropy: a single gene has multiple effects on an organism (sickle cell anemia).

Sex determination: males are XY, females are XX.

Autosomal chromosome: not involved in gender.

Fruit flies: wild-type traits are the normal phenotype; mutant traits are those that are different from normal.

Sex-linked traits: passed along the X chromosome; more common in males than females (males have only one X) (e.g., hemophilia [can't clot blood], Duchenne's muscular dystrophy [muscle weakness], colorblindness).

X inactivation: one of two X chromosomes is randomly inactivated and remains coiled as a Barr body.

Holandric trait: one that is inherited via the Y chromosome.

Linked genes: genes that lie along the same chromosome and do not follow the law of independent assortment.

- *Crossover*: a form of genetic recombination that occurs during prophase I of meiosis.
- The further apart two genes are along a chromosome, the more often they will cross over.

Linkage map: genetic map put together using crossover frequencies.

- Can determine the relative location of a set of genes according to how often they cross over.
- If two genes cross over in 20 percent of the crosses, they are 20 map units apart, etc.

Law of multiplication: To determine the probability that two random events will occur in succession, multiply the probability of the first event by the probability of the second event. (Useful in pedigree analysis!)

Pedigree: family tree used to describe genetic relationships (use pedigree diagram in review question 14 for clearer understanding). To calculate the risk a couple faces of having a child that has a recessive (bb) condition, first determine the probability that *both* parents are Bb (if neither have the condition), or the probability that one is Bb (if one *has* the condition). Once determined, multiply this probability times the probability that a Bb × Bb cross will produce a bb (¼) or that a bb × Bb will produce a bb (½).

Autosomal Recessive Disorders

Tay-Sachs: fatal, storage disease, lipid builds up in brain, mental retardation, increased incidence in eastern European Jews.

Cystic fibrosis: increased mucus buildup in lungs; untreated children die at young age; one in 25 Caucasians are carriers.

Sickle cell anemia: caused by error of single amino acid; hemoglobin is less able to carry O_2, and sickles when O_2 content of blood is low; one in 10 African Americans is a carrier. Heterozygous condition protects against malaria.

Phenylketonuria: inability to digest phenylalanine, which can cause mental retardation if not avoided in diet.

Autosomal dominant disorders: Huntington disease (nervous system disease) and achondroplasia (dwarfism).

Nondisjunction: error in which homologous chromosomes do not separate properly.

- *Monosomy*: (one copy): Turner syndrome.

- *Trisomy*: (three copies): Down syndrome (21), Patau syndrome (13), Edwards syndrome (18).

Klinefelter syndrome: XXY; XYY males, XXX females.

Chromosome disorders: deletion (cri-du-chat), inversions, duplications, and translocations (leukemia).

CHAPTER 11

Molecular Genetics

IN THIS CHAPTER

Summary: This chapter describes the various processes in cells that take DNA from gene to protein: replication, transcription, posttranscriptional modification, and translation. It also discusses the regulation of these processes before concluding with a discussion about viruses, bacteria, and genetic engineering.

Key Ideas

- ✪ DNA: adenine-thymine, cytosine-guanine—arranged in a double helix.
- ✪ RNA: adenine-uracil, cytosine-guanine—single stranded.
- ✪ DNA replication occurs during the S-phase in a semi-conservative fashion and in a 5' to 3' direction.
- ✪ Types of DNA replication mutations: frameshift, missense, nonsense.
- ✪ Transcription: mRNA is formed from a DNA template.
- ✪ Translation: process by which mRNA specified sequence of amino acids is lined up on a ribosome for protein synthesis.
- ✪ Operons act as on-off switches for transcription—allow for production of genes only when needed.
- ✪ Types of genetic recombination: transformation, transduction, and conjugation.

Introduction

Genetics has implications for all of biology. We begin our study of this subject with an introduction to DNA and RNA, followed by a description of the various processes in cells that take DNA from gene to protein: replication, transcription, posttranscriptional modification, translation, and the regulation of all these processes. The genetics of viruses and bacteria follows, and the chapter concludes with a discussion of genetic engineering.

DNA Structure and Function

Deoxyribonucleic acid, known to her peers as DNA, is composed of four **nitrogenous bases:** adenine, guanine, cytosine, and thymine. Adenine and guanine are a type of nitrogenous base called a **purine,** and contain a double-ring structure. Thymine and cytosine are a type of nitrogenous base called a **pyrimidine,** and contain a single-ring structure. Two scientists, James D. Watson and Francis H.C. Crick, spent a good amount of time devoted to determining the structure of DNA. Their efforts paid off, and they were the ones given credit for realizing that DNA was arranged in what they termed a **double helix** composed of two strands of nucleotides held together by hydrogen bonds. They noted that adenine always pairs with thymine (A=T) held together by two hydrogen bonds and that guanine always pairs with cytosine (C≡G) held together by three hydrogen bonds. Each strand of DNA consists of a sugar-phosphate backbone that keeps the nucleotides connected with the strand. The sugar is deoxyribose. (See Figure 11.1 for a rough sketch of what purine–pyrimidine bonds look like.)

Figure 11.1   Purine–pyrimidine bonds.

One last structural note about DNA that can be confusing is that DNA has something called a 5′ end and a 3′ end (Figure 11.2). The two strands of a DNA molecule run antiparallel to each other; the 5′ end of one molecule is paired with the 3′ end of the other molecule, and vice versa.

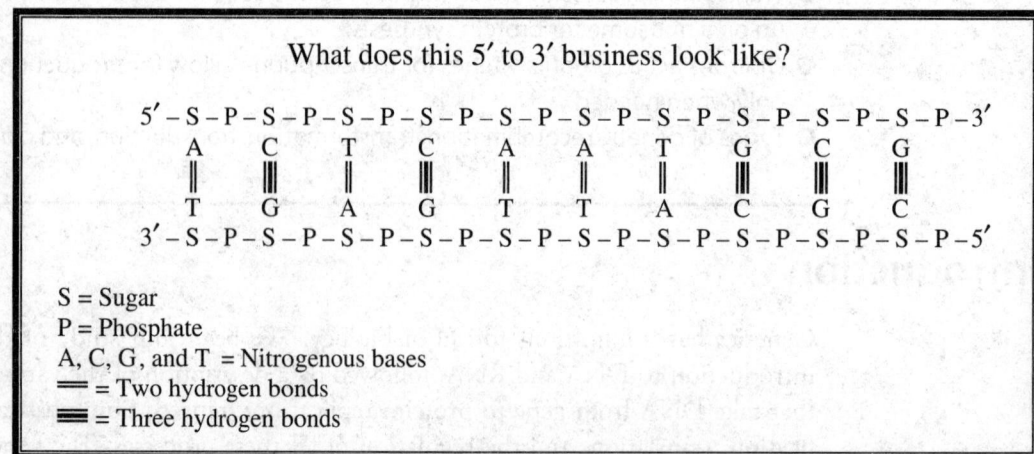

Figure 11.2   The 5′ and 3′ ends in DNA structure.

RNA Structure and Function

Ribonucleic acid is known to the world as RNA. There are some similarities between DNA and RNA. They both have a sugar-phosphate backbone. They both have four different nucleotides that make up the structure of the molecule. They both have three letters in their nickname—don't worry if you don't see that last similarity right away, . . . remember that we have been studying these things for years. These two molecules also have their share of differences. RNA's nitrogenous bases are adenine, guanine, cytosine, and **uracil.** There is no thymine in RNA; uracil beat out thymine for the job (probably had a better interview during the hiring process). Another difference between DNA and RNA is that the sugar for RNA is ribose instead of deoxyribose. While DNA exists as a double strand, RNA has a bit more of an independent personality and tends to roam the cells as a single-stranded entity.

There are three main types of RNA that you should know about, all of which are formed from DNA templates in the nucleus of eukaryotic cells: (1) messenger RNA (mRNA), (2) transfer RNA (tRNA), and (3) ribosomal RNA (rRNA).

Replication of DNA

Human cells do not have copy machines to do the dirty work for them. Instead, they use a system called **DNA replication** to copy DNA molecules from cell to cell. As we discussed in Chapter 9, this process occurs during the S-phase of the cell cycle to ensure that every cell produced during mitosis or meiosis receives the proper amount of DNA.

The mechanism for DNA replication was the source of much debate in the mid-1900s. Some argued that it occurred in what was called a "conservative" (**conservative DNA replication**) fashion. In this model, the original double helix of DNA does not change at all; it is as if the DNA is placed on a copy machine and an exact duplicate is made. DNA from the parent appears in only one of the two daughter cells. A different model called the **semiconservative DNA replication** model agrees that the original DNA molecule serves as the template but proposes that before it is copied, the DNA unzips, with each single strand serving as a template for the creation of a new double strand. One strand of DNA from the parent goes to one daughter cell, and the second parent strand to the second daughter cell. A third model, the **dispersive DNA replication model,** suggested that every daughter strand contains *some* parental DNA, but it is dispersed among pieces of DNA not of parental origin. Figure 11.3 is a simplistic sketch showing these three main theories. Watson and Crick would not be pleased to see that we did not draw the DNA as a double helix . . . but as long as you realize this is not how the DNA truly looks, the figure serves its purpose.

An experiment performed in the 1950s by Meselson and Stahl helped select a winner in the debate about replication mechanisms. The experimenters grew bacteria in a medium containing ^{15}N (a heavier-than-normal form of nitrogen) to create DNA that was denser than normal. The DNA was denser because the bacteria picked up the ^{15}N and incorporated it into their DNA. The bacteria were then transferred to a medium containing normal ^{14}N nitrogen. The DNA was allowed to replicate and produced DNA that was half ^{15}N and half ^{14}N. When the first generation of offspring replicated to form the second generation of offspring, the new DNA produced was of two types—one type that had half ^{15}N and half ^{14}N, and another type that was completely ^{14}N DNA. This gave a hands-down victory to the semi-conservative theory of DNA replication. Let's take a look at the mechanism of semi-conservative DNA replication.

During the S-phase of the cell cycle, the double-stranded DNA unzips and prepares to replicate. An enzyme called **helicase** unzips the DNA just like a jacket, breaking the hydrogen

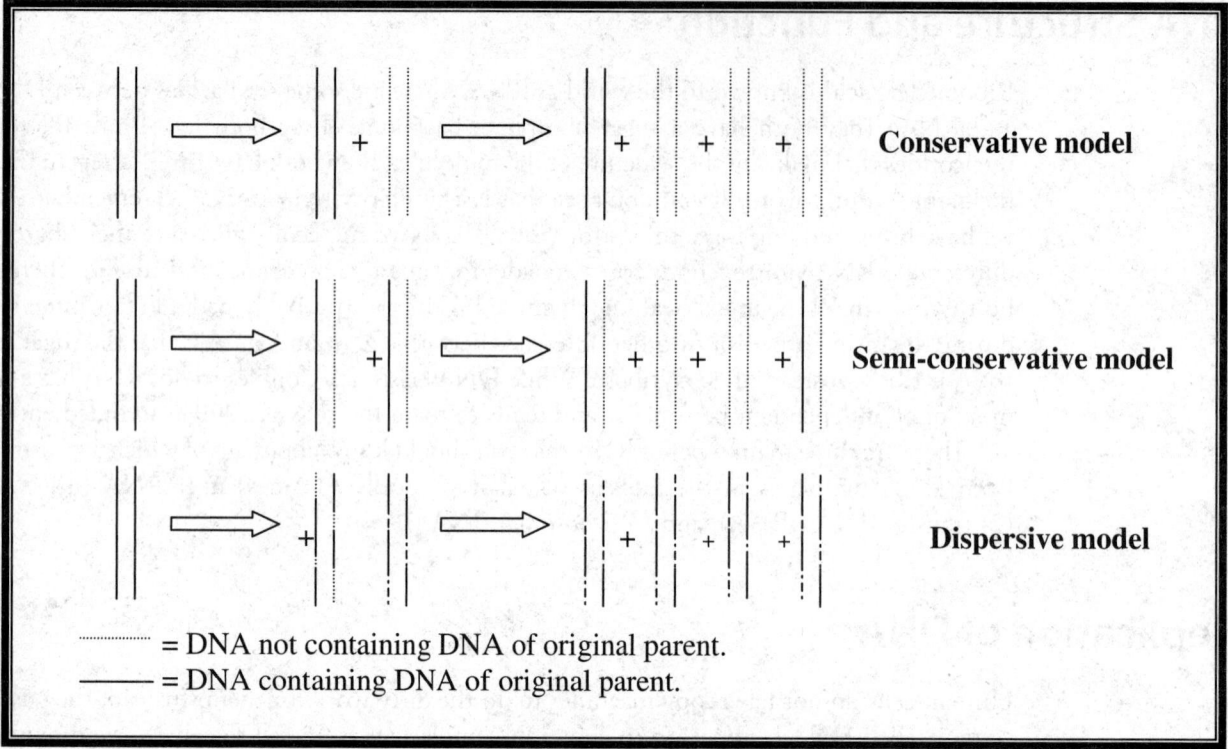

Conservative model

Semi-conservative model

Dispersive model

.... = DNA not containing DNA of original parent.
———— = DNA containing DNA of original parent.

Figure 11.3   Three DNA replication models.

bonds between the nucleotides and producing the **replication fork.** Each strand then functions as a template for production of a new double-stranded DNA molecule. Specific regions along each DNA strand serve as **primer sites** that signal where replication should originate. Primase binds to the primer, and **DNA polymerase,** the superstar enzyme of this process, attaches to the primer region and adds nucleotides to the growing DNA chain in a 5′-to-3′ direction. DNA polymerase is restricted in that it can only add nucleotides to the 3′ end of a parent strand. This creates a problem because, as you can see in Figure 11.4,

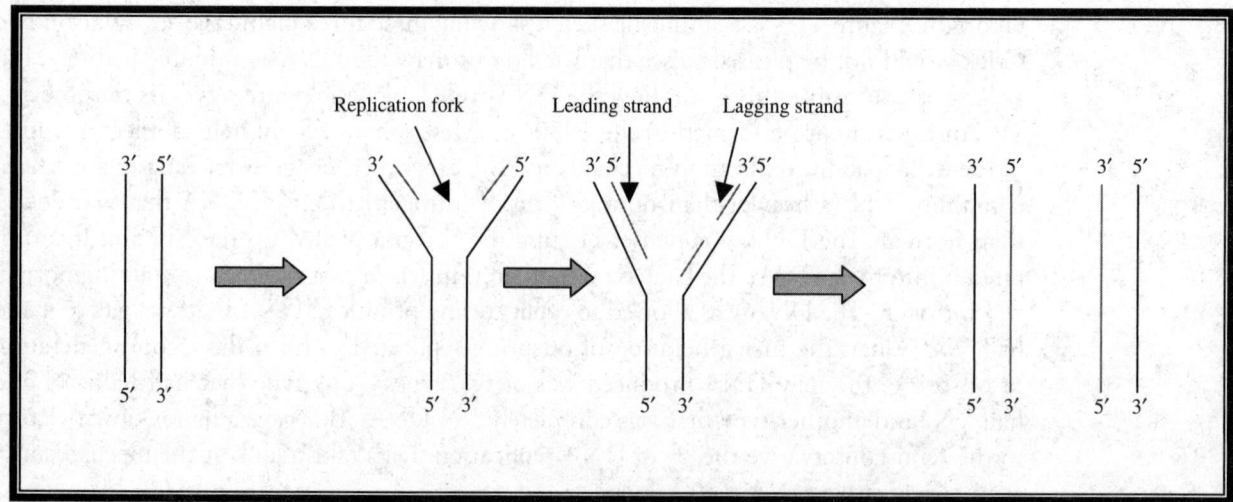

Figure 11.4   Semi-conservative DNA replication.

this means that only one of the strands can be produced in a continuous fashion. This continuous strand is known as the **leading strand.** The other strand is affectionately known as the **lagging strand.** You will notice that in the third step of the process in Figure 11.4, the lagging strand consists of tiny pieces called **Okazaki fragments,** which are later connected by an enzyme called DNA ligase to produce the completed double-stranded daughter DNA molecule. This is the semi-conservative model of DNA replication.

Unliek are worck, DNA replication is not a perfect process—mistakes are made. A series of proofreading enzymes function to make sure that the DNA is properly replicated each time. During the first run-through, it is estimated that a nucleotide mismatch is made during replication in one out of every 10,000 basepairs. The proofreaders must do a pretty good job since a mismatch error in replication occurs in only one out of every *billion* nucleotides replicated. DNA polymerase proofreads the newly added base right after it is added on to make sure that it is the correct match. Repair is easy—the polymerase simply removes the incorrect nucleotide, and adds the proper one in its place. This process is known as **mismatch repair.** Another repair mechanism is **excision repair,** in which a *section* of DNA containing an error is cut out and the gap is filled in by DNA polymerase. There are other proteins that assist in the repair process, but their identities are not of major importance. Just be aware that DNA repair exists and is a very efficient process.

Here is a short list of mutation types that you should know:

1. *Frameshift mutations.* Deletion or addition of DNA nucleotides that does not add or remove a multiple of three nucleotides. mRNA is produced on a DNA template and is read in bunches of three called **codons,** which tell the protein synthesis machinery which amino acid to add to the growing protein chain. If the mRNA reads: THE FAT CAT ATE HER HAT, and the F is removed because of an error somewhere, the frame has now *shifted* to read THE ATC ATA THE ERH AT . . . (gibberish). This kind of mutation usually produces a nonfunctional protein unless it occurs late in protein production.

2. *Missense mutation.* Substitution of the wrong nucleotides into the DNA sequence. These substitutions still result in the addition of amino acids to the growing protein chain during translation, but they can sometimes lead to the addition of *incorrect* amino acids to the chain. It could cause no problem at all, or it could cause a big problem as in sickle cell anemia, in which a single amino acid error caused by a substitution mutation leads to a disease that wreaks havoc on the body as a whole.

3. *Nonsense mutation.* Substitution of the wrong nucleotides into the DNA sequence. These substitutions lead to premature stoppage of protein synthesis by the early placement of a **stop codon,** which tells the protein synthesis machinery to grind to a halt. The stop codons are UAA, UAG, and UGA. This type of mutation usually leads to a nonfunctional protein.

4. *Thymine dimers.* Result of too much exposure to UV (ultraviolet) light. Thymine nucleotides located adjacent to one another on the DNA strand bind together when this exposure occurs. This can negatively affect replication of DNA and help cause further mutations.

Transcription of DNA

NY teacher: "Know the basic principles. They'll ask you about this process."

Up until this point, we have just been discussing DNA *replication*, which is simply the production of more DNA. In the rest of the chapter, we discuss transcription, translation, and other processes involving DNA. While DNA is the hereditary material responsible for the passage of traits from generation to generation, DNA does not directly produce the

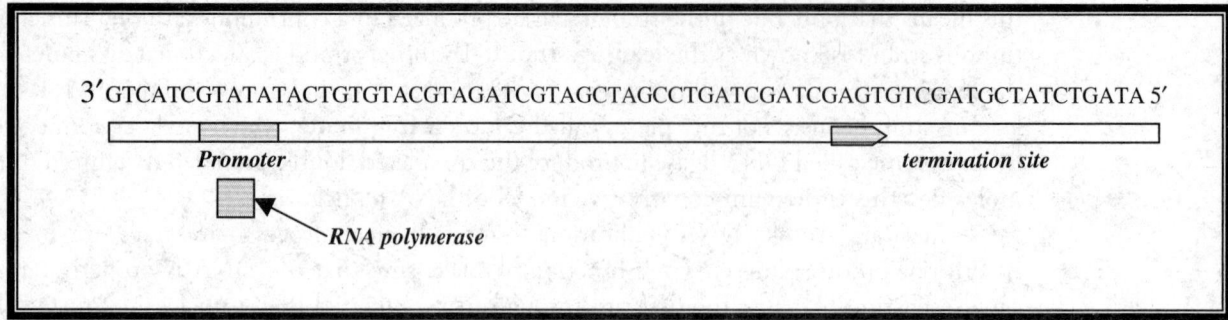

3′ GTCATCGTATATACTGTGTACGTAGATCGTAGCTAGCCTGATCGATCGAGTGTCGATGCTATCTGATA 5′

Promoter

termination site

RNA polymerase

Figure 11.5 Transcription.

BIG IDEA 3.B.1
Gene regulation results in differential gene expression, leading to cell specialization.

proteins that it encodes. DNA must first be transcribed into an intermediary: mRNA. This process is called *transcription* (Figure 11.5) because both DNA and RNA are built from nucleotides—they speak a similar language. DNA acts as a template for mRNA, which then conveys to the ribosomes the blueprints for producing the protein of interest. Transcription occurs in the nucleus.

Transcription consists of three steps: initiation, elongation, and termination. The process begins when **RNA polymerase** attaches to the promoter region of a DNA strand (initiation). A **promoter region** is simply a recognition site that shows the polymerase where transcription should begin. The promoter region contains a group of nucleotides known as the **TATA box,** which is important to the binding of RNA polymerase. As in DNA replication, the polymerase of transcription needs the assistance of helper proteins to find and attach to the promoter region. These helpers are called **transcription factors.** Once bound, the RNA polymerase works its magic by adding the appropriate RNA nucleotide to the 3′ end of the growing strand (elongation). Like DNA polymerase of replication, RNA polymerase adds nucleotides 5′ to 3′. The growing mRNA strand separates from the DNA as it grows longer. A region called the **termination site** tells the polymerase when transcription should conclude (termination). After reaching this site, the mRNA is released and set free.

RNA Processing

In bacteria, mRNA is ready to rock immediately after it is released from the DNA. In eukaryotes, this is not the case. The mRNA produced after transcription must be modified before it can leave the nucleus and lead the formation of proteins on the ribosomes. The 5′ and the 3′ ends of the newly produced mRNA molecule are touched up. The 5′ end is given a guanine cap, which serves to protect the RNA and also helps in attachment to the ribosome later on. The 3′ end is given something called a *polyadenine tail,* which may help ease the movement from the nucleus to the cytoplasm. Along with these changes, the **introns** (noncoding regions produced during transcription) are cut out of the mRNA, and the remaining **exons** (coding regions) are glued back together to produce the mRNA that is translated into a protein. This is called **RNA splicing.** We admit that it does seem strange and inefficient that the DNA would contain so many regions that are not used in the production of the gene, but perhaps there is method to the madness. It is hypothesized that introns exist to provide flexibility to the genome. They could allow an organism to make different proteins from the same gene; the only difference is which introns get spliced out from one to the other. It is also possible that this whole splicing process plays a role in allowing the movement of mRNA from the nucleus to the cytoplasm.

Translation of RNA

Now that the mRNA has escaped from the nucleus, it is ready to help direct the construction of proteins. This process occurs in the cytoplasm, and the site of protein synthesis is the ribosome. As mentioned in Chapter 5, proteins are made of amino acids. Each protein has a distinct and particular amino acid order. Therefore, there must be some system used by the cell to convert the sequences of nucleotides that make up an mRNA molecule into the sequence of amino acids that make up a particular protein. The cell carries out this conversion from nucleotides to amino acids through the use of the **genetic code.** An mRNA molecule is divided into a series of codons that make up the code. Each **codon** is a triplet of nucleotides that codes for a particular amino acid. There are 20 different amino acids, and 64 different combinations of codons. This means that some amino acids are coded for by more than one codon. For example, the codons GCU, GCC, GCA, and GCG all call for the addition of the amino acid alanine during protein creation. Of these 64 possibilities, one is a **start codon,** AUG, which establishes the reading frame for protein formation. Also among these 64 codons are three **stop codons:** UGA, UAA, and UAG. When the protein formation machinery hits these codons, the production of a protein stops.

KEY IDEA

Before we go through the steps of protein synthesis, we would like to introduce to you the other players involved in the process. We have already spoken about mRNA, but we should meet the host of the entire shindig, the **ribosomes,** which are made up of a large and a small subunit. A huge percentage of a ribosome is built out of the second type of RNA mentioned earlier, rRNA. Two other important parts of a ribosome that we will discuss in more detail later are the **A site** and the **P site,** which are tRNA attachment sites. The job of tRNA is to carry amino acids to the ribosomes. The mRNA molecule that is involved in the formation of a protein consists of a series of codons. Each tRNA has, at its attachment site, a region called the **anticodon,** which is a three-nucleotide sequence that is perfectly complementary to a particular codon. For example, a codon that is AUU has an **anticodon** that reads UAA in the same direction. Each tRNA molecule carries an amino acid that is coded for by the codon that its **anticodon** matches up with. Once the tRNA's amino acid has been incorporated into the growing protein, the tRNA leaves the site to pick up another amino acid just in case its services are needed again at the ribosome. An enzyme known as **aminoacyl tRNA synthetase** makes sure that each tRNA molecule picks up the appropriate amino acid for its anticodon.

Uh-oh . . . there is a potential problem here. There are fewer than 50 different types of tRNA molecules. But there are more codons than that. Oh, dear . . . but wait! This is not a problem because some tRNA are able to match with more than one codon. How can this be? This works thanks to a phenomenon known as **wobble,** where a uracil in the third position of an anticodon can pair with A or G instead of just A. There are some tRNA molecules that have an altered form of adenine, called inosine (I), in the third position of the anticodon. This nitrogenous base is able to bind with U, C, *or* A. Wobble allows the 45 tRNA molecules to service all the different types of codons seen in mRNA molecules.

We have met all the important players in the translation process (see also Figure 11.6), which begins when an mRNA attaches to a small ribosomal subunit. The first codon for this process is always AUG. This attracts a tRNA molecule carrying methionine to attach to the AUG codon. When this occurs, the large subunit of the ribosome, containing the A site and the P site, binds to the complex. The elongation of the protein is ready to begin. The P site is the host for the tRNA carrying the growing protein, while the A site is where the tRNA carrying the next amino acid sits. Think of the A site as the on-deck circle of a baseball field, and P site as the batter's box. So, AUG is the first codon bound, and in the P site is the tRNA carrying the methionine. The next codon in the sequence determines

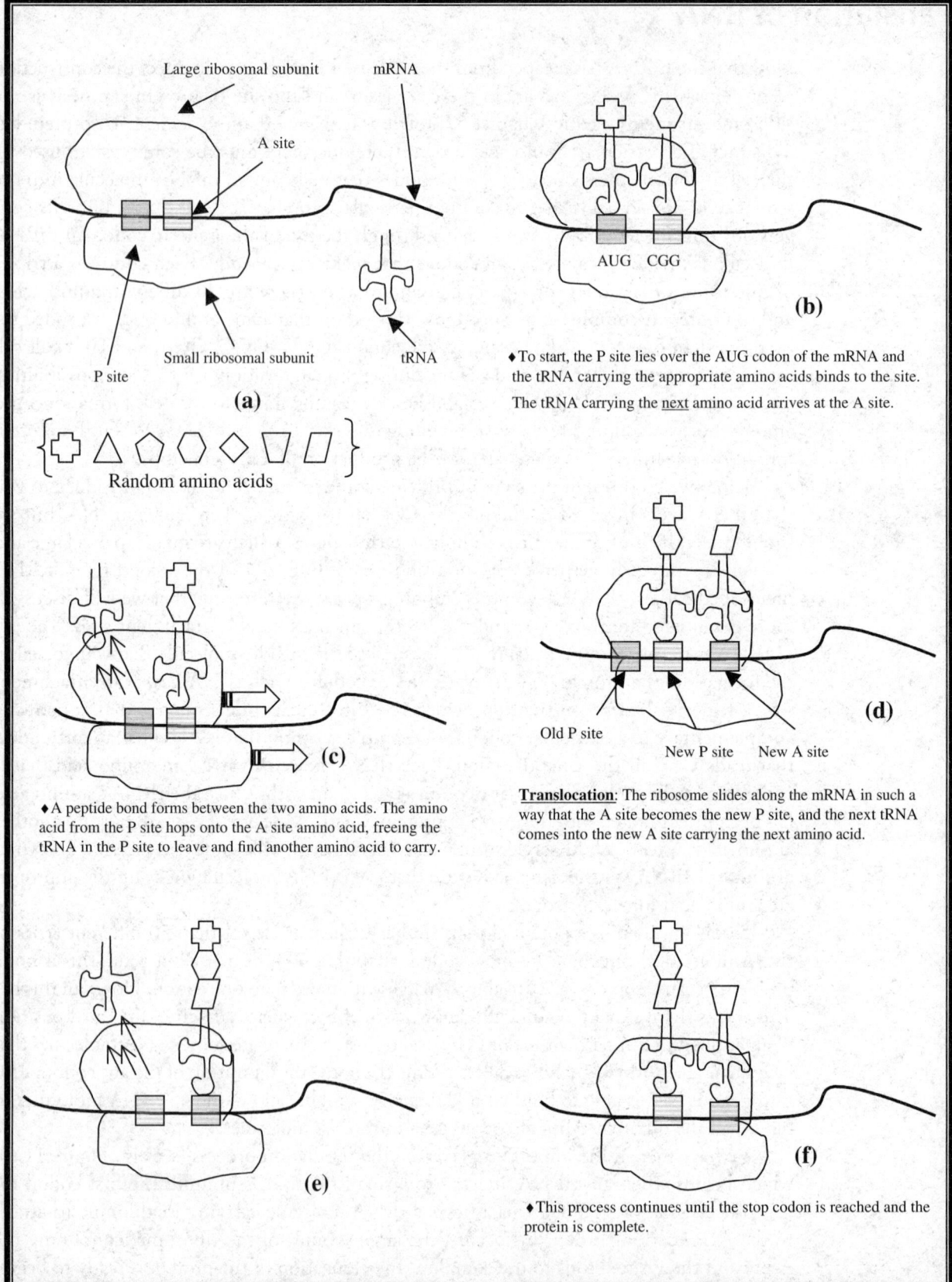

Figure 11.6   A pictorial representation of translation.

which tRNA binds next, and that tRNA molecule sits in the A site of the ribosome. An enzyme helps a peptide bond form between the amino acid on the A site tRNA and the amino acid on the P site tRNA. After this happens, the amino acid from the P site moves to the A site, setting the stage for the tRNA in the P site to leave the ribosome. Now a step called translocation occurs. During this step, the ribosome moves along the mRNA in such a way that the A site becomes the P site and the next tRNA comes into the new A site carrying the next amino acid. This process continues until the stop codon is reached, causing the completed protein to leave the ribosome.

Gene Expression

Let's cover some vocabulary before diving into this section:

Promoter region: a base sequence that signals the start site for gene transcription; this is where RNA polymerase binds to begin the process.

Operator: a short sequence near the promoter that assists in transcription by interacting with regulatory proteins (transcription factors).

CT teacher: "Be able to write about operons."

Operon: a promoter/operator pair that services multiple genes; the **lac operon** is a well-known example (Figure 11.7).

Repressor: protein that prevents the binding of RNA polymerase to the promoter site.

Enhancer: DNA region, also known as a "regulator," that is located thousands of bases away from the promoter; it influences transcription by interacting with specific transcription factors.

Inducer: a molecule that binds to and inactivates a repressor (e.g., lactose for the lac operon).

BIG IDEA 4.C.2
Environmental factors (e.g., lactose in a bacterial culture) can influence gene expression.

The control of gene expression is vital to the proper and efficient functioning of an organism. In bacteria, operons are a major method of gene expression control. The lactose operon services a series of three genes involved in the process of lactose metabolism. This contains the genes that help the bacteria digest lactose. It makes sense for bacteria to produce these genes only if lactose is present. Otherwise, why waste the energy on unneeded enzymes? This is where operons come into play—in the absence of lactose, a repressor binds to the promoter region and prevents transcription from occurring. When lactose is present, there is a binding site on the repressor where lactose attaches, causing the repressor to let go of the promoter region. RNA polymerase is then free to bind to that site and initiate transcription of the genes. When the lactose is gone, the repressor again becomes free to bind to the promoter, halting the process.

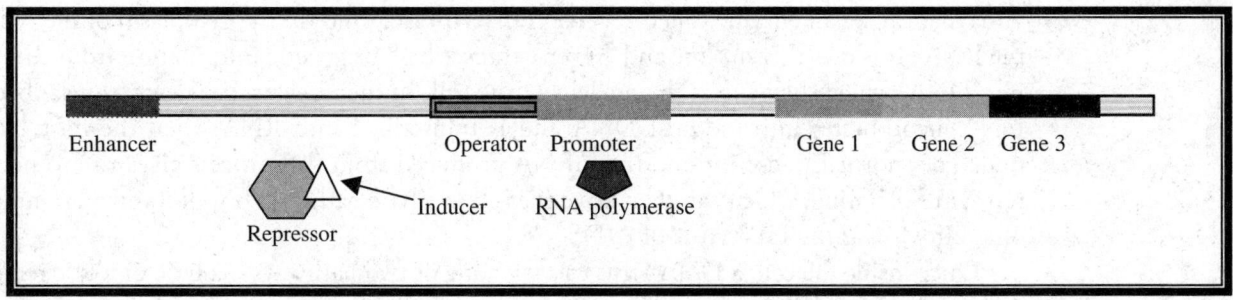

Figure 11.7 General layout of an operon.

Because gene expression in eukaryotes involves more steps, there are more places where gene control can occur. Here are a few examples of eukaryotic gene expression control:

Transcription: controlled by the presence or absence of particular transcription factors, which bind to the DNA and affect the rate of transcription.

Translation: controlled by factors that tend to prevent protein synthesis from starting. This can occur if proteins bind to mRNA and prevent the ribosomes from attaching, or if the initiation factors vital to protein synthesis are inactivated.

DNA methylation: addition of CH_3 groups to the bases of DNA. Methylation renders DNA inactive. **Barr bodies,** discussed in Chapter 10, are highly methylated.

These are only a few of the examples of gene expression control that occur in eukaryotes. Do not get lost in the specifics.

The Genetics of Viruses

A **virus** is a parasitic infectious agent that is unable to survive outside of a host organism. Viruses do not contain enzymes for metabolism, and they do not contain ribosomes for protein synthesis. They are completely dependent on their host. Once a virus infects a cell, it takes over the cell's machinery and uses it to produce whatever it needs to survive and reproduce. How a virus acts after it enters a cell depends on what type of virus it is. Classification of viruses is based on many factors:

BIG IDEA 3.A.1
DNA (and sometimes RNA) is the primary source of heritable information.

Genetic material: DNA, RNA, protein, etc.?

Capsid: type of capsid?

Viral envelope: present or absent?

Host range: what type of cells does it affect?

All viruses have a genome (DNA or RNA) and a protein coat (capsid). A **capsid** is a protein shell that surrounds the genetic material. Some viruses are surrounded by a structure called a **viral envelope,** which not only protects the virus but also helps the virus attach to the cells that it prefers to infect. The viral envelope is produced in the endoplasmic reticulum (ER) of the infected cell and contains some elements from the host cell and some from the virus. Each virus has a **host range,** which is the range of cells that the virus is able to infect. For example, the HIV virus infects the T cells of our body, and bacteriophages infect only bacteria.

A special type of virus that merits discussion is one called a retrovirus. This is an RNA virus that carries an enzyme called **reverse transcriptase.** Once in the cytoplasm of the cell, the RNA virus uses this enzyme and "reverse transcribes" its genetic information from RNA into DNA, which then enters the nucleus of the cell. In the nucleus, the newly transcribed DNA incorporates into the host DNA and is transcribed into RNA when the host cell undergoes normal transcription. The mRNA produced from this process gives rise to new retrovirus offspring, which can then leave the cell in a lytic pathway. A well-known example of a retrovirus is the HIV virus of AIDS.

Once inside the cell, a DNA virus can take one of two pathways—a lytic or a lysogenic pathway. In a **lytic cycle,** the cell actually produces many viral offspring, which are released from the cell—killing the host cell in the process. In a **lysogenic cycle,** the virus falls dormant and incorporates its DNA into the host DNA as an entity called a **provirus.** The viral

DNA is quietly reproduced by the cell every time the cell reproduces itself, and this allows the virus to stay alive from generation to generation without killing the host cell. Viruses in the lysogenic cycle can sometimes separate out from the host DNA and enter the lytic cycle (like a bear awaking from hibernation).

Viruses come in many shapes and sizes. Although many viruses are large, **viroids** are plant viruses that are only a few hundred nucleotides in length, showing that size is not the only factor in viral success. Another type of infectious agent you should be familiar with is a **prion**— an incorrectly folded form of a brain cell protein that works its magic by converting other normal host proteins into misshapen proteins. An example of a prion disease that has been getting plenty of press coverage is "mad cow" disease. Prion diseases are degenerative diseases that tend to cause brain dysfunction—dementia, muscular control problems, and loss of balance.

The Genetics of Bacteria

BIG IDEA 3.C.1
Bacteria have multiple ways to increase genetic variation.

Bacteria are prokaryotic cells that consist of one double-stranded circular DNA molecule. Present in the cells of many bacteria are extra circles of DNA called **plasmids,** which contain just a few genes and have been useful in genetic engineering. Plasmids replicate independently of the main chromosome. Bacterial cells reproduce in an asexual fashion, undergoing **binary fission.** Quite simply, the cell replicates its DNA and then physically pinches in half, producing a daughter cell that is identical to the parent cell. From this description of binary fission, it seems unlikely that there could be variation among bacterial cells. This is not the case, thanks to mutation and genetic recombination. As in humans, DNA mutation in bacteria occurs very rarely, but some bacteria replicate so quickly that these mutations can have a pronounced effect on their variability.

Transformation

An experiment performed by Griffith in 1928 provides a fantastic example of **transformation**— the uptake of foreign DNA from the surrounding environment. Transformation occurs through the use of proteins on the surface of cells that snag pieces of DNA from around the cell that are from closely related species. This particular experiment involved a bacteria known as *Streptococcus pneumoniae,* which existed as either a rough strain (R), which is nonvirulent, or as a smooth strain (S), which is virulent. A virulent strain is one that can lead to contraction of an illness. The experimenters exposed mice to different forms of the bacteria. Mice given live S bacteria died. Mice given live R bacteria survived. Mice given heat-killed S bacteria survived. Mice given heat-killed S bacteria combined with live R bacteria died. This was the kicker . . . all the other results to this point were expected. Those exposed to heat-killed S combined with live R bacteria contracted the disease because the live R bacteria underwent transformation. Some of the R bacteria picked up the portion of the heat-killed S bacteria's DNA, which contained the instructions on how to make the vital component necessary for successful disease transmission. These R bacteria became virulent.

BIG IDEA 3.C.3
Viral infection can introduce genetic variation into the host.

Transduction

To understand transduction, you first need to be introduced to something called a **phage** (Figure 11.8)—a virus that infects bacteria. The mechanism by which a phage (otherwise known as bacteriophage) infects a cell reminds me of a syringe. A phage contains within its capsid the DNA that it is attempting to deliver. A phage latches onto the surface of a cell and like a syringe, fires its DNA through the membrane and into the cell. **Transduction** is the movement of genes from one cell to another by phages. The two main forms of transduction you should be familiar with are generalized and specialized transduction.

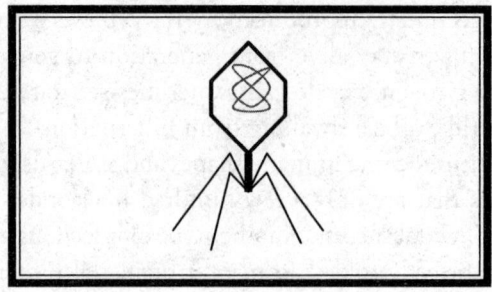

Figure 11.8   A phage.

Generalized Transduction   Imagine that a phage virus infects and takes over a bacterial cell that contains a functional gene for resistance to penicillin. Occasionally during the creation of new phage viruses, pieces of host DNA instead of viral DNA are accidentally put into a phage. When the cell lyses, expelling the newly formed viral particles, the phage containing the host DNA may latch onto another cell, injecting the host DNA from one cell into another bacterial cell. If the phage attaches to a cell that contains a nonfunctional gene for resistance to penicillin, the effects of this transduction process can be observed. After injecting the host DNA containing the functional penicillin resistance gene, crossover could occur between the comparable gene regions, switching the nonfunctional gene with the functional gene. This would create a new cell that is resistant to penicillin.

Specialized Transduction   This type of transduction involves a virus that is in the lysogenic cycle, resting quietly along with the other DNA of the host cell. Occasionally when a lysogenic virus switches cycles and becomes lytic, it may bring with it a piece of the host DNA as it pulls out of the host chromosome. Imagine that the host DNA it brought with it contains a functional gene for resistance to penicillin. This virus, now in the lytic cycle, will produce numerous copies of new viral offspring that contain this resistance gene from the host cell. If the new phage offspring attaches to a cell that is not penicillin resistant and injects its DNA and crossover occurs, specialized transduction will have occurred.

Conjugation

This is the raciest of the genetic recombinations that we will cover . . . the bacterial version of sex. It is the transfer of DNA between two bacterial cells connected by appendages called **sex pili**. Movement of DNA between two cells occurs across a cytoplasmic connection between the two cells and requires the presence of an **F-plasmid**, which contains the genes necessary for the production of a sex pilus.

Genetic Engineering

DNA technology is advancing at a rapid rate, and you need to have a basic understanding of the most common laboratory techniques for the AP Biology exam.

    Restriction enzymes are enzymes that cut DNA at specific nucleotide sequences. When added to a solution containing DNA, the enzymes cut the DNA wherever the enzyme's particular sequence appears. This creates DNA fragments with single-stranded ends called "**sticky-ends**," which find and reconnect with other DNA fragments containing the same ends (with the assistance of DNA ligase). Sticky ends allow DNA pieces from different sources to be connected, creating **recombinant DNA**. Another concept important to genetic engineering is the **vector**, which moves DNA from one source to another. Plasmids can be removed from bacterial cells and used as vectors by cutting the DNA of interest and the DNA of the plasmid with the same restriction enzyme to create DNA with similar sticky ends. The DNA can be attached to the plasmid, creating a vector that can be used to transport DNA.

Steve (12th grade): "Know this cold. It was all over my exam!"

Gel Electrophoresis

This technique is used to separate and examine DNA fragments. The DNA is cut with our new friends, the restriction enzymes, and then separated by electrophoresis. The pieces of DNA are separated on the basis of size with the help of an electric charge. DNA is added to the wells at the negative end of the gel. When the electric current is turned on, the migration begins. Smaller pieces travel farther along the gel, and larger pieces do not travel as far. The bigger you are, the harder it is to move. This technique can be used to sequence DNA and determine the order in which the nucleotides appear. It can be used in a procedure known as **Southern blotting** (after Edwin M. Southern, a British biologist) to determine if a particular sequence of nucleotides is present in a sample of DNA. Electrophoresis is used in forensics to match DNA found at the crime scene with DNA of suspects. This requires the use of pieces of DNA called *restriction fragment length polymorphisms* (RFLPs). DNA is specific to each individual, and when it is mixed with restriction enzymes, different combinations of RFLPs will be obtained from person to person. Electrophoresis separates DNA samples from the suspect and whatever sample is found at the scene of the crime. The two are compared, and if the RFLPs match, there is a high degree of certainty that the DNA sample came from the suspect. In Figure 11.9, if well A is the DNA from the crime scene, then well C is the DNA of the guilty party.

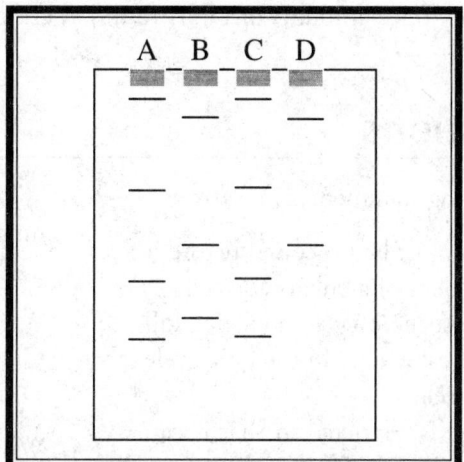

Figure 11.9   A sample gel electrophoresis.

Cloning

Sometimes it is desirable to obtain large quantities of a gene of interest, such as insulin for the treatment of diabetes. The process of cloning involves many of the steps we just mentioned. Plasmids used for cloning often contain two important genes—one that provides resistance to an antibiotic, and one that gives the bacteria the ability to metabolize some sugar. In this case, we will use a galactose hydrolyzing gene and a gene for ampicillin resistance. The plasmid and DNA of interest are both cut with the same restriction enzyme. The restriction site for this enzyme is right in the middle of the galactose gene of the plasmid. When the sticky ends are created, the DNA of interest and the plasmid molecules are mixed and join together. Not every combination made here is what the scientist is looking for. The recombinant plasmids produced are transformed into bacterial cells. This is where the two specific genes for the plasmid come into play. The transformed cells are allowed to reproduce and are placed on a medium containing ampicillin. Cells that have taken in the ampicillin resistance gene will survive, while those that have not will perish. The medium also contains a special sugar that is broken down by the galactose enzyme present in the vector to form a colored product. The cells containing the gene of interest will remain white since the galactose gene has been interrupted and rendered nonfunctional. This allows the experimenter to isolate cells that contain the desired product. Now, it is time for us to quit cloning around and move onto another genetic engineering technique.

Polymerase Chain Reaction

Think of this technique as a high-speed copy machine. It is used to produce large quantities of a particular sequence of DNA in a very short amount of time. If the cloning reaction is the 747 of copying DNA, then polymerase chain reaction (PCR) is the Concorde. This process begins with double-stranded DNA containing the gene of interest. DNA polymerase, the superstar enzyme of DNA replication, is added to the mixture along with a huge number of nucleotides and primers specific for the sequence of interest, which help initiate the synthesis of DNA. PCR begins by heating the DNA to split the strands, followed by the cooling of the strands to allow the primers to bind to the sequence of interest. DNA polymerase then steps up to the plate and produces the rest of the DNA molecule by adding the nucleotides to the growing DNA strand. Each cycle concludes having doubled the amount of DNA present at the beginning of the cycle. The cycle is repeated over and over, every few minutes, until a huge amount of DNA has been created. PCR is used in many ways, such as to detect the presence of viruses like HIV in cells, diagnose genetic disorders, and amplify trace amounts of DNA found at crime scenes.

❯ Review Questions

1. Which of the following statements is *incorrect*?

   A. Messenger RNA must be processed before it can leave the nucleus of a eukaryotic cell.

   B. A virus in the lysogenic cycle does not kill its host cell, whereas a virus in the lytic cycle destroys its host cell.

   C. DNA polymerase is restricted in that it can add nucleotides only in a 5′-to-3′ direction.

   D. During translation, the A site holds the tRNA carrying the growing protein, while the P site holds the tRNA carrying the next amino acid.

2. The process of transcription results in the formation of

   A. DNA.
   B. proteins.
   C. lipids.
   D. RNA.

3. Which of the following codons signals the beginning of the translation process?

   A. AGU
   B. UGA
   C. AUG
   D. AGG

4. Which of the following is an improper pairing of DNA or RNA nucleotides?

   A. Thymine-adenine
   B. Guanine-thymine
   C. Uracil-adenine
   D. Guanine-cytosine

5. Which of the following is responsible for the type of diseases that includes "mad cow" disease?

   A. Viroids
   B. Plasmids
   C. Prions
   D. Provirus

6. Which of the following is the correct sequence of events that must occur for translation to begin?

   A. Transfer RNA binds to the small ribosomal subunit, which leads to the attachment of the large ribosomal subunit. This signals to the mRNA molecule that it should now bind, with its first codon in the correct site, to the protein synthesis machinery, and translation begins.

   B. Messenger RNA attaches to the small ribosomal subunit, with its first codon in the correct site, thus attracting a tRNA molecule to attach to the codon. This signals to the large subunit that it should now bind to the protein synthesis machinery, and translation can begin.

   C. Messenger RNA attaches to the large ribosomal subunit with its first codon in the correct site, attracting a tRNA molecule to attach to the codon. This signals to the small subunit that it should now bind to the protein synthesis machinery, and translation can begin.

   D. Transfer RNA binds to the large ribosomal subunit, which leads to the attachment of the small ribosomal subunit. This signals to the mRNA molecule that it should now bind with its first codon in the correct site to the protein synthesis machinery, and translation begins.

7. All the following are players involved in the control of gene expression *except*

   A. episomes.
   B. repressors.
   C. operons.
   D. methylation.

8. Which of the following does *not* occur during RNA processing in the nucleus of eukaryotes?

   A. The removal of introns from the RNA molecule
   B. The addition of a string of adenine nucleotides to the 3′ end of the RNA molecule
   C. The addition of a guanine cap to the 5′ end of the RNA molecule
   D. The addition of methyl groups to certain nucleotides of the RNA molecules

9. Which of the following statements is *not* true of a tRNA molecule?

   A. The job of transfer RNA is to carry amino acids to the ribosomes.
   B. At the attachment site of each tRNA, there is a region called the *anticodon*, which is a three-nucleotide sequence that is perfectly complementary to a particular codon.
   C. Each tRNA molecule has a short lifespan and is used only once during translation.
   D. The enzyme responsible for ensuring that a tRNA molecule is carrying the appropriate amino acid is aminoacyl tRNA synthase.

For questions 10 and 11, please use the following gel:

10. Which of the DNA pieces in the gel is smallest in size?

   A. A
   B. B
   C. C
   D. D

11. If well 1 is DNA from a crime scene, which individual should contact a lawyer?

   A. Person 2
   B. Person 3
   C. Person 4
   D. Person 5

› Answers and Explanations

1. **D**—During translation, the **P site** holds the tRNA carrying the growing protein, while the **A site** holds the tRNA carrying the next amino acid. When translation begins, the first codon bound is the AUG codon, and in the P site is the tRNA with the methionine. The next codon in the sequence determines which tRNA binds next, and the appropriate tRNA molecule sits in the A site of the ribosome. A peptide bond forms between the amino acid on the A site tRNA and the amino acid on the P site tRNA. The amino acid from the P site then moves to the A site, allowing the tRNA in the P site to leave the ribosome. Next the ribosome moves along the mRNA in such a way that the A site is now the P site and the next tRNA comes into the A site carrying the next amino acid. Answer choices A, B, and C are all true.

2. **D**—The process of transcription leads to the production of RNA. RNA is not immediately ready to leave the nucleus after it is produced. It must first be processed, during which a 3′ poly-A tail and a 5′ cap are added and the introns are spliced from the RNA molecule. After this process, the RNA is free to leave the nucleus and lead the production of proteins.

3. **C**—AGG codes for the amino acid arginine. AGU codes for the amino acid serine. UGA and UAG are stop codons, which signal the end of the translation process. AUG is the start codon, which also codes for methionine.

4. **B**—Guanine does not pair with thymine in DNA or RNA. Watson and Crick discovered that adenine pairs with thymine (A=T) held together by two hydrogen bonds and guanine pairs with cytosine (C≡G) held together by three hydrogen bonds. One way that RNA differs from DNA is that it contains uracil instead of thymine. But in RNA, guanine still pairs with cytosine and adenine instead pairs with uracil. Watson and Crick also discovered that for the structure of DNA they discovered to be true, a purine must always be paired with a pyrimidine. Adenine and guanine are the purines, and thymine and cytosine are the pyrimidines.

5. **C**—Prions are the culprit for mad cow disease. *Viroids* are tiny viruses that infect plants. *Plasmids* are small circles of DNA in bacteria that are separate from the main chromosome. They are self-replicating and are vital to the process of genetic engineering. A *provirus* is that which is formed during the lysogenic cycle of a virus when it falls dormant and incorporates its DNA into the host DNA. A *retrovirus* is an RNA virus that carries an enzyme called reverse transcriptase. A classic example of a retrovirus is HIV.

6. **B**—Translation begins when the mRNA attaches to the small ribosomal subunit. The first codon for this process is always AUG. This attracts a tRNA molecule carrying methionine to attach to the AUG codon. When this occurs, the large subunit of the ribosome, containing the A site and the P site, binds to the complex. The elongation of the protein is ready to begin after the complex has been properly constructed. Answers A, C, and D are all in the incorrect order.

7. **A**—Episomes are not involved in gene expression regulation. *Episomes* are plasmids that can be incorporated into a bacterial chromosome. *Repressors* are regulatory proteins involved in gene regulation. They work by preventing transcription by binding to the promoter region. *Operons* are a promoter-operator pair that controls a group of genes, such as the lac operon. Methylation is involved in gene regulation. Barr bodies, discussed in Chapter 10, are found to contain a very high level of methylated DNA. Methyl groups have been associated with inactive DNA that does not undergo transcription. Hormones can affect transcription by acting directly on the transcription machinery in the nucleus of cells.

8. **D**—The mRNA produced after transcription must be modified before it can leave the nucleus and lead the translation of proteins in the ribosomes. Introns are cut out of the mRNA, and the remaining exons are ligated back together to produce the mRNA ready to be translated into a protein. Also, the 5′ end is given a guanine cap, which serves to protect the RNA and also helps the mRNA attach to the ribosome. The 3′ end is given the poly-A tail, which may help ease the movement from the nucleus to the cytoplasm. Methylation does not occur during posttranscriptional modification—it is a means of gene expression control.

9. **C**—tRNA does not have a short lifespan. Each tRNA molecule is released and recycled to bring more amino acids to the ribosomes to aid in translation. It is like a taxicab constantly picking up new passengers to deliver from place to place. Answer choices A, B, and D are all true.

10. **C**—Gel electrophoresis separates DNA fragments on the basis of size—the smaller you are, the farther you go. Because C went the farthest in this gel, this must be the smallest of the four selected DNA pieces. Of the four labeled, piece A must be the largest because it moved the least.

11. **C**—Person 4 should contact a lawyer. The DNA from the crime scene seems to match the DNA fingerprint from person 4. Electrophoresis is a very useful tool in forensics and can very accurately match DNA found at crime scenes with potential suspects.

› Rapid Review

Briefly review the following terms:

DNA: contains A and G (purines), C and T (pyrimidines), arranged in a double helix of two strands held together by hydrogen bonds (A with T, and C with G).

RNA: contains A and G (purines), C and U (pyrimidines), single stranded. There are three types: mRNA (blueprints for proteins), tRNA (brings acids to ribosomes), and rRNA (make up ribosomes).

DNA replication: occurs during S-phase, semi-conservative, built in 5′-to-3′ direction. Helicase unzips the double strand, DNA polymerase comes in and adds on the nucleotides. Proofreading enzymes minimize errors of process.

Frameshift mutation: deletion or addition of nucleotides (not a multiple of 3); shifts reading frame.

Missense mutation: substitution of wrong nucleotide into DNA (e.g., sickle cell anemia); still produces a protein.

Nonsense mutation: substitution of wrong nucleotide into DNA that produces an early stop codon.

Transcription: process by which mRNA is synthesized on a DNA template.

RNA processing: introns (noncoding) are spliced out, exons (coding) glued together: 3′ poly-A tail, 5′ G cap.

Translation: process by which the mRNA specified sequence of amino acids is lined up on a ribosome for protein synthesis.

Codon: triplet of nucleotides that codes for a particular amino acid: **start codon** = AUG; **stop codon** = UGA, UAA, UAG. (For specifics on translation, please flip to text for a good description.)

Promoter: base sequence that signals start site for transcription.

Repressor: protein that prevents the binding of RNA polymerase to promoter site.

Inducer: molecule that binds to and inactivates a repressor.

Operator: short sequence near the promoter that assists in transcription by interacting with transcription factors.

Operon: on/off switch for transcription. Allows for production of genes only when needed. Remember the lac operon—lactose is the inducer, when present, transcription on; when absent, it is off.

Viruses: Parasitic infectious agent unable to survive outside the host; can contain DNA or RNA, or have a viral envelope (protective coat).

- *Lytic cycle*: one in which the virus is actively reproducing and kills the host cell.
- *Lysogenic cycle*: one in which the virus lies dormant within the DNA of the host cell.

Retrovirus: RNA virus that carries with it reverse transcriptase (HIV).

Prion: virus that converts host brain proteins into misshapen proteins (mad cow disease).

Viroids: tiny plant viruses.

Phage: virus that infects bacteria.

Bacteria: prokaryotic cells; consist of one double-stranded circular DNA molecule; reproduce by binary fission (e.g., **plasmid**—extra circle of DNA present in bacteria that replicate independently of main chromosome).

Genetic Recombination

Transformation: uptake of foreign DNA from the surrounding environment (smooth vs. rough pneumococcus).

Transduction: movement of genes from one cell to another by phages, which are incorporated by crossover.

- *Generalized*: lytic cycle accidently places host DNA into a phage, which is brought to another cell.
- *Specialized*: virus leaving lysogenic cycle brings host DNA with it into phage.

Conjugation: transfer of DNA between two bacterial cells connected by sex pili.

Genetic Engineering

Restriction enzymes: enzymes that cut DNA at particular sequences, creating sticky ends.

Vector: mover of DNA from one source to another (plasmids are good vectors).

Cloning: somewhat slow process by which a desired sequence of DNA is copied numerous times.

Gel electrophoresis: technique used to separate DNA according to size (small = faster). DNA moves from: − to +.

Polymerase chain reaction (PCR): produces large quantities of sequence in short amount of time.

CHAPTER 12

Evolution

IN THIS CHAPTER

Summary: This chapter discusses evolution and the four major modes in which it occurs. It introduces you to the various forms of selection: natural, directional, stabilizing, disruptive, sexual, and artificial. It discusses the two main forms of speciation (allopatric and sympatric) and briefly touches on the theory behind how life on this planet emerged many years ago.

Key Ideas

- ✪ The four major modes of evolution are genetic drift, gene flow, mutation, and natural selection.
- ✪ Natural selection is based on three conditions: variation, heritability, and differential reproductive success.
- ✪ There are four basic patterns of evolution: co-evolution, convergent evolution, divergent evolution, and parallel evolution.
- ✪ Sources of variation within populations: mutation, sexual reproduction, and balanced polymorphism.
- ✪ Hardy-Weinberg conditions: no mutations, no gene flow, no genetic drift, no natural selection, and random mating.
- ✪ Hardy-Weinberg equations: $p + q = 1$ and $p^2 + 2pq + q^2 = 1$.
- ✪ Evidence for evolution: homologous characters, embryology, and vestigial structures.

Introduction

This chapter begins with an introduction to the concept of evolution and the four major modes in which it occurs. From there we focus more closely on natural selection and the work of Lamarck and Darwin. We then briefly touch on adaptations before looking at the various types of selection: directional, stabilizing, disruptive, sexual, and artificial selection. This is followed by a quick look at the sources of variation within populations followed by a look at the two main types of speciation: allopatric and sympatric. Next will come the yucky math portion of the chapter: the Hardy-Weinberg equation and the conditions necessary for its existence. The chapter concludes with a look at the existing evidence in support of the theory of evolution and a discussion of how life on this planet emerged so many years ago.

Definition of Evolution

How often have you heard executives report that "the idea evolved into a successful project" or popular science show narrators describe how a star "has been evolving for millions of years"? *Evolution* is no longer strictly a biological term since every academic field and nonacademic industry uses it. Such uses of the verb *evolve* reveal its meaning in its simplest form—to evolve means to change. For the AP Biology exam, however, you should remember the biological definition of evolution: *descent with modification.* Don't let the general uses of the word mislead you; a key part of this definition is *descent,* which can happen only when one group of organisms gives rise to another. When you see the word *evolution*, think of something that happens in populations, not in individuals.

More specifically, evolution describes change in allele frequencies in populations over time. When one generation of organisms (whether algae or giraffes or ferns) reproduces and creates the next, the frequencies of the alleles for the various genes represented in the population may be different from what they were in the parent generation. Frequencies can change so much that certain alleles are lost or others become fixed—all individuals have the same allele for that character. Over many generations, the species can change so much that it becomes quite different from the ancestral species, or a part of the population can branch off and become a new species (**speciation**). Why do we see this change in allele frequencies with time?

Allele frequencies may change because of random factors or by natural selection. Let's consider chance events first. Imagine a population of fish in a large pond that exhibits two alleles for fin length (short and long) and is isolated from other populations of the same species. One day a tornado kills 50 percent of the fish population. Completely by chance, most of the fish killed possess the long-fin allele, and very few of these individuals are left in the population. In the next generation, there are many fewer fish with long fins because fewer long-finned fish were left to reproduce; that allele is much more poorly represented in the pond than it was in the original parent generation before the catastrophe. This is an example of **genetic drift:** a change in allele frequencies that is due to chance events. When drift dramatically reduces population size, we call it a **bottleneck.**

Now imagine that the same pond becomes connected to another pond by a small stream. The two populations mix, and by chance, all the long-finned fish migrate to the other pond, and no long-finned fish migrate in. Again, which individuals migrated was random in this example; thus, there will be a change in the allele frequencies in the next generation. This is an example of **gene flow,** or the change in allele frequencies as genes from one population are incorporated into another.

Gene flow (also more loosely known as *migration* when the individuals are actively relocating) is random with respect to which organisms succeed, but keep in mind that we

BIG IDEA 4.C.4
The diversity of species within an ecosystem may influence the stability of the ecosystem.

could think of situations in which migration is not random. For example, if only the short-finned fish could fit in the stream connecting the two ponds, the alleles represented in the subsequent generation would *not* be random with respect to that allele. We also have not stated that the short-finned fish have an advantage by swimming to the other pond—if they did, this would be an example of natural selection, which we'll discuss below.

Finally, let's consider **mutation,** the third random event that can cause changes in allele frequencies. Mutation is *always* random with respect to which genes are affected, although the changes in allele frequencies that occur as a result of the mutation may not be. Let's say that a mutation occurs in the offspring of a fish in our hypothetical pond. The mutation creates a new allele. As a result, the allele frequencies in the offspring generation has changed, simply because we have added a new allele (remember that allele frequencies for a given gene always add up to one). As you can imagine, one mutation on its own does not have the potential to dramatically alter the allele frequencies in a population, unless this is a *really* small pond! But mutation is extremely important because it is the basis of the variation we see in the first place and it is a very strong force when it is paired with natural selection.

The four major modes of evolution are

1. Genetic drift
2. Gene flow (also called *migration*)
3. Mutation
4. Natural selection

Remember that the first three factors act randomly with respect to the alleles in the population—which alleles increase and which decrease in frequency are determined by chance events, not because some alleles are inherently better than others. We'll now turn to the fourth mode or process of evolution, natural selection, where the modification that occurs with descent is *nonrandom.*

Natural Selection

BIG IDEA 1.A.1
Natural selection is a major mechanism of evolution.

Probably the biggest mistake people make when thinking about natural selection is thinking that it is synonymous with evolution. **Natural selection** is only one process by which evolution occurs (the others are discussed in the previous section). However, it is an important process because it has been instrumental in shaping the natural world. Because of the theory of natural selection, we can explain why organisms look and behave the way they do.

Natural selection is based on three conditions:

1. *Variation:* for natural selection to occur, a population must exhibit phenotypic variance—in other words, differences must exist between individuals, even if they are slight.
2. *Heritability:* parents must be able to pass on the traits that are under natural selection. If a trait cannot be inherited, it cannot be selected for or against.
3. *Differential reproductive success:* this sounds complicated, but it's a simple concept. **Reproductive success** measures how many offspring you produce that survive relative to how many the other individuals in your population produce. The condition simply states that there must be variation between parents in how many offspring they produce as a result of the different traits that the parents have.

BIG IDEA 1.A.2
Natural selection acts on phenotypes.

It is easiest to illustrate natural selection with an example. Let's revisit our pond before the tornado came, where short- and long-finned fish inhabit murky waters. A new predator invades the pond. Fin length determines swimming speed (longer fins allow a fish to swim faster), and only the fastest fish can escape the predator. How would you expect the allele frequencies to change under these conditions? Fish with what length fin would be eaten the most? Because the short-finned fish would be the slowest, they would be featured on the menu. But the long-finned fish, able to escape this new predator, would survive and reproduce, and the frequency of the long-fin allele would increase relative to the short-fin allele. We have created a situation in which allele frequencies change as a result of a nonrandom event; the predator's presence results in a predictable decrease in the short-fin allele and a consequent increase in the long-fin allele. Remember that allele frequencies always add up to 100 percent, so the long-finned fish don't have to do particularly well for the long-fin allele to increase—they only have to do well *relative* to the short-finned fish. The actual numbers of fish could decrease for both variants of this fish species.

BIG IDEA 1.A.3
Evolutionary change is driven by random processes.

Why aren't organisms perfectly adapted to their environments? Since natural selection increases the frequencies of advantageous alleles, why don't we get to a point where all individuals have all the best alleles? For one, different alleles confer different advantages in different environments. Furthermore, remember that the environment—which includes everything from habitat, to climate, to competitors, to predators, to food resources—is constantly changing. Species are therefore also constantly changing as the traits that give them an advantage also change. In cases where a trait becomes unconditionally advantageous, we do in fact see fixed alleles; for example, all spiders have eight legs because the alternatives just aren't as good under any circumstances. But where there are heritable characters that both vary and confer fitness advantages (or disadvantages) on their host organisms, natural selection can occur.

Lamarck and Darwin

The two key figures whose research you should know for the evolution section of the AP Biology exam are Jean-Baptiste Lamarck and Charles Darwin. Lamarck proposed the idea that evolution occurs by the inheritance of acquired characters. The classic example is giraffe necks: Lamarck proposed that giraffes evolved long necks because individuals were constantly reaching for the leaves at the tops of trees. A giraffe's neck lengthened during its lifetime, and then that giraffe's offspring had a long neck because of all that straining its parents did. The key here is that change happened within organisms during their lifetimes and then the change in the trait was passed on.

What's wrong with Lamarck's theory? Try explaining to yourself how the changed character could be passed on to the offspring. The answer is that it couldn't—the instructions in the sex chromosomes that direct the production of offspring cannot be changed after they are created at the birth of an organism. Lamarck confused genetic and environmental (postconceptive) change, which is not surprising because no one had discovered genes yet.

Darwin had another idea, one that ended up being entirely consistent with Mendelian genetics (although Mendel had already written his thesis during Darwin's time, it is rumored that his book sat on Darwin's shelf, with the pages still uncut, until Darwin's death). Darwin suggested the idea of natural selection described above and coined the phrase "survival of the fittest." Although he didn't call them *genes,* he proposed a hypothetical unit of heredity that passed from parent to offspring. Incidentally, a man named Wallace also came up with the idea of natural selection during the same time, but Darwin got the publication out first and has become famous as a result.

Adaptations

An **adaptation** is a trait that if altered, affects the fitness of the organism. Adaptations are the result of natural selection and can include not only physical traits such as eyes, fingernails, and livers but also the intangible traits of organisms. For example, lifespan length is an adaptation, albeit a variable one. Mating behavior is also an adaptation—it has been selected by natural selection because it is an effective strategy. An individual with a different form of mating behavior may do better or worse than the average, but a change is likely to have some effect on reproductive success. For example, individuals whose mating strategy is to attempt to court women by running at them, arms flailing while screaming wildly, and salivating heavily, do worse than the average male.

Let's take a look at how such a behavioral adaptation can evolve. Reproductive maturity is a good example. Female chimpanzees become reproductively mature at around the age of 13. Females that mature at age 12 spend less time growing and may therefore be more susceptible to problems with pregnancy. Females that mature at 14 have lost valuable time—their earlier-maturing peers have gained a year on them. You can imagine that from generation to generation, females that matured at age 13 became better represented in the population compared to faster and slower maturers. Although there will always be individuals that differ from the mode, we can view age at reproductive maturation as an adaptation.

Types of Selection

Natural selection can change the frequencies of alleles in populations through various processes. The most commonly described are the following three:

Mike (freshman in college): "Learn these selection types . . . they make good multiple-choice questions."

1. **Directional selection.** This occurs when members of a population at one end of a spectrum are selected against, while those at the other end are selected for. For example, imagine a population of elephants with various-sized trunks. In this particular environment, much more food is available in the very tall trees than in the shorter trees. Elephants with what length trunk will survive and reproduce the most successfully? Those with the longest trunks. Those with shorter trunks will be strongly selected against (and those in the middle will also be in the middle in terms of success). Over time we expect to see an increasing percentage of elephants with long trunks (how quickly this change occurs depends on the strength of selection—if all the short-trunked elephants die, we can imagine that the allele frequencies will change very quickly). (See Figure 12.1.)

2. **Stabilizing selection.** This describes selection for the mean of a population for a given allele. A real example of this is human infant birth weight—it is a disadvantage to be really small *or* really big, and it is best to be somewhere in between. Stabilizing selection has the effect of reducing variation in a population (see Figure 12.1).

3. **Disruptive selection.** Also known as *diversifying selection,* this process can be regarded as being the opposite of stabilizing selection. We say that selection is disruptive when individuals at the two extremes of a spectrum of variation do better than the more common forms in the middle. Snail shell color is an example of disruptive selection. Imagine an environment in which snails with very dark shells and those with very light shells are best able to hide from predators. Those with an in-between shell color are gulped up like escargot at a cocktail party, creating the double-hump curve seen in Figure 12.1.

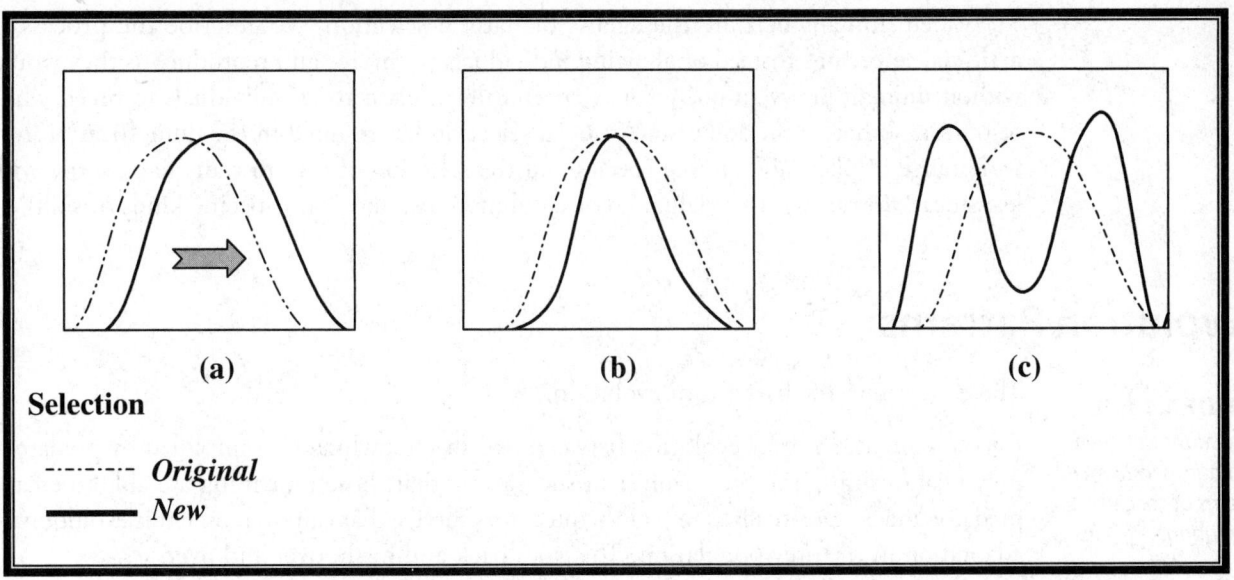

Figure 12.1   Three types of selection: (a) directional; (b) stabilizing; (c) disruptive.

These three processes describe the way in which allele frequencies can change as a result of the forces of natural selection. It is also important to remember two other types of selection that complement natural selection: sexual selection and artificial selection.

Sexual selection occurs because individuals differ in mating success. In other words, because not all individuals will have the maximum number of possible offspring, there must be some reason why some individuals have greater reproductive success than others. Think about how this is different from natural selection, which includes both reproduction and survival. Sexual selection is purely about access to mating opportunities.

Sexual selection occurs by two primary processes: **within-sex competition** and **choice.** In mammals and many nonmammalian species, females are limited in the number of off-spring they can produce in their lifetimes (because of internal gestation), while males are not (because sperm are cheap to produce and few males participate in offspring care). Which sex do you think will compete, and which sex will be choosier? In most mammals for instance, males compete and females choose. It makes sense that males have to compete because females are a limiting resource, and it makes sense that females are choosy because they invest a lot in each reproductive effort. This leads to the evolution of characters that are designed for two main functions: (1) as weaponry or other tools for male competition (e.g., large testes for sperm competition) and (2) as traits that increase mating opportunities because females prefer to mate with males who have them (e.g., colorful feathers in many birds).

On what do females base their choices? While you need not become an expert on this matter, it is important to remember that female mate choice for certain characters is not random. One hypothesis for why females choose males with colorful feathers, for example, is that colorful feathers indicate good genes, which is important for a female's offspring. Bright colors are costly, so a male with brightly colored feathers is probably healthy (which may, in turn, indicate an ability to reduce parasite load, for example). We call such sexually selected traits that are the result of female choice **honest indicators.** Keep in mind that selecting a mate for particular features does not necessarily involve conscious thought, and in most animals never does; the female does not think, "Oh! What nice feathers. He must come from good genes." Rather, females who choose males that display honest indicators have more surviving offspring than do females who don't, and as a result, the "choosing males with colorful feathers" trait increases in the population.

When humans become the agents of natural selection, we describe the process as **artificial selection.** Instead of allowing individuals to survive and reproduce as they would without human intervention, we may specifically select certain individuals to breed while restraining others from doing so. Artificial selection has resulted in the domestication of a wide range of plant and animal species and the selection of certain traits (e.g., cattle with lean meat, flowers with particular color combinations, dogs with specific kinds of skill).

Evolution Patterns

> **BIG IDEA 4.B.3**
> *Interactions between populations influence patterns of species distribution.*

There are four basic patterns of evolution:

Coevolution. The mutual evolution between two species, which is exemplified by predator–prey relationships. The prey evolves in such a way that those remaining are able to escape predator attack. Eventually, some of the predators survive that can overcome this evolutionary adaptation in the prey population. This goes back and forth, over and over.

Convergent evolution. Two unrelated species evolve in a way that makes them *more* similar (think of them as converging on a single point). They are both responding in the same way to some environmental challenge, and this brings them closer together. We call two *characters* **convergent characters** if they are similar in two species, even though the species do *not* share a common ancestor. For example, birds and insects both have wings in order to fly, despite the fact that insects are not directly related to birds.

Divergent evolution. Two related species evolve in a way that makes them *less* similar. Divergent evolution can lead to speciation (allopatric or sympatric).

Parallel evolution. Similar evolutionary changes occurring in two species that can be related or unrelated. They are simply responding in a similar manner to a similar environmental condition.

Sources of Variation

Remember that one of the conditions for natural selection is variation. Where does this variation within populations come from?

1. **Mutation.** We already discussed mutations as a mechanism by which evolution occurs. Random changes in the DNA of an individual can introduce new alleles into a population.
2. **Sexual reproduction.** Refer to Chapter 16, Human Reproduction, and the discussion of why offspring are not identical to their parents (crossover, independent assortment of homologous pairs, and the fact that all sperm and ova are unique and thus create a unique individual when joined).
3. **Balanced polymorphism.** Some characters are fixed, meaning that all individuals in a species or population have them: for example, all tulips develop from bulbs. However, other characters are polymorphic, meaning that there are two or more phenotypic variants. For example, tulips come in a variety of colors. If one phenotypic variant leads to increased reproductive success, we expect directional selection to eventually eliminate all other varieties. However, we can find many examples in the natural world where variation is prominent and one allele is not uniformly better than the others. The various ways in which balanced polymorphism is maintained are presented in Figure 12.2.

> **BIG IDEA 3.C.1**
> *Heterozygote advantage is one way biological systems can increase genetic variation.*

Mechanism	Description	Example
Heterozygote advantage	The heterozygous condition has an advantage over either homozygote, so both alleles are maintained (AA is worse off than Aa).	Sickle cell trait, a heterozygous condition, gives people in malarial environments an advantage because they are resistant to this disease.
Hybrid vigor and outbreeding	Two unrelated individuals are less likely to have the same recessive, deleterious allele than are relatives; therefore, their offspring are less likely to be homozygous for that allele; in addition, outbreeding increases the number of heterozygous alleles, increasing heterozygote advantage.	Artificially selected plants are carefully outbred in order to increase hybrid vigor; mating two inbred strains of potato will increase the number of heterozygous loci and increase the species' resistance to disease.
Frequency-dependent selection	The least common phenotype is selected for, while common phenotypes have a disadvantage.	In some fruit flies, females choose to mate with males that have the rarer phenotype, resulting in selection against the more common variants.

Figure 12.2   How balanced polymorphism is maintained.

Speciation

BIG IDEA 1.C.1
Speciation (and extinction) have occurred throughout Earth's history.

A **species** is a group of interbreeding (or potentially interbreeding) organisms. **Speciation,** the process by which new species evolve, can take one of several forms. You should be familiar with the two main forms of speciation:

1. **Allopatric speciation.** Interbreeding ceases because some sort of barrier separates a single population into two (an area with no food, a mountain, etc.). The two populations evolve independently (by any of the four processes discussed earlier), and if they change enough, then even if the barrier is removed, they cannot interbreed.

2. **Sympatric speciation.** Interbreeding ceases even though no physical barrier prevents it. This may take several forms.

Two other important terms are **polyploidy** and **balanced polymorphism:**

Polyploidy. A condition in which an individual has more than the normal number of sets of chromosomes. Although the individual may be healthy, it cannot reproduce with nonpolyploidic members of its species. This is unusual, but in some plants, it has resulted in new species because polyploidic individuals are only able to mate with each other.

BIG IDEA 1.C.2
Speciation may occur when two populations become reproductively isolated.

Balanced polymorphism. This condition (described above) can also lead to speciation if two variants diverge enough to no longer be able to interbreed (if, e.g., potential mates no longer recognize each other as possible partners).

One more term to mention before moving on is **adaptive radiation,** which is a rapid series of speciation events that occur when one or more ancestral species invades a new environment. This process was exemplified by Darwin's finches. If there are many ecological niches (see Chapter 18, Ecology in Further Detail), several species will evolve because each can fill a different niche.

When Evolution Is Not Occurring: Hardy-Weinberg Equilibrium

BIG IDEA 4.C.3
Allelic variation in a population can be modeled by the Hardy-Weinberg equation.

Evolutionary change is constantly happening in humans and other species; this seems sensible because evolution is the change in allele frequencies over time. It makes sense that these frequencies are highly variable and subject to change as the environment changes. However, biologists use a theoretical concept called the **Hardy-Weinberg equilibrium** to describe those special cases where a population is in stasis, or not evolving.

Only if the following conditions are met can a population be in Hardy-Weinberg equilibrium:

Hardy-Weinberg Conditions
1. No mutations
2. No gene flow
3. No genetic drift (and for this, the population must be large)
4. No natural selection (so that the traits are neutral; none gives an advantage or disadvantage)
5. Random mating

Notice items 1–4 in this list are the four modes of evolution, which makes sense—if we are trying to establish the conditions under which evolution does *not* occur, we must keep these processes of evolution from occurring! The fifth condition, random mating, is included because if individuals mated nonrandomly (e.g., if individuals mated with others that looked like them), the allele frequencies could change in a certain direction, and we would no longer be in equilibrium.

Determining Whether a Population Is in Hardy-Weinberg Equilibrium

Unfortunately for you, there is an equation associated with the Hardy-Weinberg equilibrium that the test writers love to put on the exam. Don't let it scare you!

$$p + q = 1$$

CT teacher: "Knowing how to do Hardy-Weinberg problems is worth 2 points to you . . . easy points."

This equation is used to determine if a population is in Hardy-Weinberg equilibrium. The symbol p is the frequency of allele 1 (often the *dominant allele*), and q is the frequency of allele 2 (often the recessive allele). Remember that the frequency of two alleles always adds up to 1 *if the population is in Hardy-Weinberg equilibrium*. For example, if 60 percent of the alleles for a given trait are dominant (p), then $p = 0.6$, and q (the recessive allele) = 1 − 0.6, or 0.4 (40 percent).

There is a second equation that goes along with this theory: $p^2 + 2pq + q^2 = 1$, where p^2 and q^2 represent the frequency of the two homozygous conditions (AA and aa). The frequency of the heterozygotes is pq plus qp or $2pq$ (Aa and aA). Since p represents the dominant allele, it makes sense that p^2 represents the homozygous dominant condition. By the same logic, q^2 represents the homozygous recessive condition.

Let's say that you are told that a population of acacia trees is 16 percent short (which is a, recessive) and 84 percent tall (which is A, dominant). What are the frequencies of the two alleles? Remember that it is not 0.16 and 0.84 because there are also the heterozygotes to consider!

In a problem like this, it is important to determine the value of q first because we know that all individuals with the recessive phenotype must be aa (q^2). You cannot begin by calculating the value of p because it is not true that all the individuals with the dominant phenotype can be lumped into p^2. Some folks displaying the dominant phenotype are heterozygous Aa (pq).

We know that $q^2 = 0.16$, so we find q by calculating $\sqrt{0.16} \rightarrow q = 0.400$. Now remember that they do not let you use a calculator. So these problems will give numbers that are fairly easy to work with. Do not despair.

What about p? Since $p + q$ is 1, and we know $q = 0.40$, then p must equal $1 - 0.40$ or 0.600.

You may also be asked to go a step further and give the percentages of the homozygous dominant and heterozygous conditions (remember, we know that the recessive condition is 16 percent—all these individuals must be aa in order to express the recessive trait). This is simple—just plug in what you know about p and q:

$$2pq = (2)\ (0.6)\ (0.4) = 0.48 \text{ or } 48\%$$
$$p^2 = (0.6)\ (0.6) = 0.36 \text{ or } 36\%$$

Now check your math: do the frequencies add up to 100 percent?

$$16 + 48 + 36 = 100$$

Why do we ever use the Hardy-Weinberg equation if it rarely applies to real populations? This can be an excellent tool to determine whether a population is evolving or not; if we find that the allele frequencies do not add up to one, then we need to look for the reasons for this (perhaps the population is too small and genetic drift is a factor, or perhaps one of the alleles is advantageous and is therefore being selected for and increasing in the population). Therefore, although the Hardy-Weinberg equilibrium is largely theoretical, it does have some important uses in evolutionary biology.

The Evidence for Evolution

Support for the theory of evolution can be found in varied kinds of evidence:

1. **Homologous characters.** Traits are said to be homologous if they are similar because their host organisms arose from a common ancestor (which implies that they have evolved). For example, the bone structure in bird wings is homologous in all bird species.

2. **Embryology.** The study of embryos reveals remarkable similarities between organisms at the earliest stages of life, although as adults (or even at birth) the species look completely different. Human embryos, for example, actually have gills for a short time during early development, hinting at our aquatic ancestry. Darwin used embryology as an important piece of evidence for the process of evolution. In 1866, the scientist Ernst Haeckel uttered the phrase, "Ontogeny recapitulates phylogeny." **Ontogeny** is an *individual's* development; **phylogeny** is a **species'** evolutionary history. What Haeckel meant was that during an organism's embryonic development, it will at some point resemble the adult form of all its ancestors before it. For example, human embryos at some point look a lot like fish embryos. The important conclusion from this is that Haeckel and others thought that embryologic similarity between developing individuals could be used to

deduce phylogenetic relationships. By the end of the nineteenth century, it was clear this law rarely holds. The real development of organisms differs in several important ways from Haeckel's schemes.

3. **Vestigial characters.** Most organisms carry characters that are no longer useful, although they once were. This should remind you of our short discussion about why organisms are not perfectly adapted to their environments (because the environment is constantly changing). Sometimes an environment changes so much that a trait is no longer needed, but is not deleterious enough to actually be selected against and eliminated. Darwin used vestigial characters as evidence in his original formulation of the process of evolution, listing the human appendix as an example.

Keep in mind that the kinds of evidence we've described are often found in the **fossil record**–the physical manifestation of species that have gone extinct (including things like bones as well as imprints). The most important thing to remember is that adaptations are the result of natural selection.

Macroevolution

Biologists distinguish between microevolution and macroevolution. **Microevolution** includes all of what we have been discussing so far in this chapter—evolution at the level of species and populations. Think of **macroevolution** as the big picture, which includes the study of evolution of groups of species over very long periods of time.

There are disagreements in the field as to the typical pattern of macroevolution. Those who believe in **gradualism** assert that evolutionary change is a steady, slow process, while those who think that evolution is best described by the **punctuated equilibria model** believe that change occurs in rapid bursts separated by large periods of stasis (no change) (see comparison in Figure 12.3). Because the fossil record is

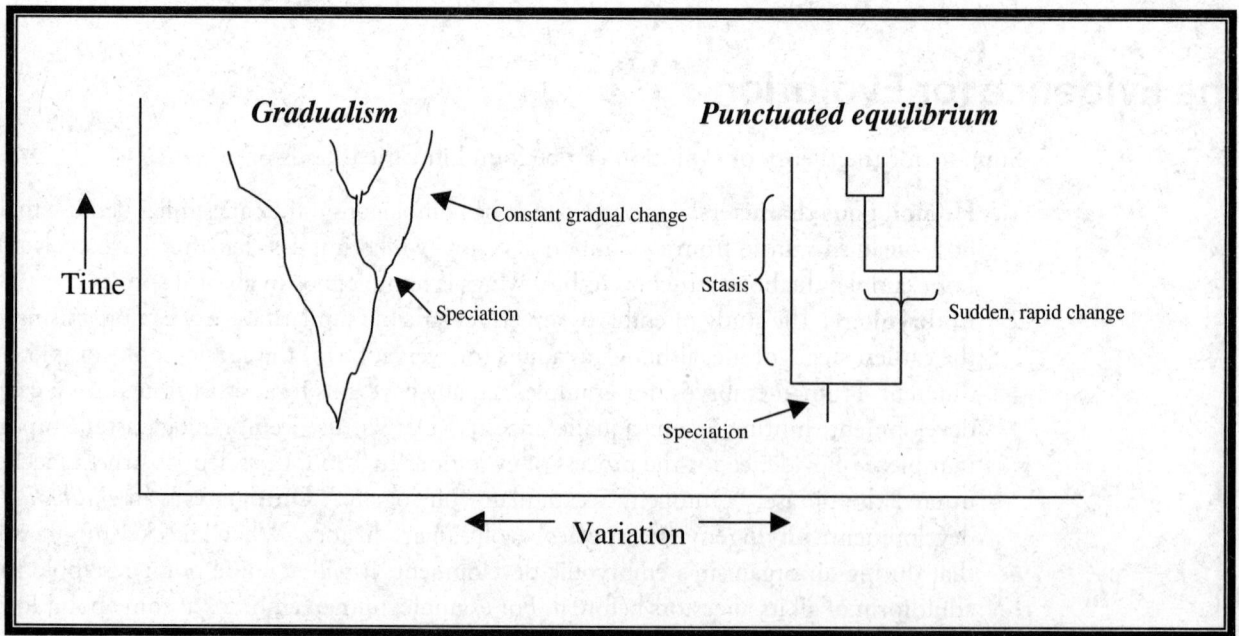

Figure 12.3   Gradualism versus punctuated equilibrium.

incomplete, it is very hard to test the two theories—if we find no fossils for a species over a contested period, how can we determine whether change was occurring? The debate therefore continues.

How Life Probably Emerged

The AP Biology exam often includes questions on how life originated. It is therefore wise to learn the steps of the **heterotroph theory** (Figure 12.4), so named because it posits that the first organisms were **heterotrophs,** organisms that cannot make their own food.

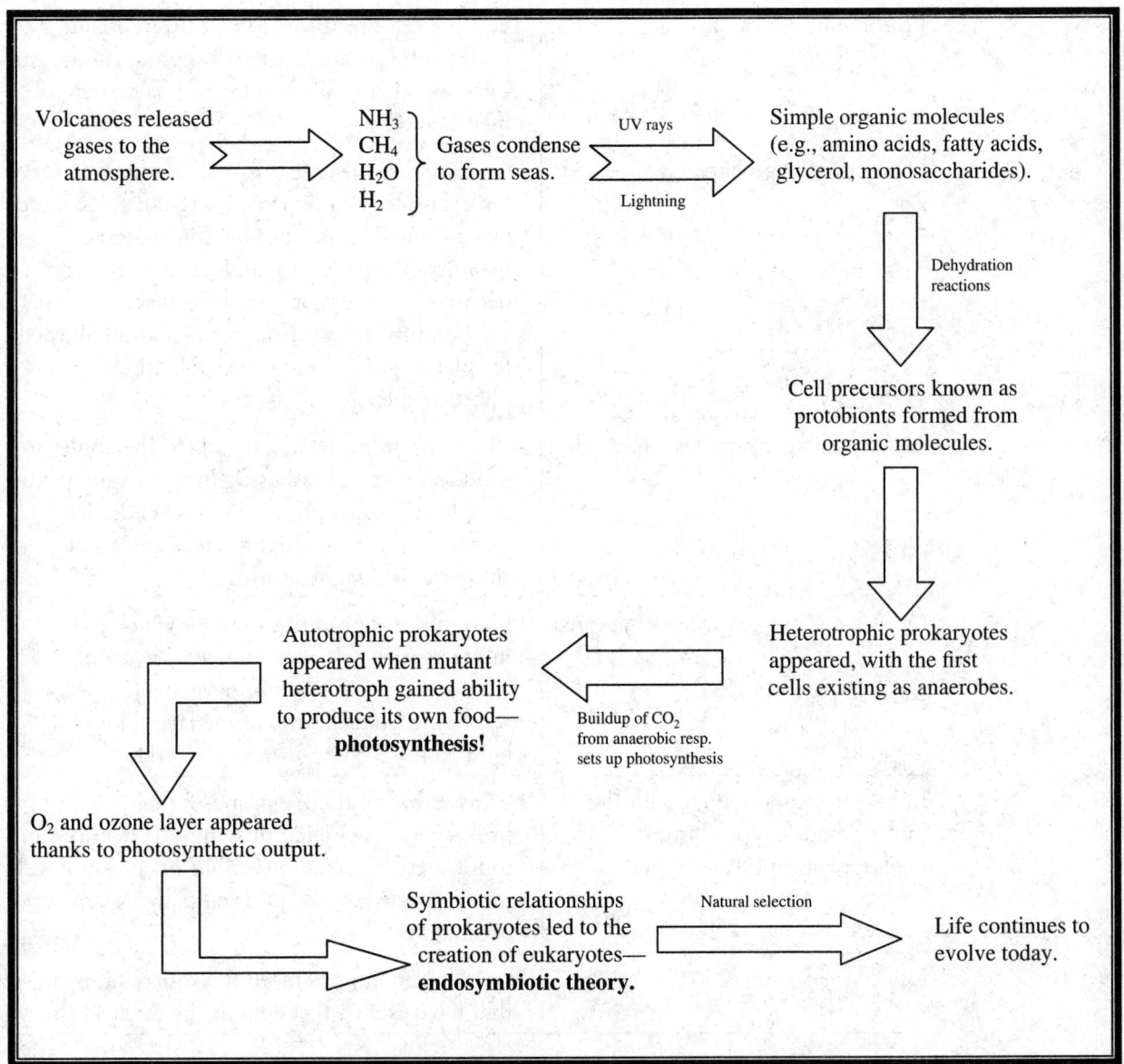

Figure 12.4   Flowchart representation of heterotroph theory.

STEP	DESCRIPTION
The earth's atmosphere formed.	Emerging from volcanoes, gases such as NH_3, CH_4, $H_2O(g)$, and H_2 (but not oxygen) invaded the atmosphere.
The seas formed.	The gases condensed to form the seas as the earth cooled.
Simple organic molecules appeared.	Energy (from UV light, lightning, heat, radioactivity) transformed inorganic molecules to organic ones, including amino acids.
Polymers and self-replicating molecules appeared.	These may have been formed through dehydration, or the removal of water molecules; e.g., proteinoids can be produced from polypeptides by dehydrating amino acids with heat.
Protobionts appeared.	These are cell precursors formed from organic molecules; they are unable to reproduce, but can carry out chemical reactions and have permeable membranes.
Heterotrophic prokaryotes appeared.	Heterotrophs consume organic substances to survive (an example is pathogenic bacteria); since there was a limited amount of organic material, heterotrophs competed and natural selection occurred—these first cells were anaerobic; thus, the buildup of CO_2 from fermentation allowed for plenty of CO_2 to be available for photosynthesis.
Autotrophic prokaryotes appeared.	A heterotroph mutated and gained the ability to produce its own food using light energy, making it a photo autotroph (e.g., photosynthetic bacteria); this was a highly successful strategy compared to the heterotroph's.
Oxygen and the ozone layer appeared.	Photosynthesis produces oxygen, which interacts with UV light to form the ozone layer—this production of oxygen allowed for aerobic respiration; the ozone layer blocks UV light from reaching the earth's surface.
Eukaryotes appeared (specifically mitochondria types and chloroplast types).	**Endosymbiotic theory** proposes that groups of prokaryotes associated in symbiotic relationships to form eukaryotes (the various organelles in cells today invaded a cell and eventually became one organism).
Life evolved.	Natural selection produced the variety of organisms that have existed throughout the earth's history.

> **BIG IDEA 1.D.1**
> *There are several hypotheses about the origin of life, each with evidence to support it.*

Why is it important that there was no oxygen to start? Alexander Oparin and J. B. S. Haldane hypothesized that oxygen would have prevented the formation of simple molecules because it is too reactive, and would have taken the place of any other element in chemical reactions. Stanley Miller and Harold Urey tested this hypothesis by simulating a primordial environment, and found that in the absence of oxygen, they were able to form organic molecules (including amino acids).

› Review Questions

1. Which of the following is an evolutionary process *not* based on random factors?

   A. Genetic drift
   B. Natural selection
   C. Mutation
   D. Gene flow

2. Which of the following is not a sexually selected trait?

   A. Fruit fly wings
   B. A male baboon's canine teeth
   C. Peacock tail feathers
   D. Male/female dimorphism in body size in many species

3. An adaptation

   A. can be shaped by genetic drift.
   B. cannot be altered.
   C. evolves because it specifically improves an individual's mating success.
   D. affects the fitness of an organism if it is altered.

4. Which of the following is *not* a requirement for natural selection to occur?

   A. Variation between individuals
   B. Heritability of the trait being selected
   C. Sexual reproduction
   D. Differences in reproductive success among individuals

5. Why can Hardy-Weinberg equilibrium occur only in large populations?

   A. Large populations are likely to have more variable environments.
   B. More individuals means less chance for natural selection to occur.
   C. Genetic drift is a much stronger force in small versus large populations.
   D. Large populations make random mating virtually impossible.

6. A population of frogs consists of 9 percent with speckles (the recessive condition) and 91 percent without speckles. What are the frequencies of the p and q alleles if this population is in Hardy-Weinberg equilibrium?

   A. $p = 0.49$, $q = 0.51$
   B. $p = 0.60$, $q = 0.40$
   C. $p = 0.70$, $q = 0.30$
   D. $p = 0.49$, $q = 0.30$

7. Frequency-dependent selection is

   A. particularly important during speciation.
   B. one way in which multiple alleles are preserved in a population.
   C. possible only when there are two alleles.
   D. most common in bacteria.

8. All of the following provide evidence for evolution *except*

   A. vestigial characters.
   B. Darwin's finches.
   C. homologous characters.
   D. mutations.

9. Why do we assume that oxygen was not present in the original atmosphere?

   A. The presence of O_2 would have resulted in the evolution of too many species too fast.
   B. Oxygen would have slowed down the rate of evolution.
   C. We know the ozone layer, which is formed by oxygen, has not been around that long.
   D. Inorganic molecules could not have formed in the presence of oxygen.

10. All these are examples of random evolutionary processes *except:*

   A. An earthquake divides a single elk species into two populations, forcing them to no longer interbreed.
   B. A mutation in a flower plant results in a new variety.
   C. An especially long winter causes a group of migrating birds to shift their home range.
   D. A mutation results in a population of trees that spread their seeds more widely than their peers, causing their population to grow.

❯ Answers and Explanations

1. **B**—Natural selection is the selective increase in certain alleles because they confer an advantage to their host organism. All other factors are random with respect to the alleles (a "bottleneck" is a type of genetic drift where a population is drastically reduced in size).

2. **A**—All fruit flies need to fly not only to find mates but also to survive. All the other characters listed are sexually selected, meaning that they have evolved because they confer specific advantages in mating (and not survival).

3. **D**—Adaptations are defined as traits that affect fitness if they are altered. Although adaptations may have evolved to increase mating success (answer C), they are not always intended for that function (e.g., they may have remained because they increase survival).

4. **C**—Natural selection can occur in asexually reproducing organisms, as long as the other three necessary conditions are met.

5. **C**—Genetic drift is change in allele frequencies as a result of random factors (e.g., natural disasters or environmental change). In small populations, genetic drift is a much more powerful force because each individual represents a greater percentage of the population's total genes than that person would in a much larger population.

Think of it this way—if you have a population of 10 cheetahs, and 3 die, you have lost 30 percent of the genes in that pool. If you have a population of 100 cheetahs, and 3 die, you have lost only 3 percent. Since Hardy-Weinberg equilibrium depends on no genetic drift, it is much more likely to occur in very large populations.

6. **C**—Remember that p and q must add up to 1 for a population to be in Hardy-Weinberg equilibrium (this eliminates answer D). Calculate q first by taking the square root of 0.09, which is 0.30. Then simply subtract 0.30 from 1 to get $p = 0.70$.

7. **B**—Frequency-dependent selection is one process by which multiple alleles are preserved in a population. For traits that are selected for or against on the basis of frequency, an allele becomes more advantageous when it is rare, and therefore increases. In this way, it is impossible for the allele to become extinct (because as soon as it gets that low, it increases again). When it gets too high, the other allele is low, and that one then increases. Frequency-dependent selection often exhibits itself in this kind of seesaw effect.

8. **D**—Mutations in and of themselves are not evidence for evolution, although they are necessary if evolution is going to occur.

9. **D**—Inorganic molecules could not have formed in the presence of oxygen because oxygen would have taken the place of other elements in every chemical reaction (because it is such a highly reactive element).

10. **D**—This is the only answer that shows evidence of natural selection, which is the *nonrandom* process by which evolution occurs. The two elk species splitting (answer A) is an example of allopatric speciation caused by a random factor (a geologic event). A mutation is also a random event (answer B); for example, if we had said that the new variety became the dominant allele in a population because it had an advantage over other variants, then that *would* be natural selection. A home range shift (answer C) is not evolution, but rather a behavioral change within an organism's lifetime.

〉 Rapid Review

There are four modes of *evolution:*

1. *Genetic drift*: change in allele frequencies because of chance events (in small populations).

2. *Gene flow*: change in allele frequencies as genes move from one population to another.

3. *Mutation*: change in allele frequencies due to a *random genetic change* in an allele.

4. *Natural selection*: process by which characters or traits are maintained or eliminated in a population based on their contribution to the differential survival and reproductive success of their "host" organisms.

There are three requirements for *natural selection* to occur:

1. *Variation*: differences must exist between individuals.

2. *Heritability*: the traits to be selected for must be able to be passed along to offspring. Traits that are not inherited cannot be selected against.

3. *Differential reproductive success*: there must be variation among parents in how many offspring they produce as a result of the different traits that the parents have.

Adaptation is a trait that, if altered, affects the fitness of an organism. Includes physical or intangible traits.

Selection types are as follows:

1. *Directional*: members at one end of a spectrum are selected against, and population shifts toward that end.

2. *Stabilizing*: selection for the mean of a population; reduces variation in a population.

3. *Disruptive (diversifying)*: selects for the two *extremes* of a population; selects against the middle.

4. *Sexual*: certain characters are selected for because they aid in mate acquisition.

5. *Artificial*: human intervention in the form of selective breeding (cattle).

Sources of *variation within populations* are

1. *Mutation*: random changes in DNA can introduce new alleles into a population.

2. *Sexual reproduction*: crossover, independent assortment, random gamete combination.

3. *Balanced polymorphism*: the maintenance of two or more phenotypic variants.

Speciation is the process by which new species evolve:

1. *Allopatric speciation*: interbreeding stops because some physical barrier splits the population into two. If two populations evolve separately and change so they cannot interbreed, speciation has occurred.

2. *Sympatric speciation*: interbreeding stops even though no physical barrier prevents it.

   • *Polyploidy*: condition in which individual has higher than normal number of chromosome sets. Polyploidic individuals cannot reproduce with nonpolyploidics.

   • *Balanced polymorphism*: two phenotypic variants become so different that the two groups stop interbreeding.

Other terms to remember are

Adaptive radiation: rapid series of speciation events that occur when one or more ancestral species invades a new environment.

Hardy-Weinberg equilibrium: $p + q = 1$, $p^2 + 2pq + q^2 = 1$. Evolution is *not* occurring. The *rules* for this are no mutations, no gene flow, no genetic drift, no natural selection, and random mating.

Homologous character: traits similar between organisms that arose from a common ancestor.

Vestigial character: character contained by organism that is no longer functionally useful (appendix).

Gradualism: evolutionary change is a slow and steady process.

Punctuated equilibria: evolutionary change occurs in rapid bursts separated by large periods of no change.

Heterotroph theory: theory that describes how life evolved from original heterotrophs.

Convergent character: traits similar to two or more organisms that do *not* share common ancestor; parallel evolution.

Convergent evolution: two unrelated species evolve in a way that makes them *more* similar.

Divergent evolution: two related species evolve in a way that makes them *less* similar.

CHAPTER > 13

Taxonomy and Classification

IN THIS CHAPTER

Summary: This chapter discusses Linnaeus's binomial system of classification and taxonomy in general. It gives information about each of the kingdoms (Monera, Protista, Plantae, Fungi, and Animalia).

Key Ideas

✪ Do not spend countless hours memorizing every detail about these various kingdoms. If you have time to burn and really want to learn all the details—go for it. If you are pressed for time, focus in on the basic and important information about each kingdom.

✪ The seven categories of classification listed from broadest to most specific: kingdom–phylum–class–order–family–genus–species.

✪ Autotrophs are the producers of the world; heterotrophs are the consumers.

✪ The endosymbiotic theory states that eukaryotic cells originated from a symbiotic partnership of prokaryotic cells.

✪ Be sure to learn the evolutionary relationships within each kingdom—this is fair game for a free-response question.

Introduction

Taxonomy is the brainchild of Linnaeus, who came up with a **binomial system of classification** in which each species was given a two-word name. The first word describes the **genus**—the group to which the species belongs. The second word is the name of the particular *species*. For example, *Homo sapiens* is the binomial system name for humans.

Taxonomy is the field of biology that classifies organisms according to the presence or absence of shared characteristics in an effort to discover evolutionary relationships among species. A *taxon* is a category that organisms are placed into and can be any of the levels of the hierarchy. There are seven common categories of classification; listed from broadest to most specific, they are kingdom, phylum, class, order, family, genus, species. A way to remember this sequence is through the use of a silly sentence such as this:

"**K**araoke **p**layers **c**an **o**rder **f**ree **g**rape **s**oda" or

"**K**ing **P**hillip **c**ame **o**ver **f**or **g**ood **s**paghetti."

Kingdom–phylum–class–order–family–genus–species.

> **BIG IDEA 1.B.2**
> *Phylogenetic trees are visual representations of ancestry.*

A **kingdom** consists of organisms that share characteristics such as cell structure, level of cell specialization, and mechanisms to obtain nutrients. Kingdoms are split into *phyla,* which are split into *classes,* which are further divided into *orders.* Orders are split into *families,* which are made up of the different *genera.* The final and most specific division is the *species.* This is the only naturally occurring taxon. These seven categories apply to many but not *all* organisms. The plant kingdom has **divisions** instead of phyla. Bacterial species tend to be placed into groups called **strains.**

Five or Six Kingdoms?

The current system of classification is a five-kingdom system that divides all the organisms of the planet into one of five kingdoms: Monera, Protista, Plantae, Fungi, and Animalia. Do not be confused or alarmed if you hear mention of a six-kingdom system. The difference in the six-kingdom system is that the kingdom Monera is split into Eubacteria and Archaebacteria. Other than that, the kingdom delineations are similar. Let's begin the tour of the various kingdoms with the kingdom Monera.

Kingdom Monera

The members of this kingdom are prokaryotes: single-celled organisms that have no nucleus or membrane-bound organelles. Since this chapter is an exercise in painful amounts of classification, subclassification, and further classification based on the previous classification of classifications, and so on, we thought we would point out a few of the many different ways that the kingdom Monera can be subdivided. The Monera kingdom can be further classified by nutritional class, reactivity with oxygen, and whether they are eubacteria or archaebacteria.

Nutritional Class

Moneran organisms can be classified as either autotrophs or heterotrophs. **Autotrophs** are the producers of the world:

1. *Photoautotrophs:* photosynthetic autotrophs (used to be called blue-green algae) that produce energy from light.
2. *Chemoautotrophs:* produce energy from inorganic substances (e.g., S bacteria).

Heterotrophs are the consumers of the world. Examples of prokaryotic heterotrophs, including parasitic bacteria that feed off hosts, and **saprobes,** such as bacteria of decay, which feed off dead organisms.

Reactivity with Oxygen

A second way to classify moneran organisms is by their ability to react with oxygen: whether they *must* react with oxygen to survive, whether they must be *without* oxygen to survive, or if they can survive with or without oxygen. There are three classes of oxygen reactivity: obligate aerobes and obligate anaerobes at the two extremes of the spectrum, and facultative anaerobes somewhere in between. **Obligate aerobes** require oxygen for respiration—they must have oxygen to grow; **obligate anaerobes** must avoid oxygen like the plague—oxygen is a poison to them; **facultative anaerobes** are happy to use O_2 when available, but can survive without it.

Archaebacteria Versus Eubacteria

There are two major branches of prokaryotic evolution: Eubacteria and Archaebacteria. **Archaebacteria** tend to live in extreme environments and are thought to resemble the first cells of the earth. The major examples you should be familiar with include (1) **extreme halophiles**—these are the "salt lovers" and live in environments with high salt concentrations, (2) **methanogens**—bacteria that produce methane as a by-product, and (3) **thermo acidophiles**—bacteria that love hot, acidic environments.

Eubacteria are categorized according to their mode of acquiring nutrients, their mechanism of movement, and their shape, among other things. The following is a list of the names of a few groups of bacteria that you should be familiar with for the AP exam:

1. Proteobacteria
2. Gram-positive bacteria
3. Cyanobacteria
4. Spirochetes
5. Chlamydias
6. Chemosynthetic bacteria
7. Nitrogen-fixing bacteria

The three basic shapes of bacteria you might want to be familiar with include:

1. *Rod-shaped bacteria:* also known as *bacilli* (e.g., *Bacillus anthracis,* the bug that causes anthrax).
2. *Spiral-shaped bacteria:* also known as *spirilla* (e.g., *Treponema pallidum,* the bug that causes syphilis).
3. *Sphere-shaped bacteria:* also known as *cocci* (e.g., *Streptococcus,* the fine bug that gives us strep throat).

To summarize, the kingdom Monera can be subdivided according to the following characteristics:

KEY IDEA

Nutrition type?	Autotroph versus heterotroph
Oxygen preference?	Obligate aerobes versus obligate anaerobes versus facultative anaerobes
Evolutionary branch?	Archaebacteria versus Eubacteria

Endosymbiotic Theory

Bill (11th grade): "Important concept to know."

The endosymbiotic theory states that eukaryotic cells originated from a symbiotic partnership of prokaryotic cells. This theory focuses on the origin of mitochondria and chloroplasts from aerobic heterotrophic and photosynthetic prokaryotes, respectively.

We can see why scientists examining these two organelles would think that they may have originated from prokaryotes. They share many characteristics: (1) they are the same size as eubacteria, (2) they also reproduce in the same way as prokaryotes (binary fission), and (3), if their ribosomes are sliced open and studied, they are found to more closely resemble those of a prokaryote than those of a eukaryote. They are prokaryotic groupies living in a eukaryotic world.

The eukaryotic organism that scientists believe most closely resembles prokaryotes is the **archezoa,** which does not have mitochondria. One phylum grouped with the archezoa is the **diplomonads.** A good example of a diplomonad you should remember is *Giardia*—an infectious agent you would do well to avoid. *Giardia* is a parasitic organism that takes hold in your intestines and essentially denies your body the ability to absorb any fat. This infection makes for very uncomfortable and unpleasant GI (gastrointestinal) issues and usually results from the ingestion of contaminated water.

Kingdom Protista

The evolution of protists from prokaryotes gave rise to the characteristics that make eukaryotes different from their prokaryotic predecessors. Protists were around a long time before fungi, plants, or animals graced our planet with their presence. Most protists use aerobic metabolism. Since this is a chapter on classification, it would be silly, if not too kind of us, to not mention how these different protists are organized. They are usually grouped into three major categories:

1. *Animal-like protists:* heterotrophic protists, also called *protozoa*
2. *Funguslike protists:* protists that resemble fungi; also called *absorptive protists*
3. *Plantlike protists:* photosynthetic protists, also called *algae*

Protists are usually unicellular or colonial. This is why they are *not* considered plants, animals, or fungi. All protists are capable of asexual reproduction. Some reproduce only asexually, and others can reproduce sexually as well. This variability in the life cycles found among various members of the protist kingdom is just one reason why they are considered to be one of the most diverse kingdoms in existence.

Animal-Like Protists (Protozoa)

This division includes protists that *ingest* foods—as do animals. As with the rest of this chapter, you do not need to become an expert on protozoans and know everything about every member. But the following is a list that contains basic information about some names that may help you on the multiple-choice section of the test. We will italicize the most important things to remember about each of them.

1. *Rhizopoda.* These *unicellular* and *asexual* organisms are also known as *amoebas.* They get from place to place through the use of **pseudopods,** which are extensions from their cells. Every living creature has to eat, and they do so through *phagocytosis.*
2. *Foraminifera.* These *marine* protists live attached to structures such as rocks and algae. Their name is derived from the word *foramen* because of the presence of calcium carbonate ($CaCO_3$) shells full of holes. Some of these protists obtain nutrients through *photosynthesis* performed by symbiotic algae living in their shells.
3. *Actinopoda.* These organisms move by *pseudopodia* and make up part of plankton, the organisms that drift near the surface of bodies of water. The two divisions of actinopoda include heliozoans and radiozoans. Just recognize the names; do not worry about anything more than that.

4. *Apicomplexa.* These *parasites* are the protists formerly known as sporozoans. They spread from place to place in a small infectious form known as a **sporozoite.** They have both *sexual* and *asexual* stages, and their life cycle requires two different host species for completion. An example of an apicomplexa is **plasmodium,** the causative agent of malaria (two hosts—mosquitoes, then humans).

5. *Zooflagellates.* These *heterotrophic* protists are known for their *flagella,* which they use to move around. Like rhizopoda, they eat by *phagocytosis* and can range from being *parasitic* to their hosts to living *mutualistically* with them. A member of this group is *trypanosoma,* which is known to cause African sleeping sickness.

6. *Ciliophora.* Their name is fitting because these protists use *cilia* to travel from place to place. They live in *water* and contain *two types of nuclei:* a **macronucleus** (which controls everyday activities) and many **micronuclei** (a function in **conjugation**). A ciliaphora you may recognize is paramecium.

Fungus-Like Protists (Slime Molds and Water Molds)

This division includes protists that resemble fungi. Once again, we are going to provide a list that contains basic information about some names that may help you on multiple-choice questions. The most important things to remember are **boldfaced** or *italicized.*

1. *Myxogastria.* These *heterotrophic,* brightly colored protists include the **plasmodial slime molds** and are not photosynthetic. Unlike the acrasidae, they do not like to eat alone— they eat and grow as a single clumped *unicellular* mass known as a **plasmodium** (same name as the causative agent of malaria, but this entity does not cause malaria). This mass ingests food by *phagocytosis.* When Mother Hubbard's cupboard is bare and there is no more food, the plasmodium stops growing and instead produces spores that allow the protist to reproduce.

2. *Acrasidae.* Known to their closer friends as **cellular slime molds,** these protists have a bit of a strange eating strategy. When there is plenty of food around, these organisms eat alone as solitary beings, but when food becomes scarce, they clump together in a manner similar to slime molds and work together as a unit.

3. *Oomycota.* These *water-mold* protists can be *parasites* or *saprobes.* They are able to munch on their surrounding environment owing to the presence of *filaments* known as *hyphae,* which release digestive enzymes. They are often multicellular, or *coenocytic.* One difference between these organisms and actual fungi is that their cell wall is made of *cellulose,* and not *chitin* as seen in fungi.

Plant-Like Protists

This division includes protists that are mostly photosynthetic. All of these organisms contain chlorophyll *a.* Focus your attention on the italicized points.

1. *Dinoflagellata.* Protists known for having *two flagella* that rest perpendicular to each other, and which allow them to swim with a funky spinning motion that makes them the envy of all other protist observers (or at least makes them really dizzy). Most dinoflagellates are *unicellular.* These protists are very important producers in many aquatic food chains.

2. *Golden algae.* Known as the *chrysophyta,* these protists move through the use of *flagella* and can also be found swimming among plankton.

3. *Diatoms.* These yellow and brown protists are also known as bacillariophyta and are a major component of plankton. They mostly reproduce in an *asexual* fashion, although they do rarely enter a *sexual* life cycle. They have ornate *walls* made of *silica* to protect them.

4. *Green algae.* Known as *chlorophyta,* they have chlorophyll *a* and *b.* Most of these protists live in freshwater and can be found among the algae that are part of the mutualistic

lichen conglomerate. Most have both *asexual* and *sexual* reproductive stages. These organisms are considered to be the ancestors of plants.

5. *Brown algae.* Known as *phaeophyta,* most of these protists are *multicellular* and live in *marine* environments. Two members to know are *kelp* and *seaweed.*

6. *Red algae.* Known as rhodophyta, they get their color from a pigment called *phycobilin.* Most of these *multicellular* protists live in the ocean and produce gametes that do not have flagella. Many live in deep waters and absorb nonvisible light via accessory pigments.

Kingdom Plantae

Classification of plants is very similar to classification of the animal kingdom, except that plants are divided into divisions instead of phyla. So, instead of "Karaoke players can order free grape soda," remember "Karaoke *dancers* can order free grape soda."

Reality again, folks . . . you do not need to become experts in the evolutionary history of plants, but you should be able to understand a phylogenetic representation of how the various plant types evolved.

Chlorophytes→bryophytes→seedless vascular plants→gymnosperms→angiosperms

Chlorophytes are green algae. Scientists have found enough evidence to conclude that they are the common ancestors of land plants. Plants are said to have experienced four major evolutionary periods since the dawn of time, described in the following sections.

CT teacher: "Know plant evolution very well. There are a lot of potential questions here. Including essays."

Bryophytes

Bryophytes were the first land plants to evolve from the chlorophytes. They include mosses, liverworts, and hornworts. Prior to bryophytes, there was no reason for these organisms to worry about water loss because they lived in water and had unlimited access to the treasured resource. But in order to survive on land, where water was no longer unlimited, two evolutionary adaptations in particular helped them survive:

1. A waxy **cuticle** cover to protect against water loss.
2. The packaging of gametes in structures known as **gametangia.**

Bryophyte sperm is produced by the male gametangia, the **antheridia.** Bryophyte eggs are produced by the female gametangia, the **archegonium.** The gametangia provide a safe haven because the fertilization and development of the zygote occur within the protected structure.

Because they lack xylem and phloem, bryophytes are also known as *nonvascular plants.* This lack of vascular tissue combined with the existence of flagellated sperm results in a dependence on water. For this reason, bryophytes must live in damp areas so they do not dry out. There are three nonvascular plants you should know about: mosses, liverworts, and hornworts. Mosses are special in that, unlike all other plants, the dominant generation in their life cycle is the haploid gametophyte. The moss sporophyte is tiny, short lived, and reliant on the gametophyte for nutritional support. One interesting fact about liverworts is that in addition to the alternation of generations life cycle, they are able to reproduce asexually.

Seedless Vascular Plants

The transition for plants from water to land was a tricky one. They needed to find a way to use the nutritional resources of the minerals and water found in soil, while not denying themselves access to the light needed for photosynthesis. Another problem facing these

early land plants was the need to find a way to distribute water and nutrients throughout the plant—not as much of an issue when the plant was submerged in water. The solution to this issue was the development of the xylem and phloem, which you will read about in Chapter 14, Plants. The **xylem** is the water superhighway for the plant, transporting water throughout the plant. The **phloem** is the sugar food highway for the plant, transporting sugar and nutrients to the various plant structures.

The first vascular plants (also referred to as **tracheophytes**) to evolve did not have seeds. Two major evolutionary changes occurred that allowed the transition from bryophytes to seedless vascular plants:

1. The switch from the gametophyte to the sporophyte as the dominant generation of the life cycle.
2. The development of branched sporophytes, increasing the number of spores produced.

The major seedless vascular plants you should know are **ferns,** which are **homosporous plants** that produce a single spore type that gives rise to bisexual gametophytes. The spores tend to exist on the underside of the fern leaves. A **heterosporous plant** produces two types of spores, some of which yield male gametophytes (**microspores**), and others produce female gametophytes (**megaspores**). The dominant generation for ferns is the sporophyte.

Seed Plants

Gymnosperm

The third major plant category to branch off the phylogenetic tree is the seed plant. Three major evolutionary changes occurred between the seedless vascular plants and the birth of seed plants:

1. Further decline in the prominence of the gametophyte generation of the life cycle.
2. The birth of pollination.
3. The evolution of the seed.

A seed is a package containing an embryo and the food to feed the developing embryo that is surrounded by a nice protective shell. The first major seed plants to surface were the **gymnosperms.** These plants are heterosporous and usually transport their sperm through the use of **pollen**—the sperm-bearing male gametophyte. Not all gymnosperms have pollen; some have motile sperm. The major gymnosperms you should remember are the **conifers,** plants whose reproductive structure is a cone. Members of this division include pine trees, firs, cedars, and redwoods. These plants survive well in dry conditions and keep their leaves year-round. They are evergreens and usually have needles for leaves.

Angiosperm

The final major plant evolutionary category to branch off the phylogenetic tree is the flowering plant. Today there are more **angiosperms** around than any other kind of plant. There are two major classes of angiosperms to know: monocots (**monocotyledons**) and dicots (**dicotyledons**). A **cotyledon** is a structure that provides nourishment for a developing plant. One distinction between monocots and dicots is that monocots have a single cotyledon, while dicots have two.

One interesting evolutionary change from the gymnosperm to the angiosperm is the adaptation of the xylem. In gymnosperms, the xylem cells in charge of water transport are the **tracheid cells,** whereas in angiosperms, the xylem cells are the more efficient **vessel elements.** Don't worry too much about this distinction, but store away in the back of your mind that vessel elements are seen in angiosperms, while tracheid cells are seen in gymnosperms.

What are flowers, really? Are they just another visually pleasing structure? No . . . they are so much more. Flowers are the main tools for angiosperm reproduction. Do not waste too much time learning every little part of a flower. Here are the most important parts to remember:

Stamen: male structure composed of an **anther,** which produces pollen.

Carpel: female structure that consists of an *ovary,* a **style,** and a **stigma.** The stigma functions as the receiver of the pollen, and the style is the pathway leading to the ovary.

Petals: structures that serve to attract pollinators to help increase the plant's reproductive success.

Below is a quick display that lists many of the major evolutionary trends observed during the phylogenetic development of plants.

> **Remember these evolutionary trends seen in plants!**
> - Dominant gametophyte generation → dominant sporophyte generation
> - Nonvascular → vascular
> - Seedless → seeds
> - Motile sperm → pollen
> - Naked seeds → seeds in flowers

Kingdom Fungi

Nearly all fungi are multicellular and are built from filamentous structures called **hyphae.** These hyphae form meshes of branching filaments known as a **mycelium,** which function as mouthlike structures for the fungus, absorbing food. Many fungi contain **septae,** which divide the hyphae filaments into different compartments. The septa have pores, which allow organelles and other structures to flow from compartment to compartment. Fungi that do not contain septae are called **coenocytic fungi.** Fungus walls are built using the polysaccharide **chitin.** As was discussed in Chapter 9, Cell Division, the fungus life cycle is predominately haploid. The only time they are diploid is as the 2*n* zygote.

The following is a list of fungus-related organisms that you should know:

1. *Zygomycota.* These *coenocytic* and *land-dwelling* fungi have very few septa and reproduce sexually. A classic example of a zygomycete is bread mold.
2. *Basidiomycota.* These club-shaped fungi are known for their haploid basidiospores and love of decomposing wood. Famous members include mushrooms and rusts.
3. *Ascomycota.* Many members of this group of saprobic fungi live as part of the symbiotic relationship called **lichen.** These fungi produce sexual **ascospores,** which are contained in sacs. Famous ascomycetes you may have heard of are yeasts and mildews. These are discussed again in Chapter 19, Laboratory Review.
4. *Lichens.* These are formed by a *symbiotic association* of photosynthetic organisms grouped together with fungal hyphae (usually an *ascomycete*). The algae member of this group tends to be *cyanobacteria* or *chlorophyta* and provides the food (sugar from photosynthesis). The fungus provides protection and drink (water).
5. *Molds.* These are *asexual, quick-growing* fungi known as *deuteromycota* or the "imperfect fungi." If you check any college refrigerator, you can find many fine samples of this organism.
6. *Yeasts.* These are *unicellular* fungi that can be asexual *or* sexual. One member of this group, *Candida,* is known to cause yeast infections in humans.

Kingdom Animalia

Animals are the final kingdom to be discussed in this chapter. There are some characteristics that separate animals from other organisms:

ADAPTATION	DESCRIPTION
Cell wall	Animals lack cell walls.
Mode of reproduction	Sexual reproduction is the norm (although there are several animals capable of asexual reproduction).
Dominant life cycle stage	The diploid stage is usually the dominant generation in the life cycle.
Motile	Most animals are mobile.
Nutritional class	Animals are multicellular heterotrophs.
Storage of energy	Animals store carbohydrates as glycogen, not starch as is seen in plants.
Special embryological events	Most animals undergo a process in which specialized tissue layers (endoderm, mesoderm, ectoderm) form during a process known as **gastrulation.**
Nervous and muscle tissue	Animals (with the exception of sponges) have specialized nervous and muscle tissue.
Cellular junctions	Animal cells contain tight junctions and gap junctions.

As is the case with all of the other kingdoms in this chapter, you do not need to become the master of animal phylogeny and taxonomy. But it is definitely useful to know the general evolutionary history of the animal kingdom and how it diversified so quickly over time (Figure 13.1).

Many people believe that the original common ancestor that started the whole process of animal evolution was most likely the **choanoflagellate.** During the evolutionary progression from choanoflagellate to the present, there have been *four* major branchpoints on which you should focus. Let's take a look at all the important changes that have allowed such diversity of life.

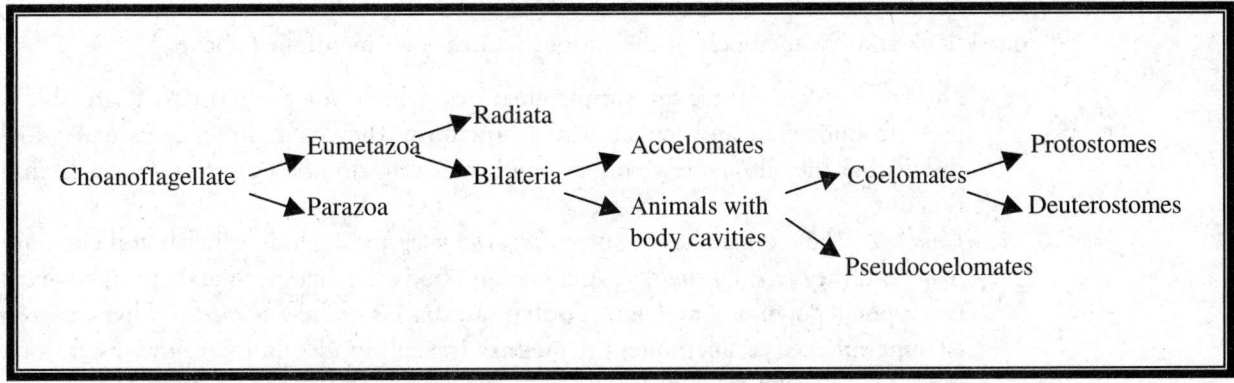

Figure 13.1 The animal phylogenetic tree.

The first major branchpoint occurred after the development of multicellularity from choanoflagellates. Off this branch of the tree emerged two divisions:

1. *Parazoa:* sponges; these organisms have no true tissues.
2. *Eumetazoa:* all the other animals with true tissue.

After this split into parazoa and eumetazoa, the second major branchpoint in animal evolutionary history occurred: the subdivision of eumetazoa into two further branches on the basis of body symmetry. The eumetezoans were subdivided into

1. *Radiata:* those that have radial symmetry, which means that they have a single orientation. This can be a top, a bottom, or a front and back. This branch includes jellyfish, corals, and hydras.
2. *Bilateria:* those that have bilateral symmetry, which means that they have a top and a bottom (dorsal/ventral) as well as a head and a tail (anterior/posterior).

The next major split in the phylogenetic tree for animal development involved the split of bilateral organisms into two further branches—one of which subdivides into two smaller branches:

1. *Acoelomates:* animals with no blood vascular system and lacking a cavity between the gut and outer body wall. An example of a member of this group is the flatworm.
2. Animals *with* a vascular system and a body cavity.
    - *Pseudocoelomates:* animals that have a fluid-filled body cavity that is *not* enclosed by mesoderm. Roundworms are a member of this branch.
    - *Coelomates:* a **coelom** is a fluid-filled body cavity found between the body wall and gut that has a lining. It comes from the mesoderm.

The final major branchpoint comes off from the coelomates. It branches into two more divisions:

1. *Protostomes:* a bilateral animal whose first embryonic indentation eventually develops into a *mouth.* Prominent members of this society include *annelids, arthropods,* and *mullusks.*
2. *Deuterostomes:* a branch that includes *chordates* and *echinoderms.* The first indentation for their embryos eventually develops into the *anus.*

These two divisions differ in their embryonic developmental stages. As already mentioned, the protostomes' first embryonic indent develops into the mouth, whereas for the dueterostome, it becomes the anus. Another difference is the *angle* of the cleavages that occur during the early cleavage division of the embryo. A third difference is the tissue from which the coelom divides.

That concludes the evolutionary development portion of this chapter. Now let's take a quick look at a few members of the various branches we mentioned above.

1. *Porifera* (*sponges*). These are simple creatures, which, for the most part, are able to perform both male and female sexual functions. They have no "true tissue," which means that they do *not* have organs, and their cells do not seem to be specialized in function.
2. *Cnidaria.* These organisms are of *radial symmetry* and include jellyfish and coral animals, and they *lack* a *mesoderm.* A cnidarian's body is a digestive sac that can be one of two types: a polyp or a medusa. A **polyp** (asexual) is *cylinder shaped* and lives *attached* to some surface (sea anemones). A **medusa** (sexual) is *flat* and roams the waters looking for food (jellyfish). Cnidarians use tentacles to capture and eat prey.

3. *Platyhelminthes.* These are *flatworms,* members of the *acoelomate* club. They have *bilateral symmetry* and a touch of *cephalization.* There are three main types of flatworms you should be familiar with:
   - *Flukes:* parasitic flatworms that alternate between sexual and asexual reproduction life cycles.
   - *Planarians:* free-living carnivores that live in water.
   - *Tapeworms:* parasitic flatworms whose adult form lives in vertebrates, including us (humans).

4. *Rotifera.* These are also members of the *pseudocoelomate* club; they have *specialized organs,* a full digestive tract, and are very tiny.

5. *Nematoda.* These are *roundworms,* found in moist environments. They have a *psuedocoelomate* body plan. Trichinosis, a disease found in humans, is caused by a roundworm that infects meat products, usually pork. Humans ingesting infected meat can become affected with this disease.

6. *Mollusca.* These creatures are members of the *protostome* division and include such species as snails, slugs, octopuses, and squids. They are *coelomates* with a full digestive system. **Bivalves,** such as clams and oysters, are mollusks that have hinged shells that are divided into two parts.

7. *Annelida.* These are segmented worms such as earthworms and leeches.

8. *Arthropoda.* This is the most heavily represented group on the planet. These creatures are *segmented, contain a hard exoskeleton* constructed out of *chitin,* and have *specialized appendages.* Some well-known members include spiders, crustaceans, and insects. One interesting tidbit about arthropods is that, like humans, some members of this group, when born, are miniature versions of their adult selves that grow in size to resemble adults. Others look completely different from adults and exist in a larva form in their youth. At some point, the larvae undergo a metamorphosis and change to the expected adult form.

9. *Echinodermata.* These are *sea stars.* These coelomates are of the dueterostome body plan. One neat characteristic of echinoderms is the presence of a **water vascular system,** which is a series of tubes and canals within the organism, that plays a role in ingestion of food, movement of the organism, and gas exchange.

10. *Chordata.* This group includes **invertebrates** (animals lacking backbones), and **vertebrates** (animals with backbones). Just in case you are asked to identify some vertebrates on a multiple-choice question, here are some members—fish, amphibians, reptiles, birds, and mammals. There are four features common to chordates you should know:
    - *Dorsal hollow nerve cord:* forms the nervous system and becomes the brain and spinal cord in some.
    - *Notochord:* long support rod that is replaced by bone in most (mesodermal in origin).
    - *Pharyngeal gill slits:* slit-containing structure, which functions in respiration and feeding, present only in the embryonic stage of most chordates.
    - *Tail:* extension past the anus that is lost by birth in many species.

› Review Questions

1. Which of the following is thought to be the common ancestor to plants?

   A. Chemoautotrophs
   B. Choanoflagellates
   C. Chordata
   D. Chlorophytes

2. Which of the following pairs of organisms is most closely interrelated?

   A. Sponge and halophile
   B. Jellyfish and coral
   C. Oyster and conifer
   D. Lichen and roundworm

3. Which of the following was an evolutionary adaptation vital to the survival of the bryophytes?

   A. The switch from the gametophyte to the sporophyte as the dominant generation of the life cycle
   B. The development of branched sporophytes
   C. The birth of pollination
   D. The packaging of gametes into gametangia

4. Which of the following is the most specific category of classification?

   A. Class
   B. Family
   C. Order
   D. Division

5. Which of the following is *not* associated with flowers?

   A. Carpel
   B. Stigma
   C. Style
   D. Hypha

6. Which of the following was the latest to branch off the animal phylogenetic tree?

   A. Radiata
   B. Acoelomates
   C. Eumetazoa
   D. Deuterostomes

For questions 7–10, please use the following answer choices:

   A. Kingdom Animalia
   B. Kingdom Fungi
   C. Kingdom Protista
   D. Kingdom Monera

7. Thermoacidophiles are grouped into this kingdom that consists of single-celled organisms lacking nuclei and membrane-bound organelles.

8. Arthropods are grouped into this kingdom whose members are multicellular heterotrophs that have the diploid stage as their dominant generation in the life cycle.

9. This kingdom is divided into plant-like, animal-like, and fungus-like divisions.

10. Molds, or deuteromycota, are grouped into this kingdom that consists of mostly multicellular organisms that are constructed out of hypha.

› Answers and Explanations

1. **D**—Chlorophytes are green algae that are the common ancestors of land plants. Chemo-autotrophs are monerans that produce energy from inorganic substances. Choanoflagellates are the organisms thought to be the starting point for the animal kingdom's phylogenetic tree. Chordata includes the invertebrates and vertebrates.

2. **B**—Jellyfish and coral are both cnidarians of the animal kingdom.

3. **D**—Since the bryophytes were the first plants to brave the land, they were still somewhat dependent on water and also needed protection for their gametes. The gametangia provided a safe haven for the gametes where fertilization and zygote development could occur. Answer choices A and B were adaptations made by seedless vascular plants. Choice C was an adaptation made by the gymnosperms.

4. **B**—**K**araoke **p**layers **c**an **o**rder **f**ree **g**rape **s**oda or **K**ing **P**hillip **c**ame **o**ver **f**or **g**ood **s**paghetti (enough said).

5. **D**—Hyphae are associated with fungi. The other parts are all associated with flowers.

6. **D**—Take a look at Figure 13.1 for this one; the deuterostomes were indeed the last to branch off.

7. **D**

8. **A**

9. **C**

10. **B**

› Rapid Review

Quickly review the following terms:

Taxonomy: Classification of organisms based upon the presence or absence of shared characteristics: kingdom → phylum (division) → class → order → family → genus → species.

Five-kingdom system: Monera → Protista → Plantae → Fungi → Animalia.

Six-kingdom system: Archaebacteria → Eubacteria → Protista → Plantae → Fungi → Animalia.

Kingdom Monera

Autotrophs (producers) versus *heterotrophs* (consumers).

Obligate aerobes (require O_2) versus *obligate anaerobes* (*no* O_2) versus *facultative anaerobes* (either or).

Archaebacteria: halophiles (salt), methanogens (methane-producers), thermoacidophiles (hot and acidic).

Eubacteria: bacteria classified according to movement, shape, nutritional methods.

Endosymbiotic theory: eukaryotes originated from a symbiotic partnership of prokaryotic cells.

Kingdom Protista

Plant like protists: photosynthetic algae; all contain chlorophyll *a*.

Animal-like protists: heterotrophic protists (protozoa).

Fungus like protists: absorptive protists that resemble fungi.

Kingdom Plantae

Chlorophytes: green algae that are the common ancestor of land plants.

Bryophytes: first land plants; two important adaptations—waxy cuticle (stop water loss), gametangia:

- *Gametangia*: protective structures to aid survival of gametes on land.
- *Mosses*: important bryophyte, dominant life cycle generation is a **haploid gametophyte.**

Seedless vascular plants: came after bryophytes and had two further changes:

- Switch from haploid gametophyte to diploid sporophyte as dominant generation.
- Development of branched sporophytes.

Ferns: important member, **homosporous** (bisexual gametophytes).

Gymnosperm: came after seedless vascular plants and had three evolutionary adaptations:

- Further increase in dominance of sporophyte generation.
- Birth of pollination.
- Evolution of the seed.

Conifers: plants whose reproductive structure is a cone.

Angiosperm: flowering plants that came after gymnosperms divided into **monocots** and **dicots.**

Kingdom Fungi

Multicellular, built from hyphae, which can be separated by septae. Fungus walls are constructed from **chitin.**

Life cycle is predominately **haploid.**

Kingdom Animalia

Important characteristics: no cell walls, $2n$ is dominant, mobile, multicellular, heterotrophic, gastrulation.

Four major branchpoints (Figure 13.1).

Common ancestor: **choanoflagellate.**

Important members (in order of split from phylogenetic tree): sponges (parazoa), jellyfish (Radiata), flatworms (Acoelomates), roundworms (Pseudocoelomate nematodes), arthropods (protostomes), humans (Chordates).

Skim the information by each subdivision of this kingdom earlier in this chapter for more information.

Plants

IN THIS CHAPTER

Summary: This chapter discusses the anatomy of plants, the mechanisms of root and shoot growth, plant hormones, tropisms, and the mechanism of water and nutrient movement from roots to shoots and back.

Key Ideas

✪ Roots are the portions of the plant that are below ground; shoots are the portions of the plant that are above ground.

✪ There are three plant tissue systems to know: ground, vascular, and dermal.

✪ Two important plant vascular structures: xylem and phloem.

✪ Regions of plant growth: root cap, zone of cell division, zone of elongation, and zone of maturation.

✪ Five important plant hormones: abscisic acid, auxin, cytokinins, ethylene, and gibberellins.

✪ Three important tropisms: gravitropism, phototropism, and thigmotropism.

Introduction

This chapter begins with a quick tour of the anatomy of plants, starting with the roots and moving to the shoots. In these two sections, the mechanisms of root and shoot growth will be examined and the important players will be identified. From there we will turn our focus to plant hormones and tropisms. A discussion on photoperiodism follows, and the chapter concludes with a look at the mechanism by which water and nutrients travel through plants from roots to shoots and back.

Anatomy of Plants

The anatomy of a plant in its most simplistic form can be divided into the roots and the shoots. **Roots** are the portions of the plant that are below the ground, while **shoots** are the portions of the plant that are above the ground. The roots wind their way through the terrain, working as an anchor to keep the plants in place. In addition, the roots work as gatherers, absorbing the water and nutrients vital to a plant's survival.

Tissue Systems

BIG IDEA 2.D.2

Homeostatic mechanisms (e.g., plants obtaining CO_2 and eliminating O_2) reflect common ancestry and divergence due to adaptation to different environments.

There are *three* plant tissue systems to know: ground, vascular, and dermal.

Ground Tissue

The ground tissue, which makes up most of the body of the plant, is found between the dermal and vascular systems and is subdivided into three cell types: **collenchyma cells,** live cells that provide flexible and mechanical support—often found in stems and leaves; **parenchyma cells,** the most prominent of the three types, with many functions—parenchyma cells found in leaves are called *mesophyll cells,* and allow CO_2 and O_2 to diffuse through intercellular spaces (owing to the presence of large vacuoles, these cells play a role in storage and secretion for plants); and **sclerenchyma cells,** which protect seeds and support the plant.

Vascular Tissue

Plant vascular tissue comes up often on the AP Biology exam. The two characters you need to be familiar with are the xylem and the phloem.

Joscelyn (12th grader): "Know these two and what their driving forces are."

Xylem. This structure has multiple functions. It is a support structure that strengthens the plant and functions as a passageway for the transport of water and minerals from the soil. One interesting (and sad) note about xylem cells is that most of them are dead and are simply there as cell walls that contain the minerals and water being passed along the plant. Xylem cells can be divided into two categories: **vessel elements** and **tracheid cells.** They both function in the passage of water, but vessel elements move water more efficiently because of structural differences that are not pertinent to this exam. ☺

Phloem. This structure also functions as a "highway" for plants, assisting in the movement of sugars from one place to another. Unlike the xylem, the functionally mature cells of the phloem, *sieve-tube elements,* are alive and well.

Dermal Tissue

Dermal tissue provides the protective outer coating for plants. It is the skin, or **epidermis.** This coating attempts to keep the bad guys (infectious agents) out, and the good guys (water and nutrients) in. Within the epidermis are cells called **guard cells,** which control the opening and closing of gaps called *stomata* that are vital to the process of photosynthesis as was discussed back in Chapter 8, Photosynthesis.

Roots

BIG IDEA 2.A.3

The high surface area of root hairs helps plants exchange matter with the environment.

Root Systems

How do plants get their nutrients? Through the hard work of roots, whose tips absorb nourishment for the plant (minerals and water) via root hairs. Most of the water and minerals are absorbed by plants at the root tips, which have **root hairs** extending from their surface. These hairs create a larger surface area for absorption in much the same way as the **brush border** does in the human intestines—improving the efficiency of nutrient and water acquisition.

A root is not just a root, for not all root structures are the same. In Chapter 13, Taxonomy and Classification, two types of angiosperm plants were mentioned: dicots and monocots. Dicots are known for having a taproot system, while monocots are associated with fibrous roots. The **taproot** (e.g., carrot) **system** branches in a way similar to the human lungs; the roots start as one thick root on entrance into the ground, and then divide into smaller and smaller branches called **lateral roots** underneath the surface, which serve to hold the plant in place. **Fibrous roots** provide plants with a very strong anchor in the ground without going very deep into the soil. The root system can be summarized as follows:

Dicots → taproot → thick entry root → division into smaller branches

Monocots → fibrous root → shallow entry into ground → strong anchor effect

Root Structure

Let's take a look at the structure of a root moving from outside to inside. The root is lined by the **epidermis,** whose cells give rise to the root hairs that plants must thank for their ability to absorb water and nutrients. Moving farther in, we come to the cortex, the majority of the root that functions as a starch storage receptacle. The innermost layer of the cortex is composed of a cylinder of cells known as the **endodermis.** These cells are important to the plant because the walls between these cells create an obstacle known as the **casparian strip,** which blocks water from passing. This is one of the mechanisms by which plants control the flow of water. Moving in through the endodermis, we come to the **vascular cylinder,** which is composed of a collection of cells known as the *pericycle.* The lateral roots of the plant are made from the pericycle, and hold the vascular tissue of the root—our friends from earlier, the xylem and phloem.

Root Growth

Plants grow as long as they are alive as a result of the presence of **meristemic cells.** Early on in the life of a plant, after a seed matures, it sits and waits until the time is right for germination. At this point, water is absorbed by the embryo, which begins to grow again. When large enough, it busts through the seed coat, beginning its journey to planthood. At the start of this journey, the growth is concentrated in the actively dividing cells of the **apical meristem.** Growth in this region leads to an increase in the length of a plant: **primary plant growth.** Later on growth occurs in cells known as the **lateral meristems,** which extend all the way through the plant. This growth leads to an increase in the width of a plant and is known as **secondary plant growth.**

Regions of Growth

Root cap: protective structure that keeps roots from being damaged during push through soil.

Zone of cell division: section of root where cells are actively dividing.

Zone of elongation: next section up along the root, where cells absorb H_2O and increase in length to make the plant taller.

Zone of maturation: section of root past the zone of elongation where the cells differentiate to their finalized form (phloem, xylem, parenchyma, epidermal, etc).

The Shoot System

Now that we have discussed roots—the part of the plant that is *in* the ground—let's take a look at shoots (leaves and stems), the parts of the plant that are *out of* the ground.

Structure of a Leaf

Leaves are protected by the waxy **cuticle** of the epidermis, which functions to decrease the transpiration rate. Inside the epidermis lies the ground tissue of the leaf, the mesophyll, which is involved in the ever-so-important process of photosynthesis. There are two important layers to the mesophyll: the **palisade mesophyll** and the **spongy mesophyll.** Most of the photosynthesis of the leaf occurs in the palisade mesophyll, where there are *many* chloroplasts. Inside a bit farther is the spongy mesophyll whose cells provide CO_2 to the cells performing photosynthesis. Important structures to successful photosynthesis are **stomata,** which are controlled by the guard cells that line the walls of the epidermis. Extending a bit farther inside the leaf, we find the *xylem,* the supplier of water to photosynthesizing cells, and the *phloem,* which carries *away* the products of photosynthesis. In C_4 plants, a second type of cell called a *bundle sheath cell* surrounds the vascular tissue to make the use of CO_2 more efficient and allow the stomata to remain closed during the hot daytime hours. These cells prevent excessive transpiration.

Structure of Stems

Again, let's travel from the outside in and discuss the basic structure. The epidermis for the stem provides protection and is covered by **cutin,** a waxy protective coat. The cortex of a stem contains the parenchyma, collenchyma, and schlerenchyma cells mentioned earlier in this chapter. You'll notice that there is no endodermis in the stem because this portion of the plant is not involved in the *absorption* of water. As a result, the next structure we see as we move inward is the vascular cylinder and our friends the xylem and phloem.

A term to know is the **vascular cambium,** which extends along the entire length of the plant and gives rise to secondary xylem and phloem. Over time, the stem of a plant will increase in width because of the secondary xylem produced each year.

Another term to know is the **cork cambium,** which produces a thick cover for stems and roots. This covering replaces the epidermis when it dries up and falls off the stem during secondary growth, forming a protective barrier against infection and physical damage.

The growth of plants is not a continuous process in seasonal environments. There are periods of dormancy in between phases of growth. Have you ever seen the rings of a tree after it has been cut down? These rings produced each year are a window into the past, and give insight into the amount of rain a tree has encountered in a given year. The wider the ring, the more water it saw.

Plant Hormones

Hormones perform the same general function for plants that they do for humans—they are signals that can travel long distances to affect the actions of another cell. There are five main plant hormones you should study for this exam.

1. *Abscisic acid.* This is the "babysitter" hormone. It makes sure that seeds do not germinate too early, inhibits cell growth, and stimulates the closing of the stomata to make sure the plant maintains enough water.
2. *Auxin.* This is a popular AP Biology exam plant hormone selection. Auxin is a hormone that performs several functions—it leads to the elongation of stems, and plays a role in phototropism and gravitropism, which we will discuss a bit later.
3. *Cytokinins.* Hormones that promote cell division and leaf enlargement. They also seem to have an element of the "fountain of youth" in them, as they seem to slow

down the aging of leaves. Supermarkets use synthetic cytokinins to keep their veggies fresh.

4. *Ethylene.* This hormone initiates fruit ripening and causes flowers and leaves to drop from trees (associated with aging).
5. *Gibberellins.* Another hormone group that assists in stem elongation. When you think gibberellins, think "grow." It is thought to induce the growth of dormant seeds, buds, and flowers.

Plant Tropisms

A **tropism** is growth that occurs in response to an environmental stimulus such as sunlight or gravity. The three tropisms you should familiarize yourself with are gravitropism, phototropism, and thigmotropism.

1. *Gravitropism.* This is a plant's growth response to gravitational force. Two of the hormones mentioned earlier play a role in this movement: **auxin** and **gibberellins.** A plant placed on its side will show gravitropic growth in which the cells on the upward-facing side will not grow as much as those on the downward side. It is believed that the relative concentrations of these hormones in the various areas of the plant are responsible for this imbalanced growth of the plant.

2. *Phototropism.* This is a plant's growth response to light. Auxin is the hormone in charge here. Auxin works its magic in the zone of elongation. While the mechanics of the phototropism process may not be vital to this exam, it is still quite interesting to know. When a plant receives light on all sides, auxin is distributed equally around the zone of elongation and growth is even. When one half of a plant is in the sun, and the other is in the shade, auxin (almost as if it feels bad for the shady portion) focuses on the darker side. This leads to unequal growth of the stem with the side receiving less light growing faster—causing the movement of the plant *toward* the light source.
3. *Thigmotropism.* This is a plant's growth response to contact. One example involves vines, which wind around objects with which they make contact as they grow.

How in the world did we figure out that auxin played such a large role in phototropism? A series of experiments performed by two scientists proved vital to the understanding of this process. Grass seedlings are surrounded by a protective structure known as the **coleoptile.** Peter Boysen-Jensen performed an experiment in which a gelatin block permeable to chemical signals was placed in between this coleoptile structure and the body of a grass seedling. When the piece of grass was exposed to light on one side, it grew toward the light. When a barrier impermeable to chemical signals was placed in between the two structures instead, this growth toward light did not occur. Another scientist, F. W. Went, came onto the scene and took Jensen's experiment a step further. Went wanted to show that it was indeed a chemical and not the coleoptile tip itself that was responsible for the phototropic response. He cut off the tip and exposed it to light while the tip was resting on an agar block that would collect any chemicals that diffused out. The block was then placed on the body of a tipless grass seedling sitting in a dark room. Even in the absence of light, a block placed more toward the right side of a seedling caused the seedling to bend to the left. A block placed more toward the left side of a seedling caused the seedling to bend to the right. Because there was no further light stimulation causing the growth, the agar block must indeed have contained a chemical that induced a phototropic response. This chemical was given the name *auxin.*

Photoperiodism

BIG IDEA 2.E.1

Timing of specific events is important in the development of an organism.

Like all of us, plants have a biological clock that maintains a **circadian rhythm**—a physiologic cycle that occurs in time increments that are roughly equivalent to the length of a day. The month of June has the longest days of the year—the most sunlight. The month of December has the shortest days of the year—the least sunlight. How is it that plants, which are so dependent on light, are able to survive through these varying conditions? This is thanks to **photoperiodism**, the response by a plant to the change in the length of days. One commonly discussed example of photoperiodism involves flowering plants (angiosperms). A hormone known as **florigen** is thought to assist in the blooming of flowers. An important pigment to the process of flowering is **phytochrome**, which is involved in the production of florigen. Because plants differ in the conditions required for flowering to occur, different amounts of florigen are needed to initiate this process from plant to plant.

One interesting application of photoperiodism involves the distinction between **short-day plants** and **long-day plants**, which flower only if certain requirements are met:

PLANT TYPE	EXAMPLE	FLOWERING REQUIREMENTS	FLOWERS DURING
Short-day plants	Poinsettias	Exposure to a night *longer* than a certain number of hours (e.g., 10 hours)	End of summer to end of winter
Long-day plants	Spinach	Exposure to a night *shorter* than a certain number of hours (e.g., 8 hours)	Late spring to early summer

Go with the Flow: Osmosis, Capillary Action, Cohesion-Tension Theory, and Transpiration

Osmosis drives the absorption of water and minerals from the soil by the root tips. Water then moves deeper into the root until it reaches the endodermis. Once there, because of the casparian strip, it can only travel through the selective endodermal cells that choose which nutrients and minerals they let through to the vascular cylinder beyond. The casparian strip essentially lets only those with a backstage pass through. Potassium has a backstage pass and can go into the vascular cylinder . . . sodium does not and gets denied. Once the water gets to the xylem, it has reached the H_2O superhighway and is ready to go all over the plant.

There are a few driving forces responsible for the movement of a plant's water supply. The three main forces we will cover here are osmosis, capillary action, and cohesion-tension theory. Of those three, the cohesion-tension theory pulls the most weight.

Osmosis

Osmosis is the driving force that moves water from the soil into xylem cells. How in the world does the plant keep the concentration gradient such that it promotes the movement of water in the appropriate direction? There are two contributing factors: (1) the water is constantly moving away from the root tips creating the space for more water to enter, and (2) osmosis is defined as the passive diffusion of water down its concentration gradient across selectively permeable membranes. It flows from a region with a high water concentration to a region with a low water concentration. There is a higher mineral concentration inside the vascular cylinder, which drives water into the xylem contained in this cylinder by a force known as **root pressure.**

Capillary Action

Capillary action is the force of adhesion between water and a passageway that pulls water up along the sides. Along with osmosis, this mechanism is a minor contributor to the movement of water up the xylem due to the counteracting force of gravity.

Cohesion-Tension Theory and Transpiration

This process is the major mover of water in the xylem. Transpiration creates a negative pressure in the leaves and xylem tissue due to the evaporative loss of water. Water molecules display molecular attraction (cohesion) for other water molecules, in effect creating a single united water molecule that runs the length of the plant. Imagine that you tie a bunch of soda cans to a rope. If you are standing in a tree, and pull up on the cans at the top of the rope, the cans at the bottom will follow—not really because they are loyal to the other cans, but because they are connected to them, they are bonded. This is similar to the movement of water through the xylem. When water evaporates off the surface of the leaf, the water is pulled up through the xylem toward the leaves—transpiration is the force pulling water through the plant.

The Changing of the Guard: Regulating Stomata Activity

The stomata are structures vital to the daily workings of a plant. When closed, photosynthesis is halted because water and carbon dioxide are inaccessible. When open, mesophyll cells have access to water and carbon dioxide. But with every reward, there is always a risk. When the stomata are open, the plant could dry out as a result of excessive transpiration. This process of opening and closing the stomata must therefore be very carefully controlled. Guard cells are the ones for the job. They surround and tightly regulate the actions of the stomata. When water flows into neighboring guard cells (leading to an increase in turgor pressure), a structural change occurs that causes the opening of the stomata. When the water flows out of the guard cells (a decrease in turgor pressure), the stomata will close. It is by this mechanism that guard cells control the opening and closing of the stomata.

"Move Over, Sugar": Carbohydrate Transport Through Phloem

The transport of carbohydrates through the phloem is called **translocation.** After their production, carbohydrates, the all-important product of photosynthesis, are dumped into the phloem (the sugar superhighway) near the site of their creation, to be distributed throughout the plant. The movement of the sugar into the phloem creates a driving force because it establishes a concentration gradient. This gradient leads to the passive diffusion of water into the phloem, causing an increase in the pressure of these cells. This pressure drives the movement of sugars and water through the phloem. As the sugars arrive at various destination sites, the sugar is consumed by plant cells, causing a reversal in the driving force for water that pushes water out of the phloem. As water exits the phloem, the increased pressure disappears and all is good once again.

› Review Questions

1. Which of the following is *not* a time when most stomata tend to be open?

   A. When CO_2 concentrations are low inside the leaf
   B. When temperatures are low
   C. When the concentration of water inside the plant is low
   D. During the day

For questions 2–5, please use the following answer choices:

   A. Abscisic acid
   B. Cytokinins
   C. Ethylene
   D. Gibberellins

2. This hormone is used by supermarkets for its "fountain of youth" effect.

3. This hormone initiates fruit ripening and works hard during the autumn months.

4. This hormone prevents seeds from germinating prematurely.

5. This hormone is known to induce growth in dormant seeds, buds, and flowers.

6. A vine is observed to wrap around a tree as it grows in the forest. This is an example of

   A. gravitropism.
   B. phototropism.
   C. thigmotropism.
   D. photoperiodism.

7. This portion of the root of a plant is responsible for the visual perception of growth:

   A. Zone of cell division
   B. Vascular cylinder
   C. Zone of elongation
   D. Endodermis

For questions 8–10, please use the following answers:

   A. Sieve-tube elements
   B. Vessel elements
   C. Guard cells
   D. Collenchyma cells

8. These cells are responsible for controlling the opening and closing of the stomata.

9. These cells are the more efficient of the two types of xylem cells.

10. These cells are live cells that function as structural support for a plant.

11. The unequal growth of the stem of a plant in which the side in the shade grows faster than the side in the sun is an example of

    A. gravitropism.
    B. phototropism.
    C. thigmotropism.
    D. photoperiodism.

〉 Answers and Explanations

1. **C**—When the concentration of water inside the plant is low, the stomata close in an effort to minimize transpiration.

2. **B**

3. **C**

4. **A**

5. **D**

6. **C**—Thigmotropism is a plant's growth in response to touch. Phototropism is growth in response to light, and gravitropism is growth in response to gravitational force. Photoperiodism is the response by a plant to the change in the length of days.

7. **C**

8. **C**

9. **B**

10. **D**

11. **B**—Phototropism, a plant's growth response to light, is controlled by auxin. This hormone is produced in the apical meristem and sent to the zone of elongation to initiate growth toward the sun.

〉 Rapid Review

The following terms and topics are important in this chapter:

Anatomy of plants: tissue systems are divided into *ground, vascular,* and *dermal.*

Ground tissue: the body of the plant is divided into three cell types:

- *Collenchyma cells*: provide flexible and mechanical support; found in stems and leaves.
- *Parenchyma cells*: play a role in storage, secretion, and photosynthesis in cells.
- *Sclerenchyma cells*: protect seeds and support the plant.

Vascular tissue: *xylem* (transports water and minerals) and *phloem* (transports sugar).

Dermal tissue: protective outer coating for plants: *epidermis.*

Roots

Types: **taproot system** (dicots)—system that divides into lateral roots that anchor the plant; **fibrous root system** (monocots)—anchoring system that does not go deep down into soil.

Structure: epidermis → endodermis (casparian strip) → vascular cylinder → xylem/phloem.

Growth: occurs for lifetime of the plant thanks to **meristem** cells:

- *Primary growth*: increased *length* of a plant (occurs in region of apical meristems).
- *Secondary growth*: increased *width* of a plant (occurs in region of lateral meristems, limited in monocots).
- *Three main growth regions*: zone of *cell division* (cells divide), zone of *elongation* (cells elongate), zone of *maturation* (cells mature to specialized form).

> ### Stems (Shoots)
>
> *Structure*: epidermis (cutin) → cortex (ground tissue) → vascular cylinder → xylem/phloem.
>
> *Vascular cambium*: gives rise to secondary xylem/phloem; runs entire length of plant.
>
> *Cork cambium*: produces protective covering that replaces epidermis during secondary growth.

> ### Leaves (Shoots)
>
> *Structure*: epidermis (cuticle) → mesophyll (photosynthesis) → vascular bundles → xylem/phloem.
>
> *C_4 plants*: leaves contain another cell type, **bundle sheath cells,** which assist in respiration in hot and dry regions.
>
> *Stomata*: structure, controlled by **guard cells,** that when open allows CO_2 in, and H_2O and O_2 out.

Plant hormones: **abscisic acid** (inhibits cell growth, helps close stomata), **auxin** (stem elongation, gravitropism, phototropism), **cytokinins** (promotes cell division, leaf enlargement, slows aging of leaves), **ethylene** (ripens fruit and causes leaves to fall), **gibberellins** (stem elongation, induces growth in dormant seeds, buds, flowers).

Plant tropisms: **gravitropism** (a plant's growth in response to gravity—auxin, gibberellins), **phototropism** (plant's growth in response to light—auxin), **thigmotropism** (plant's growth in response to touch).

Photoperiodism: response of a plant to the change in length of days; remember **florigen** and **phytochrome.**

Driving force for H_2O movement in plants: transpiration is the major driving force that draws H_2O up the xylem because of the cohesive nature of water molecules. Osmosis and capillary action are minor contributors.

Driving force for sugar movement in plants: sugar, when created, is dumped into the phloem, creating a concentration gradient that draws water in, increasing the pressure that drives the sugar through the phloem.

CHAPTER 15

Human Physiology

IN THIS CHAPTER

Summary: This chapter takes you on a tour of the human body and discusses how the various systems of the human body function on a daily basis.

Key Ideas

✪ Study this chapter well—human physiology comes up often on the AP exam.

✪ Passage of blood flow through the heart: vena cava → right atrium → right ventricle → lungs → left atrium → left ventricle → aorta → body and back.

✪ The functional unit of the lung is the alveolus.

✪ Four major thermoregulatory processes: conduction, convection, evaporation, and radiation.

✪ The CNS consists of the brain and spinal cord. The PNS is broken down into the sensory and motor divisions.

✪ Three main types of muscle: skeletal, cardiac, and smooth.

✪ Study the names, origins, and functions of the various hormones that appear in this chapter—this is a common subject for multiple-choice questions.

✪ Learn about the difference between nonspecific and specific immunity.

Introduction

BIG IDEA 4.B.2
Within multicellular organisms, specialization of organs contributes to overall function.

Welcome to the tour of the human body. During this tour, we will discuss how our bodies work. We will be making eight stops, lunch will not be served, and we don't want to hear any requests for bathroom breaks (although we will be learning about things of that nature). Buckle up—here we go.

Circulatory System

Heart

Welcome to the heart. The human heart is a four-chambered organ whose function is to circulate blood by rhythmic contraction. The heart pumps oxygenated blood from the left ventricle out to the aorta (Figure 15.1). From there it travels through **arteries** to feed the organs, muscles, and other tissues of the body. The blood returns to the heart via the **veins.** The superior and inferior vena cavae return deoxygenated blood from the body to the heart. The blood reenters the heart through the right atrium, passes through to the right ventricle, and from there to the lungs to exchange carbon dioxide for more oxygen. At this point, the blood has made a complete cycle through the body. The blood is at its most oxygenated stage just after leaving the lungs as it enters the left side of the heart and travels into the aorta. The blood is in its least oxygenated stage as it reenters the right atrium of the heart.

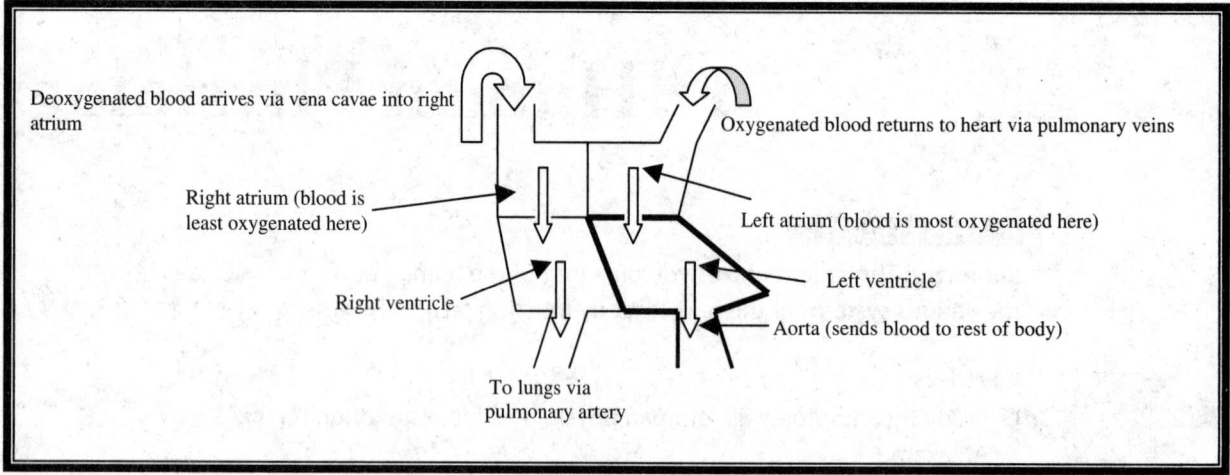

Figure 15.1 Oversimplified diagram of the heart and blood flow.

Structure–function relationships come up often on the AP Biology exam, and the circulatory system provides a good example you could add to an essay on the topic. The left ventricle of the heart is the thickest and most muscular part of the heart, and the most pressure is exerted on it. Why does this make sense functionally? Because the left ventricle is the portion of the heart that needs to pump the blood into the aorta and to the rest of the body. The left ventricle is structurally designed to fit its function. The right ventricle is smaller and less muscular because it only pumps blood a short distance to the lungs for gas exchange (the picking up of oxygen and the release of CO_2).

Blood

As we continue on our journey, if you look off to your right, you will see some of the blood and its components passing us now. If you look closely, you will see little *red blood cells*, which carry oxygen, traveling in the bloodstream. Thanks to a molecule termed **hemoglobin,** the red blood cells are able to carry and deliver oxygen throughout the body to hardworking organs and tissues. Iron is a major component of hemoglobin. If you do not have enough iron in your diet, your ability to deliver oxygen via the blood can be compromised, and you may develop **anemia.**

Blood is able to flow so efficiently because it contains primarily water. The liquid portion of the blood, the **plasma,** contains minerals, hormones, antibodies, and nutritional materials. Another common component seen in the bloodstream is the **platelet,** which is involved in the clotting of blood. You might ask, "What are the white cells flowing around?" The white blood cells are the protection system for our body. We will be seeing those up close when we talk about the immune system.

The **lymphatic system** is worth a brief mention here because it is an important part of the circulatory system. When blood flows through the capillaries of the body, proteins and fluid leak out during the exchange. The lymphatic system functions as the route by which these poor lost souls find their way back into the bloodstream. The lymphatic system also functions as a protector for the body because of the presence of structures known as **lymph nodes,** which are full of white blood cells that live to fight infection. If your neck sometimes swells when you are sick with the flu, for instance, it is probably the multiplication of white blood cells in the lymph nodes of your neck.

Diseases of the Cardiovascular System

Two diseases that you should be familiar with for the exam are *hypertension* and *arteriosclerosis. Hypertension* is high blood pressure and is a major cause of strokes and heart attacks. *Arteriosclerosis* is a big word that means hardening of the arteries. These hardened arteries become narrower and are a prime risk factor for death by embolism—the breaking off of a piece of tissue that lodges in an artery, blocking the flow of blood to vital tissues.

Respiratory System

We are going to head down to the lungs now. Please stay close because it will get a little loud in these windy tunnels. Air comes into the body through the mouth and the nose. We are currently in the nasal passages, and along with the air that came into the nose, we are being warmed and moistened in the *nasal cavity* before we head down toward the **pharynx** region, where the air and food passages cross. We will come back to this area again later on in the tour when we take the road that food uses to get from the mouth to the stomach. During inhalation, the air goes through a structure called the *glottis* into the **larynx** (human voicebox). From there, the air moves into the **trachea,** which contains rings of cartilage that help it maintain its shape. Each trachea is the tunnel that leads the air into the *thoracic cavity.* If you look outside your windows, you will notice some tiny arms waving at us as we go by. They are the **cilia,** which beat in rhythmical waves to carry foreign particles (like our tour bus) and mucus away from the respiratory tract.

BIG IDEA 2.A.3
The increased surface area of alveoli helps in gas exchange with the environment.

We are now at a fork in the road. Here the trachea divides into two separate tunnels: the two **bronchi,** which are also held open by cartilage rings, one going to the left lung, and one going to the right lung. Each bronchus divides into smaller branches, which divide into even smaller branches, which divide into tunnels called **bronchioles.** These bronchioles branch repeatedly until they conclude as tiny air pockets containing **alveoli.**

In Figure 15.2, notice how thin the walls of the alveoli are. They are usually a single cell in thickness, are covered by a thin film of water, and are surrounded by a dense bed of capillaries. You might have questioned earlier exactly where the exchange of O_2 and CO_2 actually occurs—this is the place. The alveoli are considered to be the primary functional unit of the lung. Oxygen enters the alveolus the same way we just did—it dissolves in the water lining of the wall and diffuses across the cells into the bloodstream. At the same time, the CO_2, which is carried by the blood, primarily in the form of bicarbonate (HCO_3^-), passes out of the blood in a similar manner. The O_2 moves easily into the bloodstream

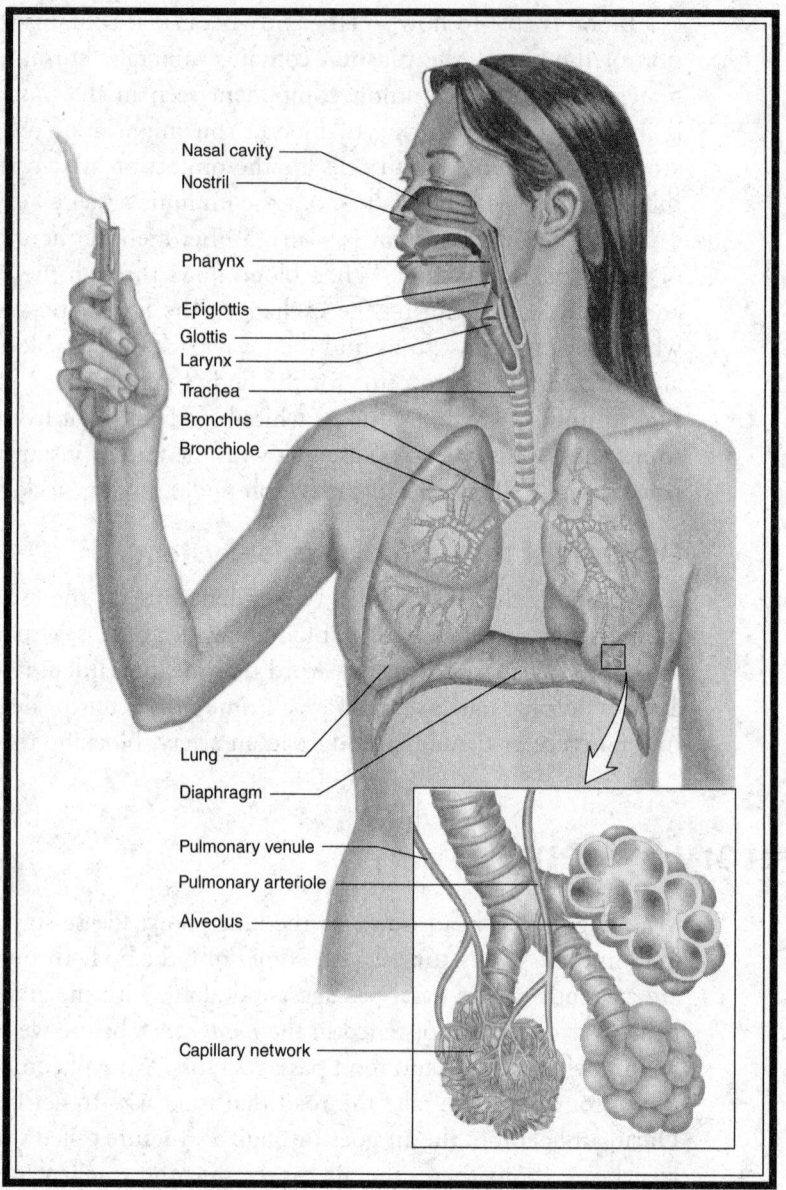

Figure 15.2 The human lungs, with close-up view of alveoli, bronchi, and bronchioles. (*From* Biology, *8th ed., by Sylvia S. Mader, © 1985, 1987, 1990, 1993, 1996, 1998, 2001, 2004 by the McGraw Hill Companies, Inc. Reproduced with permission of The McGraw-Hill Companies.*)

because it is moving down its concentration gradient. Once there, it travels with the blood to the rest of the body.

Before we move on to the digestive system, we should discuss the mechanism by which breathing actually occurs. The rib cage and the diaphragm play important roles in the breathing process. Inhalation causes the volume of the thoracic cavity to increase. As a result, the air pressure in the chest falls below that of the atmosphere, and air flows into the body. This is accompanied by a contraction of the rib-cage muscles and the diaphragm, allowing for the increase in thoracic volume. After the air exchange occurs, the muscles relax, causing the diaphragm to move up against the lungs, reducing the thoracic volume. This causes the pressure in the lungs to exceed that of the atmosphere—driving the air containing CO_2 out of the body.

Digestive System

Okay, folks, it is time to take the tour of the digestive system. Hang on tight—we are going to take a shortcut to the mouth as we are exhaled back through the system. Here we go: bronchioles, bronchi, trachea, larynx, pharynx, and mouth!

Here we sit in the oral cavity. This is where the digestion of food begins. Food is, of course, tasted in the oral cavity, and the teeth that help us chew (masticate) are performing a task called **mechanical digestion.** The liquid sloshing up against the windows of the bus is *saliva,* which contains enzymes such as **amylase** that help dissolve some of the food. Amylase breaks down the starches in our diet into simpler sugars like maltose, which are fully digested further down in the intestines. The saliva also acts as a lubricant to help the food move along the digestive pathway.

We need to carefully avoid the **tongue,** which functions to move food around while we chew and helps to arrange it into a ball that we swallow called a *bolus.* The tongue pushes the food toward the crossroad we visited during the tour of the respiratory system. You may notice that this time, as the swallowing occurs, we do not go through the glottis toward the lungs, but instead into the **esophagus,** which connects the throat to the stomach. The force created by the rhythmical contraction of the smooth muscle of the esophagus (currently pushing us toward the stomach) is called **peristalsis.**

After passing through the **esophageal sphincter,** which acts like a valve or trapdoor, food enters into the stomach, where more digestion will occur. The sphincter is usually closed in order to keep food from returning back up the esophagus to the mouth. In the stomach, the digestion occurs by a churning action that mixes the food and breaks it into smaller pieces. Folks, we would recommend that you do not step out of the bus here because the pH is way down in the 1.5–2.5 range, which provides *quite* an acidic environment. If you look closely along the edges of the stomach, you will see many glands. Some of these glands secrete gastric juice, composed of hydrochloric acid (HCl) and digestive enzymes, which helps in digestion and lowers the pH. The major enzyme of the stomach is **pepsin,** which breaks proteins down into smaller polypeptides that are handled by the intestines. The glands here secrete **pepsinogen**—the precursor to pepsin. Pepsinogen is activated into pepsin by HCl. Pepsin is picky and will function only in a particular range of pH values. This is a good thing because if it were active all the time, it would digest things it is not supposed to digest. Other glands secrete mucus to help line the stomach. It is this mucus that helps prevent the wall of the stomach from being digested along with the food.

Now we move on to the *small intestine.* To get to the small intestine, we need to pass through the Panama Canal of the body: the **pyloric sphincter.** For those of you interested in useful AP exam trivia, the small intestine is where most of the digestion and absorption occur. The terrain is a bit different in this organ. The walls are arranged into folds and ridges, which have more waving structures, this time called *villi,* similar to the cilia we saw in the respiratory tract. The walls in the small intestine contain something called a **brush border,** which is composed of a large amount of microvilli that increases the surface area of the small intestine to improve absorption efficiency. Digested nutrients absorbed in the small intestine are dumped into various veins that merge to form the hepatic portal vessel, which leads to the liver. The liver then gets first crack at the newly absorbed nutrients before they are sent to the rest of the body. As the food moves into the small intestine, it brings with it an acidity that promotes the secretion of numerous enzymes from the *pancreas* and the local glands. (***Important note to remember:*** hormones are vital to the turning on and off of the digestive glands.)

Those of you on the left side of the bus have a good view of the pancreatic duct as it expels **lipase, amylase, trypsin,** and **chymotrypsin.** Lipase is the major fat-digesting enzyme

BIG IDEA 2.A.3
Villi create high surface area, helping in exchange of nutrients with the environment.

of the body. It receives some help in the handling of the fat from a product made in the liver called **bile.** Bile contains bile salts, phospholipids, cholesterol, and bile pigments such as bilirubin. The bile is stored in the *gallbladder* and is dumped into the small intestine upon the arrival of food. The bile salts help digest the fat by *emulsifying* it into small droplets contained in water. (Emulsification is a physical change—bile does not contain any enzymes.) Amylase continues the breakdown of carbohydrates into simpler sugars. *Maltase, lactase,* and *sucrase* break maltose, lactose, and sucrose, respectively, into monosaccharides. Trypsin and chymotrypsin work together to handle the digestion of the peptides in our diet. Trypsin cuts peptide bonds next to arginine and lysine; chymotrypsin cuts bonds by phenylalanine, tryptophan, and tyrosine. Like pepsin, these two proteolytic enzymes are secreted as inactive forms: trypsinogen and chymotrypsinogen. Trypsinogen is activated first to become trypsin, which, in turn, activates chymotrypsin. Some of you might ask "If the proteolytic enzymes only cut at certain sites, how do we finish digesting the proteins?" Trypsin and chymotrypsin are examples of *enteropeptidases.* It is the **exopeptidases** that complete the digestion of proteins by hydrolyzing all the amino acids of the remaining fragments.

After the small intestine comes the large intestine (which includes the cecum, colon, and rectum). The two meet up in the lower right corner of the abdomen. The colon has three main parts: the *ascending, transverse,* and *descending colon.* There are two major functions for this part of the system—the primary function is to reabsorb water and electrolytes. A second function is to serve as a passageway for the waste material as it moves toward the rectum. The food enters the large intestine, travels up the ascending colon, across the transverse colon, down the descending colon into the rectum, where it is stored until it gets eliminated . . . but we don't need to go there. We've seen enough for now.

Control of the Internal Environment

BIG IDEA 2.D.2
Homeostatic mechanisms reflect common ancestry.

The next stop on our tour is the kidney (see Figure 15.3 for an overview of the human excretory system). The kidneys lie on the posterior wall of the abdomen. The renal artery and vein bring blood to and from the kidney, respectively. Kidneys are divided into two major regions: an outer region called the **cortex,** and an inner region called the **medulla.** These two regions are full of **nephrons,** the functional units of the kidney. The medulla is divided into structures called *renal pyramids,* which dump urine into the *major and minor calyces.* From here, the urine is sent toward the *bladder* via the *ureter.* When contracted to urinate, the bladder sends the urine through the *urethra* to the outside world.

We've pulled the bus right up to one of over a million nephrons in each kidney. The nephron is composed of a *renal corpuscle, proximal convoluted tubule, loop of Henle, distal convoluted tubule,* and *collecting duct system.* If you look closely, you will see that the renal corpuscle is made up of **glomerular capillaries** surrounded by *Bowman's capsule.*

Osmoregulation and Excretion

The blood that enters via the renal artery is sent to the various nephrons by the branching of the renal artery into smaller and smaller vessels that culminate in the capillaries of the glomerulus. The *blood pressure* is the force that leads to the movement of solutes such as water, urea, and salts into the lumen of Bowman's capsule from the glomerular capillaries. From here, the fluids pass down the proximal tubule, through the loop of Henle, and into the distal tubule, which dumps into the collecting duct. The various collecting ducts of the kidney collectively merge into the renal pelvis, which leads via the ureter to the bladder.

As we mentioned moments ago, fluid moves from the capillaries into the lumen of the nephron as a result of the force of blood pressure. During this process of **filtration,** the capillaries are able to let small particles through the pores of their endothelial linings,

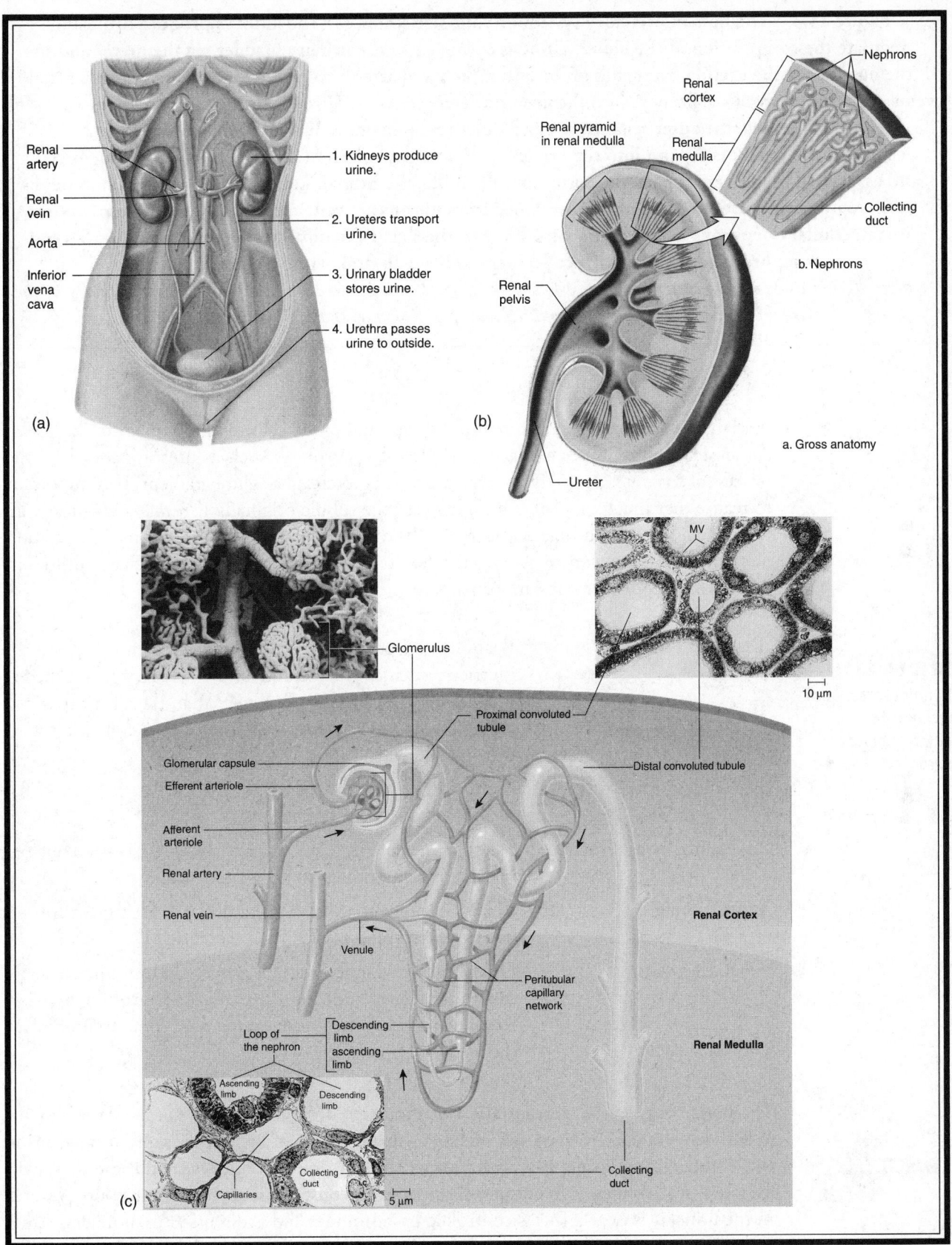

(a)

1. Kidneys produce urine.
2. Ureters transport urine.
3. Urinary bladder stores urine.
4. Urethra passes urine to outside.

Renal artery
Renal vein
Aorta
Inferior vena cava

(b)

Renal pyramid in renal medulla
Renal pelvis
Ureter

Nephrons
Renal cortex
Renal medulla
Collecting duct

b. Nephrons

a. Gross anatomy

Glomerulus

MV

10 μm

(c)

Glomerular capsule
Efferent arteriole
Afferent arteriole
Renal artery
Renal vein
Venule

Proximal convoluted tubule
Distal convoluted tubule

Peritubular capillary network

Renal Cortex

Renal Medulla

Loop of the nephron
Descending limb
ascending limb

Ascending limb
Descending limb
Capillaries
Collecting duct

Collecting duct

5 μm

Figure 15.3   (*Continued*)
For legend see the following section.

Figure 15.3 **The human excretory system on four size scales. (a) The kidneys produce urine and regulate the composition of the blood. Urine is conveyed to the urinary bladder via the ureter and to the outside via the urethra. Branches of the aorta, the renal arteries convey blood to the kidneys; renal veins drain blood from the kidneys into the posterior vena cava. (b) Urine is formed in two distinct regions of the kidney: the outer renal cortex and inner renal medulla. It then drains into a central chamber, the renal pelvis, and into the ureters. (c) Excretory tubules (nephrons and collecting ducts) and associated blood vessels pack the cortex and medulla. The human kidney has about a million nephrons, representing about 80 km of tubules. Cortical nephrons are restricted mainly to the renal cortex. Juxtamedullary nephrons have a long, hairpinlike portion that extends into the renal medulla. Several nephrons empty into each collecting duct, which drains into the renal pelvis.**
(*Adapted from* Biology, *8th ed., by Sylvia S. Mader,* © 1985, 1987, 1990, 1993, 1996, 1998, 2001, 2004 *by the McGraw Hill Companies, Inc. Reproduced with permission of The McGraw-Hill Companies.*)

but large molecules such as proteins, platelets, and blood cells tend to remain in the vessel. As the filtrate progresses along the tubule, plasma solutes such as urea are added by the process of *secretion,* a selective process that helps to create a solute gradient. It is important to realize that much of what is dumped into the tubule originally is *reabsorbed*—nearly all the sugars, water, and organic nutrients. The combination of reabsorption and secretion help the nephron to control what gets released in the urine. The following chart outlines in detail what happens in the various parts of the nephron:

BIG IDEA 2.C.1
Animals use feedback mechanisms (e.g., ADH) to maintain internal conditions.

Proximal tubule	Reabsorbs 75 percent of NaCl and water of filtrate. Nutrients such as glucose and amino acids are reabsorbed unless their concentration is higher than the absorptive capacity. Glucose in urine is an indicator of diabetes, for this reason.
Descending loop of Henle	Freely permeable to H_2O but not NaCl. Assists in control of water and salt concentrations.
Ascending loop of Henle	Freely permeable to NaCl but not water. Assists in control of salt concentration.
Distal tubule	Regulates concentration of K^+ and NaCl. Helps control pH by reabsorbing HCO_3^- and secreting H^+.
Collecting duct	Determines how much water is actually lost in urine. The osmotic gradient created in the earlier regions of the nephron allows the kidney control in the final concentration of the urine.

The body controls the concentration of the urine according to the needs of the system. When dehydrated, the body can excrete a small volume of hypertonic concentrated urine (little water in the urine; it is dark yellow). But in times of excessive fluid, the body will excrete a large volume of hypotonic dilute urine to conserve the necessary salts (lots of water in the urine; it is clear). This is controlled by hormones and is discussed in more detail in a later section, but briefly: **ADH** (antidiuretic hormone) is released by the pituitary gland; it increases permeability of the collecting duct to water, leading to more concentrated urine. **Aldosterone,** released from the adrenal gland, acts on the distal tubules to cause the reabsorption of more Na^+ and water to increase blood volume and pressure.

Thermoregulation

A fairly constant body temperature is important for many living organisms. The process by which this temperature is maintained is known as **thermoregulation.** A major organ involved in thermoregulation is the skin, which also plays a role in excretion through sweating. Four major thermoregulatory processes are conduction, convection, evaporation, and radiation. **Conduction** is the process by which heat moves from a place of higher temperature to a place of lower temperature. For example, let's say that two people are sleeping in the same bed, and that person A is cold all the time. Person A would not make it through the night if it were not for this process. Since person B tends to be warmer than person A, person A takes advantage of conduction by pulling the heat from person B's body to hers. **Convection** is heat transfer caused by airflow. Thinking about my baseline warmth (similar to that of person B), if it were not for our air conditioners in the summer, we would probably not be here today to write this book. But we curse convection in the winter as the cold wind removes heat from our bodies, making it feel that much colder outside. **Evaporation** is the process by which water leaves our bodies in the form of water vapor: sweat. Why do humid days feel so much warmer than nonhumid days? Because humidity increases the amount of water in the air, decreasing the driving force for water to leave our bodies. **Radiation** is the loss of heat through ejection of electromagnetic waves.

Before moving on to the nervous system, we must mention two more terms: endotherm and ectotherm. An **endotherm** is an organism whose body temperature is not dramatically affected by the surrounding temperature. We humans are endothermic creatures. Sure, a cold day can feel really cold, but at least it does not dramatically lower the human body temperature. **Ectothermic animals** are organisms whose body temperatures *are* affected by the surrounding temperature. Fish, reptiles, and amphibians are good examples of ectothermic organisms.

Nervous System

BIG IDEA 3.E.2
Animals have a nervous system that detects signals, transmits information, and produces responses.

The nervous system is divided into two systems: the **central nervous system** (CNS) and the **peripheral nervous system** (PNS). The CNS contains the brain and the spinal cord. The PNS can be broken down into a sensory and a motor division. The sensory division carries information *to* the CNS while the motor division carries information *away* from the CNS. The motor division can be further broken down in the **somatic nervous system** (SNS), also known as the voluntary nervous system, and the **autonomic nervous system** (ANS). As indicated by its name, the SNS controls the voluntary contraction of muscles, while the ANS controls the involuntary activities of the body: smooth muscle, cardiac muscle, and glands. The ANS is divided into the **sympathetic** and **parasympathetic** divisions.

Before delving into the various divisions of the nervous system, it is important to look at the mechanics of nerve cell transmissions (Figure 15.4). The functional unit of the nervous system is the *neuron* (nerve cell). Outside to the left of the bus is a nerve cell from the CNS. There are three main parts to a nerve cell: the cell body, the dendrite, and the axon. The **cell body** is the main body of the neuron. The **dendrite** is one of many short, branched processes of a neuron that help bring the nerve impulses toward the cell body. The **axon** is the longer extension that leaves from the neuron and carries the impulse away from the cell body toward the target cell. Some CNS nerve cells, as well as most PNS neurons, are **myelinated neurons,** which means that they have a layer of insulation around the axon, allowing for faster transmission. It is the cable Internet of the body.

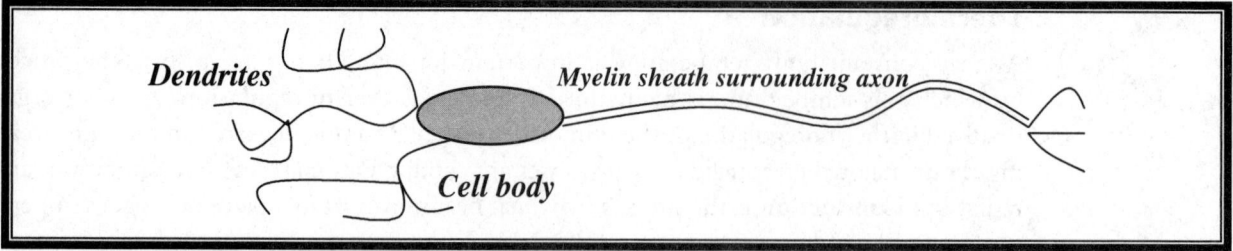

Figure 15.4 The components of a nerve cell (neuron).

The nerve cells can be divided into three main classes: sensory neurons, motor neurons, and interneurons. **Sensory neurons** receive and communicate information from the sensory environment. **Interneurons** function to make synaptic connections with other neurons. Located in the CNS, they tie together sensory input and motor output and are the intermediaries of the operation. **Motor neurons** take the commands of the CNS and put them into action as motor outputs. This relationship is the basis for the *reflex arc,* which is the basic unit of response in the CNS. A sensory neuron sends an impulse to the spinal cord, which is transmitted via a series of interneurons to a motor neuron whose impulse causes a muscular contraction.

BIG IDEA 4.A.4
Organisms exhibit complex properties due to interactions between constituent parts.

Whoa! Did you see that spark zip past just now? That was a perfect example of a nerve impulse. The membranes of these neurons all around us are full of pumps and special gated ion channels that allow the cell to change its membrane potential in response to certain stimuli. The opening of sodium channels causes the potential to become less negative, and the cell is **depolarized.** If the threshold potential is reached (electrical potential that, when reached, initiates an action potential), an action potential is triggered, which is the nerve impulse that we just saw zip by. *Action potentials* are quick changes in cell potential due to well-controlled opening and closing of ion channels. The cell also contains potassium channels that open slowly in response to depolarization. After a short period of time, the sodium channel closes, and potassium rushes out of the cell causing **repolarization** of the cell and lowering of the potential back down to its initial. Let's move farther down this axon to see where this impulse is going.

Here we are at the end of the axon, sometimes called the **synaptic knob.** This is where calcium gates are opened in response to the changing potential, which causes vesicles to release substances called **neurotransmitters** into the synaptic gap between the axon and the target cell. These neurotransmitters diffuse across the gap, causing a new impulse in the target cell. Two of the most common neurotransmitters used in the body are acetylcholine and norepinephrine. Substances called cholinesterases function to clear the neurotransmitters from the synaptic gap after an action potential by binding to the neurotransmitters and recycling them back to the neuron.

BIG IDEA 3.D.2
Cells communicate with each other using chemical signals (e.g., neurotransmitters).

The ANS regulates involuntary activities in the body. As mentioned earlier, it is subdivided into the parasympathetic and sympathetic divisions. For the most part, the parasympathetic response is one that promotes energy conservation: slower heart rate, decreased blood pressure, and bronchial muscle and urinary bladder constriction. The sympathetic response is one that prepares us for "fight or flight"—increased heart rate, dilated bronchial muscles, increased blood pressure, and digestive slowdown.

The CNS consists of the brain and spinal cord. The brain is divided into various sections that control the different regions of our bodies (Figure 15.5). The **cerebellum** is in charge of coordination and balance. The **medulla oblongata** is the control center for involuntary activities such as breathing. The **hypothalamus** is the thermostat and

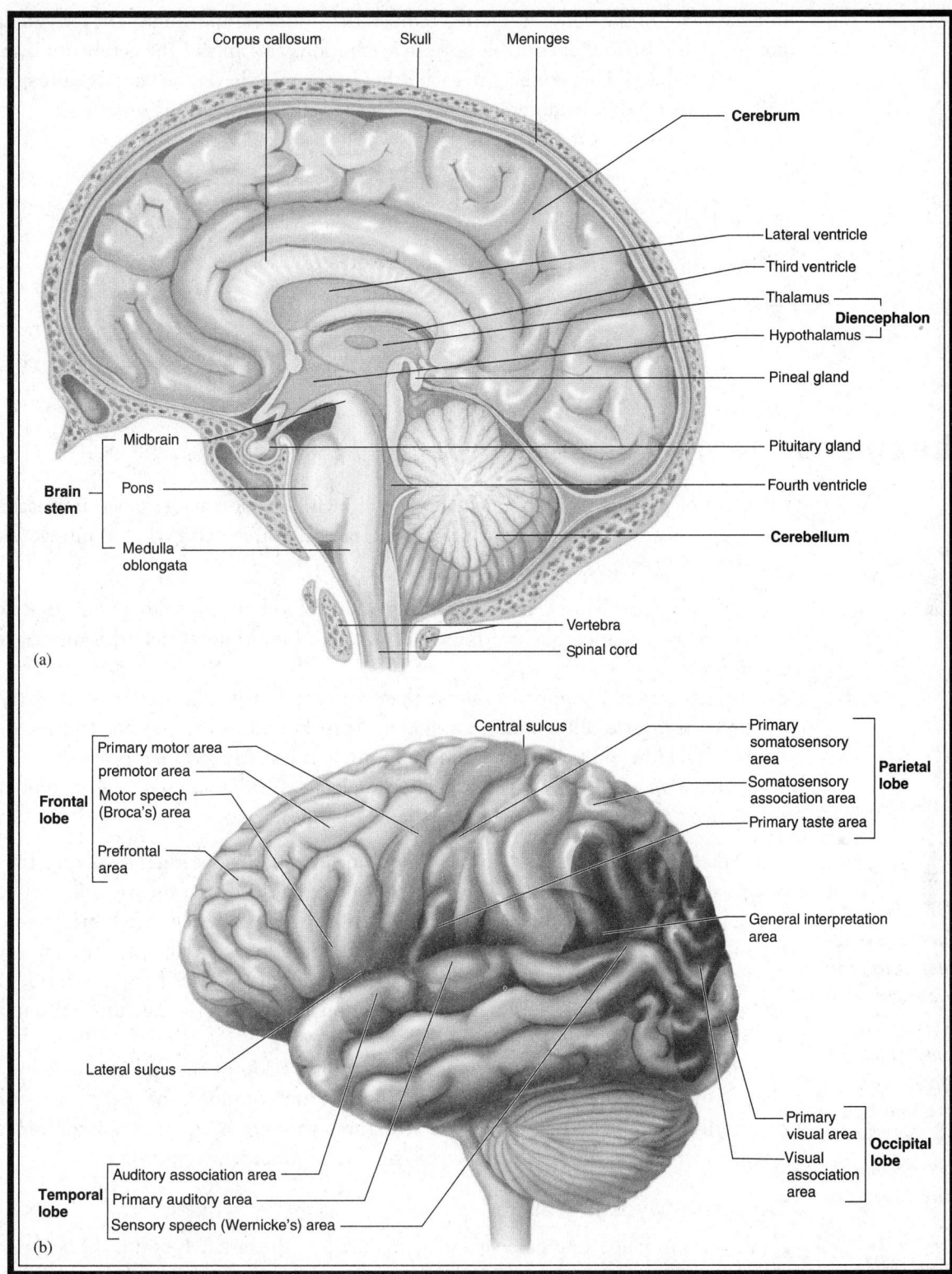

Figure 15.5 **Major structures of the human brain. (a) Of the brain's three ancestral regions, the forebrain is massively developed and contains the most sophisticated integrating centers. One of its subdivisions, the telencephalon, consists mainly of the cerebrum (cerebral hemispheres), which extends over and around most other brain centers. The diencephalon contains the thalamus and hypothalamus. The other two ancestral regions, the midbrain and hindbrain, make up the brian stem. (b) This rear view shows the bilateral nature of the brain components. The cerebral hemispheres, corpus callosum (large fiber tracts connecting the hemispheres), and basal ganglia are parts of the telencephalon.** *(From* Biology, *8th ed., by Sylvia S. Mader, © 1985, 1987, 1990, 1993, 1996, 1998, 2001, 2004 by the McGraw Hill Companies, Inc. Reproduced with permission of The McGraw-Hill Companies.)*

hunger-meter of the body, regulating temperature, hunger, and thirst. The **amygdala** is the portion of our brain that controls impulsive emotions and anger. The **cerebrum** is split into two "hemispheres" that connect to each other in the middle via the **corpus callosum.** Each half is divided into four different lobes, each specializing in various functions:

Lobes of the Brain and Their Functions	
Frontal lobe	Speech, motor cortex.
Parietal lobe	Speech, taste, reading, somatosensory.
Occipital lobe	Vision.
Temporal lobe	Hearing and smell.

Muscular System

Our tour of the muscle types of the body will include a look at the types of muscles and a quick demonstration of muscle contraction. There are three main types of muscle: **skeletal, smooth,** and **cardiac:**

1. *Skeletal muscle.* Muscle type that works when you do pushups, lift a book, and do other voluntary activities. Skeletal muscle cells contain multiple nuclei. This muscle type has a *striated* appearance.
2. *Smooth muscle.* Involuntary muscle that contracts slowly and is controlled by the ANS. Smooth muscle cells contain a single nucleus. Found in the walls of arteries, digestive tract, bladder, and elsewhere. Smooth muscle is not striated in appearance.
3. *Cardiac muscle.* Involuntary muscle of the heart. Cardiac muscle cells contain a single nucleus. Cardiac muscle cells are striated in appearance.

Muscle cells are activated by the mechanism described earlier involving the action potentials and ion channels. When an action potential reaches a muscle cell, acetylcholine is released at the **neuromuscular junction**—the space between the motor neuron and the muscle cell. This neurotransmitter depolarizes the muscle cell and, through a series of intracellular reactions, causes the release of large amounts of stored calcium inside the cell, leading to muscle contraction. Muscle contraction stops when the calcium is taken back up by the sarcoplasmic reticulum of the cell.

Folks, we are going to be treated to a demonstration of skeletal muscle contraction. Skeletal muscle consists of fiber bundles, which are composed of myofibrils. What are myofibrils? Good question. They are structures that are made up of a combination of *myofilaments* called *thin filaments* (*actin*) and *thick filaments* (*myosin*).

CT teacher: "Know the functional units of the various systems discussed in this chapter. How the structure of these functional units relates to their function could be a nice essay."

The Actin-Myosin "Tango"

It takes two to tango, and myosin and actin are up to the task. Myosin is the lead partner of this dynamic duo and powers muscle contraction. Myosin, the heart of the thick fibers, has a "head" and a "tail." The tails of the numerous myosin molecules unite to form the "thick filament" seen in Figure 15.6. The heads of the myosin molecules stick out from the thick filament and serve as the contact point with the actin. The head can exist in two forms: low and high energy. A relaxed muscle begins with the myosin heads in the low-energy form, attached to ATP. If the ATP is converted into ADP and phosphate, the myosin changes to the higher-energy form and is ready to dance. Myosin smoothly approaches its beloved partner, actin. When ready, the myosin and actin attach to each other, forming the "cross-bridge." As they get ready to slide, myosin loses its ADP and phosphate, releasing

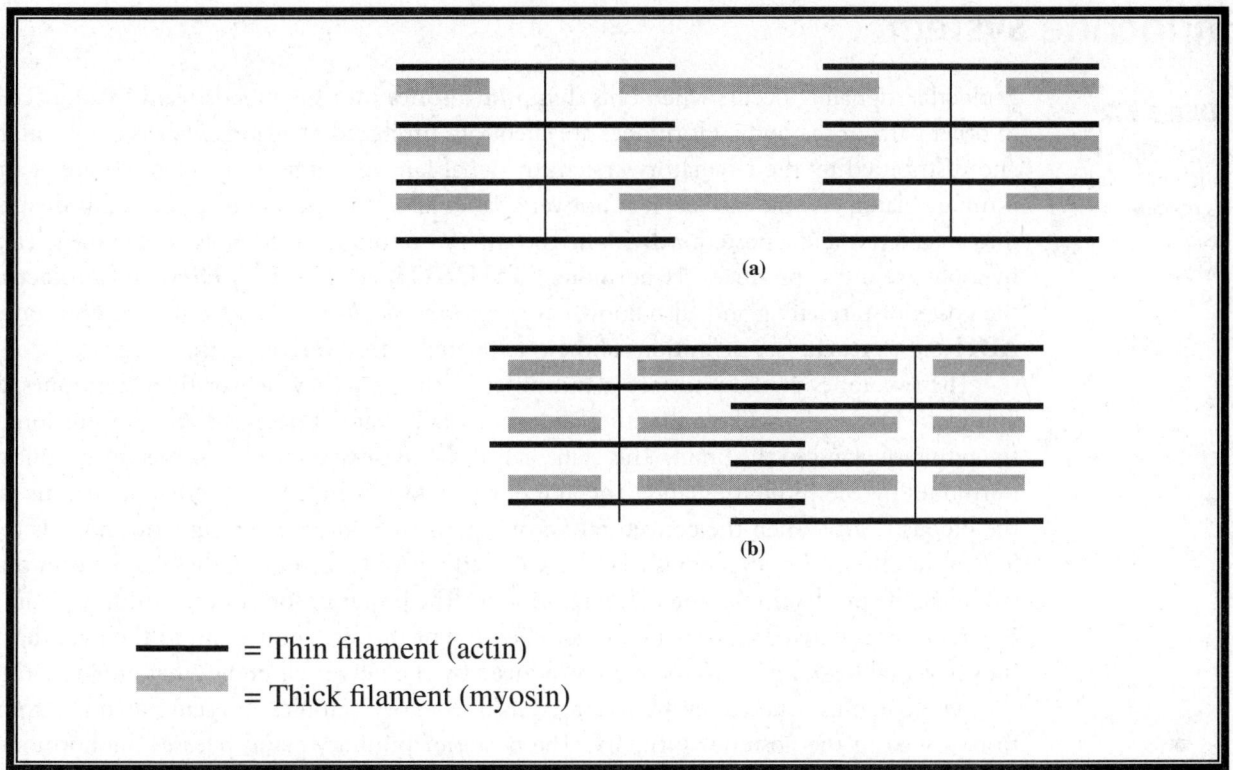

= Thin filament (actin)

= Thick filament (myosin)

Figure 15.6 Actin-myosin interaction: (a) relaxed muscle; (b) contracted muscle.

its energy, and causing it to elegantly tilt its head to one side . . . sliding the beautiful actin toward the center of the sarcomere (Figure 15.6b). The two part ways when myosin again binds to ATP, bringing us back to where we started (Figure 15.6a).

:::Applause:::

Control mechanisms are often mentioned on the AP Biology exam and make good essay material. It would be really annoying and awkward if our muscles were contracting all the time. So, it makes sense that there must be some way to control the contraction. Myosin is only able to dance with actin if a regulatory protein, known as **tropomyosin,** is not blocking the attachment site on actin. The key to the removal of tropomyosin is the presence of calcium ions. Tropomyosin is also bound to *another* regulatory protein known as troponin. Calcium causes these two to do their own little dance and shuffle away from the actin-myosin binding site. This allows the actin-myosin dance to occur and muscle contraction to follow. When the calcium is gone, the dance is complete, and the filaments separate from each other.

What causes this calcium release seen in muscle contraction? This brings us back to the neuromuscular junction mentioned not too long ago. Nervous impulses from motor neurons cause the release of acetylcholine into the neuromuscular junction. Acetylcholine binds to the muscle cell and initiates a series of reactions that culminates in the dumping of calcium from its storage facility—the sarcoplasmic reticulum. This calcium finds troponin, binds to it, and lets the dance begin.

Endocrine System

BIG IDEA 3.B.2
A variety of intercellular and intracellular signals mediate gene expression.

Endocrine signaling occurs when cells dump **hormones** into the bloodstream to affect cells in other parts of the body. Hormones are chemicals produced by glands such as the pituitary and distributed by the circulatory system to signal faraway target cells. Here we are at the pituitary gland. As you can see, it is not very big at all—it is the size of a pea and is divided into an anterior and a posterior division. The anterior pituitary gland is also called the adeno-hypophysis, and it produces six hormones: **TSH, STH, ACTH, LH, FSH,** and **prolactin;** the posterior pituitary gland, also known as the *neurohypophysis,* releases only two hormones: **ADH** and **oxytocin** (see definitions of these acronyms in the Glossary at the end of the book).

The two lobes of the pituitary gland differ in the way they deliver their hormones. If you look closely, you will see that there is a short stalk that connects the anterior portion of the pituitary gland to the brain. This stalk, called the **hypothalamus,** controls the output of hormones by the pituitary gland. The anterior pituitary is linked to the hypothalamus via the bloodstream. When the concentration of a particular anterior pituitary hormone is too low in the circulation, the hypothalamus will send releasing factors via the bloodstream that stimulate the production of the needed hormone. The posterior lobe of the pituitary gland is different—it is derived from neural tissue. Because of this, its connection to the hypothalamus is neural. ADH and oxytocin are produced by the nerve cell bodies that are located in the hypothalamus, where they are packaged into secretory granules and sent down the axons to be stored in the posterior pituitary. The posterior pituitary gland releases the hormones when appropriately stimulated by a nervous impulse from the hypothalamus. The following is a breakdown of the hormones you should be familiar with for the exam:

Hormones of the *anterior pituitary* are

CT teacher: "Have a good general understanding of these hormones and their functions."O

FSH	Follicle-stimulating hormone. A gonadotropin—stimulates activities of the testes and ovaries. In females, it induces the development of the ovarian follicle, which leads to the production and secretion of estrogen. In males, it stimulates the production of sperm.
LH	Luteinizing hormone. A gonadotropin—stimulates ovulation, formation of corpus luteum, and synthesis of estrogens and progesterone in females. In males, it stimulates the production of testosterone.
TSH	Thyroid-stimulating hormone. Works to stimulate the synthesis and secretion of thyroid hormones in the thyroid gland, which in turn regulate the rate of metabolism in the body.
STH (or HGH)	Somatotropic hormone (or human growth hormone). Stimulates protein synthesis and general growth in the body.
ACTH	Stimulates the secretion of adrenal cortical hormones, which work to maintain electrolytic homeostasis and help to cope with chronic stress.
Prolactin	Controls lactogenesis—production of milk by the breasts. Decreases the synthesis and release of GnRH (gonadotropin-releasing hormone), inhibiting ovulation.

Hormones of the *posterior pituitary* are

ADH	Stimulates reabsorption of water by the collecting ducts of the kidney.
Oxytocin	Stimulates uterine contraction and milk ejection for breastfeeding.

Hormones of the *adrenal gland* are

Cortisol	Stress hormone released in response to physiological challenges. Increases the blood glucose level in response to chronic stress.
Aldosterone	Regulates blood sodium concentration and blood volume by controlling the renal excretion of sodium.
Epinephrine	Raises blood glucose level, increases metabolic activity—"fight or flight" hormone. Also known as *adrenaline*.

Pancreatic hormones are

Insulin	Secreted in response to high blood glucose levels to promote glycogen formation. Lowers blood sugar.
Glucagon	Stimulates conversion of glycogen into glucose. Raises blood sugar.

The *parathyroid* hormone (PTH) increases serum concentration of Ca^{2+}, assisting in the process of bone maintenance.

Sex hormones are

Progesterone	Regulates menstrual cycle and pregnancy.
Estrogen	Stimulates development of secondary sex characteristics in women. Secreted in ovaries. Induces the release of LH, including the LH surge of the menstrual cycle. With progesterone, helps maintain the endometrium during pregnancy.
Testosterone	Stimulates secondary sex characteristics and the production of sperm in men. Secreted in testes.

Thyroid hormones are

Calcitonin	Lowers blood calcium. Works antagonistically to PTH.
Thyroxine	Stimulates metabolic activities.

The thymus hormone is *thymosin,* a hormone involved in the development of the T cells of the immune system.

The pineal gland hormone is *melatonin,* a hormone that is known to be involved in our biological rhythms (circadian). It is released at night.

How is the hormone secretion process of the body regulated? The two main types of regulation with which you should be familiar are negative feedback and positive feedback. **Negative feedback** occurs when a hormone acts to directly or indirectly inhibit further secretion of the hormone of interest. A good example of negative feedback involves insulin, which is secreted by the pancreas. When the blood glucose gets too high, the pancreas is stimulated to produce insulin, which causes cells to use more glucose. As a result of this activity, the blood glucose level declines, halting the production of insulin by the pancreas. **Positive feedback** occurs when a hormone acts to directly or indirectly cause increased secretion of the hormone. An example of this feedback mechanism is the LH surge that occurs prior to ovulation in females. Estrogen is released as a result of the action of FSH, and travels to the anterior pituitary to stimulate the release of LH, which acts on the ovaries to stimulate further secretion of estrogen.

BIG IDEA 3.D.1
Activity within individual cells supports function for an entire organism (e.g., epinephrine stimulation of glycogen breakdown).

BIG IDEA 3.D.2
Cells communicate with each other from a distance via hormones.

Homeostasis

NYC teacher: "This could make a nice subquestion to an essay. Understand these relationships."

Homeostasis is the maintenance of balance. Hormones can work antagonistically to maintain homeostasis in the body. Two examples we will talk about are insulin/glucagon and calcitonin/PTH:

1. *Insulin/glucagon.* Both are hormones of the pancreas and have opposing effects on blood glucose. Let's say that you eat a nice sugary snack that pushes the blood glucose above its desired level. This results in the release of insulin from the pancreas to stimulate the uptake of glucose from the blood to the liver to be stored as glycogen. It also causes other cells of the body to take up glucose to be used for energy. Sometimes if you go a long time between meals, your blood glucose can dip *below* the desired level. This sets glucagon into action and causes its release from the pancreas. Glucagon acts on the liver to stimulate the removal of glycogen from storage to produce glucose to pump into the bloodstream. When the glucose level gets back to the appropriate level, glucagon release ceases. This back-and-forth dance works to keep the glucose concentration in our bodies relatively stable over time.

BIG IDEA 2.C.1
Animals use feedback to maintain homeostasis.

2. *Calcitonin/PTH.* Like glucose, the body has a desired blood calcium (Ca^{2+}) level it tries to maintain. If it drops below this level, PTH is released by the parathyroid gland and works to increase the amount of Ca^{2+} in circulation in three major ways: it (a) releases of Ca^{2+} from bones, (b) increases absorption of Ca^{2+} by the intestines, and (c) increases reabsorption of Ca^{2+} by the kidneys. If the blood Ca^{2+} level gets too high, the thyroid gland releases calcitonin, which pretty much performs the three *opposite* responses to PTH's work: it (a) puts Ca^{2+} *into* bone, (b) decreases absorption of Ca^{2+} by the intestines, and (c) decreases reabsorption of Ca^{2+} by the kidneys.

One last distinction we want to make before we move on is to touch on the difference between protein hormones and steroid hormones.

Protein hormones are too large to move into cells and thus bind to receptors on the surface of cells. In response to the binding of a protein hormone, a change occurs in the receptor that leads to the activation of molecules inside the cell, called **second messengers,** which serve as intermediaries, activating other proteins and enzymes that carry out the mission. The second messenger to know for this exam is cyclic adenosine monophasphate (cAMP), involved in *numerous* signal cascade pathways. Protein hormones activate cAMP through a multi-step process that begins with protein–hormone activation of relay proteins such as **G proteins.** These proteins are able to directly activate a compound known as *adenyl cyclase,* which in turn produces cAMP.

Since we discussed regulatory mechanisms earlier, it is important to point out that there are G proteins that function to *inhibit* cAMP and work antagonistically to hormones that activate cAMP.

Steroid hormones are lipid-soluble molecules that pass through the cell membrane and combine with cytoplasmic proteins. These complexes pass through to the nucleus to interact with chromosomal proteins and directly affect transcription in the nucleus of cells.

Immune System

CT teacher: "Concentrate on the various cell types and the difference between specific and nonspecific defense."

What we are about to witness is an absolute treat. We just got word from the central office that the body we are touring has just received a **vaccination.** A vaccine is given to a patient in an effort to prime the immune system for a fight against a specific invader. This truly is a rare opportunity for us to see the immune system in action.

We have reentered the general bloodstream circulation of the body in an attempt to find some activity. While we are in transit, we will explain some basic immune system terms to you.

BIG IDEA 2.D.3
Organisms are affected by disruptions to their homeostasis (e.g., pathogens).

The immune system is a two-tiered defense mechanism. It consists of **nonspecific immunity** and **specific immunity.** Nonspecific immunity is exactly how it sounds—it is the nonspecific prevention of the entrance of invaders into the body. Saliva contains an enzyme called **lysozyme** that can kill germs before they have a chance to take hold. Lysozyme is also present in our tears, providing a nonspecific defense mechanism for our eyes. The skin covering the entire body is a nonspecific defense mechanism—it acts as a physical barrier to infection. The mucous lining of our trachea and lungs prevent bacteria from entering cells and actually assists in the expulsion of bacteria by ushering the bacteria up and out with a cough. Finally, remember how we told you that you did not want to get out of the bus in the stomach? That is also the case for bacteria—it is a dangerous place for them as well. The acidity of the stomach can wipe out a lot of potential invaders.

BIG IDEA 2.C.2
Organisms respond to changes in their environment (e.g., infections).

A nonspecific cellular defense mechanism is headed up by cells called **phagocytes.** These cells, *macrophages* and *neutrophils,* roam the body in search of bacteria and dead cells to engulf and clear away. Some assistance is offered to their cause by a protein molecule called **complement.** This protein makes sure that molecules to be cleared have some sort of identification displaying the need for phagocyte assistance. Complement coats these cells, stimulating phagocytes to ingest them. Cells involved in mechanisms that need cleanup assistance, such as platelets, have the ability to secrete chemicals that attract macrophages and neutrophils to places such as infection sites to help in the elimination of the foreign bacteria. They are nonspecific because they are not seeking out particular garbage . . . they are just looking for something to eat.

BIG IDEA 2.D.4
Animals have a variety of chemical defenses against infections that affect homeostasis.

A prime example of a nonspecific cellular response is inflammation. Let's say that you pick up a tiny splinter as you grab a piece of wood. Within our tissues lie cells known as mast cells. These cells contain the signal **histamine** that calls in the cavalry and initiates the inflammation response. Entrance of the splinter damages these mast cells, causing them to release histamine, which migrates through the tissue toward the bloodstream. Histamine causes increased permeability and blood flow to the injured tissue. The splinter also causes the release of signals that call in our nonspecific phagocytic cell friends, which come to the site of the injury to clear away any debris or pathogens within the tissue. The redness and warmth associated with inflammation occur because of the increase in blood flow to the area that occurs in this process.

The immune system also contains defense mechanisms, which are quite specific. One such defense mechanism involves a type of white blood cell called **lymphocytes.** There are two main flavors of lymphocytes: B cells and T cells. These cells are made in the bone marrow of the body and come from cells called **stem cells.** B cells mature in the bone marrow, and T cells mature in the thymus. B cells can differentiate into plasma cells and memory B cells, and the two main types of T cells are helper T cells and cytotoxic T cells. Cytotoxic T cells are the main players involved in cell-mediated immunity. **Helper T cells,** which assist in the activation of B cells, recognize foreign antigens on the surface of phagocytic cells and bind to these cells. After binding, they multiply to produce a bunch of T cells that pump out chemical signals, which bring in the B cells to respond.

BIG IDEA 3.D.2
Helper T cells communicate with other cells through direct contact.

We have arrived at the vaccination site in the left arm, and things are definitely heating up here. An **antigen** is a molecule that is foreign to our bodies and causes the immune system to respond. What is occurring right now is the process called the **primary immune response.** Every B cell has a specific (randomly generated) antigen recognition site on its surface. B cells patrol the body looking for a particular invader. When a B cell meets and attaches to the appropriate antigen, it becomes activated, and the B cell undergoes mitosis and differentiation into the two types of cells mentioned earlier: **plasma cells** and **memory cells.** The plasma cells are the factories that produce antibodies that function in the elimination of any cell containing on its surface the antigen that it has been summoned to kill. These antibodies, when released, bind to the antigens, immobilizing them and marking them for the macrophages to engulf and eliminate. This type of immune response falls under the category of **humoral immunity**—immunity involving antibodies.

> **BIG IDEA 4.C.1**
> *Molecular variations in F_{ab} enable cells to recognize a wider range of antigens.*

Someone had a question? How do antibodies recognize the antigen they are designed for? Excellent question. Antibodies are protein molecules with two functional regions. One end is called the *fragment antigen binding region* or F_{ab}—this is what allows an antibody to recognize a specific antigen. It is designed by the plasma cell to have an F_{ab} that binds to the antigen of interest. The other end, which binds to effector cells, is called the F_c region. There are five types of F_c regions, one for each of the five types of antibodies: IgA, IgD, IgE, IgM, and IgG. Each antibody type serves a slightly different function and is present in different areas of the body. When the antibodies bind to an antigen, complement gets involved, and this combination of antibodies and complement leads to the elimination of the invader.

We see a hand raised in the back. Yes, you are correct that we neglected to mention the memory cells. Very good. Memory cells contain the basis for the body's **secondary immune response** to invaders. Memory cells are stored instructions on how to handle a particular invader. When an invader returns to our body, the memory cells recognize it, produce antibodies in rapid succession, and eliminate the invader very quickly. The secondary immune response is much more efficient than the primary response. This is why few people are infected by sicknesses such as chicken pox after they have had them once already—their memory cells protect them. One important fact that does come up on the exam is that the secondary immune response produces a *much* larger concentration of antibodies than does the primary response.

Well, this is too good to be true . . . we just got word that this body was just recently infected by a virus. This will allow us to look at the other side of the immune response: **cell-mediated immunity.** This type of immunity involves *direct* cellular response to invasion as opposed to antibody-based defense. The virus that infected this poor sap made it past the humoral immunity system because it entered into the host's cells. This brings the cytotoxic T cells into play. The cells infected by the virus are forced to produce viral antigens, some of which show up on the surface of the cell. The cytotoxic T cells recognize these cells and wipe them out.

You might wonder how these T cells avoid killing *all* cells. All the cells of the body, except for red blood cells, have on their surface antigens called **class I histocompatibility antigens** (major histocompatibility complex [MHC]). The MHC I antigens for each person are slightly different, and the immune system accepts as friendly any cell that has the identical match for this antigen. Anything with a different MHC is foreign. This is the reason that organ donation often fails—the donor and the recipient have incompatible MHCs. There are also **class II histocompatibility antigens,** which are found on the surface of the immune cells of the body. These antigens play a role in the interaction between the cells of the immune system.

Well, we'd like to thank you for joining us on our tour of the body. We've seen a lot of things today and—whoa! We've been hit by something—and hit hard! Oh, dear. . . . Folks, we don't want you to be alarmed, but it appears that our rival tour company has played a bit of a practical joke on us. Apparently as we were observing the B cell's interaction with the vaccine, they attached a series of antigens and complement proteins to the surface of our bus. That loud noise you just heard was the sound of a macrophage taking us in . . . oh, dear, this is bad. Oh, no . . . folks, brace yourselves! The macrophage is about to ——— (transmission ended).

› Review Questions

1. In what form is most of the carbon dioxide of the body transported in the bloodstream?

   A. Complexed with hemoglobin
   B. As CO_2
   C. As HCO_3^-
   D. As CO

For questions 2–5, use the following answer choices:

   A. LH
   B. Estrogen
   C. Aldosterone
   D. TSH

2. This hormone is involved in the regulation of the body's metabolic rate.

3. This gonadotropin induces ovulation in females.

4. This hormone is involved in the regulation of the body's sodium concentration.

5. This hormone is vital to the maintenance of the endometrium during pregnancy.

6. The major emulsifier of fats in the digestive system is

   A. lipase.
   B. amylase.
   C. trypsin.
   D. bile salts.

7. Which cell type keeps humans from being infected by the same organism twice?

   A. Plasma cell
   B. Memory cell
   C. Macrophage
   D. Neutrophil

8. Which of the following muscle sites does not contain smooth muscle?

   A. Aorta
   B. Bladder
   C. Esophagus
   D. Quadriceps

9. Which of the following is the functional unit of the respiratory system?

   A. Bronchus
   B. Bronchioles
   C. Alveolus
   D. Larynx

10. Which of the following regions of the brain controls breathing?

    A. Cerebellum
    B. Medulla
    C. Cerebrum
    D. Hypothalamus

11. Which of the following is the major digestive enzyme of the stomach?

    A. Trypsin
    B. Chymotrypsin
    C. Pepsin
    D. Amylase

12. Which of the following is *not* an example of nonspecific immunity?

    A. Lysosyme of saliva
    B. Skin
    C. Mucous lining of the lungs and trachea
    D. Plasma cells

13. Which of the following is true about the filtrate of the glomerulus?

    A. It contains little or no glucose.
    B. It contains little or no protein.
    C. It contains little or no sodium.
    D. It contains little or no urea.

14. Which of the following is not a hormone secreted by the anterior pituitary?

    A. TSH
    B. FSH
    C. ADH
    D. LH

15. Which of the following scenarios would be *least* likely to initiate a response from the sympathetic nervous system of the body?

    A. Getting called on in class by the teacher when you do not know the answer
    B. Seeing a cop while you are driving too fast on the highway
    C. Walking through the woods and seeing a bear in the near distance
    D. Waking from a midafternoon nap as sunlight strikes your face

› Answers and Explanations

1. **C**—Most of the carbon dioxide traveling through the bloodstream of the body is in the form of the bicarbonate ion—HCO_3^-. Oxygen is the one that likes to complex with hemoglobin. You should try to avoid answer choice D when possible; carbon monoxide is poisonous.

2. **D**—The thyroid gland is important to the maintenance of the body's metabolic rate. An increase in TSH leads to an increase in thyroxin (thyroid hormone), which leads to an increase in the metabolic rate of the body.

3. **A**—The LH surge brought about by the combined effect of FSH and LH during the menstrual cycle leads to ovulation in females. This is essentially the release of an egg from its holding pattern in the ovary that allows it to move toward the uterus.

4. **C**—Aldosterone is released by the adrenal gland in an effort to maintain appropriate levels of sodium in the body. Its main site of action is the kidney.

5. **B**—Estrogen and progesterone work together to maintain the endometrium, which is the site of attachment for the growing fetus during pregnancy. Without these two hormones, the endometrium sloughs off and is lost.

6. **D**—Lipase is the major fat-*digesting* enzyme of our body. Bile salts help digest the fat by *emulsifying* it into small droplets contained in water. Amylase digests carbohydrates. Trypsin and chymotrypsin break down polypeptides.

7. **B**—Memory cells are produced after the body first reacts to a foreign invader. The next time the body is exposed to that invader, it can respond much more quickly and efficiently. Plasma cells produce the antibodies designed to wipe out the antigens. Macrophages and neutrophils are both types of phagocytes, which generally roam around looking for nonspecific garbage to pick up and destroy.

8. **D**—The quadriceps is the only muscle type on this list that is not a smooth muscle. It is a skeletal muscle involved in voluntary movements.

9. **C**—The alveolus is the functional unit of the lung. It is the true site of gas exchange during the respiratory process. The trachea, larynx, bronchus, and bronchioles are all tubes that the air passes through on its way to this exchange center.

10. **B**—The medulla oblongata controls the involuntary actions of the body, including respiration. The cerebellum controls balance, and the cerebrum is in charge of higher thinking. The hypothalamus monitors the concentration of many substances throughout the body, and determines when certain hormones of the pituitary should be released or cut down on.

11. C

12. D—Plasma cells are designed to produce antibodies that combat a particular antigen. They are a great example of *specific* immunity. All the other answer choices are examples of nonspecific immunity.

13. B—The filtrate in the glomerulus contains almost everything that is in the blood plasma except for large proteins, which are unable to fit through the pores. Glucose does pass into the filtrate but is usually reabsorbed if present in normal concentrations in the blood. Sodium and potassium are always present in the filtrate. Urea is one of the major waste products that the excretory system is attempting to eliminate, so it is definitely present in the filtrate.

14. C—ADH is secreted by the posterior pituitary.

15. D—A sympathetic response is one that comes in a time of fight or flight. It is designed to get you ready for action. All the other choices are things that rev you up, whereas waking from a nap as sunlight strikes your face is a rather passive and tranquil experience that doesn't usually make you want to flee the scene or fight a great battle.

› Rapid Review

The following terms are important in this chapter:

Circulatory system: blood flow—left side of heart → aorta → via arteries to organs, muscles → into the venous system of the body (vena cava) → right side of heart → lungs (pick up O_2 and release CO_2) → left side of heart.

Respiratory pathway: nose/mouth → pharynx → larynx → trachea → bronchi → bronchioles → alveoli (functional unit of the lungs; this is where gas exchange occurs).

Digestive system: digestion begins in mouth, continues in the stomach, and completes in the intestines.

- *Amylase*: enzyme that breaks down starches in the diet (mouth and small intestine).

- *Pepsin*: main digestive enzyme of the stomach that breaks down proteins.

- *Lipase*: major fat digesting enzyme of the body (small intestine).

- *Trypsin* and *chymotrypsin*: major protein digesting endopeptidases of the small intestine.

- *Bile*: contains phospholipids, cholesterol, and **bile salts** (major emulsifier of fat).

- *Maltase, lactase,* and *sucrase*: carbohydrate digesting enzymes of the small intestines.

- Most of the digestion and absorption of food occurs in the small intestine.

- Function of the large intestine is to reabsorb water and to pack the indigestible food into feces.

Excretory system: kidneys lie on the posterior wall of the abdomen. Kidney is divided into the cortex and the **medulla.** The functional unit of the kidney is the **nephron.** The medulla is divided into renal pyramids, which dump the urine produced into the minor and major calyces → renal pelvis → bladder via the ureter → out of the body via the urethra.

- Most of what is filtered out of the glomerulus is reabsorbed—nearly all the sugar, vitamins, water, and nutrients. If sugar appears in urine, it is because there is too much in the blood (diabetes).

- Two important hormones of the excretory system are **ADH** (controls water absorption) and **aldosterone** (controls sodium reabsorption).

Muscular System

MUSCLE TYPE	STRIATED?	NUCLEI?	CONTROL?	WHERE IS IT FOUND?
Skeletal	Yes	Multiple	Voluntary	Biceps, triceps, etc.
Smooth	No	Single	Involuntary	Digestive tract, bladder, arteries
Cardiac	Yes	Single	Involuntary	Heart

Endocrine System

Anterior pituitary hormones

- *FSH*: stimulates production of eggs or sperm.
- *LH*: stimulates ovulation, increases estrogen/progesterone release.
- *TSH*: increases release of thyroid hormone.
- *STH*: increases growth.
- *ACTH*: increases secretion of adrenal cortical hormones.
- *Prolactin*: controls lactogenesis, decreases secretion of GnRH.

Pancreatic hormones

- *Insulin*: increases glycogen formation.
- *Glucagon*: increases glycogen breakdown.

Parathyroid hormone (PTH) increases blood Ca^{2+} involved in bone maintenance.

Posterior pituitary hormones

- *ADH*: stimulates H_2O reabsorption in kidneys.
- *Oxytocin*: stimulates uterine contraction and milk ejection.

Adrenal gland hormones

- *Aldosterone*: regulates blood sodium concentration.
- *Cortisol*: chronic stress hormone.

Sex hormones

- *Progesterone*: involved in menstrual cycle and pregnancy.
- *Estrogen*: made in ovaries; increases release of LH (LH surge); develops female secondary sex characteristics.
- *Testosterone*: (testes): stimulates sperm production; develops male secondary sex characteristics.

Negative feedback: hormone acts to directly, or indirectly, inhibit further release of the hormone of interest.

Positive feedback: hormone acts to directly, or indirectly, cause increased secretion of the hormone.

Nervous system: divided into two parts: **central nervous system** (CNS) and **peripheral nervous system** (PNS).

- *SNS*: controls skeletal muscles and voluntary actions.

- *ANS*: controls involuntary activities of body.

- *ANS*: *sympathetic* (prepare for fight): increased heart rate, increased blood pressure, digestive slowdown, dilate bronchial muscles; *parasympathetic* (conserve energy): decreased heart rate, decreased blood pressure, bladder constriction.

- Brain: **cerebellum** (coordination/balance); **medulla** (involuntary actions such as breathing); **hypothalamus** (regulates hunger, thirst, temperature); **amygdala** (emotion control center).

Immune system:

- *Nonspecific immunity*: nonspecific prevention of entrance of invaders into the body (skin, mucus).

- *Specific immunity*: multilayered defense mechanism: (1) first line of defense—phagocytes, macrophage, neutrophils, complement; (2) second line of defense: B cells (plasma/memory), T cells (helper/cytotoxic).

- *Primary immune response*: antigen invader → B cell meets antigen → B cell differentiates into plasma cells and memory cells → plasma cells produce antibodies → antibodies eliminate antigen (**humoral immunity**).

- *Secondary immune response*: antigen invader → memory cells recognize antigen and pump out antibodies much quicker than primary response → antibodies eliminate antigen.

- *Cell-mediated immunity*: involves T cells and direct cellular response to invasion. Defense against **viruses.**

Human Reproduction

IN THIS CHAPTER

Summary: This chapter discusses differences between the sexes, reproductive anatomy in humans, and how a sperm meets up with an egg to produce an embryo. The chapter concludes with a discussion of reproductive hormones.

Key Ideas

○ Primary sex characteristics are the internal structures that assist in the process of procreation.

○ Secondary sex characteristics are the noticeable physical characteristics that differ between males and females.

○ Understand the concepts and the basics of embryology, but learn the specific details only if you have time.

○ Take the time to learn which germ layer produces which structures (endoderm, mesoderm, and ectoderm).

○ Four extraembryonic structures necessary to the healthy development of an embryo: yolk sac, chorion, allantois, and amnion.

○ Factors in cellular differentiation: cytoplasmic distribution, induction, and homeotic genes.

Introduction

Finally, the racy chapter you have all been waiting for: human reproduction! The topic was introduced in Chapter 9 in our discussion of cell division—meiosis and mitosis. This chapter begins by examining the differences between the sexes. A discussion of reproductive anatomy and the wild ride that a sperm must take to fertilize the female egg will follow. Then we will review the formation of gametes and the development of the embryo. Embryology is excessively detailed and not something you should get hung up on. You will want to know some details about development, but like glycolysis, the big picture is key. The AP Biology exam is not an embryology exam. Finally, the chapter concludes with a discussion of hormones and their effects on the reproductive system.

Sex Differences

What are the biologic differences between a man and a woman? For the purposes of *this* exam, you should keep in mind that one of the first distinctions is that boys have a Y chromosome in the nuclei of their cells, and girls do not. Another major difference lies in the sex characteristics. **Primary sex characteristics** are the structures that assist in the vital process of procreation. Among these are the testes, ovaries, and uterus. **Secondary sex characteristics** are the noticeable physical characteristics that differ between males and females such as facial hair, deepness of voice, breasts, and muscle distribution. These characteristics come into play as indicators of reproductive maturity to those of the opposite sex.

Anatomy

Since males tend to be a bit impatient, we will cover male anatomy first. The male sexual anatomy is designed for the delivery of sperm to the female reproductive system. Let's follow the journey of a sperm from the beginning to the end.

Sperm's "Wild Ride"

Here we stand in the **testis.** The male has two testes, located in a sac called the scrotum. This is the sperm factory—a portion of the testis called the **seminiferous tubules** is where the sperm are actually made. We return later to look at how these sperm are created. Notice in the other corner of the testis the structures called the **interstitial cells.** These are the structures that produce the hormones involved in the male reproductive system. Remember that the testis is the site of sperm and hormone production in the male reproductive system.

We are going to move along the production line to the **epididymis**—the coiled structure that extends from the testes. The epididymis is where the sperm completes its maturation and waits until it is called on to do its duty. From here, when called into action, the sperm moves through a tunnel called the **vas deferens.** Each epididymis connects to the **urethra** via this tunnel. The urethra is the passageway through which the sperm exits during ejaculation. Yes . . . that is indeed the same tunnel that the urine uses to get out . . . good observation in back.

We're not done yet—let's look at some other important players in this process (see also Figure 16.1). we are sure you have all heard about the **prostate gland** and how prostate cancer is currently one of the major cancers among men. But do you know what the prostate gland does? Here we are standing by this fine structure whose function in the male reproductive system is to add a basic (pH > 7) liquid to the mix to help neutralize any urine that may remain in the common urethral passage. It also helps to combat the acidity of the vaginal region of the female toward which the sperm is heading.

Follow us, everyone, more to see, more to see. . . . Here, on either side of us, are the structures called the **seminal vesicles.** These characters play an important role in the success of the sperm on its way to the female ovum. When the male ejaculates, the seminal vesicles dump fluids into the vas deferens to send along with the sperm. Think of the seminal vesicle as a convenience store. It provides three important goods to the sperm: energy by adding fructose; power to progress through the female reproductive system by adding *prostaglandins* (which stimulates uterine contraction); and mucus, which helps the sperm swim more effectively.

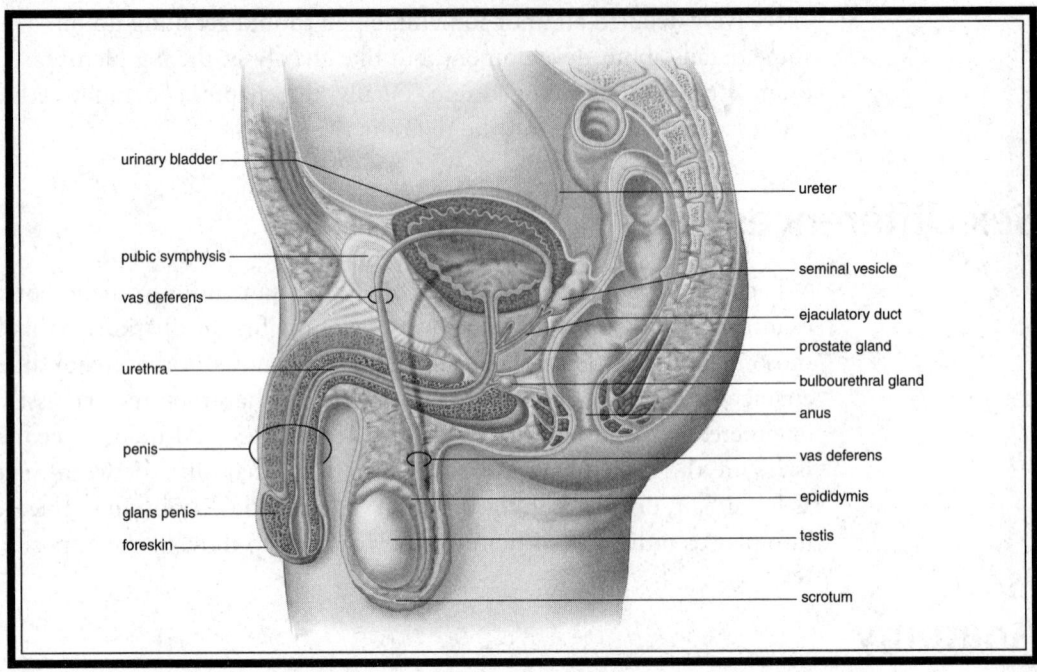

Figure 16.1 The human male reproductive system. (*From* Biology, *8th ed., by
Sylvia S. Mader, © 1985, 1987, 1990, 1993, 1996, 1998, 2001, 2004
by the McGraw Hill Companies, Inc. Reproduced with permission of
The McGraw-Hill Companies.*)

The sperm is ready to enter the female reproductive system at this point, but before we observe
the sperm as it does so, we want to take a quick tour of the female reproductive structures.

We begin in the **ovary,** the site of egg production. Females have two ovaries—one on
either side of the body. The egg leaves the ovary before it has fully matured and enters a
structure called the **oviduct.** The oviduct is also known as the **fallopian tube**—you may
be more familiar with that term. Eggs travel through here from the ovary to the **uterus.**
When fertilized by an incoming sperm in the fallopian tube, after several days' transit from
the tube to the uterus, the egg usually attaches itself to the inner wall of the uterus, which
is known as the **endometrium.** The uterus connects to the vaginal opening via a narrowed
portion called the **cervix.** As we pass through the cervical area, we now find ourselves in
the vagina, and it is here that the sperm enters the female reproductive system.

As the sperm enters, it must survive the different environment that the female body
presents (Figure 16.2). Its task is to find its way to the fallopian tube, where it must meet
the egg and penetrate its outer surface to achieve successful fertilization. The sperm works
its way through the vaginal region, up through the cervix, through the uterus, and into the
fallopian tube. Here, if the timing is appropriate, there will be a willing and waiting egg
that is hoping to meet with a sperm to produce a new diploid zygote. After successful fertilization, the new happy couple moves down to the uterus and builds a nice house in the
endometrium where it will develop into an embryo and remain until it is ready to be born.

The Formation of Gametes

In Chapter 9, we discussed cell division and mentioned the process by which gametes
are formed. Remember that the mechanics of gamete formation are different in women
and men.

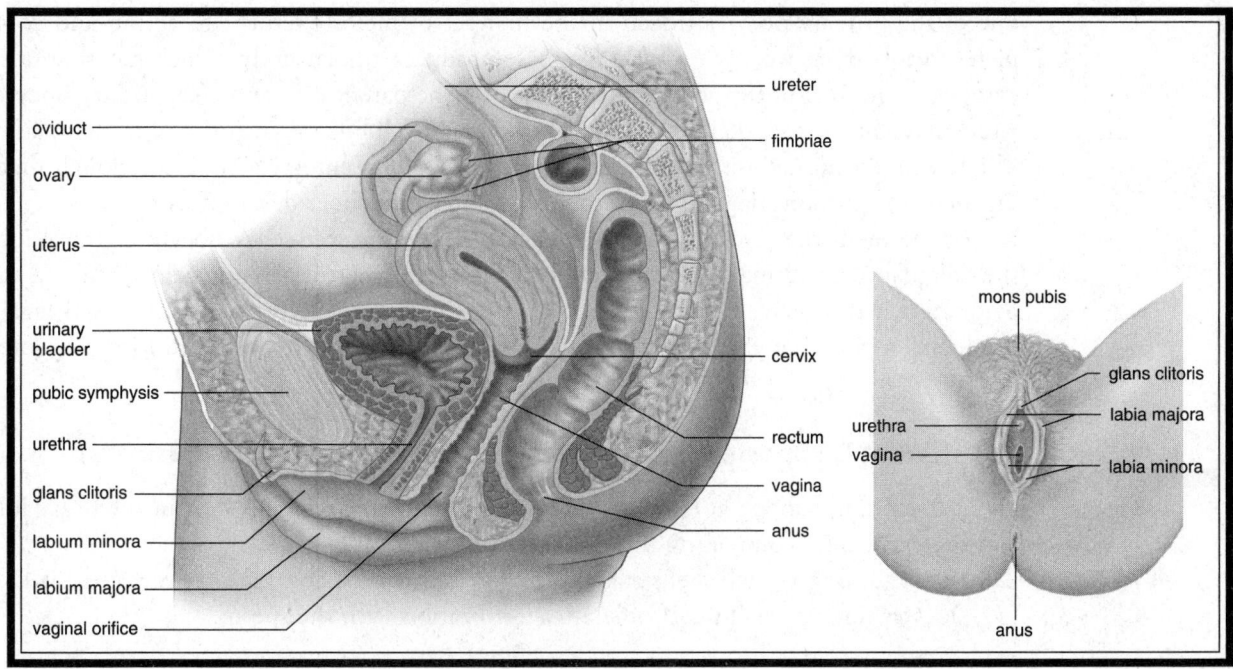

Figure 16.2   The human female reproductive system. (*From* Biology, *8th ed., by Sylvia S. Mader,*
© 1985, 1987, 1990, 1993, 1996, 1998, 2001, 2004 by the McGraw Hill Companies, Inc.
Reproduced with permission of The McGraw-Hill Companies.)

Oogenesis

In women, the process of gamete formation is called **oogenesis** (Figure 16.3), which begins
quite early—as the embryo develops. Mitotic division turns fetal cells into cells known as
primary oocytes, which begin the process of meiosis and progress until prophase I; then
the wait begins. The primary oocyte sits halted in prophase I until the host female enters
puberty a number of years later. This is where the menstrual cycle begins. Each month,

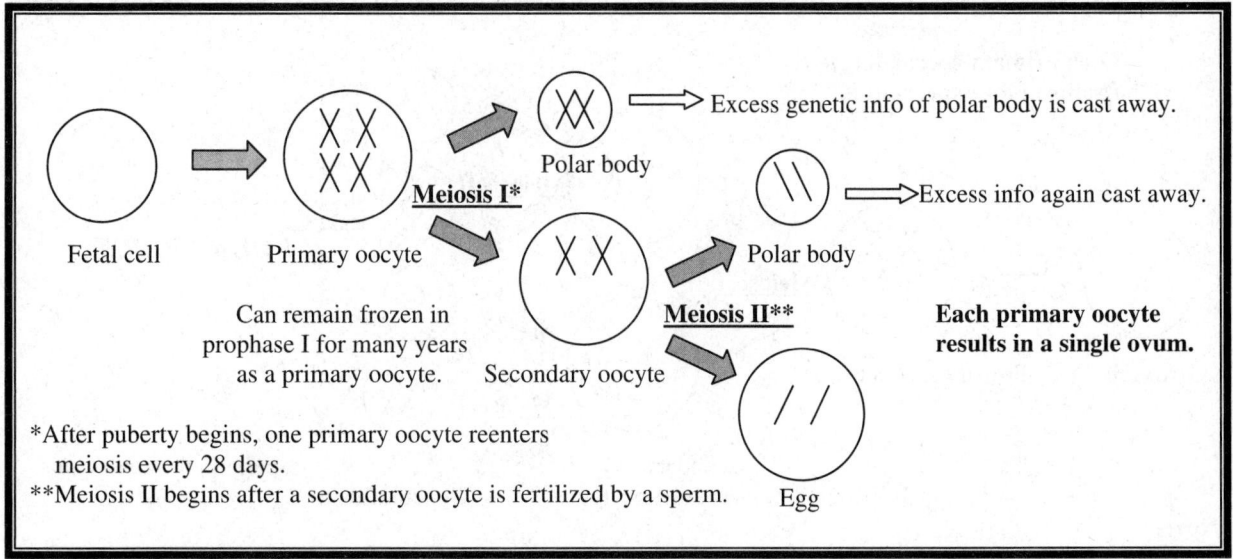

Figure 16.3   Oogenesis.

one of the primary oocytes frozen in the first act of meiosis returns to action and completes meiosis I. As we saw earlier, this phase produces a polar body, which has almost no cytoplasm and half of the genetic information of the parent cell, and a **secondary oocyte,** which has half the genetic information of the parent cell but the majority of its cytoplasm. This asymmetrical meiosis occurs because the developing embryo will need enough food, organelles, mitochondria, and other such structures for proper development.

As the menstrual cycle continues, ovulation frees the secondary oocyte to travel into the fallopian tube to make its way down to the uterus. Fertilization usually occurs in the oviduct. If a successful fertilization occurs, the secondary oocyte enters meiosis II, again producing a polar body, as well as an egg that combines with the sperm to form a zygote.

What Is Important to Remember About This Oogenesis Business?

1. It doesn't all happen at once for the ova. A primary oocyte could sit in the ovary for 40 years before completing the first stage of meiosis.
2. The beginning of each menstrual cycle causes a primary oocyte to resume meiosis I.
3. Oocytes undergo meiosis II only after fertilization with the sperm.

Spermatogenesis

For men, the process is less time-intensive. Let's face it, guys . . . we are lazy. Less effort is better. Less time makes sense and leaves us more time and energy to watch sports and play video games. Males produce gametes through a process called **spermatogenesis** (Figure 16.4). Unlike females, males do not begin forming gametes until puberty. Spermatogenesis occurs in our old friends, the seminiferous tubules. Here, **primary spermatocytes** are produced by mitotic division. These primary spermatocytes undergo meiosis I to produce two **secondary spermatocytes,** which undergo meiosis II to produce four **spermatids,** which are immature sperm. After production, they enter the epididymis, where their waiting game begins and the maturation completes.

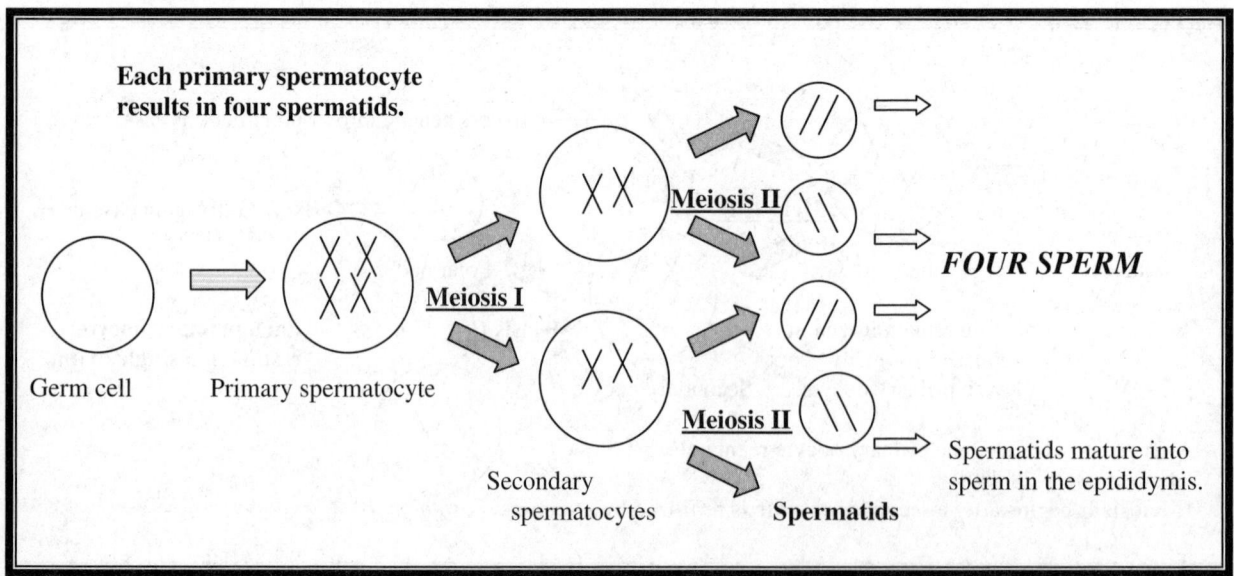

Figure 16.4   Spermatogenesis.

Embryonic Development

Embryology, the study of embryonic development, is a detailed and complex field. Fortunately, you are not taking an AP exam in embryology. Stick to the basics here and do not let the complex details bog you down. Follow along with the pretty pictures, and the review questions at the end of this chapter will give you a good indication of the level of detail required for success on the embryology questions of the AP Biology exam.

Cleavage

Embryonic development begins as soon as the egg is fertilized to produce a diploid zygote ($2n$). This zygote then divides mitotically many times without increasing the zygote's overall size. During these **"cleavage" divisions** (Figure 16.5), cytoplasm is distributed unevenly to the daughter cells but genetic information is distributed equally. This disparity exists because different cells will later produce different final products and the uneven distribution of cytoplasm plays a role in that process.

These cleavage divisions take a while in humans. The first three divisions take three days to complete. After the fourth division, the one cell has become 16 cells and is now called a **morula.** As it undergoes its next round of cell divisions, fluid fills the center of the morula

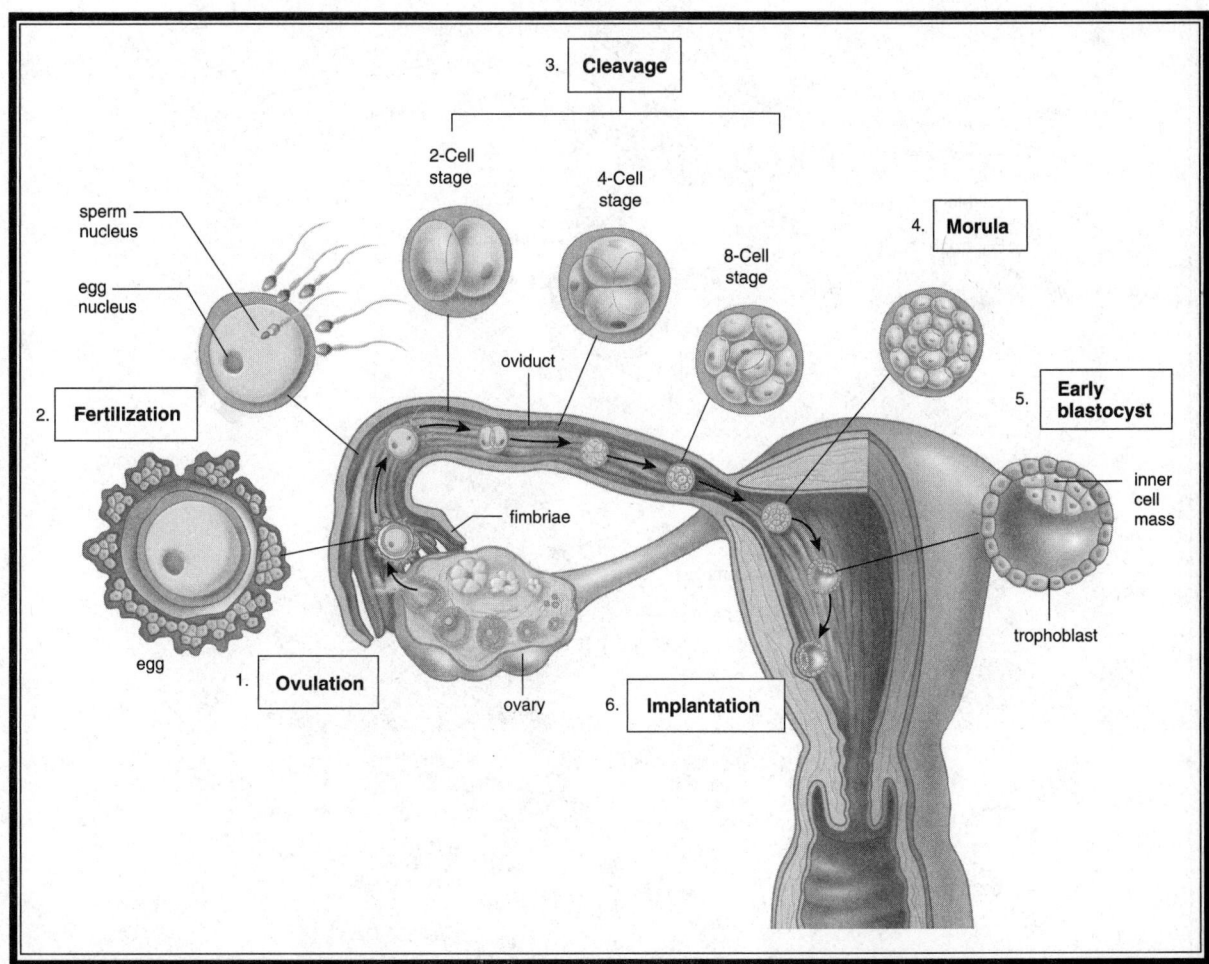

Figure 16.5   Embryonic cleavage divisions. (*From* Biology, *8th ed., by Sylvia S. Mader,* © *1985, 1987, 1990, 1993, 1996, 1998, 2001, 2004 by the McGraw Hill Companies, Inc. Reproduced with permission of The McGraw-Hill Companies.*)

to create the hollow-looking structure known to embryologists as the **blastula.** The fluid-filled cavity in the blastula is known as the blastocoel. Up to this point, much of the dividing has occurred as the zygote moves toward the uterus through the fallopian tube. By the time the blastula has formed, it has reached the uterus and has implanted on the wall. The blastula contains two parts: an **inner cell mass,** which later becomes the embryo, and a **trophoblast,** which becomes the placenta for the developing fetus and aids in attachment to the endometrium. The trophoblast also produces *human chorionic gonadotropin* (hCG), which maintains the endometrium by ensuring the continued production of progesterone and estrogen. The trophoblast later gives rise to the chorion, which we will discuss later.

Gastrulation

Okay, here's where the discussion of embryology gets a little bit tricky. The next major stage of embryonic development after cleavage is **gastrulation** (also called *morphogenesis*). During gastrulation, cells separate into three primary layers called *germ layers,* which eventually give rise to the different tissues of an adult.

Let's look at this process in a bit more detail. (See also Figure 16.6.) After the blastocyst attaches to the uterine wall, the inner cell mass divides into two major cell masses:

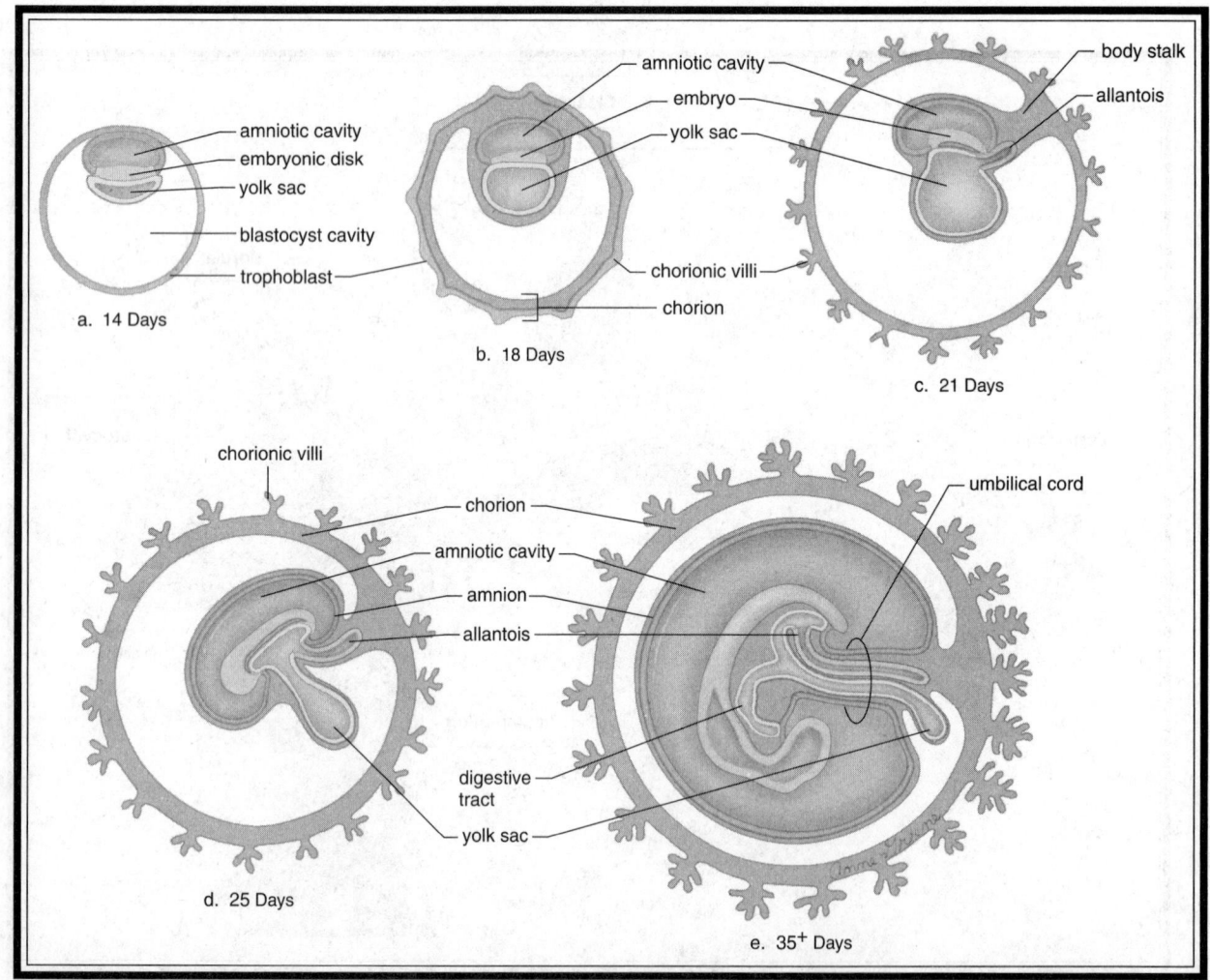

Figure 16.6   Components in the gastrulation process. (*From* Biology, *8th ed., by Sylvia S. Mader,* © 1985, 1987, 1990, 1993, 1996, 1998, 2001, 2004 by the McGraw Hill Companies, Inc. *Reproduced with permission of The McGraw-Hill Companies.*)

the **epiblast** and the **hypoblast.** The hypoblast gives rise to the yolk sac, which produces the embryo's first blood cells. In birds and reptiles, the yolk sac provides nutrients to the embryo. In humans, the **placenta** fills this role.

The epiblast develops into the three germ layers of the embryo: the **endoderm,** the **mesoderm,** and the **ectoderm.**

Endoderm: inner germ layer; gives rise to the inner lining of the gut and the digestive system, liver, thyroid, lungs, and bladder.

Mesoderm: intermediate germ layer; gives rise to muscle, the circulatory system, reproductive system, excretory organs, bones, and connective tissues of the gut and exterior of the body.

Ectoderm: outer germ layer; gives rise to nervous system and skin, hair, and nails.

The separation of cells into the three primary germ layers sets the stage for cellular differentiation by which different cells develop into different structures with different functions. As far as this specific structural and functional differentiation is concerned, keep your focus on the basic development of the nervous system.

The human nervous system derives primarily from the ectoderm, but the mesoderm contributes a structure known as the **notochord,** which serves to support the body. In vertebrates, this is present only in the embryo. The cells of the ectoderm that lie above the notochord form the **neural plate,** which becomes the **neural groove,** which eventually becomes the **neural tube.** This neural tube later gives rise to the central nervous system. One other term you should be familiar with in the development of the mammalian embryo is the **somite,** which gives rise to the muscles and vertebrae in mammals.

There are four extraembryonic structures necessary for the healthy development of the embryo:

1. *Yolk sac:* derived from the hypoblast; site of early blood cell creation in humans. Source of nutrients for bird and reptile embryos.
2. *Chorion:* formed from the trophoblast; the outer membrane of the embryo. Site of implantation onto the endometrium. Contributes to formation of the **placenta** in mammals.
3. *Allantois:* mammalian waste transporter. Later it becomes the **umbilical cord,** which carries oxygen, food, and wastes (including CO_2) back and forth from placenta to embryo.
4. *Amnion:* formed from epiblast. Surrounds fluid-filled cushion that protects the developing embryo. Present in birds, lizards, and humans, to name only a few.

How Do Cells Know What to Do?

How do the various cells of the developing embryo differentiate into cells with different functions if they come from the same parent cell? As mentioned earlier, not every cell receives the same amount of cytoplasm during the cleavage divisions. It is thought that this asymmetric distribution of cytoplasm plays a role in the differentiation of the daughter cells. Cells containing different organelles or other cytoplasmic components are able to perform different functions. Two other factors, induction and homeotic genes, contribute to cellular differentiation.

Induction is the influence of one group of cells on the development of another through physical contact or chemical signaling. Just in case you are asked to write an essay on induction, it is good to know a bit about the experiments of the German embryologist Hans Spemann. His experiments revealed that the notochord induces cells of the dorsal ectoderm to develop into the neural plate. When cells from the notochord of an embryo

---

Lindsay (12th grade): "Take the time to learn these. Know which layer produces what. It's worth a point on the exam."

BIG IDEA 2.E.1

The timing and coordination of specific events are necessary for normal development.

are transplanted to a different place near the ectoderm, the neural plate will develop in the new location. The cells from the notochord region act as "project directors," telling the ectoderm where to produce the neural tube and central nervous system.

Homeotic genes regulate or "direct" the body plan of organisms. For example, a fly's homeotic genes help determine how its segments will develop and which appendages should grow from each segment. Scientists interfering with the development of these poor creatures have found that mutations in these genes can lead to the production of too many wings, legs in the wrong place, and other unfortunate abnormalities. The DNA sequence of a homeotic gene that tells the cell where to put things is called the **homeobox.** It is similar from organism to organism and has been found to exist in a variety of organisms—birds, humans, fish, and frogs.

BIG IDEA 3.B.2

Signal transmission by homeotic genes mediates cell function.

KEY IDEA

Factors in Cellular Differentiation

Cytoplasmic distribution	Asymmetry contributes to differentiation, since different areas have different amounts of cytoplasm, and thus perhaps different organelles and cytoplasmic structures.
Induction	One group of cells influences another group of cells through physical contact or chemical signaling.
Homeotic genes	Regulatory genes that determine how segments of an organism will develop.

The Influence of Hormones

In Chapter 15 we discussed the hormones that will be included in the AP exam. A few of those play a critical role in human sexual development and reproduction. The hormones involved include LH, FSH, estrogen, progesterone, and testosterone. You do not need to know every detail, just the big picture. As proper etiquette requires, ladies first. Let's talk about the hormones involved in the female reproductive system.

Estrogen and progesterone continually circulate in the female bloodstream, and the hypothalamus monitors these levels to determine when to release certain hormones. For example, when the concentrations of estrogen and progesterone are low, the hypothalamus secretes GnRH, which travels to the anterior pituitary gland to induce the release of FSH and LH. (Just to remind you, FSH is follicle-stimulating hormone, LH is luteinizing hormone, and GnRH is gonadotropin-releasing hormone.) FSH induces the development of the follicle that contains the primary oocyte during its development. It also causes the follicular cells to release estrogen, which triggers the hypothalamus to dump more GnRH into the system. This GnRH acts on the anterior pituitary to produce the **LH surge** that initiates **ovulation**—the release of a secondary oocyte from the ovary.

BIG IDEA 2.C.1

Organisms use feedback mechanisms.

This LH surge causes further release of estrogen and progesterone from the follicular cells, which have now become a structure called the corpus luteum. The corpus luteum induces the thickening of the endometrium, the site of future fertilized egg attachment. At this point in the cycle, the levels of estrogen and progesterone elevate enough to make the hypothalamus cut off production of GnRH so that the LH and FSH levels drop back down. (This decrease in production of LH and FSH, due to high levels of estrogen and progesterone, is called **negative feedback.**) Here lies a fork in the road for the female reproductive system. If fertilization has occurred in the fallopian tube, and if the blastocyst attaches successfully to the uterine wall, hCG will be secreted, which works to keep the corpus luteum alive. As a result, the levels of estrogen and progesterone remain high and keep the endometrium intact.

If a blastocyst does not implant, production of estrogen or progesterone from the corpus luteum will cease, causing the destruction of the endometrium.

This cycle of hormonal activity is known as the *menstrual cycle.* A woman repeats this cycle, on an average, every 28 days. This cycle is disrupted when a sperm fertilizes the egg and successful implantation occurs. During pregnancy, hormone levels in the body change as a result of the presence of the corpus luteum, which maintains constant levels of estrogen and progesterone. This halts ovulation for the remainder of the pregnancy. If a sperm does not fertilize the egg, however, negative feedback reduces the levels of LH and FSH and leads to the deterioration of the endometrium, which then sloughs off during the menstrual cycle. When the levels of hormones circulating in the blood drop low enough, the cycle will begin again with the release of LH and FSH, culminating in the next menstrual cycle.

In males, as in females, GnRH causes the pituitary to release LH and FSH. The LH causes the continual production of testosterone in men. FSH and testosterone work together to assist the maturation of sperm produced during spermatogenesis. The baseline levels of testosterone are vital to the development of secondary sex characteristics in men.

❯ Review Questions

For questions 1–4, please use the following answer selections:

    A. Morula
    B. Somite
    C. Trophoblast
    D. Hypoblast

1. After the fourth cleavage division, the one cell has become 16 cells and is now given this name.

2. Gives rise to the yolk sac of the developing embryo.

3. Forms the placenta for the developing fetus.

4. Gives rise to the muscles and vertebrae in mammals.

5. Which of the following is not a structure involved in the ejaculation of sperm?

    A. Epididymis
    B. Seminal vesicles
    C. Cervix
    D. Vas deferens

6. Which of the following hormones feeds back to cause the LH surge of the menstrual cycle?

    A. Estrogen
    B. Progesterone
    C. FSH
    D. LH

7. Which of the following structures is *not* derived from the endoderm of a developing embryo?

    A. Liver
    B. Thyroid
    C. Heart
    D. Bladder

For questions 8–11, please use the following answer selections:

    A. FSH
    B. LH
    C. Testosterone
    D. hCG

8. This hormone ultimately triggers ovulation in females.

9. This hormone is produced in the interstitial cells.

10. This hormone is responsible for maintenance of the corpus luteum during early pregnancy.

11. This hormone works with testosterone to assist in maturation of the sperm produced during spermatogenesis.

12. Which structure is usually the site of fertilization in humans?

- A. Cervix
- B. Uterus
- C. Oviduct
- D. Ovary

13. Which of the following explains the mechanism by which the neural plate develops in human embryos?

- A. Induced fit
- B. Homeotic gene determination
- C. Induction
- D. Negative feedback

› Answers and Explanations

1. A

2. D

3. C

4. B

5. C—The cervix is the only structure listed here that is a part of the female reproductive anatomy. The epididymis is the site of sperm storage and maturation while it awaits ejaculation. The seminal vesicles are the convenience store, providing the sperm with the necessary materials to survive its journey from ejaculation to fertilization. The vas deferens is the tunnel connecting the epididymis to the urethra.

6. A—At the beginning of each menstrual cycle, GnRH is released from the hypothalamus and travels to the anterior pituitary gland to induce the release of FSH and LH. FSH induces the development of the follicle and causes the follicle to release estrogen, which triggers the hypothalamus to dump more GnRH into the system. This GnRH acts on the anterior pituitary to produce the LH surge, which triggers ovulation. The estrogen feeds back to the hypothalamus to induce the release of large amounts of LH that ultimately lead to increased production of even more estrogen.

7. C—The heart is part of the circulatory system and is derived from the mesoderm.

8. B

9. C

10. D

11. A

12. C—The oviduct, or the fallopian tube, is where fertilization normally occurs in humans. The uterus is where implantation and development of the embryo normally occur. The embryo usually implants on the wall of the uterus—the endometrium. The cervix is the narrow pathway from the uterus to the vaginal opening. The ovary is the site of egg production.

13. C—Remember induction. It is a concept loved by the AP Biology exam writers. *Induction* is the ability of cells to influence the development of other cells by either physical contact or chemical signals. *Homeotic genes* are genes that determine how segments of an organism will develop. *Induced fit* is how enzymes and substrates interact. *Negative feedback* is the reduction in production of a substance due to high levels already present in circulation.

❯ Rapid Review

Quickly review the following terms:

Primary sex characteristics: sexual organs that assist in reproduction.

Secondary sex characteristics: physical characteristics that differ between men and women.

Male anatomy:

- Two **testes** enclosed in the *scrotum*—site of sperm and testosterone production, which occurs in the **seminiferous tubules.**
- **Interstitial cells,** which produce testosterone involved in male reproduction.
- **Epididymis,** a coiled structure where sperm completes maturation.
- **Vas deferens,** a tunnel that connects epididymis to urethra, where sperm and urine are ejected.
- **Prostate gland,** a gland that adds basic liquid to neutralize urine acidity so that sperm don't die on the way out.
- **Seminal vesicles,** glands that produce fluid to help sperm in various ways (adds energy, power, help with swimming).

Female anatomy:

- *Ovary*: site of egg, estrogen, and progesterone production; eggs move from here through the *fallopian tube* (**oviduct**) to the **uterus,** which is where a fertilized egg attaches to the **endometrium.**
- *Cervix*: narrowed portion of the uterus that connects the uterus and vagina.

Formation of gametes:

- *Oogenesis*: formation of eggs; starts in embryonic development and doesn't finish for each egg until that egg matures during a menstrual cycle (hence, an egg could wait 40 years to finish maturation).
- *Meiosis II*: oocytes undergo this process only after fertilization by a sperm in the oviduct.
- *Spermatogenesis*: one primary spermatocyte produces four spermatids, which mature in the epididymis.

Embryology (the study of embryonic development):

- *Cleavage divisions*: mitotic divisions that occur as soon as a zygote is formed; these divisions don't increase the overall size of the zygote; cytoplasm distributed unevenly, genetic information distributed evenly.
- *Morula*: what we call the zygote when it has become 16 cells.
- *Blastula*: when a zygote has become 32 cells—by this time it is implanted in the endometrial wall.
- *Gastrulation*: cells separate into three germ layers, which give rise to different adult tissues.

  Endoderm: gives rise to inner layer; lining of gut and digestive system, liver, lungs.

  Mesoderm: gives rise to intermediate layer; muscle, circulation, bones, reproductive system.

  Ectoderm: gives rise to outer layer; nervous system, skin, hair, nails.

Factors in cellular differentiation:

1. *Cytoplasmic distribution*: different amounts of cytoplasm signal different structures.

2. *Induction*: ability of one group of cells to influence another.

3. *Homeotic genes*: regulate or direct the body plan of organisms.

Hormones play a major role in directing reproductive development and reproduction:

• *FSH*: stimulates oogenesis in females and spermatogenesis in males. Creates follicle that surrounds the primary oocyte during development.

• *LH*: stimulates the ovulation and production of estrogen and progesterone in females; stimulates production of testosterone and sperm in males. Surge in this hormone triggers ovulation (release of secondary oocyte from ovary).

• *GnRH*: causes pituitary to release LH and FSH.

• *Progesterone and estrogen*: female sex hormones involved in reproduction.

• *Testosterone*: male sex hormone involved in reproduction.

Behavioral Ecology and Ethology

IN THIS CHAPTER

Summary: This chapter focuses on the interaction between animals and their environments (ecology) and introduces you to some of the basic terms used in behavioral ecology and ethology.

Key Ideas

✪ Learn the bold-faced terms in this chapter well because they show up often on the multiple-choice portion of the exam.

✪ Types of animal learning: associative learning, fixed-action pattern, habituation, imprinting, insight learning, observational learning, and operant conditioning.

✪ Three major types of animal movement: kinesis, migration, and taxis.

✪ Behavioral patterns/concepts to know: agonistic behaviors, altruistic behaviors, coefficient of relatedness, dominance hierarchies, foraging, inclusive fitness, optimal foraging, reciprocal altruism, and territoriality.

✪ Types of animal communication: chemical, visual, auditory, and tactile.

Introduction

CT teacher: "This chapter has a lot of multiple-choice-type questions in it. Learn the general concepts. . . ."

Behavioral ecology and ethology both involve the study of animal behavior. **Behavioral ecology** focuses on the interaction between animals and their environments, and usually includes an evolutionary perspective. For example, a behavioral ecologist might ask, "Why do two bird species that live in the same environment eat two different types of seeds?" **Ethology** is a narrower field, focused particularly on animal behavior and less on ecological analysis. Historically, ethology has involved a lot of experimental work, which has given us insight into the nature of animal minds.

This chapter introduces you to some of the basic terms and concepts used in behavioral ecology and ethology.

Types of Animal Learning

Associative learning is the process by which animals take one stimulus and associate it with another. Ivan Pavlov demonstrated **classical conditioning,** a type of associative learning, with dogs. As will come to be a pattern in this chapter, some poor animals were tampered with to help us understand an important biological principle. Pavlov taught dogs to anticipate the arrival of food with the sound of a bell. He hooked up these dogs to machines that measured salivation. He began the experiments by ringing a bell just moments before giving food to the dogs. Soon after this experiment began, the dogs were salivating at the sound of the bell before food was even brought into the room. They were conditioned to associate the noise of the bell with the impending arrival of food; one stimulus was substituted for another to evoke the same response.

A **fixed-action pattern** (FAP) is an innate, preprogrammed response to a stimulus. Once this action has begun, it will not stop until it has run its course. For example, male stickleback fish are programmed to attack any red-bellied fish that come into their territory. Males do not attack fish lacking this red coloration; it is specifically the color that stimulates aggressiveness. If fake fish with red bottoms are placed in water containing these stickleback fish, there's bound to be a fight! But if fake fish lacking a red bottom are dropped in, all is peaceful.

Habituation is the loss of responsiveness to unimportant stimuli. For example, as one of us started working on this book, he had just purchased a new fish tank for his office and was struck by how audible the sound of the tank's filter was. As he sits here typing tonight about two months later, he does not even hear the filter unless he *thinks* about it; he has become habituated to the noise. There are many examples of habituation in ethology. One classic example involves little ducklings that run for cover whenever birdlike objects fly overhead. If one were to torture these poor baby ducks and throw bird-shaped objects over their heads, in the beginning they would head for cover each time one flew past them, but over time as they learned that the fake birds did not represent any real danger, they would habituate to the mean trick and eventually not react at all. One side note is that ethologists who study wild animals usually have to habituate their study subjects to their presence before recording any behavioral data.

Imprinting is an innate behavior that is learned during a critical period early in life. For example, when geese are born, they imprint on motion that moves away from them, and they follow it around accepting it as their mother. This motion can be the baby's actual mother goose, it can be a human, or it can be an object. Once this imprint is made, it is irreversible. If given an essay about behavioral ecology, and imprinting in particular, the work of Konrad Lorenz would be a nice addition to your response. He was a scientist who became the "mother" to a group of young geese. He made sure that he was around the baby geese as they hatched and spent the critical period with them creating that mother–baby goose bond. These geese proceeded to follow him around everywhere and didn't recognize their real mother as their own.

Insight learning is the ability to do something right the first time with no prior experience. It requires reasoning ability—the skill to look at a problem and come up with an appropriate solution.

Observational learning is the ability of an organism to learn how to do something by watching another individual do it first, even if they have never attempted it themselves.

An example of this involves young chimpanzees in the Ivory Coast, who watch their mothers crack nuts with rock tools before learning the technique themselves.

Operant conditioning is a type of associative learning that is based on trial and error. This is different from classical conditioning because in operant conditioning, the association is made between the animal's *own* behavior and a response. This is the type of conditioning that is important to the aposometrically colored organisms that we discuss in Chapter 18 on ecology. For example, a brightly colored lizard with a chemical defense mechanism (it can spray predators in an attempt to escape) relies on this type of conditioning for survival. The coloration pattern is there in the hope that the predator will, in a trial-and-error fashion, associate the coloration pattern with an uncomfortable chemical-spraying experience that it had in the past. This association might make the predator think twice before attacking in the future and provide the prey with enough time to escape.

Animal Movement

There are three major types of animal movement that you should familiarize yourself with for the AP exam: kinesis, migration, and taxis.

Kinesis. This is a seemingly random change in the *speed* of a movement in response to a stimulus. When an organism is in a place that it enjoys, it slows down, and when in a bad environment, it speeds up. Overall this leads to an organism spending more time in favorable environments. In Chapter 19, Laboratory Review, an example of kinesis involving pill bugs is discussed. These bugs prefer damp environments to dry ones, and when placed into a contraption that gives them the choice of being on the dry or damp side, they move quickly toward the damp side (where the speed of their movement slows).

> **BIG IDEA 2.E.3**
> *Behaviors (such as migration) are regulated by various mechanisms and are important to natural selection.*

Migration. This is a cyclic movement of animals over long distances according to the time of year. Birds are known to migrate south, where it is warmer, for the winter. It is amazing that these animals know where to go.

Taxis. These are cars taken by people who need transportation. Hmm . . . actually, *taxis,* the biological term, is a reflex movement toward or away from a stimulus. We always think about summer evenings, sitting on the porch with the bug light near by, watching the poor little moths fly *right* into the darn thing because of the taxis response. They are drawn to the light at night (**phototaxis**).

Behave Yourselves, You Animals!

There are several typical behavior patterns that you should familiarize yourself with before the exam.

1. **Agonistic behavior.** Behavior that results from conflicts over resources. It often involves intimidation and submission. The battle is often a matter of who can put on the most threatening display to scare the other one into giving up, although the displays can also be quite subtle. Agonistic behaviors can involve food, mates, and territory, to name only a few. Participants in these displays do not tend to come away injured because most of these interactions are just that: displays.
2. **Altruistic behavior.** An *altruistic* action is one in which an organism does something to help another, even if it comes at its own expense. An example of this behavior involves bees. Worker bees are sterile, produce no offspring, and play the role of hive defenders,

sacrificing their lives by stinging intruders that pose a threat to the queen bee. (Sounds to us like they need a better agent.) Another example involves vampire bats that vomit food for group mates that did not manage to find food.

3. **Coefficient of relatedness.** This statistic represents the average proportion of genes that two individuals have in common. Siblings have a coefficient of relatedness (COR) of 0.5 because they share 50 percent of their genes. This coefficient is an interesting statistic because it can be expected that an animal that has a high COR with another animal will be more likely to act in an altruistic manner toward that animal.

4. **Dominance hierarchies.** A dominance hierarchy among a group of individuals is a ranking of power among the members. The member with the most power is the "alpha" member. The second-in-command, the "beta" member, dominates everyone in the group except for the alpha. It pretty much rocks to be at the top of the dominance hierarchy because you have first dibs (choice) on *every*thing (food, mates, etc.). The dominance hierarchy is not necessarily permanent—there can always be some shuffling around. For example, in chimpanzees, an alpha male can lose his alpha status and become subordinate to another chimp if power relationships change. One positive thing about these hierarchies is that since there is an order, known by all involved, it reduces the energy wasted and the risk from physical fighting for resources. Animals that know that they would be attacked if they took food before a higher-ranking individual wait until it is their turn to eat so as to avoid conflict. Keep in mind that dominance hierarchies are a characteristic of group-living animals.

5. **Foraging.** A word that describes the feeding behavior of an individual. This behavior is not as random as it may seem as animals tend to have something called a **search image** that directs them toward their potential meal. When searching for food, few fish look for a particular food; rather, they are looking for objects of a particular size that seem to match the size of what they usually eat. This is a search image. In an aquarium at mealtime, if you watch the fish closely, you will see them zoom around taking food into their mouths as they swim. Unfortunately, sometimes the "food" they ingest is the bathroom output of another fish that happens to be the same size as the food and is floating nearby. Simply because the fish dropping is the appropriate size and fits the search image, the fish may take it into its mouth for a second before emphatically spitting it out.

6. **Inclusive fitness.** This term represents the overall ability of individuals to pass their genes on to the next generation. This includes their ability to pass their *own* genes through reproduction as well as the ability of their relatives to do the same. Reproduction by relatives is included because related individuals share many of the same genes. Therefore, helping relatives to increase the success of passage of their genes to the next generation increases the inclusive fitness of the helper. The concept of inclusive fitness can explain many cases of altruism in nature.

7. **Optimal foraging.** Natural selection favors animals that choose foraging strategies that take into account costs and benefits. For example, food that is rich in nutrients but far away may cost too much energy to be worth the extra trip. There are many potential costs to traveling a long distance for some food—the animal itself could be eaten on the way *to* the food, and the animal could expend more energy than it would gain *from* the food. You *know* that you have displayed optimal foraging behavior before. "Hey, do you want to go to Wendy's?" "Uhh . . . not really, it's a really long drive . . . let's go to Bill's Burgers down the road instead."

8. **Reciprocal altruism.** Why should individuals behave altruistically? One reason may be the hope that in the future, the companion will return the favor. A baboon may defend

an unrelated companion in a fight, or perhaps a wolf will offer food to another wolf that shares no relation. Animals rarely display this behavior since it is limited to species with stable social groups that allow for exchanges of this nature. The bats described earlier represent a good example of reciprocal altruism.

9. **Territoriality.** Territorial individuals defend a physical geographic area against other individuals. This area is defended because of the benefits derived from it, which may include available mates, food resources, and high-quality breeding sites. An individual may defend a territory using scent marking, vocalizations that warn other individuals to stay away, or actual physical force against intruders. Animal species vary in their degree of territoriality (in fact, some species are *not* territorial), and both males and females may exhibit territorial behavior.

Animal Communication

BIG IDEA 3.D.1
Communication can involve signals from other organisms or the environment.

Animals communicate in many ways. Communication need not always be vocal, and we will discuss the various communication mechanisms in this next section: visual, auditory, chemical, and tactile.

Chemical communication. Mammals and insects use chemical signals called **pheromones,** which in many species play a pivotal role in the mating game. Pheromones can be powerful enough to attract mates from miles away.

Visual communication. We mentioned a few visual communication examples earlier, such as agonistic displays. Another example of a visual display is a male peacock's feather splay, which announces his willingness to mate.

Auditory communication. This mode of communication involves the use of sound in the conveying of a message. In many parts of the United States, if one sits on one's porch on a summer night, one hears the song of night frogs and crickets. These noises are often made in an effort to attract mates.

Tactile communication. This mode of communication involves touch in the conveying of a message and is often used as a greeting (handshake in humans). A major form of primate tactile communication involves grooming behavior.

BIG IDEA 3.E.1
Individuals can act on information and communicate it to others.

Bees provide an example of communication that involves chemical, tactile, and auditory components. The beehive is a dark and crowded place, and when a worker bee returns after having found a good food source, how in the world is it going to get the attention of all of the co-workers? Unfortunately, intercom systems in hives are yet to be developed. What these bees do instead is a little dance; a dance in a tight circle accompanied by a certain wag signifies to the co-workers "Hey guys . . . food source is *right* down the street." But if the food is farther away, the bee changes the dance to one that provides directional clues as well. The bee will instead perform a different combination of funky moves. This dance provides distance and directional information to the other workers and helps them find the faraway source. The ever so pleasant chemical component to this process is the regurgitation of the food source to show the other bees what kind of food they are chasing. Imagine if humans did that . . . "Dude, I just found the greatest burger place like two miles from here . . . (burp) here . . . try this burger . . . it's delightful!"

› Review Questions

1. When horses hear an unusual noise, they turn their ears toward the sound. This is an example of

   A. a fixed-action pattern.
   B. habituation.
   C. associative learning.
   D. imprinting.

2. Why do animal behaviorists have to account for a habituation period when undertaking an observational study?

   A. They have to make sure that the study animals do not imprint on them.
   B. They have to wait until their presence no longer affects the behavior of the animals.
   C. The animals need a period of time to learn to associate the observer with data collection.
   D. Before insight learning can be observed, the animals must practice.

3. Which of the following is an example of an agonistic behavior?

   A. A subordinate chimpanzee grooms a dominant chimpanzee.
   B. Two lionesses share a fresh kill.
   C. A female wolf regurgitates food for her nieces and nephews.
   D. A blackbird approaches and takes the feeding position of another blackbird, causing it to fly away.

4. In which of the following dyads do we expect *not* to see any altruistic behavior?

   A. Two sisters who are allies
   B. Two half-brothers
   C. Two individuals migrating in opposite directions
   D. Two group members who have frequent conflicts and reconciliations

5. Which of the following is not a requirement for reciprocal altruism to occur?

   A. Ability to recognize the other individual
   B. Long lifespan
   C. Opportunity for multiple interactions
   D. High coefficient of relatedness

6. A female tamarin monkey licks her wrists, rubs them together, and then rubs them against a nearby tree. What kind of communication is this probably an example of?

   A. Chemical
   B. Visual
   C. Auditory
   D. Territorial

For questions 7–10, please use the following answers:

   A. Habituation
   B. Imprinting
   C. Associative learning
   D. Operant conditioning

7. This type of learning is the lack of responsiveness to unimportant stimuli that do not provide appropriate feedback.

8. Trial-and-error learning important to animals displaying aposometric coloration.

9. Process by which animals associate one stimulus with another.

10. Innate behavior that is learned during a critical period in life.

› Answers and Explanations

1. **A**—This is a fixed-action pattern—an innate behavior that is a programmed response to a stimulus that appears to be carried out without any thought by the organisms involved.

2. **B**—If the scientist does not allow for a period of habituation, the behavioral observations will be inaccurate since the behavior of the animal will be altered by the presence of the scientist.

3. **D**—An agonistic behavior is a contest of intimidation and submission where the prize is a desired resource. In this case, the resource is the feeding position.

4. **C**—Altruistic behavior cannot be expected from two migrating individuals for a couple of reasons: (1) there is no reason for either of them to believe that they will see the other in the future,

taking the "If I help them now, perhaps they will help me sometime in the future" element out of play; and (2) if they are migrating in different directions, it is reasonably likely that they are probably not related, which takes the "I'll help because it'll increase the chance that more of my genes get passed along" element out of play.

5. **D**—Reciprocal altruism need not occur between related individuals.

6. **A**

7. **A**

8. **D**

9. **C**

10. **B**

› Rapid Review

Quickly review the following terms:

Behavioral ecology: study of interaction between animals and their environments.

Ethology: study of animal behavior.

Types of Animal Learning

- *Fixed-action pattern*: preprogrammed response to a stimulus (stickleback fish).
- *Habituation*: loss of responsiveness to unimportant stimuli or stimuli that provide no feedback.
- *Imprinting*: innate behavior learned during critical period early in life (baby ducks imprint to mama ducks).
- *Associative learning*: one stimulus is associated with another (classical conditioning—Pavlov).
- *Operant conditioning*: trial-and-error learning (aposometric predator training).
- *Insight learning*: ability to reason through a problem the first time through with no prior experience.
- *Observational learning*: learning by watching someone else do it first.

Types of Animal Movement

- *Kinesis*: change in the speed of movement in response to a stimulus. Organisms will move faster in bad environments and slower in good environments.
- *Migration*: cyclic movement of animals over long distances according to the time of year.
- *Taxis*: reflex movement toward or away from a stimulus.

Animal Behaviors

- *Agonistic behavior*: conflict behavior over access to a resource. Often a matter of which animal can mount the most threatening display and scare the other into submission.
- *Dominance hierarchies*: ranking of power among the members of a group; subject to change. Since members of the group know the order, less energy is wasted in conflicts over food and resources.
- *Territoriality*: defense of territory to keep others out.
- *Altruistic behavior*: action in which an organism helps another at its own expense.
- *Reciprocal altruism*: animals behave altruistically toward others who are *not* relatives, hoping that the favor will be returned sometime in the future.
- *Foraging*: feeding behavior of an individual. Animals have a search image that directs them to food.
- *Optimal foraging*: natural selection favors those who choose foraging strategies that maximize the differential between costs and benefits. If the effort involved in obtaining food outweighs the nutritive value of the food, forget about it.
- *Inclusive fitness*: the ability of individuals to pass their genes not only through the production of their own offspring, but also by providing aid to enable closely related individuals to produce offspring.
- *Coefficient of relatedness*: statistic that represents the average proportion of genes two individuals have in common. The higher the value, the more likely they are to altruistically aid one another.

Communication

- *Chemical*: communication through the use of chemical signals, such as pheromones.
- *Visual*: communication through the use of visual cues, such as the tail feather displays of peacocks.
- *Auditory*: communication through the use of sound, such as the chirping of frogs in the summer.
- *Tactile*: communication through the use of touch, such as a handshake in humans.

CHAPTER 18

Ecology in Further Detail

IN THIS CHAPTER

Summary: This chapter covers the main concepts of ecology, including population growth, biotic potential, life history strategies, and predator–prey relationships. This chapter also discusses concepts such as succession, trophic levels, energy and biomass pyramids, biomes, and biogeochemical cycles.

Key Ideas

✪ Three main types of dispersion patterns: clumped, uniform, and random.

✪ Two main types of population growth: exponential (J-shaped) and logistic (S-shaped.)

✪ Two primary life history strategies: *K*-selected and *R*-selected populations.

✪ Three main symbiotic relationships: commensalism, mutualism, and parasitism.

✪ Defense mechanisms: aposematic coloration, Batesian mimicry, cryptic coloration, deceptive markings, and Müllerian mimicry.

✪ Biomes that come up on the AP exam: desert, savannah, taiga, temperate deciduous forest, temperate grassland, tropical forest, tundra, and water.

✪ Have a general understanding of the biogeochemical cycles (carbon, nitrogen, and water).

Introduction

Ecology is the study of the interaction of organisms and their environments. This chapter covers the main concepts of ecology, including population growth, biotic potential, life history "strategies," and predator–prey relationships. The chapter will also look at within-community and between-community (intra- and intercommunity) interactions. Finally we will talk about succession, trophic levels, energy pyramids, biomass pyramids, biomes, and biogeochemical cycles.

Population Ecology and Growth

Like many fields of biology, ecology contains hierarchies of classification. A **population** is a collection of individuals of the same species living in the same geographic area. A collection of populations of species in a geographic area is known as a **community.** An **ecosystem** consists of the individuals of the community and the environment in which it exists. Ecosystems can be subdivided into abiotic and biotic components: **biotic components** are the living organisms of the ecosystem, while **abiotic components** are the *nonliving* players in an ecosystem, such as weather and nutrients. Finally, the **biosphere** is the entire life-containing area of a planet—all communities and ecosystems.

Three more terms for you: (1) the **niche** of an organism, which consists of all the biotic and abiotic resources used by the organism; (2) **population density,** which describes how many individuals are in a certain area; and (3) **distribution,** which describes how populations are dispersed over that area. There are three main types of dispersion patterns that you should know (see also Figure 18.1):

1. *Clumped:* The individuals live in packs that are spaced out from each other, as in schools of fish or herds of cattle.
2. *Uniform:* The individuals are evenly spaced out across a geographic area, such as birds on a wire sitting above the highway—notice how evenly spaced out they are.
3. *Random:* The species are randomly distributed across a geographic area, such as a tree distribution in a forest.

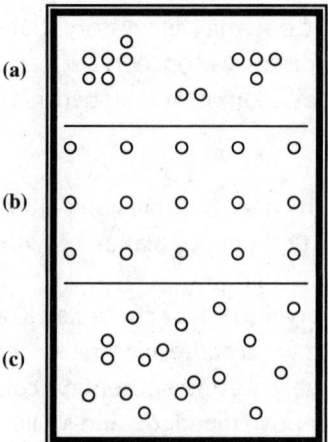

Figure 18.1   Distribution patterns: (a) clumped; (b) uniform; (c) random.

Population ecology is the study of the size, distribution, and density of populations and how these populations change with time. It takes into account all the variables we have mentioned already and many more. The size of the population, symbolized N, indicates how many individuals of that species are in a given area. **Demographers** study the theory and statistics behind population growth and decline. The following is a list of demographic statistics you should be familiar with for the AP Biology exam:

Birth rate   Offspring produced per time period. Highest among those in the middle of the age spectrum.

Death rate   Number of deaths per time period. Highest among those at two extremes of the age spectrum.

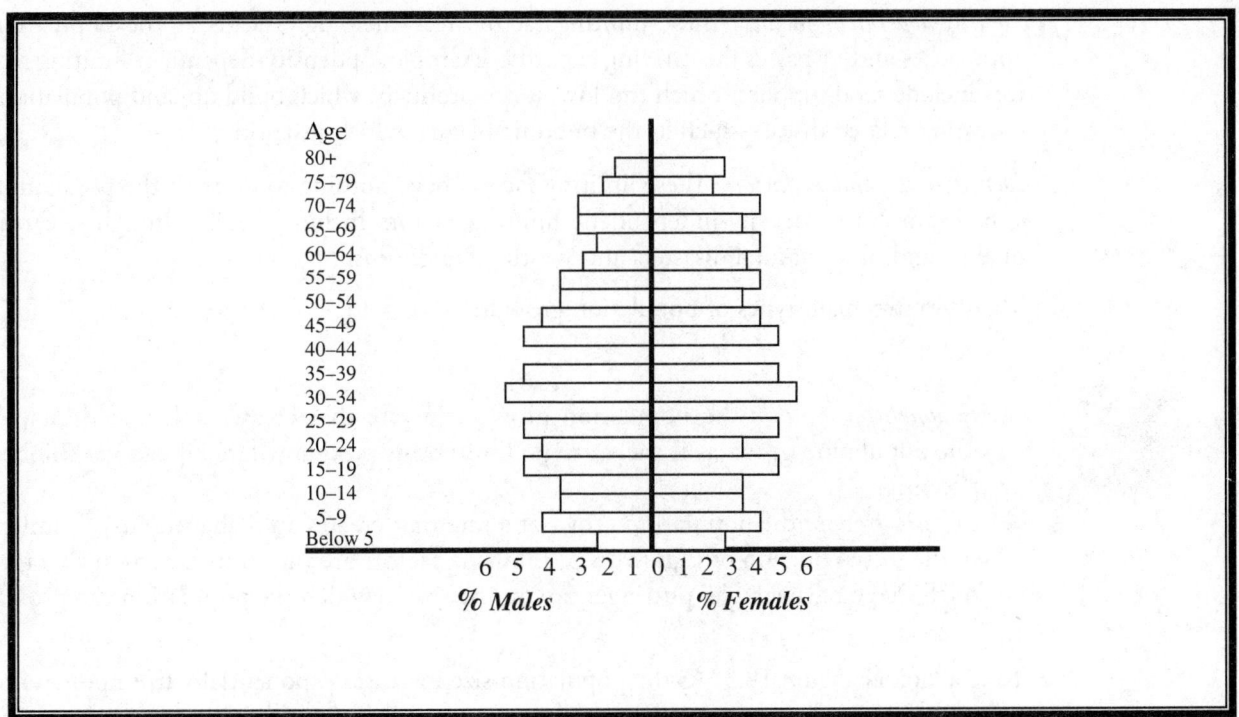

Figure 18.2   A typical age structure chart.

Sex ratio	Proportion of males and females in a population.
Generation time	Time needed for individuals to reach reproductive maturity.
Age structure	Statistic that compares the relative number of individuals in the population from each age group (Figure 18.2).
Immigration rate	Rate at which individuals relocate into a given population.
Emigration rate	Rate at which individuals relocate out of a given population.

Liz (college freshman): "Know how to read these charts."

All these statistics together determine the size and growth rate of a given population. Obviously, a higher birth rate and a lower death rate will give a faster rate of population growth. A high female sex ratio could lead to an increase in the number of births in a population (more females to produce offspring). A short generation time allows offspring to be produced at a faster rate. An age structure that consists of more individuals in the middle of their reproductive years will grow at a faster rate than one weighted toward older people.

Population Growth and Size

Biotic potential is the maximum growth rate of a population given unlimited resources, unlimited space, and lack of competition or predators. This rate varies from species to species. The **carrying capacity** is defined as the maximum number of individuals that a population can sustain in a given environment.

If biotic potential exists, then why isn't every inch of this planet covered with life? Because of the environment in which we live, numerous **limiting factors** exist that help control population sizes. A few examples of limiting factors include predators, diseases, food supplies, and waste produced by organisms. There are two broad categories of limiting factors:

Density-dependent factors. These limiting factors rear their ugly heads as the population approaches and/or passes the carrying capacity. Examples of density-dependent limiting factors include food supplies, which run low; waste products, which build up; and population-crowding-related diseases such as the bubonic plague, which just stink.

Density-independent factors. These limiting factors have nothing to do with the population size. Examples of density-independent limiting factors include floods, droughts, earthquakes, and other natural disasters and weather conditions.

There are two main types of population growth:

1. *Exponential growth:* the population grows at a rate that creates a J-shaped curve. The population grows as if there are no limitations as to how large it can get (biotic potential).
2. *Logistic growth:* the population grows at a rate that creates an S-shaped curve similar to the initial portion of Figure 18.3. Limiting factors are the culprits responsible for the S shape of the curve, putting a cap on the size to which the population can grow.

Take a look at Figure 18.3. As the population size increases exponentially from point *A* to point *C*, there seem to be enough natural resources available to allow the growth rate to be quite high. At some point, however, natural resources, such as food, will start to run out. This will lead to competition between the members of the population for the scarce food. Whenever there is competition, there are winners and losers. Those who win survive; those who lose do not. Notice that the population rises above the carrying capacity. How can this be? This is short-lived, as the complications of being overpopulated (lack of food, disease from increased population density, buildup of waste) will lead to a rise in the death rate that pushes the population back down to the carrying capacity or below. When it drops below the carrying capacity, resources replenish, allowing for an increase in the birth rate and decline in the death rate. What you are looking at in Figure 18.3 is the phenomenon known as a **population cycle.** Often, as seen in the figure, when the population size dips below the carrying capacity, it will later come back to the capacity and even surpass it.

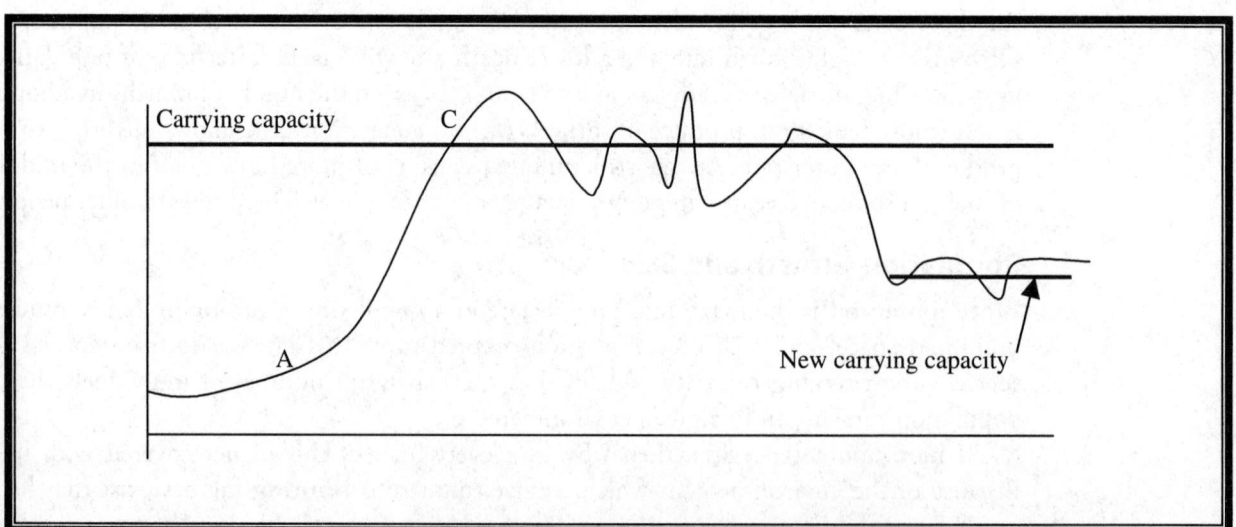

Figure 18.3   Carrying capacity.

However, another possibility shown in this figure is that when a population dips below the carrying capacity due to some major change in the environment, when all is said and done, it may equilibrate at a new, lower carrying capacity.

Life History Strategies

You should be familiar with two primary life history "strategies," which represent two extremes of the spectrum:

K-selected populations: populations of a roughly constant size whose members have low reproductive rates. The offspring produced by these *K*-selected organisms require extensive postnatal care until they have sufficiently matured. Humans are a fine example of a *K*-selected population.

R-selected populations: populations that experience rapid growth of the J-curve variety. The offspring produced by *R*-selected organisms are numerous, mature quite rapidly, and require very little postnatal care. These populations are also known as **opportunistic populations** and tend to show up when space in the region opens up as a result of some environmental change. The opportunistic population grows fast, reproduces quickly, and dies quickly as well. Bacteria are a good example of an *R*-selected population.

Survivorship Curves

Survivorship curves (Figure 18.4) are another tool used to study the population dynamics of species. These curves show the relative survival rates for population members of different ages.

Type I individuals live a long life until an age is reached where the death rate in the population increases rapidly, causing the steep downward end to the type I curve. Examples of type I organisms include humans and other large mammals.

Type II individuals have a death rate that is reasonably constant across the age spectrum. Examples of type II species include lizards, hydra, and other small mammals.

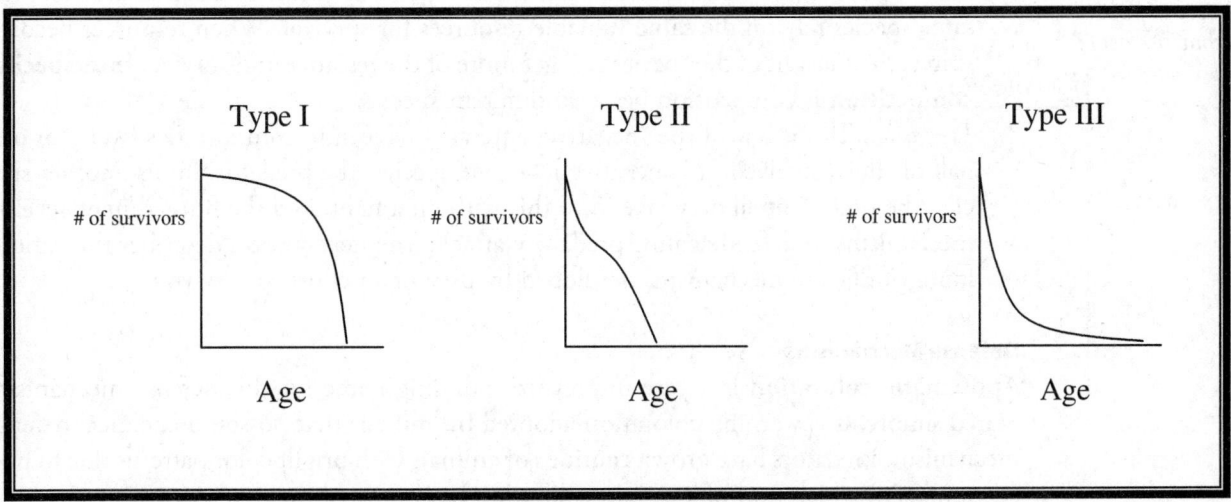

Figure 18.4   Survivorship curves.

Type III individuals have a steep downward curve for those of young age, representing a death rate that flattens out once a certain age is reached. Examples of type III organisms include many fishes, oysters, and other marine organisms.

Community and Succession

Community

Most species exist within a community. Because they share a geographic home, they are bound to interact. These interactions range from positive to neutral to negative.

Del (12th grade): "Know this for the multiple-choice questions. I should have. . . ."

Forms of Species Interaction

1. *Symbiosis.* A symbiotic relationship is one between two different species that can be classified as one of three main types: commensalism, mutualism, or parasitism.
   A. *Commensalism.* One organism benefits while the other is unaffected. Commensalistic relationships are rare, and examples are hard to find. Cattle egrets feast on insects that are aroused into flight by cattle grazing in the insects' habitat. The birds benefit because they get food, but the cattle do not appear to benefit at all.
   B. *Mutualism.* Both organisms reap benefits from the interaction. One popular example of a mutualistic relationship is that between acacia trees and ants. The ants are able to feast on the yummy sugar produced by the trees, while the trees are protected by the ants' attack on any potentially harmful foreign insects. Another example involves a lichen, which is a collection of photosynthetic organisms (fungus and algae) living as one. The fungus component pulls its weight by helping to create an environment suitable for the lichen's survival, while the algae component supplies the food for the fungus. Without each other's contribution, they are doomed.
   C. *Parasitism.* One organism benefits at the other's expense. A popular example of a parasitic relationship involves tapeworms, which live in the digestive tract of their hosts. They reap the benefits of the meals that their host consumes by stealing the nutrients and depriving the host of nutrition. Another less well-known example of parasitism involves myself and my younger brother's Playstation 2 console.
2. *Competition.* Both species are harmed by this kind of interaction. The two major forms of competition are intraspecific and interspecific competition. **Intraspecific competition** is *within*-species competition. This kind of competition occurs because members of the same species rely on the same valuable resources for survival. When resources become scarce, the most fit of the species will get more of the resource and survive. **Interspecific competition** is competition between different species.
3. *Predation.* This is one of the "negative" interactions seen in communities (well, for one half of those involved, it is negative.) ☺ One species, the predator, hunts another species, the prey. Not all prey give in to this without a fight, and the hunted may develop mechanisms to defend against predatory attack. The next section describes the various kinds of defense mechanisms developed by prey in an effort to survive.

BIG IDEA 2.D.1

Everything from cells to ecosystems is affected by interactions involving the exchange of matter and energy.

BIG IDEA 4.A.5

Communities are composed of populations that interact in complex ways.

Defense Mechanisms

Aposematic coloration is a very impressive-sounding name for this defense mechanism. Stated simply, it is warning coloration adopted by animals that possess a chemical defense mechanism. Predators have grown cautious of animals with bright color patterns due to past encounters in which prey of a certain coloration have sprayed the predator with a chemical defense. It is kind of like the blinking red light seen in cars with elaborate alarm systems.

Burglars notice the red light and may think twice about attempting to steal that car because of the potential for encountering an alarm system.

In **Batesian mimicry,** an animal that is harmless copies the appearance of an animal that is dangerous to trick predators. An example of this is a beetle whose colors closely resemble those of bees. Predators may fear that the beetle is a bee and avoid confrontation.

In **cryptic coloration,** those being hunted adopt a coloring scheme that allows them to blend in to the colors of the environment. It is like camouflage worn by army soldiers moving through the jungle. The more you look like the terrain, the harder you are to see.

Some animals have patterns called **deceptive markings,** which can cause a predator to think twice before attacking. For example, some insects may have colored designs on their wings that resemble large eyes, causing individuals to look more imposing than they truly are.

In **Müllerian mimicry,** two species that are aposematically colored as an indicator of their chemical defense mechanisms mimic each other's color scheme in an effort to increase the speed with which their predators learn to avoid them. The more often predators see dangerous prey with this coloration, the faster the negative association is made.

Looking at Figure 18.5, we can see how the predator–prey dance plays out. When the prey population starts to decrease because of predation, there is a reactionary reduction in the predator population. Why does this happen? Because the predators run low on a valuable resource necessary to their survival—their prey. Notice in the figure that as the predator population declines, an increase in the population of the prey begins to appear because more of those prey animals are able to survive and reproduce. As the prey population density rises, the predators again have enough food available to sustain a higher population, and their population density returns to a higher level again. Unless disturbed by a dramatic environmental change, this cyclical pattern continues.

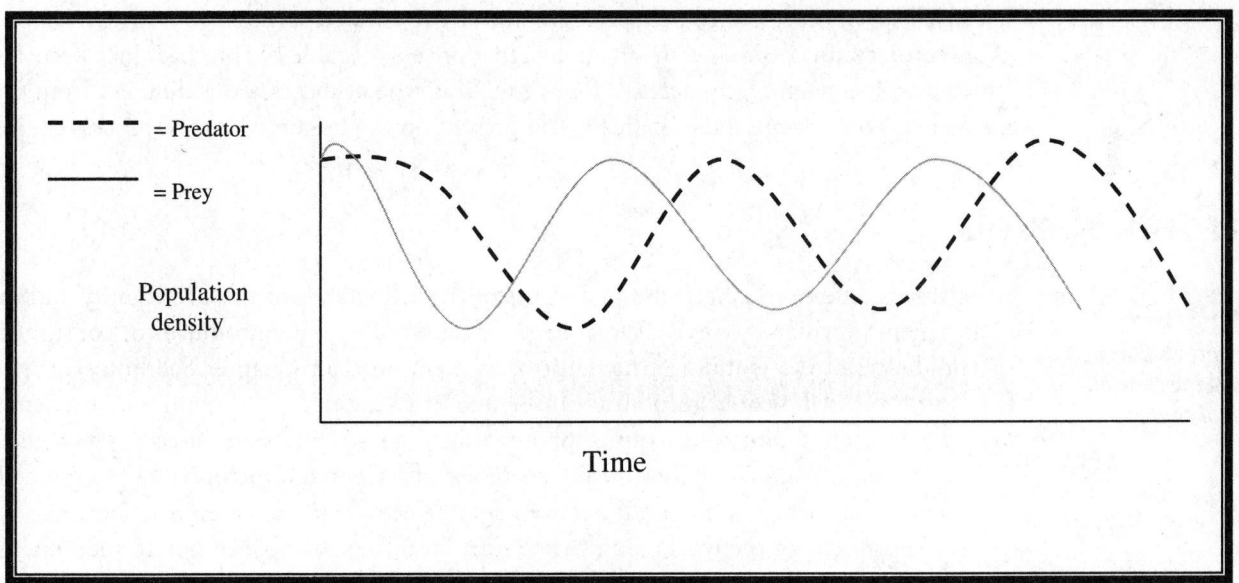

Figure 18.5 Predator–prey population curves.

Coevolution is mutual evolution between two species and is often seen in predator–prey relationships. For example, imagine that the hunted prey adapts a new character trait that allows it to better elude the predator. In order to survive, the predator must evolve so that it can catch its victim and eat.

KEY IDEA

Succession

When something happens to a community that causes a shift in the resources available to the local organisms, it sets the stage for the process of **succession**—the shift in the local composition of species in response to changes that occur over time. As time passes, the community goes through various stages until it arrives at a final stable stage called the **climax community.** Two major forms of succession you should know about are primary and secondary succession.

Primary succession occurs in an area that is devoid of life and contains no soil. A **pioneer species** (usually a small plant) able to survive in resource-poor conditions takes hold of a barren area such as a new volcanic island. The pioneer species does the grunt work, adding nutrients and other improvements to the once uninhabited volcanic rock until future species take over. As the plant species come and go, adding nutrients to the environment, animal species are drawn in by the presence of new plant life. These animals contribute to the development of the area with the addition of further organic matter (waste). This constant changing of the guard continues until the **climax community** is reached and a steady-state equilibrium is achieved. **Bare-rock succession** involves the attachment of lichen to rocks, followed by the step-by-step arrival of replacement species up to the climax community. **Pond succession** is kicked off when a shallow, water-filled hole is created. As time passes, animals arrive on the scene as the pioneer species deposit debris, encouraging the growth of vegetation on the pond floor. Over time, plants develop whose roots are underwater and whose leaves are above the water. As these plants begin to cover the entire area of the pond, the debris continues to build up, transforming the once empty pond into a marsh. When enough trees fill into the area, the marsh becomes a swamp. If the conditions are appropriate, the swamp can eventually become a forest or grassland, completing the succession process. One trivia fact to take out of primary succession is that usually the pioneer species is an *R*-selected species, while the later species tend to be *K*-selected species.

Secondary succession occurs in an area that once had stable life but has since been disturbed by some major force such as a forest fire. This type of succession is different from primary succession because there is already soil present on the terrain when the process begins.

> **BIG IDEA 4.C.4**
>
> *The diversity of species within an ecosystem may influence the stability of that ecosystem.*

Trophic Levels

> **BIG IDEA 2.A.1**
>
> *All living systems require the constant input of energy.*

As we discussed earlier, an ecosystem consists of the individuals of the community and the environment in which they exist. Organisms are classified as either producers or consumers. The producers of the world are the autotrophs mentioned in Chapter 8, Photosynthesis. The autotrophs you should recognize can be one of two types: photosynthetic or chemosynthetic autotrophs. **Photoautotrophs** (photosynthetic autotrophs) start the earth's food chain by converting the energy of light into the energy of life. **Chemoautotrophs** (chemosynthetic autotrophs) release energy through the movement of electrons in oxidation reactions.

The consumers of the world are the heterotrophs. They are able to obtain their energy only through consumption of other living things. One type of consumer is a **herbivore,** which feeds on plants for nourishment. Another consumer, the **carnivore,** obtains energy and nutrients through the consumption of other animals. A third consumer, the **detritivore,** obtains its energy through the consumption of dead animals and plants. A special subcategory of this type of consumer includes decomposers, which also consume dead animal and plant matter, but then release nutrients back into the environment. The decomposer subcategory includes fungi, bacteria, and earthworms.

Here comes another hierarchy for you to remember. The distribution of energy on the planet can be subdivided into a hierarchy of energy levels called **trophic levels.** Take a look

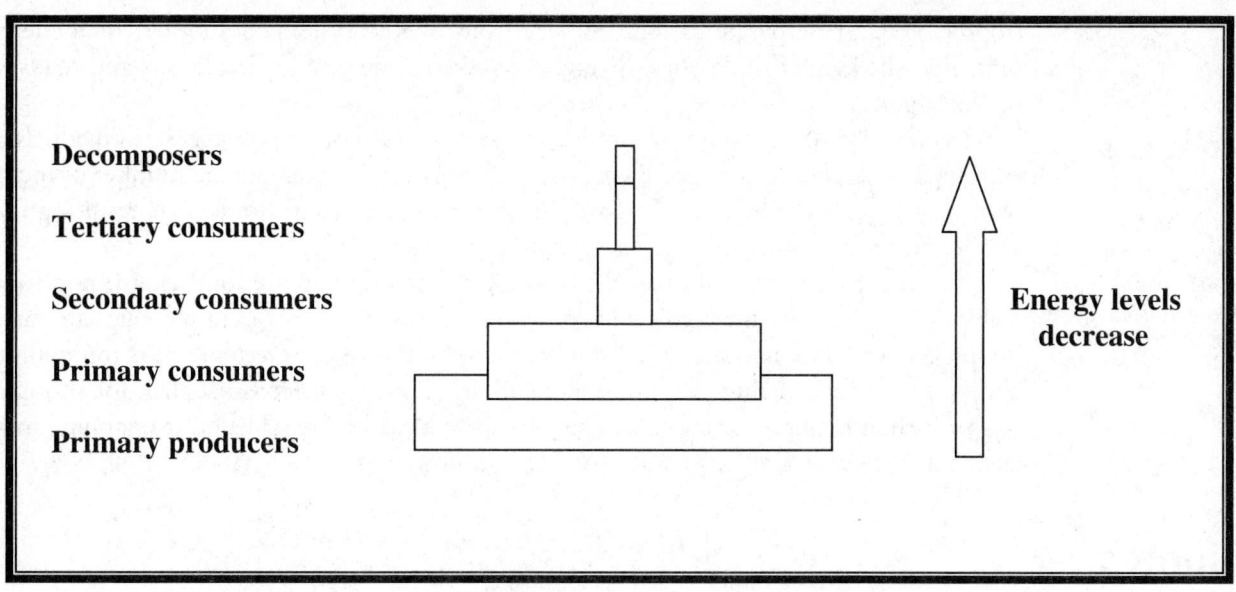

Decomposers

Tertiary consumers

Secondary consumers

Primary consumers

Primary producers

Energy levels decrease

Figure 18.6   Energy pyramid, indicating decrease in energy level.

at the energy pyramid in Figure 18.6. The primary producers make up the first trophic level. The next trophic level consists of the organisms that consume the primary producers: the herbivores. These organisms are known as **primary consumers.** The primary consumers are consumed by the **secondary consumers,** or primary carnivores, that are the next trophic level. These primary carnivores are consumed by the secondary carnivores to create the next trophic level. This is an oversimplified yet important basic explanation of how trophic levels work. Usually there are only four or five trophic levels to a food chain because energy is lost from each level as it progresses higher.

The energy pyramid is not the only type of ecological pyramid that you might encounter on the AP Biology exam. Be familiar with a type of pyramid known as a *biomass pyramid* (Figure 18.7), which represents the cumulative weight of all of the members at a given

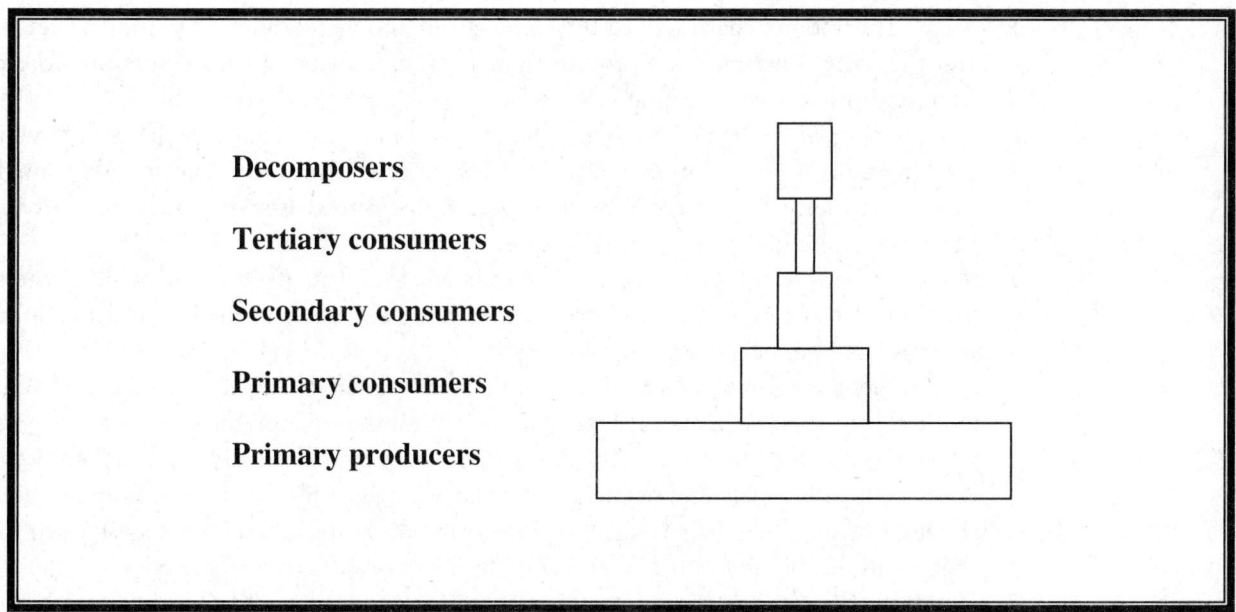

Decomposers

Tertiary consumers

Secondary consumers

Primary consumers

Primary producers

Figure 18.7   Biomass pyramid.

trophic level. These pyramids tend to vary from one ecosystem to another. Like energy pyramids, the base of the biomass pyramid represents the primary producers and tends to be the largest.

BIG IDEA 4.A.6

Interactions among organisms and with their environment result in movement of matter and energy.

There is also the **pyramid of numbers,** which is based on the *number* of individuals at each level of the biomass chain. Each box in this pyramid represents the number of members of that level. The highest consumers in the chain tend to be quite large, resulting in a smaller number of those individuals spread out over an area.

Two more terms to cover before moving on to the biomes are **food chains** and **food webs.** A *food chain* is a hierarchical list of who snacks on who. For example, bugs are eaten by spiders, who are eaten by birds, who are eaten by cats. A *food web* provides more information than a food chain—it is not so cut and dry. Food webs recognize that, for example, bugs are eaten by more than only spiders. Food webs can be regarded as overlapping food chains that show all the various dietary relationships.

Biomes

The various geographic regions of the earth that serve as hosts for ecosystems are known as **biomes.** Read through the following list so that you will be able to sprinkle some biome knowledge into an essay on ecological principles.

BIG IDEA 4.B.4

Distribution of local and global ecosystems changes over time.

1. *Deserts.* The driest land biome of the group, **deserts** experience a wide range of temperature from day to night and exist on nearly every continent. Deserts that do not receive adequate rainfall will not have any vegetative life. However, plants such as cacti seem to have adjusted to desert life and have done quite nicely in this biome, given enough water. Much of the wildlife found in deserts is nocturnal and conserves energy and water during the heat of the day. This biome shows the greatest daily fluctuation in temperature due to the fact that water moderates temperature.

2. *Savanna.* **Savanna** grasslands, which contain a spattering of trees, are found throughout South America, Australia, and Africa. Savanna soil tends to be low in nutrients, while temperatures tend to run high. Many of the grazing species of this planet (herbivores) make savannas their home.

3. *Taiga.* This biome, characterized by lengthy cold and wet winters, is found in Canada and has gymnosperms as its prominent plant life. **Taigas** contain coniferous forests (pine and other needle-bearing trees).

4. *Temperate deciduous forests.* A biome that is found in regions that experience cold winters where plant life is dormant, alternating with warm summers that provide enough moisture to keep large trees alive. **Temperate deciduous forests** can be seen in the northeastern United States, much of Europe, and eastern Asia.

5. *Temperate grasslands.* **Temperate grasslands** are found in regions with cold winters. The soil of this biome is considered to be among the most fertile of all. This biome receives less water than tropical savannas.

6. *Tropical forests.* Found all over the planet in South America, Africa, Australia, and Asia, **tropical forests** come in many shapes and sizes. Near the equator, they can be rainforests, whereas in lowland areas that have dry seasons, they tend to be dry forests. Rainforests consist primarily of tall trees that form a thick cover, which blocks the light from reaching the floor of the forest (where there is little growth). Tropical rainforests are known for their rapid recycling of nutrients and contain the greatest diversity of species.

7. *Tundras.* The **tundra** biome experiences extremely cold winters during which the ground freezes completely. The upper layer of the ground is able to thaw during the summer months, but the land directly underneath, called the **permafrost,** remains

frozen throughout the year. This keeps plants from forming deep roots in this soil and dictates what type of plant life can survive. The plant life that tends to predominate is short shrubs or grasses that are able to withstand difficult conditions.

8. *Water biomes.* Both freshwater and marine **water biomes** occupy the majority of the surface of the earth.

The general distribution of biomes on the earth's surface is shown in Figure 18.8.

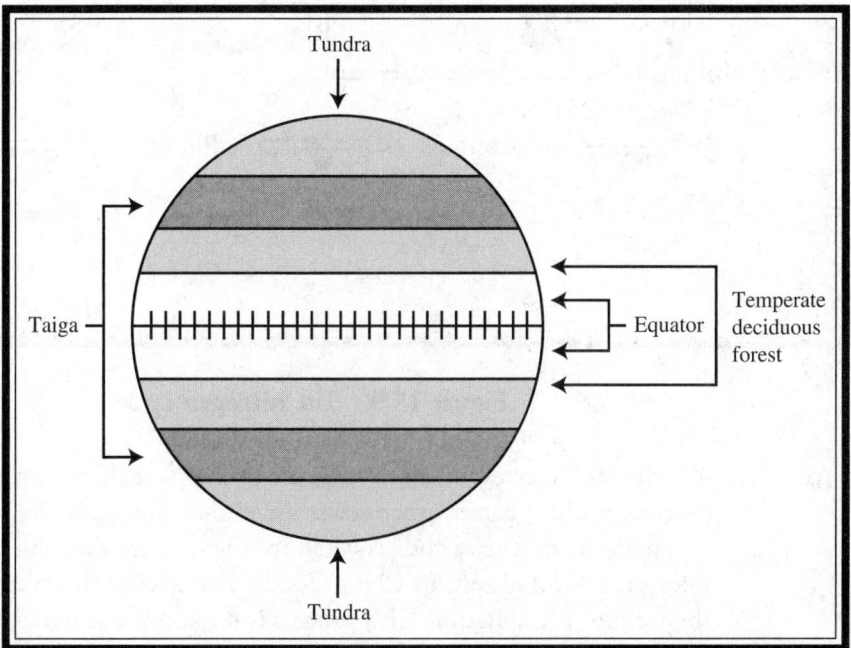

Figure 18.8   General distribution of biomes on the earth's surface. (The other land biomes such as grassland and desert are interspersed in temperate and tropical regions with water as the limiting factor.)

Biogeochemical Cycles

One last topic to briefly cover before we wave goodbye to ecology is that of **biogeochemical cycles.** These cycles represent the movement of elements, such as nitrogen and carbon, from organisms to the environment and back in a continuous cycle. Do not attempt to become a master of these cycles, but you should understand the basics.

Carbon cycle. Carbon is the building block of organic life. The **carbon cycle** begins when carbon is released to the atmosphere from volcanoes, aerobic respiration (CO_2), and the burning of fossil fuels (coal). Most of the carbon in the atmosphere is present in the form of CO_2. Plants contribute to the carbon cycle by taking in carbon and using it to perform photosynthetic reactions, and then incorporating it into their sugars. The carbon is ingested by animals, who send the carbon back to the atmosphere when they die.

Nitrogen cycle. Nitrogen is an element vital to plant growth. In the **nitrogen cycle** (Figure 18.9), plants have nitrogen to consume thanks to the existence of organisms that perform the thankless task of **nitrogen fixation**—the conversion of N_2 to NH_3 (ammonia). The only source of nitrogen for animals is the plants they consume. When these organisms die, their remains become a source of nitrogen for the remaining members of the environment. Bacteria and fungi (decomposers) chomp at these organisms and break down any nitrogen remains. The NH_3 in the environment is converted by bacteria into NO_3 (nitrate), and this NO_3 is taken up

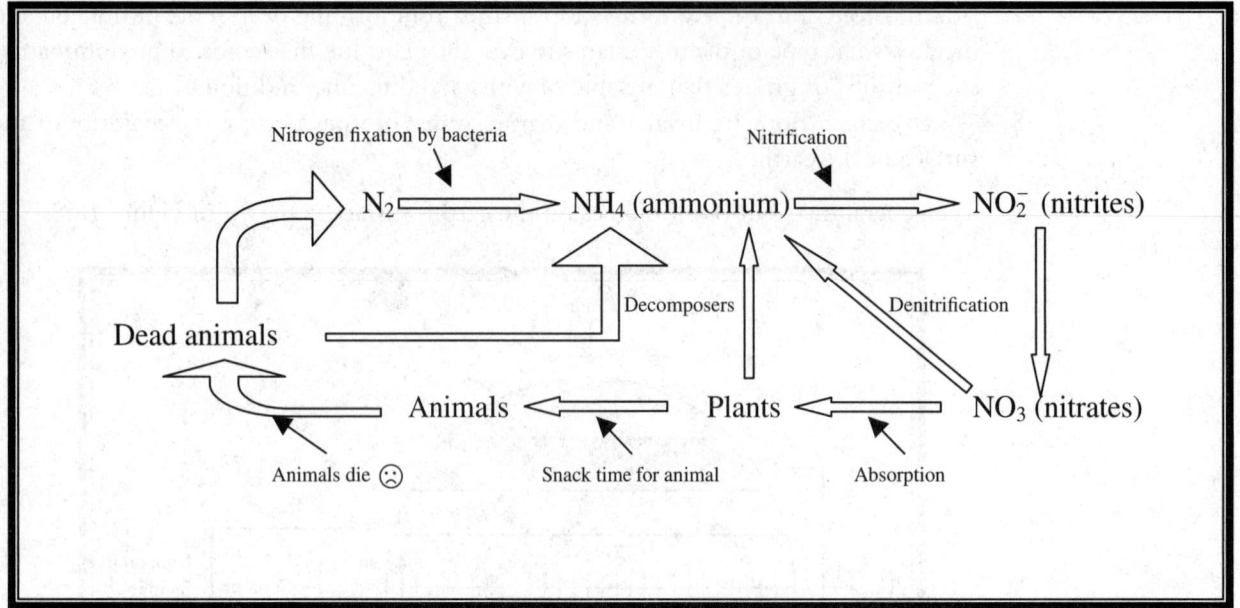

Figure 18.9   The nitrogen cycle.

by plants and then eventually by animals to complete the nitrogen cycle. **Denitrification** is the process by which bacteria themselves use nitrates and release N_2 as a product.

Water cycle. The earth is covered in water. A considerable amount of this water evaporates each day and returns to the clouds. Eventually, this water is returned to the earth in the form of precipitation. This process is termed the **water cycle.**

❭ Review Questions

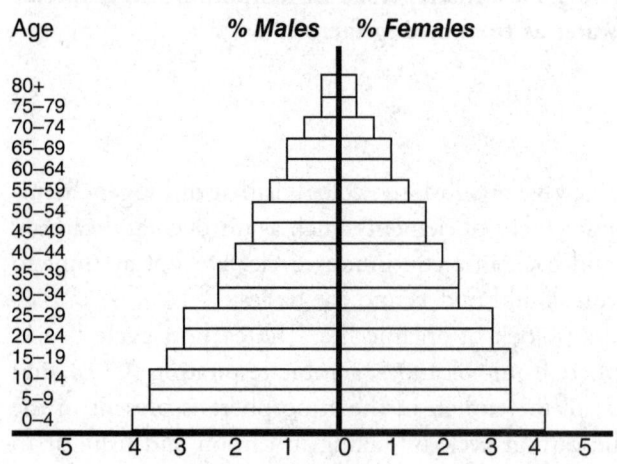

1. How would you describe the population depicted in the age structure graph shown here?

   A. Growing rapidly
   B. Growing slowly
   C. Not growing at all
   D. Experiencing slow negative growth

2. Carbon is most commonly present in the atmosphere in what form?

   A. CCl_4
   B. CO
   C. CO_2
   D. CH_2

3. Which of the following is a density-dependent limiting factor?

   A. Flood
   B. Drought
   C. Earthquake
   D. Famine

4. The process by which bacteria themselves use the nitrate of the environment, releasing N_2 as a product, is called

   A. nitrogen fixation.
   B. abiotic fixation.
   C. denitrification.
   D. chemosynthetic autotrophism.

For question 5, please use the following curve:

5. At what point on the graph does the decline in rabbit population act as a limiting factor to the survival of the foxes, leading to a decline in their population size?

   A. A
   B. B
   C. C
   D. D

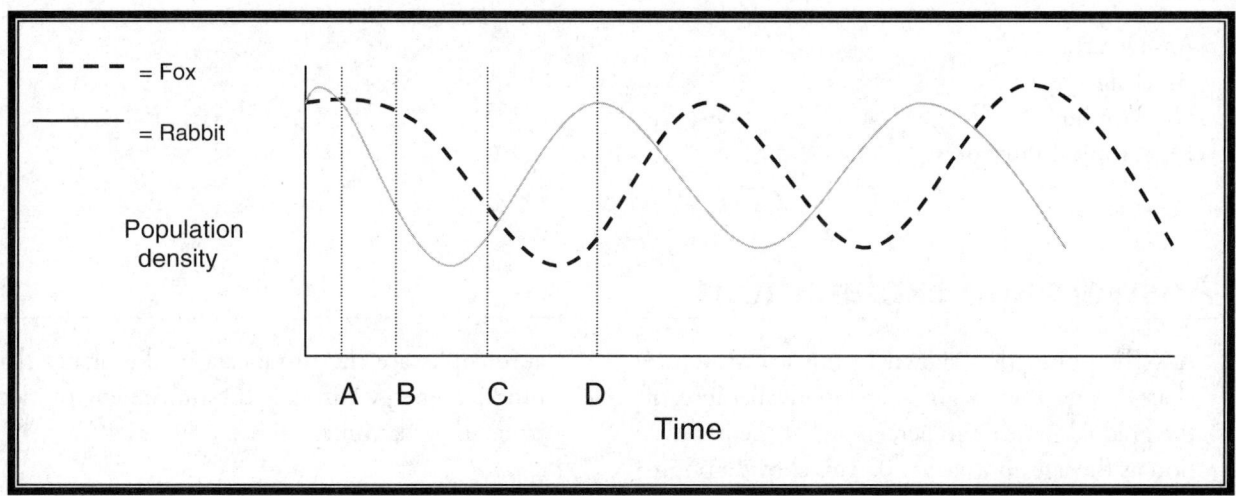

6. A collection of all the individuals of an area combined with the environment in which they exist is called a/an

   A. population.
   B. community.
   C. ecosystem.
   D. biosphere.

For questions 7–10, please use the following answer choices:

   A. Aposematic coloration
   B. Batesian mimicry
   C. Müllerian mimicry
   D. Cryptic coloration

7. A beetle that has the coloration of a yellow jacket is displaying which defense mechanism?

8. A moth whose body color matches that of the trees in which it lives is displaying which defense mechanism?

9. Two different lizard species, each possessing a particular chemical defense mechanism and sharing a similar body coloration, are displaying which defense mechanism?

10. A lizard with a chemical defense mechanism has a bright-colored body as a warning to predators that it is one tough customer is displaying which defense mechanism?

11. Which of the following is *not* a characteristic of a *K*-selected population?

   A. Populations tend to be of a relatively constant size.
   B. Offspring produced tend to require extensive postnatal care.
   C. Primates are classified as *K*-selected organisms.
   D. Offspring are produced in large quantities.

12. Which of the following would have the survivorship curve shown in the following diagram?

    A. Humans
    B. Lizards
    C. Oysters
    D. Fish

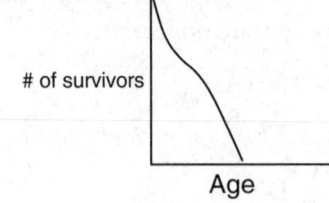

13. This biome is known for having the most diverse variety of species.

14. This biome is the driest of the land biomes.

15. The predominate plant life of this biome is short shrubs or grasses.

16. This biome is known for its cold, lengthy, and snowy winters and the presence of coniferous forests.

For questions 13–16, please use the following answer choices:

    A. Desert
    B. Taiga
    C. Tundra
    D. Tropical rain forest

› Answers and Explanations

1. **A**—The population shown in this age structure chart is one that is growing rapidly because of the gradual increase in percentage of the population as the age approaches 0. This shows a population that has a high birth rate and a reasonable life expectancy.

2. **C**—CO_2 is the dominant form of carbon present in the atmosphere.

3. **D**—Density-dependent limiting factors show up as the population approaches and/or passes the carrying capacity. Examples of density-dependent limiting factors include availability of food resources, waste buildup, and density-induced diseases. The other three choices are examples of density-independent factors, which affect population size regardless of how large or small it may be.

4. **C**—*Denitrification* is defined as the process by which bacteria themselves use nitrates and release nitrogen gas as a product. Bacteria also perform the necessary task of nitrogen fixation, which takes atmospheric nitrogen and converts it to NH_3. They later take this NH_3 and convert it to nitrate, which plants require for photosynthetic success. (*Abiotic fixation* is a term that we made up because it sounded cool.) Chemiosynthetic autotrophs are the producers of the planet that produce energy through the movement of electrons in oxidation reactions.

5. **B**—At this point, the population of rabbits has declined to the point where the foxes are starting to feel the reduction in their food supply. The fox survival curve soon begins its decline, which leads to the revival of the rabbits.

6. **C**—An *ecosystem* consists of all the individuals in the community and the environment in which they exist. A *population* is a collection of individuals of the same species living in the same area. A *community* is a collection of all the different populations of the various species in a geographic area. A *biosphere* is the collection of all the life-containing areas of the planet.

7. **B**—An animal that is harmless copies the appearance of an animal that *is* dangerous as a defense mechanism to make predators think twice about attacking.

8. **D**—Cryptic coloration is the animal kingdom's version of army clothes. Their coloration matches that of their environment so they can blend in and hide from their predators.

9. **C**—Two species that are aposematically colored as an indicator of their chemical defense mechanism mimic each other's color scheme in an effort to increase the speed with which their predators learn to avoid them. This, of course, requires a predator that can learn based on experience.

10. **A**—This defense mechanism is warning coloration adopted by animals that possess a chemical defense mechanism. Ideally, predators will learn to avoid the species, helping the prey survive longer.

11. **D**—*K*-selected populations tend to be populations of a roughly constant size, with low reproductive rates and whose offspring require

extensive postnatal care until they have sufficiently matured. *R*-selected populations tend to produce many offspring per birth.

12. **B**—Lizards follow a type II survivorship curve as illustrated in the diagram in review question 12. Humans (answer A) follow a type I curve, while oysters and fish (answers C and D) follow a type III survivorship curve.

13. **D**

14. **A**

15. **C**

16. **B**

〉 Rapid Review

The following terms are important in this chapter:

Population: collection of individuals of the same species living in the same geographic area.

Community: collection of populations of species in a geographic area.

Ecosystem: community + environment.

Biosphere: communities + ecosystems of planet.

Biotic components: living organisms of ecosystem.

Abiotic components: nonliving players in ecosystem.

Dispersion patterns: **clumped dispersion** (animals live in packs spaced from each other—cattle), **uniform distribution** (species are evenly spaced out across an area, e.g., birds on a wire), **random distribution** (species are randomly distributed across an area, e.g., trees in a forest).

Biotic potential: maximum growth rate for a population.

Carrying capacity: maximum number of individuals that a population can sustain in a given environment.

Limiting factors: factors that keep population size in check: **density-dependent** (food, waste, disease), **density-independent** (weather, natural disasters).

Population growth: **exponential growth** (J-shaped curve, unlimited growth), **logistic growth** (S-shaped curve, limited growth).

Life history strategies: *K*-**selected populations** (constant size, low reproductive rate, extensive postnatal care—humans); *R*-**selected populations** (rapid growth, J-curve style, little postnatal care, reproduce quickly, die quickly—bacteria).

Survivorship curves: show survival rates for different-aged members of a population:

* *Type I*: live long life, until age is reached where death rate increases rapidly—humans, large mammals.

- *Type II*: constant death rate across the age spectrum—lizards, hydra, small mammals.
- *Type III*: steep downward death rate for young individuals that flattens out at certain age—fish, oysters.

Forms of Species Interaction

- *Parasitism*: one organism benefits at another's expense (tapeworms and humans).
- *Commensalism*: one organism benefits while the other is unaffected (cattle egrets and cattle).
- *Mutualism*: both organisms reap benefits from the interaction (acacia trees and ants, lichen).
- *Competition*: both species are harmed by the interaction (**intraspecific** vs. **interspecific**).
- *Predation*: one species, the predator, hunts the other, the prey.

Defense Mechanisms

- *Cryptic coloration*: coloring scheme that allows organism to blend into colors of environment.
- *Deceptive markings*: patterns that cause an animal to appear larger or more dangerous than it really is.
- *Aposematic coloration*: warning coloration adopted by animals that possess a chemical defense mechanism.
- *Batesian mimicry*: animal that is harmless copies the appearance of an animal that is dangerous.
- *Müllerian mimicry*: two aposemetrically colored species have a similar coloration pattern.

Primary succession: occurs in area devoid of life that contains no soil; **pioneer species** come in, add nutrients, and are replaced by future species, which attract animals to the area, thus adding more nutrients; constant changing of guards until the **climax community** is reached and a steady-state equilibrium is achieved.

Secondary succession: occurs in area that once had stable life but was disturbed by major force (fire).

Biomes: The Special Facts

We recommend that you read the biome material in the chapter for more detail.

- *Desert*: driest land biome.
- *Taiga*: lengthy cold, wet winters; lots of conifers.
- *Temperate grasslands*: most fertile soil of all.
- *Tundra*: permafrost, cold winters, short shrubs.
- *Savanna*: grasslands, home to herbivores.
- *Deciduous forest*: cold winters/warm summers.
- *Tropical forest*: greatest diversity of species.
- *Water biomes*: freshwater and marine biomes of earth.

Trophic levels: hierarchy of energy levels on a planet; energy level decreases from bottom to top (Figure 18.7); primary producers (bottom) → primary consumers (herbivores) → secondary consumers → tertiary consumers → decomposers.

Laboratory Review

IN THIS CHAPTER

Summary: This chapter covers the 13 laboratory experiments that are included in the AP Biology curriculum.

Key Ideas

✪ Hands-on lab work and understanding the process of science are central parts of AP Biology. Translation—LEARN THESE WELL!

✪ Read the summaries found here and review the work that you did on the labs during the year.

✪ If you missed one of these labs in class, or just do not feel comfortable with the material even after reading this chapter, ask your teacher to go over the lab with you.

Introduction

In this chapter we take a look at each of the 13 lab experiments that are included in the AP Biology curriculum. We summarize the major objectives from each experiment and the major skills and conclusions that you should remember. This chapter is important, so do not just brush it aside if lab experiments are not your cup of tea. Experimental (data) analysis will be heavily emphasized on the exam, in both the multiple-choice and the essay sections. Of course, the questions will not be an exact duplication of the experiment, but they will test your understanding of the objectives and main ideas that are discussed in this chapter. So, only 13 experiments separate us and the end of the review material for this exam.

All of the investigations in this chapter have multiple parts, including the opportunity for you to go crazy and create your own investigation. We have no idea what kind of mad-scientist experiment you might design, so we will instead focus on the more straightforward portions of these labs, including a summary of what the key ideas are from each investigation.

Investigation 1: Artificial Selection

BIG IDEA 1
Evolution

This lab focuses on the role of *differential reproduction* in natural selection, meaning some organisms in a population reproduce more than others and leave more offspring. But instead of it being "natural" selection, it's "artificial" because *you* get to choose which organisms are allowed to reproduce!

Basic Setup

For natural selection to occur, first there needs to be variation in a population, right? Well, look closely at the Wisconsin Fast Plants that you'll be working with. Do you see any trait that you could easily measure (e.g., leaf color, hairiness, height)? Are there any variations in this particular trait? It should not be something that is a clear-cut yes or no, but rather a trait that exhibits a range. Now you get to make selection decisions! You will choose the top (or bottom) 10 percent of your plants with this trait, and those lucky few are the ones allowed to reproduce. You will transfer pollen between this pool of "winners" and, once the seeds develop, plant and grow your second generation of plants. Once again, you will measure your chosen trait in this second population.

Results

In this experiment you are essentially choosing which genes are passed to the next generation. By artificially selecting, say, only the purplest of the plants, you are ensuring that the next generation will have inherited those "purpley" genes. You will hopefully observe an increase (or decrease, depending on your investigation) of your chosen trait in the second population of plants. This is called *directional selection*. Considering that one of the requirements of this class is your ability to graph and analyze data, it would probably be an excellent idea for you to create a bar graph to compare the quantity of your trait between these two generations. Are the means significantly different?

Don't forget to keep this a controlled experiment! Did you measure the trait of your first-generation plants when they were nine days old? Remember to measure the second generation *at the same age, using the same method.*

Key Skills

- Graph your data.
- Explain how natural selection acts on phenotypes.
- Use data to show how a measurable trait is changing in your plant population.

Investigation 2: Mathematical Modeling: Hardy-Weinberg

BIG IDEA 1
Evolution

This investigation lets you build upon what you learned from Investigation 1: the idea of natural selection and how it changes a population. If you truly wanted to see if a population was evolving, you would track the frequency of alleles and how they change from generation to generation. To do so, you first need to determine what your population's alleles look like *right now*, before any funky evolutionary stuff happens. This information can then be used as a point of comparison to see if the allelic frequencies are indeed changing in your population. The Hardy-Weinberg equilibrium is used to describe a population that is in stasis, or not evolving. Your goal in this lab is to model how allele frequencies change in a generation of some imaginary population, and you will do this using a computer model.

Basic Setup

On the AP Biology exam, will you have to open up a spreadsheet file and correctly enter a formula? No. Will you have to understand how to use the Hardy-Weinberg equilibrium and how to correctly analyze the data obtained? You bet! The idea to understand is how the fitness of an allele affects its frequency in a population. For example, there are two alleles for a given gene: A and a. If a population is in Hardy-Weinberg equilibrium (i.e., not evolving), and the frequency of both alleles is 0.5 (meaning one half of the alleles in this population's gene pool is the dominant A form, whereas the other half is in the recessive a form), then it will remain that way for gazillions of generations. But how could you make that ratio change? That, my friend, is evolution, and that is the point of this lab. Using tools such as computer programs and spreadsheets, you can model how a hypothetical gene pool changes from generation to generation.

Results

Though the bulk of this lab was dedicated to creating your spreadsheet, the real investigation begins when you get to tweak your non-evolving population. The equations you have to know for this experiment are $p + q = 1$ and $p^2 + 2pq + q^2 = 1$. Chapter 12 lists the five conditions required for the existence of Hardy-Weinberg equilibrium:

1. No mutations
2. No gene flow
3. No genetic drift (large population size)
4. No natural selection (so that the traits are neutral; none gives an advantage or disadvantage)
5. Random mating

If any of these five conditions does not hold true, then the population will experience microevolution, and the frequencies of the alleles will be subject to change.

Using your computer model, you can design an experiment to measure the effect of selection, heterozygote advantage, and genetic drift:

- *Selection.* Imagine that an individual homozygous recessive for a condition does not survive to reproduce. Because the aa offspring would not survive to reproduce, this will cause a shift in allele frequencies to include more A children and fewer a children.
- *Heterozygote advantage.* This is a situation in which being heterozygous for a condition provides some benefit (e.g., sickle cell allele in malarial regions). In this case, the allele will still decrease, but not as fast as in the selection example.
- *Genetic drift.* Imagine that 60 percent of your hypothetical population were killed in some horrific environmental disaster. This would leave the remaining 40 percent to continue breeding and passing on genes to the next generation. The random nature in which organisms are eliminated can lead to a shift in the allele frequency and the p and q will probably change depending on the genotype of those who are left behind.

There are two questions to ponder as you finish this experiment:

1. *Why is it so difficult to eliminate a recessive allele?* It is difficult because the allele remains in the population, hidden as part of the heterozygous condition, safe from selection, which can act only against genes that are expressed. So, although the q for a population may decline, it will not disappear completely because of the pq individuals.

2. *Why does heterozygote advantage protect recessive genes from being eliminated?* Those who are heterozygous for the condition are receiving some benefit. For example, those who have sickle trait are protected against malaria. This positive benefit for heterozygous individuals helps keep the recessive condition alive in the population.

Key Skills

- Use data from a changing population and analyze it using the Hardy-Weinberg equation.
- Explain how data from using this equation demonstrates genetic drift and the effects of selection.

Investigation 3: Comparing DNA Sequences to Understand Evolutionary Relationships with BLAST

BIG IDEA 1
Evolution

Say you found a brand-new fossilized creature buried in your backyard, and you want to find its closest living relative. Or maybe you identified a single gene that causes disease in hedgehogs and you want to know if that same gene is found in humans. This lab focuses on the use of BLAST (Basic Local Alignment Search Tool) as a tool to answer such questions. In addition, it incorporates the use of cladograms. A cladogram is a visual representation of the evolutionary relatedness of a species. In this investigation, you will use BLAST to generate the information needed to construct a cladogram.

Basic Setup

Given a genetic sequence, you are required to use the online BLAST software to compare it to other gene sequences already in their gigantic database. Results will show a ranking of the most closely related organisms (and what percentage of their base pairs actually match up). Just as in the previous lab, you won't have a computer available to you during the AP exam, so no, you won't have to actually know how to use BLAST while taking the test. You will, however, most likely need to analyze data obtained from a hypothetical BLAST query and, from those results, generate a cladogram depicting evolutionary relatedness.

Results

By determining the percent similarity of an unknown gene with those from other organisms, you should be able to then place your unknown creature within a cladogram to show evolutionary relatedness. For example, say you had a table showing the percent similarity of "gene X" in humans versus four other species (see Table 19.1).

If you drew a cladogram showing the evolutionary relationship, it would look something like Figure 19.1.

Table 19.1   Percent similarity between gene X in humans and other species.

SPECIES	GENE PERCENT SIMILARITY COMPARED TO HUMANS
A	98%
B	91%
C	70%
D	52%

Figure 19.1   Cladogram for percent similarity between gene X in humans and other species. The closer two species reside on a clade, the closer they are genetically related.

Key Skills

- Explain the relationship between genetic sequences and evolutionary relatedness.
- Draw and/or analyze a cladogram that shows evolutionary relationships.

Investigation 4: Diffusion and Osmosis

> **BIG IDEA 2**
>
> *Cellular Processes: Energy, Communication, and Homeostasis*

This investigation draws on information covered in Chapter 6, Cells. If you feel uncomfortable with this material, take a few moments to flip back to Chapter 6 and scan through the information about diffusion, osmosis, and cell transport. In summary, osmosis occurs from an area of high water potential to an area of low water potential. In a given solution, the higher the solute concentration, the lower that solution's water potential.

Part 1: Surface Area and Cell Size

Basic Setup for Part 1

Besides turning your fingers blue, this lab will demonstrate the relationship between surface area and volume and how this ratio affects diffusion rates in a cell. Your cell model is a block of agar that contains an indicator dye that changes color when the pH drops. You're given a chunk of this blue agar to carve into three different block sizes, each with differing surface area–to–volume ratios (SA:V). Each block is dropped into a solution, and as the liquid diffuses into the agar, the pH causes a change in agar color. This enables you to easily track the amount of time it takes for diffusion to be completed.

Results for Part 1

It's all about a large surface area–to–volume ratio. The block with the biggest SA:V ratio wins the race. For example, say you have three sizes of agar blocks:

> block 1 = 1 cm × 1 cm × 1 cm
> block 2 = 2 cm × 2 cm × 2 cm
> block 3 = 1 cm × 1 cm × 8 cm

You should be able to calculate both the volume (cm^3) and the surface area (cm^2) for each of these blocks. (Remember: formulas will be provided for you on the AP exam!)

BLOCK	VOLUME (cm^3)	SURFACE AREA (cm^2)	SA:V
1	1	6	6
2	8	24	3
3	8	34	4.25

Notice that even though blocks 2 and 3 have the same volume, their surface areas are different. This results in diffusion taking longer in block 2 than it does in block 3.

Key Concept

- A high SA:V ratio is important for any cell that relies on a high diffusion rate. If you were a tiny bacterium, your health and well-being would be dependent on quickly getting good stuff in (glucose for cellular respiration!) and bad stuff out (metabolic waste). The linings of your small intestine and lungs have many folds in order to create the highest surface area possible in the smallest amount of space and thereby facilitate diffusion of food monomers or oxygen molecules.

Part 2: Modeling Diffusion and Osmosis

Basic Setup for Part 2

Now you get to create a model of a cell using dialysis tubing. Just like a real cell, the tubing is selectively permeable to water and some solutes. The point of this lab investigation is to use different solutions to model how water potential influences osmosis.

Results for Part 2

Say you filled your dialysis bag with a 1 Molar (1 M) sucrose solution, weighed it, and placed it in a beaker of 1 M NaCl solution. After 30 minutes, you weigh the bag again and—voilà!—it got lighter! That means it lost some water, right? Can you use water potential to show why that makes sense? Recall that you can calculate the solute potential for a solution with this equation:

$$\Psi_S = iCRT, \text{ where i = ionization constant and C = molarity}$$

The molarities are equal for both of these solutions, so the ionization constant is the deciding factor. NaCl ionizes and sucrose does not! So for NaCl, i = 2, whereas for sucrose i = 1. Therefore, the NaCl solution has a higher solute potential; or, in other words, it is a hypertonic solution compared to your dialysis tubing "cell." Therefore, water will diffuse out of the bag into the surrounding NaCl solution.

Key Concepts

- Osmosis occurs from an area of high water potential to low water potential.
- A cell's environment allows you to make predictions about molecular movement through cell membranes.

Part 3: Observing Osmosis in Living Cells

Basic Setup for Part 3

Here you get to work with pretty, color-coded (unlabeled) sucrose solutions ranging from 0.0 M up to 1.0 M, and use potato cores to figure out the relative concentrations of these solutions. To take it one step further, you can then calculate percent change in weight of your potato cores and determine the water potential of the potato tissue. Remember that the bigger the difference in water potential between a cell and the solution, the bigger the movement of water (either into or out of the cells).

Results for Part 3

Once you calculate the potatoes' percent change in weight for each of the unknown solutions, you can arrange them from most negative to most positive. A supernegative percent change in weight indicates a significant loss of water; a highly hypertonic solution increases water loss from cells. The more negative the number, the higher the molarity of the solution! The same is true for superpositive percent change in weight. That means the potato cores gained a lot of water, which happens in a hypotonic solution. The greater the weight gain, the lower the molarity of the solution.

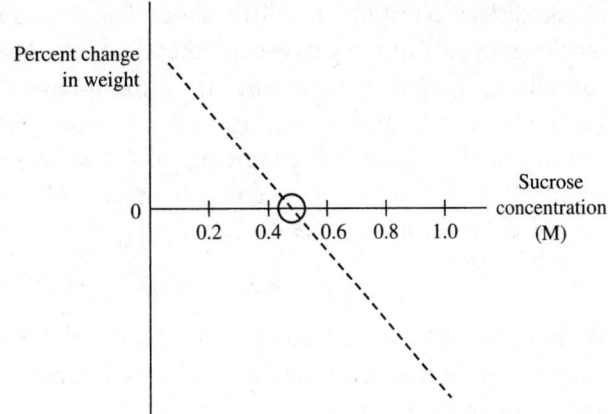

Figure 19.2   Potato core change in weight.

What if you wanted to determine the actual water potential (molarity) of the potato? It's easy, once you remember that if the water potential of the solution equals that of the cells, there is no net change in weight. If you graph your percent changes in weight, you can estimate the potato's water potential (see Figure 19.2).

The point where the line crosses the *x*-axis indicates the molarity when there would be no net change in weight. Therefore, 0.5 M is the approximate molarity (or, in this case, water potential) of your potato!

One final thought about your data: Although we often focus on quantitative (numerical) measurements in our labs, qualitative observations are still very important. When you removed your potato cores from the solution, did they feel different? Floppy and bendy? That would suggest that the cells lost water because they were in a hypertonic solution (the higher molarities). Was the potato core rigid, and would it snap if you bent it? That would suggest that it was in a hypotonic (low molarity) solution and water flowed into the cells, increasing their turgor pressure.

Key Concepts (for All Three Procedures)

- A high surface area–to–volume ratio increases diffusion rates.
- A cell that relies on diffusion would evolve to have a high SA:V ratio.
- Water diffuses from an area of high to low water potential.

Investigation 5: Photosynthesis

BIG IDEA 2

Cellular Processes: Energy, Communication, and Homeostasis

Photosynthesis is a complex (and possibly confusing) metabolic process through which autotrophs generate glucose by first converting the sun's light energy into the chemical form that all living cells use (ATP). If you wish to design a lab to track the rate of photosynthesis, how would you do it? Measure glucose production? Carbon dioxide use? Maybe focus on the light reaction's reduction of the electron carrier NAD+ into its reduced form (NADH) as in the DPIP lab? Well, some of the best experiments are the simplest, so let's watch little pieces of a leaf float in water as oxygen is produced as a by-product of photosynthesis.

Basic Setup

This is a cool way to measure photosynthetic rates, based on the amount of oxygen produced. Little leaf disks are put in a large syringe with some slightly soapy water (this helps break surface tension). The little disks float on top of the water, which introduces the challenging part of the lab: getting them to sink. A vacuum must be created in the syringe to pull out the atmospheric gases from the spongy mesophyll layer in the leaf tissue. This takes a bit of trial and error, but once it is accomplished, the disks will slowly drift to the bottom of the syringe. The contents of the syringe are dumped into a cup filled with a sodium bicarbonate solution and put under light. As more photosynthesis occurs, more oxygen is produced:

$$6CO_2 + 6H_2O \rightarrow C_6H_{12}O_6 + 6O_2$$

If you look closely, you can see tiny bubbles forming on your leaf disks! Once enough oxygen is produced (and caught within the internal leaf space), the little disks will begin to rise to the top very slowly.

Here's a question: if your leaf pieces are photosynthesizing, where are they getting the necessary carbon dioxide? When sodium bicarbonate ionizes in water, it provides an alternative source of carbon dioxide for the plant.

Results

The investigative part of the lab allows you to explore variables that you think might influence photosynthesis in your leaf disks. Do the levels of CO_2 effect photosynthesis? How about amount of light? Regardless of your choice of variable, perform the same leaf disk analysis and compare the amount of time it takes for half of your disks to rise (ET_{50}, or estimated time it takes 50 percent of the disks to float) in both your control and experimental groups.

Key Concepts

- A lot of photosynthesis means a lot of oxygen production.
- Light increases the rate of photosynthesis.
- Carbon dioxide was provided by dissolved sodium bicarbonate.

Investigation 6: Cellular Respiration

BIG IDEA 2

Cellular Processes: Energy, Communication, and Homeostasis

If you would like to see how different environmental conditions affect an organism's respiration rate, this is the lab for you! In this investigation you will use a respirometer (or microrespirometer) to track the respiration rate of seeds. Based on the equation for cellular respiration, $C_6H_{12}O_6 + 6O_2 \rightarrow 6CO_2 + 6H_2O$, how would you measure respiration rates?

There are, in fact, three ways to measure respiration:

1. *Oxygen consumption:* how much O_2 is actually consumed
2. *Carbon dioxide production:* how much CO_2 is actually produced
3. *Energy released during respiration:* how much energy is released

Basic Setup

This experiment examines germinating peas by measuring the volume of gas that surrounds the peas at certain intervals in an effort to determine the rate of respiration. Two gases contribute to the volume around the pea: O_2 and CO_2. How can we use the amount of oxygen consumed during respiration as our measuring point if CO_2 is present as well? Something needs to be done with the CO_2 released during respiration. Otherwise we would not get a true representation of how much the volume is changing as a result of oxygen consumption. The CO_2 would skew the numbers by making it appear as if less O_2 were being consumed.

The CO_2 problem can be handled by adding potassium hydroxide, which reacts with CO_2 to produce K_2CO_3. This reaction allows us to limit the number of variables that could be affecting the volume around our beloved peas to

1. Change in the volume of oxygen
2. Change in the temperature (PV = nRT)
3. Change in the pressure of the surrounding atmosphere

Aerobic respiration requires and uses oxygen. So, one would expect the volume of oxygen around the pea to decline as respiration occurs. The reactions of interest for this experiment occur in a tubelike device known as a **respirometer**. To calculate the change in volume that occurs with these peas, one first has to measure the initial volume around the peas. A control group must then be set up that consists of peas that are not currently germinating and will have a rate of respiration lower than that of germinating seeds. This will give the experimenter a baseline with which to compare the respiration rate of the germinating seeds. Since temperature and pressure are also able to affect the volume around the peas, it is important to set up another control group that can calculate the change in volume that is due to temperature and pressure as opposed to respiration. Any changes in this control group should be subtracted from the changes found in the germinating seeds to determine how much of the volume change is actually due to oxygen consumption and respiration.

Just a side thought: Can you imagine how awkward it could have been if one of Mendel's lab partners had decided to run this experiment? I can see it now: Mendel walks into the lab and asks, "Has anyone seen my peas? After seven long years, I've nearly completed my research. Just need to tally up that last generation of peas. . . . Very exciting. . . . Hmm. . . . I thought my peas were sitting here on this desk by my respirometer."

Results

1. Germinating seeds consume *more* oxygen than do nongerminating seeds. This makes sense, because they have more reactions going on.
2. Seeds germinating at a lower temperature consume *less* oxygen than do seeds germinating at a higher temperature.
3. You can determine how much oxygen is consumed by watching how much water is drawn into the pipettes as the experiment proceeds. (Refer to your classroom lab manual if you are confused by the pipette portion of this lab.) This water is drawn in as a result of the drop in pressure caused by the consumption of oxygen during respiration.

Key Concepts

- A respirometer measures respiration rates by tracking the amount of oxygen being used in cellular respiration.
- Warm conditions usually speed up cellular respiration; cold slows it down.

Investigation 7: Cell Division: Mitosis and Meiosis

BIG IDEA 3

Genetics and Information Transfer

This experiment draws on information found in Chapter 9, Cell Division.

Part 1: Onion Roots Treated with a Mitosis-Inducing Chemical

Basic Setup for Part 1

Your goal is to see if there is a greater number of cells undergoing mitosis in root cells treated with lectin, a chemical that induces mitosis. Either you or your teacher will prepare slides of these root cells, and you will then count the number of cells either in interphase or in mitosis. Since you need a point of comparison, you will do similar counts with root cells that have not been treated with this chemical (the control).

Results for Part 1

So, how are you supposed to estimate how much time cells on a slide in front of you spend in either mitosis or interphase? Say, for example, that you record your findings and get the following breakdown: For your control, of 300 cells examined, 268 are in interphase and 32 cells are in one of the stages of mitosis (prophase, metaphase, anaphase, or telophase). This would mean that the cell spent 89.3 percent of its time in interphase. At any moment in time, 89.3 percent of the cells are in interphase. Here's how to get that number. Take the number of cells in interphase, 268, and divide that by the number of cells examined, 300. The result is 0.893. Move the decimal point two places to the right to get the percentage, 89.3 percent. By the same logic, these data also show that 10.7 percent are in mitosis. For comparison, let's say the chemically treated slide had 210 cells in interphase and 40 in mitosis (for a total of 250 cells examined).

Now, once you count your mitotic versus interphase cells for both treated and untreated roots, you need to use chi-square analysis to check if the difference is significant:

$$x^2 = \sum \frac{(o-e)^2}{e}$$

Do not panic! Even though that equation may seem intimidating, it's really not that bad. First, determine how many of your treated cells would be in mitosis *if the chemical didn't have any effect*. In other words, if 10.7 percent of your control cells were stuck in mitosis, you'd expect that same percentage in your treated group: (250 treated cells) × (0.107) = ~27 cells in mitosis. That leaves the remaining 223 cells in interphase (if you didn't expect that mitosis-inducing chemical to do its job). So now you use chi-square analysis to compare what you actually saw in your chemically treated cells (40 in mitosis and 210 in interphase) to see if there are, in fact, significantly more cells stuck in mitosis. In other words, your null hypothesis is that the treatment did not make a difference. If you find that the chi-square value is greater than the critical value, you reject this null hypothesis in favor of the experimental hypothesis (the chemical likely *did* make a difference). See Table 19.2.

As you can see, your chi-square value is 0.758 + 6.26 = 7.02. To determine your critical value, you must choose a p value (usually 0.05) and the degrees of freedom. The degrees of freedom (df) equals the number of groups minus one. In this lab, there are two groups, interphase and mitosis; therefore, df = 2 − 1, or 1. Based on the chi-square table (which will be provided for you on the AP exam), your degrees of freedom equals 3.38. Since your calculated chi-square value (7.02) was bigger than 3.38, you can reject the null hypothesis that said the treatment made *no* difference. The chemical did increase the number of cells in mitosis.

Table 19.2 Chi-Square Table for Investigation 7.

	# OBSERVED (o)	# EXPECTED (e)	(o − e)	(o − e)²	(o − e)²/e
Interphase cells	210	223	−13	169	0.758
Mitosis cells	40	27	13	169	6.26

Key Skill

• Analyze data using chi-square analysis. You can be sure that the AP exam will have at least one question asking you to do this. This lab is excellent practice for such a question.

Part 2: Meiosis and Crossover in *Sordaria*

Basic Setup and Results for Part 2

The title to this section makes *Sordaria* sound like some posh vacation spot in Europe. In reality it is a haploid ascomycete fungus. Anyway, the final portion of this experiment looks at the crossover that occurs during meiosis of this fungus and briefly discusses how recombination maps can be created using such data. Meiosis in *Sordaria* results in the formation of eight haploid **ascospores,** each of which can develop into a new haploid fungus. Crossover in *Sordaria* can be observed by making hybrids between wild-type and mutant strains. Wild-type *Sordaria* have black ascospores, and mutants have different col-ored ascospores (e.g., tan). When mycelia of these two strains come together and undergo meiosis, and if no crossover occurs, the asci that develop will contain four black and four tan ascospores in a 4:4 pattern. If crossover occurs, the ratio will change to either 2:2:2:2 or 2:4:2.

Chapter 10, Heredity, discusses gene maps constructed from crossover frequencies. You would construct the map here by first determining the percentage of asci that showed crossover. Referring to Figure 19.3, count the number of 2:2:2:2 and 2:4:2 asci and divide that sum into the total number of offspring. This result multiplied by 100 will give the crossover percentage. This number can then be used to determine how far away the gene is from the centromere. The crossover percentage is divided by 2 to determine this distance because a crossover involves only half the spores in each ascus.

Key Skill

• Explain how meiosis and crossing over leads to increased genetic diversity.

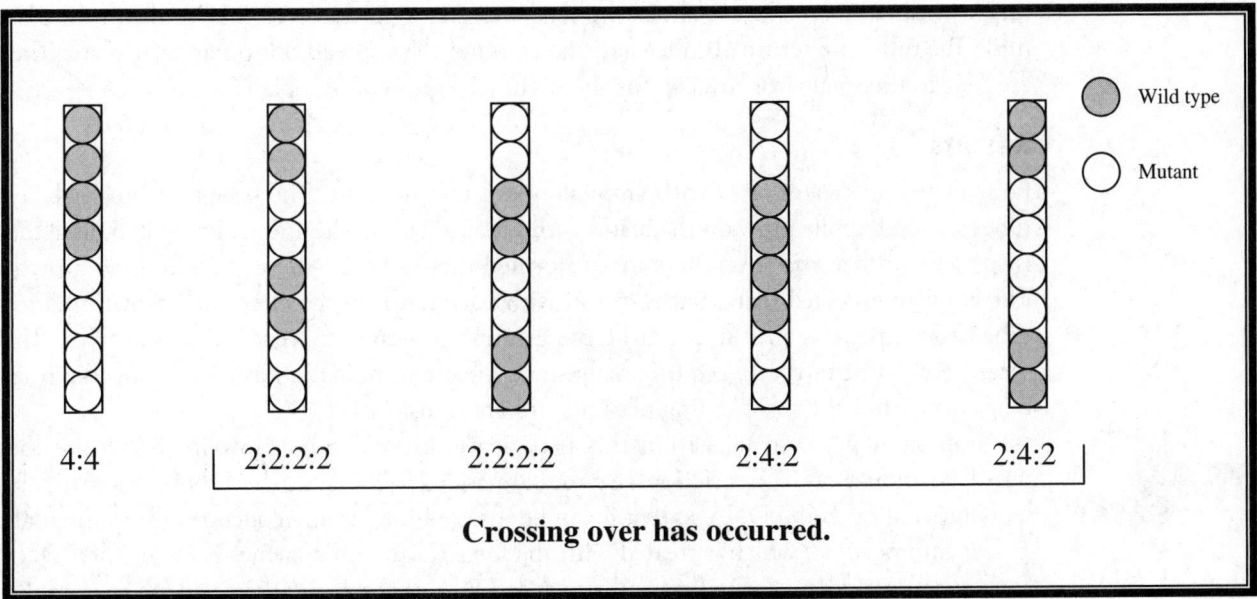

Figure 19.3 Crossover patterns in *Sordaria*.

Investigation 8: Biotechnology: Bacterial Transformation

BIG IDEA 3
Genetics and Information Transfer

This experiment deals with material from Chapter 11, Molecular Genetics. This is the kind of experiment that can make you feel like a biotech junkie. Here, you use plasmids to move DNA from one cell to another cell—**transformation.** You get to play with restriction enzymes, *E. coli* (*Escherichia coli*—eww), and gel electrophoresis.

Full understanding of this experiment requires a basic knowledge of

1. What vectors are and how they are made
2. What gel electrophoresis is and how it works
3. What a restriction enzyme is and why it is so important to the field of biotechnology

You will find all this information waiting for you in Chapter 11. We are not going to cave in and explain to you now what those things are. That is something you should do on your own.

OK, we'll tell you now. . . . *Escherichia coli* (usually abbreviated *E. coli*) is a bacteria that is present in everyone's intestinal tract. It grows in the laboratory as well and contains extrachromosomal DNA circles called **plasmids.** This experiment deals with the process of *transformation*: the uptake of foreign DNA from the surrounding environment. This is made possible by the presence of proteins on the surface of cells that snag pieces of DNA from around the cell; these DNA pieces are from closely related species.

The goal of this experiment is to take a bacterial strain that has ampicillin resistance, and transfer the gene for this resistance to a strain that dies when exposed to ampicillin. After attempting to transform the bacteria, the experimenter can check to see if it was successful by growing the potentially transformed bacteria on a plate containing ampicillin. If it grows as if all is well, the transformation has succeeded. If nothing grows, something has gone wrong.

Basic Setup

A colony of *E. coli* is added to each of two test tubes. In one tube a solution is added that contains a plasmid that carries the ampicillin-resistance gene; the other tube receives no such plasmid. The waiting game follows, and after 15 minutes on ice, the two tubes are quickly heated in an effort to shock the cells into taking in the foreign DNA from the plasmid. The tubes are returned to ice and the colonies then spread out on an agar plate. They are sent to the incubator to sleep for the night and grow on the plate.

Results

Four plates are created: two with ampicillin and two without. The bacteria from both test tubes should happily grow on the plates without ampicillin. The ampicillin-coated plate that is spread with bacteria from the nontransformed tube is bare—there is, indeed, no growth. The ampicillin-coated plate that is spread with bacteria from the attempted-transformation tube shows growth . . . it may not be the greatest growth ever seen, but it is growth. This means that some of the *E. coli* originally susceptible to ampicillin have picked up the resistance gene from the surrounding plasmid and are transformed.

KEY IDEA

Important point to take from this part of the experiment: "How in the world does transformation work?" Restriction enzymes are added, which cut the DNA at a particular sequence and open the DNA so that it can be inserted into another such region in the main *E. coli* chromosome, which is treated with the *same* restriction enzyme. If the opened DNA from the plasmid happens to find and attach to DNA of the *E. coli* that is added to the tube, hallelujah, transformation occurs. In order for this transformation to succeed, the *E. coli* must be **competent,** which means ready to accept the foreign DNA from the environment.

This competence is ensured by treating the cells with calcium or magnesium. Don't worry too much about how this competence business really works. Just know that bacteria must be competent for transformation to occur.

Key Concepts

- DNA works the same for all cells, both eukaryotic and prokaryotic.
- By adding a gene (changing an organism's genotype), you can change how it looks (its phenotype).
- Environmental factors can affect gene expression! If lactose is present, *E. coli*'s lac operon will turn on.

Investigation 9: Biotechnology: Restriction Enzyme Analysis of DNA

BIG IDEA 3
Genetics and Information Transfer

The three activities in this lab all work together to analyze and compare DNA sequences. For example, after cutting DNA samples from two different people with the same restriction enzymes, you would see that the RFLP patterns produced by gel electrophoresis are different. Do you have no idea what that last sentence even means? Read on . . .

Activity 1: Restriction Enzymes

Restriction enzymes are special because they are very picky about their job—they cut DNA at very specific sequences, called *restriction sites*. Many restriction sites are a 4- to 10-nucleotide base pair (bp) palindrome, a sequence that reads the same from either direction. If a restriction enzyme cuts exactly in the center of the restriction site, it will create blunt ends; if it cuts the backbone in two places, the pieces will have single-stranded overhanging "sticky" ends with exposed hydrogen bonds. If you cut two different DNA sequences with the same restriction enzyme, and if sticky ends are created, you could use ligase to then glue two sequences together, even if the DNA was not originally from the same organism! That is called a recombinant DNA molecule, and it is the basis of many biotechnological wonders. For example, if you isolate the human insulin gene with a restriction enzyme, and use that same enzyme to cut open a bacterial plasmid, you could glue the human gene into the plasmid. That's how therapeutic insulin is produced today (thank you, *E. coli*).

Activity 2: DNA Mapping Using Restriction Enzymes

Say you wanted to identify somebody based on his or her DNA. You hear about it all the time, but how is it actually done? Using those restriction enzymes we just talked about, you can cut up a sample of DNA and look at the sizes of the distinct little pieces you have created (this requires gel electrophoresis—more on that in a bit). Everyone has a unique pattern of different lengths of DNA fragments. Restriction mapping is a way to create an organism's unique genetic "fingerprint." These unique DNA fragments are called restriction fragment length polymorphisms (RFLPs). But how do you arrange these little pieces in such a way that you can compare the DNA of two or more people? Once again, read on . . .

Activity 3: Gel Electrophoresis

Another important biotechnological tool is gel electrophoresis. Gel electrophoresis is a lab technique used to separate DNA on the basis of size. When there is an electric current running from one end of the gel to the other, the fragments of DNA dumped into the wells at the head of the gel will migrate to the other side, with the smaller pieces moving the fastest. The more voltage there is running through the gel, the *faster* the DNA will migrate. The longer the voltage is run through the gel, the *farther* the DNA will migrate. The more DNA cut by the same restriction enzymes you put into each well, the *thicker* the bands will be on the gel. If you reverse the flow of the current on the gel, the DNA will migrate in the opposite direction. The DNA just wants to go toward the positive charge . . . optimists, we suppose.

> ### Important Facts About Electrophoresis
> 1. DNA migrates from negative to positive charges.
> 2. Smaller DNA travels faster than larger DNA.
> 3. The DNA migrates only when the current is running.
> 4. The more voltage that runs through the gel, the faster the DNA migrates.
> 5. The more time the current runs through the gel, the farther the DNA goes.

Key Concepts

- Understand how to use restriction enzymes and gel electrophoresis to create genetic profiles.
- The pattern made by RFLP using gel electrophoresis will look different for each individual.

Investigation 10: Energy Dynamics

BIG IDEA 4
Interactions

You will create a simple model of an ecosystem, with a single producer (plant) and a single consumer (caterpillars). Producers are so important because they capture the sun's energy and convert it into a form that can be used by us nonphotosynthetic organisms (consumers). The term **gross productivity** refers to the total amount of energy captured by producers. The **net productivity** is the amount of that energy that is actually stored by the plant (and thus is available for consumers to munch on).

As you may recall, the second law of thermodynamics says that energy transfer is never 100 percent efficient. This lab demonstrates that fact by tracking energy as it travels through a food chain. Specifically, how much of a plant's energy is actually used by the caterpillars who eat it? How much is applied to the caterpillar's growth, and how much is burned up in cellular respiration? Also, be aware that this lab has the best procedure direction of the entire year: you get to mass the frass (more on that in a bit).

Basic Setup

You will determine the total weight of all your caterpillars at the beginning of the investigation and then, after they feed for three days, weigh them again. Their change in mass was fueled by the plants they ate. The question is what percentage of that plant's energy was actually turned into caterpillar mass? If you determine the plant energy consumed by each larva, and also take into consideration the amount of their food that wasn't actually used (caterpillar poop, also called "frass"), then you're left with the amount of the producer's energy that was used for the caterpillar's metabolism. Furthermore, if you knew the amount of plant energy consumed by the larva, and subtracted from that both the energy lost in the poop and energy used for the caterpillar's increase in mass, what you're left with is the energy used in respiration.

Results

You should find that, no, energy transfer isn't perfect. All of that plant's energy was not, in fact, transferred to and used by the caterpillars.

Key Concepts

- Understand how this lab relates to the idea of how living organisms use free energy.
- Biomass is the mass of living tissue minus any water weight.

Investigation 11: Transpiration

BIG IDEA 4
Interactions

This experiment takes the concepts found in Chapter 6 of the text and applies them to the material in Chapter 14, Plants. You might want to review the material on plant anatomy and vascular tissue before you begin.

Here is just a quick reminder of how water moves from the soil to the leaves and branches of a plant. Three minor players in the transport of water are capillary action, osmosis, and root pressure. Water is drawn into the xylem (the water superhighway for the plant) by osmosis. The osmotic driving force is created by the absorption of minerals from the soil, increasing the solute concentration within the xylem. Once in the xylem, root pressure aids in pushing the water a small way up the superhighway. The main driving force for the movement of water in a plant from root to shoot is transpiration. When water evaporates from the plant, it causes an upward tug on the remaining water in the xylem, pulling it toward the shoots. The cohesive nature of water molecules contributes to this transpiration-induced driving force of water through the xylem of the plants. Water molecules like to stick together, and when one of their kind is pulled in a certain direction, the rest seem to follow.

This experiment examines various environmental factors that affect the rate of transpiration: air movement, humidity, light intensity, and temperature. The rate of transpiration increases with increased air movement, decreased humidity, increased light intensity, and increased temperature. It is not hard to remember that increased temperature leads to increased transpiration—think about how much more you sweat when it is hot. It also makes sense that decreased humidity would lead to an increase in the rate of transpiration. When it is less humid, there is less moisture in the air, and thus there is more of a driving force for water to leave the plant. Imagine that you are standing with a 40-watt bulb shining on your neck, and then a 100-watt bulb shining on your neck. The higher-wattage bulb will probably cause you to sweat more. The same thing with plants: the higher the intensity of the light, the more transpiration that occurs. Air movement is less obvious. If there is good airflow, then evaporated water on leaves is removed more quickly, increasing the driving force for more water to transpire from the plant.

Basic Setup

One easy and straightforward way to measure water loss is by measuring the entire plant's mass every day for about a week. This "whole plant" method requires you to tightly seal a plastic sandwich bag around the root ball so the only water loss is through the leaves. Furthermore, if the poor plant is even *thinking* about flowering, you need to ensure that it does not do so (pull off any flowers or buds). Once you understand this basic setup, the real fun begins: inquiry! Think of some variables that may affect transpiration from your poor plants. Sun? Wind? It's up to you. One plant will be your control, and every other plant will be assigned a single variable. Take the weights of your little guys as soon as they're all ready to go; this will be your *time zero* weights. Then measure the weights again 24 hours later, for as many days as your teacher indicates. Remember that if a leaf falls off during this experiment, it has to stay with the plant for subsequent weighings. When your data collection is over, you need to determine the best way to compare results between treatments. Just looking at the total change in weight doesn't really get you anywhere; it's hard to compare if the initial plant weights were different to begin with. Calculating percent change would help. But what if you need to determine the total surface area (cm^2) of your leaves? The idea of outlining each and every leaf on a piece of grid paper makes even the most dedicated AP Biology student weep, so here's a suggestion: Calculate the surface area for only one lucky little leaf, and then weigh it. Now you have a conversion ratio (SA/g) you can use to determine the (approximate) surface area for all the leaves. All you need to do is determine how much all those leaves weigh. Easy!

Another method of measuring water loss is by using a device called a potometer. This tracks transpiration from only part of a plant that has been inserted into a water-filled tube with a pipette stuck on the other end. As water evaporates from the leaves, the water is pulled down the pipette, allowing you to track changes in volume.

Results

Ideally, any treatment that increased water loss through either more photosynthesis (e.g., light) or more evaporation from the leaf surfaces (e.g., wind) would decrease your plant's weight. On the flip side, if you slow down transpiration by creating a humid environment (e.g., misting your plant) or slow down photosynthesis (e.g., stick the poor plant in the dark), you would expect water loss to be slowed.

Key Concepts

- The higher the leaf surface area, the greater the rate of transpiration.
- The more stomata, the more water loss.
- An increase in water potential of the environment would slow evaporation; a decrease in water potential would increase evaporation.

Investigation 12: Fruit Fly Behavior

BIG IDEA 4
Interactions

This experiment draws on information found in Chapter 17, Behavioral Ecology and Ethology. This experiment is basically an exercise in messing with fruit flies' heads. You get to stick them in a choice chamber and explore environmental factors that either attract or repel them.

Basic Setup

First, get to know your flies. For example, males have a darker abdomen whereas females' abdomens are pale and rounder. Next, you get to create something called a choice chamber. In this experiment the chamber consists of two plastic bottles with their bottoms cut off and joined together with tape. Each end of the chamber will have one of the substances you decide to test. You can also use the chamber to investigate the flies' response to other variables, such as light or gravity. No matter what you're interested in, wrangle about 25 of those little creatures in there and let them get used to their new digs. Place a cotton ball with a few drops of water in the cap at one end (control) and a few drops of the substance you're testing at the other end. The flies will exhibit positive chemotaxis if they move toward the substance you're testing, negative chemotaxis if they move away from it.

Results

It is not important that you take away from this experiment that fruit flies enjoy the scent of one type of substance over another. What is important is that you recognize how to set up an experiment such as this one involving the choice chamber to measure chemotaxis in animals.

Key Skills

- Design a controlled experiment to determine environmental factors that either attract or repel your fruit flies.
- Analyze your data to identify the effect of environmental factors on your flies' behavior.

Investigation 13: Enzyme Activity

BIG IDEA 4
Interactions

This experiment draws on information from Chapter 5, Chemistry. The experiment is designed to practice the calculation of the rate of enzyme-catalyzed reactions through the measurement of the products produced. In this particular experiment, the enzyme **peroxidase** is used to convert hydrogen peroxide to water and oxygen, and the products are measured to assist in the determination of the rate of reaction. If you do not feel comfortable with your knowledge of enzyme-substrate interactions, refer to Chapter 5 before continuing this section.

The Nitty-Gritty About Experiment 2

The reaction of interest in this experiment is as follows:

$$2H_2O_2 \rightarrow 2H_2O + O_2$$

This reaction does indeed occur without the assistance of peroxidase, but it occurs at a slow rate. When our friend peroxidase is added to the mix, the reaction occurs at a much faster clip. Take a look at the enzymatic activity curve in Figure 19.4. Notice the constant rate of reaction in the first six minutes of the experiment.

However, after the sixth minute, the rate slows, as if the enzyme has become tired. This is because as the reaction proceeds, the number of substrate molecules remaining declines, which means that fewer enzyme-substrate interactions can occur. When calculating the **rate of reaction,** it is the constant linear portion of the curve that matters. That is the accepted rate value for the enzyme. Do not attempt to factor in the slowing portion of the curve.

Basic Setup

In this particular experiment, turnip peroxidase is added to a beaker that holds H_2O_2 and is allowed to react for a certain period of time. After the reaction stops, the amount of O_2

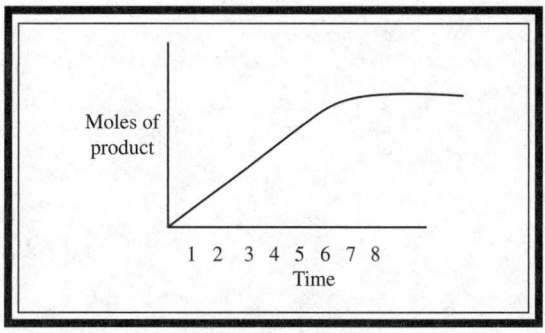

Figure 19.4   Enzyme-activity curve.

produced is measured using the color indicator guaiacol. Guaiacol readily grabs and binds to oxygen, forming tetraguaiacol, a brown chemical. The greater the amount of oxygen produced, the darker brown your solution becomes. The relative amount of oxygen is determined by comparing the color of the tube to a turnip peroxidase color chart (a previously made series of dilutions of the oxygen-guaiacol reaction). Once you're comfortable with the experimental setup, you will investigate at what pH peroxidase works its best.

Results

You'll have six test tubes, each with a different pH buffer. Once the reaction has proceeded long enough to produce a nice color spectrum among all the different pH solutions, record the color for each tube. Once you use your lab manual's turnip peroxidase color chart to help you quantify the relative amounts of oxygen produced, you can graph your data as color intensity versus pH. Peroxidase is found in many different forms with optimum pHs ranging from 4 to 11 depending on the source. Turnip peroxidase, for example, tends to work best at pH 5.

Key Concepts

- The reaction rate can be affected by four major factors: pH, temperature, substrate concentration, and enzyme concentration.
- The rate of reaction can be found by measuring either the appearance of product or the disappearance of reactant. Either measure can provide insight into the effectiveness of an enzyme's presence.
- When calculating the rate of reaction, remember that the rate is actually the portion of the graph with a constant slope.
- To determine the ideal pH at which an enzyme functions, run the enzyme reaction at a series of different pH values and measure the various reaction rates.

› Review Questions

1. If a dialysis bag with a solute concentration of 0.6 M is placed into a beaker with a solute concentration of 0.4 M, in which direction will water flow?

    A. Water will flow from the dialysis bag to the beaker.
    B. Water will flow from the beaker into the dialysis bag.
    C. Water will first flow out of the bag, and then back into the bag.
    D. The solution is already in equilibrium, and water will not move at all.

2. What is the rate of reaction for the enzyme–substrate interaction shown in the graph below?

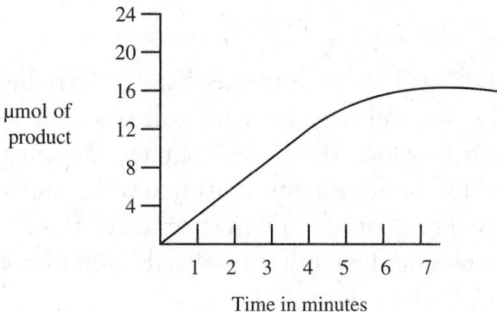

    A. 6 μmol/min (micromoles per minute)
    B. 5 μmol/min
    C. 4 μmol/min
    D. 3 μmol/min

3. In an experiment involving *Sordaria,* an ascomycete fungus, it was found that of 450 offspring produced, 58 yielded a 2:2:2:2 ratio and 32 a 2:4:2 ratio. Approximately how far apart is the gene from the centromere?

    A. 10.0 map units
    B. 15.0 map units
    C. 20.0 map units
    D. 25.0 map units

4. A plant would show the highest rate of transpiration under which of the following conditions?

    A. High humidity
    B. Low temperature
    C. High light intensity
    D. Low air movement

5. Which of the following will result in a quicker rate of DNA migration on an electrophoresis gel?

    A. Increase in temperature of the gel
    B. Increase in amount of DNA added to the well
    C. Reversal of charge of gel, switching positive and negative sides
    D. Increase in current flowing through the gel

6. A lab experiment is set up in which the participants are heterozygous individuals (Aa). After the F_1 generation is produced, 40 percent of the participants are randomly removed from the experiment and the remaining 60 percent are left to continue breeding. This experiment would be used to show what phenomenon?

    A. Natural selection
    B. Genetic drift
    C. Gene flow
    D. Mutation

7. You are studying a population of pea plants with flower colors ranging from white to dark pink. You selected only those plants with the darkest pink flowers to use in cross-pollination. Once you plant the seeds and grow your new generation of pea plants, what would you expect to see?

    A. The relative numbers of flower colors would remain unchanged.
    B. You would see disruptive selection.
    C. Your results would show directional selection.
    D. The relative numbers of white flowers would increase.

8. Which of the following would indicate you successfully transformed your *E. coli* culture with the plasmid containing the gene for ampicillin resistance?

   A. The ampicillin-containing agar plates would show growth from your control culture (*E. coli* without the plasmid), but not your transformed culture.
   B. The ampicillin-containing agar plates would show growth from your transformed culture, but not the control.
   C. The transformed culture would not grow on the agar-only plates.
   D. Both the transformed *E. coli* and the untransformed *E. coli* would grow on the plain agar plates.

〉 Answers and Explanations

1. **B**—The water will flow into the dialysis bag because the solute concentration in the bag is higher than that of the beaker. This creates an osmotic driving force that moves water into the bag in an effort to equalize the discrepancy in solute concentrations.

2. **D**—The rate of reaction can be approximated by calculating the slope of the straight portion of the graph. In this case it is 15 μmol of product produced in 5 minutes for an approximate rate of 3 μmoles/min.

3. **A**—The distance between the gene and the centromere in *Sordaria* is determined by adding up the number of crossovers that occur and dividing that by the number of offspring produced. This quotient should be multiplied by 100, and that product represents the percent of the offspring that experienced crossover. This percentage should be divided by 2 to obtain the distance from the centromere to the gene of interest.

4. **C**—The factors that increase the rate of transpiration are high light intensity, high temperature, low humidity, and high airflow.

5. **D**—The more current you put through the gel, the faster the DNA will migrate. Adding more DNA will result in thicker bands. Reversing the positive and negative ends will swap the direction in which the DNA migrates. Running the gel for a longer amount of time will increase the distance that the DNA fragments travel, and increasing the temperature really won't have too much of an effect.

6. **B**—This is an example of genetic drift, in which a random chunk of the population is eliminated resulting in a potential change in the frequencies of the alleles being studied.

7. **C**—If you allow only the plants with the dark-pink flower genes to reproduce, those are the genes that will be passed on to the next generation. This will shift the average flower color towards the darker end of the spectrum, an example of directional selection.

8. **B**—By successfully transforming your *E. coli*, you are giving it the gene that enables it to survive in the presence of ampicillin (something the bacteria are unable to do otherwise). Therefore, you have successfully transformed your culture if it grows on ampicillin-containing agar, but the control culture without the plasmid dies.

› Rapid Review

Investigation 1: Artificial Selection

- To demonstrate evolution in a plant population, choose which traits are selected for and cross-pollinate only between those selected plants. Once the offspring (seeds) are planted and grown, check this trait to see if it is more prevalent in the new population.

- This is an example of directional selection, when members of a population at one end of a spectrum are selected for, whereas the trait at the other end of the spectrum becomes rarer.

Investigation 2: Mathematical Modeling: Hardy-Weinberg

- The Hardy-Weinberg equation is used to check the frequencies of alleles in a population that is not evolving. This "snapshot" of the population is used as a point of comparison, to see if evolution does occur (and changes the allelic frequencies).

- For a given gene, there is the p allele and the q allele. Therefore, $p + q = 1$.

- For that same gene, organisms can be homozygous dominant (pp), homozygous recessive (qq), or heterozygous (pq or qp). Therefore, $p^2 + 2pq + q^2 = 1$.

- By altering any of the five conditions required for a non-evolving Hardy-Weinberg population, you can cause a change in your population's gene pool.

Investigation 3: Comparing DNA Sequences to Understand Evolutionary Relationships with BLAST

- BLAST is a computer program used to compare specific genes from different organisms.

- The more similar the nucleotide base sequence between two genes, the closer the evolutionary relationship.

- A cladogram is a visual representation of the evolutionary relatedness of a species.

Investigation 4: Diffusion and Osmosis

- Water flows from **hypotonic** (low solute) to **hypertonic** (high solute).

- To measure diffusion and osmosis, take dialysis bags containing solutes of varying concentrations, place them into beakers containing solutions of various concentrations, and record the direction of flow during each experiment.

Investigation 5: Photosynthesis

- To experimentally determine the photosynthetic rate of various plants in various environments, first remove the air from leaf disk samples and add the samples to water containing sodium bicarbonate (a source of carbon dioxide). They will sink to the bottom of the cup.

- As the leaf tissue photosynthesizes, oxygen is released, causing the disks to rise to the surface. Expose different plant samples to different environmental conditions, measure how much photosynthesis occurs (ET_{50}), and then compare.

Investigation 6: Cell Respiration

- To experimentally determine the rate of respiration in peas, use a respirometer to calculate the change in volume that occurs around the peas. Set up (1) a control group of nongerminating peas that will have a lower baseline respiration rate, (2) a control group that measures the change in oxygen due to pressure and temperature changes, and (3) an experimental group that contains the group whose respiration rate you want to measure.

Investigation 7: Cell Division: Mitosis and Meiosis

- To determine experimentally the percentage of cells in a particular stage of the cell cycle, examine an onion root slide and count the number of cells per stage. Divide the number in each stage by the total number of cells to determine the relative percentages.

- To determine how far a gene for an ascomycete fungus is from its centromere, cross a wild-type strain with a mutant and examine the patterns among the ascospores. A ratio of 4:4 means no crossover occurred, whereas ratios of 2:2:2:2 or 2:4:2 indicate crossing over did occur. Total number of crossover divided by total number of offspring equals the percent crossover. Divide this by 2 to get distance from the centromere.

Investigation 8: Biotechnology: Bacterial Transformation

- To run a transformation, add ampicillin-sensitive bacteria to two tubes, and to only one of the two, add a plasmid containing both the gene you would like to transform and the gene for ampicillin resistance. The other tube is the control. Ice the two tubes for 15 minutes, then quickly heat-shock the cells into picking up foreign DNA. Ice the tubes again, spread the bacteria out on ampicillin-coated plates, and incubate overnight. If transformation occurs, your bacteria will grow on the ampicillin plate.

Investigation 9: Biotechnology: Restriction Enzyme Analysis of DNA

- Gel electrophoresis can be used in court to determine if an individual committed a crime or if an individual is the parent of a particular child. Each person has a particular DNA fingerprint. When that individual's DNA is cut with restriction enzymes and run on an electrophoresis gel, it will show a unique pattern that only that person has. By matching a person's DNA fingerprint with that of the child of interest or the evidence from the crime scene, proper identifications can be made.

Investigation 10: Energy Dynamics

- A simple model system can be used to track how much energy is transferred from a single producer (plant) to a single consumer (caterpillars).

- By weighing the amount of plant eaten by the caterpillars (and the amount of the plant excreted), it is possible to calculate the percent of the plant's energy that was either incorporated into the caterpillar's body or used in cellular respiration.

- These are methods for estimating the efficiency of transfer of energy from producer to consumer.

Investigation 11: Transpiration

- To design an experiment to test the effects of various environmental factors on the rate of transpiration, measure the amount of water that evaporates from the surface of plants over a certain amount of time under normal conditions. You can do this using the whole-plant method or by using a piece of equipment known as a potometer, a device that measures water loss by plants. Compare the normal rate with the rates obtained when the temperature, humidity, airflow, or light intensity is altered. If you run an experiment of this nature, it is important to measure the surface area of the leaves involved because larger surface areas can transpire more water more quickly.

Investigation 12: Fruit Fly Behavior

- To study kinesis of an insect such as a fruit fly, create a contraption known as a choice chamber, which is designed to study which of two substances an organism prefers. For example, one-half of the choice chamber may contain banana extract, the other distilled water. Place the organism of interest into the choice chamber and record how many of that organism are on each side of the chamber every 30 seconds. This procedure can also be performed for a choice chamber that has differing temperatures, humidities, light intensities, salinities, and other parameters.

Investigation 13: Enzyme Activity

- Enzyme reaction rate is affected by pH, temperature, substrate concentration, and enzyme concentration.

- To test the rate of reactivity of an enzyme and the difference it makes compared to the speed of the normal reaction, run the reaction without an enzyme, then run it with your enzyme, and compare.

- To determine the ideal pH (or temperature) for an enzyme, run the reaction at varying pH values (or temperatures) and compare.

STEP 5

Build Your Test-Taking Confidence

AP Biology Practice Exam 1
AP Biology Practice Exam 2

Answer Sheet for AP Biology Practice Exam 1

PART A: MULTIPLE-CHOICE QUESTIONS

1 Ⓐ Ⓑ Ⓒ Ⓓ	22 Ⓐ Ⓑ Ⓒ Ⓓ	43 Ⓐ Ⓑ Ⓒ Ⓓ
2 Ⓐ Ⓑ Ⓒ Ⓓ	23 Ⓐ Ⓑ Ⓒ Ⓓ	44 Ⓐ Ⓑ Ⓒ Ⓓ
3 Ⓐ Ⓑ Ⓒ Ⓓ	24 Ⓐ Ⓑ Ⓒ Ⓓ	45 Ⓐ Ⓑ Ⓒ Ⓓ
4 Ⓐ Ⓑ Ⓒ Ⓓ	25 Ⓐ Ⓑ Ⓒ Ⓓ	46 Ⓐ Ⓑ Ⓒ Ⓓ
5 Ⓐ Ⓑ Ⓒ Ⓓ	26 Ⓐ Ⓑ Ⓒ Ⓓ	47 Ⓐ Ⓑ Ⓒ Ⓓ
6 Ⓐ Ⓑ Ⓒ Ⓓ	27 Ⓐ Ⓑ Ⓒ Ⓓ	48 Ⓐ Ⓑ Ⓒ Ⓓ
7 Ⓐ Ⓑ Ⓒ Ⓓ	28 Ⓐ Ⓑ Ⓒ Ⓓ	49 Ⓐ Ⓑ Ⓒ Ⓓ
8 Ⓐ Ⓑ Ⓒ Ⓓ	29 Ⓐ Ⓑ Ⓒ Ⓓ	50 Ⓐ Ⓑ Ⓒ Ⓓ
9 Ⓐ Ⓑ Ⓒ Ⓓ	30 Ⓐ Ⓑ Ⓒ Ⓓ	51 Ⓐ Ⓑ Ⓒ Ⓓ
10 Ⓐ Ⓑ Ⓒ Ⓓ	31 Ⓐ Ⓑ Ⓒ Ⓓ	52 Ⓐ Ⓑ Ⓒ Ⓓ
11 Ⓐ Ⓑ Ⓒ Ⓓ	32 Ⓐ Ⓑ Ⓒ Ⓓ	53 Ⓐ Ⓑ Ⓒ Ⓓ
12 Ⓐ Ⓑ Ⓒ Ⓓ	33 Ⓐ Ⓑ Ⓒ Ⓓ	54 Ⓐ Ⓑ Ⓒ Ⓓ
13 Ⓐ Ⓑ Ⓒ Ⓓ	34 Ⓐ Ⓑ Ⓒ Ⓓ	55 Ⓐ Ⓑ Ⓒ Ⓓ
14 Ⓐ Ⓑ Ⓒ Ⓓ	35 Ⓐ Ⓑ Ⓒ Ⓓ	56 Ⓐ Ⓑ Ⓒ Ⓓ
15 Ⓐ Ⓑ Ⓒ Ⓓ	36 Ⓐ Ⓑ Ⓒ Ⓓ	57 Ⓐ Ⓑ Ⓒ Ⓓ
16 Ⓐ Ⓑ Ⓒ Ⓓ	37 Ⓐ Ⓑ Ⓒ Ⓓ	58 Ⓐ Ⓑ Ⓒ Ⓓ
17 Ⓐ Ⓑ Ⓒ Ⓓ	38 Ⓐ Ⓑ Ⓒ Ⓓ	59 Ⓐ Ⓑ Ⓒ Ⓓ
18 Ⓐ Ⓑ Ⓒ Ⓓ	39 Ⓐ Ⓑ Ⓒ Ⓓ	60 Ⓐ Ⓑ Ⓒ Ⓓ
19 Ⓐ Ⓑ Ⓒ Ⓓ	40 Ⓐ Ⓑ Ⓒ Ⓓ	61 Ⓐ Ⓑ Ⓒ Ⓓ
20 Ⓐ Ⓑ Ⓒ Ⓓ	41 Ⓐ Ⓑ Ⓒ Ⓓ	62 Ⓐ Ⓑ Ⓒ Ⓓ
21 Ⓐ Ⓑ Ⓒ Ⓓ	42 Ⓐ Ⓑ Ⓒ Ⓓ	63 Ⓐ Ⓑ Ⓒ Ⓓ

PART B: GRID-IN QUESTIONS

AP Biology Practice Exam 1: Section I

PART A: MULTIPLE-CHOICE QUESTIONS

Time—1 hour and 30 minutes (for Parts A and B)

For the multiple-choice questions that follow, select the best answer
and fill in the appropriate letter on the answer sheet.

1. Which of the following characteristics would allow you to distinguish a prokaryotic cell from an animal cell?

    A. Ribosomes
    B. Cell membrane
    C. Chloroplasts
    D. Cell wall

2. Which of the following is the source of oxygen produced during photosynthesis?

    A. H_2O
    B. H_2O_2
    C. CO_2
    D. CO

3. An organism exposed to wild temperature fluctuations shows very little, if any, change in its metabolic rate. This organism is most probably a

    A. ectotherm.
    B. endotherm.
    C. thermophyle.
    D. ascospore.

4. Which of the following is a frameshift mutation?

    A. CAT HAS HIS → CAT HAS HIT
    B. CAT HAS HIS → CAT HSH ISA
    C. CAT HAS HIS → CAT HIS HAT
    D. CAT HAS HIS → CAT WAS HIT

5. A researcher conducts a survey of a biome and finds 35 percent more species than she has found in any other biome. Which biome is she most likely to be in?

    A. Tundra
    B. Tiaga
    C. Tropical rainforest
    D. Temperate deciduous forest

6. On the basis of the following crossover frequencies, determine the relative location of these four genes:

m & n	→	15%
p & f	→	20%
n & f	→	30%
m & f	→	45%
n & p	→	10%

    A. f   p   m   n

    B. m   n   f   p

    C. m   n   p   f

    D. n   m   p   f

7. A man contracts the same flu strain for the second time in a single winter season. The second time he experiences fewer symptoms and recovers more quickly. Which cells are responsible for this rapid recovery?

    A. Helper T cells
    B. Cytotoxic T cells
    C. Memory cells
    D. Plasma cells

8. Which of the following are traits that are affected by more than one gene?

    A. Heterozygous traits
    B. Pleiotropic traits
    C. Polygenic traits
    D. Blended alleles

9. A lizard lacking a chemical defense mechanism that is colored in the same way as a lizard that has a defense mechanism is displaying

   A. aposometric coloration.
   B. cryptic coloration.
   C. Batesian mimicry.
   D. Müllerian mimicry.

10. Crossover would most likely occur in which situation?

   A. Two genes (1 and 2) are located right next to each other on chromosome A.
   B. Gene 1 is located on chromosome A, and gene 2 is on chromosome B.
   C. Genes 1 and 2 are located near each other on the X chromosome.
   D. Gene 1 is located on chromosome A; gene 2 is located far away but on the same chromosome.

11. Imagine an organism whose $2n = 96$. Meiosis would leave this organism's cells with how many chromosomes?

   A. 192
   B. 96
   C. 48
   D. 24

12. A student conducts an experiment to test the efficiency of a certain enzyme. Which of the following protocols would probably not result in a change in the enzyme's efficiency?

   A. Bringing the temperature of the experimental setup from 20°C to 50°C
   B. Adding an acidic solution to the setup
   C. Adding substrate but not enzyme
   D. Placing the substrate and enzyme in a container with double the capacity

13. You observe a species that gives birth to only one offspring at a time and has a relatively long lifespan for its body size. Which of the following is probably *also* true of this organism?

   A. It lives in a newly colonized habitat.
   B. It is an aquatic organism.
   C. It requires relatively high parental care of offspring.
   D. The age at which the offspring themselves can give birth is relatively young.

14. Which of the following is an example of a detritivore?

   A. Cactus
   B. Algae
   C. Bat
   D. Fungus

15. In a certain population of squirrels that is in Hardy-Weinberg equilibrium, black color is a recessive phenotype present in 9 percent of the squirrels, and 91 percent are gray. What percentage of the population is homozygous dominant for this trait?

   A. 21 percent
   B. 30 percent
   C. 49 percent
   D. 70 percent

16. Refer to question 15 for details on the squirrel population. Which of the following conditions is required to keep this population in Hardy-Weinberg equilibrium?

   A. Random mating
   B. Genetic drift
   C. Mutation
   D. Gene flow

17. A reaction that includes energy as one of its reactants is called a(n)

   A. exergonic reaction.
   B. hydrolysis reaction.
   C. endergonic reaction.
   D. redox reaction.

18. To which of the following labeled trophic levels would a herbivore most likely be assigned?

   A. A
   B. B
   C. C
   D. D

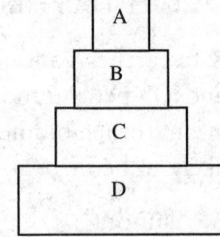

19. A population undergoes a shift in which those who are really tall and those who are really short decrease in relative frequency compared to those of medium size, due to a change in the availability of resources. This is an example of

    A. directional selection.
    B. stabilizing selection.
    C. disruptive selection.
    D. sympatric speciation.

20. Which of the following statements is correct?

    A. Water flows from hypertonic to hypotonic.
    B. Germinating seeds use less oxygen than do nongerminating seeds.
    C. The rate of transpiration decreases with an increase in air movement.
    D. Smaller DNA fragments migrate more rapidly than do larger DNA fragments on gel electrophoresis.

21. Which of the following is not a form of interspecies interaction?

    A. Commensalism
    B. Succession
    C. Mutualism
    D. Parasitism

22. Sickle cell anemia is a disease caused by the substitution of an incorrect nucleotide into the DNA sequence for a particular gene. The amino acids are still added to the growing protein chain, but the symptoms of sickle cell anemia result. This is an example of a

    A. frameshift mutation.
    B. missense mutation.
    C. nonsense mutation.
    D. thymine dimer mutation.

For questions 23–26, please refer to the following structures:

23. This represents the backbone of a structure that is vital to the construction of many cells and is used to produce steroid hormones.

24. This structure plays a vital role in energy reactions.

25. This structure is a purine found in DNA.

26. This structure was synthesized in the ribosome.

For questions 27–30, please refer to the following answers:

    A. Glycolysis
    B. Chemiosmosis
    C. Fermentation
    D. Calvin cycle

27. When oxygen becomes unavailable, this process regenerates NAD^+, allowing respiration to continue.

28. This process leads to the net production of two pyruvate, two ATP, and two NADH.

29. This process couples the production of ATP with the movement of electrons down the electron transport chain by harnessing the driving force created by a proton gradient.

30. This process has as its products $NADP^+$, ADP, and sugar.

For questions 31–34, please refer to the following answers:

    A. Desert
    B. Tundra
    C. Taiga
    D. Deciduous forests

31. This biome has cold winters and is known for its pine forests.

32. This biome is the driest of the land biomes and experiences the greatest daily temperature fluctuations.

33. This biome contains trees that drop their leaves during the winter months.

34. This biome contains plants whose roots cannot go deep due to the presence of a permafrost.

Questions 35–36: A behavioral endocrinologist captures male individuals of a territorial bird species over the course of a year to measure testosterone (T) levels. In this population, males may play one of two roles: (1) they may stay in their natal group (the group they were born in) and help raise their younger siblings, or (2) they may leave the natal group to establish a new territory. Use this information and the two histograms that follow to answer the following questions.

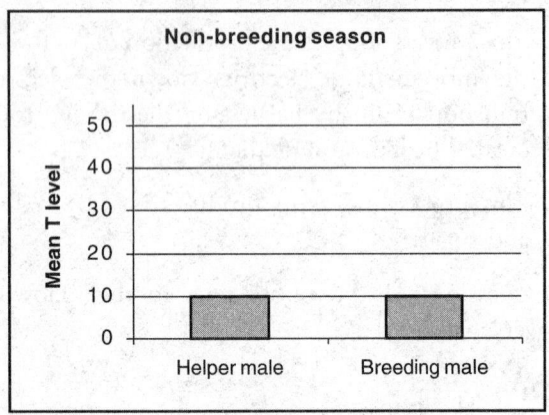

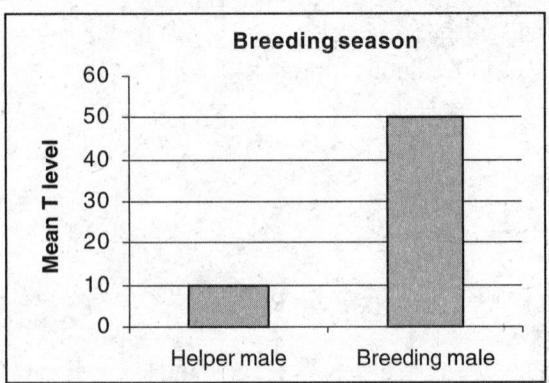

35. Testosterone level in this population may be an example of

A. adaptive radiation.
B. an adaptation.
C. divergent selection.
D. development.

36. What can you infer about the role of testosterone in reproduction in this species?

A. It is detrimental to breeding.
B. It aids adult males only.
C. It ensures that all males reproduce equally.
D. It aids in breeding.

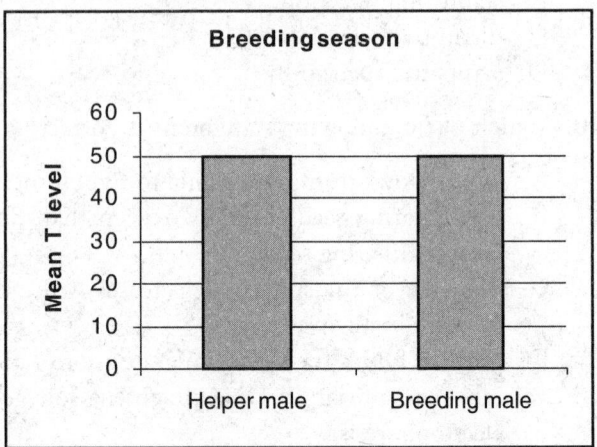

37. Which of the following is the best explanation of the results presented in the preceding graph, collected from the same population in a different year?

A. The so-called helper males are actually breeding.
B. The population has stopped growing.
C. Females are equally attracted to adult and helper males.
D. Testosterone level is affected by many processes.

Questions 38–41: A researcher grows a population of ferns in her laboratory. She notices, after a few generations, a new variant that has a distinct phenotype. When she tries to breed the original phenotype with the new one, no offspring are produced. When she breeds the new variants, however, offspring that look like the new variant result.

38. What originally caused the change in the variant?

A. Karyotyping
B. Balance polymorphism
C. Mutation
D. Polyploidy

39. What kind of speciation does this example illustrate?

    A. Allopatric
    B. Sympatric
    C. Isolated
    D. Polyploidy

40. Which of the following could possibly characterize the new variant?
    A. Adaptive radiation
    B. Divergent selection
    C. Equilibrium
    D. Polyploidy

41. Which of the following is likely to exhibit the process described earlier?

    A. Fallow deer
    B. Fruit flies
    C. Grass
    D. Spotted toads

For questions 42–44, please refer to the following answers:

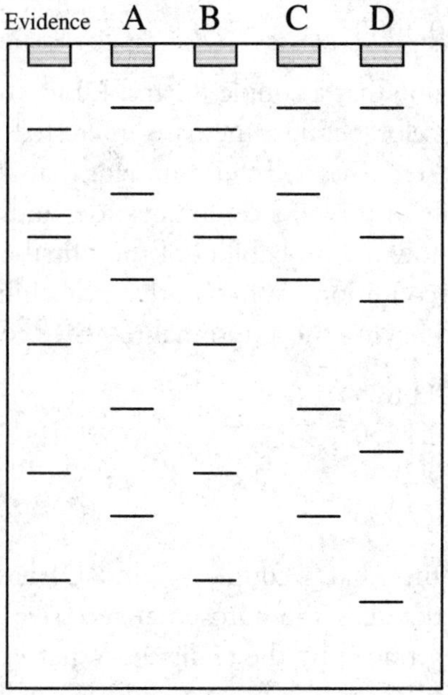

42. The DNA placed in this electrophoresis gel separates as a result of what characteristic?

    A. pH
    B. Charge
    C. Size
    D. Polarity

43. If this gel were used in a court case as DNA evidence taken from the crime scene, which of the following suspects appears to be guilty?

    A. Suspect A
    B. Suspect B
    C. Suspect C
    D. Suspect D

44. Which two suspects, while not guilty, could possibly be identical twins?

    A. A and B
    B. A and C
    C. B and C
    D. B and D

Questions 45–48: The frequency of genotypes for a given trait are given in the accompanying graph. Answer the following questions using this information:

AA	Aa	aa
36%	45%	?%

45. What is the frequency of the recessive homozygote?

    A. 15 percent
    B. 19 percent
    C. 25 percent
    D. 40 percent

46. What would be the approximate frequency of the heterozygote condition if this population were in Hardy-Weinberg equilibrium?

    A. 20 percent
    B. 45 percent
    C. 48 percent
    D. 72 percent

47. Is this population in Hardy-Weinberg equilibrium?

    A. Yes
    B. No
    C. Cannot tell from the information given
    D. Maybe, if individuals are migrating

48. Which of the following processes may be occurring in this population, given the allele frequencies?

    A. Directional selection
    B. Homozygous advantage
    C. Hybrid vigor
    D. Allopatric speciation

Questions 49–51: An eager AP Biology student interested in studying osmosis and the movement of water in solutions took a dialysis bag containing a 0.5 M solution and placed it into a beaker containing a 0.6 M solution.

49. After the bag has been sitting in the beaker for a while, what would you expect to have happened to the bag?

    A. There will have been a net flow of water out of the bag, causing it to decrease in size.
    B. There will be have been a net flow of water into the bag, causing it to swell in size.
    C. The bag will be the exact same size because no water will have moved at all.
    D. The solute will have moved out of the dialysis bag into the beaker.

50. If this bag were instead placed into a beaker of distilled water, what would be the expected result?

    A. There will be a net flow of water out of the bag, causing it to decrease in size.
    B. There will be a net flow of water into the bag, causing it to swell in size.
    C. The bag will remain the exact same size because no water will move at all.
    D. The solute will flow out of the dialysis bag into the beaker.

51. Which of the following is true about water potential?

    A. It drives the movement of water from a region of lower water potential to a region of higher water potential.
    B. Solute potential is the only factor that determines the water potential.
    C. Pressure potential combines with solute potential to determine the water potential.
    D. Water potential *always* drives water from an area of lower pressure potential to an area of higher pressure potential.

Questions 52–54 all use the following pedigree, but are independent of each other:

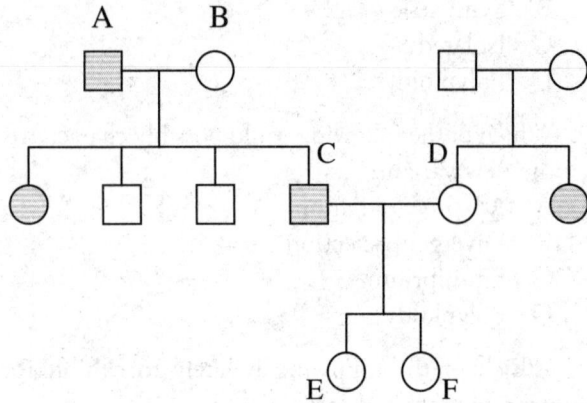

52. If the pedigree is studying an autosomal recessive condition for which the alleles are A and a, what was the probability that a child produced by parents A and B would be heterozygous?

    A. 0.0625
    B. 0.1250
    C. 0.2500
    D. 0.5000

53. Imagine that a couple (C and D) go to a genetic counselor because they are interested in having children. They tell the counselor that they have a family history of a certain disorder and they want to know the probability of their firstborn having this condition. What is the probability of the child having the autosomal recessive condition?

    A. 0.0625
    B. 0.1250
    C. 0.2500
    D. 0.3333

54. Imagine that a couple (C and D) have a child (E) that has the autosomal recessive condition being traced by the pedigree. What is the probability that their second child (F) will have the autosomal recessive condition?

    A. 0.0625
    B. 0.1250
    C. 0.2500
    D. 0.5000

For questions 55–56, please refer to the following diagram:

55. The bold line that point *C* intersects is known as the

A. biotic potential.
B. carrying capacity.
C. limiting factor.
D. maximum attainable population.

56. On the basis of what happens at the end of this chart, what is the most likely explanation for the population decline after point *E*?

A. The population became too dense and it had to decline.
B. There was a major environmental shift that made survival impossible for many.
C. Food became scarce, leading to a major famine.
D. The population had become too large.

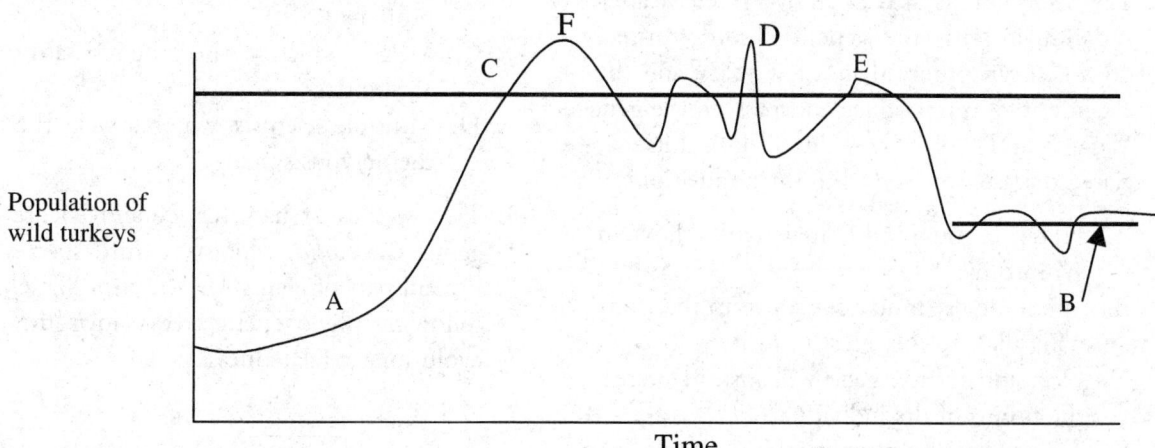

Questions 57 and 58: The solutions in the two arms of this U-tube are separated by a membrane that is permeable to water and sodium chloride, but not to sucrose. Side A is filled with a solution of 0.6 M sucrose and 0.2 M sodium chloride (NaCl), and side B is filled with a solution of 0.2 M sucrose and 0.3 M NaCl. Initially, the volume on both sides is the same.

57. At the beginning of the experiment,

A. Side A is hypertonic to side B.
B. Side A is hypotonic to side B.
C. Side A is isotonic to side B.
D. Side A is hypotonic to side B with respect to sucrose.

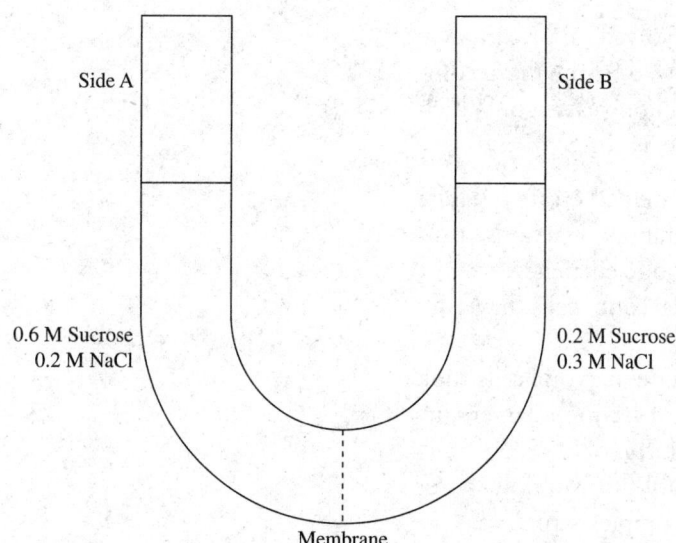

58. If you examine side A after a couple of days, you will see

  A. an increase in the concentration of NaCl and sucrose and an increase in water level.
  B. a decrease in the concentration of NaCl, an increase in water level, and no change in the concentration of sucrose.
  C. no net change.
  D. an increase in the concentration of NaCl and an increase in the water level.

59. Tay-Sachs is a disease caused by a recessive allele. Individuals with the genetic disorder usually do not survive more than a few years, and thus are not able to reproduce and pass on the gene. What would explain how this allele and its associated disease is preserved in the population?

  A. Heterozygous individuals will show no symptoms.
  B. Spontaneous mutation converts the dominant allele to the recessive form.
  C. Occasionally the gene will instead increase the fitness of the individual.
  D. Tay-Sachs is asymptomatic in people who are homozygous recessive.

60. A new plant was discovered and determined to have an unusually low number of stomata on the undersides of its leaves. For what environment would this plant most likely be best adapted?

  A. Cold and rainy
  B. Humid and sunny
  C. Hot and humid
  D. Hot and dry

61. The first simple cells evolved approximately 3.5 billion years ago, followed by the more complex eukaryotic cells 2.1 billion years ago. Which of the following statements is correct?

  A. Eukaryotic organelles helped create separate environments for metabolic reactions, thus increasing their metabolic efficiency.
  B. Prokaryotic and eukaryotic cells have no structural similarities.
  C. The organelles in larger eukaryotic cells took care of the problems of having a larger surface area–to–volume ratio.
  D. Eukaryotic cells are able to multiply faster based on their more complex structure.

62. Easily produced genetic variation is key to the rapid evolution of viral and microbial populations. Furthermore, pathogens that need to escape the immune system rely on this variation to generate new surface antigens that go unrecognized by the host's immune system. Which of the following is an example of this antigenic variation?

  A. HIV, which can remain integrated into the host genome for many years
  B. The flu virus, which changes its envelope proteins
  C. MRSA, which has become resistant to many antibiotics
  D. Multiple sclerosis, which attacks the cells of the nervous system

63. Two species of hamster (X and Y) are in the genus *Cricetulus*, whereas a third species (Z) is instead part of genus *Mesocricetus*. Which of the following phylogenetic trees shows the correct evolutionary relatedness?

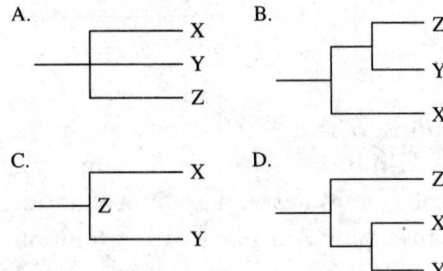

PART B: GRID-IN QUESTIONS

Calculate the correct answer and enter it on the top line of the grid-in area with each number/symbol in a separate column. Then fill in the correct circle below each number/symbol you entered (only one filled-in circle per column).

1. In a certain species of plant, the allele to produce green melons (G) is dominant over the allele to produce yellow melons (g). A student performed a cross between a plant that produced green melons and a plant that produced yellow melons. When the student observed the next generation, the 94 seeds that were produced from the cross matured into 53 plants with green melons and 41 plants with yellow melons. Calculate the chi-squared value for the null hypothesis that the green-melon parent was heterozygous for the melon-color gene.

2. In a population of grasshoppers, the allele for tan color is dominant to the allele for green color. A drastic increase in rainfall leads to selection against the tan phenotype. When the rainy season ends, 23 percent of the remaining grasshoppers have the green phenotype. If this population is now in Hardy-Weinberg equilibrium, what will the frequency of the tan allele be in the next generation?

3. The bacteria that cause pimples can be grown in the lab using a suitable nutrient broth, where they will eventually achieve exponential growth. Using the graph that follows, calculate the mean rate of growth, in millions of bacteria per hour, during their exponential phase.

4. What is the water potential for a solution that is 0.1 M at 20°C? The solution is in an open container. The equation for water potential is:

$$\text{water potential } (\Psi) = \text{pressure potential } (\Psi_P) + \text{solute potential } (\Psi_S)$$

The equation for solute potential is:

$$\Psi_S = -iCRT$$

where:

    i = ionization constant (assume that it is 1)

    C = molar concentration

    R = pressure constant (R = 0.0831 liter MPa/mole K)

    T = temperature in Kelvin (assume a room temperature of 293 K)

5. Determine the surface area–to–volume ratio for a cube that has a side length of 2.5 cm. The volume of a cube = $(l)(w)(h)$. The surface area = 6 × area of a single side.

6. If $C_iV_i = C_fV_f$, where i is the initial solution concentration and f is the final concentration, how many milliliters of a 0.5 M glucose solution would you need in order to make 250 milliliters of a 0.1 M glucose solution?

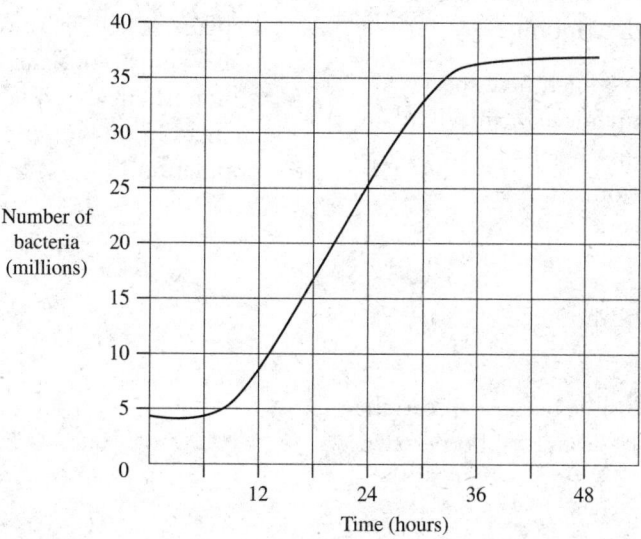

Number of bacteria (millions)

Time (hours)

AP Biology Practice Exam 1: Section II

FREE-RESPONSE QUESTIONS

Time—1 hour and 30 minutes

(The first 10 minutes is a reading period. Do not begin writing until the 10-minute period has passed.)
Questions 1 and 2 are long free-response questions that should require about 20 minutes each.
Questions 3–8 are short-response questions that should require about 6 minutes each.
Outline form is not acceptable. Answers should be in essay form.

1. A murder trial court case ended up ruling against the defendant because of DNA evidence found at the crime scene and analyzed in the forensics lab.

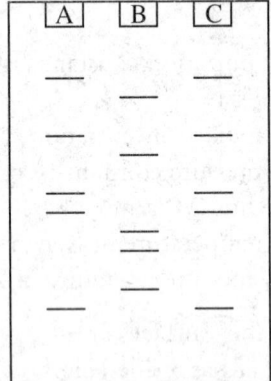

A. Describe how a gel electrophoresis experiment works and is set up, why things move the way they do, and why the gel would be able to prove, beyond a shadow of a doubt, that the defendant was indeed guilty as charged.

B. Gel electrophoresis is also used to determine court paternity cases. Describe how a gel could be used to prove whether an individual is the father of a particular baby. Include all the pertinent experimental laboratory procedures in your description.

2. Speciation, the process by which new species are formed, can occur by many mechanisms. Explain how *three* of the following are involved in the process of species formation.

A. Geographic barriers
B. Polyploidy
C. Balanced polymorphism
D. Reproductive isolation

3. Life on Earth is made possible because of certain unique characteristics of water. Choose **two** characteristics of water.

A. For each characteristic that you choose, identify and define the property.

B. Describe one example of how the property affects the functioning of living organisms.

4. Evolution is the change in allele frequencies in a population over time. This can occur through a variety of mechanisms, three of which are listed below.

  • Natural selection
  • Genetic drift
  • Mutation

A. Define **two** of the three forces of evolution listed above and give an example.

B. You are studying a population of field mice that includes individuals with light and dark brown coats. Every six months you perform capture/recapture experiments to census the proportion of light and dark individuals. The following numbers indicate the percentage of dark-coat individuals caught in each successive census over the course of five years:

96, 94, 95, 91, 93, 95, 74, 73, 77, 76

Explain which of the three processes of evolution is most consistent with this data, and give a hypothetical explanation for the observed changes in phenotypic frequencies in this mouse population.

5. Homeostasis, or the maintenance of a steady-state environment, is a characteristic of all living organisms. For each of the following physiological parameters describe how homeostasis is maintained:

   A. Blood glucose levels
   B. Body temperature
   C. Blood calcium levels

6. Membranes are vital to the transport of substances into and out of cells. Three important forms of cellular transport include:

   A. Active transport
   B. Endocytosis and exocytosis
   C. Facilitated diffusion

For each of the forms listed above, explain how the organization of the cell membranes functions in the movement of specific molecules across membranes and explain the significance of each type of transport to a specific cell.

7. Skin is coated with sebum, an oily substance that slows water loss and inhibits growth of some microorganisms.

   A. Briefly explain how sebum is able to perform its function.
   B. Explain why lungs are more vulnerable to infection than skin. Include the idea of surface area in your answer.

8. The complete oxidation of a mole of glucose produces 686 kcal of free energy. The oxidation of a mole of glucose in a cell generates a maximum of 38 moles of ATP. Each mole of ATP stores about 7.3 kcal of energy. The efficiency of the ATP energy yield from the complete aerobic respiration of glucose is about 40 percent.

   A. Using the laws of thermodynamics, explain what happens to the rest of the energy.
   B. How do humans benefit from this energy loss?
   C. Why would hibernating animals possess an adaptation to reduce efficiency of cellular respiration even further?

› Answers and Explanations for AP Biology Practice Exam 1

PART A: MULTIPLE-CHOICE QUESTIONS

1. **D**—Cell walls are present in prokaryotes but not eukaryotic animal cells. Ribosomes and cell membranes are present in both of them. Chloroplasts and large central vacuoles are not seen in either of them. Animal cells have small vacuoles.

2. **A**—The oxygen released by plants is produced during the light reactions of photosynthesis. The main inputs to the light reactions are water and light. Water is the source of the oxygen.

3. **B**—Endotherms are organisms whose metabolic rates do not respond to shifts in environmental temperature.

4. **B**—A frameshift mutation is one in which the reading frame for the protein construction machinery is shifted. It is a deletion or addition of nucleotides in a number that is *not* a multiple of 3. Often this can lead to premature stop codons, which lead to nonfunctional proteins.

5. **C**

6. **C**—We can see from the data that m and f have the highest crossover frequency. They must therefore be farthest apart of any pair along the chromosome. This leaves only answer choice C.

7. **C**—Memory B cells are able to recognize foreign invaders if they come back into our systems and lead to a more rapid and efficient attack on the invader.

8. **C**—Polygenic traits are traits that require the input of multiple genes to determine the phenotype. Skin color is a classic example of a polygenic trait; three genes combine to provide the various shades of skin tone seen in humans.

9. **C**—This is a classic example of Batesian mimicry.

10. **D**—Crossover is most likely to occur between two genes that are located far away from each other on the same chromosome.

11. **C**—Meiosis reduces the number of chromosomes in an individual by half: $96 \div 2 = 48$.

12. **D**—The volume of the container is not a major factor that affects enzyme efficiency.

13. **C**—The original question describes an organism that can be classified as a *K*-selected population. Individuals of this class tend to have fairly constant size, low reproductive rates, and offspring that require extensive care.

14. **D**—A detritivore is an organism that includes the subcategory of decomposers. Fungi are decomposers.

15. **C**—If 9 percent of the population is homozygous recessive, this means that $q^2 = 0.09$, and that the square root of $q^2 = 0.30 = q$. This means that $p = 0.70$ since $p + q = 1$. Thus, the percentage of the population that is homozygous dominant: $p^2 = (0.7)^2 = 0.49$ or 49 percent.

16. **A**—All the other answer choices are violations of the Hardy–Weinberg equilibrium.

17. **C**—Exergonic reactions give off energy, and hydrolysis reactions are reactions that use water to break apart a compound. Redox reactions are reactions that involve the movement of electrons.

18. **D**—Herbivores tend to be the primary consumers of trophic pyramids, and thus would take up the first level up from the bottom.

19. **B**—Stabilizing selection tends to eliminate the extremes of a population, directional selection is a shift toward one of the extremes, and disruptive selection is the camel-hump selection in which the two extremes are favored over the middle. Sympatric speciation is the formation of new species due to an inability to reproduce that is not caused by geographic separation.

20. **D**—This is a lab experiment question based on the material in Chapter 19. We threw it in here just to remind you that you should not ignore the concepts of this very important chapter. You will be asked about these concepts on the exam.

21. **B**—Succession is an ecological process in which landforms evolve over time in response to the environmental conditions. Commensalism is when one organism benefits while the other is unaffected. Mutualism is when both organisms

reap benefits from the interaction. Parasitism is when one organism benefits at the other's expense.

22. **B**

23. **A**—Cholesterol is one of the lipids that serves as the starting point for the synthesis of sex hormones.

24. **C**

25. **D**—Purines have a double-ring structure; pyrimidines, a single-ring one.

26. **B**—The ribosome is the site of protein synthesis.

27. **C**

28. **A**

29. **B**

30. **D**

31. **C**

32. **A**

33. **D**

34. **C**

35. **B**—Testosterone level is an adaptive trait in this population, one that has been molded by natural selection (or possibly sexual selection; we cannot determine this from the question) to aid in reproduction. Adaptive radiation is a process by which many speciation events occur in a newly exploited environment and does not apply here. This is not an example of divergent selection because both breeding and nonbreeding males have low testosterone levels during at least one part of the year; if the two male types always differed in testosterone level, this population could eventually split into two populations. Development and sperm production may be related to testosterone but are not addressed in this experiment.

36. **D**—Since testosterone levels are increased only during the breeding season, we can infer that testosterone has some role in breeding. Since reproductive males express higher testosterone levels only during the breeding season, we hypothesize that testosterone is beneficial, as opposed to detrimental, to breeding.

37. **A**—Since testosterone seems to be linked with reproduction, we infer from the new data that the "nonbreeding" males are actually breeding

and therefore have elevated testosterone levels. Females, population growth, and number of offspring produced are not considered in this example. Finally, although testosterone does affect many physiological processes, none of these are discussed or illustrated in this example.

38. **C**—Although several processes can affect the frequency of a new phenotype or genotype, once it is in place, the original genetic change must have been the result of a mutation (probably a chromosomal aberration).

39. **B**—No physical barrier separated the two populations; this is therefore an example of sympatric, not allopatric speciation. The other answer choices are not types of speciation.

40. **D**—Polyploidy is the only answer that can describe an *individual*. All the others are processes or states that describe *population* events. Polyploidy is the duplication of whole chromosomes that leads to speciation because the new variety can no longer breed with the original.

41. **C**—Polyploidy is much more common in plants; mutations such as the duplication of whole chromosomes are usually lethal to animals.

42. **C**—Gel electrophoresis separates DNA on the basis of size. Smaller samples travel a greater distance down the gel compared to larger samples.

43. **B**—His DNA fingerprint seems to exactly match that of the evidence DNA sample.

44. **B**—A and C seem to share the exact same restriction fragment cut of their DNA. Perhaps they are messing with our heads and added the DNA from the same individual twice.

45. **B**—$100 - 45 - 36 = 19$ percent.

46. **C**—36 percent of the population is AA. Taking the square root of 0.36, we find the frequency of the A allele to be 0.6. This means that the a allele's frequency must be $1 - 0.6$, or 0.4. From these numbers, we can calculate the *expected* Hardy-Weinberg heterozygous frequency is $2pq = 2(A)(a) = 2(0.6)(0.4) = 48.0$ or 48 percent.

47. **B**—The expected heterozygous probability does not match up with the actual. This population is not in Hardy–Weinberg equilibrium.

48. **B**—The homozygous frequency is higher than expected; one explanation for this is that the homozygotes are being selected for.

49. **A**—Water will flow *out* of the bag because the solute concentration of the beaker is hypertonic compared to the dialysis bag. Osmosis passively drives water from a hypotonic region to a hypertonic region.

50. **B**—Water would now flow *into* the bag because the solute gradient has been reversed. Now the beaker is hypotonic compared to the dialysis bag. Water thus moves into the bag.

51. **C**—Water potential = pressure potential + solute potential. Water passively moves from regions with high water potential toward those with lower water potential.

52. **D**—The mother (person B) must be heterozygous Aa because she and her husband (aa) have produced children that have the double recessive condition. This means that person B (the mother) must have contributed an a and that the cross is Aa × aa—and the probability is ½.

53. **D**—To answer this question, we must first determine the probability that person D is heterozygous. We know she is not aa because she does not have the condition. Since we know that the father *has* the condition, we know for certain that his genotype is aa. Both of mother D's parents must be heterozygous since neither of them have the condition, but they have produced a child with the condition. The probability that mother D is heterozygous Aa is ⅔. The probability that a couple with the genotypes Aa × aa have a double recessive child is ½. The probability that these two will have a child with the condition is ½ × ⅔ = ⅓ = 0.3333.

	A	a
A	AA	Aa
a	Aa	aa

54. **D**—If the couple has a child (person E) with the recessive condition, then we know for certain that mother D must be heterozygous. It is definitely an aa × Aa cross, leaving a 50 percent chance that their child will be aa.

55. **B**

56. **B**

57. **A**—The total solute potential for side A is 1.0 MPa (remember that for NaCl, i = 2), and the total solute potential for side B is 0.8 MPa. Therefore, side A has a higher concentration of solute (hypertonic).

58. **D**—Water will move from a hypotonic solution (side B) toward a hypertonic solution (side A). Sodium will diffuse from a region of more sodium (side B) to a region of less sodium (side A).

59. **A**—Heterozygous individuals carry the recessive gene but are themselves healthy.

60. **D**—Low numbers of stomata help to reduce water loss, helpful in hot and dry regions.

61. **A**—Prokaryotic and eukaryotic cells *do* have similar structures, the organelles in eukaryotic cells took care of having a *smaller* surface area–to–volume ratio, and eukaryotic cells are not able to multiply faster.

62. **B**—Changing envelope proteins are created because of genetic variation in the genes that code for these proteins.

63. **D**—This cladogram shows a closer relationship between X and Y.

PART B: GRID-IN QUESTIONS

1. **1.53**—If the green-melon parents were Gg, you would expect a cross with a yellow-melon plant (gg) to produce 50 percent Gg and 50 percent gg offspring. What you actually observed was 53 green and 41 yellow. Based on a total number of 94 offspring, your expected half-and-half ratios would be 47 of each color.

	# OBSERVED (o)	# EXPECTED (e)	(o − e)	(o − e)^2	(o − e)^2/e
green-melon plant	53	47	6	36	0.766
yellow-melon plant	41	47	−6	36	0.766

The chi-square value is 1.53 (less than the critical value of 3.84), so the null hypothesis is accepted.

2. **0.52**

tan = p; green = q
green phenotype = q^2 = 0.23; frequency of green allele = $\sqrt{0.23}$ = 0.48
Since $p + q = 1$, the tan allele (p) = 1 − 0.48 = 0.52.

3. 1.27—Logarithmic growth takes place during the time where the slope is the greatest, approximately between 12 and 30 hours. During that time (18 hours), the bacterial population started at 10 million and increased to 33 million (a difference of 23 million). Therefore, 23 million divided by 18 hours gives a rate of 1.27 million bacteria per hour.

		1	.	2	7
⊖		⊘	⊘	⊘	
	⊙	⊙	●	⊙	⊙
		⓪	⓪	⓪	⓪
	①	●	①	①	①
	②	②	②	●	②
	③	③	③	③	③
	④	④	④	④	④
	⑤	⑤	⑤	⑤	⑤
	⑥	⑥	⑥	⑥	⑥
	⑦	⑦	⑦	⑦	●
	⑧	⑧	⑧	⑧	⑧
	⑨	⑨	⑨	⑨	⑨

4. –2.4—The solute potential is $-(1) \times (0.1 \text{ M}) \times (0.00831 \text{ MPa/mole K}) \times (293 \text{ K}) = -0.24 \text{ MPa}$. The pressure potential is zero because the solution is in an open container. Therefore $(-0.24) + 0 = -0.24 \text{ MPa}$.

–			2	.	4
●		⊘	⊘	⊘	
	⊙	⊙	⊙	●	⊙
		⓪	⓪	⓪	⓪
	①	①	①	①	①
	②	②	●	②	②
	③	③	③	③	③
	④	④	④	④	●
	⑤	⑤	⑤	⑤	⑤
	⑥	⑥	⑥	⑥	⑥
	⑦	⑦	⑦	⑦	⑦
	⑧	⑧	⑧	⑧	⑧
	⑨	⑨	⑨	⑨	⑨

5. 2.4

$$SA = 6 \times (2.5 \text{ cm} \times 2.5 \text{ cm}) = 37.5 \text{ cm}^2$$
$$V = (2.5 \text{ cm})^3 = 15.6 \text{ cm}^3$$
$$SA/V = 37.5/15.6 = 2.4$$

			2	.	4
⊖		⊘	⊘	⊘	
	⊙	⊙	⊙	●	⊙
		⓪	⓪	⓪	⓪
	①	①	①	①	①
	②	②	●	②	②
	③	③	③	③	③
	④	④	④	④	●
	⑤	⑤	⑤	⑤	⑤
	⑥	⑥	⑥	⑥	⑥
	⑦	⑦	⑦	⑦	⑦
	⑧	⑧	⑧	⑧	⑧
	⑨	⑨	⑨	⑨	⑨

6. 50

$$(0.5 \text{ M})(V_i) = (0.1 \text{ M})(250 \text{ mL})$$
$$V_i = 50 \text{ mL}$$

				5	0
⊖		⊘	⊘	⊘	
	⊙	⊙	⊙	⊙	⊙
		⓪	⓪	⓪	●
	①	①	①	①	①
	②	②	②	②	②
	③	③	③	③	③
	④	④	④	④	④
	⑤	⑤	⑤	●	⑤
	⑥	⑥	⑥	⑥	⑥
	⑦	⑦	⑦	⑦	⑦
	⑧	⑧	⑧	⑧	⑧
	⑨	⑨	⑨	⑨	⑨

› Free-Response Grading Outline

1. Gel electrophoresis question (10 points)

   A. Electrophoresis experiment (maximum 5 points)
      - Mentioning that smaller particles travel faster. (1 point)
      - Mentioning that the fragments of DNA are placed into wells at the head of the gel to begin their migration to the other side. (1 point)
      - Mentioning that the DNA migrates only as electric current is passed through the gel. (1 point)
      - Mentioning that the DNA migrates from negative charge to positive charge. (1 point)
      - Mentioning that when DNA samples from different individuals are cut with restriction enzymes, they show variations in the band patterns on gel electrophoresis known as *restriction fragment length polymorphisms* (RFLPs). (1 point)
      - Mentioning that DNA is specific to each individual, and when it is mixed with restriction enzymes, different combinations of RFLPs will be obtained from person to person. (1 point)
      - Definition of a DNA fingerprint as the combination of an individual's RFLPs inherited from each parent. (1 point)
      - Mentioning that if an individual's electrophoresis pattern identically matches that of the crime scene evidence, the DNA has spoken and shown the individual to be the perpetrator, since the probability of two people having an identical set of RFLPs is virtually non-existent. (1 point)

   B. Paternity (maximum 5 points)
      - Mentioning that DNA samples would need to be taken from the disputed child and the potential parents involved. (1 point)
      - Definition of a restriction enzyme as an enzyme that cuts DNA at a particular sequence and creates open fragments of DNA called "sticky ends." (1 point)
      - Mentioning that the DNA from all the different individuals involved must be cut by the same restriction enzyme(s) so that the RFLPs created can be compared with each other. (1 point)
      - Mentioning that each sample of DNA must be placed into a different well at the top of the gel plate. (1 point)
      - Mentioning that the DNA will migrate from negative charge to positive charge, once the current is applied, to create an RFLP pattern specific for each individual—this is a look at the DNA fingerprint of an individual. (1 point)
      - Mentioning that some sort of dye should be added to the DNA samples that will allow for proper viewing of the bands after the current is disconnected. (1 point)
      - Mentioning that one of the two DNA cuts from the child's fingerprint should match up with one of the two DNA cuts from the father's fingerprint and one from the mother's fingerprint as well, because the child inherits one chromosome of each homologous pair from the mother and one from the father. (1 point)

2. Speciation question (here, you can obtain 4 points from a couple of the answers; if 4 points are obtained for an answer, a maximum of 3 points can be obtained from each of the other 2 answers)

   A. Geographic barriers (maximum 4 points)
      - Mentioning how geographic barriers can lead to reproductive isolation of members from the same species. (½ point)
      - Mentioning that if these geographically separated species are moved into regions that have different environments, natural selection might favor different characteristics from the same species in the different environments. (1 point)
      - Mentioning that this is an example of allopatric speciation—interbreeding ceases because some sort of barrier separates a single population into two. (1 point)
      - Definition of divergent evolution as the evolution of two species farther apart from each other as they are exposed to different environmental challenges. (1 point)

- Mentioning the Galapagos finches as an example of geographic barriers leading to reproductive isolation and divergent evolution. (½ point)
- Mentioning that if after a long period of time, these divergent species come back together and are unable to reproduce, they have become a new species. (1 point)

B. Polyploidy (maximum 4 points)
- Definition of polyploidy as a condition in which an individual has more than the normal number of sets of chromosomes. (1 point)
- Description of how polyploidy initially occurs—an accident during cell division could double the chromosome number in the offspring, producing a tetraploid ($4n$) organism. (1 point)
- Alternate description of how polyploidy could initially occur—the breeding of two individuals from different species leads to a hybrid that is usually sterile and contains chromosomes that are not able to pair up during meiosis because they are not homologous. (1 point)
- Definition of an autopolyploid—organism with more than two chromosome sets all from the same species. (½ point)
- Definition of an allopolyploid—organism with more than two chromosome sets that come from more than one species. (½ point)
- Mentioning that although an individual may be healthy, it cannot reproduce with nonpolyploidic members of its species. (1 point)
- Mentioning that polyploidic individuals are able to mate only with other individuals who have the same polyploidic chromosomal makeup. (1 point)

C. Balanced polymorphism (maximum 3 points)
- Definition of balanced polymorphism—some characters have two or more phenotypic variants, such as tulip color. (1 point)
- Mention of the fact that if one phenotypic variant leads to increased reproductive success, directional selection will eventually eliminate all other varieties because only those who have the particular phenotypic variant of choice will survive to be able to reproduce, and thus only their genes will be passed along. (1 point)
- Mentioning that this requirement for a particular variant of the trait in order to survive reproductively isolates individuals of the same species from each other, opening the door for sympatric speciation. (1 point)
- Mentioning that if the balanced polymorphism causes the two variants to diverge enough to no longer be able to interbreed, speciation has occurred. (1 point)
- Citing an example of balanced polymorphism. (1 point)

D. Reproductive isolation (maximum 4 points)
- Mentioning that any barrier that prevents two species from producing offspring can be categorized as reproductive isolation. (½ point)
- Definition of prezygotic barriers as reproductive barriers that make the fertilization of the female ovum impossible. (1 point)
- Mentioning, as an example of prezygotic barriers, any of the following (½ point each, up to 1 point total for prezygotic barrier examples): (a) *habitat isolation*—two species live in different habitats (they just don't see each other, so they cannot reproduce); (b) *temporal isolation*—two species mate at either different times of the year or different times of the day (either way, they are isolated from each other because they do not mate at the same time); (c) *behavioral isolation*—two species have different mating behaviors that do not mix well (members of the other species do not understand the actions of the other as mating signals—a simple communication breakdown ☺); (d) *mechanical isolation*—mating may actually be attempted, but the physical sexual structures do not function together properly (they are incompatible).
- Definition of postzygotic barriers as reproductive barriers that prevent a properly formed hybrid between two species from reproducing themselves. (1 point)

- Mentioning, as an example of postzygotic barriers, any of the following (½ point each, up to 1 point total for postzygotic barrier examples): (a) *hybrid breakdown*—sometimes the first generation of hybrids produced are able to reproduce with each other, but after that the wheels come off and the next generation is infertile; (b) *reduced hybrid viability*—the two different species are able to mate physically and the hybrid zygote is formed, but problems arise during the development of the hybrid that lead to prenatal death of the individual; (c) *reduced hybrid fertility*—the two different species are able to mate physically and produce a viable offspring, but the offspring is infertile.

3. Life on earth is made possible because of certain unique characteristics of water. (maximum 4 points for entire question)

A. Properties of water (maximum 2 points)
- Mentioning that hydrogen bonding holds water molecules together (cohesion). (1 point)
- Mentioning that water has high specific heat (water changes its temperature less than most substances when it absorbs or loses a certain amount of heat). (1 point)
- Mentioning that the solid form of water is less dense than its liquid form. (1 point)
- Mentioning water acts as a solvent for so many substances. (1 point)

B. Effects on living organisms (maximum 2 points)
- Mentioning that hydrogen bonding allows for flow of water through plants (xylem). (1 point)
- Mentioning that water's high specific heat means large bodies of water store heat and leads to milder climates in coastal areas. (1 point)
- Noting that water's unusual density means ice floats. If it sank, all bodies of water would freeze solid from the bottom up, and sustainable life on earth would not be possible. (1 point)
- Mentioning that water's ability as a solvent allows for many reactions to occur in the cell. (1 point)

4. Evolution is the change in allele frequencies in a population over time. (maximum 4 points for entire question)

A. Definition and examples (maximum 2 points)
- Defining natural selection. (maximum 1 point)
  a. Mentioning it is the process by which certain alleles increase in frequency in a population because of the survival or reproduction benefit they give to those individuals who possess them. (½ point)
  b. Possible example: sickle cell allele persists in populations where malaria is present (having sickle-shaped red blood cells makes you less likely to contract malaria). (½ point)
  c. Defining genetic drift. (maximum 1 point)
  d. Describing how random processes can change allele frequencies. (½ point)
  e. Possible example: allele frequencies in a new population are dependent on which alleles are present in the founders of that population (founder effect). (½ point)
- Defining mutation.
  a. Mentioning that changes in DNA create genetic variation and new alleles. (½ point)
  b. Mentioning that evolution by "neutral mutations" can occur even if the new alleles are not acted on by natural selection. (½ point)
  c. Possible example: eye color gene mutates to a different color without any change in vision or behavior as a result of the mutation. (½ point)

B. Explanation of data (maximum 2 points)
- Mentioning the changes could not be the gradual process of natural selection because they occurred rapidly between two censuses. (1 point)
- Indicating that the changes could be caused by genetic drift. (1 point)
- Indicating that the changes could be caused by some environmental event (flood, fire) that randomly killed many dark-coated mice. (1 point)

5. Homeostasis, or the maintenance of a steady-state environment, is a characteristic of all living organisms. (maximum 4 points for entire question)

A. Blood glucose levels (maximum 1½ points)
   - Mentioning insulin/glucagon is released from the pancreas. (½ point)
   - Mentioning insulin stimulates uptake of glucose from the blood to the liver. (½ point)
   - Mentioning insulin causes glucose to be stored as glycogen in the liver. (½ point)
   - Mentioning insulin signals body cells to take up glucose for energy use. (½ point)
   - Mentioning glucagon stimulates the liver to release glucose into the bloodstream. (½ point)

B. Body temperature (maximum 1½ points)
   - Describing how body insulation (hair, fat, feathers) reduces heat loss. (½ point)
   - Mentioning that vasodilation results in increased blood flow and increased heat loss. (½ point)
   - Mentioning that vasoconstriction results in decreased blood flow and decreased heat loss. (½ point)
   - Mentioning that sweating results in evaporative cooling. (½ point)
   - Mentioning that shivering generates energy. (½ point)

C. Blood calcium levels (maximum 1½ points)
   - Mentioning that parathyroid hormone (PTH) is released by the parathyroid gland. (½ point)
   - Mentioning that PTH increases the amount of calcium in circulation. (½ point)
   - Mentioning that PTH causes release of calcium from bones. (½ point)
   - Mentioning that PTH leads to increased absorption of calcium by the intestines and kidneys. (½ point)
   - Mentioning that calcitonin is released by the thyroid gland. (½ point)
   - Mentioning that calcitonin decreases the amount of calcium in circulation. (½ point)
   - Mentioning that calcitonin promotes reabsorption of calcium by the bones. (½ point)
   - Mentioning that calcitonin leads to decreased absorption of calcium by the kidneys and intestines. (½ point)

6. Membranes are vital to the transport of substances into and out of cells. (maximum 4 points for entire question)

A. Active transport (maximum 1½ points)
   - Describing active transport as the movement of a particle against its concentration gradient (from low concentration to high concentration), which requires input of energy. (½ point)
   - Mentioning that it allows the cell to concentrate substances within the cell membrane. (½ point)
   - Mentioning that it is performed by protein pumps in the membrane. (½ point)
   - Possible example: sodium-potassium pump moves potassium into the cell and sodium out of the cell. (½ point)

B. Endocytosis and exocytosis (maximum 2 points)
   - Mentioning that endocytosis brings a substance into a cell by enclosing it within a membrane-created vesicle. (½ point)
   - Mentioning that the vesicle then fuses with lysosome (contains hydrolytic enzymes). (½ point)
   - Possible example: phagocytes (white blood cells) of the immune system engulf foreign invaders. (½ point)
   - Mentioning that receptor-mediated endocytosis uses proteins embedded in a membrane that contains receptors for specific molecules. (½ point)
   - Mentioning that exocytosis expels waste substances for export by enclosing these substances in a vesicle that fuses with the membrane. (½ point)
   - Possible examples: cells expelling waste or a pancreatic cell exporting insulin protein into the bloodstream. (½ point)

C. Facilitated diffusion (maximum 1½ points)
   - Describing facilitated diffusion as the diffusion of particles with the assistance

of membrane transport proteins. (½ point)

- Mentioning that transport proteins are specific and have a binding site for the specific molecule of interest. (½ point)
- Mentioning that it does not require energy. (½ point)
- Mentioning that osmosis occurs from a hypotonic solution to a hypertonic solution. (½ point)

7. Skin is coated with sebum, an oily substance that slows water loss and inhibits growth of some microorganisms. (maximum 4 points for entire question)

  A. How sebum works (maximum 2 points)
  - Mentioning that sebum (or any oily substance) is composed of lipids. (1 point)
  - Mentioning that lipids are hydrophobic (repel water). (1 point)
  - Mentioning that sebum creates a hydrophobic barrier on skin that slows water loss. (1 point)

  B. Why lungs are more vulnerable to infection (maximum 2 points)
  - Mentioning that lungs provide a moist environment, ideal for microbial growth. (1 point)
  - Mentioning that lungs have a highly folded surface (high surface area). (1 point)
  - Mentioning that a higher surface area provides more opportunities for invasion. (1 point)

8. The complete oxidation of a mole of glucose produces 686 kcal of free energy. (maximum 4 points for entire question)

  A. Loss of energy (maximum 3 points)
  - Mentioning that energy cannot be created or destroyed but only transformed from one form to another (first law of thermodynamics). (1 point)
  - Mentioning that every energy transformation results in some energy loss as heat (second law of thermodynamics). (1 point)
  - Mentioning that the remaining 60 percent energy from glucose oxidation is lost as heat. (1 point)

  B. Benefits from loss of energy (maximum 1 point)
  - Mentioning that humans use some of the heat to maintain body temperature. (1 point)

  C. Adaptation of hibernating animals (maximum 2 points)
  - Mentioning that hibernating animals don't need a lot of ATP because they are inactive. (1 point)
  - Mentioning that they must still maintain internal body heat. (1 point)
  - Mentioning that lower efficiency means heat generation without much ATP being produced. (1 point)

Scoring and Interpretation
AP BIOLOGY PRACTICE EXAM 1

Multiple-Choice Questions:

number of correct answers: _____
number of incorrect answers: _____
number of blank answers: _____

Grid-In Questions:

number of correct answers: _____
number of incorrect answers: _____
number of blank answers: _____

_____ + _____ = _____
multiple-choice   grid-in   Section I
number correct   number correct   raw score

Free-Response Questions:

1. ____ / 10   3. ____ / 4   6. ____ / 4
2. ____ / 10   4. ____ / 4   7. ____ / 4
                   5. ____ / 4   8. ____ / 4

Add up the total points accumulated in the eight questions and multiply the sum by 1.57 to obtain the free-response raw score: _____ × 1.57 = _____
                                         free-response points   Section II raw score

CALCULATE YOUR SCORE

Now combine the raw scores from the multiple-choice and free-response sections to obtain your new raw score for the entire practice exam. Use the ranges listed below to determine your grade for this exam. Don't worry about how we arrived at the following ranges, and remember that they are rough estimates on questions that are not actual AP exam questions . . . do not read too much into them.

Raw Score	Approximate AP Score
83–138	5
63–82	4
48–62	3
26–47	2
0–25	1

Answer Sheet for AP Biology Practice Exam 2

ANSWER SHEET FOR MULTIPLE-CHOICE QUESTIONS

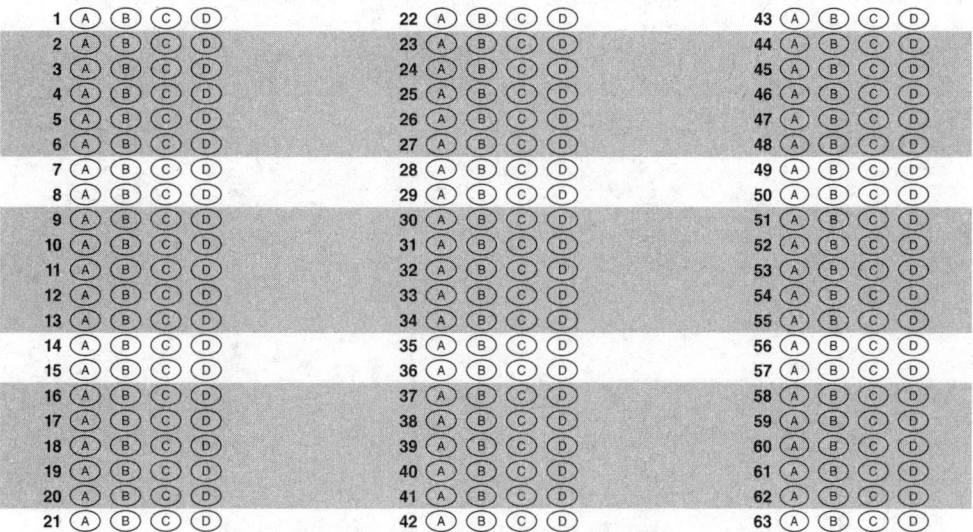

PART B: GRID-IN QUESTIONS

AP Biology Practice Exam 2: Section I

PART A: MULTIPLE-CHOICE QUESTIONS

Time–1 hour and 30 minutes (for Parts A and B)

For the multiple-choice questions to follow, select the best answer
and fill in the appropriate letter on the answer sheet.

1. A baby duck runs for cover when a large object is tossed over its head. After this object is repeatedly passed overhead, the duck learns there is no danger and stops running for cover when the same object appears again. This is an example of

   A. imprinting.
   B. fixed-action pattern.
   C. agonistic behavior.
   D. habituation.

2. In a population of giraffes, an environmental change occurs that favors individuals that are tallest. As a result, more of the taller individuals are able to obtain nutrients and survive to pass along their genetic information. This is an example of

   A. directional selection.
   B. stabilizing selection.
   C. sexual selection.
   D. disruptive selection.

3. The relatives of a group of pelicans from the same species that separated from each other because of an unsuccessful migration are reunited 150 years later and find that they are unable to produce offspring. This is an example of

   A. allopatric speciation.
   B. sympatric speciation.
   C. genetic drift.
   D. gene flow.

4. A cell is placed into a hypertonic environment and its cytoplasm shrivels up. This demonstrates the principle of

   A. diffusion.
   B. active transport.
   C. facilitated diffusion.
   D. plasmolysis.

5. Which of the following is a biotic factor that could affect the growth rate of a population?

   A. Volcanic eruption
   B. Glacier melting
   C. Destruction of the ozone layer
   D. Sudden reduction in the animal food resource

6. Which of the following is not a way to form recombinant DNA?

   A. Translation
   B. Conjugation
   C. Specialized transduction
   D. Transformation

7. Chemiosmosis occurs in
   I. Mitochondria
   II. Nuclei
   III. Chloroplasts

   A. I only
   B. II only
   C. III only
   D. I and III

8. Which of the following theories is based on the notion that mitochondria and chloroplasts evolved from prokaryotic cells?

   A. Fluid mosaic model
   B. Endosymbiotic model
   C. Taxonomic model
   D. Respiration feedback model

9. Which of the following is *not* known to be involved in the control of cell division?

   A. Cyclins
   B. Protein kinases
   C. Checkpoints
   D. Fibroblast cells

10. Which of the following statements about post-transcriptional modification is incorrect?

    A. A poly-A tail is added to the 3′ end of the mRNA.
    B. A guanine cap is added to the 5′ end of the mRNA.
    C. Introns are removed from the mRNA.
    D. Posttranscriptional modification occurs in the cytoplasm.

11. In a certain pond, there are long-finned fish and short-finned fish. A horrific summer thunderstorm leads to the death of a disproportionate number of long-finned fish to the point where the relative frequency of the two forms has drastically shifted. This is an example of

    A. gene flow.
    B. natural selection.
    C. genetic drift.
    D. stabilizing selection.

12. Which of the following cells is most closely associated with phagocytosis?

    A. Neutrophils
    B. Plasma cells
    C. B cells
    D. Memory cells

13. Which of the following statements about photosynthesis is *incorrect*?

    A. H_2O is an input to the light-dependent reactions.
    B. CO_2 is an input to the Calvin cycle.
    C. Photosystems I and II both play a role in the cyclic light reactions.
    D. O_2 is a product of the light-dependent reactions.

14. If a couple has had three sons and the woman is pregnant with their fourth child, what is the probability that child 4 will *also* be male?

    A. ½
    B. ¼
    C. ⅛
    D. ¹⁄₁₆

15. Which of the following is an *incorrect* statement about gel electrophoresis?

    A. DNA migrates from positive charge to negative charge.
    B. Smaller DNA travels faster.
    C. The DNA migrates only when the current is running.
    D. The longer the current is running, the farther the DNA will travel.

16. You are told that in a population of guinea pigs, 4 percent are black (recessive) and 96 percent are brown. Which of the following is the frequency of the heterozygous condition?

    A. 16 percent
    B. 32 percent
    C. 40 percent
    D. 48 percent

17. Which of the following is known to be involved in the photoperiodic flowering response of angiosperms?

    A. Auxin
    B. Cytochrome
    C. Phytochrome
    D. Gibberellins

18. Which of the following tends to be highest on the trophic pyramid?

    A. Primary consumers
    B. Herbivores
    C. Primary carnivores
    D. Primary producers

19. A form of species interaction in which one of the species benefits while the other is unaffected is called

    A. parasitism.
    B. mutualism.
    C. commensalism.
    D. symbiosis.

20. The transfer of DNA between two bacterial cells connected by sex pili is known as

    A. specialized transduction.
    B. conjugation.
    C. transformation.
    D. generalized transduction.

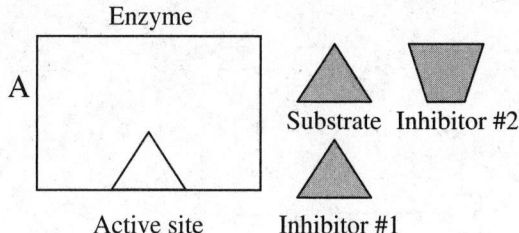

Enzyme

A

Active site   Inhibitor #1

Substrate Inhibitor #2

For questions 21–22, please use the preceding diagram:

21. If inhibitor 1 is able to bind to the active site and block the attachment of the substrate to the enzyme, this is an example of

    A. noncompetitive inhibition.
    B. competitive inhibition.
    C. a cofactor.
    D. a coenzyme.

22. Which of the following is *not* a change that would affect the efficiency of the enzyme shown above?

    A. Change in temperature
    B. Change in pH
    C. Change in salinity
    D. Increase in the concentration of the enzyme

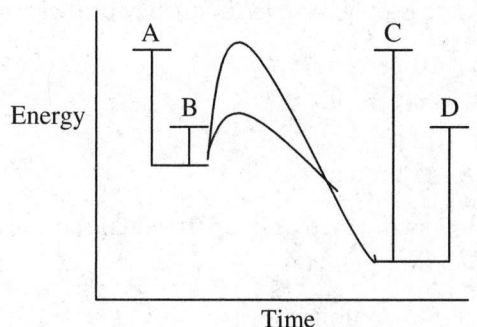

Energy

A

B

C

D

Time

23. Which of the following points on the preceding energy chart represents the activation energy of the reaction involving the enzyme?

    A. A
    B. B
    C. C
    D. D

For questions 24–27, please use the following answers:

    A. Aposomatic coloration
    B. Batesian mimicry
    C. Deceptive markings
    D. Cryptic coloration

24. Those being hunted adopt a coloring scheme that allows them to blend in to the colors of the environment.

25. An animal that is harmless copies the appearance of an animal that is dangerous as a defense mechanism to make predators think twice about attacking.

26. Warning coloration adopted by animals that possess a chemical defense mechanism.

27. Some animals have patterns that can cause a predator to think twice before attacking.

Questions 28–31 refer to the following choices:

    A. Enhancer
    B. Repressor
    C. Operator
    D. Promoter

28. Short sequence by promoter that assists transcription by interacting with regulatory proteins.

29. Protein that prevents the binding of RNA polymerase to the promoter site.

30. Transcription-affecting DNA region that may be located thousands of basepairs away from the promoter.

31. Basepair sequence that signals the start site for gene transcription.

Questions 32–35 refer to the following choices:

    A. Divergent evolution
    B. Convergent evolution
    C. Parallel evolution
    D. Coevolution

32. Two unrelated species evolve in a way that makes them more similar.

33. Similar evolutionary changes occurring in two species that can be related or unrelated.

34. The tandem back-and-forth evolution of closely related species, which is exemplified by predator-prey relationships.

35. Two related species evolve in a way that makes them less similar.

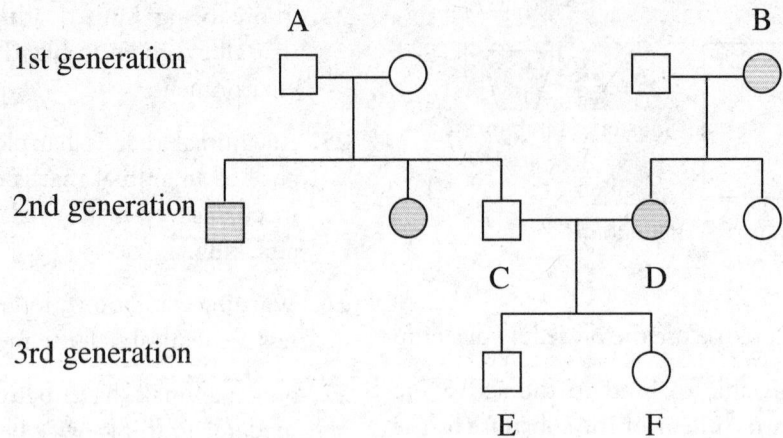

A   B

1st generation

2nd generation

3rd generation

C   D

E   F

Questions 36–39 refer to the preceding pedigree.

36. What kind of inheritable condition does this pedigree appear to show?

   A. Autosomal dominant
   B. Autosomal recessive
   C. Sex-linked dominant
   D. Sex-linked recessive

37. What is the probability that couple C and D will produce a child that has the condition?

   A. 0
   B. 0.125
   C. 0.250
   D. 0.333

38. Which of the following conditions could show the same kind of pedigree results?

   A. Cri-du-chat syndrome
   B. Turner syndrome
   C. Albinism
   D. Hemophilia

39. If child E does in fact have the condition, what is the probability that child F will also have it?

   A. 0
   B. 0.250
   C. 0.500
   D. 0.750

Questions 40–42: An experiment involving fruit flies produced the following results:

Vestigial wings are wild type, crumpled wings are mutant.

Gray body is dominant, black body is mutant.

525 vestigial, gray-bodied flies	V = vestigial
555 crumpled, black-bodied flies	v = crumpled
75 crumpled, gray flies	G = gray
45 vestigial, black-bodied flies	g = black

40. From the data presented above, one can conclude that these genes are

   A. sex-linked.
   B. epistatic.
   C. holandric.
   D. linked.

41. What is the crossover frequency of these genes?

   A. 10 percent
   B. 20 percent
   C. 30 percent
   D. 35 percent

42. How many map units apart would these genes be on a linkage map?

   A. 5 map units
   B. 10 map units
   C. 20 map units
   D. 30 map units

Questions 43–45: A laboratory procedure involving plants presents you with the data found in the following 2 charts:

Pigment	R_f
Beta carotene	1.251
Chlorophyll *a*	1.015
Chlorophyll *b*	0.985
Xanthophyll	1.125

Transpiration Rate → 1.0 = Control Rate (All Leaves Have the Same Surface Area)

PLANT	T^*10°C	T 15°C	T 20°C	HUMIDITY 20%	HUMIDITY 15%	HUMIDITY 10%	WIND 5 MPH†	WIND 10 MPH	WIND 15 MPH
A	1.042	1.105	1.211	1.121	1.130	1.205	1.001	1.025	1.100
B	0.600	0.800	1.000	0.851	0.910	0.950	0.760	0.785	0.810
C	1.240	1.245	1.251	1.411	1.519	1.550	1.214	1.240	1.301

*Temperature
†Miles per hour

43. From the transpiration rate data, it appears that transpiration rate rises as

A. temperature ↑, wind speed ↓, humidity ↓
B. temperature ↑, wind speed ↑, humidity ↓
C. temperature ↑, wind speed ↑, humidity ↑
D. temperature ↓, wind speed ↑, humidity ↑

44. According to the R_f values given in the preceding smaller table, which pigment would migrate the fastest on chromatography paper?

A. Xanthophyll
B. Chlorophyll *a*
C. Chlorophyll *b*
D. Beta carotene

45. From the transpiration rate data presented in the preceding larger table, which of the following plants appears to be most resistant to transpiration?

A. Plant A
B. Plant B
C. Plant C
D. Plants B and C are similarly resistant

Questions 46–48: A population of rodents is studied over the course of 100 generations to examine changes in dental enamel thickness. Species that are adapted to eat food resources that require high levels of processing have thicker enamel than do those that eat softer, more easily processed foods. Answer the following questions using this information and the curves that follow.

46. How is average enamel thickness changing in this population?

A. There is no real change.
B. The color and size are changing.
C. It is increasing.
D. It is decreasing.

47. You randomly pick one data point from all three sets of data (all three generations), and the individual's enamel thickness score is 15. Which of the following can be inferred?

A. The individual comes from generation 1.
B. The individual comes from generation 50.
C. The individual comes from generation 100.
D. The individual could be from any of these generations.

48. What inference can you make about this species' diet?

A. Its food resources are getting softer and easier to process.
B. Its food resources are getting harder and more difficult to process.
C. The population is growing.
D. The population is shrinking.

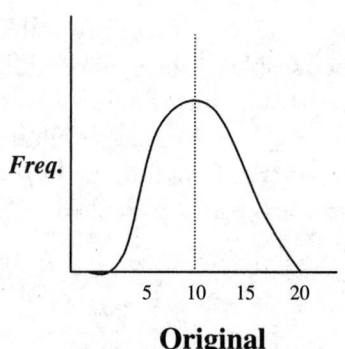

Original

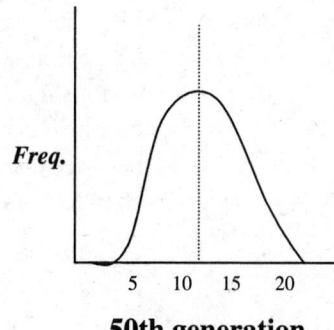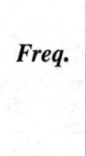

50th generation

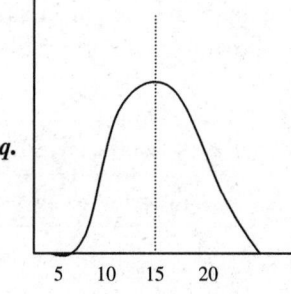

100th generation

Questions 49–52: A student sets up a lab experiment to study the behavior of slugs. She sets up a large tray filled with soil that measures 1 square meter and has four sets of conditions, one in each quadrant:

Low salinity, high temperature	Low salinity, low temperature
High salinity, high temperature	High salinity, low temperature

She places 20 slugs in the tray, 5 in each quadrant. Use this information to answer the following questions:

49. What is this lab setup called?

   A. A gel sheet
   B. A choice chamber
   C. A potometer
   D. An incubation chamber

50. After 5 minutes, there are 5 slugs in each quadrant. Which of the following is not a viable explanation for this finding?

   A. The slugs haven't had time to move yet.
   B. The slugs have no preference for temperature or salinity conditions.
   C. The slugs can't move from one area of the tray to another.
   D. The slugs do not like to live in high-temperature areas.

51. After 20 minutes, 20 slugs are in the high-temperature, low-salinity quadrant. What kind of animal behavior has this experiment displayed?

   A. Kinesis
   B. Taxis
   C. Survival
   D. Feeding

52. A classmate has set up a similar experiment in the following manner:

Low salinity, low temperature
High salinity, high temperature

Of the 20 slugs that she puts in her tray, 18 move to the high-salinity, high-temperature section within one hour, while the other 2 move to the low-salinity, low-temperature section. She concludes that slugs prefer conditions of high salinity and temperature. What is wrong with this conclusion?

   A. She didn't specify what the two temperatures or salinities were.
   B. The slugs may not have been able to move where they wanted.
   C. Crowding may have affected the behavior of the slugs, causing the 2 others to move to the other section.
   D. She is measuring two variables at once with no control, and therefore can't conclude anything about slug tastes.

53. Viral transduction is the process by which viruses carry bacterial DNA from one bacterial cell to another. In what way does this process play a role in bacterial evolution?

   A. By making the bacterial cell more resistant to predators
   B. By directly creating new species of bacteria
   C. By increasing genetic variation of the bacteria
   D. By selecting for viruses better able to infect bacteria

54. ADH is a hormone secreted by the kidneys that reduces the amount of water excreted in the urine. ADH is released in times of dehydration. This is an example of

   A. innate behavior.
   B. maintaining homeostasis.
   C. failure to respond to the environment.
   D. positive feedback.

For questions 55–57 refer to the information and graph that follows.

Five dialysis bags, made from a semipermeable membrane that is impermeable to glucose, were filled with various concentrations of glucose and placed in separate beakers containing 0.5 M glucose solution. The bags were weighed every 10 minutes and the percent change in mass for each bag was graphed:

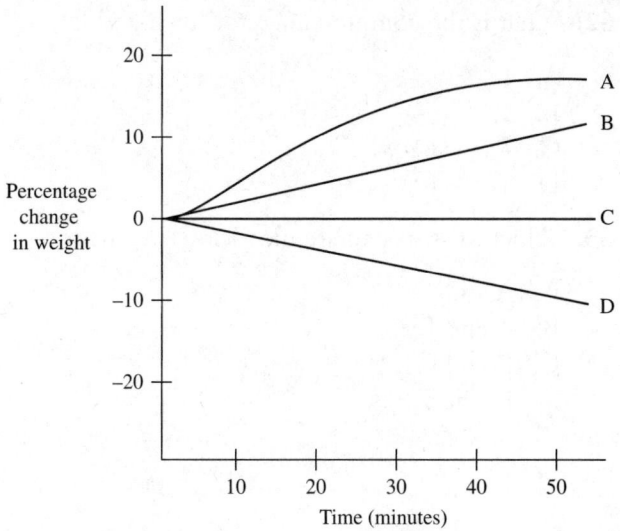

55. Which line represents the bag that contained a solution isotonic to the 0.5 M solution?

A. A
B. B
C. C
D. D

56. Which line represents that bag with the highest initial concentration of glucose?

A. A
B. B
C. C
D. D

57. Which line or lines represent bags that contain a solution that is hypertonic at 50 minutes?

A. A and B
B. B
C. C
D. D and E

58. A mutation in a bacterial enzyme changed a previously polar amino acid into a nonpolar amino acid. This amino acid was located at a site distant from the enzyme's active site. How might this mutation alter the enzyme's substrate specificity?

A. By changing the enzyme's pH optimum
B. By changing the enzyme's location in the cell
C. By changing the shape of the protein
D. An amino acid change away from the active site cannot alter the enzyme's substrate specificity.

Use the following picture of DNA to answer questions 59 and 60:

template strand   5'_____ 3'
complementary strand   3'_____ 5'

59. Based on the preceding picture, which direction would RNA polymerase move?

A. 3' → 5' along the template strand
B. 3' → 5' along the complementary strand
C. 5' → 3' along the template strand
D. 5' → 3' along the complementary strand

60. If the DNA segment is a transcriptional unit, where would the promoter be located?

A. To the left of the complementary strand
B. To the right of the template strand
C. To the left of the template strand
D. To the right of the complementary strand

61. A single gene from five related species of leafhopper was compared, and the nucleotide differences between the genes are as shown in the table:

Nucleotide Differences

Species	1	2	3	4	5
1	—	1	8	19	7
2		—	8	20	9
3			—	19	2
4				—	18
5					—

Which of the following phylogenetic trees best shows the correct evolutionary relationship between the leafhoppers?

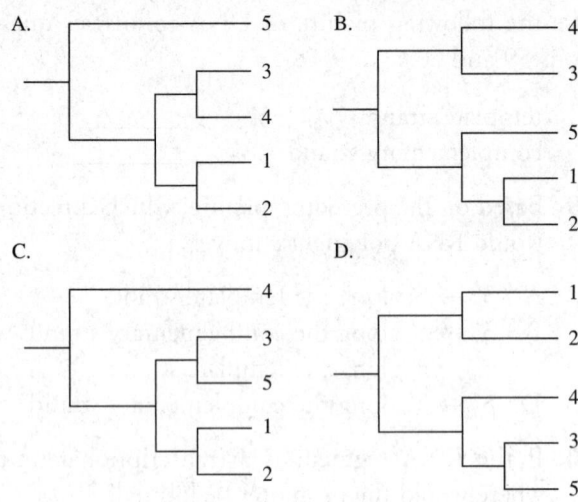

62. What is the common ancestor for B and E?

    A. 1
    B. 2
    C. 3
    D. 4

63. Which two species are most closely related?

    A. A and E
    B. A and B
    C. B and C
    D. D and E

Answer questions 62 and 63 based on the following cladogram:

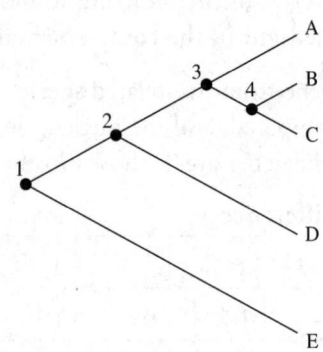

PART B: GRID-IN QUESTIONS

Calculate the correct answer and enter it on the top line of the grid-in area with each number or symbol in a separate column. Then fill in the correct circle below each number or symbol you entered (only one filled-in circle per column).

1. Twenty people decide to start a new population, totally isolated from anyone else. Two of the individuals are heterozygous for a recessive allele, which in homozygotes causes cystic fibrosis. Assuming this population is in Hardy-Weinberg equilibrium, what fraction (expressed as a decimal) of people in this new population will have cystic fibrosis?

2. A certain mutation found in fruit flies (*Drosophila melanogaster*) is hypothesized to be autosomal recessive. The experimenter crossed two *Drosophila* flies that were heterozygous for the trait. The next generation produced 70 wild-type males, 65 wild-type females, 36 males with the mutation, and 40 mutant females. Calculate the chi-squared value for the null hypothesis that the mutation is autosomal recessive.

3. If the pH of a solution is calculated using the equation $pH = -\log[H^+]$, what is the pH of a solution with a hydrogen ion concentration of 1.33×10^{-8}?

4. A cell is in equilibrium with its surroundings. The molarity of the surrounding solution at 20°C is 0.8 M. Calculate the solute potential of the surrounding solution.

   The equation for solute potential is $\Psi_s = -i\,CRT$ where

   i = ionization constant (assume that it is 1)
   C = molar concentration
   R = pressure constant (R = 0.0831 liter MPa/mole K)
   T = temperature in kelvins (room temperature is 293 K)

5. Treatment of tomato plants with a growth hormone yielded the following weights of tomatoes: 100 g, 86 g, 123 g, 98 g, 104 g, 71 g. What is the average weight of a tomato after treatment?

6. After seven days of growth, a plant's weight was 14.3 grams. The percent biomass of that plant was determined to be 23.1 percent. What amount of energy (in kcal) is stored in the plant, if the amount of stored energy = (g biomass) × 4.35 kcal?

AP Biology Practice Exam 2: Section II

FREE-RESPONSE QUESTIONS

Time—1 hour and 30 minutes

(The first 10 minutes is a reading period. Do not begin writing until the 10-minute period has passed.)
Questions 1 and 2 are long free-response questions that should require about 20 minutes each.
Questions 3–8 are short-response questions that should require about 6 minutes each.
Outline form is not acceptable. Answers should be in essay form.

1. The immune system is the body's defense against foreign invaders and is divided into specific and nonspecific immunity, and humoral and cell-mediated immunity. Answer three of the following four questions:

   A. Describe the primary immune response and how an invading antigen is met, dealt with, and eliminated. Describe the cells involved and how they are created.

   B. Describe the mechanism by which the immune system deals with viruses, invaders that make it *inside* our *cells*.

   C. Define nonspecific immunity, and list three examples of nonspecific defense mechanisms in humans.

   D. Define the term *vaccination*, and describe how a vaccination works.

2. You just started working at a local laboratory and are usually given the grunt-work lab assignments to perform. Design and describe how you would do the following experiments:

   A. Describe how you would design an experiment to prove the theory that photosynthesis requires both light and chloroplasts. Describe what equipment you would use, what your control would be, and how your expected outcome would support your hypothesis.

   B. You are told that you need to determine how the following factors affect the rate of transpiration in plants: temperature, humidity, light intensity, and air movement. Describe how you would perform an experiment that could accomplish that task, and give your prediction of the expected results. Be sure to describe your experimental setup.

3. The phenotype for scale color in gila monsters is determined by a specific locus. The dominant allele (black) is represented by G and the recessive allele (brown) is represented by g. The cross between a male gila monster with black scales and a female gila monster with brown scales produced the following F_1 generation:

   • Black-scaled gila monsters: 52
   • Brown-scaled gila monsters: 55
   • White-scaled gila monsters: 1

   The black-scaled females and brown-scaled males from the F_1 generation were then crossed to produce the following F_2 generation:

   • Black-scaled gila monsters: 53
   • Brown-scaled gila monsters: 54
   • White-scaled gila monsters: 0

   A. Based on the data presented here, determine the P-generation genotypes. Provide Punnett squares that support your answer.

   B. The white-scaled female in the F_1 generation resulted from a mutational change. Explain what a mutation is and discuss a type of mutation that might have produced the white-scaled female in the F_1 generation.

4. The idea of surface area is an important concept in biology. Explain how surface area plays a critical role in the digestive system.

5. The following table includes data from scan samples conducted on a fictional mammal called a googabear every 10 minutes over the course of 42 hours. At each scan, it was noted whether the googabear was active or inactive. The percentage of active (feeding, moving, engaging in social behavior) and inactive (resting or sleeping) scans recorded for each time period are shown in the table. Describe the pattern of activity for the googabear and discuss possible reasons for this pattern.

TIME	0600–1200	1200–1800	1800–2400	0000–0600	0600–1200	1200–1800	1800–2400
% active	83	75	22	5	93	89	15
% inactive	17	25	88	95	7	11	85

6. In earth's early history, the evolution of photosynthesis in simple cells occurred before the evolution of more complex cells. Briefly describe the significance of photosynthesis being present first.

7. What evidence supports the theory that chloroplasts and mitochondria are evolved from prokaryotic cells?

8. You are asked to estimate if a certain species of plant could live in a salt marsh. You collect the following data:

- The overall Ψ of the soil (Ψ_{soil}): −2.2 MPa
- Solute concentration of plant cell contents: 0.08 M (assume i = 1, and 12°C
- Pressure potential of the plant cells: −1.2 MPa
- R = 0.00831 liter MPa/mole K

Do you think the plant could grow in this environment? Why or why not? Show your work.

› Answers and Explanations for Practice Exam 2

PART A: MULTIPLE-CHOICE QUESTIONS

1. **D**—Habituation is the loss of responsiveness to unimportant stimuli or stimuli that do not provide appropriate feedback. This is a prime example of habituation.

2. **A**—Directional selection occurs when members of a population at one end of a spectrum are selected against, while those at the other end are selected for. Taller giraffes are being selected for; shorter giraffes are being selected against.

3. **A**—When interbreeding ceases because some sort of barrier separates a single population into two (an area with no food, a mountain, etc.), the two populations evolve independently, and if they change enough, then, even if the barrier is removed, they cannot interbreed. This is allopatric speciation.

4. **D**—Chapter 19, despite being last, is a very important chapter. The experiments are very well represented on the AP Biology exam, and you should read this chapter carefully and learn how to design and interpret experiments.

5. **C**

6. **A**

7. **D**

8. **B**—The endosymbiotic theory proposes that mitochondria and chloroplasts evolved through the symbiotic relationship between prokaryotic organisms.

9. **D**—Fibroblast *growth factor* is said to be involved, but fibroblast cells are not.

10. **D**—Posttranscriptional modification actually occurs in the nucleus.

11. **C**—Genetic drift is a change in allele frequencies that is due to chance events. When drift dramatically reduces population size, it is called a "bottleneck."

12. **A**—Neutrophils are phagocytic cells of the immune system. They roam the body looking for rubbish to clear.

13. **C**—Only photosystem I is involved in the cyclic reactions. Photosystem II is not.

14. **A**—Genetics has no memory . . . it will be ½ forever.

15. **A**—DNA migrates from a negative charge to a positive charge. The rest are true.

16. **B**—$0.04 = q^2$. Therefore, the square root of $0.04 = q = 0.20$ and $p + q = 1$. So $p + 0.20 = 1$. Therefore, $p = 0.80$, and $2pq$ is the frequency of the heterozygote condition: $2(0.20)(0.80) = 0.320 = 32$ percent.

17. **C**—Phytochrome is an important pigment to the process of flowering. Of its two forms, the active form, P_{fr}, is responsible for the production of the hormone florigen, which is thought to assist in the blooming of flowers.

18. **C**—Primary carnivores > primary consumers = herbivores > primary producers.

19. **C**—The example to know is the cattle egrets that feast on insects aroused into flight by cattle grazing in the insects' habitat. The birds benefit because they get food, but the cattle do not appear to benefit at all.

20. **B**—Conjugation is the sexual reproduction of bacteria.

21. **B**—In competitive inhibition, an inhibitor molecule resembling the substrate binds to the active site and physically blocks the substrate from attaching.

22. **C**—This is the only factor that is not a major factor affecting enzyme efficiency.

23. **B**—The activation energy of a reaction is the amount of energy needed for the reaction to occur. Notice that the activation energy for the enzymatic reaction is much lower than the nonenzymatic reaction.

24. **D**

25. **B**

26. A

27. C

28. C

29. B

30. A

31. D

32. B

33. C

34. D

35. A

36. **B**—It is not autosomal dominant because in order for the second generation on the left to have those two individuals with the condition, one parent would need to display the condition as well. It is probably not sex-linked because it seems to appear as often in females as in males. Autosomal recessive seems to be the best fit for this disease.

37. **D**—One first needs to determine the probability that person C is heterozygous (Bb). We know that person D is double recessive because she has the condition. We know that the parents for person C must be Bb and Bb because neither of them has the condition, but they produced children with the condition. The probability of person C being heterozygous is ⅔, because a monohybrid cross of his parents (Bb × Bb) gives the following Punnett square:

	B	**b**
B	BB	Bb
b	Bb	bb

Since you know that he doesn't have the condition, he cannot be bb. This leaves just three possible outcomes, two of which are Bb. A cross must then be done between the father (person C) Bb and the mother (person D) bb. The chance of their child being bb is 50 percent or ½. This means that the chance of these two having a child with the condition is ⅔ × ½ or ⅓.

38. **C**—Albinism is the only autosomal recessive condition on this list.

39. **C**—It is ½, because finding out that one of their children has the condition lets us know that the father (person C) is *definitely* Bb. This changes the probability of ⅔ to 1, meaning that the probability of the two having another child with this condition is simply the result of the Punnett square of Bb × bb, or ½.

40. **D**—When you see a ratio like the one in this problem—7:7:1:1 (approximately)—the genes are probably linked. The reason the crumpled, gray, and vestigial black flies exist at all is because crossover must have occurred.

41. **A**—To determine the crossover frequency in a problem like this, simply add up the total number of crossovers (75 + 45 = 120) and divide that sum by the total number of offspring (120 + 555 + 525 = 1200). This results in 120/1200 or 10 percent.

42. **B**—One map unit is equal to a 1 percent recombination frequency.

43. **B**—The data in the table show you that this answer is the correct choice.

44. **D**—The larger the value of R_f for a bunch of pigments dissolved in a particular chromatography solvent, the faster the pigments will migrate. Beta carotene has the highest R_f value.

45. **B**—Across the board it seems to have the lowest rate of transpiration. You can make this leap because, as mentioned on top of the larger chart, all the leaves have the same surface area, allowing you to compare their transpiration values.

46. **C**—The average enamel thickness started at 10, increased to 12, and then increased to 15. It is therefore increasing overall.

47. **D**—The average enamel thickness does not describe the range of possible values; an individual with a thickness of 15 could reasonably come from any of the three generations (if we took into account probability, we could say that the individual most likely came from the 100th generation because this population has the highest frequency of individuals with this thickness; however, the question does not ask for probabilities).

48. **B**—Because thicker enamel in this species indicates foods that are more difficult to process, the answer is B.

49. **B**—Experimental setups where individuals are given a choice as to where to move are called "choice chambers."

50. **D**—All the answers except D are possible, and are important things to consider when setting up an experiment. For example, it is important to allow your study animals enough time to move and/or get used to their new surroundings and conditions before drawing conclusions about their behavior. D is not a good answer because half of the slugs started in a high-temperature area and haven't moved.

51. **A**—Kinesis is the movement of animals in response to current conditions; animals tend to move until they find a favorable environment, at which point their movement slows.

52. **D**—It is important to try to measure only one variable at once. The 18 slugs may have moved to the higher-temperature, higher-salinity conditions because they need high temperatures to survive, even if they dislike high salinity, and vice versa. The original experiment circumvents this problem by giving a choice for all the possible combinations of variables.

53. **C**—New genes are introduced into the bacterium through viral transduction.

54. **B**—When the body has too little water, ADH works to increase the amount of water available. This drive to maintain a stable condition is an example of homeostasis.

55. **C**—Line C showed no net change in weight, indicating the concentration of the solution inside the bag was the same (isotonic) as the solution in the beaker.

56. **A**—The most water would diffuse into the most hypertonic solution; line A shows the biggest increase in weight.

57. **B**—Line B still shows an increase in weight at 50 minutes, whereas line A has leveled out and is isotonic at 50 minutes.

58. **C**—Even though an amino acid doesn't have direct contact with the substrate, it still plays a role in the overall shape of the enzyme.

59. **A**—As RNA polymerase adds new nucleotides to the 3′ end of the new strand, it is moving toward the 5′ end of the (antiparallel) template strand.

60. **B**—The promoter would be located upstream from where transcription would begin.

61. **C**—There are few nucleotide differences between species 1 and 2, indicating they would reside close to one another on the cladogram. The same holds true for species 3 and 5. There are large numbers of differences between species 4 and all others, indicating it would be positioned on its own branch.

62. **A**—Both B and E branches originate from point 1.

63. **C**—Species B and C reside the closest to one another.

PART B: GRID-IN QUESTIONS

1. **.0025**—For this specific gene in this specific population, there are a total of 40 alleles, two of which are the recessive cf allele ($2/40 = 0.05 = q$). Since you need to be homozygous recessive to have cystic fibrosis, $(q) \times (q) = q^2 = (0.05)^2 = .0025$. In other words, 25 out of 10,000 people (0.25 percent) will have cystic fibrosis.

2. **13.33**—If both parents were heterozygous and if this trait is indeed recessive, you would expect the next generation to show 75 percent normal-looking flies and 25 percent of the flies with the recessive trait. Based on a total of 211 flies, that would mean you would expect 158 normal flies and 53 recessive flies. Your observed numbers were, instead, 135 normal flies and 76 recessive flies.

	# OBSERVED (O)	# EXPECTED (e)	(o − e)	(o − e)²	(o − e)²/e
wild-type flies	135	158	−23	529	3.35
recessive flies	76	53	23	529	9.98

Since your chi-squared value (13.33) is higher than the critical value of 6.64 (based on 1 degree of freedom), you have to reject your hypothesis. Something other than an autosomal recessive trait is going on.

3. 7.88—pH = −log(1.33 × 10⁻⁸) = 7.88

		7	.	8	8
⊖		⊘	⊘	⊘	⊘
	⊙	⊙	●	⊙	⊙
		⓪	⓪	⓪	⓪
	①	①	①	①	①
	②	②	②	②	②
	③	③	③	③	③
	④	④	④	④	④
	⑤	⑤	⑤	⑤	⑤
	⑥	⑥	⑥	⑥	⑥
	⑦	●	⑦	⑦	⑦
	⑧	⑧	⑧	●	●
	⑨	⑨	⑨	⑨	⑨

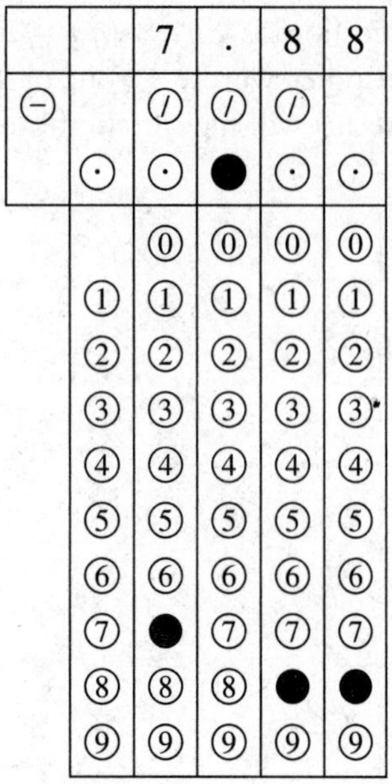

4. −19.5—Ψ_s = −(1)(0.8 M)(0.0831 L bars/mole K)(294 K) = −19.5 MPa

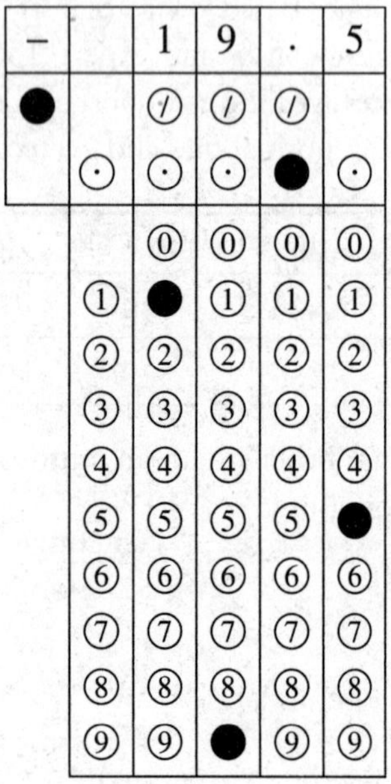

−		1	9	.	5
●		⊘	⊘	⊘	
	⊙	⊙	⊙	●	⊙
		⓪	⓪	⓪	⓪
	①	●	①	①	①
	②	②	②	②	②
	③	③	③	③	③
	④	④	④	④	④
	⑤	⑤	⑤	⑤	●
	⑥	⑥	⑥	⑥	⑥
	⑦	⑦	⑦	⑦	⑦
	⑧	⑧	⑧	⑧	⑧
	⑨	⑨	●	⑨	⑨

5. 97—Add the weight of all tomatoes and divide by the number of tomatoes. The average is 97 grams.

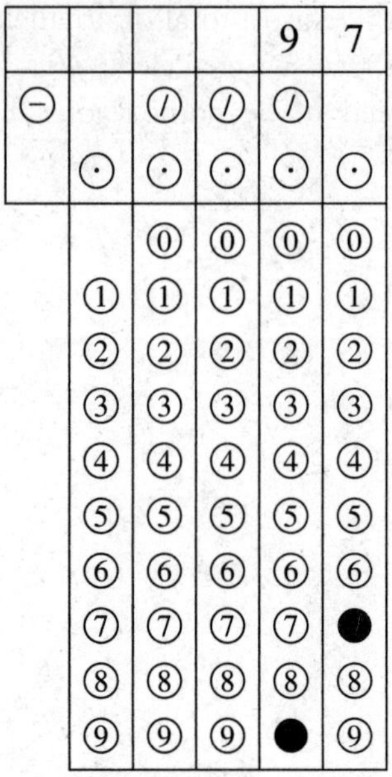

				9	7
⊖		⊘	⊘	⊘	
	⊙	⊙	⊙	⊙	⊙
		⓪	⓪	⓪	⓪
	①	①	①	①	①
	②	②	②	②	②
	③	③	③	③	③
	④	④	④	④	④
	⑤	⑤	⑤	⑤	⑤
	⑥	⑥	⑥	⑥	⑥
	⑦	⑦	⑦	⑦	●
	⑧	⑧	⑧	⑧	⑧
	⑨	⑨	⑨	●	⑨

6. 14.4—The computation is shown below:

(14.3 g)(0.231) = 3.30 g biomass

(3.30 g biomass)(4.35 kcal) = 14.4 kcal

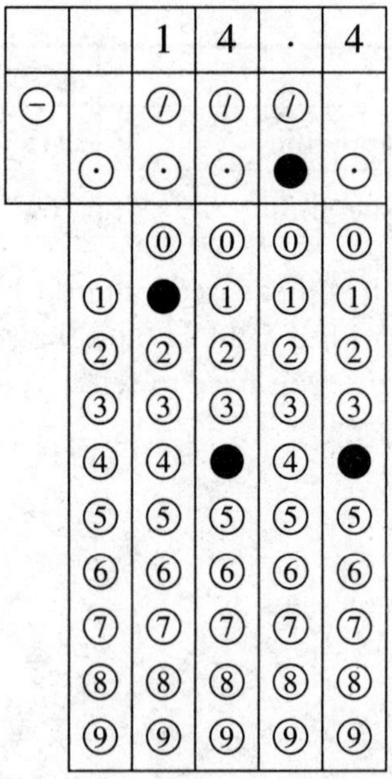

		1	4	.	4
⊖		⊘	⊘	⊘	
	⊙	⊙	⊙	●	⊙
		⓪	⓪	⓪	⓪
	①	●	①	①	①
	②	②	②	②	②
	③	③	③	③	③
	④	④	●	④	●
	⑤	⑤	⑤	⑤	⑤
	⑥	⑥	⑥	⑥	⑥
	⑦	⑦	⑦	⑦	⑦
	⑧	⑧	⑧	⑧	⑧
	⑨	⑨	⑨	⑨	⑨

› Free-Response Grading Outline

1. Immune system question (here, the student can obtain 4 points from two of the answers; if 4 points are awarded for an answer, a maximum of 3 points can be obtained for each of the remaining answers)

A. (maximum 4 points)
- Definition of an antigen as a molecule foreign to the body. (½ point)
- Mentioning that the primary immune response is an example of humoral immunity. (½ point)
- Description of a B cell and how each B cell has a specific antigen recognition site on its surface that will match up with only *one* antigen. (1 point)
- When B cells meet and attach to the appropriate antigen, they become activated and undergo mitosis and differentiation into two types of cell. (1 point)
- The two types of cell are the memory cells and plasma cells. (½ point)
- Definition of plasma cells as the cells that produce the specific antibodies. (½ point)
- Definition of memory cells as the cells that head up the secondary immune response. (½ point)
- Description of how an antibody recognizes a particular antigen, including the fact that antibodies have two functional regions: F_{ab}, which binds to the antigen; and F_c, which binds to the effector cells, and later comes in and cleans up the trash left behind. (1 point)
- Mentioning that complement is the one that binds to the antigen–antibody complex and aids in the quicker removal of the complex from the body. (½ point)

B. (maximum 3 points)
- Mentioning that this portion of the immune system is known as *cell-mediated immunity.* (½ point)
- Mentioning that the major player involved here is the cytotoxic T cell. (1 point)

- Mentioning that the cells infected by a virus are forced to produce viral antigens, some of which show up on the surface of the cell, and that it is these antigens that cytotoxic T cells recognize and attack. (1 point)
- Mentioning that all cells of the human body (except red blood cells) have class I histocompatibility antigens (MHC I) on their surfaces. (1 point)
- Further discussion of MHC—mentioning that MHC I antigens are slightly different for each person and the immune system accepts any cell that has the identical MHC I as friendly, and any cell that has a different form of MHC on its surface as an enemy. (1 point)

C. (maximum 4 points)
- Definition of nonspecific immunity as the nonspecific prevention of the entrance of invaders into the human body. (1 point)
- Examples (each example is worth 1 point)
  a. Lysozyme in the saliva can kill germs before they have the chance to take hold.
  b. The skin covering the body is a major form of nonspecific protection against invasion.
  c. The mucous membrane lining the trachea and lungs prevent bacteria from entering cells and actually assist in the expulsion of bacteria by ushering them up and out with a cough.
  d. The low pH of the stomach (acidity) is a nonspecific defense mechanism because it is able to kill a lot of bacteria that enter the body that cannot handle such an acidic environment.

D. (maximum 4 points)
- Definition of a vaccination as something given to an individual in an effort to prime the immune system to be prepared to fight a specific sickness if confronted again in the future. (1 point)

- Recognition that a vaccination is the injection of an antigen into the system (human body). (½ point)
- Description of how the reception of an antigen by a B cell causes B-cell differentiation into memory and plasma cells. (½ point)
- Mentioning that at the time of the vaccination, the plasma cells will produce antibodies to wipe out the small dose of antigen presented during the vaccination, and that the memory cells will remember the antigen and be ready to react later if necessary. (1 point)
- Definition of a secondary immune response. Memory cells are stored instructions on how to handle a particular invader. When the invader returns to the body, the memory cells recognize it and produce antibodies in rapid fashion. (1 point)
- Mentioning that the secondary immune response is faster and more efficient than the primary immune response. (½ point)
- Mentioning that the principle of a successful vaccination rests on the belief that the secondary immune response will succeed and wipe out the sickness if the individual is exposed in the future. (½ point)

2. Plant laboratory question

A. (maximum 5 points)
- Mentioning that the products of the light reactions of photosynthesis are ATP, NADPH, and oxygen. (½ point)
- Mentioning that in this experiment, the $NADP^+$ would be replaced by a compound known as DPIP. (½ point)
- Mentioning that normally this compound DPIP has a nice blue color, but when reduced, it changes to a colorless solution. (½ point)
- Mentioning that a machine called a *spectrophotometer* will be used to measure the amount of light that can pass through various samples. (½ point)

- Description of the experiment.
  a. Set aside three beakers—one with boiled chloroplasts, two with unboiled chloroplasts. (1 point)
  b. Take initial reading on spectrophotometer to determine how much light passes through the unboiled chloroplasts *before* the experiment begins. (½ point)
  c. Take one sample (unboiled chloroplasts) and measure how much photosynthesis occurs while it sits in a dark environment. After a certain amount of time, use the spectrophotometer to measure how much light can pass through the solution. (1 point)
  d. Take a second sample (unboiled chloroplasts) and measure how much photosynthesis occurs when it is exposed to light. After a certain amount of time, use the spectrophotometer to measure how much light can pass through the solution. (1 point)
- Mentioning that they would now compare the two samples to see the effect of light on photosynthesis. (1 point)
- Take a third sample (boiled chloroplasts) and expose it to light, and after a certain period of time, measure how much light can pass through the solution. (1 point)
- Mentioning that they would now compare the third sample and the second sample to see the effect of the presence or absence of chloroplasts on photosynthesis. (1 point)

B. (maximum 5 points)
- Definition of transpiration as the evaporative water loss from plants. (1 point)
- Mentioning that they will use a potometer to measure the amount of water loss from plants. (1 point)
- Mentioning that the surface area of a leaf is important to the measurement of transpiration rate in an experiment of this nature. (½ point)

- Description of experiment.
  a. Begin by measuring the amount of water that evaporates from the surface of a plant over a certain amount of time under normal conditions. Use this as the control. (1 point)
  b. Change the temperature, humidity, light intensity, and air movement that the plant is exposed to by 5-degree increments, and measure the amount of transpiration that occurs at the various temperatures. (1 point for each variable mentioned up to a maximum of 2 points)
  c. Mention that these values will be compared to the control to determine the effect of temperature, humidity, light intensity, and air movement. (½ point for each variable mentioned up to a maximum of 1 point)
- Mentioning that transpiration increases with an increase in temperature, decrease in humidity, increase in light intensity, and increased air movement. (1 point for each, up to a maximum of 2 points)

3. The phenotype for scale color in gila monsters is determined by a specific locus. (maximum 4 points for entire question)

   A. P-generation genotypes (maximum 2 points)
   - Creating the correct Punnett square, as shown here (1 point):

	g	g
G	Gg	Gg
g	gg	gg

   - Mentioning that genotype of P-generation = Gg (heterozygous) crossed with gg (homozygous recessive). (1 point)

   B. Explanation for mutation (maximum 3 points)
   - Mentioning that mutation is a random event that causes change in allele frequencies. (1 point)

- Possible explanation: scale-color gene is tied to another gene that controls pigment distribution (gene at one locus alters phenotypic expression of a gene at another locus). (1 point)
- Using the term *epistasis* correctly. (1 point)
- Possible explanation: point mutation occurred as DNA responsible for the production of protein that determines scale color was undergoing replication. (1 point)

4. The idea of surface area is an important concept in biology. Explain how surface area plays a critical role in the digestive system. (maximum 4 points for entire question)
   - Mentioning that majority of absorption occurs in small intestine. (1 point)
   - Mentioning that numerous folds and ridges increase surface area. (1 point)
   - Mentioning that brush border and microvilli increase surface area. (1 point)
   - Mentioning that large surface area leads to greater absorption of nutrients. (1 point)
   - Mentioning that chewing (mastication) breaks up food into smaller pieces. (1 point)
   - Mentioning that higher surface area gives greater access to salivary amylase. (1 point)

5. The following table includes data from scan samples conducted on a fictional mammal called a googabear every 10 minutes over the course of 42 hours. (maximum 4 points for entire question)
   - Mentioning that googabears are more active from 6 a.m. until 6 p.m. (during daylight hours). (1 point)
   - Mentioning that they decrease activity from 6 p.m. to 6 a.m. (when it is dark). (1 point)
   - Mentioning that googabears' food source is available during daylight. (1 point)
   - Mentioning that googabear predators are nocturnal (out at night), so it is safest for googabears to remain hidden at night. (1 point)
   - Mentioning that googabears rely on collective body heat at night (huddling); activity of huddled group is low. (1 point)

6. In earth's early history, the evolution of photosynthesis in simple cells occurred before the evolution of more complex cells. (maximum 4 points for entire question)
   - Mentioning that photosynthesis releases oxygen as a by-product. (1 point)
   - Mentioning that photosynthesis led to an increase in atmospheric oxygen. (1 point)
   - Mentioning that the presence of more oxygen in the atmosphere allowed the evolution of cellular respiration. (1 point)
   - Mentioning that oxygen allowed cells to generate more energy and grow larger and more complex. (1 point)
   - Mentioning that the first photosynthetic cells were prokaryotic. (1 point)
   - Mentioning that eukaryotic cells could not evolve until there was a higher level of atmospheric oxygen. (1 point)

7. What evidence supports the theory that chloroplasts and mitochondria are evolved from prokaryotic cells? (maximum 4 points for entire question)
   - Mentioning that chloroplasts and mitochondria have their own DNA. (1 point)
   - Mentioning that chloroplast and mitochondrial DNA consist of a single, circular molecule (like bacterial DNA). (1 point)
   - Mentioning that chloroplast and mitochondrial DNA are not associated with histones (like bacterial DNA). (1 point)
   - Mentioning that chloroplasts and mitochondria replicate by a process similar to prokaryotes. (1 point)
   - Mentioning that the inner membranes of both organelles have enzymes homologous to those found in prokaryotes. (1 point)

8. You are asked to estimate if a certain species of plant could live in a salt marsh. (maximum 4 points for entire question)
   - Calculate $\Psi_{plant\ cell}$:
     Ψ = pressure potential + solute potential solute potential of plant cell = Ψ_s = $-iCRT$ = $-(1)(0.08\ M)(.00831)(273 + 12)$ = -0.189 MPa (1 point)
     Ψ = -1.2 MPa (pressure potential) + -0.189 MPa (solute potential) = -1.39 MPa (1 point)
   - Mentioning that the plant cell's water potential (-1.39 MPa) is higher than that of the soil (-2.2 MPa). (1 point)
   - Mentioning that water would flow out of the plant cell (hypotonic) into soil (hypertonic). (1 point)
   - Mentioning that the plant cell would not survive. (1 point)

Scoring and Interpretation
AP BIOLOGY PRACTICE EXAM 2

Multiple-Choice Questions:

number of correct answers: _____
number of incorrect answers: _____
number of blank answers: _____

Grid-In Questions:

number of correct answers: _____
number of incorrect answers: _____
number of blank answers: _____

_____ + _____ = _____
multiple-choice   grid-in   Section I
number correct   number correct   raw score

Free-Response Questions:

1. _____ / 10   3. _____ / 4   6. _____ / 4
2. _____ / 10   4. _____ / 4   7. _____ / 4
                     5. _____ / 4   8. _____ / 4

Add up the total points accumulated in the eight questions and multiply the sum by 1.57 to obtain the free-response raw score: _____ × 1.57 = _____
                                                    free-response points   Section II raw score

CALCULATE YOUR SCORE

Now combine the raw scores from the multiple-choice and free-response sections to obtain your new raw score for the entire practice exam. Use the ranges listed below to determine your grade for this exam. Don't worry about how we arrived at the following ranges, and remember that they are rough estimates on questions that are not actual AP exam questions . . . do not read too much into them.

Raw Score	Approximate AP Score
83–138	5
63–82	4
48–62	3
26–47	2
0–25	1

Futuyma, Douglas J. *Evolutionary Biology.* 3d ed. Sunderland, MA: Sinauer Associates, Inc., 1998.

Kotz, John C., Paul M. Treichel, and John Townsend. *Chemistry and Chemical Reactivity.* 8th ed. Stamford, CT: Brooks/Cole, 2011.

Reece, Jane B., Lisa A. Urry, and Michael L. Cain. *Campbell Biology.* 9th ed. San Francisco: Benjamin Cummings, 2011.

Starr, Cecie, Christine Evers, and Lisa Starr. *Biology: Concepts and Applications.* 8th ed. San Francisco: Brooks/Cole, 2011.

Strauss, Eric, and Marylin Lisowski. *Biology: The Web of Life.* Teacher's ed. Menlo Park, CA: Addison-Wesley Longman, 1998.

Wilbraham, Antony C. *Chemistry.* 5th ed. New York: Pearson, 2000.

WEBSITES

Here is a list of websites that contain information and links that you might find useful to your preparation for the AP Biology exam:

- http://www.campbellbiology.com
- http://www.collegeboard.com
- http://www.africangreyparrott.com/teach.html
- http://faculty.washington.edu/herronjc/ SoftwareFolder/AlleleA1.html
- http://blast.ncbi.nlm.nih.gov

abiotic components The *nonliving* players in an ecosystem, such as climate and nutrients.

abscisic acid Plant hormone that inhibits cell growth, prevents premature germination, and stimulates closing of the stomata.

achondroplasia Autosomal dominant form of dwarfism seen in one out of 10,000 people.

ACTH See **adrenocorticotropic hormone.**

active site Part of the enzyme that interacts with the substrate in an enzyme–substrate complex.

active transport The movement of a particle across a selectively permeable membrane *against* its concentration gradient. This movement requires the input of energy, which is why it is termed "active" transport.

adaptation A trait that, if altered, affects the fitness of the organism. Adaptations are the result of natural selection and can include not only physical traits such as eyes and fingernails but also the intangible traits of organisms, such as lifespan.

adaptive radiation A rapid series of speciation events that occur when one or more ancestral species invades a new environment.

ADH See **antidiuretic hormone.**

adrenocorticotropic hormone (ACTH) A hormone that stimulates the secretion of adrenal cortical hormones, which work to maintain electrolytic homeostasis in the body.

aerobic respiration Energy-producing reactions in animals that involve three stages: glycolysis, the Krebs cycle, and oxidative phosphorylation. Requires oxygen.

age structure Statistic that compares the relative number of individuals in the population from each age group.

agonistic behavior Behavior that results from a conflict of interest between individuals; often involves intimidation and submission.

alcohol Organic compound that contains a hydroxyl (—OH) functional group.

alcohol fermentation Occurs in fungi, yeast, and bacteria. Pyruvate is converted in two steps to ethanol, regenerating two molecules of NAD^+.

aldehyde Carbonyl group in which one R is a hydrogen and the other is a carbon chain. Hydrophilic and polar.

aldosterone Released from the adrenal gland, this hormone acts on the distal tubules to cause the reabsorption of more Na^+ and water. This increases blood volume and pressure.

allantois Transports waste products in mammals to the placenta. Later it is incorporated into the umbilical cord.

allele A variant of a gene for a particular character.

allopatric speciation Interbreeding ceases because some sort of barrier separates a single population into two (an area with no food, a mountain, etc.). The two populations evolve independently, and if they change enough, then, even if the barrier is removed, they cannot interbreed.

alternation of generations Plant life cycle, so named because during the cycle, plants sometimes exist as a diploid organism and at other times as a haploid organism.

altruistic behavior Behavior pattern that reduces the overall fitness of one organism while increasing the fitness of another.

alveoli Functional unit of the lung where gas exchange occurs.

amines Compounds containing amino groups.

amino acid A compound with a carbon center surrounded by an amino group, a carboxyl group, a hydrogen, and an R group that provides an amino acid's unique chemical characteristics.

aminoacyl tRNA synthetase Enzyme that makes sure that each tRNA molecule picks up the appropriate amino acid for its anticodon.

amino group A functional group that contains —NH_2 and that acts as a base; an example is an amino acid.

amnion Structure formed from epiblast that encloses the fluid-filled cavity that helps cushion the developing embryo.

amygdala The portion of the human brain that controls impulsive emotions and anger.

amylase Enzyme that breaks down the starches in the human diet to simpler sugars such as maltose, which are fully digested farther down in the intestines.

anaerobic respiration Energy-producing reactions, known as *fermentation,* that do not involve oxygen. It begins with glycolysis and concludes with the formation of NAD⁺.

anemia Illness in which a lack of iron causes red blood cells to have a diminished capacity for delivering oxygen.

aneuploidy The condition of having an abnormal number of chromosomes.

angiosperm Flowering plant divided into monocots and dicots (monocotyledons and dicotyledons).

anion Ion with a negative charge that contains more electrons than protons.

anterior pituitary gland Structure that produces six hormones: TSH, STH (or HGH), ACTH, LH, FSH, and prolactin.

anther Pollen-producing portion of a plant.

antheridia Male gametangia in bryophytes and ferns designed to produce flagellated sperm that swim to meet up with the eggs produced by the female gametangia.

anticodon Region present at a tRNA attachment site; a three-nucleotide sequence that is perfectly complementary to a particular codon.

antidiuretic hormone (ADH) A hormone produced in the brain and stored in the pituitary gland; it increases the permeability of the collecting duct to water, leading to more concentrated urine content.

antigen A molecule that is foreign to our bodies and causes our immune systems to respond.

apical meristem Region at the tips of roots and shoots where plant growth is concentrated and many actively dividing cells can be found.

apoplast pathway Movement of water and nutrients through the nonliving portion of cells.

aposematic coloration Warning coloration adopted by animals that possess a chemical defense mechanism.

archaebacteria One of two major prokaryotic evolutionary branches. These organisms tend to live in extreme environments and include halophiles, methanogens, and thermoacidophiles.

archegonium Female gametangia in bryophytes, ferns, and gymnosperms.

archezoa Eukaryotic organism that allegedly most closely resembles prokaryotes.

arteries Structures that carry blood away from the heart.

artificial selection When humans become the agents of natural selection (breeding of dogs).

ascospores Haploid meiotic products produced by certain fungi.

A site Region on protein synthesis machinery that holds the tRNA carrying the next amino acid.

associative learning Process by which animals take one stimulus and associate it with another.

atom The smallest form of an element that still displays its unique properties.

ATP synthase Enzyme that uses the flow of hydrogens to drive the phosphorylation of an adenosine diphosphate molecule to produce adenosine triphosphate.

auditory communication Communication that involves the use of sound in the conveying of a message.

autonomic nervous system (ANS) A subdivision of the peripheral nervous system (PNS) that controls the involuntary activities of the body: smooth muscle, cardiac muscle, and glands. The ANS is divided into the sympathetic and parasympathetic divisions.

autosomal chromosome One that is not directly involved in determining gender.

autotroph An organism that is self-nourishing. It obtains carbon and energy without ingesting other organisms.

auxin Plant hormone that leads to elongation of stems and plays a role in phototropism and gravitropism.

axon A longer extension that leaves a neuron and carries the impulse away from the cell body toward target cells.

balanced polymorphism When there are two or more phenotypic variants maintained in a population.

bare-rock succession The attachment of lichen to rocks, followed by the step-by-step arrival of replacement species.

Barr bodies Inactivated genes on X chromosomes.

Batesian mimicry An animal that is harmless copies the appearance of an animal that is dangerous as a defense mechanism to make predators think twice about attacking.

behavioral ecology Science that studies the interaction between animals and their environments from an evolutionary perspective.

bile Substance that contains bile salts, phospholipids, cholesterol, and bile pigments such as bilirubin, is stored in the gallbladder, and is dumped into the small intestine on the arrival of the food.

bile salts Help to mechanically digest fat by emulsifying it into small droplets contained in water.

binary fission Mechanism by which prokaryotic cells divide. The cell elongates and pinches into two new daughter cells.

binomial system of classification System created by Linnaeus in which each species is given a two-word name: Genus + species (e.g., *Homo sapiens*).

biogeochemical cycles Cycles that represent the movement of elements, such as nitrogen and carbon, from organisms to the environment and back in a continuous cycle.

biomass pyramid *Biomass* represents the cumulative weight of all of the members at a given trophic level.

biome The various geographic regions of the earth that serve as hosts for ecosystems.

biosphere The entire life-containing area of a planet—all ecosystems and communities.

biotic components Living organisms of an ecosystem.

biotic potential The maximum growth rate for a population given unlimited resources, unlimited space, and lack of competition or predators.

birth rate Offspring produced per a specific time period.

bivalves Mollusks with hinged shells such as oysters and clams.

blastula As a morula undergoes its next round of cell divisions, fluid fills its center to create this hollow-looking structure.

"blending" hypothesis Theory that the genes contributed by two parents mix as if they are paint colors and the exact genetic makeup of each parent can never be recovered; the genes are as inseparable as blended paint.

bottleneck A dramatic reduction in population size that increases the likelihood of genetic drift.

bronchi Tunnels that branch off the trachea that lead into the individual lungs and divide into smaller branches called bronchioles.

bronchioles Tiny lung tunnels that branch repeatedly until they conclude as tiny air pockets containing alveoli.

brush border Large numbers of microvilli that increase the surface area of the small intestine to improve absorption efficiency.

bryophytes The first land plants to evolve from the chlorophytes. Members of this group include mosses, liverworts, and hornworts.

bundle sheath cells Cells that are tightly wrapped around the veins of a leaf. They are the site for the Calvin cycle in C_4 plants.

C_4 photosynthesis Photosynthetic process that alters the way in which carbon is fixed to better deal with the lack of CO_2 that comes from the closing of the stomata in hot, dry regions.

C_4 plant Plant that has adapted its photosynthetic process to more efficiently handle hot and dry conditions.

Calvin cycle A name for the light-independent (dark) reactions of photosynthesis.

CAM (crassulacean acid metabolism) photosynthesis Plants close their stomata during the day, collect CO_2 at night, and store the CO_2 in the form of acids until it is needed during the day for photosynthesis.

capsid A protein shell that surrounds genetic material.

carbohydrate Organic compound used by the cells of the human body in energy-producing reactions and as structural material. The three main types of carbohydrates are monosaccharides, disaccharides, and polysaccharides.

carbon cycle The movement of carbon from the atmosphere to living organisms and back to the environment in a continuous cycle.

carbon fixation The attachment of the carbon from CO_2 to a molecule that is able to enter the Calvin cycle, assisted by rubisco.

carbonyl group A functional group that is hydrophilic and polar. It has a central carbon connected to R groups on either side. If both Rs are carbon chains, it is a ketone. If one R is a hydrogen and the other a carbon chain, it is an aldehyde.

carboxyl group An acidic functional group (COOH). This functional group shows up along with amino groups in amino acids.

cardiac muscle Involuntary muscle of the heart that is striated in appearance and contains multiple nuclei.

carnivore A consumer that obtains energy and nutrients through consumption of other animals.

carotenoid A photosynthetic pigment.

carrying capacity The maximum number of individuals a population can sustain in a given environment.

casparian strip Obstacle that blocks the passage of water through the endodermis of plants.

catalase Enzyme that assists in the conversion of hydrogen peroxide to water and oxygen. Found in peroxisomes.

catalysts Molecules that speed up reactions by lowering the activation energy of a reaction.

cation Ion with a positive charge that contains more protons than electrons.

cell body The main body of the neuron.

cell cycle A cycle that consists of four stages: G_1, S, G_2, and M. G_1 and G_2 are growth stages, S is the part of the cell cycle in which the DNA is duplicated, and the M phase stands for mitosis—the cell division phase.

cell-mediated immunity This type of immunity involves *direct* cellular response to invasion as opposed to antibody-based defense.

cell plate Plant cell structure constructed in the Golgi apparatus composed of vesicles that fuse together along the middle of the cell, completing the separation process.

cellular slime molds Protists with a unique eating strategy. When plenty of food is available, they eat alone. When food is scare, they clump together and form a unit.

cellulose Polysaccharide composed of glucose used by plants to form cell walls.

cell wall Wall that functions to shape and protect cells. Present in plant but not animal cells.

central nervous system (CNS) The CNS is made up of the brain and the spinal cord. The CNS controls skeletal muscles and voluntary movement.

cephalization The concentration of sensory machinery in the anterior end of a bilateral organism.

cerebellum Portion of brain in charge of coordination and balance.

cerebrum Portion of the brain that controls functions such as speech, hearing, sight, and motor control. Divided into two hemispheres and four lobes per hemisphere.

cervix The uterus connects to the vaginal opening via this narrowed region.

CF See **cystic fibrosis.**

character A heritable feature, such as flower color, that varies among individuals.

checkpoints Stop points throughout the cell cycle where the cell verifies that there are enough nutrients and raw materials to progress to the next stage of the cycle.

chemical communication Mammals and insects communicate through the use of chemical signals called *pheromones.*

chemiosmosis The coupling of the movement of electrons down the electron transport chain with the formation of ATP using the driving force provided by a proton gradient. Seen in both photosynthesis and respiration.

chemoautotrophs Autotrophs that produce energy through oxidation of inorganic substances.

chitin Polysaccharide that is an important part of the exoskeletons of arthropods such as insects, spiders, and shellfish.

chlorophyll A photosynthetic pigment.

chlorophytes Green algae that are probably the common ancestors of land plants.

chloroplast The site of photosynthesis and energy production in plant cells and algae.

choanoflagellate Accepted to be the common ancestor of the animal kingdom.

choice Refers to the selection of mates by one sex (in mammals, it is usually females who exercise choice over males).

choice chamber Chamber used in scientific experiments to study kinesis.

cholesterol Steroid that is an important structural component of cell membranes and serves as a precursor molecule for steroid sex hormones.

chorion Formed from the trophoblast, it is the outer membrane of the embryo and the site of implantation onto the endometrium. It contributes to formation of the placenta in mammals.

chromatin The raw material that gives rise to the chromosomes (genetic material is uncoiled).

chromosomal translocations Condition in which a piece of one chromosome is attached to another, nonhomologous chromosome.

chromosome duplication Error in chromosomal replication that results in the repetition of a genetic segment.

chromosome inversion Condition in which a piece of a chromosome separates and reattaches in the opposite direction.

chronic myelogenous leukemia A cancer affecting white blood cell precursor cells. In this disease, a portion of chromosome 22 has been swapped with a piece of chromosome 9.

chymotrypsin Enzyme that cuts protein bonds in the small intestine.

cilia Structures that beat in rhythmical waves to carry foreign particles and mucus away from the lungs.

circadian rhythm A physiologic cycle that occurs in time increments that are roughly equivalent to the length of a day.

class I histocompatibility antigens The surface of all the cells of the human body, except for red blood cells, have these antigens, which are slightly different for each individual. The immune system accepts any cell that has the identical match for this antigen as friendly. Anything with a different major histocompatibility complex is foreign.

class II histocompatibility antigens Antigens found on the surface of the immune cells of the body. These antigens play a role in the interaction between the cells of the immune system.

classical conditioning Type of associative learning that Ivan Pavlov demonstrated with his experiments involving salivation in dogs.

cleavage divisions Developing embryo divides; cytoplasm is distributed unevenly to the daughter cells while the genetic information is distributed equally.

cleavage furrow Groove formed in animal cells between the two daughter cells; this groove pinches together to complete the separation of the two cells after mitosis.

climax community Final stable stage at the completion of a succession cycle.

clumped dispersion Scenario in which individuals live in packs that are spaced out from each other.

codominance Both alleles express themselves fully in a heterozygous organism.

codon A triplet of nucleotides that codes for a particular amino acid.

coefficient of relatedness Statistic that represents the average proportion of genes that two individuals have in common.

coelom Fluid-filled body cavity found between the body wall and the gut that has a lining and is derived from the mesoderm.

coelomates Animals that contain a true coelum.

coenocytic fungi Fungi that do not contain septae.

coevolution The mutual evolution between two species, which is exemplified by predator–prey relationships.

coleoptile Protective structure found around a grass seedling.

collenchyma cells Live plant cells that provide flexible and mechanical support.

commensalism One organism benefits from the relationship while the other is unaffected.

community A collection of populations of species in a given geographic area.

competent Describes a cell that is ready to accept foreign DNA from the environment.

competition Both species involved are harmed by this kind of interaction. The two major forms of competition are intraspecific and interspecific competition.

competitive inhibition Condition in which an inhibitor molecule resembling the substrate binds to the active site and physically blocks the substrate from attaching.

complement A protein that coats cells that need to be cleared, stimulating phagocytes to ingest them.

compounds Two or more elements combined to form an entity.

conduction Process by which heat moves from a place of higher temperature to a place of lower temperature.

conifers Gymnosperm plants whose reproductive structure is a cone.

conjugation The transfer of DNA between two bacterial cells connected by appendages called *sex pili*.

conservative DNA replication The original double helix of DNA does not change at all; it is as if the DNA is placed on a copy machine and an exact duplicate is made. DNA from the parent appears in only one of the two daughter cells.

convection Heat transfer caused by airflow.

convergent characters Characters are convergent if they look the same in two species, even though the species do *not* share a common ancestor.

convergent evolution Two unrelated species evolve in a way that makes them *more* similar. They both respond the same way to some environmental challenge, bringing them closer together.

cork cambium Area that produces a thick cover for stems and roots. It produces tissue that replaces dried-up epidermis lost during secondary growth.

cork cells Cells produced by the cork cambium that die and form a protective barrier against infection and physical damage.

corpus callosum Bridge that connects the two hemispheres of the brain.

cortex Outer region of the kidney or adrenal gland.

cortisol Stress hormone released in response to physiological challenges.

cotyledon Structure that provides nutrients for a developing angiosperm plant.

cri-du-chat syndrome This syndrome occurs with a deletion in chromosome 5 that leads to mental retardation, unusual facial features, and a small head. Most die in infancy or early childhood.

crossover Also referred to as "crossing over." When the homologous pairs match up during prophase I of meiosis, complementary pieces from the two homologous chromosomes wrap around each other and are exchanged between the chromosomes. This is one of the mechanisms that allows offspring to differ from their parents.

cryptic coloration Those being hunted adopt a coloring scheme that allows them to blend in to the colors of the environment.

cuticle Waxy covering that protects terrestrial plants against water loss.

cutin Waxy coat that protects plants.

cyclic light reactions Pathway that produces only ATP and uses only photosystem I.

cyclin Protein that accumulates during interphase; vital to cell cycle control.

cystic fibrosis (CF) A recessive disorder that is the most common lethal genetic disease in the United States. A defective version of a gene on chromosome 7 results in the excessive secretion of a thick mucus, which accumulates in the lungs and digestive tract. Left untreated, children with CF die at a very young age.

cytokinesis The physical separation of the newly formed daughter cells during meiosis and mitosis. Occurs immediately after telophase.

cytokinin Plant hormone that promotes cell division and leaf enlargement, and slows down the aging of leaves.

cytoskeleton Provides support, shape, and mobility to cells.

death rate Number of deaths per time period.

deceptive markings Patterns that can cause a predator to think twice before attacking. For example, some insects may have colored designs on their wings that resemble large eyes, making individuals look more imposing than they are.

decomposer See **detritivore**.

dehydration reaction A reaction in which two compounds merge, releasing H_2O as a product.

deletion A piece of the chromosome is lost in the developmental process.

demographers Scientists who study the theory and statistics behind population growth and decline.

dendrite One of many short, branched processes of a neuron that help send the nerve impulses toward the cell body.

denitrification The process by which bacteria use nitrates and release N_2 as a product.

density-dependent inhibition When a certain density of cells is reached, cell growth will slow or stop. This is because there are not enough raw materials for the growth and survival of more cells.

density-dependent limiting factors Factors related to population size that come into play as population size approaches or passes the carrying capacity. Examples of density-dependent limiting factors include food, waste, and disease.

density-independent limiting factors Factors that limit population growth that have nothing to do with the population size, such as natural disasters and weather.

depolarization The electric potential becomes less negative inside the cell, allowing an action potential to occur.

desert The driest land biome on earth, which experiences a wide range of temperatures from day to night and exists on nearly every continent.

detritivore Also known as *decomposer*. A consumer that obtains its energy through the consumption of dead animals and plants.

dicot (dicotyledon) An angiosperm plant that has two cotyledons.

diffusion The movement of molecules down their concentration gradients without the use of energy. It is a passive process during which molecules move from a region of higher concentration to a region of lower concentration.

dihybrid cross The crossing of two different characters (BbRr × BbRr). A dihybrid cross between heterozygous gametes gives a 9:3:3:1 phenotype ratio in the offspring.

diploid (2n) An organism that has two copies of each type of chromosome. In humans, this refers to the pairs of homologous chromosomes.

diplomonads A phylum that is associated with the archezoan eukaryotes.

directional selection Occurs when members of a population at one end of a spectrum are selected against and/or those at the other end are selected for.

disaccharide A sugar consisting of two monosaccharides bound together. Common disaccharides include sucrose, maltose, and lactose.

dispersive DNA replication A theory that suggests that every daughter strand contains *some* parental DNA, but it is dispersed among pieces of DNA not of parental origin.

disruptive selection Selection is disruptive when individuals at the two extremes of a spectrum of variation do better than the more common forms in the middle.

distribution Describes the way populations are dispersed over a geographic area.

divergent evolution Two related species evolve in a way that makes them less similar, sometimes causing speciation.

division The classification category that replaces the phylum in plant classification.

DNA methylation The addition of CH_3 groups to the bases of DNA, rendering DNA inactive.

DNA polymerase The main enzyme in DNA replication that attaches to primer proteins and adds nucleotides to the growing DNA chain in a 5′-to-3′ direction.

DNA replication The process by which DNA is copied. This process occurs during the S phase of the cell cycle to ensure that every cell produced during mitosis or meiosis receives the proper amount of DNA.

dominance hierarchy A ranking of power among the members of a group of individuals.

double helix The shape of DNA—two strands held together by hydrogen bonds.

Down syndrome A classic aneuploid syndrome affecting one of every 700 children born in the United States. It most often involves a trisomy of chromosome 21, and leads to mental retardation, heart defects, short stature, and characteristic facial features.

Duchenne muscular dystrophy Sex-linked disorder caused by the absence of an essential muscle protein that leads to progressive weakening of the muscles combined with a loss of muscle coordination.

ecosystem All the individuals of a community and the environment in which it exists.

ectoderm Outer germ layer that gives rise to the nervous system, skin, hair, and nails.

ectothermic animal Animal whose basic metabolic rates increase in response to increases in temperature.

Edwards syndrome The presence of trisomy 18, which occurs in one out of every 10,000 live births and affects almost every organ of the body.

electron transport chain (ETC) The chain of molecules, located in the mitochondria, that passes electrons along during the process of chemiosmosis to regenerate NAD^+ to form ATP. Each time an electron passes to another member of the chain, the energy level of the system drops.

element The simplest form of matter.

embryology The study of embryonic development.

emigration rate Rate at which individuals relocate *out of* a given population.

endergonic reaction A reaction that requires *input* of energy to occur. A + B + energy → C.

endocytosis Process by which substances are brought into cells by enclosure into a membrane-created vesicle that surrounds the substance and escorts it into the cell.

endoderm Inner germ layer that gives rise to the inner lining of the gut, digestive system, liver, thyroid, lungs, and bladder.

endodermis Cells that line the innermost layer of the cortex in plants that give rise to the casparian strip.

endometrium Inner wall of the uterus to which the embryo attaches.

endopeptidases Enzymes that initiate the digestion of proteins by hydrolyzing all the polypeptides into small amino acid groups.

endosymbiotic theory Proposes that groups of prokaryotes associated in symbiotic relationships to form eukaryotes (mitochondria and chloroplasts).

endothermic animal Animal whose body temperature is relatively unaffected by external temperature.

enhancer DNA region, also known as a "regulator," that is located thousands of bases away from the promoter that influences transcription by interacting with specific transcription factors.

enzymes Catalytic proteins that are picky, interacting only with particular substrates. However, the enzymes can be reused and react with more than one copy of their substrate of choice and have a major effect on a reaction.

epiblast Develops into the three germ layers of the embryo: the endoderm, the mesoderm, and the ectoderm.

epidermis (plants) The protective outer coating of plants.

epididymis The coiled region that extends from the testes. This is where the sperm completes its maturation and waits until it is called on to do its duty.

episomes Plasmids that can be incorporated into a bacterial chromosome.

epistasis A gene at one locus alters the phenotypic expression of a gene at another locus. A dihybrid cross involving epistatic genes produces a 9:4:3 phenotype ratio.

esophageal sphincter Valvelike trapdoor between the esophagus and the stomach.

esophagus Structure that connects the throat to the stomach.

estrogen Hormone made (secreted) in ovaries that stimulates development of sex characteristics in women and induces the release of luteinizing hormone (LH) before the LH surge.

ETC See **electron transport chain.**

ethology The study of animal behavior.

ethylene Plant hormone that initiates the ripening of fruit and the dropping of leaves and flowers from trees.

eubacteria One of two major prokaryotic evolutionary branches. Categorized according to their mode of nutritional acquisition, mechanism of movement, shape, and other characteristics.

eukaryotic cell Complex cell that contains a nucleus, which functions as the control center of the cell, directing DNA replication, transcription, and cell growth. Organisms can be unicellular or multicellular and contain many different membrane-bound organelles.

evaporation Process by which a liquid changes into a vapor form. Functions in thermoregulation for humans when water leaves our bodies in the form of water vapor—sweat.

evolution Descent with modification. Evolution happens to populations, not individuals, and describes change in allele frequencies in populations with time.

excision repair Repair mechanism for DNA replication in which a section of DNA containing an error is cut out and the gap is filled by DNA polymerase.

exergonic reaction A reaction that *gives off* energy as a product. A + B → energy + C.

exocytosis Process by which substances are exported out of the cell. A vesicle escorts the substance to the plasma membrane, fuses with the membrane, and ejects its contents out of the cell.

exons Coding regions produced during transcription that are glued back together to produce the mRNA that is translated into a protein.

exopeptidases Enzymes that complete the digestion of proteins by hydrolyzing all the amino acids of any remaining fragments.

exponential growth A population grows at a rate that creates a J-shaped curve.

extreme halophiles Archaebacteria that live in environments with high salt concentrations.

F_1 The first generation of offspring, or the first "filial" generation in a genetic cross.

F_2 The second generation of offspring, or the second "filial" generation in a genetic cross.

facilitated diffusion The diffusion of particles across a selectively permeable membrane with the assistance of transport proteins that are specific in what they will carry and have a binding site designed for molecules of interest. This process requires no energy.

facultative anaerobe Organisms that can survive in oxygen-rich or oxygen-free environments.

fallopian tube See **oviduct.**

fats Lipids, made by combining glycerol and fatty acids, used as long-term energy stores in cells. They can be saturated or unsaturated.

fatty acid Long carbon chain that contains a carboxyl group on one end that combines with glycerol molecules to form lipids.

fermentation Anaerobic respiration pathway that occurs in absence of oxygen. Produces less ATP than aerobic respiration.

ferredoxin Molecule that donates the electrons to $NADP^+$ to produce NADPH during the light reactions of photosynthesis.

fibrous root system Root system found in monocots that provides the plant with a very strong anchor without going very deep into the soil.

filtration Capillaries allow small particles through the pores of their endothelial linings, but large molecules such as proteins, platelets, and blood cells tend to remain in the vessel.

fixed-action pattern An innate behavior that seems to be a programmed response to some stimulus.

florigen Hormone thought to assist in the blooming of flowers.

fluid mosaic model Model that states that the membrane is made of a phospholipid bilayer with proteins of various lengths and sizes, interspersed with cholesterol.

fluke Parasitic flatworm that alternates between sexual and asexual reproductive cycles.

follicle-stimulating hormone (FSH) A gonadotropin that stimulates activities of the testes and ovaries. In females, it induces the development of the ovarian follicle, leading to the production and secretion of estrogen, and in males it stimulates the production of sperm.

food chain A hierarchical list of who snacks on who. For example, bugs are eaten by spiders, who are eaten by birds, who are eaten by cats.

food web Can be regarded as overlapping food chains that show all the various dietary relationships in an environment.

foraging The behavior of actively searching for and eating a particular food resource.

fossil record The physical manifestation of species that have gone extinct (e.g., bones and imprints).

F-plasmid Plasmid that contains the genes necessary for the production of a sex pillus.

frameshift mutations Deletion or addition of DNA nucleotides that does not add or remove a multiple of three nucleotides. Usually produces a nonfunctional protein unless it occurs late in protein production.

frequency-dependent selection Alleles are selected for or against depending on their relative frequency in a population.

FSH See **follicle-stimulating hormone.**

functional groups The groups responsible for the chemical properties of organic compounds.

G₁ phase The first growth phase of the cell cycle, which produces all the necessary raw materials for DNA synthesis.

G₂ phase The second growth phase of the cell cycle, which produces all the necessary raw materials for mitosis.

gametangia Protective covering that provides a safe haven for the fertilization of the gametes and the development of the zygote in bryophytes, ferns, and some gymnosperms.

gametes Sex cells produced during meiosis in the human life cycle.

gametophyte A haploid multicellular organism.

gastrulation Cells separate into three primary layers called *germ layers,* which eventually give rise to the different tissues of an adult.

gene flow The change in frequencies of alleles as genes from one population are incorporated into those from another.

generalized transduction Transduction caused by the accidental placement of host DNA into a phage instead of viral DNA during viral reproduction. This host DNA may find its way into another cell where crossover could occur.

generation time Time needed for individuals to reach reproductive maturity.

genetic code Code that translates codons found on mRNA strands into amino acids.

genetic drift A change in allele frequencies that is due to chance events.

genotype An organism's genetic makeup for a given trait. A simple example of this could involve eye color, where B represents the allele for brown and b represents the allele for blue. The possible genotypes include homozygous brown (BB), heterozygous brown (Bb), and homozygous blue (bb).

genus Taxonomic group to which a species belongs.

gibberellin Plant hormone that assists in stem elongation and induces growth in dormant seeds, buds, and flowers.

glomerular capillaries The early portion of the nephron where the filtration process begins.

glucagon Hormone that stimulates conversion of glycogen into glucose.

glycerol Three-carbon molecule that combines with fatty acids to produce a variety of lipids.

glycogen Storage polysaccharide made of glucose molecules used by animals.

glycolysis Occurs in the cytoplasm of cells and is the beginning pathway for both aerobic and anaerobic respiration. During glycolysis, a glucose molecule is broken down through a series of reactions into two molecules of ATP, NADH, and pyruvate.

glycoprotein Protein that has been modified by the addition of a sugar.

Golgi apparatus Organelle that modifies proteins, lipids, and other macromolecules by the addition of sugars and other molecules to form glycoproteins. The products are then sent to other parts of the cell.

G-proteins Proteins vital to signal cascade pathways. These proteins directly activate molecules such as adenyl cyclase to assist in a reaction.

gradualism The theory that evolutionary change is a steady, slow process.

grana Flattened channels and disks arranged in stacks found in the thylakoid membrane.

gravitropism A plant's growth response to gravitational force. Auxin and gibberellins are involved in this response.

gross productivity The difference over time between the dissolved oxygen concentrations of the light and dark bottles calculated in primary productivity experiments.

growth factors Assist in the growth of structures.

guard cells Cells within the epidermis of plants that control the opening and closing of the stomata.

gymnosperm First major seed plant to evolve. Heterosporous plant that *usually* transports its sperm through the use of pollen. Conifers are the major gymnosperm to know.

habituation Loss of responsiveness to unimportant stimuli that do not provide appropriate feedback.

haploid (*n*) An organism that has only one copy of each type of chromosome.

Hardy-Weinberg equilibrium A special case where a population is in stasis, or not evolving.

helicase Enzyme that unzips DNA, breaking the hydrogen bonds between the nucleotides and producing the replication fork for replication.

helper T cell Immune cells that assist in activation of B cells.

hemoglobin Molecule that allows red blood cells to carry and deliver oxygen throughout the body to hardworking organs and tissues.

hemophilia Sex-linked disorder caused by the absence of a protein vital to the clotting process. Individuals with this condition have difficulty clotting blood after even the smallest of wounds.

herbivore Consumer that obtains energy and nutrients through consumption of plants.

heterosporous plant Plant that produces two types of spores, male and female.

heterotroph An organism that must consume other organisms to obtain nourishment. They are the consumers of the world.

heterotroph theory Theory that posits that the first organisms were heterotrophs (organisms that cannot produce their own food).

heterozygote advantage The situation, such as sickle cell anemia in malarial regions, in which being heterozygous for a condition provides some benefit.

heterozygous (hybrid) An individual is heterozygous (or a hybrid) for a gene if the two alleles are different (Bb).

histamine Chemical signal responsible for initiation of the inflammation response of the immune system.

holandric trait A trait inherited via the Y chromosome.

homeobox DNA sequence of a homeotic gene that tells the cell where to put body structures.

homeotic genes Genes that regulate or "direct" the body plan of organisms.

homologous characters Traits are said to be homologous if they are similar because their host organisms arose from a common ancestor.

homologous chromosomes Chromosomes that resemble one another in shape, size, function, and the genetic information they contain. They are not identical.

homosporous plant Plants that produce a single spore type that gives rise to bisexual gametophytes.

homozygous (pure) An individual is homozygous for a gene if both of the given alleles are the same (BB or bb).

honest indicators Sexually selected traits that are the result of female choice and signal genetic quality.

hormones Chemicals produced by glands such as the pituitary and used by the endocrine system to signal distant target cells.

host range The range of cells that a virus is able to infect. For example, HIV infects the T cells of our body.

humoral immunity Immunity involving antibodies and circulating fluids.

Huntington's disease An autosomal dominant degenerative disease of the nervous system that shows itself when a person is in their 30s or 40s and is both irreversible and fatal.

hybrid vigor Refers to the fact that hybrids may have increased reproductive success compared to inbred strains. This is due to the fact that inbreeding increases the likelihood that two deleterious, recessive alleles will end up in the same offspring.

hydrolysis reaction A reaction that breaks down compounds by the addition of H_2O.

hydrophilic Water-loving.

hydroxyl group A hydrophilic and polar functional group (—OH) that is present in compounds known as *alcohols*.

hypercholesterolemia Recessive disorder (hh) that causes cholesterol levels to be many times higher than normal and can lead to heart attacks in children as young as two years old.

hypertonic Characterizes a solution that has a higher solute concentration than does a neighboring solution.

hypha Filament found in fungi made of chitin that separates fungi into multicellular compartments.

hypoblast Forms the yolk sac, which produces the embryo's first blood cells.

hypothalamus The thermostat and "hunger meter" of the body, regulating temperature, hunger, and thirst.

hypotonic Characterizes a solution that has a lower solute concentration than a neighboring solution.

immigration rate Rate at which individuals relocate *into* a given population.

imprinting Innate behavior that is learned during a critical period early in life.

inclusive fitness An individual's fitness gain that is a direct result of his or her contribution to the reproductive effort of closely related kin. This results from the fact that close kin share copies of identical genes.

incomplete dominance Blending inheritance. The heterozygous genotype produces an intermediate phenotype rather than the dominant phenotype; neither allele dominates the other.

induced-fit model Theory that suggests that when an enzyme and a substrate bind together, the enzyme is *induced* to alter its shape for a tighter active-site/substrate attachment, which places the substrate in a favorable position to react more quickly.

inducer Molecule that binds to and inactivates a repressor.

induction The ability of one group of cells to influence the development of another. This influence can be through physical contact or chemical signaling.

inner cell mass Portion of the blastula that develops into the embryo.

inorganic compounds For the most part, compounds containing no carbon. There are some exceptions such as carbon dioxide, carbon monoxide, and others.

insight learning The ability to do something correctly the first time even with no prior experience.

insulin Hormone secreted in response to high blood glucose levels to promote glycogen formation.

integral proteins Proteins that are implanted within the bilayer and can extend part way or all the way across the membrane.

intermediate filaments Substances constructed from a class of proteins called keratins; function as reinforcement for the shape and position of organelles in a cell.

intermediate inheritance An individual heterozygous for a trait (Yy) shows characteristics not exactly like those of *either* parent. The phenotype is a "mixture" of both of the parents' genetic input.

interneurons Function to make synaptic connections with other neurons. They work to integrate sensory input and motor output.

interphase The first three stages of the cycle, G_1, S, and G_2. Accounts for approximately 90 percent of the cell cycle.

interspecific competition Competition between different species that rely on the same resources for survival.

interstitial cells The structures that produce the hormones involved in the male reproductive system.

intraspecific competition *Within*-species competition that occurs because members of the same species rely on the same valuable resources for survival.

introns Noncoding regions produced during transcription that are cut out of the mRNA.

invertebrate Animal without a backbone.

ion An atom with a positive or negative charge.

isotonic solution Solution that has the same solute concentration as surrounding solutions.

karyotype A chart that organizes chromosomes in relation to number, size, and type.

ketone Carbonyl group in which both Rs are carbon chains; hydrophilic and polar.

kinesis A random change in the speed of movement in response to a stimulus. Organisms speed up in places they don't like and slow down in places they do like.

kingdom The broadest of the classification groups.

Klinefelter syndrome (XXY) Syndrome in which individuals have male sex organs but are sterile and display several feminine body characteristics.

Krebs cycle Energy-producing reaction that occurs in the matrix of the mitochondria, in which pyruvate is broken down completely to H_2O and CO_2 to produce 3 NADH, 1 $FADH_2$, and 1 ATP.

***K*-selected populations** Populations of a roughly constant size whose members have low reproductive rates. The offspring produced by *K*-selected organisms require extensive postnatal care.

lac operon Operon that aids in control of transcription of lactose metabolizing genes.

lactic acid fermentation Occurs in human muscle cells when oxygen is unavailable. Pyruvate is directly reduced to lactate by NADH to regenerate the NAD^+ needed for the resumption of glycolysis.

lagging strand The discontinuous strand produced during DNA replication.

larynx Passageway from the pharynx to the trachea. Commonly called the "voicebox."

lateral meristems Cells that extend all the way through the plant from roots to shoots and provide the secondary growth that increases the girth of a plant.

lateral roots Roots that serve to hold a plant in place in the soil.

law of dominance When two opposite pure-breeding varieties (homozygous dominant vs. homozygous recessive) of an organism are crossed, all the off-spring resemble one parent. This is referred to as the "dominant" trait. The variety that is hidden is referred to as the "recessive" trait.

law of independent assortment Members of each pair of factors are distributed independently when the gametes are formed. In other words, inheritance of one particular trait or characteristic does not interfere with inheritance of another trait (in unlinked genes). For example, if an individual is BbRr for two genes, gametes formed during meiosis could contain BR, Br, bR, or br. The B and b alleles assort *independently* of the R and r alleles.

law of multiplication Law that states that to determine the probability that two random events will occur in succession, you simply multiply the probability of the first event by the probability of the second event.

law of segregation Every organism carries pairs of factors, called *alleles,* for each trait, and the members of the pair segregate out (separate) during the formation of gametes. For example, if an individual is Bb for eye color, during gamete formation one gamete would receive a B and the other made from that cell would receive a b.

leading strand The continuous strand produced during DNA replication.

LH See **luteinizing hormone.**

LH surge Giant release of LH that triggers ovulation—the release of a secondary oocyte from the ovary.

lichen A symbiotic collection of organisms (fungus and algae) living as one.

life cycle Sequence of events that make up the reproductive cycle of an organism.

limiting factors Environmental factors that keep population sizes in check (predators, diseases, food supplies, and waste).

linkage map A genetic map put together using cross-over frequencies.

linked genes Genes along the same chromosome that tend to be inherited together because the chromosome is passed along as a unit.

lipase The major fat-digesting enzyme of the human body.

lipids Hydrophobic organic compounds used by cells as energy stores or building blocks. Three important lipids are fats, steroids, and phospholipids.

logistic growth A population grows at a rate that creates an S-shaped curve.

long day plants Plants, such as spinach, which flower if exposed to a night that is shorter than a critical period.

luteinizing hormone (LH) A gonadotropin that stimulates ovulation and formation of a corpus luteum, as well as the synthesis of estrogen and progesterone.

lymphatic system Important part of the circulatory system that functions as the route by which proteins and fluids that have leaked out of the bloodstream can return to circulation. The lymphatic system also functions as a protector for the body because of the presence of lymph nodes.

lymph nodes Structures found in the lymphatic system that are full of white blood cells, which live to fight infection. These nodes often swell up during infection as a sign of the body's fight against the infectious agent.

lymphocyte White blood cell. There are two main types of lymphocyte: B cells and T cells. These cells are formed in the bone marrow of the body and arise from stem cells.

lysogenic cycle The virus falls dormant and incorporates its DNA into the host DNA as an entity called a *provirus.* The viral DNA is quietly reproduced by the cell every time the cell reproduces itself, and this allows the virus to stay alive from generation to generation without killing the host cell.

lysosome Membrane-bound organelle that specializes in digestion and contains enzymes that break down proteins, lipids, nucleic acids, and carbohydrates.

lysozyme An enzyme, present in saliva and tears, that can kill germs before they have a chance to take hold.

lytic cycle The cell actually produces many viral off-spring, which are released from the cell, killing the host cell in the process.

macroevolution The big picture of evolution, which includes the study of evolution of groups of species over very long periods of time.

macronucleus A nucleus present in some protists (Ciliophora) and which controls the everyday activities of organisms.

macrospores Female gametophytes produced by heterosporous plants.

map unit Also termed *centigram.* Unit used to geographically relate the genes on the basis of crossover frequencies. One map unit is equal to a 1 percent recombination frequency.

matter Anything that has mass and takes up space.

mechanical digestion The physical breakdown of food that comes from chewing.

medulla Inner region of the kidney.

medulla oblongata The control center for involuntary activities such as breathing.

medusa A cnidarian that is flat and roams the waters looking for food (e.g., jellyfish).

melatonin Hormone that is known to be involved in our biological rhythms (circadian).

memory cells Stored instructions on how to handle a particular invader. When an invader returns to the body, the memory cells recognize it, produce antibodies in rapid fashion, and eliminate the invader very quickly.

meristemic cells Cells that allow plants to grow indeterminately.

mesoderm Intermediate germ layer that gives rise to muscle, the circulatory system, the reproductive system, excretory organs, bones, and connective tissues of the gut and exterior of the body.

mesophyll Interior tissue of a leaf.

mesophyll cells Cells that contain many chloroplasts and host the majority of photosynthesis.

methanogens Archaebacteria that produce methane as a by-product.

microevolution Evolution at the level of species and populations.

microfilaments Substances built from actin that play a major role in muscle contraction.

micronucleus A nucleus present in some protists (Ciliophora) and which functions in conjugation.

microspores Male gametophytes produced by heterosporous plants.

microtubules Substances constructed from tubulin; play a lead role in the separation of cells during cell division; are also important components of cilia and flagella.

migration This is a cyclic movement of animals over long distances according to the time of year.

mismatch repair Process during DNA replication by which DNA polymerase replaces an incorrectly placed nucleotide with proper nucleotide.

missense mutation Substitution of the wrong nucleotides into the DNA sequence. These substitutions still result in the addition of amino acids to the growing protein chain during translation, but they can sometimes lead to the addition of *incorrect* amino acids to the chain.

mitochondrion Double-membraned organelle that specializes in the production of ATP; host organelle for the Krebs cycle (matrix) and oxidative phosphorylation (cristae).

mitotic spindle Apparatus constructed from microtubules that assists in the physical separation of the chromosomes during mitosis.

monocot (monocotyledon) Angiosperm with a single cotyledon.

monohybrid cross A cross that involves a single character in which both parents are heterozygous (Bb × Bb). A monohybrid cross between heterozygous gametes gives a 3:1 phenotype ratio in the offspring.

monosaccharide The simplest form of a carbohydrate. The most important monosaccharide is glucose, which is used in cellular respiration to provide energy for cells.

morula A structure formed during the cleavage divisions of the zygote.

motor neurons Nerve cells that take the commands from the central nervous system (CNS) and put them into action as motor outputs.

M phase mitosis This is the stage during which the cell separates into two new cells.

Müllerian mimicry Two species that are aposematically colored as an indicator of their chemical defense mechanism; they mimic each other's color scheme in an effort to increase the speed with which predators learn to avoid them.

mutant phenotypes Characters that are not the wild-type strain in fruit flies and other organisms.

mutation A random event that can cause changes in allele frequencies. It is *always* random with respect to which genes are affected, although the changes in allele frequencies that occur as a result of the mutation may not be.

mutualism Scenario in which two organisms benefit from an interaction or relationship.

mycelium Meshes of branching filaments formed from hyphae that function as mouthlike structures for fungi.

myelinated neurons Neurons with a layer of insulation around the axon, allowing for faster transmission. They form the cable Internet of the body.

natural selection The process by which characters or traits are maintained or eliminated in a population based on their contribution to the differential survival and reproductive success of their "host" organisms.

negative feedback Occurs when a hormone acts to directly or indirectly inhibit further secretion of the hormone of interest.

nephron The functional unit of the kidney.

net productivity Difference between the concentration of dissolved oxygen for the initial and light bottle in a primary productivity experiment.

neural plate Structure that becomes the neural groove, which eventually becomes the neural tube. This neural tube later gives rise to the central nervous system.

neural tube Embryonic structure that gives rise to the central nervous system.

neuromuscular junction The space between the motor neuron and the muscle cell.

neurotransmitter Chemical released by neurons that functions as a messenger, causing a nearby cell to react and continue the nervous impulse.

niche Term used to describe all the biotic and abiotic resources used by the organism.

nitrogen cycle The shuttling of nitrogen from the atmosphere, to living organisms, and back to the atmosphere in a continuous cycle.

nitrogen fixation The conversion of N_2 to NH_3 (ammonia).

nitrogenous bases Monomers such as adenine, guanine, cytosine, thymine, and uracil out of which DNA and RNA are constructed.

noncompetitive inhibition Condition in which an inhibitor molecule binds to an enzyme away from the active site, causing a change in the shape of the active site so that it can no longer interact with the substrate.

noncyclic light reactions Pathway that produces ATP, NADPH, and O_2. Uses both photosystem I and II.

nondisjunction The improper separation of chromosomes during meiosis, which leads to an abnormal number of chromosomes in offspring. Examples include Down syndrome, Turner syndrome, and Klinefelter's syndrome.

nonsense mutation Substitution of the wrong nucleotides into the DNA sequence. These substitutions lead to premature stoppage of protein synthesis by the early placement of a stop codon. This type of mutation usually leads to a nonfunctional protein.

nonspecific immunity The nonspecific prevention of the entrance of invaders into the body.

notochord Structure that serves to support the body. Found in the embryos of chordates.

nucleic acid Macromolecule composed of nucleotides, sugars, and phosphates that serves as genetic material of living organisms (DNA and RNA).

nucleoid Region of a prokaryotic cell that contains the genetic material.

nucleolus Eukaryotic structure in which ribosomes are constructed.

nucleus The control center of eukaryotic cells that is the storage site of the genetic material (DNA). It is the site of replication, transcription, and post-transcriptional modification of RNA.

obligate aerobe Organism that requires oxygen for respiration.

obligate anaerobe Organism that only survives in oxygen-free environments.

observational learning The ability of an organism to learn how to do something by watching another individual do it first.

oil Type of lipid.

Okazaki fragments The lagging DNA strand consists of these tiny pieces that are later connected by an enzyme, DNA ligase, to produce the completed double-stranded daughter DNA molecule.

ontogeny The development of an individual.

oogenesis Process by which female gametes are formed. Each meiotic cycle leads to the production of a single ovum, or egg.

operant conditioning Type of associative learning that is based on trial and error.

operator A short sequence near the promoter that assists in transcription by interacting with regulatory proteins (transcription factors).

operon A promoter/operator pair that services multiple genes.

opportunistic populations *R*-selected organisms that tend to appear when space in the region opens up due to some environmental change. They grow fast, reproduce quickly, and die quickly as well.

optimal foraging Theory that predicts that natural selection will favor animals that choose foraging strategies that maximize the differential between benefits and costs.

organic compounds Carbon-containing compounds. Important examples include carbohydrates, proteins, lipids, and nucleic acids.

osmosis The passive diffusion of water down its concentration gradient across selectively permeable membranes. It will flow from a region with a lower solute concentration (hypotonic) to a region with a higher solute concentration (hypertonic).

outbreeding Mating between unrelated individuals of the same species.

ovary The site of egg production. In animals, females often have two, one on either side of the body. Plants *usually* only have one ovary.

oviduct Known also as the *fallopian tube,* this is the site of fertilization and connects the ovary to the uterus. Eggs move through here from the ovary to the uterus (in animals only).

ovulation Stage of menstrual cycle in which the secondary oocyte is released from the ovary.

oxaloacetate Compound that plays an important role in C_4 photosynthesis of plants and the Krebs cycle in animals.

oxidative phosphorylation Aerobic process in which NADH and $FADH_2$ pass their electrons down the electron transport chain to produce ATP.

oxytocin Hormone that stimulates uterine contraction and milk ejection for breastfeeding.

P_1 The parent generation in a genetic cross.

palisade mesophyll Host to many chloroplasts and much of the photosynthesis of a leaf.

parallel evolution Similar evolutionary changes occurring in two either related or unrelated species that respond in a similar manner to a similar environment.

parasitism Scenario in which one organism benefits at the other's expense.

parasympathetic nervous system Branch of autonomic nervous system that shuts down the body to conserve energy.

parathyroid hormone (PTH) Hormone that increases serum concentration of Ca^{2+}, assisting in the process of bone maintenance.

parenchyma cells Plant cells that play a role in photosynthesis (mesophyll cells), storage, and secretion.

Patau syndrome Presence of trisomy 13, which occurs in about one out of every 12,000–16,000 live births and causes serious brain and circulatory defects.

pedigrees Family trees used to describe the genetic relationships within a family. One use of a pedigree is to determine whether parents will pass certain conditions to their offspring.

pepsin The major enzyme of the stomach, which breaks down proteins into smaller polypeptides to be handled by the intestines.

pepsinogen The precursor to pepsin that is activated by active pepsin (a small amount of which normally exists in the stomach).

peripheral nervous system (PNS) The PNS can be broken down into a sensory and a motor division. The sensory division carries information *to* the CNS while the motor division carries information *away* from the CNS.

peripheral proteins Proteins, such as receptor proteins, not implanted in the bilayer, which are often attached to integral proteins of the membrane.

peristalsis The force created by the rhythmic contraction of the smooth muscle of the esophagus and intestines.

permafrost Frozen layer of soil just underneath the upper soil layer, found in the tundra biome.

peroxisome Organelle that functions to break down fatty acids, and detoxify.

petals Structures that serve to attract pollinators.

PGAL (phosphoglyceraldehyde) Molecule important to energy-producing reactions photosynthesis and respiration.

phage A virus that infects bacteria.

phagocytes Immune cells (macrophages and neutrophils) that use endocytosis to engulf and eliminate foreign invaders.

pharynx Tube through which both food and air pass after leaving the mouth.

phenotype The physical expression of the trait associated with a particular genotype. Some examples of the phenotypes for Mendel's peas were round or wrinkled, green or yellow, purple flower or white flower.

phenylketonuria (PKU) An autosomal recessive disease caused by a single gene defect that leaves a person unable to break down phenylalanine, which results in a by-product that can accumulate to toxic levels in the blood and cause mental retardation.

pheromones Chemical signals important to communication.

phloem Important part of plant vascular tissue that functions to transport sugars from their production site to the rest of the plant.

phosphate group An acidic functional group that is a vital component of molecules that serve as cellular energy sources: ATP, ADP, and GTP.

phospholipid Lipid with both a hydrophobic tail *and* a hydrophilic head; the major component of cell membranes with the hydrophilic phosphate group forming the outside portion and the hydrophobic tail forming the interior of the wall.

photoautotrophs Photosynthetic autotrophs that produce energy from light.

photolysis Process by which water is broken up by an enzyme into hydrogen ions and oxygen atoms. Occurs during the light reactions of photosynthesis.

photoperiodism The response by a plant to the change in the length of days.

photophosphorylation Process by which ATP is made during the light-dependent reactions of photosynthesis. It is the chloroplast equivalent of oxidative phosphorylation.

photorespiration Process by which oxygen competes with carbon dioxide and attaches to RuBP. Plants that experience photorespiration have a lowered capacity for growth.

photosynthesis The process by which plants generate energy from light and inorganic raw materials. This occurs in the chloroplasts and involves two stages: the light-dependent reactions and the light-independent reactions.

photosystem Cluster of light-trapping pigments involved in the process of photosynthesis.

phototaxis Reflex movement toward light at night.

phototropism A plant's growth in response to light. Auxin is the hormone involved with this process.

phycobilin Photosynthetic pigment.

phylogeny The evolutionary history of a species.

phytochrome Important pigment in the process of flowering. Leads to the production of florigen.

pigment A molecule that absorbs light of a particular wavelength.

pioneer species A species that is able to survive in resource-poor conditions and takes hold of a barren area such as a volcanic island. Pioneer species do the grunt work, adding nutrients and other improvements to the once-uninhabited volcanic rock until future species take over.

PKU See **phenylketonuria.**

placenta In humans, this structure provides the nutrients for the developing embryo.

planarians Free-living platyhelminthe carnivores that live in the water.

plasma The liquid portion of the blood that contains minerals, hormones, antibodies, and nutritional materials.

plasma cells The factories that produce antibodies that eliminate any cell containing on its surface the antigen that the plasma cell has been summoned to kill.

plasma membrane Selective barrier around a cell composed of a double layer of phospholipids that controls what is able to enter and exit a cell.

plasmids Extra circles of DNA in bacteria that contain just a few genes and have been useful in genetic engineering. Plasmids replicate independently of the main chromosome.

plasmodial slime molds Nonphotosynthetic heterotrophic funguslike protists. They eat and grow as a unified clumped unicellular mass known as a *plasmodium.*

plasmodium This word has two meanings in this book. It can be the causative agent of malaria, or it can be the clumped unicellular mass that fungi form under certain feeding conditions.

plasmolysis The shriveling of the cytoplasm of a cell in response to loss of water in hypertonic surroundings.

platelet Blood cell involved in the clotting of blood.

pleiotropy A single gene has multiple effects on an organism.

PNS See **peripheral nervous system.**

polar A molecule that has an unequal distribution of charge, which creates a positive and a negative side to the molecule.

polar body Castaway cell produced during female gamete formation that contains only genetic information.

pollen Sperm-bearing male gametophyte of gymnosperms and angiosperms.

polygenic traits Traits that are affected by more than one gene (e.g., eye color).

polymerase chain reaction Technique used to create large amounts of a DNA sequence in a short amount of time.

polyp Cylinder-shaped cnidarian that lives attached to a surface (e.g., sea anemone).

polyploidy A condition in which an individual has more than the normal number of sets of chromosomes.

polysaccharide A carbohydrate usually composed of hundreds or thousands of monosaccharides, which acts as a storage form of energy, and as structural material in and around cells. Starch and glycogen are storage polysaccharides; cellulose and chitin are structural polysaccharides.

pond succession Process by which a hole filled with water passes through the various succession stages until it has become a swamp, forest, or grassland.

population A collection of individuals of the same species living in the same geographic area.

population cycle When a population size dips below the carrying capacity, it will later come back to the capacity and even surpass it. However, the population could dip below the carrying capacity as a result of some major change in the environment and equilibrate at a new, lower carrying capacity.

population density The number of individuals per unit area in a given population.

population ecology The study of the size, distribution, and density of populations and how they change with time.

positive feedback Occurs when a hormone acts to directly or indirectly cause increased secretion of a hormone.

posterior pituitary gland Structure that produces only two hormones: ADH and oxytocin.

potometer Lab apparatus used to measure transpiration rates in plants.

predation Scenario in which one species, the predator, hunts another species, the prey.

primary consumers The consumers that obtain energy through consumption of the producers of the planet. Known as *herbivores*.

primary immune response When a B cell meets and attaches to the appropriate antigen, it becomes activated and undergoes mitosis and differentiation into plasma cells and memory cells.

primary oocytes Cells that begin the process of meiosis and progress until prophase I, where they sit halted until the host female enters puberty.

primary plant growth Increase in the length of a plant.

primary productivity Rate at which carbon-containing compounds are stored.

primary sex characteristics The sexual organs that assist in the vital process of procreation; include the testes, ovaries, and uterus.

primary spermatocytes Produced by mitotic division, these cells immediately undergo meiosis I to produce two secondary spermatocytes, which undergo meiosis II to produce four spermatids.

primary structure The sequence of the amino acids that make up a protein.

primary succession Succession that occurs in an area that is devoid of life and contains no soil.

primer sites DNA segments that signal where replication should originate.

prion Incorrectly folded form of a brain cell protein that works by converting other normal host proteins into misshapen proteins. Prion diseases tend to cause dementia, muscular control problems, and loss of balance.

progesterone Hormone involved in menstrual cycle and pregnancy.

prokaryotic cell A *simple* cell with no nucleus, or membrane-bound organelles; divides by binary fission and includes bacteria—both heterotrophic and autotrophic types.

prolactin Hormone that controls the production of milk and leads to a decrease in the synthesis and release of GnRH, thus inhibiting ovulation.

promoter region A recognition site that shows the polymerase where transcription should begin.

prostate gland Structure whose function in the male reproductive system is to add a basic (pH > 7) liquid to the mix to help neutralize the acidity of the urine that may remain in the common urethral passage.

protein Organic compound composed of chains of amino acids that function as structural components, transport aids, enzymes, and cell signals, among other things.

protein hormones Hormones too large to move inside a cell, and which bind to receptors on the surface of the cell instead.

protein kinase Protein that controls the activities of other proteins through the addition of phosphate groups.

provirus A virus genome that is integrated into the DNA of a host cell that can be transmitted from one generation to the next without causing lysis.

pseudocoelomate Animal that has a fluid-filled body cavity that is not enclosed by mesoderm.

...ds Extensions from protists (organisms of ... kingdom Protist) that assist in collection of nutrients.

P site Region in protein synthesis machinery that holds the tRNA carrying the growing protein.

PTH See **parathyroid hormone.**

punctuated equilibria model Theorizes that evolutionary change occurs in rapid bursts separated by large periods of stasis (no change).

purine A nitrogenous base that contains a double ring structure (adenine, guanine).

pyloric sphincter The connection point between the stomach and the small intestine.

pyramid of numbers Pyramid based on the *number* of individuals at each level of the biomass chain. Each box in this pyramid represents the number of members of that level. The highest consumers in the chain tend to be quite large, resulting in a smaller number of those individuals spread out over a given area.

pyrimidine A nitrogenous base that contains a single ring structure (cytosine, thymine).

Q_{10} value Statistic that shows how an increase in temperature affects the metabolic activity of an organism.

quaternary structure The arrangement of separate polypeptide "subunits" into a single protein. Seen only in proteins with more than one polypeptide chain.

radiation The loss of heat through ejection of electromagnetic waves.

random distribution Random distribution of species in a given geographic area.

rate of reaction Rate at which a chemical reaction occurs.

reaction centers Control centers made up of pigments.

reciprocal altruism Altruistic behavior performed with the expectation that the favor will be returned.

recombinant DNA DNA that contains DNA pieces from multiple sources.

red blood cells Cells in body that contain hemoglobin and serve as the oxygen delivery system in the body.

red-green colorblindness Sex-linked condition that leaves those afflicted unable to distinguish between red and green colors.

redox reaction A reduction–oxidation reaction involving the transfer of electrons.

replication fork Fork opened in DNA strand that allows DNA replication to occur.

repolarization The lowering of the potential back down to its initial level, stopping the transmission of neural signals at that point.

repressor Protein that prevents the binding of RNA polymerase to the promoter site.

reproductive success A measure of how many surviving offspring one produces relative to how many the other individuals in one's population produce.

RER See **rough endoplasmic reticulum.**

respirometer Machine that can be used to calculate the respiration rate of a reaction.

restriction enzymes Enzymes that cut DNA at specific nucleotide sequences. This results in DNA fragments with single-stranded ends called "sticky ends," which find and reconnect with other DNA fragments containing the same ends (with the assistance of DNA ligase).

retrovirus An RNA virus that carries an enzyme called *reverse transcriptase* that reverse-transcribes the genetic information from RNA into DNA. In the nucleus of the host, the newly transcribed DNA incorporates into the host DNA and is transcribed into RNA when the host cell undergoes normal transcription.

reverse transcriptase Enzyme carried by retroviruses that function to convert RNA to DNA.

R_f Variable that indicates the relative rate at which one molecule migrates compared to the solvent of a paper chromatograph.

ribosomes Host organelle for protein synthesis composed of a large subunit and a small subunit. Ribosomes are built in the nucleolus.

RNA polymerase Enzyme that runs transcription and adds the appropriate nucleotides to the 3′ end of the growing strand.

RNA splicing Process that removes introns from newly produced mRNA and then glues exons back together to produce the final product.

root Portion of the plant that is below the ground.

root cap Protective structure found around the apical meristem of a root that keeps it together as it pushes through the soil.

root hairs Hairs extending off the surface of root tips that increase the surface area for absorption of water and nutrients from the soil.

root pressure Driving force that contributes to the movement of water through the xylem of a plant.

rough endoplasmic reticulum (RER) Membrane-bound organelle with ribosomes on the cytoplasmic surface of the cell. Proteins produced by RER are often secreted and carried by vesicles to the Golgi apparatus for further modification.

rRNA Ribosomal RNA, which makes up a huge portion of ribosomes.

***R*-selected populations** Populations that experience rapid growth of the J-curve variety. The offspring produced by *R*-selected organisms are numerous, mature quite rapidly, and require very little postnatal care.

rubisco Enzyme that catalyzes the first step of the Calvin cycle in C_3 plants.

saprobe Organism that feeds off dead organisms.

saturated fat Fat that contains no double bonds. It is associated with heart disease and atherosclerosis.

savanna Grassland that contains a spattering of trees found all over South America, Australia, and Africa. Savanna soil tends to be low in nutrients, while temperatures tend to run high.

sclerenchyma cells Plant cells that function as protection and mechanical support.

search image Mental image that assists animals during foraging. It directs them to food of interest.

secondary consumers Consumers that obtain energy through consumption of the primary consumers.

secondary immune response Memory cells are the basis for this efficient response to invaders.

secondary oocyte An oocyte that has half the genetic information of the parent cell, but the majority of its cytoplasm.

secondary plant growth Growth that leads to an increase in plant girth.

secondary sex characteristics The noticeable physical characteristics that differ between males and females such as facial hair, deepness of voice, breasts, and muscle distribution.

secondary spermatocyte Cells formed during spermatogenesis that give rise to spermatids and eventually sperm.

secondary structure The three-dimensional arrangement of a protein caused by hydrogen bonding.

secondary succession Succession in an area that previously had stable plant and/or animal life but has since been disturbed by some major force such as a forest fire.

second messenger Molecule that serves as an intermediary, activating other proteins and enzymes in a chemical reaction.

semiconservative DNA replication Before the parent strand is copied, the DNA unzips, with each single strand serving as a template for the creation of a new double strand. One strand of DNA from the parent goes to one daughter cell; the second parent strand goes to the second daughter cell.

seminal vesicles Structures that dump fluids into the ejaculatory duct to send along with the sperm, providing three important advantages to the sperm: energy by adding fructose; power to progress through the female reproductive system by adding prostaglandin (which stimulates uterine contraction); and mucus, which helps the sperm swim more effectively.

seminiferous tubules Actual site of sperm production.

sensory neurons Nerve cells that receive and communicate information from the sensory environment.

septae Structures that divide the hypha filaments of fungi into different compartments.

SER See **smooth endoplasmic reticulum.**

sex pili bacterial appendage vital to process of conjugation.

sex ratio Proportion of males and females in a given population.

sexual selection The process by which certain characters are selected for because they aid in mate acquisition.

shoots Parts of a plant that are above the ground.

short-day plants Plants, such as poinsettias, that flower if exposed to nighttime conditions longer than a critical period of length.

sickle cell anemia A recessive disease caused by the substitution of a single amino acid in the hemoglobin protein of red blood cells, leaving hemoglobin less able to carry oxygen and also causing the hemoglobin to deform to a sickle shape when the oxygen content of the blood is low. The sickling causes pain, muscle weakness, and fatigue.

sieve-tube elements Functionally mature cells of the phloem that are alive.

sink Site of carbohydrate consumption in plants.

skeletal muscle Striated muscle that controls voluntary activities and contains multiple nuclei.

smooth endoplasmic reticulum (SER) Membrane-bound organelle involved in lipid synthesis, detoxification, and carbohydrate metabolism; has no ribosomes on its cytoplasmic surface.

smooth muscle Involuntary muscle that contracts slowly and is controlled by the autonomic nervous system (ANS).

potassium pump A mechanism that actively moves potassium *into* the cell and sodium *out of* the cell against their respective concentration gradients to maintain appropriate levels inside the cell.

solute A substance dissolved in a solution.

somatotropic hormone (STH) A hormone that stimulates protein synthesis and growth in the body.

somite Structure that gives rise to the muscles and vertebrae in mammals.

source Site of carbohydrate creation in plants.

Southern blotting Procedure used to determine if a particular sequence of nucleotides is present in a sample of DNA.

specialized transduction Transduction involving a virus in the lysogenic cycle that shifts to the lytic cycle. If it accidentally brings with it a piece of the host DNA as it pulls out of the host chromosome, this DNA could find its way into another cell.

speciation The process by which new species evolve.

species A group of interbreeding (or potentially interbreeding) organisms.

specific immunity Complicated multilayered defense mechanism that protects a host against foreign invasion.

spectrophotometer Machine used to determine how much light can pass through a sample.

spermatids Immature sperm that enter the epididymis, where their waiting game begins and maturation is completed.

spermatogenesis Process by which the male gametes are formed. Four haploid sperm are produced during each meiotic cycle. This does not begin until puberty, and it occurs in the seminiferous tubules.

S phase The DNA is copied so that each daughter cell has a complete set of chromosomes at the conclusion of the cell cycle.

spongy mesophyll Region of a plant where the cells are more loosely arranged, aiding in the passage of CO_2 to cells performing photosynthesis.

sporophyte The diploid multicellular stage of the plant life cycle.

sporozoite Small infectious form that apicomplexa protists take to spread from place to place.

stabilizing selection This describes selection for the mean of a population for a given allele; has the effect of reducing variation in a given population.

stamen Male structure of a flower that contains the pollen-producing anther.

starch Storage polysaccharide made of glucose molecules; seen in plants.

start codon (AUG) Codon that establishes the reading frame for protein formation.

stem cells Cells that give rise to the immune cells of the human body.

steroid hormones Lipid-soluble molecules that pass through the cell membrane and combine with cytoplasmic proteins. These complexes pass through to the nucleus to interact with chromosomal proteins and directly affect transcription in the nucleus.

steroids Lipids composed of four carbon rings. Examples include cholesterol, estrogen, progesterone, and testosterone.

STH See **somatotropic hormone.**

sticky ends Single-stranded DNA fragments formed when DNA is treated with restriction enzymes. These fragments find and reconnect with other fragments with the same ends.

stigma Flower structure that functions as the receiver of pollen.

stomata Structure through which CO_2 enters a plant, and water vapor and O_2 leave.

stop codons (UGA, UAA, UAG) Codons that stop the production of a protein.

storage diseases Diseases such as Tay-Sachs that are caused by the absence of a particular lysosomal hydrolytic enzyme.

strain Groups into which bacterial species are placed.

stroma The inner fluid portion of the chloroplast that plays host to the light-independent reactions of photosynthesis.

style Pathway in flower that leads to the ovary.

substrates Substances that enzymes act upon.

succession Shift in the local composition of species in response to changes that occur over time.

sulfhydryl group A functional group that helps stabilize the structure of many proteins.

survivorship curves A tool used to study the population dynamics of species.

symbiosis A relationship between two different species that can be classified as one of three main types: commensalism, mutualism, and parasitism.

sympathetic nervous system Branch of the autonomic nervous system that gets the body ready to move.

sympatric speciation Interbreeding ceases even though no physical barrier prevents it. Can occur as a result of polyploidy and balanced polymorphism.

symplast pathway Movement of water and nutrients through the living portion of plant cells.

synaptic knob The end of the axon. This is where calcium gates are opened in response to the changing potential, which causes vesicles to release substances called *neurotransmitters* (NTs) into the synaptic gap between the axon and the target cell. These NTs diffuse across the gap, causing a new impulse in the target cell.

tactile communication Communication that involves the use of touch in the conveying of a message.

taiga Biome characterized by lengthy, cold, and wet winters. This biome is found in Canada and has gymnosperms as its prominent plant life. This biome contains coniferous forests (pine and other needle-bearing trees).

tapeworm Parasitic flatworm whose adult form lives in vertebrates.

taproot system System of roots found in many dicots that starts as one thick root and divides into many smaller lateral roots, which serve as an anchor for the plant.

TATA box Group of nucleotides found in the promoter region that assists in binding of RNA polymerase to the DNA strand for transcription.

taxis The reflex movement toward or away from a stimulus.

taxonomy The field of biology that classifies organisms according to the presence or absence of shared characteristics in an effort to discover evolutionary relationships between species.

Tay-Sachs disease A fatal genetic storage disease that renders the body unable to break down a particular type of lipid.

temperate deciduous forest A biome that is found in regions that experience cold winters where plant life is dormant, alternating with warm summers that provide enough moisture to keep large trees alive.

temperate grasslands Found in regions with cold winter temperatures. The soil of this biome is considered to be among the most fertile of all.

termination site Region of DNA that tells the polymerase when transcription should conclude.

territoriality Scenario in which territorial individuals defend their territory against other individuals.

tertiary structure The 3D (three-dimensional) arrangement of a protein caused by interaction among the various R groups of the amino acids involved.

test cross Crossing of an organism of unknown dominant genotype with an organism that is homozygous recessive for the trait, resulting in offspring with observable phenotypes. Test crosses are used to determine the unknown genotype.

testis The site of sperm and testosterone production in animals; males have two testes, located in the scrotum.

testosterone Sex hormone produced in testes that stimulates the growth of male sex characteristics.

thermoacidophiles Archaebacteria that live in hot, acidic environments.

thermoregulation The process by which temperature is maintained.

thigmotropism A plant's growth in response to touch.

thylakoid membrane system Inner membrane that winds through the stroma of a chloroplast. Site of the light-dependent reactions of photosynthesis.

thymine dimers Thymine nucleotides located adjacent to one another on the DNA strand bind together when excess exposure to UV light occurs. This can negatively affect replication of DNA and assist in the creation of further mutations.

thymosin Hormone involved in the development of the T cells of the immune system.

thyroid-stimulating hormone (TSH) A hormone that stimulates the synthesis and secretion of thyroid hormones, which regulate the rate of metabolism in the body.

thyroxin Hormone released by the thyroid gland that functions in the control of metabolic activities in the body.

tongue Structure that functions to move food around while we chew and helps to arrange the food into a swallowable bolus.

trachea The tunnel that leads air into the thoracic cavity.

tracheid cells Xylem cells in charge of water transport in gymnosperm.

tracheophytes Vascular plants.

transcription factors Helper proteins that assist RNA polymerase in finding and attaching to the promoter region.

transduction The movement of genes from one cell to another by phages.

transformation The transfer of genetic material from one cell to another, resulting in a genetic change in the receiving cell.

translocation Movement of the ribosome along the mRNA in such a way that the A site becomes the P site and the next tRNA comes into the new A site carrying the next amino acid.

...tion (plants) Movement of carbohydrates ...ough the phloem.

transpiration Process by which plants lose water by evaporation through their leaves.

trichinosis Disease found in humans caused by a roundworm that infects meat products.

trophic levels Hierarchy of energy levels that describe the energy distribution of a planet.

trophoblast Forms the placenta for the developing fetus, and aids in attachment to the endometrium. This structure also produces human chorionic gonadotropin (hCG), which maintains the endometrium by ensuring the continued production of progesterone.

tropical forests These forests consist primarily of tall trees that form a thick cover, which blocks the light from reaching the floor of the forest (where there is little growth). Tropical rainforests are known for their rapid recycling of nutrients and contain the greatest diversity of species.

tropism Plant growth that occurs in response to an environmental stimulus such as sunlight or gravity.

tropomyosin Regulatory protein known to block the actin–myosin binding site and prevent muscular contraction in the absence of calcium.

trypsin Enzyme that cuts protein bonds in the small intestine.

TSH See **thyroid-stimulating hormone.**

tundra This biome experiences extremely cold winters during which the ground freezes completely. Short shrubs or grasses that are able to withstand the difficult conditions dominate.

Turner syndrome Affects females who are missing an X chromosome.

umbilical cord Structure that transports oxygen, food, and waste (CO_2) between the embryo and the placenta.

uniform distribution Scenario in which individuals are evenly spaced out across a given geographic area.

unsaturated fat Fat that contains one or more double bonds; found in plants.

uracil The nucleotide that replaces thymine in RNA.

urethra Exit point for both urine and sperm from males and urine for females.

uterus Site of embryo attachment and development in mammals.

vaccination Inoculation of medicine into a patient in an effort to prime the immune system to be prepared to fight a specific sickness if confronted in the future.

vacuole A storage organelle that is large in plant cells but small in animal cells.

vascular cambium A cylinder of tissue that extends the length of the stem and root and gives rise to the secondary xylem and phloem.

vascular cylinder Structure in plants that is composed of cells that produce the lateral roots of the plant.

vas deferens Tunnel that connects the epididymis to the urethra.

vector Agent that moves DNA from one source to another.

veins Structures that return blood to the heart.

vena cava system System of veins that returns deoxygenated blood from the body to the heart to be reoxygenated in the lungs.

vertebrate Animal with a backbone.

vessel elements Xylem cells in charge of water transport in angiosperms. More efficient than tracheid cells.

vestigial characters Characters that are no longer useful, although they once were.

viral envelope Protective barrier that surrounds some viruses but also helps them attach to cells.

viroids Plant viruses that are only a few hundred nucleotides in length.

virus A parasitic infectious agent that is unable to survive outside a host organism. Viruses do not contain enzymes for metabolism or ribosomes for protein synthesis.

visual communication Communication through the use of the visual senses.

water biomes Both freshwater and marine biomes, which occupy the majority of the surface of the earth.

water cycle The earth is covered in water. A lot of this water evaporates each day and returns to the clouds. This water is then returned to the earth in the form of precipitation.

water potential The force that drives water to move in a given direction. Combination of solute potential and pressure potential.

water vascular system Series of tubes and canals within echinoderms that play a role in ingestion of food, movement, and gas exchange.

wild-type phenotype The normal phenotype for a characteristic in fruit flies and other organisms.

within-sex competition Competition for mates between members of the same sex.

wobble Nucleotides in the third position of an anticodon are able to pair with many nucleotides instead of just their normal partner.

X-inactivation During the development of the female embryo, one of the two X chromosomes in each cell remains coiled as a Barr body whose genes are not expressed. A cell expresses the alleles of the active X chromosome only.

xylem The "superhighway," or important part of the vascular tissue in plants, through which water and nutrients travel throughout the plant. Also functions as a support structure that strengthens the plant.

yolk sac Derived from the hypoblast, this is the site of early blood cell formation in humans and the source of nutrients for bird and reptile embryos.

zone of cell division Region at the tip of a root formed by the actively dividing cells of the apical meristem.

zone of elongation Cells of this region elongate tremendously during plant growth.

zone of maturation Region in the plant where cells differentiate into their final forms.

Study Smarter and Manage Your Time Better

Create Your Own Personal Study Schedule

Download Your BONUS McGraw-Hill Education AP Planner App

5 Steps to a 5: AP Biology 2018
Now with extra AP practice questions

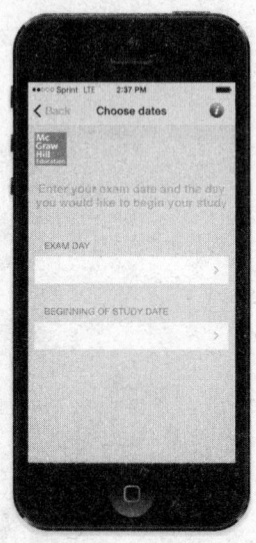

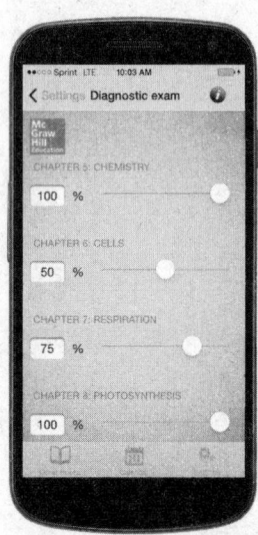

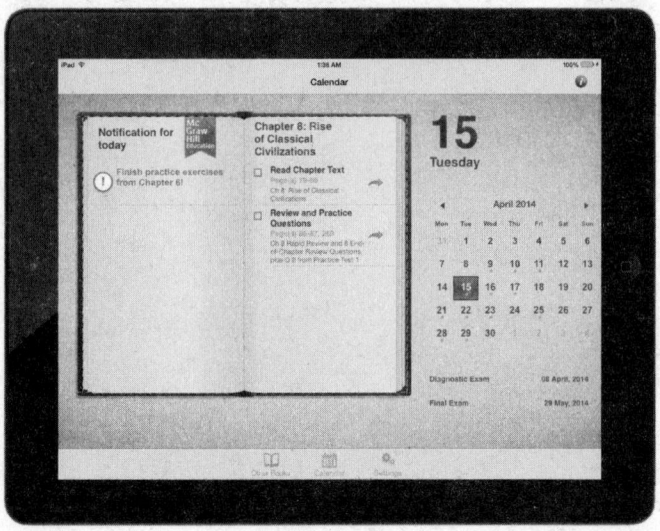

Select your exam date

Create your own customized study schedule based on diagnostic test results

Get a complete, day-by-day study schedule with review and practice assignments

✔ *Flaming,* or being fervently disparaging of other people or other Web pages

✔ Posting offensive material on your page without some kind of warning label

Netiquette is an amorphous and evolving area of online behavior, so you may want to join a Web-oriented newsgroup where you can ask questions before publishing. Also, check out this site for in-depth info:

```
www.albion.com/netiquette/corerules.html
```

Yet, within the bounds of netiquette, you still need to publicize your site. Nothing is more frustrating than putting up a site that no one visits.

Fortunately, publicizing your site is not hard. Add your site to the popular indexes, for example, through the Submit-It site at `www.submit-it.com`. (Like many other such services, the Submit-It site charges a fee.)

You can also send e-mail to appropriate blogs, put out a press release, send e-mail to friends and business contacts, or shout from the rooftops.

DO Ask for Feedback

Put your e-mail address on your home page and ask for comments. You'll be amazed by what people say about your pages. (Some of the comments may even be complimentary!) People who have never before seen your site can offer a good, fresh perspective and give you feedback on things that you may not have previously thought about.

After you have your site working the way you want it to, experiment. Try weird things. Keep asking for feedback. Never be afraid to figure out complex and hard stuff. (It's only complex and hard because you don't understand it *yet!*)

Everyone can benefit from outside input. Criticism by your prospective audience is not only useful, it's also educational. You can learn a lot about what people expect and want. Criticism can't hurt anything but your pride, and listening to it almost always improves your site.

Whether from outside input or your own research and ideas, you can find so much neat stuff out there that can make your Web-publishing efforts even more exciting — JavaScript, multimedia, new browsers and publishing tools, Net-based games, and online business infrastructure. All this new stuff *is* understandable and usable by normal folks like you and me. Don't be intimidated. You can use all of it. (If you've come this far, you've got what it takes!)

DON'T Let Your Site Get Stale

A static site is a boring site. True, it works for some purposes, but in general, if you want people to keep revisiting your site, you must keep it updated. The best sites are those that continually provide new and interesting content. Include pointers to information that's frequently updated, such as "Thought for the day" or "Links to new, cool sites." Let users know how often to expect updates and be sure to showcase new content. A "New" icon next to recently added or updated content can work wonders.

You can easily add a blog piece to your site. Some packages make this automatic; or, use your knowledge of HTML to easily update your site with new commentary every few days.

In addition to updating your site, update yourself! Broadening your knowledge of Web design, new trends and technologies, and what's "cool" at the moment can only help improve your site.

Chapter 17

Ten Places to Host Your Page

• •

*W*here to host your Web site is always a good question. And these days, with so many different kinds of Web services, the very definition of a Web site is under question.

Is a Facebook page a Web site? Is a set of photos you've unloaded to Flickr? Literally speaking, yes.

But a true standalone Web site, built from the ground up, not only offers you more choices — it can also knit together all your other online involvements in a coherent whole, a kind of control panel for your online life.

So here are ten places to host "real" Web sites — though I include two blogging sites, as blogs can so easily be expanded into complete sites.

Google Page Creator

Google Page Creator is a very flexible page creation service, described in Chapter 3. It will hold your hand in setting up a simple site — or simply give you space to put up as complicated and customized site as you want.

How to use it: Go to `pages.google.com` and log in or sign up for an account.

Network Solutions

Network Solutions is the original provider of Web URLs and still one of the biggest. Network Solutions also offers easy-to-use Web-page creation tools and Web hosting. It's on the expensive side, and they are quite good at selling services. But there's a lot of functionality available.

If you look for a Web URL on Network Solutions, they can apparently "lock down" the URL for a few days — so if you search for it again, it seems to be gone, but actually it's just being held. Consider doing your domain name searches at another site, such as www.123reg.com, to avoid this.

How to use it: Go to www.netsol.com and look at the services on offer.

Fasthosts

Fasthosts is a U.K.-based hosting provider that's like a slightly less polished — and slightly less expensive — Network Solutions. I've used their services and like them.

How to use it: Go to www.fasthosts.co.uk and check out what's available.

AOL

Say what? Yes, America Online. AOL may be well known as a business failure, a company that once was big enough to merge with Time Warner and is now being sold off in chunks to various other companies around the world, but there's more to the story.

They developed good Web-page creation services at their peak, and the offerings are still there.

How to use it: Go to www.aol.com and look carefully at the offerings; there are several levels of service available, so check carefully before committing.

Yahoo!

Yahoo! is one of the original founding companies of the Web, and many people still weave in and out of the Yahoo! site and various Yahoo! services several times a day. And they have good Web-page creation offerings that fit with their other services. The leader is GeoCities, which was bought by Yahoo! some years ago and is still a major player in free Web pages.

How to use it: Go to www.yahoo.com and sign up for an account, then look at some of their existing Web pages and sites. Or go straight to www.geo cities.com if you want to skip the Yahoo! site, though you'll still need a Yahoo! account to use GeoCities.

Blogger

Blogger is a very early provider of free blogging. Since being purchased by Google a few years ago, they've stabilized their platform and have grown steadily. (Using Blogger is described in some detail in Chapter 4.)

How to use it: Go to www.blogger.com and see what's there, though you'll need a Google account to use Blogger.

WordPress

WordPress is gradually emerging as the serious alternative to blogger. Word Press offers free services, but many of its users pay at least something — more, it seems, than on many other blogging sites — and they seem happy to do so. Don't expect total ease of use, though; a business whose catchphrase is "code is poetry" hardly shies away from offering power tools.

How to use it: Go to www.wordpress.org and give a careful look around before committing.

MobileMe

If you are a Mac user or an iPhone owner, you simply have to consider MobileMe, which until recently was called .Mac ("dot-Mac"). MobileMe will cost you — $99 a year in the U.S. — but more than a million users say it's worth it. MobileMe offers not only Web-page creation and hosting but all sorts of related services such as calendaring, e-mail, and more. All in the easy-to-use interface you expect from Apple.

Apple — and its users — suffered serious teething problems in the transition from .Mac to MobileMe; a very small percentage (but still a large number) of users lost some stored e-mails. The optimistic view of the aftermath can be summed up as, "they've gotten that out of their system"; the pessimistic view, "once bitten, twice shy."

How to use it: Go to www.apple.com/mobileme and look at the offerings carefully; consider not only the cost but the hassle of transitioning to MobileMe from products, many of them likely to be free, that you already use.

Weebly

Weebly is based on Ajax, the Web 2.0 technology that's helping bring many sites to life with interaction and animation. Weebly is relatively new, but already quite popular. Consider it seriously, especially if you like social-networking tools such as Facebook, Flickr, and YouTube.

How to use it: Go to www.weebly.com and see if you like the look of their users' pages more than what you see at the better-established competitors.

Ning

Different from the rest, Ning is actually for *creating your own social network,* not just your own Web site. If you like Facebook but have exhausted all its capabilities and want to do more, or want a Web page that's anything but boring, consider Ning.

How to use it: Go to www.ning.com and try the idea of being a social-networking guru on for size.

Chapter 18

Ten Ways to Make Your Page a Site

. . . .

Creating a Web page is a real thrill, but once the excitement dies down, you might be left feeling a bit anxious. How to convert your fun Web page into an interesting and enduring site?

Here are ten techniques for making the leap to a lasting, interesting Web site you'll be proud of.

Specialize

The tendency when you create a Web page is to mention several things, or even everything that interests you. It's your Web page, so it should be about you, right?

Maybe, but when you expand to a Web site you should consider specializing. People go to Web sites for what the site offers, and people expect the site to be like a mosaic, with each page contributing to an overall picture. Unless you're so famous, or so fascinating, that people really want to build up a picture of you just because you're you, they probably want to learn about some company or topic. Focus your efforts into a coherent site with a single overarching theme. (Even if you keep the focus on yourself, consider choosing an aspect such as your career, family, or creative use of the online world across various other sites.)

Let Go of Your Tool

Tools such as Google Page Creator are great for getting started. You do everything online, so there's no worry about getting your pages hosted; they're hosted for you even as you're creating them.

However, the only way to have real flexibility in the design and development of your site is to move away from online tools and templates to your own chosen approach. The quickest way to get there is to move to a more independent model: developing your site on your own computer, and then uploading files to the Web to bring them to life.

Copy Your Page to Your Hard Drive

Even if you leave your page or site in an online tool for a while, you can still benefit from keeping, and working on, a local copy. It's nerve-wracking to be working in an online tool with little or no backup, knowing you can wreck your site with a few poorly chosen keystrokes and mouse clicks.

Copy your Web site to your hard drive, a page at a time, and then work on the copy of your site that lives on your own computer. This will increase your understanding and capability very quickly. Then copy and paste from your work on your own machine into the tool that makes changes in your live site. Soon you'll be ready to bypass the tool and upload entire pages (and their graphics) files directly to your Web host.

Use FTP

The all-too-frequently seen FTP, or File Transfer Protocol, has done more to discourage Web-page authors than perhaps any other aspect of Web publishing. With FTP, you have to log in to a remote site, and then transfer files in a process that feels more like trying to keep up with the nerds in the computer lab than, say, updating your Facebook profile.

Still, you have to learn it. Use the tools available on your host (which are just FTP with a pretty face) or download an FTP program from CNET's excellent `download.com` site to get going, and take the time to learn how to use it. You'll be glad you did.

Get a URL

Having your own URL — that is, an independent Web address for your site, not `mysite.geocities.com` but `www.mysite.com` — is a big step that will make your site feel very "real" indeed. You don't need to do this on Day 1; in fact, getting a URL can actually distract you from getting started. But as your Web page takes on a life of its own, getting and using a URL becomes a necessary step in your site's growing up. Use the services described in the previous chapter to find and purchase a URL and, if needed, Web hosting.

Add a Blog

I was slow to warm to blogs — I even found the name offputting. But they've proven themselves to be the single simplest and best way to steadily expand a site with fresh content. (Blogging will do a lot to give you ideas for other, structural additions to your site as well.)

You can even blog from your mobile phone. Use the tools in Chapter 17 (or other tools) to add a blog to your site, and keep using them so your site gradually expands and improves.

Add Other Tools

Many Web hosts offer fun tools to add to your site, such as online polling, message boards, news feeds, and such. Or use RSS — Really Simple Syndication — to bring in news or other information. There are hundreds of things you can do; look around at sites you like and figure out how to add your favorite features from those sites to your own site. (If nothing else, this effort will make you steadily better at Web searching.)

Add Navigation

Keep working on your site navigation — extending it, improving it, or making it easier to use. Navigation is what makes a Web site hold together, like the covers and binding of a book. Unlike a hard-copy book, however, a Web site can gradually improve, especially as you refine your navigation to make your Web site better and better with time.

Quote Others

Bring in quotes, contributions, and material written or drawn by others. Link to relevant videos on YouTube. (Even if you have to create them yourself — but include the comments others make about your video on YouTube.) Keep getting in outside opinion.

Keep Plugging Away

Keep adding little things here and there. It took months before my wife and I got the site for her business, at `batcs.co.uk`, into decent shape — but, to my worry, something was still missing. As we gradually added press coverage, information about courses, and a few frequently asked questions, suddenly the site seemed to become more solid, real, and interesting. We reached a tipping point in which there was enough valuable content to be interesting, and even a bit impressive. Keep plugging away at the details, adding content and functionality, and you will too.

Part VI
Appendixes

The 5th Wave   By Rich Tennant

"Okay, I think I forgot to mention this, but we now have a Web management function that automatically alerts us when there's a broken link on The Aquarium's Web site."

In this part . . .

Often appendixes are the miscellaneous extra bits of a book — but these are useful enough that they deserve their own section: A glossary of Web-publishing terms, a guide to basic HTML tag definitions, and all you need to know about the CD-ROM included with this book.

Appendix A

Web Words Worth Knowing

* *

*T*his glossary defines important terms used in this book. To see where a term is used in the book, check the index.

56K. 56 kilobits per second, a standard speed for dialup Internet access used by most current modems. Actual online access speeds are limited by U.S. government regulation to a top speed of about 53 Kbps, and your 56K modem may not achieve even that speed reliably, depending on the quality of the connection you get when you dial in.

absolute address. A description of a file's location that starts with the domain name, machine name, or disk name on which the file is located. See also *pathname* and *relative address*.

ActiveX. A Microsoft technology for distributing executable files called *ActiveX controls* (programs that can change your file system directly) over the Internet. ActiveX is powerful, but it only works on Windows — and it triggers warning messages from security software even on that operating system, so beginning Web authors should avoid it.

anchor. One end of a link between two files. When you look at a Web page, the underlined, colored text that you see is an anchor at one end of a hypertext link. Clicking the text brings up another Web page, which is the anchor at the other end of the link.

animated GIF. A GIF graphic that includes several slightly different images in sequence. Browsers that support animated GIFs display the graphics one at a time to create an animation.

attribute. In HTML, an attribute is a qualifier added within an HTML tag. The attribute modifies the tag's purpose. For example, in the tag `<IMG SRC="budpic.jpg">`, the attribute is `SRC` (short for "source"). See also *tag*.

blog. Short for "Web log," a form of Web site in which the author's frequent postings are recorded, usually with the newest posting first. Site visitors are often allowed to comment. Web logs use special software to prevent the user from having to set up or manage the Web page.

broadband. Any kind of fast Internet access, whether by cable modem, DSL, or other connection significantly faster than the 56K top speed of a modem. Broadband connections are typically "always on" and do not require dialing in.

browser. A program used to look at World Wide Web documents. Mosaic was the first popular browser, followed by Netscape Navigator; Microsoft Internet Explorer is the current market leader.

bulleted list. See *unordered list.*

cable modem. A form of broadband access to the Internet that uses a cable TV connection. (If the local cable company that serves your house offers this service, it's worth a look.)

Cascading Style Sheets (CSS). A language used to control the look of a Web page (colors, fonts, and so on), whereas HTML is used to control the structure of the content (headings, paragraphs, and so on).

clickable image map. A graphic that includes areas called *hot spots,* which, when clicked, take you to different Web pages or different locations within a Web page. Some large Web sites use clickable image maps on their home pages to entice the users to move farther into the site.

Common Gateway Interface script (CGI script). A kind of program often used to transfer data from an HTML form to an application. The CGI script runs on the server that hosts the Web page with the form. See also *form.*

compression. Storing a file in less space than previously required. *Lossless* compression creates a file from which the original file can be exactly re-created. *Lossy* compression eliminates some (hopefully less important) data from the original file in order to allow the compressed file to be smaller.

definition list. A type of HTML list in which terms occupy a column on the left side of the screen and definitions occupy a wider column on the right side.

DHTML (Dynamic HTML). DHTML is not a markup language (as is HTML); the term refers to the use of three languages together in Web design: HTML, CSS, and JavaScript.

domain name. A name that represents a Web site to the outside world. In the United States, the domain name can end in `.com` (for businesses), `.edu` (for educational institutions), `.org` (for nonprofit organizations), or the prestigious `.net` (for organizations that are part of the structure of the Web itself). Newly added suffixes, which haven't necessarily caught on yet, include `.biz` and `.firm`. When visiting a domain that was created for an organization outside the United States, you may see different suffixes that have been added to represent a country or region. For example, `.uk` signifies that the domain was created for the United Kingdom. The part of the domain that precedes the suffix, such as `stanford` in `stanford.edu`, is either the name of the group that puts up the Web site, or a name that attracts people to the site. Domain names can start with www if desired, but it's not always necessary.

DSL. Digital Subscriber Line, a type of *broadband* Internet access that uses a phone line. (Not available in some areas, but worth serious consideration if it's available to you.)

electronic mail (e-mail). A message sent over a network from one computer user to another computer user. The most popular service on the Internet. Used as a noun ("I just got an e-mail.") and a verb ("E-mail me on that, will you?"). Also used as singular ("I just deleted an e-mail.") and plural ("I just deleted all my e-mail.").

embed. To place a reference to a file of a type not directly supported by the HTML specification in a Web page, using the `embed` HTML command. Multimedia files are the ones most commonly embedded. The file is then played back by a helper program such as RealPlayer, QuickTime, or Windows Media Player.

File Transfer Protocol (FTP). An Internet service for transferring files between different machines, including those that run different operating systems. It's a commonly used mechanism for uploading Web pages to a Web site.

firewall. Hardware, software, or a combination that protects a network from unauthorized access while allowing authorized access.

form. An HTML-defined way to specify text boxes and pull-down menus to enable users of a Web page to enter data. The data from the form must be processed on the Web server by a program such as a *CGI script.*

freeware. Software that can be used for free, though often with a license that contains some restrictions on its use. See also *shareware.*

Graphic Interchange Format (GIF). Can be pronounced "jiff" or (my preference) "giff." A format for encoding less complex images, such as computer-generated graphics, for transfer among machines. GIF format is the most popular means for storing images for transfer over the Internet and is supported by all graphical Web browsers. An image stored in GIF format is often referred to as "a GIF." See also *JPEG, transparent GIF.*

Graphical User Interface (GUI). Software that enables users to interact with a computer by using a mouse and keyboard to manipulate images and menus on the computer's screen. The Windows and Macintosh user interfaces are both examples of GUIs.

hexadecimal. What the witch did to her accountant so her tax bill would be more favorable. (Just kidding.) Actually, a way of counting that uses 16 "digits," 0 through 9 plus A through F, instead of the 10 digits that common decimal numbering uses. Hexadecimal numbers are often used to describe values stored inside a computer — in particular, colors used in Web pages.

In hexadecimal numbering, 0 through 9 have their normal values, but A represents 10, B represents 11, and so on through F, which represents 15. Place values are also different; each successive place represents the next greater power of 16. For example, 2F in hexadecimal translates to 47 in decimal; the 2 represents two 16s, and the F represents fifteen 1s.

hit. This is what you hope your Web site will become. Also, a successful connection, file transfer, and disconnection between a Web client and a Web server. Accessing a single, text-only page generates one hit; accessing a single page with three graphics on it generates four hits. Hits can be counted fairly easily and are a crude measure of the popularity of a Web site. When you see a site that advertises "a million hits a week," remember that the number of hits may be many times greater than the number of different people who visited. See also *Web client* and *Web server*.

home page. A Web page that you intend users to come to directly when they visit your Web site. If a Web site has multiple pages, the home page usually serves as the front door to the rest of your site, and the guide to all the other pages housed there.

HTML 4.01. Currently the most broadly used version of *Hypertext Markup Language,* invented by Tim Berners-Lee (now, not coincidentally, Sir Tim Berners-Lee) in the late 1980s. All browsers available today support this version of HTML, though different browsers may interpret some tags differently.

Hypertext Markup Language (HTML). The language used to annotate, or "mark up" text documents so they can be formatted appropriately and linked to other documents for use on the World Wide Web. See *tag*.

Hypertext Transfer Protocol (HTTP). The agreed-upon format used by Web programs to exchange messages among World Wide Web servers and between Web servers and clients.

image map. See *clickable image map*.

Integrated Services Digital Network (ISDN). Sometimes jokingly spelled out as "It Still Does Nothing," this special type of phone line is available to many businesses and homes as a *broadband* connection option that supports faster transmission of data than standard phone lines.

Internet. The hardware and software that together support the interconnection of most existing computer networks, allowing a computer anywhere in the world to communicate with any other computer that's also connected to the Internet. The Internet supports a variety of services, including the World Wide Web.

Internet Protocol (IP). The networking specification that underlies the Internet. IP's most important feature is its support for routing of the packets — small chunks of information that make up a communication — across multiple connections to the final destination.

Internet service provider (ISP). A company that offers connection to the Internet and support for Internet services such as the World Wide Web. An ISP may also provide Web site storage space and related services to customers.

intranet. An internal network used for distributing information broadly within an organization, but not to the general public. Many intranets work just like the Internet and World Wide Web, only on a smaller scale.

Java. A programming language that supports the creation of distributed programs, called *applets,* whose functionality can be easily and flexibly split between a client computer and the server that it's connected to. Java provides a way for the Web to support easy sharing of programs and data and, unlike ActiveX, Java is cross-platform. Java has become less widely used within Web pages, but it is widely used on Web servers and corporate networks.

JavaScript. Largely unrelated to Java (except through their common parent, C), JavaScript is often used to add interaction or some dynamic quality to a page (a calculator, a menu) through lines of text commands placed in the document or in a separate, linked file.

Joint Photographic Experts Group (JPEG). A format for storing compressed images. JPEG images were once supported by helper applications but are now directly supported by nearly all browsers. JPEG is the best format for most photographs. See *GIF.*

link. A connection between two documents on the Web, usually specified by an *anchor* in an HTML document.

mirroring. Keeping a copy of data on additional servers to make data available more quickly and to a greater number of simultaneous users.

MP3 and MPEG. Formats created by the Motion Picture Experts Group (or MPEG) for storing compressed sounds (MP3) and movies (MPEG). These files can be played back by a variety of helper applications but are not directly supported by browsers. See *JPEG.*

multimedia. Literally means "many media," and in this sense, a Web page with graphics is multimedia. However, multimedia is usually understood to mean either more than two types of media or, alternatively, time-based media such as animation, sound, or video and space-based media such as 3-D and virtual reality. On the Web, multimedia is also used to mean any extension of the Web beyond the basics of text, hyperlinks, GIF graphics, and JPEG graphics. Multimedia is beyond the basics, so it usually requires a special plug-in or player to support it.

newsgroup. An ongoing exchange of electronic messages about a specific topic, such as pets, restaurants, or Web authoring. To access newsgroups, users must use special software called news reader software, which is available on the Web and also included as a feature of current browsers.

numbered list. See *ordered list.*

online service. Also referred to as a "traditional" or "proprietary" online service to differentiate from the Internet, which is seen as an "open" online service. Traditional online services, such as America Online and CompuServe, package access and content into a single branded product. The Internet and the Web have eroded the boundaries between online services by allowing cross-service functionality, such as e-mail between subscribers of different online services. The online service providers are further eroding these boundaries by offering Internet access, Web access, and Web-authoring support.

ordered list. A numbered list. A type of HTML list in which each item is given a number, in sequence, when the list displays. The author of the list can rearrange the items as needed, and the numbers adjust accordingly because the numbers are assigned only when the list appears onscreen. See *unordered list.*

page-description language. A defined format for specifying the appearance of a document when displayed or printed. Adobe's PostScript, used by many programs and in many laser printers, is a page-description language; it's not a structural markup language such as HTML or SGML.

pathname. A description of the location of a file. Pathnames can be specified by absolute addressing or relative addressing.

plug-in. A small program that works with a Web browser to allow multimedia files to be displayed in a Web page, or that otherwise extends the capabilities of the browser.

protocol. An agreed-upon format for exchanging data, such as *FTP* (file-transfer protocol).

QuickTime. A multiplatform standard from Apple Computer, Inc., for multi-media. See also *multimedia, QuickTime plug-in,* and *QuickTime VR.*

QuickTime plug-in. A *plug-in* for Firefox and Microsoft Internet Explorer that supports user interaction with QuickTime and QuickTime VR content embed-ded in a Web page. See also *QuickTime* and *QuickTime VR.*

QuickTime VR. A multiplatform standard for image-based virtual reality. See also *QuickTime* and *QuickTime plug-in.*

relative address. The path from a base document, such as an HTML docu-ment, to another document on the same computer, such as another Web page on the same site. See also *pathname* and *absolute address.*

shareware. Software that can be used for free for a limited period of time, after which the user is requested (though usually not forced) to pay a fee for continued use. See *freeware.*

shrink-wrapped software. (No, this is not software developed and packaged by psychiatrists.) Shrink-wrapped software is sold as a product and packaged in a box (rather than offered as a download over the Internet); the user pays up front before taking possession of the software. See also *freeware* and *shareware.*

site management. Capabilities in a Web-authoring package that help authors work on characteristics of an entire Web site, instead of just one page at a time. Site-management capabilities include maintenance of links between Web pages (and offering notification when links are no longer functional), spell-checking, built-in uploading of Web pages to a server, and easy search and replace across an entire site.

standard. An agreed-upon way to do something, such as building a computer system (for example, the IBM-compatible standard) or exchanging data (for example, the ASCII standard). Many different standards exist, ranging from those created by a single manufacturer for its own purposes (the DOS standard) to those created by internationally recognized standards bodies such as ISO (the International Standards Organization). In other words, in computing, the definition of standard is not very standard.

Standard Generalized Markup Language (SGML). A full-featured specifica-tion for describing the content and structure of documents but not their exact appearance when displayed. *HTML* is a subset of SGML.

syntax. A fee paid for moral or legal violations (no, wait, that's a "sin tax"). In computer languages and protocols, the syntax is the ordering of the elements that make up the instructions to the computer, as with *HTML.*

system operator (sysop). Pronounced "siss-op." A person responsible for some part of the operations of a computer system, including online services. A sysop's responsibilities can vary from the technical, such as backing up a computer hard drive, to the nontechnical, such as monitoring a newsgroup for inappropriate or irrelevant content and removing it if found.

tag. Part of an HTML document that contains information besides the actual document content, such as formatting information or an anchor. For example, the <b> tag starts bolding the characters that follow it, and the </b> tag ends bolding. So to make a word or phrase bold, surround it with the <b> and </b> tags.

text editor. A program that allows text to be entered and edited but not formatted for display. Text editors save their files without proprietary formatting information, so the files are portable across different application programs and different computer systems. Examples are Notepad (Windows), BBEdit (Macintosh), and vi (Unix).

thumbnail. A small graphical image that serves as a preview of a larger image.

Transmission Control Protocol/Internet Protocol (TCP/IP). A communications *protocol* that was developed under contract from the U.S. Department of Defense in the 1970s to connect different systems and different networks. TCP/IP is the protocol on which the Internet is based.

transparent GIF. A file stored in Graphic Interchange Format and modified so that one color — usually, the color of the area around the objects of interest — is assigned transparency. This capability makes the rectangular frame around the objects seem to disappear so that the graphic appears to float over the page on which it appears.

Uniform Resource Locator (URL). A specification for identifying any file on the Internet. The URL is made up of the name of the protocol by which the file should be accessed, the name of the server that the file is stored on, and the pathname of the file on the server. Here is a sample URL for an HTML file named MyCruise, to be accessed by using the Web protocol http, which is stored on a server called www.bigweb.com in the Travel directory:

```
http://www.bigweb.com/Travel/MyCruise.html
```

If no filename is given at the end of the path, a default file, typically index.htm or index.html, is returned.

unordered list. A bulleted list. A type of HTML list in which each item is displayed next to a symbol such as a bullet.

Web authoring. Creating documents for use on the World Wide Web. This process includes creating text documents with HTML tags, as well as creating or obtaining suitable graphics and sound or video files for inclusion in the Web page — and putting them in.

Web browser. See *browser.*

Web client. A computer that connects to the World Wide Web and downloads Web pages and other data from it.

Web page. An online text document that uses HTML tags to specify formatting and includes links from the document to other content, including documents, graphics, and sound or video files.

Web publishing. The entire process of creating and maintaining a Web site, from creating text documents with HTML tags and graphics, to putting the documents on a server, to revising the documents over time.

Web server. A computer that connects to the World Wide Web and hosts HTML-tagged text documents, graphics, and multimedia files to be downloaded by *Web clients.*

Web site. One or more linked Web pages accessed through a *home page.* The URL of the home page is made available to users on other Web sites, and often through other advertising and marketing means as well.

wiki. A Web site that can be cooperatively updated to capture the knowledge of a number of people and share it — with the original authors and possibly with others. The most famous example is Wikipedia (`www.wikipedia.org`), an extensive and popular online encyclopedia maintained via modified wiki principles.

word processor. A program for creating and editing text files with formatting. Files created by a word processor contain formatting codes and cannot be used on the Web unless specifically saved in *text-only* or *plain-text* format, without the proprietary codes that word processors embed in the file to indicate formatting.

World Wide Web (also known as the Web). An Internet service that provides files from servers linked by *Hypertext Transfer Protocol* (HTTP). The Web specification allows formatted text and graphics to be viewed directly by a Web browser and allows other kinds of files to be opened separately by helper applications specified in the Web browser's setup. After e-mail, the Web is the most popular Internet service, partly because it can also be used to access other Internet services, such as newsgroups and FTP.

Appendix B

A Quick Guide to HTML Tags

One of the best resources on the Web is *The Bare Bones Guide to HTML*. At this writing, this excellent reference lists nearly all the tags in the most widely supported version of HTML, Version 4.0, plus Netscape extensions.

This site was developed and is maintained by Kevin Werbach, a Harvard Law School graduate and former FCC attorney in Washington who has invested a lot of time and thought in Web authoring. You can find out an awful lot about Web authoring from the thoughts, resources, and examples on the *Bare Bones Guide* home page at `http://werbach.com/barebones`.

The Bare Bones Guide lists tags from the different versions of HTML, with notes describing which version of HTML a given tag supports. I thought that splitting the HTML tags into separate tables, organized by the version of HTML they support, would help you zero in on the ones you need.

In the version of *The Bare Bones Guide* in this book, I include only HTML tags from HTML versions through Version 4.0. For frames only, I use HTML 4.0 tags; see Table B-26 at the end of this chapter. I do this because HTML 4.0 tags are the most commonly used by the broad range of Web pages and Web browsers out there. The online version of *The Bare Bones Guide to HTML* lists tags up to the current version of the HTML standard at the time that you access the site.

The original *The Bare Bones Guide to HTML*, from which I adapted this version, is copyrighted (©1995–2008) to Kevin Werbach. You can reproduce the original, as long as you include this statement:

> *Copyright ©1995–2008 Kevin Werbach. Distribution is permitted, as long as there is no charge and this document is included without alteration in its entirety. This Guide is not a product of Bare Bones Software. More information is available at* `http://werbach.com/barebones`.

For more on HTML, you may also want to visit the World Wide Web consortium, the organization with the most responsibility for Web standards. A good starting point is the HTML4 area at `www.w3.org/TR/html4/`.

Just a few things to keep in mind about *The Bare Bones Guide to HTML:*

- ✔ **It's not affiliated with Bare Bones Software,** makers of the BBEdit text editor for the Macintosh (www.barebones.com).

- ✔ **I got Kevin's permission to use it.** And it's everywhere (see the accompanying sidebar), but it's handy to have in this book.

- ✔ **HTML is not case-sensitive.** You'll notice that Kevin uses UPPERCASE characters in HTML tags. I decided to use lowercase characters throughout this book, in keeping with current HTML standards.

Versions of HTML

The tags in this table are part of the HTML 4.0 standard and are supported by all up-to-date browsers. So if you aren't worried about ancient history — in Web terms, that's anything that happened more than a year ago — and aren't worried about the stubborn few users of your Web pages who may still have old browsers, you can ignore this section and go straight to the tables. But if you really want to know the details, read on.

The versions of HTML I describe in this appendix are

- ✔ **HTML 2.0:** All browsers available today support this basic version of HTML. However, some tags are interpreted differently by different browsers. For example, a top-level heading, marked by an <H1> tag, may be formatted somewhat differently in different browsers.

- ✔ **Netscape Navigator 1.0, 1.1:** These early versions of Netscape Navigator fueled the first huge surge in the growth of the Web. These were the first browsers to provide support for centered text, floating graphics, and colored text and backgrounds by using new "extensions" to HTML 2.0. Other browsers and HTML 3.2 have adopted many of the features and new tags introduced by Netscape in Netscape Navigator 1.0 and 1.1.

Twenty-two world languages in *The Bare Bones Guide*

Online, you find versions of *The Bare Bones Guide* in English in plain text, formatted text, and table versions, as well as translations into additional languages: Chinese (two versions), Danish, Dutch, Estonian, Finnish, French, German, Hebrew, Icelandic, Indonesian, Italian, Japanese, Korean, Norwegian, Portuguese, Romanian, Russian (three versions), Slovenian, Spanish, Swedish, and Turkish.

- ✔ **HTML 3.2:** This is a widely supported version of the HTML standard. Many of the ideas originally included in the HTML 3.0 proposal, such as tables and paragraph alignment, were first supported by Netscape Navigator 1.0 and 1.1.

- ✔ **Netscape Navigator 2.0:** This years-old used version of Netscape Navigator implements a few minor features, plus a major one: frames, which are specific areas within the browser window that contain different content and can be updated separately.

- ✔ **HTML 4.0 and later browser versions:** HTML 4.0 is the latest standardized version of HTML. It includes some features that were introduced by Microsoft and Netscape in their own browsers. However, HTML 4.0 includes some complex features that are not consistently implemented in current browser versions.

Over time, browsers are updated and improved to support a wider range of tags. However, a few users still have the old version of their browser. So don't assume that just because a new version of a browser supports specific tags, all users of that browser will upgrade and gain the ability to view those tags correctly.

How to Use This Appendix

To use this appendix when creating your own pages, start with the first table, a basic list of HTML 2.0– and HTML 3.2–compliant tags that work with almost any browser. If you use only the tags in this list, your pages will be as widely usable as possible. Then you can selectively spice up your pages by using tags from the different sets of HTML extensions listed in the later tables. You can also use this list to create separate versions of your pages: one version for all browsers and another for browsers that support the specific extensions that you use.

This appendix includes HTML tags that I did not discuss in the text of this book. To find out more about a specific tag, experiment with it in your Web text and your browser. If you need more information than you can get by experimenting, buy a more advanced book on HTML, such as *HTML 4 For Dummies,* 5th Edition, by Ed Tittel and others (Wiley).

Reading the Tables

Within the tables you may see some tags that are not preceded by a dash, followed by tags preceded by a dash, such as

Tag Name	*Tag*	*Notes*
Preformatted	`<PRE></PRE>`	Display text spacing as-is
- Width	`<PRE WIDTH=?></PRE>`	Width in characters

The tags with descriptions that start with a dash are actually options within other tags. These optional tags modify the effect of the tag that they appear with. You will always see the option listed with the tag that it modifies, so that you can see how to use it in your own HTML-tagged text.

The use of the dash symbol to indicate optional tags and other symbols in the tables are described in Table B-1.

Note: In order to align columns correctly, some tags are broken. At the points that these tags break, I placed a downward, left-curving arrow (⤶) to indicate the break.

Table B-1	Symbols Used in the Tables
Symbol	*Meaning*
URL	URL of an external file (or just filename if in the same directory)
?	Arbitrary number (for example, `<H?>` means `<H1>`, `<H2>`, `<H3>`, and so on)
%	Arbitrary percentage (for example, `<HR WIDTH=%>` means `<HR WIDTH=50%>`, and so on)
***	Arbitrary text (for example, `ALT="***"` means fill in with text)
$$$$$$	Arbitrary hexadecimal number* (for example, `BGCOLOR="#$$$$$$"` means `BGCOLOR="#00FF1C"`, and so on)
|	Alternatives (for example, `ALIGN=LEFT|RIGHT|CENTER` means pick one of these)
- *Option*	An option within a tag

*For an explanation of hexadecimal numbering, see Appendix A.

Widely Supported Tags

The tags in Table B-2 through Table B-10 are in all versions of HTML since 2.0 (in some cases) or 3.2 (in others) and should work in all browsers.

Table B-2	Generally All HTML Documents Should Have These Tags	
Tag Name	*Tag*	*Notes*
Document Type	`<HTML></HTML>`	Beginning and end of file
Title	`<TITLE></TITLE>`	Must be in header
Header	`<HEAD></HEAD>`	Descriptive info, such as title
Body	`<BODY></BODY>`	Bulk of the page

Table B-3	Structural Definition: Apearance Controlled by the Browser's Preferences	
Tag Name	*Tag*	*Notes*
Heading	`<H?></H?>`	The HTML 2.0 specification defines six levels
Block Quote	`<BLOCKQUOTE>`	Usually indented `</BLOCKQUOTE>`
Emphasis	`<EM></EM>`	Usually displayed as italic
Strong Emphasis	`<STRONG></STRONG>`	Usually displayed as bold
Citation	`<CITE></CITE>`	Usually italics
Code	`<CODE></CODE>`	For source code listings
Sample Output	`<SAMP></SAMP>`	
Keyboard Input	`<KBD></KBD>`	
Variable	`<VAR></VAR>`	
Author's Address	`<ADDRESS></ADDRESS>`	

Table B-4	Presentation Formatting: Author Specifies Text Appearance	
Tag Name	**Tag**	**Notes**
Bold	`<B></B>`	
Italic	`<I></I>`	
Typewriter	`<TT></TT>`	Displayed in a monospaced font
Preformatted	`<PRE></PRE>`	Displays text spacing as-is
- Width	`<PRE WIDTH=?>↵ /PRE>`	Width in characters

Table B-5	Links and Graphics	
Tag Name	**Tag**	**Notes**
Link	`<A HREF="URL"></A>`	
Link to Target	`<A HREF="URL#***"></A>`	If in another document
	`<A HREF="#***"></A>`	If in current document
Define Target	`<A NAME="***"></A>`	
Display Image	`<IMG SRC="URL">`	
- Alignment	`<IMG SRC="URL" ALIGN↵ =TOP|BOTTOM|MIDDLE|↵ RIGHT|LEFT>`	HTML 3.2 and beyond only
- Alternate	`<IMG SRC="URL" ALT="***">`	
- Imagemap	`<IMG SRC="URL" ISMAP>`	Requires a script

Table B-6	Dividers	
Tag Name	**Tag**	**Notes**
Paragraph	`<P>`	See Table B-14 for more info
Line Break	` `	A single carriage return
Horizontal Rule	`<HR>`	HTML 3.2 only

Table B-7	**Lists: Can Be Nested**	
Tag Name	*Tag*	*Notes*
Unordered List	`<UL><LI></UL>`	`<LI>` before each list item
Ordered List	`<OL><LI></OL>`	`<LI>` before each list item
Definition List	`<DL><DT><DD></DL>`	`<DT>` = term, `<DD>` = definition

Table B-8	**Special Characters: Must All Be Lowercase**	
Tag Name	*Tag*	*Notes*
Special Character	`&#?;`	Where ? is the ISO 8859-1 code for the character
<	`&lt;`	
>	`&gt;`	
&	`&amp;`	
"	`&quot;`	
Registered TM	`&reg;`	
Copyright	`&copy;`	

See a complete list of special characters at `www.bbsinc.com/symbol.html`.

Table B-9	**Forms: Generally Require a Script on Your Server**	
Tag Name	*Tag*	*Notes*
Define Form	`<FORM ACTION="URL" METHOD=GET|POST></FORM>`	
Input Field	`<INPUT TYPE="TEXT|PASSWORD|CHECKBOX|RADIO|IMAGE|HIDDEN|SUBMIT|RESET">`	
- Field Name	`<INPUT NAME="***">`	
- Field Value	`<INPUT VALUE="***">`	
- Checked?	`<INPUT CHECKED>`	Check boxes and radio buttons
- Field Size	`<INPUT SIZE=?>`	In characters
- Max Length	`<INPUT MAXLENGTH=?>`	In characters
Selection List	`<SELECT></SELECT>`	

(continued)

Table B-9 *(continued)*

Tag Name	Tag	Notes
- Name of List	`<SELECT NAME="***">`↵ `</SELECT>`	
- # of Options	`<SELECT SIZE=?>`↵ `</SELECT>`	
- Multiple Choice	`<SELECT MULTIPLE>`	Can select more than one
Option	`<OPTION>`	Items that can be selected
- Default Option	`<OPTION SELECTED>`	
Input Box Size	`<TEXTAREA ROWS=? COLS=?>`↵ `</TEXTAREA>`	
- Name of Box	`<TEXTAREA NAME="***">ccc` `</TEXTAREA>`	

Table B-10   Miscellaneous

Tag Name	Tag	Notes
Comment	`<!-- *** -->`	Not displayed by the browser
Prologue	`<!DOCTYPE HTML`↵ `PUBLIC"-//IETF//`↵ `DTD HTML 2.0//EN">`	
URL of This File	`<BASE HREF="URL">`	Must be in header
Relationship	`<LINK REV="***"`↵ `REL="***"HREF="URL">`	In header
Meta Information	`<META>`	Must be in header

Other Widely Used Tags

The tags in Table B-11 through Table B-17 work with nearly all the browsers currently in use. For a frequently updated list of widely used tags, see *The Bare Bones Guide to HTML* at the URL listed at the beginning of this chapter.

Table B-11 — **Structural Definition: Appearance Controlled by the Browser's Preferences**

Tag Name	Tag	Notes
- Align Heading	`<H? ALIGN=LEFT|↩ CENTER|RIGHT></H?>`	HTML 3.2 Option within the HTML 2.0–compliant Heading tag
Division	`<DIV></DIV>`	HTML 3.2
- Align Division	`<DIV ALIGN=LEFT|↩ RIGHT|CENTER|↩ JUSTIFY></DIV>`	HTML 3.2
Large Font Size	`<BIG></BIG>`	HTML 3.2
Small Font Size	`<SMALL></SMALL>`	HTML 3.2

Table B-12 — **Presentation Formatting: Author Specifies Text Appearance**

Tag Name	Tag	Notes
Subscript	`<SUB></SUB>`	HTML 2.0
Superscript	`<SUP></SUP>`	HTML 2.0
Center	`<CENTER></CENTER>`	Netscape 1.0. widely implemented; for both text and images

Table B-13 — **Links and Graphics**

Tag Name	Tag	Notes
Dimensions	`<IMG SRC="URL"↩ WIDTH= "?"HEIGHT=↩ "?">`	HTML 3.2. Image width and height in pixels

Table B-14	Dividers	
Tag Name	*Tag*	*Notes*
Paragraph	`<P></P>`	HTML 3.2. Paragraph tag, `<P>`, redefined as a container tag, `</P>` is optional
- Align Text	`<P ALIGN=LEFT│↩ CENTER│RIGHT│↩ JUSTIFY></P>`	HTML 3.2
- No Line Breaks	`<P NOWRAP></P>`	Internet Explorer only

Table B-15	Backgrounds and Colors	
Tag Name	*Tag*	*Notes*
Tiled Background	`<BODY BACKGROUND=↩ "URL">`	HTML 3.2
Background Color	`<BODY BGCOLOR=↩ "#$$$$$$">`	HTML 3.2. Color order, red/green/blue
Text Color	`<BODY TEXT=↩ "#$$$$$$">`	HTML 3.2. Color order, red/green/blue
Link Color	`<BODY LINK=↩ "#$$$$$$">`	HTML 3.2. Color order, red/green/blue
Active Link	`<BODY ALINK=↩ "#$$$$$$">`	HTML 3.2. Color order, red/green/blue
Visited Link	`<BODY VLINK=↩ "#$$$$$$">`	HTML 3.2. Color order, red/green/blue

You can find more info at `www.werbach.com/web/wwhelp.html`.

Table B-16	Tables	
Tag Name	*Tag*	*Notes*
Define Table	`<TABLE></TABLE>`	HTML 3.2
- Table Border	`<TABLE BORDER>↩ </TABLE>`	HTML 3.2. Either on or off
- Table Border	`<TABLE BORDER>↩ </TABLE>`	HTML 3.2. Can set the border width in pixels

Tag Name	Tag	Notes
-Cell Spacing	`<TABLE CELLSPACING=?>`	HTML 3.2
- Cell Padding	`<TABLE CELLPADDING=?>`	HTML 3.2
- Desired Width	`<TABLE WIDTH=?>`	HTML 3.2. In pixels
- Width Percent	`<TABLE WIDTH=%>`	HTML 3.2 Percentage of page
Table Row	`<TR></TR>`	HTML 3.2
- Alignment	`<TR ALIGN=LEFT|RIGHT|↵ CENTER|JUSTIFY VALIGN=TOP|↵ MIDDLE|BOTTOM>`	HTML 3.2
Table Cell	`<TD></TD>`	HTML 3.2. Must appear within table rows
- Alignment	`<TD ALIGN=LEFT|↵ RIGHT| CENTER↵ VALIGN=TOP|MIDDLE|↵ BOTTOM>`	HTML 3.2
- No Line Breaks	`<TD NOWRAP>`	HTML 3.2
- Columns to Span	`<TD COLSPAN=?>`	HTML 3.2
- Rows to Span	`<TD ROWSPAN=?>`	HTML 3.2
- Desired Width	`<TD WIDTH=?>`	HTML 3.2. In pixels
- Width Percent	`<TD WIDTH=%>`	HTML 3.2 Percentage of table
- Desired Height	`<TD HEIGHT=?>`	HTML 3.2. In pixels
- Height Percent	`<TD HEIGHT=%>`	HTML 3.2 Percentag_
Table Header	`<TH></TH>`	HTM_
- Alignment	`<TH ALIGN=LEFT|RI_ CENTER|JUSTIF_ VALIGN=TO_ MIDDLE|_`	
- No Line Breaks	`<TH N_`	
- Columns to Span	`<TH COL_`	

_ontinued)

Table B-16 *(continued)*

Tag Name	Tag	Notes
- Rows to Span	`<TH ROWSPAN=?>`	HTML 3.2
- Desired Width	`<TH WIDTH=?>`	HTML 3.2. In pixels
- Width Percent	`<TH WIDTH=%>`	HTML 3.2. Percentage of table
- Desired Height	`<TH HEIGHT=?>`	HTML 3.2. In pixels
- Height Percent	`<TH HEIGHT=%>`	HTML 3.2. Percentage of page
Table Caption	`<CAPTION></CAPTION>`	HTML 3.2
- Alignment	`<CAPTION ALIGN=TOP | BOTTOM>`	HTML 3.2. Above/below table

Table B-17   Miscellaneous

Tag Name	Tag	Notes
Script	`<SCRIPT></SCRIPT>`	
- Location	`<SCRIPT SRC="URL"></SCRIPT>`	
- Type	`<SCRIPT TYPE="***"></SCRIPT>`	
- Language	`<SCRIPT LANGUAGE="***"></SCRIPT>`	
Java Applet	`<APPLET>`	HTML 3.2
- Applet Name	`<APPLET NAME="***">`	HTML 3.2
- Alternate Text	`<APPLET ALT="***">`	HTML 3.2
- Applet Code Location	`<APPLET CODE="URL">`	HTML 3.2
- Code Base Directory	`<APPLET CODEBASE="URL">`	HTML 3.2
- Applet Window Height	`<APPLET HEIGHT=?>`	HTML 3.2. In pixels
- Width	`<APPLET WIDTH=?>`	HTML 3.2. In pixels
- ...ntal Offset	`<APPLET HSPACE=?>`	HTML 3.2. In pixels

Tag Name	Tag	Notes
- Alignment	`<APPLET` `ALIGN=[left|` `right|top|` `middle|bottom]>`	HTML 3.2
Applet Parameter	`<PARAM>`	HTML 3.2
- Parameter Name, Value	`<PARAM NAME="applet` `name", VALUE="` `parameter value">`	HTML 3.2
3.2 Prologue	`<!DOCTYPE HTML` `PUBLIC"- //W3C//DTD` `HTML3.2 FINAL//EN">`	HTML 3.2

Less Frequently Used Tags

Some Netscape Navigator-only tags were slow to be adopted by non-Netscape browsers. However, most of the tags in Table B-18 through Table B-26 can be used with up-to-date browsers. HTML 4.0-specific tags are only supported by relatively recent browsers.

Table B-18	Structural Definition: Appearance Controlled by the Browser's Preferences	
Tag Name	**Tag**	**Notes**
Defined Content	`<SPAN></SPAN>`	HTML 4.0
Quote	`<Q></Q>`	HTML 4.0. For short quotations
- Citation	`<Q CITE="URL"></Q>`	HTML 4.0
Insert	`<INS></INS>`	HTML 4.0. Marks additions in a new version
- Time of Change	`<INS DATETIME=":::"></INS>`	HTML 4.0
- Comments	`<INS CITE="URL"></INS>`	HTML 4.0
Delete	`<DEL></DEL>`	HTML 4.0. Marks deletions in a new version

(continued)

Table B-18 *(continued)*

Tag Name	Tag	Notes
- Time of Change	`<DEL DATETIME=":::">` `</DEL>`	HTML 4.0
- Comments	`<DEL CITE="URL">` `</DEL>`	HTML 4.0
Acronym	`<ACRONYM></ACRONYM>`	HTML 4.0
Abbreviation	`<ABBR></ABBR>`	HTML 4.0

Table B-19   Presentation Formatting: Author Specifies Text Appearance

Tag Name	Tag	Notes
Blinking	`<BLINK></BLINK>`	Navigator 1.0. Most derided tag ever
Font Size	`<FONT SIZE=?>` `</FONT>`	HTML 3.2. Ranges from 1–7
Change Font Size	`<FONT SIZE=+|-?>` `</FONT>`	HTML 3.2
Base Font Size	`<BASEFONT SIZE=?>`	HTML 3.2. From 1–7; default is 3
Font Color	`<FONT COLOR=` `"#$$$$$$"> </FONT>`	HTML 3.2
Underline	`<U></U>`	HTML 2.0
Strikeout	`<S></S>`	HTML 2.0
Select Font	`<FONT FACE="***">` `</FONT>`	HTML 4.0

Table B-20   Links, Graphics, and Sounds

Tag Name	Tag	Notes
- Target Window	`<A HREF="URL"` `TARGET="***"></A>`	HTML 4.0
Action on Click	`<A HREF="URL"` `ONCLICK="***"></A>`	HTML 4.0
Mouseover Action	`<A HREF="URL"` `ONMOUSEOVER="***"></A>`	HTML 4.0

Tag Name	Tag	Note
Mouseover Action	`<A HREF="URL" ONMOUSEOUT="***"></A>`	HTML 4.0
- Alignment	`<IMG SRC="URL" ALIGN= LEFT|RIGHT| TEXTTOP|ABSMIDDLE| BASELINE| ABSBOTTOM>`	Navigator 1.0. Option within the HTML 2.0–compliant Display Image tag
- Image Map	`<IMG SRC="URL" USEMAP="URL">`	HTML 3.2. Option within the HTML 2.0–compliant Display Image tag
- Map	`<MAP NAME="***"> </MAP>`	HTML 3.2. Describes the map. Option within the HTML 2.0–compliant Display Image tag
- Section	`<AREA SHAPE="RECT" COORDS="#,#,#,"HREF= "URL"|NOHREF>`	HTML 3.2. Option within the HTML 2.0–compliant Display Image tag
- Border	`<IMG SRC="URL" BORDER=?>`	HTML 3.2
Runaround Space	`<IMG SRC="URL" HSPACE= ? VSPACE=?>`	HTML 3.2. In pixels
Low-Res Proxy	`<IMG SRC="URL" LOWSRC= "URL">`	
N1.1 Client Pull	`<META HTTP-EQUIV= "Refresh" CONTENT= "?; URL=URL">`	HTML 2.0
Embed Object	`<EMBED SRC="URL">`	Navigator 2.0. Insert object into page
- Object Size	`<EMBED SRC="URL" WIDTH ="?" HEIGHT= "?">`	Navigator 2.0, Internet Explorer
Object	`<OBJECT></OBJECT>`	Navigator 4.0
Parameters	`<PARAM>`	Navigator 4.0

Table B-21 Dividers

Tag Name	Tag	Notes
- Clear Text Wrap	`<BR CLEAR=LEFT | RIGHT|ALL>`	HTML 3.2. Option within the HTML 2.0–compliant Line Break tag
- Alignment	`<HR ALIGN=LEFT | RIGHT|CENTER>`	HTML 3.2. Option within the HTML 2.0–compliant Horizontal Rule tag
- Thickness	`<HR SIZE=?>`	HTML 3.2. In pixels. Option within the HTML 2.0–compliant Horizontal Rule tag
- Width	`<HR WIDTH=?%>`	HTML 3.2. In pixels. Option within the HTML 2.0–compliant Horizontal Rule tag
- Width Percent	`<HR WIDTH=?%>`	HTML 3.2. As a percentage of page width. Option within the HTML 2.0–compliant Horizontal Rule tag
- Solid Line	`<HR NOSHADE>`	HTML 3.2. Without the 3-D cutout look. Option within the HTML 2.0–compliant Horizontal Rule tag
No Break	`<NOBR></NOBR>`	Navigator 1.0. Prevents line breaks
Word Break	`<WBR>`	Navigator 1.0. Where to break a line if needed

Table B-22 Lists: Can Be Nested

Tag Name	Tag	Notes
- Bullet Type	`<UL TYPE=DISC | CIRCLE| SQUARE>`	HTML 3.2. For the whole list. Option within the HTML 2.0–compliant Unordered List tag
	`<LI TYPE=DISC | CIRCLE| SQUARE>`	HTML 3.2. This and subsequent list items. Option within the HTML 2.0–compliant Unordered List tag

Tag Name	Tag	Notes
- Numbering Type	`<OL TYPE=A|a|I|i|1>`	HTML 3.2. This and subsequent list items. Option within the HTML 2.0–compliant Ordered List tag
	`<LI TYPE=A|a|I|i|1>`	HTML 3.2. This and subsequent list items. Option within the HTML 2.0–compliant Ordered List tag
- Starting Number	`<OL START=?>`	HTML 3.2
- Count	`<OL VALUE=?>`	HTML 3.2 For the whole list. Option within the HTML 2.0–compliant Ordered List tag

Table B-23	Forms: Generally Require a CGI Script on Your Server	
Tag Name	**Tag**	**Notes**
- File Upload	`<FORM ENCTYPE="multi part/form-data"></FORM>`	HTML 4.0
- Wrap Text	`<TEXTAREA WRAP=OFF|VIRTUAL|PHYSICAL></TEXTAREA>`	HTML 2.0
Button	`<BUTTON></BUTTON>`	HTML 4.0
- Button Name	`<BUTTON NAME="****"></BUTTON>`	HTML 4.0
- Button Type	`<BUTTON TYPE="SUBMIT|RESET|BUTTON"></BUTTON>`	HTML 4.0
- Default Value	`<BUTTON VALUE="****"></BUTTON>`	HTML 4.0
Label	`<LABEL></LABEL>`	HTML 4.0
- Item Labeled	`<LABEL FOR="****"></LABEL>`	HTML 4.0
Option Group	`<OPTGROUP LABEL="****"></OPTGROUP>`	HTML 4.0

(continued)

Table B-23 *(continued)*

Tag	Tag Names	Notes
Group Elements	`<FIELDSET></FIELDSET>`	HTML 4.0
Legend	`<LEGEND></LEGEND>`	HTML 4.0. Caption for fieldsets
- Alignment	`<LEGEND ALIGN="TOP|BOTTOM|LEFT|RIGHT"></LEGEND>`	HTML 4.0

Table B-24   **Tables**

Tag Name	Tag	Notes
- Table Alignment	`<TABLE ALIGN=LEFT|RIGHT|CENTER>`	HTML 4.0
- Table Color	`<TABLE BGCOLOR="$$$$$$"></TABLE>`	HTML 4.0
- Table Frame	`<TABLE FRAME=VOID|ABOVE|BELOW|HSIDES|LHS|RHS|VSIDES|BOX|BORDER></TABLE>`	HTML 4.0
- Table Rules	`<TABLE RULES=NONE|GROUPS|ROWS|COLS|ALL></TABLE>`	HTML 4.0
- Desired Width	`<TD WIDTH=?>`	HTML 4.0. In pixels
- Cell Color	`<TD BGCOLOR="#$$$$$$">`	HTML 4.0
- Desired Width	`<TH WIDTH=?>`	HTML 4.0. In pixels
- Cell Color	`<TH BGCOLOR="#$$$$$$">`	HTML 4.0
Table Body	`<TBODY>`	HTML 4.0
Table Footer	`<TFOOT></TFOOT>`	HTML 4.0. Must come before `<THEAD>`
Table Header	`<THEAD></THEAD>`	HTML 4.0

Tag Name	Tag	Notes
Column	`<COL></COL>`	HTML 4.0. Groups column attributes
- Columns Spanned	`<COL SPAN=?></COL>`	HTML 4.0
- Column Width	`<COL WIDTH=?></COL>`	HTML 4.0
- Width Percent	`<COL WIDTH="%"></COL>`	HTML 4.0
Group columns	`<COLGROUP></COLGROUP>`	HTML 4.0. Groups column structure
- Columns Spanned	`<COLGROUP SPAN=?>↩` `</COLGROUP>`	HTML 4.0
- Group Width	`<COLGROUP WIDTH=?>↩` `</COLGROUP>`	HTML 4.0
- Width Percent	`<COLGROUP WIDTH="%">↩` `</COLGROUP>`	HTML 4.0

Table B-25	Frames: Define and Manipulate Specific Regions of the Screen	
Tag Name	**Tag**	**Notes**
Frame Document	`<FRAMESET></FRAMESET>`	HTML 4.0. Instead of `<BODY>`
- Row Heights	`<FRAMESET ROWS=↩` `#,#,#,> </FRAMESET>`	HTML 4.0. Pixels or percent
- Row Heights	`<FRAMESET ROWS=*>↩` `</FRAMESET>`	HTML 4.0. * = relative size
- Column Widths	`<FRAMESET COLS=↩` `#,#,#,> </FRAMESET>`	HTML 4.0. Pixels or percent
- Column Widths	`<FRAMESET COLS=*>↩` `</FRAMESET>`	HTML 4.0. * = relative size

- Borders	`<FRAMESET FRAMEBORDER=`
	`"yes|no"↩`
	`</FRAMESET>`
		HTML 4.0

- Border Width	`<FRAMESET BORDER=?>↩` `</FRAMESET>`	HTML 4.0

(continued)

Table B-25 *(continued)*

Tag Name	Tag	Notes
- Border Color	`<FRAMESET ORDERCOLOR= "******"⤸ </FRAMESET>`	HTML 4.0
Define Frame	`<FRAME>`	HTML 4.0. Contents of an individual frame
- Display Document	`<FRAME SRC="URL">`	HTML 4.0
- Frame Name	`<FRAME NAME="***"⤸ _blank |_self⤸ _parent|_top>`	HTML 4.0
- Margin Width	`<FRAME MARGINWIDTH=?>`	HTML 4.0. Left and right margins
- Margin Height	`<FRAME⤸ MARGINHEIGHT=?>`	HTML 4.0. Top and bottom margins
- Scroll bar?	`<FRAME SCROLLING=⤸ "YES |NO|AUTO">`	HTML 4.0
- Not Resizable	`<FRAME NORESIZE>`	HTML 4.0
Borders	`<FRAME FRAMEBORDER="yes|no">`	HTML 4.0
Border Color	`<FRAME BORDERCOLOR="#$$$$$$">`	HTML 4.0
Inline Frame	`<IFRAME></IFRAME>`	HTML 4.0. Takes same attributes as FRAME
Dimensions	`<IFRAME WIDTH=? HEIGHT=?></IFRAME>`	HTML 4.0
Dimensions	`<IFRAME WIDTH="%" HEIGHT="%"></IFRAME>`	HTML 4.0
Unframed Content	`<NOFRAMES></NOFRAMES>`	HTML 4.0 For non-frames browsers

Note: *Frame tags introduced prior to HTML 4.0 are not supported by all browsers.*

Table B-26	Miscellaneous	
Tag Name	*Tag*	*Notes*
- Prompt	`<ISINDEX PROMPT=⏎ "***">`	HTML 2.0. Text to prompt input
Base Window Name	`<BASE TARGET="***">`	HTML 2.0. Must be in header
Other Content	`<NOSCRIPT></ NOSCRIPT>`	HTML 4.0. If scripts not supported
Base Window Name	`<BASE TARGET="***">`	HTML 4.0. Must be in header
Bidirect Off	`<BDO DIR=LTR|RTL> </BDO>`	HTML 4.0. For certain character sets

Appendix C

About the CD-ROM

*T*his handy appendix gets you started using the book's CD to create and improve your Web site (which is, after all, why you got the book, right?). You'll find system requirements, installation instructions, and an overview of the CoffeeCup trial software included on the disc. Enjoy! (Well, okay, *install.*)

System Requirements

Make sure that your computer meets the minimum system requirements shown in the following list. If your computer doesn't match up to most of these requirements, you may have problems using the software and files on the CD. For the latest and greatest information, please refer to the ReadMe file located at the root of the CD-ROM.

- A PC running Microsoft Windows
- An Internet connection
- A CD-ROM drive

If you need more information on the basics, check out these books published by Wiley Publishing, Inc.: *PCs For Dummies* by Dan Gookin, as well as *Windows XP For Dummies* and *Windows Vista For Dummies,* both by Andy Rathbone.

Using the CD

To install the items from the CD to your hard drive, follow these steps:

1. **Insert the CD into your computer's CD-ROM drive.**

   The license agreement appears.

   Note to Windows users: The interface won't launch if you have autorun disabled. In that case,

   a. *Choose Start⇨Run.*

      For Windows Vista, choose Start⇨All Programs⇨Accessories⇨Run.

   b. *In the dialog box that appears, type* **D:\Start.exe.**

      Replace *D* with the proper letter if your CD drive uses a different letter. If you don't know the letter, see how your CD drive is listed under My Computer.

   c. *Click OK.*

2. **Read through the license agreement and then click the Accept button if you want to use the CD.**

   The CD interface appears. The interface allows you to browse the contents and install the programs with just a click of a button (or two).

What You'll Find on the CD

Well, if you hold it up to the light at an angle, you'll see lovely rainbow patterns on the surface . . . oh, you want to know what *files* you'll find on the CD after you put it in your computer's CD or DVD drive? Okay, then, here goes.

The CD holds three very useful programs from the nice people at CoffeeCup Software: **HTML Editor, Visual Site Designer,** and **Website Color Schemer.**

These three programs are described in some detail in Part IV, which steps you through creating your Web site in CoffeeCup software. What follows is a brief description of each program to help you make up your mind as to whether you want to install one, two, or all three of them.

These programs are Windows-only. If you have a Macintosh (or a Linux box, for that matter), you'll have to use something else that supports Windows. I'm sorry not to have Mac tools here, but the market for low-cost Mac tools is very slender — partly because there are fewer Macs (I know, more all the time), but also because so many Mac users already have a higher-priced tool. One strong alternative is the online suite that Apple offers, for a small price, to Mac owners. Another favorite you may want to check out is BBEdit, at `www.bare bones.com`.

Now for a word about CoffeeCup Software, which is one of the cooler Windows-only software companies around. There has been ongoing upheaval in the world of free or inexpensive Web-page creation software, chronicled over the many editions of *Creating Web Pages For Dummies* going back more than ten years. I even skipped including a CD in the previous edition of the book (call it sheer exhaustion).

That's because my horses kept getting shot out from under me, to use a metaphor from Westerns. FrontPage Express, for example — a nice little free program from Microsoft — disappeared. Netscape Navigator became Mozilla, then Firefox, losing Web-authoring capability along the way. Even a program whose creation was led by a former Apple coworker of mine, and that I wrote a whole book about — Pagemill — was hoovered up by Adobe, and then disappeared.

Most Web page authors have been affected by these changes. Microsoft FrontPage, the most popular Web page creation tool ever, was often available for US$100 or so. It's now been pulled from the market, replaced with Microsoft Expression Web — a much more powerful but more complicated tool that costs hundreds of dollars, and that's part of a suite that costs several times more.

About CoffeeCup

All this time, CoffeeCup has been making good software, steadily improving it, listening to users, and ending up with what is now widely considered great software. True techies, yet customer-friendly, they create tools they'd like to have, buff them up to make them into products, release them to users, then steadily upgrade them.

Again it's like a Western: When the smoke clears, they are among the last ones standing with capable, easy-to-use, sensible tools that do what the vast majority of us need, plus some nice extras that are bundled into the main tools, offered separately, or both.

CoffeeCup combines highly rated software with good technical support and great licensing terms. You can use any of their programs for free for several weeks, and then pay a reasonable fee to buy them permanently. And that really does mean forever — once you pay to make the program your own, you get free upgrades for life! (No, I don't work for CoffeeCup. But their software sure serves the purposes of this book.)

The three programs included on the CD are just a few of the many made by CoffeeCup, all of which share free trial versions, a reasonable purchase price, and lifetime free upgrades.

To learn more about the company and to see the latest versions of CoffeeCup programs, visit their Web site at www.coffeecup.com.

However, you should try using the program versions on this book's CD first. Why? Well, for openers, they have a longer free licensing period than the versions available online. And the CD versions exactly match the figures and instructions in the book, so you don't have to figure out why and how things look different (because they won't).

The standalone Web Site Color Schemer even comes with a long free licensing period. Then, when you reach the end of that time frame, you get a code to use. The code converts a downloaded, new version of Web Site Color Schemer to a fully paid-for one, at no cost to you.

CoffeeCup HTML Editor

CoffeeCup HTML Editor combines two tools that work together like two sides of a coin. The Code Editor allows you to write "pure" HTML while using menus and toolbar buttons. It organizes and "pretties up" your HTML code, a real boon when you set a page aside for a while, then have to come back to it and figure out what's going on.

At any point, you can switch to the Visual Editor. This lets you work in a version of what your Web page will look like when it's actually published, just like a word processor does for your printed documents. Changes you make in one Editor automatically appear in the other.

CoffeeCup HTML Editor even includes CSS support, an advanced feature which, among other good effects, pulls even old greybeards like myself kicking and screaming into the modern era. (And me kicking and screaming is not a pretty site — pun intended.)

CoffeeCup HTML Editor draws positive reviews from the big magazines and Web sites, including from reviewers who actually know how to use Microsoft Expression Web, Dreamweaver, and such — as well as glowing user comments year in and year out. Its customers include a wide range of people who want to stay close to their code but still be productive, without spending a lot of money — all of which describes a large and growing range of people.

CoffeeCup Visual Site Designer

CoffeeCup Visual Site Designer breaks the user's dependency on pure HTML. It lets you design a page using drag and drop and free-form text entry. It creates nicely formatted, sensible HTML behind the scenes — but doesn't let you edit it directly in the tool like the CoffeeCup HTML Editor does.

CoffeeCup Visual Site Designer includes Web site templates, graphics, page backgrounds, and more. It really makes it easy to create a polished Web page.

This book emphasizes staying close to the code, at least while you're learning. But Visual Site Designer is another big step in productivity and only a small step away from the code.

What you can do, and how you do it, are still determined by the capabilities of, and even the spirit behind HTML. You can always bring the HTML code into a text editor or CoffeeCup HTML Editor and give it a good, long working over.

CoffeeCup Color Schemer

CoffeeCup Color Schemer was probably created by one of the talented Web programming gurus at CoffeeCup in about, well, two cups of coffee. Then, of course, it's been gradually improved until it's a powerful, flexible tool that just about anyone can both use and have fun with.

CoffeeCup Color Schemer lets you build a Web site design using any color on the famous color wheel (of millions of colors) along with colors you "pick" from any graphic on your computer's screen, including, amazingly, icons on your desktop. And it shows you what the colors look like in combination.

Color Schemer is one of the few tools out there that gives an ordinary Web user-turned-site-designer a fighting chance of actually creating a decent-looking Web page from colors you select yourself.

Color Schemer is built into CoffeeCup HTML Editor, so you don't need to download Color Schemer if you use the HTML Editor.

But if you don't use the other tools, Color Schemer is a standalone tool worth having, even if — especially if — you're a purist who works in straight HTML typed into a text editor. (Or chiseled into solid rock with a hammer and a die-punch, if a text editor isn't basic enough for you.)

Troubleshooting

I tried my best to pull together programs that work on most computers with the minimum system requirements. Alas, your computer may differ, and some programs may not work properly for some reason.

The two likeliest problems are that you don't have enough memory (RAM) for the programs you want to use, or you have other programs running that are affecting installation or running of a program. If you get an error message such as `Not enough memory` or `Setup cannot continue`, try one or more of the following suggestions, and then try using the software again:

- ✔ **Turn off any antivirus software running on your computer.** Installation programs sometimes mimic virus activity and may make your computer incorrectly believe that it's being infected by a virus.

- ✔ **Close all other running programs.** The more programs you have running, the less memory is available to other programs. Installation programs typically update files and programs; so if you keep other programs running, installation may not work properly.

- ✔ **Have your local computer store add more RAM to your computer.** This is, admittedly, a drastic and somewhat expensive step. However, adding more memory can really help the speed of your computer and allow more programs to run at the same time.

Customer Care

If you have trouble with the CD-ROM, please call Wiley Product Technical Support at 800-762-2974. Outside the United States, call 1-317-572-3993. You can also contact Wiley Product Technical Support at `http://support.wiley.com`. Wiley Publishing will provide technical support only for installation and other general quality control items. For technical support on the applications themselves, consult the program's vendor or author.

To place additional orders or to request information about other Wiley products, please call 877-762-2974.

Index

• *I* •

• *X* •

• *Y* •

Wiley Publishing, Inc.
End-User License Agreement

5. Limited Warranty.

(a) WPI warrants that the Software and Software Media are free from defects in materials and workmanship under normal use for a period of sixty (60) days from the date of purchase of this Book. If WPI receives notification within the warranty period of defects in materials or workmanship, WPI will replace the defective Software Media.

(b) WPI AND THE AUTHOR(S) OF THE BOOK DISCLAIM ALL OTHER WARRANTIES, EXPRESS OR IMPLIED, INCLUDING WITHOUT LIMITATION IMPLIED WARRANTIES OF MERCHANTABILITY AND FITNESS FOR A PARTICULAR PURPOSE, WITH RESPECT TO THE SOFTWARE, THE PROGRAMS, THE SOURCE CODE CONTAINED THEREIN, AND/OR THE TECHNIQUES DESCRIBED IN THIS BOOK. WPI DOES NOT WARRANT THAT THE FUNCTIONS CONTAINED IN THE SOFTWARE WILL MEET YOUR REQUIREMENTS OR THAT THE OPERATION OF THE SOFTWARE WILL BE ERROR-FREE.

(c) This limited warranty gives you specific legal rights, and you may have other rights that vary from jurisdiction to jurisdiction.

6. Remedies.

(a) WPI's entire liability and your exclusive remedy for defects in materials and workmanship shall be limited to replacement of the Software Media, which may be returned to WPI with a copy of your receipt at the following address: Software Media Fulfillment Department, Attn.: *Creating Web Pages For Dummies, 9th Edition*, Wiley Publishing, Inc., 10475 Crosspoint Blvd., Indianapolis, IN 46256, or call 1-800-762-2974. Please allow four to six weeks for delivery. This Limited Warranty is void if failure of the Software Media has resulted from accident, abuse, or misapplication. Any replacement Software Media will be warranted for the remainder of the original warranty period or thirty (30) days, whichever is longer.

(b) In no event shall WPI or the author be liable for any damages whatsoever (including without limitation damages for loss of business profits, business interruption, loss of business information, or any other pecuniary loss) arising from the use of or inability to use the Book or the Software, even if WPI has been advised of the possibility of such damages.

(c) Because some jurisdictions do not allow the exclusion or limitation of liability for consequential or incidental damages, the above limitation or exclusion may not apply to you.

7. U.S. Government Restricted Rights.
Use, duplication, or disclosure of the Software for or on behalf of the United States of America, its agencies and/or instrumentalities "U.S. Government" is subject to restrictions as stated in paragraph (c)(1)(ii) of the Rights in Technical Data and Computer Software clause of DFARS 252.227-7013, or subparagraphs (c)(1) and (2) of the Commercial Computer Software - Restricted Rights clause at FAR 52.227-19, and in similar clauses in the NASA FAR supplement, as applicable.

8. General.
This Agreement constitutes the entire understanding of the parties and revokes and supersedes all prior agreements, oral or written, between them and may not be modified or amended except in a writing signed by both parties hereto that specifically refers to this Agreement. This Agreement shall take precedence over any other documents that may be in conflict herewith. If any one or more provisions contained in this Agreement are held by any court or tribunal to be invalid, illegal, or otherwise unenforceable, each and every other provision shall remain in full force and effect.